Reviews by aca
politicians & 1

What is refreshing about Macgregor's book is that it's not merely an identification of the ills of democracy and how they came about, but it goes on to propose detailed remedies to overcome them, and does so without needing to resort to left or right politics but rather to a fundamentally citizen-centric view.

It is a highly ambitious book, meticulously researched and well argued.

— Author Mike Muntisov at *LibraryThing*

It explains so much (just about everything, really) about the present sorry state of human affairs. And it has put politics into a manageable perspective for me.

I sense, at last, that there is a way out of the straightjacket we find ourselves in.

— Ross Roache

It is a formidable effort, very learned and extremely wide-ranging... The illustrations are excellent.

It has certain family resemblances to The Dawn of Everything by David Graeber and David Wengrow, Yuval Noah Harari's three volumes, and books by Steven Pinker and Jared Diamond.

— Dr Barry Jones, former president of the Australian Labor Party, Minister for Science, and author of *Sleepers, Wake!* (a global best-seller on the future of work)

If Karl Marx had someone reading his notes as they came off the table at the British Museum, and then saw how those notes later affected the world: that's how I feel reading this book. Very timely and powerful.

— Douglas Wakefield

Fascinating and inspiring. I agree about the energising and unifying potential of the idea of a new constitution, addressing the problems he so clearly describes. I also agree he has identified the main points. My hope is that someone with the talents of a demagogue or an advertising guru will catch on and help the idea spread.

— Dr David Erdal, evolutionary psychologist, CEO and author

John Macgregor outlines a series of practical yet powerful ways in which we, the people, can be reconnected to the machinery of our own government. In doing so, he paints a picture of Democracy as a living, evolving thing whose development we can all actively share in.
This is a much needed book for our political times.

— Jon Puckridge, author

Unlike the typical online manifesto, full of bold yet incoherent mandates, this book clearly defines, contextually situates, supports, and suggests how to operationalize its ideas...

I'm impressed by how he presented his thesis in a non-partisan tone. He has chosen quotes and examples that demonstrate the core issues are trans-partisan, including the capture of government by corporate and plutocratic actors. The book should appeal to thoughtful readers across the political spectrum.

The Bill of Change and associated enabling and bolstering mechanisms strike me as very well considered. The lens is optimistic, seeing in humanity the capacity to cognitively reframe and organize our way out of the agency-capture dilemma that has so far characterized us. Such optimism is necessary if we are to change anything.

I especially find value in the toolkit he introduces—the cognitive tools, including null corner and the upstream principle—which help us think productively about the key issues.

Despite the potential Gordian knot of our animal nature, I see every reason to push for a third draft democracy program of change in every way possible, as quickly as possible. He highlights some of the most pervasive challenges to success and offers an interlocking system of structural remedies. I'm unaware of any other proposals recognizing and addressing the failure points as systemically.

Third draft democracy offers great and timely value and I want to see it in as many thoughtful hands as possible.

This is such a critical topic and fine piece of work.

— Major Mark Harris, PhD,
knowledge analyst, US Air Force

The Mechanics of Changing the World

POLITICAL ARCHITECTURE
TO ROLL BACK STATE &
CORPORATE POWER

JOHN MACGREGOR

Worldwork Press

Website: thirddraftdemocracy.com

Substack: https://johnmacgregor.substack.com

X: @JohnMMacgregor

Facebook: Third Draft Democracy

MeWe: mewe.com/i/johnmacgregor6

Mastodon: @JohnMacgregor@newsie.social

Instagram: www.instagram.com/johnmmacgregor/

Rumble (videos): JohnMMacgregor

Published by Worldwork Press, 2024

ISBN 978-0-6459483-0-1 (paperback)

ISBN 978-0-6459483-1-8 (ebook)

This book is available on Amazon in print or Kindle and is distributed to bookshops worldwide by IngramSpark.

Typeset by Robert Harrison in Adobe Garamond, licensed from Vellum.

Greek Circle image licensed from Shutterstock/Kyne Skywalker.

For Dara

Contents

Part Three

Decontamination

Part Four

Isegoria

Part Five

Renovating the democratic machinery

Part Six
Teaching the democratic arts

Part Seven
The invisible consensus

Part Eight
The Bill of Change

Part Nine
Strategy

Part Ten
Striking at the root

Preface

The subject of democratic decline has now begun making its way up humanity's ever-growing list of anxieties. Hundreds of books, articles and TED Talks on the state of democracy tell us where we are—A—in contrast to where we should be (B). However, none suggest with any precision how to get from one to the other: C. I thought it was time for a book about C.

First, a few words about words.

The centrepiece of this book is a raft of constitutional legislation I call the Bill of Change. Here, the term 'bill' means 'list', as it does in the Bill of Rights.

Given my subject matter—the governance of billions of humans over thousands of years—I need to generalize. In the Introduction, for example, I say, 'Our nations' founding documents are rooted in a world that no living person can remember.' That's not exactly true—most East Timorese will remember the world of 2002. And when I say something like 'our constitution' or 'the constitution', I'm usually generalizing again, to mean 'most constitutions', or the type of constitution that the context suggests. Given that, in 2024, the UN has 193 member states, the reader will not want me to blot the page with footnotes, or qualify every statement. Ditto prime minister/president, state/province, parliament/congress, MP/congressperson, liberal/progressive and other synonyms I tend to use interchangeably.

We lack a language for the state of the present world, and equally for the world we want—the former because the words in use tend to describe it superficially; the latter because few people have envisaged it. So I've coined some new terms—such as *tableau*, *blind sector* and *secular optimism*. I tend to italicize (and explain) these first time round. They're also defined in the glossary at the end of the book.

Two words that recur a lot are *inequality* and *monopoly*. Please consider them shorthand for 'tendencies'. (Equality of opportunity is desirable, but equality of outcomes impossible; a literal monopoly is rare.)

A third shorthand I use often is *neoliberalism*. This word is now used only by neoliberalism's opponents. Its *proponents* continue to privatize, cut taxes on the rich, deregulate, lower trade barriers, weaken trade unions, advocate lower wages, financialize the economy and offshore profits—but all of this now lacks a name. As the phenomenon itself hasn't gone anywhere, I've stuck with *neoliberalism*.

A word I employ even more frequently is *plutocracy*. As I use it, the word more often describes a tacit confluence of interests than a well-orchestrated conspiracy—closer to blind, opportunistic natural selection than an *Illuminati* flowchart. My use of the word doesn't imply criticism of wealth: but of wealth controlling politics and society. As this is our present reality—the first cause of our inequality, ignorance and ravaged environment—I've had little choice but to use the word repeatedly. Also, *plutocracy* has more explanatory power than *oligarchy*. Indeed monarchies, tyrannies and oligarchies are all usually plutocracies—making *plutocracy* a good catch-all.

'Free market' in quotes means the present global system of market pantheism, not its opposite, the free market. I sometimes use 'democracy' in the same fashion.

As for the countable noun *democracy*—i.e., a nation practising democracy—few of these are democracies by my definition.

However, that's how they're generally described, so for simplicity I tend to term them as such.

When I use the word *corporation*, I mean a large corporation—not small- or medium-sized businesses, which do little harm to anyone, and have no effect on government policy.

I'm afraid you'll have to live with my English—a mixture of the Australian, American and British dialects.

I've divided the book into 'parts'—Part One to Part Ten. Each part deals with a major theme. The 76 chapters distributed among them deal with the nitty-gritty.

I cite all kinds of nations to illustrate my arguments—but I cite the United States the most. This is because: (i) it's in the US that plutocratic rule is most highly developed—it's our 'anti-model'; (ii) no country affects the world as much as the US does, via war, culture and finance; (iii) the US has by far the best data.

Whilst the book's subject matter is the mechanics of changing the world, not all these mechanics will be interesting to every reader. So (for example) if you're already convinced that money has contaminated democratic politics, you may not need to read every word of Part Three. When the mood strikes, *skim*! It's more important to understand the principles in play than how preferential votes are calculated in Tasmania.

No reader will agree with everything I've written. And to hope for this would be at odds with the spirit of the book. Indeed, some of my facts will prove wrong, along with some of my conclusions. Human judgement is trifling against the vastness of the world.

I'll update the book as readers' corrections come in. All I ask of each critique is: do better.

Introduction

That whenever any Form of Government becomes destructive of these ends, it is the Right of the People to alter or to abolish it, and to institute new Government, laying its foundation on such principles and organizing its powers in such form, as to them shall seem most likely to effect their Safety and Happiness.

— US Declaration of Independence

It's sometimes thought that we haven't cracked the problem of governance in complex societies because the answers lie buried within too many variables—complex societies are *too* complex.

I propose a different answer: our problems only become too complex when encountered too far 'downstream'. That is, we need to address the challenges of environmental breakdown, war, inequality—farm failure, surveillance, debt—at the appropriate level: the level of democratic design. Attacking them singly, within an impossibly skewed system, has not gone well.

Under an onslaught of large problems, numerous problems, and limitless data, we've been paralyzed by a forest of signposts—and have not spotted the well-defined, navigable path lying at our feet.

Redesigning democracy will require lengthy debate and complex design work—but not so lengthy or so complex as building a rocket that can leave the solar system, halving the global birth rate, or wiping out smallpox—all of which we've done.

Threats to entrenched power can be identified by the aura of silence that surrounds them. For the last half-century, the premise of the media-government network seems to be that democracy's evolution has reached its natural limits. The expansion of democracy is never broached out loud, let alone acted on. Accordingly, ordinary people see the constitution as immovable —like a vast national monument. There is ceaseless analysis of daily politics, and none of the rules and institutions that make it what it is.

Our environmental, social and economic issues are, at bottom, a democratic issue. Until we address them at the level of the system that gives them their shape, we're combating consequences, not causes.

COVID has shown us that new thinking is possible. In the pandemic's all-but-forgotten early days, the sense of being one world seemed—very briefly—closer to the surface than at any time since the 'blue planet' photos of 1969. Whole countries mobilized in a way not seen since World War Two. Social divisions and polarization dropped sharply.[1]

The pandemic was a dress rehearsal for the true crises coming our way: a foretaste of the states of emergency, shortages, economic depressions and lifestyle disruptions that will follow the various, pending crunches that environmental overshoot and misgovernment are walking us toward.

But the post-pandemic world requires much more than the inspired troubleshooting of hand-sewn surgical gowns and 15-hour shifts. It requires architecture.

Constitutional obduracy

Contemporary democracy seems conceptually exhausted.[2]

— Irfan Ahmad (Indian author)

Introduction

The 'COVID Recession', the Global Financial Crisis that preceded it, and the Dotcom Bust before that, were named after their precipitating events. But whilst our recurring economic crises may have diverse and unconnected triggers—the IT industry, New York banks, a virus—triggers are not causes. Recurring crises with similar symptoms have their roots in the system.

These crisis-prone systems of ours are often characterized in economic terms, but the first cause is political: leaders and regulators who no longer govern in our interests. Our economic crises arise from a policy regime (cheap money, rentierism, monopoly, deregulation, designed-in middle class debt) that merely awaits a credit crunch, a sector downturn—a pandemic—to blow down the Potemkin village.

Ultimately, this occurs because our constitutions—those documents that suggest our national character, and spell out the rules by which our decisions are made—are products of their era. They don't address the modern world because they know nothing of it. A constitution's growing ignorance of the present means that time can transmute it into a Pandora's box, releasing 'strife, care, pride, hatred and despair' on society—or, more correctly, polarization, inequality and war. It's worthy to go after these 'plagues'—but our real attention should be on the box.

The divisions and depressions of the 21st Century are not cosmic mysteries: they arose on the back of a democratic withering. Our nations' founding documents are rooted in a world no living person can remember. Most enshrine hard-won liberties, a separation of powers and regular elections—all of which should be jealously guarded. But in the gaps—what they don't describe—an unseemly raft of afflictions has sprung up.

Democracy has been captured proactively. But it has also been left almost untouched by the treasury of knowledge on human nature that has accumulated since 1789. The result of these twin deficits is not pretty.

Seventy-five percent of Americans believe that 'corruption is widespread throughout government in this country'.[3] As Gallup CEO Jim Clifton emphasized, 'Not incompetence, but corruption'.[4] (One could add: Not occasional, but widespread.)

The same perception is shared throughout the world's democracies—France (64%), Israel (74%), Taiwan (77%), Poland (78%), Czech Republic (83%), Spain (84%), Portugal (86%) and Lithuania (90%).[5] This is a broad hint that the problem is the reigning democratic model, not the policies of any one country.

Western voters now understand that the currency in which the wealthy support politicians is money, and the currency in which they are repaid is policy. The result is a disenchanted populace, and a professional political class that rules the democratic void. Strongman plutocrats, masquerading as populists—who promise to 'burn down the system'—are gaining increasing vote-shares where there are free elections.[6]

The same trend to plutocracy is underway in the 'socialist' states such as China—governed now by wealthy families and Communist Party 'princelings'—and the Indochinese nations, where an ocean of blood spilt for national sovereignty has resulted —two generations on—in rule by small groups of kleptocrats.

Both types of jurisdiction—democratic capitalist and party-run communist—have devolved into plutocracy because there are insufficient 'brake' institutions to prevent it: feeble checks and balances, token democratic cultures, information cornered by the few. Generally, there is only the ideology of the market or the party. Missing is the capacity to evolve, arising from the all-important mechanics of popular control.

If we are to survive the 21st Century, our task is to fashion a system that confers power without selling it, facilitates information without creating it, efficiently subtracts bad leaders from the political equation, and tethers the mutability of our era to a series of dynamic constitutional experiments.

Interlocking reforms

This book rests on these premises:

- Our daily politics is a kind of neurosis—a 'displacement activity'—substituting for the system redesign that can resolve our crises. War, inequality and

environmental overshoot are insoluble within the
current framework.

- Power is deployed more adroitly, more fairly and more
  safely when it is dispersed.

- For a well-functioning society, we need not to swing
  right or left: we require a political system by which
  informed majorities can craft a policy mosaic.

- Our present, inefficient form of democracy is likely to
  be replaced by authoritarianism, which is increasingly
  efficient. Reinventing democracy is not only desirable:
  it's a condition for its survival.

Popular institutions are the key to making these things a reality. Their absence—whether in a G20 member or a poor Asian
country—makes plutocracy inevitable. The best constitutions have
always pre-empted clamorous attempts at cure with the sweet
silence of prevention.

Democracy is not a single thing. It's not 'voting'; it's not 'free
information'; it's not 'civic engagement'. Because it's a web with
many threads, reform, too, must be a web. Change that survives
requires reforms that protect and strengthen each other.

I would argue that four spheres—monopoly media, political
money, skewed electoral machinery and civic alienation—are
democracy's present-day choke points. They're not the only
impediments to a happy society; they may not even be the
most important. But they're at the top of the chain of causation
—the ones we need to fix first if anything downstream is to be
fixed.

Democracy, civilization's flower, has an historical timetable
that can be extended. If the Athenian legal architecture of the 6th
Century BC was our first shot, and the democratizations of the
last century or two were our second, we might call the new model
'third draft democracy'.

At the core of the third draft is the Bill of Change—a set of articles of constitutional law that relate to each other via an underlying principle.

What is the principle?

It is that the power of special interests has expanded, and democracy has not: that new institutions are required to undo the plutocracy that has grown up around our democracy, like the brambles round Sleeping Beauty's castle.

The Bill is designed to shape a society that satisfies progressives and conservatives alike with its stability, its faith in itself, and its equality of political opportunity. Our present factionalism will not be resolved by one side winning—but by the arrival of decision-making that all respect. Division ends with the birth of a new idea.

Part One
Why democracy was invented

By using a mirror of brass, you may see to adjust your hat. By using antiquity as a mirror, you may learn to foresee the rise and fall of empires.

— Chinese Emperor T'ai Tsung

Chapter 1
Human egalitarianism

I
f we anchor our idea of democracy in empirically weak or
romantic notions of human nature, we'll probably come
unstuck. So it may be good to begin by looking at how
human groups have actually behaved throughout most of the
human timeline. That would give us some idea of the extent to
which democracy is a 'fit' with our human make-up.

The earliest known remains for our species, *Homo sapiens*, are
roughly 300,000 years old. These were discovered in Morocco in
1961, and were identified much later, by the paleoanthropologist
Jean-Jacques Hublin, who published his findings in 2017.[1] Older
remains than this may yet be found. But for the moment, it seems
that *we* might have become *us* something like 300,000 years ago.

The other period of interest is the ten thousand years or so
since agriculture and human settlement began. For simplicity, I've
called the culture of this era—actually a series of thousands of
cultures—the *Myriade*.[a] (Myriad meaning 'ten thousand' and *–ade*
'product of'.)

---

[a] No existing term quite works. 'Civilization' began well after agriculture;
'Holocene' is a geological term; and 'ten kiloyears', 'ten millennia', etc, characterize
time but not the unprecedented 'settlement' culture of the *Myriade*, or its novel forms
of governance and technology.

3

Chapter 1

The 30 symbols below represent the *Homo sapiens* timeline in 10,000-year increments:

+++++++++++++++++++++++++++++++*

The first 29 of them make up our hunter-gatherer era. The asterisk at the end is the *Myriade*: the time since we began cropping systematically and settled down. It's obvious that nearly all of our genetic endowment pre-dates the era of fixed human settlement.

There's been a little frank evolution during the *Myriade*—blue eyes for some, dairy tolerance for others—but most of our human DNA was established in our time as nomadic hunter-gatherers living in bands.

These bands contained ever-fluctuating numbers—commonly 20 to 50—with a collection of bands, by the late Stone Age, frequently forming a larger 'ethnolinguistic group' or network of maybe 1,500 people.[2] The picture varied greatly from savannah to coast to forest to Arctic—and from ice age to warmer 'interglacial' times: but often a network would extend 200 to 400 kilometres from edge to edge. Its larger population and spread allowed information, resources and ideas to be shared widely. It also maximized co-operation in such things as food processing technology and hunting strategies.[3]

Fig. 1.1: Stone Age rock art in Zimbabwe, showing a hunt scene

The emerging 'network' model made the entire society more resilient.[4] From about 45,000 years ago, groups in the Mediterranean Basin, for example, had much increased their 'demographic robustness': they had higher populations, a wider geographical spread and much greater cultural diversity. Body ornaments, decorated tools and art joined the human repertoire.

High-status individuals in stratified, hierarchical societies tend to leave behind 'prestige possessions' and evidence of conspicuous consumption. They live in fancier abodes, and are buried with well-ornamented 'grave goods'.[5] None of these things have been found in the campsites of small-scale, pre-agricultural societies. This meshes quite well with our knowledge of the 'counter-dominant' culture of hunter-gatherers of recent times.

This particular simian offshoot didn't permit alpha males, and took down bigshots.[6] This was something quite new to the great ape family. In place of the hyper-competition of its ape cousins, *Homo sapiens* had learned co-operation.

Some of the foundational work in this field has been done by anthropologist Christopher Boehm, who cites the example of a South American Yanomamo chief observed by one of Boehm's colleagues. Seeing the need to tidy up the centre of the village in advance of a visit by a neighboring village, the chief

> went out and began to rake it himself. Others saw him and began to follow his example, at which point he retired to let them finish the job. He was obliged to lead by example.[7]

Decision-making in many hunter-gatherer societies is more evenly shared between women and men than in traditional agricultural societies.[8]

Broadly, anthropology finds that whilst human individuals do have 'hierarchical' or 'dominant' tendencies, such traits tend to be overcome by a range of pressures from the group. As the economic anthropologist Harold Schneider put it:

> All men seek to rule, but if they cannot rule they prefer to be equal.[9]

Chapter 1

Homo sapiens' tendency to co-operate and share is encapsulated by Dr Michael Tomasello, of the Max Planck Institute:

> It is inconceivable that you would ever see two chimpanzees carrying a log together.[10]

Indeed, one survey of the hunter-gatherer literature concludes that humans, uniquely in the animal kingdom, are 'ultrasocial' —possessing

> the ability to care about the welfare of others (other-regarding concerns), to 'feel into' others (empathy), and to understand, adhere to, and enforce social norms (normativity).[11]

Another worldwide survey found that 'relatively few hunter-gatherer societies have well-defined social strata or politico-religious offices' (though people with special skills are highly respected).[12] They tend to have low to modest wealth differences—and 'social insurance', where the less advantaged are taken care of by the group. Humans probably ended up this way, the survey concludes, because, over time 'strict hierarchical structures became maladaptive'.[13]

This idea is seconded by David Erdal and Andrew Whiten, of the University of St Andrews in Scotland:

> Counterdominance ('no one is going to get away with more than I') is an economically efficient predisposition: it ensures that sharing takes place, and, given the risk profile of hunting, sharing rather than attempted dominance is the efficient strategy.[14]

Intriguingly, in the midst of all this egalitarian co-operation, individualism somehow assumes a key role. Whilst equality was the highest value for the group, for the individual it was autonomy —or what modern Americans call 'freedom'. Humans did not evolve to live as a homogenous mass.

Individualism, according to anthropologist Tim Ingold, is a

'fundamental value which ethnology [the comparative study of cultures] consistently attributes to hunters and gatherers'.[15]

Erdal and Whiten write that to recognize good performance, and defer to those who achieve it, is a 'cross-culturally stable tendency'—all cultures do it. Individualism, which they see as 'grounded in inherited tendencies', probably had an adaptive advantage by 'structuring groups around effective individuals'.[16]

In short—Christopher Boehm writes—humanity's '"democratic" origins...are not recent and historical, but evolutionary and ancient. They date from well back in the Paleolithic era, and were intimately involved with the development of human nature itself.'[17]

When hunter-gatherer groups *do* have 'leaders', they're much less powerful than those in modern political groups, and more easily removed. Of 48 such societies surveyed by Christopher Boehm, 38 had removed an unsatisfactory leader—11 of them by assassination.[18]

British anthropologist Susan Kent goes so far as to suggest that hunter-gatherer 'leaders' were only 'situational, temporary and nonbinding "leaders" who are "leaders" only because ethnographers and others have labeled them as such'.[19]

When bossy people and power junkies cropped up—anthropologists call them 'upstarts'—human groups worldwide developed a suite of actions to keep them in their place. These included:

Rebuffs
Rebukes
Criticism
Ridicule
Satire
'Cutting down'
'Shouting down'
Disobedience
Exile

Thus, if a chief of the Iban tribe in the Philippines gives a command, he's likely to be 'sharply rebuffed'. The Mbuti Pygmies 'shout down' a successful hunter who becomes over-assertive, as do the South American Shavante. If an individual among the Nuer (Nile Valley), Inuit (Arctic), Arapaho (North America), Bedouin (Arabia) and Chaco (South America) attempts to give orders, he is disobeyed or simply ignored.[20]

In most groups, would-be autocrats are routinely fired. Others are deserted: the band picks up its tools, food and children, and goes to live elsewhere, leaving the 'leader' to cope by himself. Homicide is not uncommon: several groups simply kill off men who try to dominate them.

From the Arctic to the tropics, behaviors that merit such forms of overthrow include:

Monopolizing resources
Lying
War-mongering
Meanness
Incest
Employing clan-members to work for oneself
Giving orders
Being over-assertive
Indecision
Greed
Partiality
Self-aggrandizement
Aggressive behavior
Dominating others
Making deals with outsiders
Not protecting the group from disaster
Boasting
Trying to over-rule the wishes of the group [21]

Though *Homo sapiens* emerged within the hierarchy-conscious great ape family, she turned the great ape social model on its head.

In *The Western Illusion of Human Nature*, the anthropologist Morton Sahlins argues that modern ideas in both economics and biology play into the mistaken idea of an incorrigibly selfish human nature:

> For the greater part of humanity, self interest as we know it is unnatural in the normative sense; it is considered madness, witchcraft or some such grounds for ostracism, execution or at least therapy... Such avarice is generally taken for a loss of humanity.[22]

Similar rank-and-file attitudes toward wealth and power exist today[23]—only today there's less scope for deploying them. We'll look at ourselves (literate moderns) in more detail in Part Seven.

Finally, if hunter-gatherers displayed political harmony within the band, what about relations *between* groups? What about our famous propensity for war?

Christopher Boehm believes that some larger recent-era groups engaged in feuds and 'strings of revenge killings', which added up to quite a lot of victims over time.[24] And it may be that large-scale warfare increased when late Stone Age tribes were expanded by trade—as when the South American sweet potato was introduced to Papua-New Guinea in the 17th Century: suddenly there was a food surplus to fight over.[25]

But whilst there was a certain amount of homicide in ancient populations,[26] a survey of the archeological evidence of prehistoric warfare, by the American anthropologist Brian Ferguson, found no proven large death tolls from 'intergroup violence'. Ferguson, whose expertise lies in the anthropology of war, finds no evidence that Stone Age humans were prone to war, or that making war is an evolved human tendency.[27]

In summary, the record of our time on Earth tells us that, under the right conditions, we're a co-operative, egalitarian and amiable-enough species. We are highly social; we value individual autonomy; we don't have much time for leaders.

With that distinguished backstory, something like democracy might have been inevitable.

Chapter 2
The long march

Because tools of mass control were discovered before tools of mass co-operation, the human itinerary since the Stone Age at first took us away from egalitarianism.

That is, social hierarchies as we now know them seem to have begun some time after the arrival of agriculture and settlement—and it was only later, as we developed the tools of philosophy and science, of civil rights and democracy, that we began, incrementally, our reversion to type.

Whilst agriculture is colloquially dated to the Neolithic Revolution in the Middle East around 10000 BC, in fact it had at least 11 independent centres of origin, including China, Turkey, Pakistan, the Andes, New Guinea, the Sahel in Africa, and Mesopotamia—the earliest being in the Levant about 11,500 years ago.

Still-emerging evidence on Australian Aboriginals may push it well beyond that.

But the conventional timeline—farming led to settlement; settlement led to civilization—now looks more messy. Britons, who'd begun cropping by the time of Stonehenge, later abandoned it.[1] And excavations at Gobekli Tepe in southern Turkey reveal that the late Stone Age people at this site erected twenty-ton megaliths, and gathered in large numbers, from around 9000 BC—long before they turned to agriculture.[2] Until recently, hunter-gatherers weren't supposed to do things like this.

Fig. 1.2: Excavation at Gobekli Tepe, showing T-shaped monoliths arranged in circular patterns, each carved with animal figures & abstract symbols.

Gobekli is thought to be the world's oldest ceremonial site. It's likely that the first wheat was domesticated, only 20 miles away, well after the complex began. This makes a case that humans first met in large numbers principally for ritual and social purposes, not economic ones.[3]

Egalitarianism seems to have survived into the Neolithic, a couple of millennia later—when hunting and gathering were giving way to farming. Another Turkish site, Catalhoyuk, dating from around 7000 BC, is a dense collection of mudbrick houses that contained 5,000 to 7,000 people. Catalhoyuk's ritual and social life was highly organized, and its community was mutually dependent and tightknit. Its excavator, British archeologist Ian Hodder, writes:

You might have thought that all of this organization—this large number of people living together—necessitated some sort of central hierarchy. But that's not what we find at Catalhoyuk. We think Catalhoyuk is an aggressively egalitarian society, where showing difference was not really allowed… In fact we can find no chiefly house or chiefly centre—or high status house or high status centre. Everybody seems to be about the same. Everybody has the same amount of storage, the same amount of productive facility, and so on. This is a very egalitarian society.[4]

Gender equality too, Hodder says, survived at Catalhoyuk, where 'the same social stature was given to both men and women'.[5]

Human nature is often conceptualized via a 'split model'. Religion gives us 'lower nature' v. selflessness; anthropology has 'dominance' v. 'counter-dominance'; and psychology has 'anti-social' v. 'pro-social' traits. Since we emerged from the Stone Age, our religion and our philosophy have repeatedly emphasized this choice between hierarchy and equality.

As we'll see in the chapters ahead, it's the social design that coaxes one or the other forward.

Humanity's hallmark egalitarianism arose from a suite of biological and cultural adaptations[6]—you might call them the 'democratic instinct'. So it's not surprising that the first kings and prelates had to work hard to keep this instinct in check. The written history of humankind is the history of opulent aristocracies, toiling masses, and regular rebellions.

Where and when the trek toward democracy began is much debated. The safe answers are 'Eurasia' and 'a long time ago'.

Limited kinds of assembly had existed in early Sumerian cities, millennia before the Greek Golden Age. There is no record of land ownership in Neolithic or Copper Age Europe up till about 1700 BC—all was communal—which hints that decision-making might also have been communal.[7]

Local assemblies that advised princes seem to have originated in Syria, Iraq and Iran, then spread west through Phoenician cities such as Sidon and Byblos,[8] and made their way to Greece.[9]

The main form of political organization in the ancient era was the city-state. Long before their democratic experiment, the Greeks enacted the first city-state constitution. The event was surrounded by notable symbolism. Firstly, in a male-dominated culture, this constitution was decreed by a woman. And secondly, it was delivered *underground*—to the ancients, the source of 'big dreams' that conferred an expanded view of life: the place of self-renewal.[10]

The receiver was Lycurgus, the leader of Sparta in around the 9th Century BC. The giver was the priestess at the Temple of Apollo at Delphi—the spiritual centre of the ancient European world.

According to the historian Plutarch, writing in the 1st Century AD, Lycurgus had realized that his fractious people and unstable state required a revolution:

> He was convinced that a partial change of the laws would be of no avail whatsoever, but that he must proceed as a physician would with a patient who was debilitated and full of all sorts of diseases; he must reduce and alter the existing temperament by means of drugs and purges, and introduce a new and different regimen.[11]

The Delphic priestess, channelling Apollo, god of order and harmony—the divine law-maker—instructed Lycurgus to establish a council of 28 nobles, which could propose and rescind laws. Significantly, the council's reach was to be tempered by assemblies of the people. The power of Sparta's two kings was no longer absolute.[12]

Plutarch tells us this 'gave steadiness and safety to the commonwealth', and 'always kept things in a just equilibrium; the twenty-eight always adhering to the kings so far as to resist democracy, and, on the other hand, supporting the people against the establishment of absolute monarchy'.[13] Indeed this watering down of kingly power ensured that Sparta's kings escaped the fates of neighboring ones, whose tight grip on power led to successful revolutions.

Such parries against oligarchy arose in several Greek cities thereafter. One scholar has counted 18 cities that employed semi-popular or quasi-democratic government before 480 BC. Democracy, you could say, was born into a receptive family of city-states.

Sometimes this expansion of freedom stalled or went into reverse, and sometimes it remained stable for years. On one occasion it projected an entire society into the future overnight, in a dramatic paradigm shift.

Athens

I would take the Tube, by myself, at the age of about 13, and visit the British Museum. I would walk through the cat-headed Egyptians, and the cloven-hoofed Babylonians, and the type-writer-bearded Assyrians—and all the other savage and ludicrous near-Eastern divinities—until I penetrated the sanctum sanctorum—the innermost and holiest shrine of London's greatest cultural temple, the Duveen Galleries…

You go into that room and you feel that you are in a new and better world. You've left behind the totalitarian tyrannies, with their rigid and robotic processions of prisoners, their undifferentiated armies, their scenes of humiliation and massacre… You notice a change in mood. It's not just the quality of the sculpture, though that's taken a hyper-leap forward, with a new accuracy and fluency in the modelling: it's in the attitude towards the subject. You look at the riders of the Panathenaic Frieze…and you realise that the sculptors were trying to say something new.

These people were idealised certainly—but they were meant to be the real people of Athens, the ordinary people. And in their scale and in the attention to detail, they were just as important as anyone else on that frieze. No smaller—just as big and just as carefully rendered—as the Olympian gods themselves. And so after thousands of years of civilisation, and after centuries of abject quivering before fish gods and cow gods and sky gods, you are seeing the arrival of the individual: centre-stage at last in the story of humanity.[14]

The long march

— Boris Johnson (classical scholar and former British prime minister)

In ancient Greece, an important task of the oracle was to represent the community's future thoughts to it. She—a temple priestess channelling a goddess or god—suggested new technology, new forms of government, new moral outlooks: better ways of being human.

The priestess took the role of the 'unacknowledged legislator' that Percy Shelley later claimed for the poet: a mirror of 'the gigantic shadows which futurity casts upon the present'.[15]

An oracular priestess generally dealt with a procession of supplicants—kings, merchants, philosophers, paupers—which gave her unique insight into her era's social currents. Able to sense what lay in the psychic shadows, and draw it into the daylight, she nudged civilization forward.

The most influential of these priestesses was at Delphi. The classicist FWH Myers writes:

> It is from Delphi that reverence for oaths, respect for the life of slaves, of women, derive in great measure their sanction and strength.[16]

In her *adyton*, or underground chamber, the Delphic priestess sat in a kind of bronze cauldron. This was held aloft on a tripod—which symbolized the collective strength of the community.[17] As Greece's Classical Era drew nearer, the rights of ordinary people were more often cited, and the priestess increasingly marshalled her society-shaping grandiloquence against tyranny. She famously told one rich visitor that his costly offering was not worth the cake offered by a poor man. Several tyrants were given the brush-off.[18]

Fig. 1.3: Design on 5th Century BC bowl. The Delphi
priestess sits atop a tripod structure. Her supplicant is a
visiting king.

In the early 6th Century BC, Athens was in uproar. Common
people increasingly refused to accept the steep inequality in their
polis, or city-state. Athens, Plutarch tells us, 'was on the verge of
revolution, because of the excessive poverty of some citizens, and
the enormous wealth of others'.[19] As Aristotle described it:

> [T]here was contention for a long time between the upper
> classes and the populace. Not only was the constitution at this
> time oligarchical in every respect, but the poorer classes, men,
> women, and children, were the serfs of the rich... The whole
> country was in the hands of a few persons, and if the tenants
> failed to pay their rent they were liable to be hauled into slavery,
> and their children with them. All loans secured upon the
> debtor's person, a custom which prevailed until the time of
> Solon, who was the first to appear as the champion of the
> people.[20]

Solon was a poet and merchant—a noble, though not a wealthy one—who was trusted by all sides for his sagacity. He was chosen by the majority of citizens in this modestly successful city-state to devise a constitution that would end the ructions that threatened social implosion.

Solon did what people tended to do when faced with an impossible problem: he went to Delphi. There, the priestess—a peasant girl in a land ruled by aristocratic men, sitting underground beside a large, smooth stone representing the navel of the Earth—instructed him not to flinch from establishing the first proto-democracy:

> Seat yourself now amidships
> For you are the pilot of Athens.
> Grasp the helm fast in your hands:
> You have many allies in your city.[21]

If this event occurred as recorded, it's a moment as remarkable as Prometheus stealing fire from the gods to kindle civilization. Our debt to this unnamed girl has never been acknowledged.

Returning to Athens, Solon cancelled all debts, and outlawed debt servitude. He released debtors from slavery, and from prison, and brought them back from exile.[22] Plutocracy was terminated at a stroke. The poor and the middle classes once again had a future they could contemplate without dread.

In one of his poems, Solon wrote:

> I stood with a mighty shield in front of both classes,
> And suffered neither of them to prevail unjustly.[23]

According to Athenians writing in later centuries, Solon established the jury system (still in use around the world today) and allowed any citizen to prosecute a crime.[24] He also decreed that certain public office-holders be chosen by lot—the 'sortition' system now being revived in some 21st Century democracies.[25] (Part Five.)

Solon's motto was: 'Equality prevents war'.

The Solonic reforms were revolutionary for the time—though this was not yet democracy. Some retrograde laws were kept on, and the aristocratic Areopagus council remained the guardian of the constitution.

Soon after, the populace, happy with their lot, 'went back to farming'—metaphorically, the mistake populaces have been making ever since—and left politics to city-based experts. As a result of this neglect, after three decades Solon's constitution was overtaken by a *tyranny*: government by a single ruler, or *tyrannos*.

But because the atmosphere of Athens had changed, even the 'tyrant', whose name was Peisistratos, invoked egalitarian ideas, and was neither violent nor overly greedy. He subjected himself to the law like any citizen.

There was a half-century interregnum in which Peisistratos ruled, and then his sons. The latter were less competent than their father, and crueller. One was assassinated; the other was eventually forced to abdicate.

We're now at 508 BC, nearly nine decades after Solon's revolution. That year saw the rise of Cleisthenes, Athens' second lawgiver. A leading citizen—chosen, like Solon, for his judgement and lack of self-interest—Cleisthenes was given the authority to broker a deal to end the chaos accompanying the end of the tyranny.

Aristotle tells us that 'the populace flocked together' to support him.[26]

Fig. 1.4: Bust of Cleisthenes in the Ohio state Capitol building

Cleisthenes created ten new clans, both to replace the fractious old clans and to expand the franchise. He sent (or went) to Delphi for advice on their names. The priestess obliged, naming the clans after ten national heroes—in so doing, giving her blessing to the most radical social experiment of the ancient world.

The Oracle functioned for at least 1,200 years—a long succession of priestesses conveying the evolving thoughts of Apollo, protector of music and poetry, provider of roads and homes. It was she who inspired the three most important constitutions of the Greek world—Sparta's, then the Athenian constitutions of Solon and Cleisthenes. In such ways, in the heart of a patriarchal age, did a humble village girl prod the Greek era toward democracy.

Cleisthenes restored Solon's reforms, and extended them. He institutionalized and broadened sortition for the awarding of government posts. And he introduced ostracism—ten years of exile—to get budding tyrants and coup-plotters out of the way. Cleisthenes further broke up old power bases by enrolling foreigners and even slaves as citizens.[27] Hereditary privilege, the blight of the age, was pulled out by its roots.

The people's Assembly now became the prime law-making body. It met on a hill named the *Pnyx*. Typically, six thousand citizens met there about 40 days per year. The new regime even allowed Athenians to elect their own generals. What we now call 'direct democracy' had arrived in Athens.

Fig. 1.5: The world's first democratic space. The *Pnyx* in Athens today, with the *bema* or speaker's platform to the left.

Chapter 2

Eighteen years after Cleisthenes' reforms, Athens won the Battle of Marathon against Persia, the regional superpower. Thereafter, confidence in democracy grew—and the Athenian *demos*, or citizen body, began selecting its nine *archons* (chief administrators) for the first time. Archonships had traditionally been reserved for aristocrats. Now, five hundred candidates were elected by popular vote, and from these the nine were chosen by lot.

From this point on, the ownership of property had diminishing import for political power.[28] Increasingly, it was the citizenry that drove change, decided policy and shaped the *polis*.

What resulted was not mob rule, chaos, or the reign of the lowest common denominator. Nor did the citizens bankrupt the *polis* by awarding themselves perks and benefits. Instead, the years that followed Cleisthenes' reforms produced many of the elements of what we now think of as civilization. This Greek Classical era, centred on Athens, saw the invention or reinvention of philosophy, logic, rhetoric, poetry, aesthetics, education, historiography, social security, constitutional law, politics, sculpture, pottery, drama, viticulture, fitness training, archeology, architecture, physics, optics, harmonics, mathematics, geometry, astronomy, medicine, pharmacology, biology, botany and zoology.

The Athenian experiment gave us Aeschylus, Sophocles, Euripides, Aristophanes, Themistocles, Xenophon, Thucydides, Herodotus, Diogenes, Demosthenes, Epicurus, Hippocrates, Pericles, Socrates, Plato and Aristotle. How many of our names will be lower-case adjectives 2,500 years from now?

The era furnished us with further adjectives via its philosophical schools—not only the Platonists and Epicureans, but the Sophists, Skeptics, Peripatetics, Cynics and Stoics.

In the decades that followed Cleisthenes' democratic reforms, the Parthenon was built, Plato speculated that the Earth was round, and tiny Greece expelled the Persian superpower from the region. The existence of gods was questioned, and Plato suggested that women could become philosophers and heads of government[29]—ideas that reached their flowering only in our own era.

Through the 5th and 4th centuries BC, the experiment spread

through much of Greece. Trade, philosophy, science and the arts blossomed, and a middle class was able to flourish. Classicist Josiah Ober writes that, because of its 'distinct approach to politics'—a level playing field, and rules the people made themselves—Greece experienced 'an historically unusual period of sustained economic growth'.[30]

When silver was discovered in Attica, the region surrounding Athens, the proceeds were deemed to be community money, and were used to build one hundred *trireme* warships. The trireme got its first test at the Battle of Salamis in 480 BC, which the Greeks fought against the invading Persians. It was a massacre. The democracy had thrown up a master strategist, Themistocles, who boxed the Persians up in narrow straits, where their vastly superior numbers were neutralized.

As Professor Paul Cartledge puts it: 'If there wasn't a notion of the power of the people—as against dictatorship and tyranny—before the Persian invasion, there was after.'[31] The Athenians soon began characterizing their invention with the feminine nouns *isegoria* (equality of speech) or *demokratia* (*demos* = people; *kratos* = power).[32]

As the democracy proved itself, it became more democratic. In 462, at the instigation of the leading citizen Ephialtes, the aristocratic Areopagus council—which had till then had oversight of laws and magistrates—had its powers reduced to the trial of homicides.

Ephialtes' protégé, Pericles, became the foremost political leader in the years 461 to 429, instigating many expansions of the democracy—such as pay for jury service, and a reduced property qualification for archonship.[33] Pericles was the great orator of the era: probably trained in the art by his remarkable lover, Aspasia. (Aspasia also trained the young Socrates in rhetoric. In our age, she would probably be at the top of at least one profession, if not a national leader.)

In his famed 'Funeral Oration', Pericles explained what made Athens tick:

Our constitution does not copy the laws of neighbouring states; we are rather a pattern to others than imitators. It is called a democracy, because not the few but the many govern. If we look to the laws, they afford equal justice to all in their private differences; advancement in public life falls to reputation for capacity, class considerations not being allowed to interfere with merit; nor again does poverty bar the way...[34]

Fig. 1.6: Bust of Pericles, with the inscription 'Pericles, son of Xanthippus, Athenian'.

In the same speech (which Plato believed was written by Aspasia), Pericles articulated the Athenian attitude to personal liberty:

> Freedom is a feature of our daily life; and as for suspicion of one
> another in our daily private pursuits, we do not frown on our
> neighbor if he behaves to please himself...[35]

The Athenians fell woefully short on what we now call human
rights and gender equality—to say nothing of international law.
They kept women out of civic life; they owned slaves; they invaded
other city-states, or coerced them into what amounted to an
Athenian empire. In the ancient world, where honor and survival
tended to trump empathy, such attitudes were part of the psychological furniture. Human society was not to make serious progress
on these fronts for another 2,000 years.

But when we compare Athens to the other societies of its era—
rather than to developed, liberal societies in the modern world—it
is in a class of one.

The Athenians were the first to employ democracy systematically: to apply it to the management of a state. They codified it
through ceaseless law-making, and participated in it *en masse*. They
fought and died for it in battle, taught it to their children, developed a body of philosophy around it, and proactively exported it
to other lands. They even deified it: in time, *Demokratia* became a
goddess.

For all their flaws, the Athenians resolved the dilemma that has
thwarted nearly every society since: they reconciled the classes.

Even the wealthy grew happier. Before his reforms, Solon
observed that 'riches too great are poured upon men of unbalanced
soul'.[36] After two centuries of democratic expansion, Pericles was
able to say that 'wealth, to us, is not mere material for vainglory'.
The rich had grasped the advantages of working with other citizens
in a body, rather than lording it over them. The scholar LaRue Van
Hook noted of the Periclean era:

> In the city, the house of the rich man and that of the poor man
> differed little in appearance.[37]

Constitutional change, it seems, was moulding character.
As the democracy matured, over its two centuries, citizens

gained the right to sue the state, and sometimes did so successfully. Social mobility was uncommon, but at least possible. At the beginning of the 4th Century, the richest man in Athens was Pasion the banker—originally a slave, then a *metic* (resident foreigner), and finally a citizen.[38]

The notions of equality and liberty were distinguished from each other, but in rhetoric and conversation they were often twinned. As the doyen of today's Greek scholars, Mogens Herman Hansen, writes:

> The constant interplay of the two concepts is characteristic of Athenian democratic ideology and shows…the close affinity between modern democracy and Athenian demokratia…

The Assembly, Plato writes, was comprised of 'blacksmiths, shoemakers, merchants, shippers, rich, poor, the grand, and the humble'; or, according to Xenophon, 'fullers, shoemakers, carpenters, smiths, countrymen, merchants and market traders'.

When a decree was made, it began, *Edoxe toi demo*—'This was decided by the people'.

Pericles, a staunch democrat from an aristocratic family, dominated the Assembly for most of his adult life: Thucydides wrote that Athens was 'in name a democracy, but in fact under the rule of the first man'.[39]

That was true in the sense that the Athenians greatly esteemed *arete*—excellence—and Pericles rose to prominence due to his brilliance, first as a military strategist, then as a statesman. But he could not rule by edict. He had no troops at his private command, and could not make decisions of state off his own bat.

According to one description, the high-prestige individual in hunter-gatherer societies is

> listened to, [and] their opinions are heavily weighed (not obeyed) because the person enjoys credit, estimation or standing in general opinion.[40]

That was Pericles. There was no parallel between his position and that of King Xerxes across the water in Persia. As with Britain in 1940, the democracy had produced a kind of genius, but the genius remained beholden to the democracy.

When the self-regard of any Athenian leader grew too great, he was put in his place with tactics such as disobedience and satire. In 490 BC, after Athens won the Battle of Marathon, Miltiades, the victorious general, asked the Assembly for a crown of olives. A cranky citizen stood up and said, 'Let Miltiades ask for such an honor for himself when he has conquered the barbarian single-handed'.[41] The Assembly agreed.

Pericles himself was mercilessly satirized in the public drama. Throughout the democracy, what Boris Johnson calls 'Athens' archaic spirit of insubordination' eclipsed the halo of rank.[42]

As the democratic decades ticked by, citizens became more civically literate.[43] 'Policy' had a mosaic quality: it was a quilt of what we'd now call conservative and progressive influences.

Once Pericles died in 429, leaders in the democracy's remaining century were more often lower-born small businessmen —most notably the tanner Kleon, the lamp-maker Hyperbolos and the lyre-maker Kleophon. According to the Classical scholars Raaflaub, Ober and Wallace:

> In the end the demos was able to pick its leaders from among its own ranks; from being followers of the powerful, the common people evolved into a community of the powerful.[44]

Throughout Greece, the democratic idea caught on by 'organic conquest': dozens of city-states imitated the model.[a] In Athens, the locals came to believe that Solon had discovered democracy, rather than invented it—as if, all along, it had lain just beyond the cusp of human awareness.[45]

As occurred later with Rome, Britain and the United States, empire and war eventually loomed large in the undoing of Athens. As a cultural and economic florescence arrived on the coat-tails of democracy, Athens developed the habits of imposing ruinous trade

---

[a] New terms are defined in the glossary at the end of the book.

treaties on smaller rivals, of turning allies into vassals, and of exacting cruel reprisals when those vassals rebelled. This made Athens' rival, Sparta, nervous enough to want to challenge her power. The two city-states formally went to war in 431 BC.

When this Peloponnesian War was over, 27 years later, Athens had lost her fleet, her walls, a third of her population, her civic cohesion, her prosperity and her power.[46] The state that had defeated the Persian empire became, briefly, a Spartan vassal whose citizens were lashed in the streets by 'whip squads' for any disrespect to the new overlords.

As a regional force, Athens never recovered. But even as geopolitical power drained away, the Athenians increased their efforts to develop their constitution. (This was never a single document—but rather the ever-evolving 'rules defining the powers of the organs of state'.[47]) To guard against populism, the Assembly was weakened. Laws were now made by 'boards' selected by sortition. The system was rational and efficient: there was, for example, little conflict between laws as they multiplied.[48] Through the 4th Century, on the back of this smooth civic machinery, arrived much of the science, philosophy, literature and drama we now associate with Classical Greece.

Remarkably for such a philosophical race, the Greeks were not yet cured of war—which continued between the city-states for much of the century. This finally brought on a collective exhaustion that opened the door to Alexander the Great, to the north in Macedon, who conquered all of Greece near the end of the 4th Century, and much else besides.

In 322 BC, the Macedonians dissolved Athens' democratic institutions, setting it down the road to centuries as a Roman, Byzantine, Latin, Aragonese, Florentine and Ottoman colony. Democracy survived in bits of Greece into the 'Hellenistic' era that came between Alexander and Rome. Thereafter, the country did not know democracy again till the 20th Century. According to classicist and political scientist Josiah Ober, it took 2,300 years for Greece to return to the level of material wellbeing that had accompanied the democracy.[49]

The temple at Delphi went on into the Christian era, with

reduced influence, until it was shut down by a Roman emperor in the 4th Century AD. It was subsequently buried by earthquakes and landslides. When the 17th Century French traveller Jacob Spon rediscovered the site, he was startled to find that a miserable village named Castri now sat over it:

> What I found stranger still was that the most famous place in the world had suffered such a reversal of fortune that we were obliged to look for Delphi in Delphi itself, and enquire after the whereabouts of Apollo's Temple even as we stood on its foundations.[50]

Fig. 1.7: The Apollo temple at Delphi today

Today, Delphi is a tourist town, struggling, even before the pandemic, with Greece's second Great Depression in 100 years. At its beautiful central café, situated between its two main streets under a giant plane tree, a waiter named Yannis will tell you that in Greece, since the austerity imposed by the European Union in 2015, 'There is no democracy. Democracy is dead.'

In Athens, a couple of hours east by road, the Pnyx—the world's first democratic space—is used mostly by dog-walkers. The site of Plato's Academy is bestrewn with the bedding of the homeless.

Athenian democracy is not forgotten. In Washington, the buildings of the Capitol, Supreme Court and Library of Congress display Greek columns in its honor, as do public buildings in most Western cities.

It was in between its two historical phases—the Greek and the modern—that democracy endured its long sleep.

Chapter 3
The long sleep

For 1,500 years, democracy existed for the most part only on paper. To the new, monotheistic world, it was a Greek archaism less interesting than the squabbles amongst the gods on Mount Olympus, which at least provided good children's stories. Works documenting the discarded idea lay in libraries such as those of Alexandria, Antioch, Pergamon and Ephesus, mostly unread, alongside the more popular Greek manuscripts on science, medicine and warfare.

Bits of democracy popped up from time to time. Influenced by the Greek example, early Christian churches of the gnostic kind selected their clergy by drawing lots.[1] This resulted in less emphasis on hierarchy and more on the inner life—and in women deacons, priests and bishops. But these groups were annihilated once the pagan emperor Constantine gained control of the Church in 325 AD.

From the 5th Century, the Byzantine Empire kept alive Greek mathematics, medicine, science and philosophy, and built on them substantially. The other great culture-preserver was the Islamic Golden Age, centred in Baghdad, which lasted from the 8th to the 13th centuries. A succession of caliphs, and the scholars they retained in such institutions as the House of Wisdom, translated and preserved the surviving Greek works. This at least ensured that a record of the Greek democratic period remained in existence.

Islam in this era placed strong emphasis on equality. Councils checked the power of rulers; monopolies were outlawed; land was given to the landless; and endowments were made to the poor by the wealthy.[2] But institutional democracy wasn't practised anywhere. Only the idea survived—via a fragile continuity. Amid the comings and goings of the Macedonian, Roman, Byzantine and Islamic empires, there was never a time when barbarism ruled everywhere. As one high culture collapsed, scholars would flee to another, their manuscripts hidden away in bags and donkey carts.

Chapter 4
Scattered reappearance of democratic practices

When Adam delved and Eve span, who was then the gentleman?[1]

> — Radical priest John Ball, emphasizing the natural equality of all people to a crowd during the Peasants' Revolt (1381). The saying spread through Britain and Europe in the medieval period.

Roughly a millennium and a half after the eclipse of democratic Athens, in one part of Europe and another there were occasional signs that the democratic instinct was stirring.

The incrementalism of these changes makes it impossible to say when the new, parliamentary form of democracy 'began': that would depend on how both 'parliament' and 'democracy' are defined.

The Icelandic Althing, for example—a gathering mostly of district chieftains—met annually to make laws from 930 AD. From the 13th Century, numerous Swiss city-states used a popular assembly—the *Landsgemeinde*—to pass and amend laws.[2]

Chapter 4

In 1188, Prince Alfonso IX of Leon in the Iberian Peninsula put together a *Curia Regis*—an advisory council of nobles, bishops and the urban middle class. Its bourgeois members were 'elected', though we're not sure by whom. Nonetheless, UNESCO believes this was the first time something resembling a parliament came into being. Alfonso's reform was derisory by today's standards. Democracy's second incarnation, unlike its first, began with fairy steps.

A generation after the *Curia*, England was home to another questionable starting point. Magna Carta, in 1215, granted a set of rights to nobles and free males: introducing *habeas corpus*, limiting King John's taxing powers, and for the first time putting the monarch within the law. Like every evolution toward democracy till the 20th Century, its rights went to a minority—but it did serve as the thin end of the wedge. The Charter bolstered the power of wealthy males: which, paradoxically, opened the door to reducing that power over time.

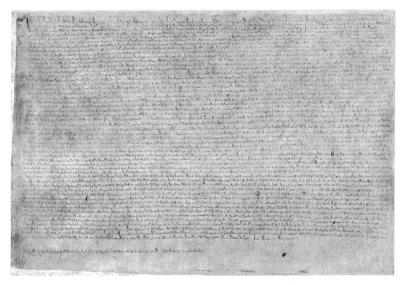

Fig. 1.8: *Magna Carta Libertatum* or the Great Charter of Liberties, 1215
—written on parchment with iron gall ink, in medieval Latin.

Kings, the quintessential plutocrats, do not give up their

prerogatives gracefully. Forced to sign the Charter, John, much vexed, threw himself to the ground...

...gnashed his teeth, rolled his eyes, grabbed sticks and straws and gnawed them like a madman.[3]

Over the ensuing centuries, elements of Magna Carta were repealed, reinstated, replaced, improved on... The Charter was less a sea change than a vague but unmistakable warning to monarchs: an intimation of their disposability.

Two years after Magna Carta, in 1217, the Charter of the Forest—less famous but possibly more consequential—re-established the rights of ordinary people to land that had been 'enclosed' for the king's use.

Near the end of the next century, in 1381, England's Peasants' Revolt protested foreign war and draconian labor laws: demanding self-regulating local communities, and an end to serfdom. Armies of peasants and artisans marched through the kingdom opening up gaols, and beheading unpopular officials—including the Archbishop of Canterbury, the Lord High Treasurer and the Chief Justice. It was a near-run thing. But the rebels were, in time, either defeated in battle or mollified by a raft of concessions from the king.

Most of the concessions were revoked the moment the peasants stood down and 'went back to farming'. But, like many failed rebellions, the Peasants' Revolt had lasting effects. The king wound back the war in France, and a poll tax raised to finance it was scrapped. For the next century, peasants pointedly reminded tax collectors of the revolt. No monarch dared again to raise taxes too high.[4]

When an elite uses its control of politics to shift wealth upwards—as it generally does—you'd expect that common people would fight back: and that world history, therefore, would be a history of peasants' revolts.

Indeed it is. From the 3rd millennium BC to the 21st Century, they occurred in China, Egypt, France, Denmark, Lithuania, Hungary, Japan, Catalonia, Poland, the Netherlands, Italy, the

WHEN ADAM DELVED AND EVE SPAN,
WHO WAS THEN THE GENTLEMAN?

Fig. 1.9: Adam delving & Eve spinning, 1888, by Edward Burne-Jones. The illustration harks back to the Peasants' Revolt. It was used by the English socialist William Morris in his novel, *A Dream of John Ball,* about the centuries-old struggle for equality.

Roman, Byzantine, Ottoman and Dutch empires, Vietnam, Germany, Sweden, Russia, Taiwan, Switzerland, Austria, Korea, Brazil, Romania, Albania, India, El Salvador, Yugoslavia, Kenya, Cuba, Nigeria, Thailand, Ethiopia and Mexico.[5]

In 1647—brandishing pamphlets on the Peasants' Revolt of three centuries earlier—the English 'Levellers' helped to convene what looks remarkably like a constitutional convention.[6] Over two weeks, during these 'Putney Debates', the Levellers pushed for manhood suffrage, jury trials and a new constitution for England— with power vested in the House of Commons. This was all written into an 'Agreement of the People'.

The Levellers were crushed. But again, it was a near-run thing —and again there were long-term effects. English Leveller Richard Rumbold voiced the view that God had not

> made the greater part of mankind with saddles on their backs and bridles in their mouths, and some few booted and spurred to ride the rest.[7]

One hundred and forty years later, Thomas Jefferson wrote that

> the mass of mankind has not been born with saddles on their backs, nor a favoured few booted and spurred, ready to ride them...[8]

Just as the Peasants' Revolt had influenced the Levellers, so did the Levellers influence the design of the United States Constitution.

Set-ups like the Peasants' Revolt and the Levellers might be thought of as *tableaus*: public consciousness changes first; concrete reform comes much later. (In solitaire, a *tableau* is an opening pile from which better combinations are later made.)

Recurring century after century, *tableaus* remind us of the deep drive to equality inherent in human groups—but also of how hard it has been, since the Paleolithic, to enact that equality in one lifetime.

The main design obstacles, perhaps, have been our large numbers and our geographical dispersion. It's hard for millions of disparate people to reach agreement, especially as special interests —few in numbers, better resourced, with a built-in consensus— will usually be first to the drawing board.

But as we'll see in the chapters ahead, the democratic tools now exist to reverse this disadvantage. Self-governance is possible at scale.

Chapter 5
Why democracy was reinvented (the second draft)

It was in the 18th Century that democracy began to wake from its twenty centuries of stony sleep.

As the Enlightenment took root, thinkers met in coffee houses, salons and debating clubs, formed their own societies, and communicated through their own journals and books—the 'Republic of Letters'. For the first time in centuries, the ideas that guided society were no longer the monopoly of rulers and religious authorities.

With the advent of long-distance sea travel, there was a two-way traffic in ideas between Old World and New. Benjamin Franklin took American scientific and political ideas to Europe—suggesting paper money to the British and religious tolerance to the French. The Declaration of Independence, penned mostly by Thomas Jefferson, was replete with the ideas of the European Enlightenment—such as the equality of man and John Locke's 'consent of the governed'.

On both sides of the Atlantic, the Enlightenment also addressed the problem of business monopoly—where one player eliminates the others from an economic sphere, in order to set its terms and prices. This kind of general market control was seen to be as dangerous to liberty as total government control. Indeed, monopoly enterprises were often compared to monarchs. (Adam Smith more tactfully described them as 'a great enemy to good management'.[1])

Thus Samuel Adams not only set up the 'Committees of Correspondence'—a strategic matrix that linked thousands of Patriots in the 13 American colonies—but in December 1773 he called a mass meeting in Boston to protest the Tea Act, passed to protect the world's largest business monopoly, the East India Company.

Some of that meeting's attendees boarded a Company ship, and dumped 342 chests of tea into Boston Harbor. And here followed another oft-seen pattern in reform campaigns: an extreme government response catalyzing resistance, and turning the middle ground in favor of change. The British responded to the Boston Tea Party with a heavy-handedness that blew up in their faces. Within months of their closing the port of Boston and limiting public assembly, the 'alternative government' of Massachusetts was training a militia outside Boston. In September 1774, the first Continental Congress met.

Two generations after the American Revolution, when Britain's 'Chartists' appeared, the British authorities fell into the same trap on home turf.

The Chartists were a working men's movement—with thousands of women working in the background—and were so-named because in 1838, in the spirit of the Levellers, they convened to draw up a 'People's Charter'.

The Chartists were no mere 'protest movement'. Like the Americans, they itemized their demands for constitutional change, and presented them for enactment. Like thoughtful reformers throughout history, they focused on parliamentary and electoral reform: reasoning that a legislative bounty would flow from that.

The Chartists also grasped that a successful reform movement needed a broad base. So rather than insisting on ideological purity, they drew disparate groups from up and down the country into a great coalition. A chronicler in one of these groups wrote:

There were [radical] associations all over the county, but there was a great lack of cohesion. One wanted the ballot, another manhood suffrage and so on... The radicals were without unity of aim and method, and there was but little hope of accomplishing anything. When, however, the People's Charter was drawn up...clearly defining the urgent demands of the working class, we felt we had a real bond of union; and so transformed our Radical Association into local Chartist centres...[2]

The Chartists were Britain's most strategically savvy reform movement till the Suffragettes burst on the scene 65 years later. They had six demands—a vote for every man, a secret ballot, an end to the parliamentary property qualification, payment of MPs (allowing working men to serve), equal constituencies, and annual elections.

Most Chartists *did* want more: for example, an end to slavery, child labor and workhouses—to say nothing of better wages. But by confining the Charter to political rights, they drew in millions. In a 'quickening' era not unlike our own, people understood that electoral reform was the pathway to much more.

The Chartists also grasped the historical continuity of constitutional reform movements. They had the face of Wat Tyler, leader of the Peasants' Revolt 450 years earlier, painted on their banners.

Chartism's national convention in 1839 saw itself as an alternative parliament. The House of Commons voted not to receive the reform petition that came out of it, which had been signed by 1.3 million people. A second petition in 1842, with over three million signatures, met the same fate.

Anger boiled over, and there was a series of armed risings. Hundreds of Chartists were jailed. In 1842, 58 men—nearly the whole Chartist national executive—were prosecuted, with the Attorney General himself conducting the case. (It failed.) When the Chartists established a land company, and bought land to allot to members, the government shut it down. The newspapers crusaded relentlessly against the movement.

Fig. 1.10: Chartist meeting in London, 1848

When the Chartist movement expired in the 1850s, it had not achieved one of its goals.

But Chartism, too, was a *tableau*. The injustices it had established in the public mind set change quietly in motion. In 1867, urban working men got the vote. In 1872, the secret ballot arrived. In 1911, the payment of MPs was introduced. Full manhood suffrage was enacted in 1918, and the property qualification abolished. By that year, the only Chartist demand that had not been met was annual elections (which may not have been much of an idea anyway).

The effects of the movement did not end in England. Many Chartists were jailed and transported to Australia—about as close to a definition of 'failure' as you could find in the mid-19th Century.

But, once there, they helped to foment the rebellions against the extortionate 'miner's right'—a levy on digging for gold—on the Victorian goldfields. The Ballarat Reform League, for example (which advocated a representative political system) was led by Welsh Chartist John Humffray.[3]

Once again, many of these risings were put down violently. The most famous was at the Eureka Stockade in Ballarat, which was stormed by British forces, who killed perhaps 60 'diggers'.

Again, a highly publicized 'failure' had the effect of radically changing public opinion. The phoenix of change soon rose from the ashes of Eureka. Within two years of the rebellion, the Victorian government replaced the 'miner's right', and introduced the secret ballot and near-universal male suffrage.

Fig. 1.11: Remnant of the original five-starred Eureka flag, now in the Ballarat Fine Art Gallery. Today the design is often proposed as the flag of an Australian republic.

Mark Twain called Eureka 'a victory won by a lost battle' (as good a definition of a *tableau* as any).[4] As a result of the rebellion, in 1920, decades after the guns had fallen silent, my grandmother was able to purchase her miner's right on the Victorian goldfields for the very reasonable sum of one shilling and threepence.

These factors—organic conquest, a tight focus on constitutional change, and victory forming in the smoke of a lost battle— were again on display when the British Suffragettes materialized at the turn of the 20th Century.

One more feature that recurred with the Suffragettes was their perception of historical continuity with other movements. The Suffragettes' founder, Emmeline Pankhurst, wrote in her autobiography:

> One of my earliest recollections is of a great bazaar which was held in my native city of Manchester, the object of the bazaar being to raise money to relieve the poverty of the newly emancipated negro slaves in the United States. My mother took an active part in this effort, and I, as a small child, was entrusted with a lucky bag by means of which I helped to collect money.
>
> Young as I was—I could not have been more than five years —I knew perfectly well the meanings of the words slavery and emancipation.[5]

Emmeline read the *Odyssey* at nine, and was an ardent suffragist by 14. When she was sent to school in Paris (her daughter Sylvia wrote), she made a French playmate and

> was delighted to discover that she had been born on the anniversary of the destruction of the Bastille, and was proud to tell her friend that her own grandmother had been an earnest politician, and one of the earliest members of the Anti-Corn Law League, and that her grandfather had narrowly escaped death on the field of Peterloo.[6]

Emmeline's lawyer husband, Richard (a staunch supporter of women's suffrage) had been a Chartist in his youth. He was an advocate of public sanitation (one of the great political struggles of the 19th Century), freedom of speech and public education. Ahead of his time, he was active in promoting arbitration to replace war as the means for settling international disputes.

In her history of the Suffragettes, Sylvia Pankhurst introduces each activist, as she enters the story, with a character sketch. Like many of their American counterparts, these women had all been active in campaigns for the poor, for factory workers, for temperance, for education, for prison reform... Like most successful movements, suffragism did not see itself in narrow terms. The

Suffragettes were very focused on the constitutional goal—votes for all women, which they achieved in 1928—but they also grasped that they were part of a broader movement for humankind. (And, thanks to them, the writing was on the wall for 'mankind'.)

Fig. 1.12: Emmeline Pankhurst under arrest (again)— outside Buckingham Palace, 1914.

As with many reform movements, the 'radical' ideal for which the Suffragettes shed so much blood, sweat and tears was in time assimilated into popular thinking. This might be illustrated by one obscure event:

After Cambodia came out of its Khmer Rouge dark age, at the first national elections in 1993, there was no debate on whether women should be given the franchise. Even in a patriarchal society which had never before had a free election, no man stood on a rostrum to denounce the idea, and no newspaper editorial predicted the end of civilization (or even Cambodian culture) if women were given the vote. A right for which women had for years been imprisoned, tortured and pilloried by the press was accorded without a second thought.

Democracy was reinvented for the same reason it was originally devised: to separate power from wealth.

The struggles that brought about its reinvention had many things in common:

- They drew inspiration, and copied tactics, from predecessor movements.
- They drew in diverse groups by limiting demands to high-yield issues.
- They grasped that monopoly was a block to liberty.
- They provoked establishment over-reaction, which helped to win over the middle.
- Their victories often arrived indirectly, via *tableaus*.
- Their ideas caught on from one jurisdiction to the next via 'organic conquest'.
- They focused on reforming the machinery of law-making: prioritizing constitutional law over ordinary law.

In this context, a striking feature of modern protest is its atomization—a thousand reform movements attacking a thousand separate ills. The atomization is 'vertical' as well as 'horizontal': unlike the Levellers, the Chartists and the Suffragettes, today's causes rarely grasp that they are in a centuries-old lineage.

Few modern movements are linked to their siblings, and few to their ancestors.

Chapter 6
The two thousand-year counter-revolution

I n ancient Jewish tradition there's a place named *Otzar* (the 'treasury of souls') where the unborn await their time on Earth.[1]

Metaphorically, in the 18th and 19th centuries, the beasts that ravage today's democracies still slept in *Otzar*. For instance, the purchase of legislation, the cornering of information by the wealthy, wars driven by corporations, and the surveillance state, were not on the mental map of early constitution-writers.

As a result, the second democratic model—the Euro-American —reached its zenith in the mid-20th Century, then was slowly overpowered by lines of attack its designers could not have fore-seen. Twenty-five centuries after the Greeks formulated it, democ-racy—the ideal that people should govern themselves—still evoked the most ingenious establishment resistance.

It's not clear why plutocrats prefer unlimited accumulation of wealth and power over living in a more engaged and happy society. Possibly, evolution placed no upper limit on the power urge because none was needed: any Stone Age assertions of power were swiftly curbed by peers. In the Stone Age, moreover, opportunities for power, like those for carbohydrates, were more limited.

With agriculture came big populations, currency, writing and (you could say) the invention of secrecy. For the first time, a skilled player could pile up all the tokens in his corner: he didn't have to be good at anything else. Our successful hunter, now an ambitious miller, could accumulate produce.

Thus did the machinery of civilization permit co-operation and equality to be nudged aside by competition and hierarchy. Those who gained control over grain wasted no time in donning the soldier's helmet, the king's crown and the bishop's mitre, to gain control over people.

The post-Stone Age *deconstraint* of the power impulse has never sat well with a species grounded in equality. It's probably why the history of human settlement is the history of protest, rebellion and revolution.

So, how to put the power urge back in its box?

In the West, Cleisthenes was the first to intuit that the shape of the system counted for more than laws and policies. He understood that until rule by the wealthy is replaced by a rational mechanics of government, just about any leader—benevolent or cruel, well-intended or selfish—will be moulded by that system.

Thus third draft democracy has no 'policies' beyond the shape of the system. It doesn't compete with the political ideologies—not with socialism, nor capitalism, nor today's 'free market' dogma. It will undoubtedly allow elements of several ideologies into governance, from one jurisdiction to the next. But it isn't comparable to any of them, as it's not, finally, a set of decisions, but a system of decision-making.

No *ism* has the versatility to combat the risks of our era. As we'll see in Part Seven, humans are not ideological creatures anyway. Like sleep and waking—male and female—our 'conservatism' and 'progressivism' are not warring tendencies: they exist to co-exist.

The universality of this pattern is nicely captured by the Taoist *taijitu* (yin-yang) symbol—which was also, by other names, on the shields of the Western Roman infantry,[2] and indeed goes back to Neolithic Europe. In the *taijitu,* the white

and black zones curve into each other, as if they're trying to merge. Light and darkness stake a claim in the middle of each other's territory—with a white dot in the black zone, and a black dot in the white. The *taijitu* suggests that what appears to be 'opposite' might actually be 'complementary'.

Democracy is so lethal to special interests that it has been subject to a kind of permanent counter-revolution. That millennia-long crusade suggests that it remains the most radical idea in society.

But a vehicle built in the 18th Century, however elegant, cannot bear the heavy freight of the modern age. Constitutional redesign is more pressing than reforming banks, halting wars or reducing ocean pollution, as ignoring it ensures that victories on these fronts will continue to be hard-won, costly and occasional.

Part Two
The upstream principle

Now is the seed-time of Continental union... The least fracture now will be like a name engraved with the point of a pin on the tender rind of a young oak; the wound would enlarge with the tree, and posterity read it in full-grown characters.[1]

— Thomas Paine in *Common Sense*
(January 1776)

Chapter 7
A problem has a family tree

An ailment is best understood when you see the full cycle of events that generated it. So it's an important exercise to look beyond the bad policy and mediocre leaders that shape our era: to the collared information, legislative capture and public disengagement that permitted them to multiply. Causes, too, have causes. If you want to end a problem (or prevent it from ever leaving *Otzar*) it pays to go upstream in the cascade of events.

To make a society function more rationally, how far upstream would that be?

Psychotherapy or brainwashing for an entire population would be well upstream—but they are, respectively, impossible and undesirable. Getting everyone to join the same religion, or political party, is probably both.

If we want to change the way a society functions, to the benefit of the largest number, a pragmatic place to begin is the constitution: the law that gives rise to the laws that shape the society that envelops the individual.

To illustrate the point: slaughterhouse workers in the US have seen their real wages fall by fifty percent since the dawn of the neoliberal revolution in 1975. Work conditions have also plummeted, and accident rates have soared.[1] [2] It's technically correct—

but meaningless—to say that all this flowed from changes to company policies. The journey toward low slaughterhouse wages began well before that—in the decision made by corporations to invest in politics. That journey, in turn, was made possible by the US and the state constitutions, which place no meaningful limits on the purchase of government legislation.[3] Thus, legislatures have passed laws that promote deregulation, industry consolidation and union busting—which, in turn, gave firms the power to depress wages and conditions.[4]

The decision to invest in politics was not specific to slaughtermen. It was made much higher up the decision-tree, and has affected nearly every part of national life. For instance, it gave rise to the mass foreclosures of the Global Financial Crisis, which in turn converted millions of home-owners to renters—which, years later during the pandemic, led to a surge of evictions.[5]

Plutocracy, the capture of political power by organized wealth, works 'horizontally'—across hundreds of overlapping issues—but also 'vertically' in time: producing event-cascades that last for decades. Thus problems like slaughtermen's wages have many ancestors and siblings.

You can't generally fix these 'families' of problems within the system that generated them. If a problem becomes system-wide—or persists for years, against the public interest, and defying all logic—it's probably the system that is causing it.

Event-cascades can also be rational and positive—the chapters ahead are filled with examples—and the idea of third draft democracy is to seed these positive cascades in place of our existing ones, which are approaching disorder. The proportional representation voting system (PR), for example (which we look at in Part Five) captures more 'nuance' in the voter's intention—leading to:

Small parties and outsiders doing better at the polls →
→ Because voters see this, significantly more of them show up to vote →
→ Both those things lead to power being shared more widely, often via stable coalition governments →

→ Which in turn yield more fiscal surpluses, and less income inequality, carbon emissions and military spending.

An 'upstream' approach to decisions—to making good ones and preventing bad ones—may be less exciting than the vivid brawls of daily politics. But it will create policy that is cheaper, better-supported and more durable.

Carl Jung wrote:

> I have frequently seen people become neurotic when they content themselves with inadequate or wrong answers to the questions of life.[6]

One reason our politics is so frustrating—indeed so neurotic—is that it's bogged down in issues no-one can solve at the level on which they're being addressed.

Because of this downstream focus, the role of democracy—once forward-looking and creative—is now to administer social, economic and environmental patch-ups. It has morphed into the ambulance following the neoliberal parade.

This is the *architecture of repair*—a trillion-dollar infrastructure to mend what was preventable: collapsed banks, oil spills, terrorism, poverty, and free-wheeling pandemics.

Let's look at the three most prominent crises of the last generation—the War on Terror, the Global Financial Crisis and the COVID-19 pandemic—and try to trace them to their roots.

Chapter 8
The war on terror

Fig. 2.1: Arlington National Cemetery, Virginia, at Christmas

Wars are always profitable, but multi-decade quagmires —such as the Indochina War, and more recently the War on Terror—can lock in cashflow for as long as a generation.

To better illuminate its causal chain, I'll work *backwards* through the War on Terror: from its downstream effects up to its execution; and then from its execution back to its causes.

Downstream

When much of Syria rose against its government in 2011, the conflagration was soon joined by ISIS—the 'Islamic State'. ISIS had made its way across the border from Iraq, where it had grown in strength as a result of the US occupation, and the ensuing civil war.

By 2014, ISIS controlled most of Syria's oil and gas production, and one-third of Iraq's territory, and had metastasized to 18 countries worldwide. It captured major cities, destroyed heritage sites, began a genocide against the Yazidi people, and perpetrated some of the cruellest mass executions since the Middle Ages.

ISIS cells also killed hundreds in terror attacks in Tunis, Suruç (Turkey), Beirut, Paris, Aden, Brussels, Nice, Kabul, Istanbul, St Petersburg, Manchester and Tehran.[1] Attacks inspired by ISIS included a fatal siege in Sydney, and bombings in New York.[2] In the process of murdering 49 people in an Orlando nightclub in 2016, Omar Mateen posted to Facebook:

> You kill innocent women and children by doing us airstrikes. Now taste the Islamic state vengeance.[3]

Back on its home turf, ISIS produced a booklet on the management of female sex slaves, which prescribed when a prepubescent girl could be raped.[4] When in control of Mosul and Raqqa, it put captive women on display in slave markets with price tags, and advertised them on WhatsApp.[5] In 2017, the group was denounced for 'extremism'—by al-Qaeda.

In such a fashion had the invasion of Iraq multiplied fanatics.

About 4.5 million people had died in America's 'post-9/11 warzones' by 2023—not only from direct violence, but from food insecurity, destruction of health infrastructure, environmental contamination, and economic collapse.[6]

For the developed world, the invasion set off a long train of costly 'repair' events that continue to the present. There was not only the worldwide effort to defend against *jihadis*, and to mop up the damage they caused, but the enormous job of rebuilding Iraq.

Another such effort was (and is) the resettlement of refugees. For the well-connected, this can be as lucrative as flattening their cities of origin. For example, in 2021 the Australian company Canstruct, a donor to the governing Liberal Party, was awarded its eighth contract to run a detention centre for asylum-seekers—many from 'War on Terror' countries.[7] These contracts are neither open nor competitive; over the objections of the auditor-general, their values were sometimes unilaterally increased by the government by such multiples as 4,500%.

Their total cost to date is $AU1.5 billion.[a] In July 2021, the Canstruct centre held 108 asylum-seekers: a cost to the taxpayer of $AU8,800 per day per inmate.[8]

For me, the War on Terror incarnates in Dara, a ten-year-old Kurdish girl I met in in the Moria refugee camp on the Greek island of Lesbos. Dara had seen her home town of Kobane, in northern Syria, occupied by ISIS, then levelled in the fighting to recapture it.[9] In her six months on Lesbos, she'd taught herself English and Greek. She was not only extremely bright but very sweet-natured. Despite fasting from dawn till dusk (it was Ramadan) she constantly brought me snacks and cups of tea.

On the phone they shared, Dara's family showed me video of the town's rubble, replete with dead babies and body parts. They'd spent a month on the road to Greece, in which time Dara hadn't eaten a full meal.

There are many Daras. By 2021, when the Syrian Civil War entered its 11th year, it had produced 6.6 million refugees, and 6.7 million internally displaced people.[10] It's impossible to say what portion of this was caused by ISIS, and other factors that grew from the US occupation of Iraq. But the Iraqi Civil War (an explicit by-product of the War on Terror) had created 4.7 million refugees by 2008: perhaps 16% of Iraq's population. Seventeen

---

a   The value of 1 Australian dollar has averaged about 70 US cents since 2018.

years after the American invasion there were still 1.4 million internally displaced Iraqis.[11]

A study by Brown University, published in September 2020, found that the eight most violent of the wars against terror in which the US was involved—in Afghanistan, Pakistan, Iraq, Libya, Syria, Yemen, Somalia and the Philippines—have displaced between 37 and 59 million people.[12]

Immediate costs

No plausible estimate of Iraqi deaths from the 2003 invasion puts the toll lower than the World Health Organization's 150,000 to mid-2006.[13] The Iraq Body Count project put it near 200,000 to 2019, though it acknowledges this may be an undercount.[14,b]

Come on, let us shoot!

Fig. 2.2: Baghdad, 2007: US helicopter attack that killed 12 to 18 civilians. (From a US military video leaked to WikiLeaks.)

A study by *The Lancet* estimated 655,000 'excess Iraqi deaths as a consequence of the war', again to mid-2006.[15] This nationwide study had families produce death certificates to validate claims. It

---

b 'Sources for Figures' at the back of the book tells you where photos, illustrations etc come from. Where relevant, the listing will give you the citation number for the information in the caption.

was described as 'close to best practice' by the Chief Scientific Advisor to the UK Defence Ministry.[16]

In 2015, Physicians for Social Responsibility conducted a 'meta-study' of all existing data, to gain as 'realistic an estimate as possible of the total body count in the three main war zones Iraq, Afghanistan and Pakistan during 12 years of "war on terrorism"'.[17] It found

> that the war has, directly or indirectly, killed around 1 million people in Iraq, 220,000 in Afghanistan and 80,000 in Pakistan, i.e. a total of around 1.3 million. Not included in this figure are further war zones such as Yemen... And this is only a conservative estimate. The total number of deaths in the three countries named above could also be in excess of 2 million.[18]

Then there are the financial costs:

To 2014, the War on Terror—in Iraq, Afghanistan and elsewhere—had cost the US government $1.6 trillion,[c] according to the Congressional Research Service.[19]

Nobel Prize-winning economist Joseph Stiglitz and his colleague, Linda Bilmes, did an analysis of the Iraq War's costs that included those the government had overlooked or hidden—for instance the cost of borrowing money to fund the war, and of caring for grievously injured soldiers. Their total was more than $3 trillion. They estimated that the war probably cost the rest of the world the same amount again.[20]

Stiglitz and Bilmes point out that *one* trillion dollars would have paid for

> 8 million housing units, or 15 million public school teachers, or healthcare for 530 million children for a year, or scholarships to university for 43 million students. Three trillion could have fixed America's social security problem for half a century.[21]

A third study, done in 2018 at Brown University in Rhode

---

[c] Unless otherwise stated, all dollar amounts in the book are USD.

Island, estimates the costs and future obligations of America's wars in Iraq, Syria, Afghanistan and Pakistan at $5.9 trillion.[22]

In 2011 dollars, World War Two cost the United States $4 trillion.[23]

Root causes

It's harder to get rich and powerful in Washington during peace-time, so our leaders have a built-in bias for war.[24]

— Tucker Carlson

How was the War on Terror launched—and why?

Single-issue explanations for big events are obviously suspect. For example, the centrepiece of the war—the occupation of Iraq—had numerous causes, including media groupthink, and the influences of biblical prophecy, racism and jingoism.

A bit more clarity emerges if we apply the ancient criterion of *cui bono*—'who benefits?'

It doesn't seem to have been ordinary Iraqis, or ordinary Americans. In Iraq, perhaps 5% of the population was killed, perhaps 16% became refugees, and no democracy worthy of the name was established. ISIS created mayhem in western Iraq until 2017—many of its units led by men radicalized by the US invasion.[25]

In the United States after 2003, terrorism worsened, surveillance of the public intensified, and by mid-2024 the federal budget had blown out to a degree once deemed unthinkable.

So, who *did* benefit? That story might begin in early 2003, when Lawrence Wilkerson compiled a dossier for his boss, Secretary of State Colin Powell. The dossier was an array of evidence in three subject areas: Saddam Hussein's supposed mobile biological laboratories, chemical weapons stocks and active nuclear program. It also claimed that Saddam was harboring al-Qaeda leader Abu Al-Zarqawi.[26]

Before laying these claims before the UN Security Council in February 2003, Powell was warned by his department that many of them were 'weak', 'not credible' or 'highly questionable'.[27] But, under pressure from the President and Vice President, Powell went to the UN:

> My colleagues, every statement I make today is backed up by sources, solid sources. These are not assertions. What we're giving you are facts and conclusions based on solid intelligence.[28]

Wilkerson later reflected:

> My participation in that presentation at the UN constitutes the lowest point in my professional life. I participated in a hoax on the American people... The three most essential parts of that presentation turned out to be absolutely false.[29]

So did the claim that Saddam was harboring Abu Al-Zarqawi.

Much of the intelligence that Wilkerson, Powell and Bush relied on flowed from a small group inside the Pentagon, calling itself 'the Cabal'. The 'Cabal's' influence, according to journalist Seymour Hersh,

> rivalled both the CIA and the Pentagon's own Defense Intelligence Agency, the DIA, as President Bush's main source of intelligence regarding Iraq's possible possession of weapons of mass destruction and connection with Al Qaeda.[30] [d]

The 2003 invasion was given a series of changing public rationales: WMD, curbing terrorism, ending human rights abuses, bringing democracy—none of which ultimately survived scrutiny. What was the true rationale?

---

[d] A similar extra-Constitutional cabal—dubbed 'the Enterprise'—took shape in the White House in the 1980s, to establish and fund the murderous Nicaraguan *Contras*. The group was described by journalist Bill Moyers as 'creating that unsupervised power so feared by the framers of our Constitution'. Some of its members had been part of the cabal that overthrew the democratic government of Iran in 1953. These cabals (another was Richard Nixon's Watergate 'Plumbers') repeatedly escape detection, cause mayhem around the world, and are a strong argument for the failure of the presidential system, and of second draft democracy generally.

One place to find answers would be the Project for the New American Century (PNAC), founded in 1997. PNAC was a think tank bankrolled by foundations funded by companies involved in ammunition and chemicals,[31] industrial automation,[32] banking, media, and oil.[33]

In 1997, PNAC issued a document calling for large-scale re-armament and 'global military domination' by the US, as well as beefed-up defence of the 'American homeland'. In 1998, it called for a military strategy aimed 'above all, at the removal of Saddam Hussein's regime from power'.[34] In 2000, a PNAC document stated that 'the unresolved conflict with Iraq provides the imme-diate justification' for the United States 'to play a more permanent role in Gulf regional security'.[35]

PNAC's ideas percolated into the mind of George W Bush in the years leading up to his presidency, usually via others, such as his brother Jeb, and Richard Cheney—both PNAC foundation signatories. As Bush prepared to take office, Vice President-elect Cheney was put in charge of the transition. As a result, PNAC 'names' such as Wolfowitz, Cohen, Rumsfeld, Libby, Bolton, Abrams and Perle were appointed to manage the administration's foreign policy.[36]

So it was that Paul Wolfowitz, Assistant Defense Secretary under Donald Rumsfeld, established 'the Cabal'—the group providing the administration with a steady stream of false informa-tion on Iraqi WMD.[37]

Corporate-sponsored think tanks across the political spectrum supported the cause. For example, the Brookings Institution worked on liberal journalists and politicians: ultimately making the war a bipartisan effort backed by many leading Democrats.

And, in the words of General William Odom, former director of the National Security Agency:

> It's pretty hard to imagine us going into Iraq without the strong lobbying efforts from AIPAC and the neocons.[38]

The financial supporters of AIPAC—the American Israel Public Affairs Committee—are not declarable, but there appear to be only two major ones, who donate in the tens of millions of dollars.[39]

The War on Terror underlined the difficulty in distinguishing politics, business and think tanks from each other. In personnel terms, there was often little difference. In the think tanks that conceived the Iraq invasion, the administration that launched it, and the corporations that gained from it, the same names recur. Richard Cheney (Halliburton, PNAC, White House) and Donald Rumsfeld (various defense contractors, PNAC, White House[40]) are only the best-known. Richard Perle was involved in planning the War on Terror inside PNAC, implementing it in the Bush Administration, and profiting from it as a businessman.[41]

Just before the invasion, Cheney's former company, Halliburton, was awarded a secret, no-bid contract to restore and operate Iraq's oil fields.[42]

The 70 companies engaged to reconstruct Afghanistan and Iraq received a total of $8 billion in contracts—Halliburton being the top recipient.[43] The politician to whom the 70 had contributed the most money was George W Bush.[44]

General Wesley Clark, former supreme commander of NATO, observed:

> This country was taken over by a group of people with a policy coup—Wolfowitz and Cheney and Rumsfeld. And you could name another half-dozen collaborators from the Project for the New American Century.[45]

In the lead-up to war, MSNBC—a key media cheerleader— was owned by GE, which supplied and maintained many of the weapons systems deployed in Iraq. Nearly all the experts MSNBC interviewed were pro-war. In February 2003, when the host of its top-rated show, *Donahue,* expressed skepticism about the war, his show was cancelled. This (a leaked memo revealed) was to remove from the airwaves 'a home for the liberal anti-war agenda'.[46]

The one-sided narrative was not confined to MSNBC. In American TV coverage overall, 64% of interviewees were pro-war and 10% opposed.[47]

The notion—popular at the time—that the Coalition had failed to do any serious planning for post-war Iraq was not true for the oil industry.[48] Shortly before the invasion, investigative journalist Greg Palast was leaked a Bush Administration plan for Iraq's post-invasion economy. The plan was written by the State Department, and banking, chemical and oil industry men. It was, he writes:

> A highly detailed program, begun years before the tanks rolled, for imposing a new regime of low taxes on big business, and quick sales of Iraq's banks and bridges—in fact, 'ALL state enterprises'—to foreign operators…
>
> [T]he secret team included executives from Royal-Dutch Shell and ChevronTexaco… The oil section of the Plan…calls for Iraqis to sell off to 'IOCs' (international oil companies) the nation's 'downstream' assets—that is, the refineries, pipelines and ports that, unless under armed occupation, a Mideast nation would be loathe to give up.[49]

After the invasion, the Americans cancelled the promised early elections, so there would be no democratic interference in the project of relieving Iraq of its oil assets.

In line with the PNAC blueprint, Bush in 2007 pressured the Iraqi government to pass an oil law that would, in the words of *The New York Times*, 'allow much (if not most) of Iraq's oil revenues to flow out of the country and into the pockets of international oil companies'.[50]

As British journalist Greg Muttitt described it:

> Bush was talking to [Iraqi prime minister] Maliki every two weeks, and he was constantly saying, 'Where is our oil law?'… Maliki said in around March of 2007 he understood very clearly from American officials that if they didn't get their oil law they would be looking to remove him from office.[51]

The operation was not inconsistent with American history.

Chapter 8

Major General Smedley Butler, the most highly decorated Marine Corps officer of his era, wrote in 1935:

> I helped make Mexico and especially Tampico safe for American oil interests in 1914. I helped make Haiti and Cuba a decent place for the National City Bank boys to collect revenues in. I helped in the raping of half a dozen Central American republics for the benefit of Wall Street. The record of racketeering is long. I helped purify Nicaragua for the international banking house of Brown Brothers 1909-12. I brought light to the Dominican Republic for American sugar interests in 1916. I helped make Honduras 'right' for American fruit companies in 1903. In China in 1927 I helped see to it that Standard Oil went its way unmolested.
>
> During those years, I had, as the boys in the back room would say, a swell racket. I was rewarded with honors, medals, promotion. Looking back on it, I feel I might have given Al Capone a few hints. The best he could do was to operate his racket in three districts. I operated on three continents.[52]

Fig. 2.3: Butler in China, 1901, helping to put down the Boxer Rebellion. After Britain, France, Japan, Germany & Russia carved China into 'spheres of influence', the 'Boxers' (a coalition of societies practising martial arts) rose up to expel the foreigners. An international expeditionary force, including Americans, defeated the rebellion.

After Butler's time, super-profits continued through the Korea and Indochina wars, and numerous smaller ones—most featuring the same corporations that later made windfall profits in Iraq.

Chief among them, in this era, was Brown & Root—since swallowed by Halliburton—which financed the political career of Lyndon Baines Johnson. Once he became president, Johnson simultaneously escalated the Indochina War and steered contracts to the company to build ports, airports and military bases in Vietnam.

In that tragic enterprise, writes historian Barbara Tuchman, America's Congressmen, too, 'were in large part willing captives of the giant identified by Eisenhower as the military-industrial complex'.[53]

This model, then, has been in place for a long time. Were there alternatives?

Had Western politics been conducted rationally, Iraq would still be under a disarmed Saddam (he would have turned 87 in 2024) or a successor. Instead of a 20-year interlude of slaughter, corruption and incompetence, Afghanistan would have endured the years 2001 to 2021 under the Taliban.

These are miserable scenarios, but they're better than what eventuated. ISIS would likely never have existed. Most of the million people who died in Iraq (including 4,400 US service personnel) would have lived. Millions of Iraqis, Afghans and others now in refugee camps would be in their homes.

It was the War on Terror, perhaps more than any other event, that caused much of the world to cease buying the Western narrative—seeing its talk of democracy and human rights as little more than hypocrisy. In this, it achieved what three-quarters of a century of communist propaganda had failed to do.

Coda

A massive study of how the United States went to war in Indochina, conducted by the Pentagon…led its 30 to 40 authors and researchers to many broad conclusions and specific findings, including the following:

Chapter 8

That the Johnson Administration, though the President was reluctant and hesitant to take the final decisions, intensified the covert warfare against North Vietnam and began planning in the spring of 1964 to wage overt war, a full year before it publicly revealed the depth of its involvement and its fear of defeat.[54]

— *New York Times*, June 13, 1971

A confidential trove of government documents obtained by The Washington Post reveals that senior U.S. officials failed to tell the truth about the war in Afghanistan throughout the 18-year campaign, making rosy pronouncements they knew to be false and hiding unmistakable evidence the war had become unwinnable.[55]

— Washington *Post*, December 9, 2019

Examining the financial incentives in modern American wars—and discarding the rhetoric that surrounds them—seems to unveil Establishment thinking with some clarity: a long war is better than a short one, a loss is as good as a win, and public opposition means little so long as it comes late enough. When risk is wholly outsourced, national unity and public revenue—even military victory and political reputation—can be gambled away for commercial success.

In the War on Terror, many of the same companies

- sponsored the think tanks that designed it
- bankrolled the leaders who launched it
- supplied the weaponry it was fought with
- and rebuilt the countries that weaponry destroyed.

The war planning that began inside PNAC in the 1990s—a decade before she was born—led eventually to Dara living, in 2018, in a hepatitis-prone refugee camp thousands of miles from her home.

Behind the armies that dispossessed her walked another army

—of oil men with draft action plans and check books. Behind them lay a constitutional landscape that legitimated what they did, and ensured it would be subject to little public scrutiny.

The chain of events from this constitutional system to Dara is the Upstream Principle.

Chapter 9
The global financial crisis

A second, shorter illustration of the principle is the Global Financial Crisis (GFC) that began in 2007-8.

There were numerous causes of the GFC—though a flowchart depicting its central ones might look something like this:

After holding hearings, and reviewing millions of documents, the Senate Subcommittee on Investigations identified all of those causes but the first.[1]

The committee did draw attention to the Office of Thrift Supervision—which described the banks it was meant to regulate as 'constituents'; and the regulator of credit rating agencies, which allowed Wall Street firms to pay the agencies to rate them. An agency could thus be 'run out of town' for not providing a AAA rating. Ninety percent of AAA ratings the agencies gave to subprime mortgage-backed securities were later downgraded to junk.

Unmolested by regulators, banks sold complex, risky financial products to investors who did not understand them—then placed 'short' bets on these products, profiting handsomely when their values fell and their clients lost money. Goldman Sachs went one better: arranging for short bets on its own products, and *then* selling them to clients—in one case earning $1.7 billion in the process.

The finance sector is the largest donor of federal campaign funding in the US—handing over hundreds of millions of dollars each election cycle.[2] For example, between 1990 and 2007 it gave $6.9 million to the influential Senator Joe Biden—who proved a reliable vote in the repeal of the Glass-Steagall Act. Glass-Steagall had separated the ownership of financial institutions from that of risky investment firms. Its repeal is seen by many as a key cause of the GFC.[3]

Another factor in the crisis was revolving door employment between government and banks.

By exerting political influence in the years to 2009, Lawrence Summers—a hedge fund manager—had intervened to prevent regulation of derivatives, and Robert Rubin (26 years at Goldman Sachs) was instrumental to the Glass-Steagall repeal. On his election, Barack Obama appointed them both as key economic advisors—just in time to devise a response to the Global Financial Crisis for which they were significantly responsible.[4]

A second report on the GFC was produced by the Financial Crisis Inquiry Commission. Topping its list of causes was 'widespread failures in financial regulation and supervision':

> The sentries were not at their posts, in no small part due to the widely accepted faith in the selfcorrecting nature of the markets and the ability of financial institutions to effectively police themselves. More than 30 years of deregulation and reliance on selfregulation by financial institutions, championed by former Federal Reserve chairman Alan Greenspan and others, supported by successive administrations and Congresses, and actively

pushed by the powerful financial industry at every turn, had stripped away key safeguards.[5]

A UN report on the crisis worldwide found 'poor governance' to be at its core.[6] Simon Johnson, the IMF's chief economist in 2007 and 2008, compared the crisis to the various national bailouts he'd taken part in:

> Typically, these countries are in a desperate economic situation for one simple reason—the powerful elites within them over-reached in good times and took too many risks... They reckon —correctly, in most cases—that their political connections will allow them to push onto the government any substantial problems that arise.[7]

The 2008 crisis arose, Johnson wrote, for the same reasons: the 'confluence of campaign finance, personal connections, and ideology' brought 'a river of deregulatory policies'. The result was 'an ever-increasing volume of transactions founded on a relatively small base of actual physical assets'. When the crash came, government responded with 'delay, lack of transparency and an unwillingness to upset the financial sector'—which, he added, has 'a veto over public policy'. Thus:

> The second problem the U.S. faces—the power of the oligarchy —is just as important as the immediate crisis of lending.[8]

In a rational system, the public could expect dramatic action to ensure that such a crisis could never happen again. As campaign finance expert Thomas Ferguson noted, in 2009 many people vested such hopes in the incoming US President, Barack Obama. The voters, Ferguson observed in 2010, 'had elected a Democratic president on a promise of "Change", with both houses of Congress solidly Democratic'. Instead

> the administration lavished aid on the financial sector. The spectacle of the government aiding bankers, who turned around and

paid themselves record bonuses, has just been unbearable for millions of people…

The Obama campaign's dependence on money and personnel from the financial sector was clear to anyone who looked, even before he won the nomination. For years I've promised people that I'll tell you who bought your candidate before you vote for him or her, by simply applying my 'investment theory of political parties'. When I analyzed the early money in Obama's campaign in March 2008, it was impossible not to see that many of the people responsible for the financial crisis were major Obama supporters.

As I wrote, serious financial reform would not be on President Obama's agenda.[9]

The US recession beginning in 2008 led to lost output of up to $10 trillion by 2009. By 2011, the value of home equity had dropped by $9.1 trillion,[10] and 8.7 million jobs had been lost.[11]

Fines were levied on some offending financial institutions, at a fraction of their fraudulently obtained profits. No prosecutions of Wall Street offenders were launched. Indeed, many of the architects of the 2008 crash were hired not only into the first and second Obama administrations, but the Trump[12] and Biden[13] administrations thereafter.

Chapter 10
The COVID pandemic

In 2019, medical historian Frank Snowden wrote, rather presciently:

> Epidemic diseases are not random events that affect societies capriciously and without warning... To study them is to understand that society's structure, its standard of living, and its political priorities.[1]

For anyone making such an argument, COVID-19 certainly delivered.

By 2024, the year this book went to press, many aspects of the pandemic—viral origins, masks, lockdowns, vaccines—had become subject to fierce dispute, even among experts. Whilst the results of the War on Terror and the GFC can now be clearly judged, there's still little consensus on how well our governments managed the pandemic.

But third draft democracy is *metapolitics*—to do with how decisions are made, not what they should be. And we *can* examine how those pandemic decisions were made: these facts are not that contentious.

Examining the entire pandemic would require a book in itself, so I'll select vaccines—probably the highest-profile of the pandemic issues—as a case study. We'll look at (i) the incentives within each stage of vaccine development and (ii) how transparent each stage is.

The way society develops, regulates, promotes and prescribes the chemicals that are legally injected into our bloodstreams should tell us much about how governance constellates above us, information around us, and perceptions within us.

1. Incentives for vaccine-makers

The incentive for every player in the vaccine development game is of course money—profits, salaries, fees, kickbacks, gifts, and so on. The further you go down the development pipeline (below), the less visible this incentive is. So with vaccine-makers— at the top of the pipeline—the incentive is in the plainest sight.

For these manufacturers, revenue flows from two sources—or, rather, from one source wearing two hats: the taxpayer and the consumer.

The taxpayer: The US government's contribution to developing the COVID vaccines was $18-23 billion, $19.3 billion or $39.5 billion—depending on which estimate you read.[2] This support goes back to the vaccines' pre-history—the early 2000s— when the mRNA technology was developed at the University of Pennsylvania with government funding.[3]

Little of the money had conditions attached. Drug companies held onto the patents, and banked most of the profits.[4]

The consumer: By the end of 2021, the top three COVID vaccine-makers were between them making profits of $65,000 a minute—totalling $34 billion for the year.

A good portion of these profits flowed from vaccine supply contracts that indemnified the companies against 'adverse events' (side effects).[5] [6] Pharma had gained such powers over government (according to a study in the *Journal of Pharmaceutical Policy and Practice*) via 'state capture'.[7]

Transparency was scarce:

For example, Moderna in the US was contractually obliged to

disclose the extent of its taxpayer funding. But it declined to heed the contract—and the government declined to enforce it.[8] When the EU's first COVID vaccine supply contract was made public, nearly every bit of useful information (e.g. the price per dose and the rollout schedule) had been redacted.

Fig. 2.5: A released page from AstraZeneca's COVID vaccine supply contract with the UK Government (2021)

Most vaccine supply contracts didn't get that far. Transparency International surveyed 182 of them. Only 13 had been made public—most heavily redacted.[9]

Although very few indemnity clauses made it into public view, in those that did, the vaccine-maker was rendered immune from any liability for causing death, illness, disability or injury—mental or physical. The taxpayer would be paying for vaccine harms, not the vaccine-maker.

In Latin America, Pfizer made governments put up national assets such as central bank reserves, military bases and embassy buildings, to cover it against claims for vaccine side effects. These included any claims against the company for 'negligence, fraud or malice'. This only came out via leaks.[10]

Secrecy likewise surrounded EU President Ursula von der Leyen's negotiation of the world's largest COVID vaccine deal—for 900 million Pfizer doses.[11] Europe's Parliament,[12] its Court of Auditors,[13] its Public Prosecutor[14] and the European Ombudsman[15] all investigated. They had no success: von der Leyen was not talking. Critics were curious to know how it came about that the contracts she negotiated paid Pfizer €31 billion above the vaccines' production cost.[16]

In summary: The incentive of revenue proved a rational one, at least for drug companies: by the start of 2022, COVID vaccines were among the most lucrative products in history. Pfizer's revenues alone were greater than those of most nations.[17]

.

2. Incentives for clinical trial researchers

Those running COVID vaccine trials were mostly paid by the vaccine manufacturer. This enabled the company to set the ground rules, interpret the data, and bury the results if they were disappointing.

(It's probably for that reason that only 45% of COVID vaccine trial results were ever disclosed.[18])

By way of example, the *British Medical Journal* (*BMJ*) reported that

> Pfizer's pivotal covid vaccine trial was funded by the company and designed, run, analysed and authored by Pfizer employees.[19]

The majority of drug and vaccine trials overall are funded this way: 63%,[20] 68%[21], 75%[22] or 87%[23]—depending on study. Curiously, company-sponsored trials are much more successful than independent ones. Meta-analyses of hundreds of trials find that those sponsored by industry succeed between two and 20 times more often.[24]

Even more curiously, the opposite seems to be true for side effects. Company-sponsored trials report *less* of these. For example, company-sponsored trials of the Pfizer vaccine did not report a fraction of the side effects that an independent team found in Denmark in 2023.

The latter analysed the records of 10.8 million doses: finding that side effects were batch-dependent—with one batch causing them in 1-in-20 patients.[25][26] Neither Pfizer nor the regulator had noticed this.

Transparency:

The path from corporate check to scientific result is camouflaged by many factors. One of these is trial design. Richard Smith —former editor-in-chief of the *BMJ*—wrote in 2005:

> The companies seem to get the results they want not by fiddling the results, which would be far too crude…but by asking the 'right' questions… I must confess that it took me almost a quarter of a century editing for the *BMJ* to wake up to what was happening.[27]

Few COVID vaccine-makers made their trial 'protocols' (designs) public—and then only late, after public pressure.[28] When Transparency International (TI) analyzed 86 COVID vaccine trials, they found that 76 of them kept the protocol secret. This meant there was no way to spot design flaws that could have skewed results.[29]

As for the 'clinical study reports'—which describe the trial's methods and results—only two of the nine jurisdictions that TI studied mandated that these be shared with the public. The US and the UK, for example, did not.[30]

When it came to the more detailed 'raw' or 'patient-level' data —which would allow independent researchers to confirm the accuracy of the results—most of this was also suppressed. The *BMJ* lamented that

> despite the global rollout of covid-19 vaccines and treatments, the anonymised participant level data underlying the trials for these new products remain inaccessible to doctors, researchers, and the public—and are likely to remain that way for years to come.[31]

Thereafter, if any avenues of free disclosure remain, they can be chilled by court action. For example, when the European Medicines Agency began releasing even basic trial reports, drug companies launched lawsuits to try to stop it.[32] And if a trial scientist voices public concern about a drug, he can be sued by the maker for breach of contract.[33]

3. Incentives for contract research organizations (CROs)

Trials are often hived off to a 'contract research organization'. There are thousands of CROs worldwide, with a collective value of $73 billion.[34]

These entities have a built-in 'incentive' problem—as medical investigative journalist Jeanne Lenzer explains:

> CROs face a fundamental conflict of interest—if they do not please their commercial clients, they may be less likely to get more work from them.[35]

The weight of this incentive became clear in September 2021, when it emerged that a part of the US Pfizer vaccine trial was riddled with errors, malpractice and falsification of data. Samples were mislabeled, data retrospectively changed, and 'adverse events' not followed up. Staff who flagged these irregularities were 'targeted' by management at Ventavia, the CRO responsible.

Ventavia kept the findings to itself: management was concerned the company would be exposed by a Food and Drug Administration (FDA) inspection. They needn't have worried. Because of the FDA's own incentive structure (section 7., below), physical inspections of trials are now rare.

The Ventavia malpractice was only revealed when a regional director reported it to the FDA, then leaked it to the press. (She was fired within hours.)

Even then the FDA did not investigate. Three months later the agency approved the vaccine for emergency use—the irregularities were nowhere to be found in its report—and Pfizer went on to re-hire Ventavia to run four new COVID trials.[36]

4. Incentives for the trial committees

A drug or vaccine trial generally has an *independent data monitoring committee* (IDMC) to analyze data as it comes in—and to keep an eye on patient safety, and a trial's evolving endpoints.

Notwithstanding the word 'independent', the IDMC is usually appointed by the vaccine-maker—which drafts the committee's mission statement, and pays its members, and can replace the latter at will.[37]

A trial also has an *ethics committee*—to ensure the 'rights, safety and wellbeing of human subjects'. And it will, at times, need an *endpoint adjudication committee* and/or a *steering committee*—to ensure scientific integrity.

All of these are typically bankrolled by the vaccine-maker.[38]

5. Incentives for medical journals

Five large corporations own most medical journals—ownership concentration akin to that of mainstream media.[39] Shareholders of the five are mostly international investment houses and fund managers of the BlackRock and Vanguard variety—not companies or people whose principal interest is science or medicine.[40] [41] [42]

Medical journals are one of the most lucrative sectors of the publishing industry. *The Lancet,* for example, has an estimated annual revenue of $71 million.[43]

The journals make much of their income—sometimes all of it —from drug company advertising.[44] This gives pharma a lot of say over content: submissions that pass the editorial test can sometimes be vetoed by a journal's marketing department.[45] In narrow commercial terms, this can be prudent. When the *Annals of Internal Medicine* published a study showing that ads in journals were often inaccurate, drug companies withdrew their advertising. The journal lost between $1 and $1.5 million, and its two co-editors resigned.[46]

Journals are not only hit with sticks but fed with carrots. A journal that runs an article favorable to a vaccine may be rewarded with an order for glossy reprints, to be distributed to doctors as advertising. Such deals can yield a million dollars apiece.

Some journals need none of these incentives, as they are secretly owned by a drug company for the purpose of spruiking its drugs.[47] [48]

Transparency of authorship:

Many articles in medical journals are penned by *ghostwriters*. Studies with differing definitions and methods have put the incidence at 1%, 8%, 11%, 50%, 70%, 75% and 91%.[49]

Commonly, a ghostwriter is paid by the drug company to write a paper favorable to its drug or vaccine.[50] As he lacks scientific credentials, his paper will be credited to the scientists named as the 'principal authors'. The arrangement is kept from the public: even as far back as the paper's original Word document, all data that identifies the true author is stripped from the file properties.[51]

The 'medical communications' company DesignWrite starts with a first draft, sends it to the drug- or vaccine-maker for comment, then writes the second. Only thereafter is the paper's academic 'author' brought in. As the academic may not know anything about what he has 'authored', he'll get crib notes from DesignWrite so he can respond to peer reviewers' questions.[52]

Peer review itself—which might have shone light on such malfeasance—has not done so, according to former *BMJ* editor Richard Smith:

> Research into peer review has mostly failed to show benefit but has shown a substantial downside (slow, expensive, largely a lottery, wasteful of scientific time, fails to detect most errors, rejects the truly original, and doesn't guard against fraud).[53] [54] [55]

6. Incentives for the editors of medical journals

As with clinical trials, medical journals have a double layer of incentives. Not only are the journals themselves paid by drug- and vaccine-makers, but so are many of their editors.

A study of 52 influential American journals found that more than 50% of editors (senior, managing, associate, deputy and executive, as well as editors-in-chief) were being paid directly by the drug industry. The average annual payment was $27,500. The monies were for items like 'enrolling patients in a study', and 'food and beverage, royalties, honorariums, consulting fees, travel and entertainment'.[56]

Specialist journals are notably favored. Citing a study in the *BMJ*, Nephrologist Jason Fung wrote that in 2014:

> Each editor of the *Journal of the American College of Cardiology* received, on average $475,072 personally and another $119,407 for 'research'. With 35 editors, that's about $15 million in bribes to doctors. No wonder the *JACC* loves drugs and devices.[57]

7. Incentives for regulatory bodies

With trial scientists and medical journals compromised, one might hope that accountability—and objective judgement— would kick in when the vaccine reaches a regulator.

But the pharmaceutical industry has left little to chance. If even one player gives the wrong message, public skepticism might stir. A 'chorus' is required.

As regulators are such a critical part of the 'chorus', here there is a triple layer of incentives:

Firstly, national medicine regulators are mostly financed by the pharmaceutical industry in the form of fees.[58]

The regulator in the United States (the FDA) receives 65% of its funding from the industry. In Japan, the figure is 85%, in the UK 86%, and in Europe 89%. Australia's Therapeutic Goods Administration gets 96% of its funding from the drug and vaccine industry.[59]

Generally, a regulator doesn't have to work too hard for its fees. When the Australian regulator approved the Pfizer vaccine, for instance, standard practice applied: the TGA didn't read the patient data from the relevant study, and relied on a summary supplied by Pfizer.

The *BMJ* wonders whether this arrangement might have some-thing to do with the rash of drug and device scandals of recent years: opioids, joint prostheses, breast and contraceptive implants, cardiac stents, pacemakers, et al.[60] Under our present form of democracy, and the 'non-disclosure' that cloaks its workings, we will probably never know.

Secondly, a regulator will typically be advised by armslength bodies which supposedly critique its decisions objectively. For advice on COVID vaccine approvals, for example, Britain's regulator has the Commission on Human Medicine (CHM)—which it describes as an 'independent body'. It's not clear why, as the CHM is wholly funded by 'medicines licensing fees' from the drug industry.

A CHM subcommittee, the Paediatric Medicines Expert Advisory Group, is 'an independent advisory committee' that provides 'impartial advice' on child vaccines and medicines. Its impartial advice is funded by the drug industry.[61]

Thirdly, there are incentives for the individuals working in these agencies. In four separate studies of departing FDA employees, for instance, half to two-thirds went to work for a company whose drug they had approved.[62]

Transparency:

Regulatory assessments tend to be kept secret till they're of little use. The Australian Government published its January 2021 assessment of the Pfizer vaccine more than two years later, in March 2023—and then only because of a Freedom of Information request, which it fought for months. The eventual release was heavily redacted.

In response to a lawsuit seeking the data from its own Pfizer vaccine assessment, the FDA offered a staged release—one small section per month—till the year 2097. The plaintiffs declined the offer, on the ground that those involved in the case will by then 'have died of old age'.[63]

8. Incentives for those working in the biomedical research agencies

The US Government's biomedical research system disburses $30 billion from taxpayers to scientific grantees each year.

Hundreds of millions of these dollars flow back from corporations to government: and to individual government scientists and bureaucrats, for work they've done on a drug's development. Between 2009 and late 2023, Pfizer made 265 such grants to National Institutes of Health scientists, and Moderna 207.[64]

Transparency:

This definitive conflict-of-interest scenario unfolds amid sepulchral secrecy.[65]

In 2022, the watchdog group *OpenTheBooks* won a court order to get details of the 1,700 government employees who'd received such payments. The National Institutes of Health responded by supplying data to 2014 only—with corporation names and dollar amounts redacted. This included 23 payments to senior bureaucrat Anthony Fauci.[66]

9. Incentives for politicians

I do, yes—it's ten thousand sterling.[67]

> — Matt Hancock, the British health secretary (2018-21) who oversaw the COVID response —on being asked in 2023 if he had a daily rate for serving on a corporate advisory board. The interview was by fake 'recruiters'. Ex-chancellor Kwasi Kwarteng likewise agreed to a £10,000 daily payment. Both men were serving MPs.

The politicians who make decisions on vaccine development and rollout—and how much the public should know about each —appoint the health regulators, and also the bureaucrats who decide on government vaccine subsidies. They sign off on public health rules and messaging. They also sign off on large grants to drug companies for vaccine R&D.

And they influence whether a law is enforced. For instance, the FDA does not dispute that it's legally obliged to make its COVID vaccine assessments public. But, knowing that the political class has its back, it declines to do so.[68]

Members of this political class often go to a job at the vaccine-maker on retirement, or have come to government from such a company—and often enough both. (The latter are known as 'serial revolvers'.)

Australia's politicians and regulators, and the drug companies they shuttle to and from, work 'collaboratively', and resemble a well-established, sprawling family.[69] Some of Britain's top government health and science positions—including Chief Scientific Advisor—are occupied by former drug company executives.[70]

Under the Trump administration, the Health and Human Services secretary was the former president of Lilly USA, and the chief of the FDA resigned to take up a position at Pfizer. At the former's confirmation hearing, Senator Elizabeth Warren opined that his résumé 'reads like a how-to manual for profiting from government service'.[71]

The Biden administration, too, is replete with drug industry lobbyists, executives, lawyers and stock-holders.[72] Flowing the other way, nearly 340 former congressional staffers work for drug companies and their lobbyists. Many once staffed key pharma-related committees.[73]

This is plutocracy's cardio-vascular system: a continuous flow of personnel from corporation to government and back again.

10. Incentives in the vaccine injury reporting process

In 2021, Britain's regulator, the MHRA, moved to improve its vaccine 'adverse event' reporting by appointing Commonwealth Informatics—a 'pharmacovigilance' company. In the US, Commonwealth was already performing this task for the FDA's Adverse Event Reporting System.[74]

Commonwealth serves large pharmaceutical companies world-wide, including four of the top ten. Its owner, Qinesca Solutions, is a corporate giant with a slew of pharma clients of its own, including Pfizer.[75] A British MP gave a crisp summation of the incentive structure in this arrangement:

The contract has been given by the MHRA—who are 86% funded themselves by Big Pharma—to a company which is funded by Big Pharma, to investigate complaints against Big Pharma.[76]

11. Incentives for media

I've written a lot of things over the last few years—*The Daily Mail, The Telegraph, The Express*, and lots of other publications. For the first year or two [of the pandemic] we could write nothing about the origin of the virus... [And] the minute I questioned the efficacy of the vaccine—even though it had been edited in the usual *Daily Mail* style, it would get crushed at the last minute. I was expecting it to come out—and I was told by the editor, 'Something more important came up.' This was the trend that happened all over the place...

I was invited onto the BBC to do a program about the origin of the virus... They edited my contribution so it looked like I agreed that it came from an animal. Russian and Chinese radio and TV stations would have been proud of it.[77]

— Professor Angus Dalgleish, British physician, oncologist and pathologist

With trial scientists, trial committees, contract research organizations and medical journals (and their individual editors) largely on the drug company payroll: along with regulatory bodies (and those working in them), biomedical research agencies, politicians, and the vaccine injury reporting agencies: a late check on a COVID vaccine's safety and efficacy might have been media reportage.

But media, too, is part of the drug industry 'chorus'.

Pharmaceutical ad spending in the US was one billion dollars per month in 2022.[78] It made up 75% of the total ad spend on television.[79] During the pandemic, the US Government added to this sum by paying millions to *The Washington*

Post, *The LA Times*, NBC, CNN and Fox News to advertise COVID vaccines. Notably, potential critics such as BuzzFeed and Newsmax were also paid, along with hundreds of local newspapers and TV stations. *Blaze media*, which broke this story in 2022, reported that, collectively, these outlets went on to produce

> countless articles and video segments that were nearly uniformly positive about the vaccine in terms of both its efficacy and safety.[80]

As usual, the expenditure was kept secret from those who paid for it, and had to be unearthed via freedom of information requests.[81]

In December 2023, Tucker Carlson was asked if financial pressure from advertisers 'shaped things' on the news—or if this idea was just 'a boogie man that doesn't exist?':

> Oh, it not only exists but it defines news coverage. Especially on pharma. Because pharma is the biggest advertiser on television. If Pfizer is sponsoring your show, you're not going to question the facts. It's that simple. And, of course, that's why they're the biggest advertiser—so they can shape news coverage. That's the point.[82]

12. Incentives for social media companies

> Hey folks-Wanted to flag the below tweet and am wondering if we can get moving on the process of having it removed ASAP.[83]
>
> — Email to Twitter from the White House COVID-19 team, on a tweet from Robert F Kennedy Jr questioning COVID vaccine safety (2021)

Not to sound like a broken record, but how much content is

being demoted, and how effective are you at mitigating reach, and how quickly? [84]

> — Email from the White House director of
> digital strategy, asking Facebook about alleged
> COVID misinformation (2021)

Take some of the stuff around COVID… Unfortunately I think a lot of the Establishment…asked for a bunch of things to be censored that in retrospect ended being more debatable—or true. [85]

> — Mark Zuckerberg (2023)

For a social media company, an elementary goal is survival: so there is a strong incentive to stay on the right side of the government—which has the power to apply laws, including anti-monopoly law.

The central incentive, of course, is revenue—which rests almost solely on happy advertisers.

Global pharma and healthcare advertising on social media is worth $15.3 billion annually. For example, four of the top ten spenders on the Facebook app are drug advertisers. (The less effectual a drug is the more is spent to promote it.) [86] [87] [88]

These advertisers are also campaign contributors. Pharma contributed $4.7 billion to US federal politics between 1999 and 2018. [89] It gives to more than two-thirds of the members of the US Congress, [90] [91] and 2,400 state lawmakers. [92] The revolving door is also involved: many legislators, civil servants and ex-law enforcement officials have moved to drug companies and their 'anti-misinformation' arms since the pandemic began. For instance, Moderna's 'global intelligence' division is headed by Nikki Rutman, who spent nearly 20 years as an FBI analyst. in May 2023, Jonathan Van-Tam, Britain's former deputy chief medical officer—who oversaw supply contracts for COVID shots, and the investments in manufacturing—took a senior advisory role with Moderna. [93]

All this may shed light on why government officials were so quick to ask social media to censor posts that went against drug sector interests, and why the social media companies so readily obliged.

The Public Good Projects, an NGO funded by Pfizer and Moderna, co-ordinates many of these efforts. With the help of artificial intelligence, Moderna and PGP monitor 150 million websites, including MSM, independent media, social media and gaming sites. The focus is on dissident voices such as Michael Shellenberger, Russell Brand and Alex Berenson.

On Substack, Lee Fang reported that PGP helped with the deletion of posts from numerous social media platforms through 2021 and 2022—including accurate content that had 'the potential to fuel vaccine hesitancy':

> Emails from that period show that PGP routinely sent Excel lists of accounts to amplify on Twitter and others to de-platform.[94] [95]

PGP also 'helped Twitter to formulate its pandemic-related speech policies', Fang reported.

Thus, when Jay Bhattacharya, Professor of Medicine at Stanford University, published a study showing that the World Health Organization had originally overstated the COVID fatality rate by a factor of 17 times, he was put on a Twitter 'trends blacklist'—a tweak to the algorithm that ensured his posts would not trend.[96] [97] (His paper became the 55th most-read scientific paper in history.)

Transparency:

None of this information was released voluntarily—it all arrived in the public space via leaks. Indeed, Twitter in this period claimed, 'We do not shadow ban'—when in fact it had run a 'search blacklist', engaged in 'visibility filtering', and issued 'recent abuse strikes' and 'do not amplify' edicts.[98]

The existence of co-ordinated corporate-government COVID censorship of those from the left and right reached the ears of the public only after Elon Musk bought Twitter in late 2022, and released the relevant files. This is only the tip of what is now emerging as a large iceberg: a corporate and 'all-of-government' censorship partnership whose targets extend well beyond COVID critics (Part Five).

13. Incentives for doctors

Unsurprisingly, drug company monetary incentives percolate through the process we've been looking at right down to the level of prescribing doctors.

'Opinion leader' doctors do the best: receiving large consulting and speaking fees to promote specific drugs. In the five years to 2019, 700 US doctors received more than one million dollars each for such services.[99]

Regular MDs do not miss out. A company will often pay for a doctor's continuing professional education (which typically features the sponsor's drugs), or underwrite expensive holidays thinly disguised as conferences. Then there are more prosaic items like 'gifting branded as office supplies'.[100]

Such largesse, when it flowed from Purdue Pharma to encourage doctors to prescribe OxyContin, helped to kick-start the American opioid epidemic.[101]

In Britain, doctors on average receive £10,000 in 'education' from drug companies annually.[102] In 2016, 631,000 doctors— covering 65% of American patients—were given gifts such as travel, speaking fees and drug company stock. The total value was $8.2 billion.[103]

'Industry-physician interactions'—lunches, trips, gifts, speaking engagements, and so on—lead doctors worldwide not only to over-prescribe,[104] but to prescribe the donor's drug over cheaper, generic alternatives.[105]

The indoctrination of doctors by drug companies begins in medical school.[106] In 2004 Purdue Pharma funded a Canadian medical school course on pain management, wrote the textbook, and supplied the lecturer. The text described Purdue's drug OxyContin as a 'weak opioid'. As a result of this kind of marketing, Canada has its own opioid epidemic, which causes thousands of deaths per year.[107]

14. Incentives for patient advocacy groups, non-profits, professional associations, government health services

A modern plutocracy lives or dies by the *chorus effect*. Its messages, whether about a war, a financial system or a vaccine, flow to the public ear from an array of sources—expected and unexpected, central and marginal, official and unofficial—to create the impression of broad, diverse support. All this is achieved by a financial inducement for every player in the system, and even at its edges.

Those at its edges, indeed, are among the most useful—as entities such as patient groups, NGOs, professional associations and public health agencies are *presumed* to be giving their opinions freely, for no reward. This adds a vital layer of credibility.

So, how freely given are these opinions?

Patient groups: Various studies have found between 20% and 83% of these to be funded by pharma.[108] For instance, the American Heart Association receives tens of millions of dollars annually from Pfizer, AstraZeneca, GlaxoSmithKline, and other drug- and vaccine-makers.[109] In the US there's no requirement to report these payments—so they're seldom disclosed.[110]

To flesh out the *chorus effect*, pharma funds not only large patient groups such as the American Diabetes Association, but small, obscure ones like the Caring Ambassadors Program.

Drug companies are overt in pressuring patient group boards and staff to act in the company's interests.[111] This seems to have stopped many groups from complaining about high drug prices.[112] Indeed, industry-funded patient groups have lobbied the US Congress to *not* allow the import of cheaper drugs from Canada—in the interests of 'safety'.[113]

A patient group will also be paid to lobby a regulator to approve a drug or vaccine. Or it might assemble an 'expert panel' to pass judgement on it on the public's behalf. (The panel will be a group of doctors who are likewise on the industry payroll.)[114]

If a drug or vaccine is not government-subsidized, patient groups will be paid to complain about this—on 'affordability' grounds—via social media posts, press releases and submissions to government. A PR firm is then hired to generate media stories about the 'complaints'.[115]

Investing in patient groups is a significant part of drug company business. Studies reveal €6.4 million paid out in Sweden (2014-2018), €8.8 million in Denmark (2014–2019), $AU34 million in Australia (2013-2016), £57 million in Britain (2012-2016), and $680 million in the US in 2018 alone.[116]

The biggest contributors included companies that went on to make COVID vaccines, such as Merck, Johnson & Johnson and AstraZeneca.

Non-profits (NGOs) are another beneficiary of drug company generosity. For example, the US National Consumers League and the Immunization Partnership were given hundreds of thousands of dollars by Pfizer to lobby for mandatory COVID vaccinations (and were instructed to keep the donations quiet). Other beneficiaries are 'dark money' non-profits, or 'action networks', that lobby politicians on drug prices, alert the public to the 'dangers' of importing cheaper drugs, and get pro-pharma politicians elected. Pharma's US trade association gave more than half a billion dollars to these non-profits in 2020.[117]

Journalist Lee Fang writes that the *professional associations* for pharmacists and practitioners of preventive medicine, managed care, clinical pathology and emergency medicine

> signed a letter in support of the Biden administration mandate to require employers with 100 or more employees to require their employees to be fully vaccinated or tested at least weekly. The organizations all received individual grants from Pfizer.[118]

In Britain, the royal colleges—of general practitioners, physicians, surgeons, et al—received more than £9 million in donations from drug and device companies between 2015 and 2022. Pfizer was the largest donor.[119]

Finally, drug companies contribute millions of pounds to parts of Britain's *National Health Service*, and to individual NHS doctors. The money is to fund the 'redesign of patient services'— usually to maximize the purchase of the companies' drugs.[120]

End-to-end containment

This is an impressive state of anarchy.

How might one 'follow the science' in a regime like this?

And how many of these scenarios—perverse incentives, no transparency—apply to the other elements of the COVID response?

By mid-2024, official accounts of that response were being undermined by independent studies, a series of exposés, an unexplained global rise in 'excess deaths', and some humbling concessions by the WHO. Narratives on viral origins, school closures, the effectiveness of masks and prolonged intubation, the wisdom of vaccine mandates, and the reliability of government data, were shown to have been often dubious, sometimes wrong, and occasionally fraudulent. [121] [122] [123] [124] [125] [126] [127] [128] [129] [130] [131] [132]

No consensus has yet emerged on the safety and efficacy of the vaccines themselves. But by looking upstream, as we've done, it's clear they were evaluated in compromised circumstances. From lab to jab, every stage was sponsored by the one party with an overwhelming financial interest in the outcome.

You might call this *end-to-end containment*.

A plutocracy develops end-to-end containment in each major economic sector. The 'just war' narrative, for example, is built through investment in politicians, media, think tanks, schools, universities, astroturfing and lobbying (Part Three). As with vaccines, even the peripheral players are catered for: intelligence agencies put journalists on the payroll;[133] the military works with studios to make it look good in movies; the funds of independent media critics are frozen so they lose their platforms…[134]

A similar 'chorus' was assembled post-2008, to fumigate the reputation of the financial sector.

In each case, the goal is an ensemble of voices that support a certain viewpoint. Any critic who then arises seems 'uninformed'.

End-to-end containment is imposed on any narrative that significantly affects the disposition of wealth. (There are few attempts to condition the populace about nutrition or personal morals.) This is less a centralized conspiracy than money sponta-neously filling the holes in a dated constitutional order.

The lure of this money—high profits, generous salaries, large campaign donations—draws all players in the same direction: as a cold snap causes fuel companies to raise production, road repair teams to work overtime, and householders to shut their curtains—without anyone co-ordinating them.

Upstream of this approach to power and information is the political capture we'll encounter shortly, in Part Three.

Downstream of it, we have spin in place of news, war in place of peace, bubble economies in place of stability, and favors in place of governance.

Leaving the real world: the replication crisis

The story of the COVID vaccines is not unique in the field of biomedicine. The development of nearly every device, drug or vaccine is shaped by a similar list of incentives, and is likewise shielded from view by a meticulous regime of secrecy.

This lays the ground for the hundred tricks—woven through the process—by which something can be 'made true'. For example, in a trial report, an inconvenient dataset can be left out;[135] or a new 'expected outcome' can be inserted retrospectively, if the first one didn't deliver. (This 'outcome switching' is rife.)

Simpler again, inadequate endpoints can be set in the first place. In 2020, a *BMJ* analysis of four major COVID vaccine trial protocols found that none of them were designed to detect impor-tant outcomes—such as hospital admission or death. Instead,

> these mega-trials all set a primary endpoint of symptomatic covid-19 of essentially any severity… These studies seem designed to answer the easiest question in the least amount of time, not the most clinically relevant questions.[136]

Any study showing a drug or vaccine to have no efficacy, or dangerous side effects, is likely to be 'bottom-drawered'. It never sees light of day.[137] The resulting 'publication bias' has had lethal results. New companies can trial the drug, tweak the methodology to show it to 'work', and get it approved for market. Heart anti-arrhythmic drugs killed 100,000 Americans this way.[138]

Ninety-four percent of published antidepressant trials are successful. But when—in a rare feat of scholarship—researchers dug out all the unpublished trials, the overall success rate dropped to 51%.[139] In the published literature, the benefits of antidepressants are large; in reality, they're of 'small magnitude'.[140] [141]

You might guess that science arrived at in these ways would be fragile and inconsistent—would be wrong much of the time.

Over the last decade or two, a few curious researchers tried to replicate the findings of a range of existing studies, using improved and unbiased methodologies. The results were dismal. In two of the best-known analyses, the 'replication rates' of preclinical studies were 25% and 11%.[142] The first, in the journal *Nature*, was titled 'Believe it or not'. The second attempted to confirm 53 'landmark' studies in oncology—on which much modern cancer therapy is built. It succeeded in replicating only six.

In a survey by *Nature*, 67% of medical researchers, 77% of biologists and 87% of chemists had at one time or another tried and failed to reproduce another scientist's results. For all that, studies that can't be replicated are cited more often than those that have been.[143]

To find evidence of medical misrepresentation at scale, you don't need to look to the Old West or the New Age.[144] The authority of the august medical journals, the well-credentialed researchers, the 'gold standard' science, the 'stringent' government regulation, the media 'watchdogs', crumbles to the touch.

This radically pessimistic view is shared by many with the deepest knowledge and longest experience:

> It is simply no longer possible to believe much of the clinical research that is published, or to rely on the judgment of trusted physicians or authoritative medical guidelines. I take no pleasure in this conclusion, which I reached slowly and reluctantly.[145]

> — Marcia Angell, former editor-in-chief of *The New England Journal of Medicine* (2009)

Sadly I followed the same path and spelt out my disillusionment in my book. I wrote it in 2004, and since then my pessimism has deepened.[146]

> — Richard Smith, former editor of the *British Medical Journal* and chief executive of the BMJ Publishing Group—commenting in 2010 on the above quote from Marcia Angell.

Journals have devolved into information laundering operations for the pharmaceutical industry.

The case against science is straightforward: much of the scientific literature, perhaps half, may simply be untrue.[147]

> — Richard Horton, editor-in-chief of *The Lancet* (2015)

Our prescription drugs are the third leading cause of death after heart disease and cancer. Our drugs kill around 200,000 people in America every year…

Much of what the drug industry does fulfils the criteria for organized crime in US law. They behave in many ways like the Mafia does. They corrupt everyone they can corrupt. They have bought every type of person—even including ministers of health in some countries… The drug industry buys the professors first. Then chiefs of department, then chief physicians, and so on.[148]

> — Professor Peter Gøtzsche, co-founder of *The Cochrane Collaboration*

We like to imagine that medicine is based on evidence, and the results of fair tests. In reality, those tests are often profoundly flawed. We like to imagine that doctors are familiar with the research literature, when in reality much of it is hidden from them by drug companies. We like to imagine that doctors are well-educated, when in reality much of their education is funded by industry. We like to imagine that regulators only let effective drugs onto the market, when in reality they approve hopeless drugs, with data on side effects casually withheld from doctors and patients.[149]

> — Dr Ben Goldacre, in his best-seller *Bad Pharma* (2012)

There is increasing concern that in modern research, false findings may be the majority or even the vast majority of published research claims. However, this should not be surprising. It can be proven that most claimed research findings are false.[150]

National and federal research funds are funneled almost exclusively to research with little relevance to health outcomes.[151]

> — John Ioannidis, holder of four professorships at Stanford University, including Statistics and Medicine

Chapter 11
Throwing away our advantages

Between them, and in less than a generation, the War on Terror, the GFC and the pandemic brought about the greatest redistribution of global wealth since the 1930s. Millions of words have been written about each—however the political system that made them inevitable generally went unmentioned. With all three crises, the critiques (the articles, the books, the podcasts) focused on the decisions, rather than the system of which those decisions were a natural consequence.

If we want to reverse a recurring failure, it needs to be at the first level—the level of the system—not at the level of each individual failure. Until it makes that shift, a civilization that has made a Level 1 error will see a procession of Level 2 solutions crash and burn.

> Donald Trump and Barack Obama both ran on the platform that they were going to fundamentally alter American foreign policy. They were going to reduce our commitments around the world, they were going to get out of the Forever Wars, not start any more Forever Wars, and so on. Both of them were defeated in the end by the foreign policy establishment.[1]
>
> — Political scientist John Mearsheimer

So it was with COVID: no commentary ventured upstream, to note that the pandemic in general and vaccines in particular would have been managed better, and more cost-effectively, had decisions been:

- Discussed within an information system not shaped by organized money
- Made by experts not beholden to corporate largesse
- Driven by an informed populace, not a secretive elite.

The Western policy failures that caused our three crises confirmed to China's democracy cynics that Western governments are hamstrung by an idealistic political system that doesn't work in practice. To the Chinese, the idea of emulating this system is laughable.[2]

Democracy is supposed to be imbued with such advantages as responsive government, transparency and an open public debate. Eliminating conflict-of-interest is its *raison d'être*.

Each of our case studies was a medium-term crisis that laid bare long-term arrangements. All three showed that democracies work only when they don't throw away their advantages.

Chapter 12
The spending cascade

The strategy of shifting investment risk onto others was employed by the military-industrial complex in 2003, by the financial sector in 2008, and by the pharmaceutical industry in the pandemic. Having captured media, regulators and political class, these sectors were able to take large risks—outsourcing those risks, on each occasion, to the public.

Each of our examples—a war, a financial crisis, a pandemic—triggered what you might term a *spending cascade*. This is an event-complex (such as a war) manufactured to require the transfer of public funds to corporations; or a natural event (such as a pandemic) that can be opportunistically moulded to that end.

A spending cascade has a very high return-on-investment, as it's comprised of many events that *each* requires a large slice of public and private money. For instance, the profits made via the pandemic—which US market observer Jim Cramer described as 'one of the greatest wealth transfers in history'[1]—were earned not only from medical care, but from the supply of protective equipment, from mass testing, from vaccine development, from the shift in retail to the online behemoths, from the creation of 'misinformation experts'… Essentially, money was made by anyone close enough to the system to lobby it for the benefits it could bestow.

The spending cascade

In Britain, Conservative Party donors were given massive COVID contracts—unadvertised, with no competing bids—that were not disclosed to press or public. A no-bid contract for testing kits, worth £347 million, went to the health care company Randox, which employed a government MP as a £100,000 per year consultant.[2] This was after Randox's previous contract—for £133 million—yielded contaminated kits, requiring 750,000 to be recalled.

Consultants for such firms as Deloitte, who earned up to £6,250 per day, became wealthy almost overnight.[3][4]

As early as September 2020, Britain's test-and-trace program—managed largely by such consultants—was judged by the Scientific Advisory Group for Emergencies to be having 'a marginal impact on transmission',[5] and was expected to cost the country the equivalent of four aircraft carriers.[6]

This is *market pantheism*: the superstition that the market does everything best, has requirements that eclipse all others, and is immanent, as a kind of organizing principle, in all things.

The rationale for market pantheism has always been that it rewards initiative and brings efficiency. If that argument had not been sunk by the GFC, it was certainly dispatched by COVID.

A classical spending cascade, such as the Iraq War, tends to have three stages:

- Research and development
- Execution
- Remediation of damage

What makes it a *cascade* is that each event necessitates the next. Thus, the war made spending on anti-terrorism unavoidable, spending on homeland defense a political necessity, and spending on reconstruction a moral duty.

Chapter 13
Eternal protest

The Iraq War entrenched more deeply the psychology of *eternal protest*. Millions of people formed activist groups, took to the streets, mounted petitions, wrote to newspapers—then watched, helpless, as their direst predictions came true. They may as well have written letters to the Sphinx.

The same helplessness prevailed during the GFC—the same inability of ordinary people to influence even the most irrational policies. No regulator was jailed, and the responsible bankers received pay rises, golden handshakes and Cabinet posts.

Some of geographer Jared Diamond's large environmental threats—things that (in his words) can 'do us in'—are over-population, habitat destruction, loss of biodiversity, depletion of natural resources, soil loss, freshwater pollution, environmental toxins and climate change.[1] Diamond points out that we need to solve *all* of these:

> Because if we solve eleven and we fail to solve the twelfth we are in trouble. For example, if we solve our problems of water and soil and population but don't solve our problem of toxics, then we are in trouble.[2]

Fig. 2.6: London, February 15, 2003: one of 800 protests worldwide against the Iraq War—judged by scholars to collectively be 'the largest protest event in human history'. In London perhaps one million turned out; in Rome it was three million.

Presently, is reversing all of these perils plausible? Could a political architecture that cannot rid the world of nuclear weapons —the original and perhaps the worst—be expected to neutralize the dozen other existential threats we have on the books?

If we spotted a scenario like ours in a history book—a society facing multiple lethal risks—we could be pretty sure that, in the pages ahead, it would either opt for structural change or would vanish.

Yet it remains rare for an existential threat to be viewed as a product of our political arrangements. Each is tackled on the assumption that the system will respond if enough fact, logic and popular pressure are thrown at it. This assumption has under-pinned the campaigns against fracking since the early 2000s, against climate change since the 1970s, and against nuclear prolif-eration since the 1950s—with similar results.

With climate change (for instance) debate tends to focus on atmospheric carbon and its main driver: rising consumption in developed countries.[3] So far so good. But it's not generally stated that the policy failures permitting this arise from a constitutional order that is slow, hierarchical, secretive, and very bad at realizing the wishes of its principals. Even if we assume that climate change is unimpeachably real (Part Five suggests a rigorous, public-driven means of testing this claim), those who suspect fraud can hardly be blamed. That is what they observed in Iraq, in the GFC, in the pandemic—in a string of crises going back to Vietnam.

The chain of causation is important in tort law (where a loss may have two or more successive causes), in Buddhism (where 'feeling conditions craving, craving conditions clinging, clinging conditions becoming', and so on), and in philosophy ('if A had not occurred, D could not have occurred'). However, it's little used in political science.

As a result of today's downstream focus, we have today's tread-mill politics. For first order problems like Diamond's, we have only second order responses.

Society can't make wise choices if we don't address the schema by which knowledge develops, and the rules by which decisions are made. That's the matrix in which our options come into being, and without a good matrix we won't have good options.

Chapter 14
Grapes from brambles

Figs are not gathered from thorn bushes, nor grapes from brambles.[1]

— Gospel of Matthew

As we'll see in Part Seven, majorities worldwide believe that the democratic political system is 'broken'. Yet amid this global landscape, even those organizations with *democracy* in their name have no systematic proposal to reform democracy—neither Democracy Now! (progressive), nor the Democratic Party in the US (centrist), nor Ireland's Democratic Unionist Party (conservative), nor the US National Endowment for Democracy (government)—nor the United Nations Democracy Fund (international).

The Bill of Change—the subject matter of this book—seeks to deal with our problems at the top of the causal chain. Graphically, such an intervention would look like your great-great-grandfather at the top of the family tree.

In the next four Parts, I propose a series of constitutional reforms by which this can be done. None of them require diminishing the institutions, or the hard-won freedoms, in our constitutions. The connection of war, depression and inequality to these elderly parchments lies not in what they contain but in what they omit. Over a period in which society changed beyond recognition, democracy changed very little. Fences built to repel the foxes of the 18th Century have not kept out the monsters of the 21st.

Fig. 2.7: Veterans Row, Los Angeles. Most of these men and women served in the War on Terror; many were made homeless by the GFC; some were killed by the pandemic. The US Veterans Administration is charged with housing them—but has instead made 'improper and illegal' leases of the allocated land to political donors & developers.

Part Three
Decontamination

All for ourselves, and nothing for other people, seems, in every age of the world, to have been the vile maxim of the masters of mankind.[1]

— Adam Smith (1776)

I hope we shall crush in its birth the aristocracy of our monied corporations which dare already to challenge our government to a trial by strength, and bid defiance to the laws of our country.[2]

— Thomas Jefferson, 3rd US president (1816)

The real difficulty is with the vast wealth and power in the hands of the few and the unscrupulous who represent or control capital... This is a government of the people, by the people, and for the people no longer. It is a government of corporations, by corporations, and for corporations.[3]

— Rutherford B Hayes, 19th US president (1888)

Behind the ostensible government sits enthroned an invisible government, owing no allegiance and acknowledging no responsibility to the people. To destroy this invisible government, to dissolve the unholy alliance between corrupt business and corrupt politics is the first task of the statesmanship of the day.[4]

— Theodore Roosevelt, 26th US president (1912)

If the government is to tell big business men how to run their business, then don't you see that big business men have to get closer to the government even than they are now? Don't you see that they must capture the government, in order not to be restrained too much by it? Must capture the government? They have already captured it.

— Woodrow Wilson, 28th US president (1913)

I had a nice talk with Jack Morgan [banker J.P. Morgan] the other day and he seemed more worried about [Assistant Secretary of Agriculture Rexford] Tugwell's speech than about anything else, especially when Tugwell said, 'From now on property rights and financial rights will be subordinated to human rights.'… The real truth of the matter is, as you and I know, that a financial element in the larger centers has owned the Government ever since the days of Andrew Jackson.[5]

— Franklin Roosevelt, 32nd US president (1933)

There is no question in the world that money has control.[6]

— Senator Barry Goldwater (1986)

When these political action committees give money, they expect something in return other than good government…

Poor people don't make political contributions. You might get a different result if there were a poor-PAC up here.[7]

— Senator Robert Dole (1986)

One question, among many raised in recent weeks, had to do with whether my financial support in any way influenced several political figures to take up my cause. I want to say in the most forceful way I can: I certainly hope so.[8]

— Charles Keating, head of the collapsed Lincoln Savings (1989)

Well, the plutocracy…is when money has ceased just entertaining itself with leveraged buyouts and all the stuff they did in the '80s, and really takes over politics. And takes it over on both sides, when money not only talks, money screams. When you start developing philosophies in which giving a check is a First Amendment right. That's incredible. But what you've got is that this is what money has done. It's produced the fusion of money and government.[9]

— Kevin Phillips, former chief political strategist for President Nixon (2002)

Number one, money is the Lord your Savior. You, both candidate and manager, shall have no other Lord.[10]

— Democratic consultant Jeffrey Pollock (2006)

I would say to [the Congressman], 'When you're done working on the Hill, we'd very much like you to consider coming to work for us.' The moment I said that...we owned them. And what does that mean? Every request from our office, every request of our clients, everything that we want, they're gonna do.[11]

— Former lobbyist Jack Abramoff (2011)

As for President Obama, what is there to be said? Goldman Sachs was his number-one private campaign contributor. He put a Citigroup executive in charge of his economic transition team, and he just named an executive of JP Morgan Chase, the proud owner of $7.7 million in Chase stock, his new chief of staff.[12]

— Journalist Matt Taibbi (2011)

American democracy has been hacked... [Congress] is now incapable of passing laws without permission from the corporate lobbies and other special interests that control their campaign finances.[13]

— Al Gore (2013)

When some think tank comes up with the legislation and tells you not to fool with it, why are you even a legislator anymore? You just sit there and take votes and you're kind of a feudal serf for folks with a lot of money.[14]

— Dale Schultz, Wisconsin Republican, former state Senate majority leader (2013)

The alliance of money and the interests that it represents, the access that it affords to those who have it at the expense of those who don't, the agenda that it changes or sets by virtue of its power, is steadily silencing the voice of the vast majority of Americans.[15]

— Senator John Kerry (2013)

If you ask me pro forma where does it [power over US foreign policy] exist today—it exists more in the National Security Council and its staff than it does anywhere else—certainly anywhere else in the Cabinet. So, what I'm saying is it is centralized in the White House. But what does that mean?... Who's behind the White House, and who's therefore behind US foreign policy, more or less? I think the answer today is the oligarchs, which would be the same answer incidentally—ironically—for Putin and Russia: the people who own the wealth, the people who therefore have the power, and who more or less—and I'm not being too facetious here I don't think—buy the President, and thus buy American foreign policy.[16]

— Col. Lawrence Wilkerson, former chief of staff
to secretary of state Colin Powell (2014)

Now it's just an oligarchy, with unlimited political bribery being the essence of getting the nominations for president or to elect the president. And the same thing applies to governors and US senators and congress members. So now we've just seen a complete subversion of our political system as a payoff to major contributors.[17]

— Jimmy Carter, 39th US president (2015)

He [Jeb Bush] raises $100 million, so what does $100 million mean? $100 million means he's doing favors for so many people. It means lobbyists, it means special interests, it means donors. Who knows it better than me? I give to everybody. They do whatever I want. It's true.

Many of Hillary's donors are the same donors as Jeb Bush's—all rich, will have total control. Know them well.[18]

— Donald Trump, 45th US president (2015)

Using a new and more comprehensive dataset built from government sources, the paper shows that the relations between money and votes cast for major parties in elections for the US Senate and House of Representatives from 1980 to 2018 are well approximated by straight lines.[19]

— Economists Thomas Ferguson, Paul Jorgensen and Jie Chen (2022)

They frankly own the place.[20]

— Democratic Senator Dick Durban, on the banks' relationship with Congress (2016)

Cash on hand.[21]

— Senator Mitch McConnell, on the three most important words in politics (2016)

In the early 1990s there was no difference between our two major political parties in their assessment of what we now call climate change. They had different notions of what you should do about it—but they all understood that it was man-made and that it was something serious that needed attention. By 2013 or 2014, only eight of 278 Republicans in Congress would admit that climate change was man-made. That is the donor network.[22]

— Professor Nancy McLean (2017)

I am scrambling to make sure I am not the third monkey headed into Noah's Ark. You got to hustle like hell before the flood hits.[23]

> — Jack Howard, lobbyist for the US Chamber of Commerce, on the 18-page wishlist he sent to Congress for corporate pandemic relief (2020).

So there is an implicit bribe in civil service: you act as a servant to industry, say Monsanto, and they take care of you later on. They do not do it out of a sense of honor: simply, it is necessary to keep such a system going and encourage the next guy to play by the rules.[24]

> — Nassim Nicholas Taleb (2018)

Boris Johnson has received a donation of £1m from a Thai-based British businessman, the newly released register of MPs' interests has shown.

Christopher Harborne, a tech industry investor... handed the £1m donation to Johnson's personal office, set up after he left No 10.[25]

> — *The Guardian* (2023)

Chapter 15
Ariadne's thread

In one of the old Greek legends, the god Poseidon settles a dispute over the throne of Crete by providing a magnificent white bull to a prince named Minos, to signify that he, Minos, is the true king. The bull is handed over on the condition that Minos immediately sacrifice it to the god.

But the new king kept the bull for himself.

Long story short, Poseidon punished Minos by making his queen fall in love with the bull. Consequently, she gave birth to a half-bull, half-man—the violent, unnatural monster known as the Minotaur. Once he grew a little, the Minotaur started laying waste to the land. With no natural source of sustenance, he began to eat people.

So the King asked Daedalus, his scientist and engineer, to build a massive labyrinth around the Minotaur, so complex that it could never find its way out. Hedging his bets, Minos decreed that the monster should also be fed with seven young women and seven young men, every year.

According to the comparative mythologist Joseph Campbell, had King Minos sacrificed the bull as required, he would have been 'divested of his private character and clothed in the mantle of his vocation'.[1] Instead, he used his public office for personal gain

—and the Minotaur materialized. The king, Campbell wrote, thereby 'cut himself as a unit off from the larger unit of the community.'

Campbell had discovered the tyrant-monster in mythologies all round the world:

> He is the hoarder of the general benefit. He is the monster avid for the greedy rights of 'my and mine'... The inflated ego of the tyrant is a curse to himself and his world—no matter how his affairs may seem to prosper.

The king's daughter, Ariadne—the story continues—was given a ball of thread by Daedalus, the engineer who'd built the maze. At its entrance, Ariadne hands the thread to Theseus, one of the sacrificial victims. Theseus ties one end to the maze entrance, and in he goes.

Fig. 3.1: Theseus, awaiting the Minotaur, holding thread & sword

Theseus finds his way to the centre of the labyrinth, slays the Minotaur (needless to say), and finds his way out with the thread.

So, when Minos sequesters the bull—a community resource—for his own use, its progeny literally consumes the future. When Theseus employs human ingenuity for the good of the *demos*, the kingdom is saved. You don't need to be religious to see some pretty good symbolism here—and maybe to wonder what kind of 'thread' it will be that delivers us from the bane of self-interest in public life.

Chapter 16
An inter-tribal issue

That bane existed in Athens,[1] and it crops up today in every country. In undeveloped ones, it more usually recurs as 'brown paper bag' corruption; in the Anglosphere, the 'election-industrial complex' produces roughly the same result. We don't call the latter *corruption*, as it's mostly done within the law. So, to distinguish it from developing world systems, I'll call it *contamination*.

Contamination both distorts the free market and breeds inequality. Hence it is reviled by people across the political spectrum—it's 'inter-tribal':

> We are ruled by mercenaries who feel no long-term obligation to the people they rule. They're day traders. Substitute teachers. They're just passing through. They have no skin in this game, and it shows.[2]
>
> — Tucker Carlson on Fox News

Without sufficient public scrutiny, all political systems degenerate into the service of wealth. All end up controlled by the few with the cash, not the many with the votes. The primary democratic task is to break the nexus of money and power.[3]

— George Monbiot in *The Guardian*

Plutocracy is the control of policy by wealth—a kind of 'dyad' in which the goals of organized money merge with those of politics. Plutocracy will emerge even when the wealthy have good intentions, if there are no *demotic institutions* to prevent this. (We look at these institutions in Part Five.)

This distortion of policy generates a slew of secondary symptoms. An important one of these is economic *stasis*. For example, start-ups can't afford political influence, but old money uses it to protect itself against innovation. That also advantages the old over the young.

Thus the Pentagon these days sources few goods or services from the entrepreneurs and university spin-offs it once favored. Its procurement is almost wholly from big corporations that sponsor legislators and employ retired generals.

Plutocracy does not protect economic vitality—only itself. Harvard law professor Lawrence Lessig provides another example:

> Look to Wall Street: Never has an industry been filled with more rabid libertarians; but never has an industry more successfully engineered government handouts when the gambling of those libertarians went south.[4]

The institution of campaign finance, moreover, favors the worst corporate citizens. Companies that tend to cause harm—producers of tobacco, oil, coal, pharmaceuticals, gambling machines, junk food and dodgy financial products—have less public credibility than, say, software or solar panel makers. They'll also attract more interest from regulators. Therefore, they need to contribute more heavily to politics than others, to keep government at bay. The result can be policies that favor the worst companies over the best.[5]

In the field of environment policy, this is called the 'pollution paradox': the worst polluters make the largest political contributions, as they have greater public pressure to overcome. One US study found that contributions increase in line with the unpopularity of an industry;[6] and a study of investment banks by the International Monetary Fund found a high correlation between 'intensity of lobbying' and 'high-risk trading'.[7]

According to the official report, BP's Deepwater Horizon disaster, the largest-ever marine oil spill, resulted from risky practices by the corporate giants—and top political contributors—BP, Halliburton and Transocean. The risky practices were enabled by 'regulatory oversight' so lax that the report called for 'fundamental reform'.[8]

The US economist Thomas Ferguson believes the effect of political finance 'is to cement parties, candidates, and campaigns into the narrow range of issues that are acceptable to big donors':

> Running for major office in the US is fabulously expensive. In the absence of large scale social movements, only political positions that can be financed can be presented to voters. On issues on which all major investors agree (think of the now famous 1 percent), no party competition at all takes place, even if everyone knows that heavy majorities of voters want something else.[9]

To ensure parties stay 'cemented' into this narrow range of issues, when one major party makes noises about regulating a donor's industry, the donor can increase contributions to the other. Through such warning shots has the gaming industry in Australia kept regulation at bay.

Minor parties, which are more inclined to regulate abuses, get little campaign money. Moreover, *OpenSecrets*, which tracks political donors, finds that

> incumbents get vastly more than challengers, committee chairmen and legislative leaders get more than rank-and-file members, and parties in power get more than parties in the minority.[10]

So corporate investment in politics also centralizes power and works against change.

All of this tends to keep the debate focused on issues that corporations care little about, such as same-sex marriage and abortion.[11]

This situation is opposed by virtually everyone who is not paid to support it. It persists because nothing in the free market compares with the return-on-investment (ROI) garnered by political donations:

> In the mid-1990s, American oil and gas corporations contributed $10.3 million to politicians, who responded with $4 billion in tax breaks.[12] This was an ROI of 388 to 1.

In Australia between 2012 and 2015, the three major parties received $AU3.7 million from the fossil fuel industry, which yielded $AU7.7 billion in subsidies—an ROI of more than two thousand to one.[13]

An investigation published by *Forbes* magazine found that, in the four years to 2017, America's Fortune 100 companies spent $2 billion in lobbying and yielded $399 billion in federal contracts and grants—an ROI of nearly 20,000%.[14]

Another study, on the American Jobs Creation Act—a one-off tax break in 2009—found that 'for each dollar spent on lobbying for it, a corporation received $220 in U.S. income tax savings'—an ROI of 22,000%.[15]

Only artificial markets such as Ponzi schemes generally bring results of this order.

The damage isn't limited to lost public revenue: it's also bad for capitalism. As Luigi Zingales, a business professor at the University of Chicago, puts it:

> Once you get these kinds of returns, companies will not invest in R&D, they will not invest in new organizational forms, they will not invest in new technology, they will not invest in new plant and equipment. They will invest in lobbying.[16]

Because every political campaign is defined by 'cash on hand', every electoral cycle begins with what Lawrence Lessig calls the 'money primary'. This, he says, 'determines which candidates are allowed to run':

> Members of Congress and candidates for Congress spend between 30 and 70 percent of their time 'dialing for dollars'— calling people all across the country to get the money they need to run their campaigns or to get their party back into power...
>
> BF Skinner gave us this wonderful image of the Skinner Box, where any stupid animal could learn which buttons it needs to push for its sustenance. This is a picture of the life of the modern American congressperson.[17]

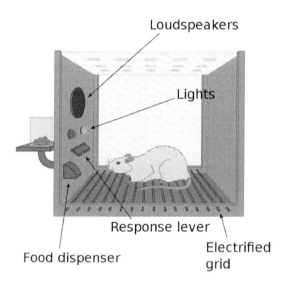

Fig. 3.2: An 'operant conditioning chamber' or Skinner Box

All this probably explains why in the first quarter of 2011, when the United States had two wars, high unemployment and a budget crisis to deal with, Congress spent more time discussing bank swipe fees—what percentage banks get when a debit card is used —than any of these issues.[18]

Wikipedia defines the *free market* as

> a system in which the prices for goods and services are set freely by consent between vendors and consumers, in which the laws and forces of supply and demand are free from any intervention by a government, price-setting monopoly, or other authority.

Around the world, people prefer the free market system, when given a choice.[19] However, thanks largely to political contamination, the free market is not something we've lived in for some time. Because of airline clout with legislators, consumers can't even use their market power to increase the legroom in planes.[20]

As we've seen, in 2008 economist Thomas Ferguson predicted that the significant bank money pouring into Barack Obama's campaign would ensure Obama would not only be elected, but would engage in no meaningful reform of the finance industry.[21] To the dismay of Obama activists, who'd campaigned under the banner of 'change we can believe in', he proved to be right. Obama chose as his running mate Joe Biden, a long-standing ally of the banking and credit card industries.[22]

The 2008 crisis produced overwhelming evidence of felonies by Wall Street executives—none of which were ever prosecuted. Instead, as Matt Taibbi wrote in *Rolling Stone* in 2009, Obama

> ship[ped] even his most marginally progressive campaign advisers off to various bureaucratic Siberias, while packing the key economic positions in his White House with the very people who caused the crisis in the first place.[23]

None of this would have surprised those who'd been keeping up with the political science. In 2005, a now-famous study by

Chapter 16

Princeton scholar Martin Gilens, based on 2,000 survey questions, had found that

> when Americans with different income levels differ in their policy preferences, policy outcomes strongly reflect the preferences of the most affluent but bear virtually no relationship to the preferences of poor or middle income Americans...
>
> Whether or not elected officials and other decision makers 'care' about middle-class Americans, influence over actual policy outcomes appears to be reserved almost exclusively for those at the top of the income distribution.[24]

Gilens and a colleague, Benjamin Page, published a second study in 2014, which canvassed 1,179 policy issues:

> When the preferences of economic elites and the stands of organized interest groups are controlled for, the preferences of the average American appear to have only a minuscule, near-zero, statistically non-significant impact upon public policy.[25]

Historically, plutocrats who are spoiled to this degree tend to gain a swollen sense of their own entitlement. When Xerxes the Great of Persia had his bridges across the Hellespont destroyed by a storm in 480 BC, he 'had the sea whipped as punishment'.[26] And say no more about King John.

In 2016, the senior banker Hank Paulson wrote:

> Anyone, whether Republican or Democrat, who has studied our entitlement programs and can do basic math knows they are unsustainable in their present form... It doesn't surprise me when a socialist such as Bernie Sanders sees no need to fix our entitlement programs. But I find it particularly appalling that Trump, a businessman, tells us he won't touch Social Security, Medicare and Medicaid.[27]

The crash of 2008, which relocated many Americans to trailer parks, was partly brought on by various 'fragile' securities created by Goldman Sachs during Hank Paulson's tenure as CEO. By no small irony, Paulson was thereafter appointed President Obama's treasury secretary, to oversee the rescue of the banks that caused the crisis. Goldman itself was loaned $589 billion—a beneficiary of America's largest socialist project since the New Deal.

If the tyrants of the ancient world were why the Greeks invented democracy, Hank Paulson is why it needs to be reinvented.

Chapter 17
A feedback loop

Astudent of physics or chemistry might by now have picked up that politics is locked in a positive feedback loop with corporate money. No matter how unethical the corporate practice, or how irrational the government decision, because of the feedback loop, unethical practices and irrational decisions are inevitable. If a corporation wishes to stay competitive, or a politician to stay in office, they must preserve the system.

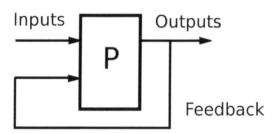

Fig. 3.3: In a feedback loop, a system's outputs return to become inputs

The loop's inescapability can produce bizarre results. Barack Obama, despite having campaigned against lobbyists, took no substantial action against them as president—and saw his climate bill sunk by lobbyists.[1]

Donald Trump—having promised to drain the Washington swamp—appointed a shipping heiress to run the Department of Transportation, an oil lobbyist to run the Interior Department, a pharmaceutical executive to run the Department of Health and Human Services, an investment banker to run the Treasury, and a coal lobbyist to run the Environmental Protection Agency—to identify just the tip of the iceberg.[2]

In 2019, during his presidential campaign, Joe Biden addressed an audience of wealthy donors:

> We can disagree in the margins but the truth of the matter is it's all within our wheelhouse and nobody has to be punished. No one's standard of living will change, nothing would fundamentally change. Because when we have income inequality as large as we have in the United States today, it brews and ferments political discord and basic revolution… It allows demagogues to step in and say the reason we're where we are is because of 'the other'. You're not 'the other'. I need you very badly. I hope if I win this nomination, I won't let you down. I promise you.[3]

As it panned out, Biden received nearly $1.4 billion in contributions[4]—his top donors being two hedge funds, a mall operator, a real estate magnate, a billionaire investor, the owner of a venture capital firm, and a hotelier.[5]

As he took office in January 2021, there was a flurry of anti-lobbying rhetoric from Biden. By year's end, Washington's lobbyists were making never-before-seen incomes via the new president's spending programs.[6] During the first full financial quarter of Biden's presidency (Q2 of 2021), one lobbyist—the brother of a top Biden aide—took in $850,000.[7] In the same three-month period, two others—both former Biden aides—took in $1 million and $1.7 million, respectively.

Circularity is one of lobbying's hallmarks: personnel migrate from Congress to lobby firm and back again. But there's also a circular flow of money. For example:

The RAND Corporation, a military-oriented think tank, is part-funded by the US government →
→ RAND persuades government officials to increase military spending →
→ This increases profits for arms manufacturers →
→ The manufacturers contribute to those same government officials →
→ Who increase funding for the RAND Corporation.

In another example of the loop's circularity, Lockheed Martin sells jets to developing countries, then lobbies the US government to buy more such jets itself—because of the threat now posed by developing countries owning them.[8]

In many domains, a positive feedback loop can only end badly:

Positive feedback tends to cause system instability. When the loop gain is positive and above 1, there will typically be exponential growth, increasing oscillations, chaotic behavior or other divergences from equilibrium... Thermal runaway is a type of positive feedback that can destroy semiconductor junctions. Positive feedback in chemical reactions can increase the rate of reactions, and in some cases can lead to explosions... Out of control, it can cause bridges to collapse.[9]

As the loop reaches its zenith, we generally see the disconnection of 'warning lights'.

In Washington, the monitoring of lobbyists is now the job of two small congressional offices, neither of which has the power to investigate breaches of the Lobbying Disclosure Act. The US Attorney's office in Washington *does* have the power to pursue breaches—but is yet to pursue one. The office has one full-time employee in its lobbying section: a paralegal responsible for data entry.[10]

The government which found trillions of dollars to destabilize the Middle East cannot afford one investigator for its 100,000 lobbyists. As a result, wealth redistribution is practised more vigorously in the US than in any socialist country, though with a different class of beneficiaries.

In February 2016, the Australian Labor Senator Sam Dastyari observed that 'ten large companies' control the political debate in Canberra:

> The entire political debate has become so dominated by the interests that they're pushing, and the agenda that they're pushing. And [we've] ended up with this complete crowding out of a proper political discourse in this country because there is one sectional interest that is so much louder than every other voice out there combined.[11]

Seven months later, Dastyari demonstrated this system's universality—that it can be utilized by anyone with the funds, whatever their ideology—when he was forced to resign from the front bench for taking money from firms linked to the Chinese Government.

Outside the Anglosphere, the feedback loop contains less contamination and more frank corruption: though the two are generally only cosmetically different, and have comparable ROIs. (We'll compare the two models in the next chapter.)

Woven through both the corruption and contamination models is the illicit offshoring of money. Estimates of the untaxed sums lost to offshoring range up to $36 trillion.[12] British financial journalist John Lanchester wrote in 2018 that a large fraction of the world's 'balance sheet' is missing—and that there has been no effort to repair this:

> Effective legal instruments to prevent offshore tax evasion are incredibly simple and could be enacted overnight, as the United States has just shown with its crackdown on oligarchs linked to Putin's regime. All you have to do is make it illegal for banks to enact transactions with territories that don't comply with rules on tax transparency.[13]

Politically, the result of all this is *stasis*. Public pressure produces little: the system can't respond: and in time the public ceases expecting it to.

In the US, majorities oppose offshore drilling,[14] the repeal of net neutrality,[15] and withdrawal from the intermediate-range nuclear forces treaty.[16] Americans also desire most of the items we look at in Part Five, including citizen commissions to draw electoral districts, proportional representation and ranked-choice voting.[17] If you discounted political capture, you'd be hard-pressed to find a reason these things aren't enacted.

A system like this can't be reformed with 'new regulations'. Any government forced to make them would probably soon work quietly to dilute them—and its successor to repeal them. Nor will media exposure do the job: media is part of the loop. Plutocracy is the world's best-kept secret because plutocrats own the newspapers.

Millennia of civilization have taught us that elites of any kind —royal or republican; 'democratic' or communist; progressive or conservative; theocratic or atheist—bring self-interest at best, and corruption at worst. Any analysis of politics along one of these spectrums needs to shift up a level.

Unless we believe there's an elite somewhere that can be trusted to make our decisions for us, the way to end this capture is to place leaders under popular control, and to empower citizens to make decisions themselves.

As we'll soon see, the tools by which we can do this are now abundant.

Chapter 18
The plutocratic armory

The best available estimates say that the top 0.00001 percent's share of total wealth today is almost 10 times what it was four decades ago.[1]

— Economist Paul Krugman (2022)

While the 1% tends to gain its ascendancy via proxies in legislatures and presidential palaces, it would be counterproductive for it to broadcast this. A plutocracy needs, instead, to create the appearance of broad social backing.

For that purpose, it underwrites a supporting 'chorus'. We've seen the *chorus effect* writ small in Part Two, in connection with vaccine production. Here we'll see it writ large—across the face of society.

The most powerful chorus member is the mainstream media (Part Four). But there are numerous other public-facing institutions—such as lobby organizations, think tanks and astroturfing outfits—whose role, broadly speaking, is to make dubious facts seem plausible and wrongdoing seem upright.

There is quite a profusion of these vehicles of influence; the same people can wear several hats; and players tend to move from industry or lobby group to government and back again with some regularity. David Urban was the lobbyist most influential on President Trump—but he was also a presidential fund-raiser, campaign manager, appointee, head-hunter and advisor: and a national media figure.[2] Joe Biden's campaign in 2020 hired a slew of corporate lobbyists,[3] and in 2021 his administration drew in people from think tanks, 'strategic consultancies' (glorified lobby organizations) and industry—notably the military-industrial complex and the oil sector.[4] One 'strategic consultant' became Biden's secretary of state, and two others became his national security advisor and director of national intelligence. A former director of the arms giant Raytheon was given the defense portfolio.[5]

That's Washington—but the influences we look at herein (Part Three) occur across the democratic world: affecting executive, legislative and judicial branches; the local, state, national and regional tiers of government; civil services and 'qangos' (government-NGO hybrids)—and their staffs and their families.

Because the vectors of political contamination are many, we'll look first at straight-out political money—then progress through the 'chorus'.

Political contributions

I've had my people let him know that every minute late he is, is one less minute he will have with me.[6]

> — Uber founder Travis Kalanick, when kept
> waiting by US Vice President Joe Biden at the
> World Economic Forum, 2016

In the developing world, the head of a patronage network will usually be a prime minister or president—handing out jobs, contracts and military rank in return for cash and loyalty. Because it's filled by family members, yes-men and those who've bought a ministry, the cabinet of such a nation will generally be low in competence. Competence, though, isn't the goal. Throughout much of Africa, the Middle East and Southeast Asia, entering politics is not a chance to serve society or even to administer anything: it's an investment. The payoff system trickles down to the lowliest public servant or soldier—who will typically pay for his job,[a] and thereafter share a portion of its takings (e.g. government fees) with his superiors. All this breaks the law, so the law is never enforced.

In the West, the reverse pattern applies. The patron is usually a businessperson, the client a public official, and their relationship perfectly legal. The businessperson sets the terms of the arrangement, and tends to be the dominant party. British MP Stephen Byers spoke for many a modern politician when he described himself as a 'cab for hire'.[7]

By these mechanics, corporations contribute millions of dollars to Western politicians, and claim no ulterior motive. Politicians award the corporations billions of dollars in contracts, which they claim have no connection to the contributions.

The doors this arrangement opens for a company are the stuff of dreams.

Over the first decade of the 21st Century, the Royal Bank of Scotland (RBS)—then the world's largest bank—was permitted to get away with many risky liquidity practices, and had a large takeover waved through—which dangerously lowered its capital levels.[8] RBS had for decades helped to illegally manipulate the inter-bank 'Libor' rate for profit, unmolested by regulators. This caused 'a cascade of mispriced financial assets throughout the entire global financial system'.[9] The value of the manipulated contracts—everything from household mortgages to commercial loans—was $300 trillion.[10] A small tweak of one basis point (.01%) could yield the manipulator millions of dollars.[11] The eventual cost to national, state and municipal bodies—and to individuals, including pensioners[12]—was in the multiple billions.[13]

As court transcripts later made clear, the rigging of the Libor

---

[a] For example, in an Asian country I have lived in, a little over $12,000 will purchase a job as a medic in the army. A one-star rank in the traffic police is $15,000, and a two-star $20,000. A colonel's rank in the Iraqi army toward the end of the US occupation cost about $200,000.

rate was not the work of rogue traders, but was institutionally supported by RBS.[14]

In 2008, the bank showed how valuable political protection can be when a company that has overplayed its risks teeters on oblivion. On the morning of October 7, the British chancellor of the exchequer, Alistair Darling, was phoned by the RBS chairman, Tom McKillop, who told him (Darling later recalled) that the bank was 'haemorrhaging money, and asked what we were going to do about it'.[15]

Darling enquired how long RBS could last. 'Until the beginning of the afternoon,' he was told.

The government quickly calculated that a chain reaction would soon crash Barclays, then Lloyds, and then possibly all the large British banks. Darling thought 'we faced a situation where the banking system right across the world, never mind Britain, could have collapsed'.

The possibility that cash machines, and the ability to buy food, might soon cease across the country was kept under wraps. For several days and nights, multi-millionaire bankers and government officials alike sat along the floors of the Treasury building—it had run out of chairs—looking for a solution.[16]

In the end, the taxpayer was obliged to pitch in: taking a £46 billion stake in RBS—84% of the company—on which, to 2020, she had incurred a £32 billion loss.[17]

Financial journalist Jill Treanor estimates that total losses from the bank's 'disastrous lending, over-paying for takeovers, fines and legal bills' would total more than £90 billion.[18]

In its report, the UK's Financial Services Authority (FSA) found, to no-one's surprise, that RBS had been poorly regulated. It discovered many of the bank's questionable practices to be the work of CEO Fred Goodwin—who'd been permitted to reward himself on its collapse with a £700,000 golden handshake. The FSA took no criminal action against Goodwin, or any RBS employee.[19]

Little of this is rational. How could it have occurred?

British investment banks contribute to political parties largely via low-interest loans with no end date—packaged with an offer of additional loans to finance the interest on the existing one. (The kind of arrangement that, in any other context, would cause an auditor to fall off her chair.) RBS was Britain's largest such political lender. Along with two other banks—HSBC and the Bank of Scotland—it loaned a total of £871 million to the major British parties in the years before the crisis: 2004 to 2007.

The three banks subsequently became the chief beneficiaries of the Asset Protection Scheme: Britain's bailouts.[20]

Corruption v. contamination

Whilst politicians benefit personally under both developing world and Western models, in the West the benefits accrue more gradually: via donations for election and re-election, and a future containing directorships, consultancies and speaking engagements.

Thus, where Thomas Jefferson wrote, in his retirement, that 'banking establishments are more dangerous than standing armies',[21] in *his* retirement, his distant successor Barack Obama gives $400,000 speeches to bankers.[22]

The balance of power between business and politics tends to vary from poor countries to rich—from the 'corruption' model to the 'contamination' one.

Where a developing world oligarch will tend to kowtow to the politician, in the West it's generally the politician who kowtows to the oligarch.

It's a *bit* more complicated than that. Even in the West the political half of the dyad *will* discipline the corporate half when their shared interests are imperilled—for example via social media censorship. Moreover, Western-style contamination has a tendency to *evolve* into corruption: as rules are incrementally discarded, and 'breaches' develop into 'norms'.

With those caveats in mind, let's look at 'corruption' v. 'contamination'.

2015 saw the revelation of Brazil's 'Car Wash'—a scandal that had spread through much of Latin America. Billions of dollars were involved, along with 20 political parties—left, right and centre. Essentially, executives at Brazil's state-owned oil company, Petrobas, took bribes in return for awarding contracts to construction firms. The value of the contracts was inflated by up to 3%, which was kicked back to those executives—with a cut passed on to the politicians who'd appointed them.

The scheme was certainly rewarding. On exposure, one *third-tier* Petrobas executive (who reported to the director for engineering and services) agreed to return $100 million.[23] Petrobas as a whole wrote off $17 billion to graft and over-valued assets.[24]

By mid-2018, politicians in ten countries—including the president of Peru and three ex-presidents, and the vice president of Ecuador—had been disgraced. A lead prosecutor stated that in one element of the scandal alone—the 'Odebrecht' case—

> there are many reasons for you to become speechless. How a company created a whole system only to pay bribes, and how many public agents were involved. This case implicated almost one-third of Brazil's senators and almost half of all Brazil's governors.
>
> One sole company paid bribes in favour of 415 politicians and 26 political parties in Brazil. It makes the Watergate scandal look like a couple of kids playing in a sandbox.[25]

The amounts lost in 'Car Wash' could have paid for a million nurses, or the teaching of 17 million children, for a year. The scandal is believed to have knocked 3.5% off Brazil's GDP. It helped to take unemployment from 7.1% to 13%, and ushered in the worst recession in decades.

Both the 'contamination' and 'corruption' feedback loops can culminate in the election of a strongman with policies so bizarre he would have been unelectable in any other era: the noise that finally overwhelms the democratic signal. In the wake of 'Car Wash', and on the strength of his promises to clean up corruption, Jair Bolsonaro was elected president of Brazil.

(Bolsonaro took office in 2019, and by 2020 he'd been named 'Person of the Year' by the Organized Crime and Corruption

Reporting Project—a global network of investigative journalists—for 'his role in promoting organized crime and corruption'.[26])

The scandal surrounding '1MDB'—Malaysia's state development fund—likewise conformed largely to the 'corruption' model. Also beginning in 2015, the scandal saw the theft of $4.5 billion from the fund—$731 million of which turned up in prime minister Najib Razak's bank account.

In addition, the prime minister and his wife acquired luxury items worth $273 million—including 1,400 necklaces, 567 handbags, 423 watches, 2,200 rings, 1,600 brooches and 14 tiaras. There was so much cash found inside the couple's properties that it took 22 officials with bill-counting machines three days to count it.[27]

Under the 'contamination' model, all this is achieved more gracefully, under a patina of law. For example, in place of bagmen and kleptocrats, Canada has 6,800 lobbyists,[28] Brussels 30,000,[29] and the US 100,000.[30] Thirty percent of European MPs go to work for lobbying firms when they leave office.[31]

These lobbyists do not busy themselves in pushing for a fairer society, or less plastic in the oceans. Each round of contamination deletes more laws and regulations, enabling larger profits, and so further contamination, in the next: a snowballing capture of government.

In our globalized era, the two systems frequently interact. For example, in 2014 in Iraq, the majority of soldiers defending the collapsing northern stronghold of Mosul against ISIS turned out to be 'phantoms'. ISIS took Mosul because only one in three of its presumed defenders was actually there. The phantom soldiers' salaries—provided by the US taxpayer—had been pocketed by the commanders.[32]

A kind of flimsy deniability is important to both systems. In Iraq, though everyone knows what's going on, it's poor form to discuss the arrangements openly. In Australia there's a 'declarations regime' for political contributions, but it contains enough loopholes to render it meaningless—and it is never enforced.[33]

(For example, a minister who goes into lobbying within 18 months of leaving office is to be sanctioned with a 'loss of ministerial responsibility'. Literally: after leaving office she is to lose office.[34])

The two models also overlap in Europe's farm subsidies, which are so generous that Saudi princes and Russian oligarchs invest ill-gotten gains in European land, just to receive them. The subsidies are not available to smallholders—only to those who own large parcels of land. To qualify for a farm subsidy, one doesn't need to farm—only to own farm land. Because ponds, reed beds and forests are not eligible, they sometimes need to be destroyed for the land to qualify. Farm subsidies—which create higher taxes and higher prices for Europeans[35]—amount to 40% of the EU budget. They're one of the largest socialist schemes in the world (though this is socialism for the rich).[36]

There's nothing rational about Europe's farm subsidies, but they can be explained. Most members of the EU's agriculture committee—which sets the subsidy rates—'have business or personal links to the farming sector they are charged with regulating'.[37]

The passivity toward corrupt rulers within the developing world now permeates the developed world too. Western publics not only know they're being robbed—they have come to take it for granted.

In a 2013 Pew survey, 69% of Americans said that economic decisions since 2008 had benefited banks and large financial institutions the most, and 71% that government had done nothing to benefit the middle class.[38]

In 2015, 76% thought government was 'run by a few big interests'—which (Pew said) 'has long been the view of most Americans, with majorities consistently saying this for much of the past 15 years'.[39] The view is held even more widely by conservatives than by liberals.

The global polling organization *Worldpublicopinion.org* found the belief that government is run by and for 'a few big interests' is pervasive in France (59%), Britain (60%), Argentina (71%), Nigeria and South Korea (78%), the United States (80%), Mexico (83%), and Ukraine (84%)—all 'democracies'.

The revolving door

> If they say, 'Can you hang on a second, I want to close my door,'
> or 'Can I call you back from my cell phone?', you know they're
> interested.[40]
>
> — Washington recruiter John Hesse, on feeling
> out congressional staffers for lobbying jobs.

Of those who left politics for non-government work after the 115th
United States Congress (2017-19), 59% became lobbyists. These
included a woman who launched her lobbying company before
she left Congress, and a man who'd urged the House to authorize a
gold-copper mine in Alaska, then went to work for the mining
company.[41]

One firm stands alone as a supplier of senior government
personnel. In the words of progressive media outlet *Common
Dreams*:

> Goldman Sachs has been a conspicuous presence at the scene of
> one disaster after another in the past half century. The bank is a
> leader in a Wall Street business model that relies on market
> manipulation and unsustainable financial bubbles to enrich a
> few insiders, but that produces disastrous consequences for the
> rest of us.[42]

Goldman's long-standing misbehavior could only be sustained
were its influence present at the top of the power structure, as it
usually is. Former Goldman employees include past or present finance
ministers of Spain, Nigeria and Sweden; prime ministers of Australia,
Britain and Italy; reserve bank governors of England, Greece, South
Africa, Australia, Canada and Europe; president of the World Bank;
along with four secretaries of the US treasury, and an array of regulators, senior civil servants and ministers worldwide.[43] The chairman of
Goldman Sachs International is José Manuel Barroso, whose previous
job was President of the European Commission.

Donald Trump appointed numerous Goldman executives to key posts in his administration,[44] as did Joe Biden after him.[45] The practice goes back to World War Two: Trump and Biden did nothing that Obama, Bush, Clinton, Johnson, Eisenhower, Truman and Roosevelt hadn't done before them.[46]

Law professor James Kwak writes that Goldman's pre-2008 illegalities—a substantial contributor to the GFC—were pursued by a mere handful of Justice Department investigators, who 'didn't try very hard' and were 'reined in by their politically appointed bosses'.[47]

This was the 'dyad' model again: the exchange of personnel between banks and government had created a merging of interests. Accused financial firms, Kwak writes, simply recruited star prosecutors from the Justice Department to defend them:

> Increasingly, the prosecutors and the defense attorneys on opposite sides of the table are the same people, just at different points in their careers.
>
> Executives who bend the rules are 'good people who have done one bad thing', in the words of one SEC lawyer reluctant to bring charges against individuals. Prosecutors no longer punish lawbreakers, but instead make corporations promise to behave better in the future.[48]

Keen to acquire influence of their own, the tech companies too have embraced the model. Google's hiring of government officials stepped up sharply in 2011, after the EU began an investigation into its antitrust violations. In the US, there have been more than 250 revolving door jobs between the company and the federal government.[49] There has also been a significant exodus of FBI and CIA agents to high-salary jobs at Twitter/*X*,[50] of congressional staffers to Facebook,[51] and of intelligence, cybersecurity, law enforcement and military people to Amazon.[52]

The larger salaries these men and women earn commonly allow them to donate money to their former political bosses. The 'revolvers' have other uses as well. The FBI's general legal counsel went to Twitter in 2020, for example, and—against the advice of

Twitter's in-house security expert—he framed the Hunter Biden laptop controversy as 'Russian disinformation'.[53]

'The degree to which Twitter was simply an arm of the government was not well understood by the public,' Elon Musk later stated. 'It was a state publication. Republicans were suppressed at ten times the rate of Democrats.'[54]

Older industries continue to make good use of the methods they helped to pioneer. In the US, nine of the last ten commissioners of the Food and Drug Administration went on to jobs linked to Big Pharma.[55] In Australia, the New South Wales government's chief environmental regulator became the deputy director of the Australian Coal Association; and the Association's executive director was once Australia's negotiator for the Kyoto Protocols.[56]

In Washington, presumably lobbying is the most common career choice for retiring legislators because the average increase in income is 1,452%.[57]

Fig. 3.4: Under Secretary of Defense for Acquisitions, 'Pete' Aldridge (right), with his boss—Defense Secretary Donald Rumsfeld—in 2001. Aldridge's career hopscotched from defense contractors such as LTV Aerospace & McDonnell Douglas to senior Administration jobs such as Director of the National Reconnaissance Office & Under Secretary of the Air Force. One of his purchases whilst in government was Lockheed Martin's F-35 combat aircraft. As of late 2023, the F-35 had cost $1.7 trillion (80% over-budget) and was ten years late.

Think tanks

Imperative that we should give no indication in our literature that we are working to educate the Public along certain lines which might be interpreted as having a political bias. In other words, if we said openly that we were re-teaching the economics of the free-market, it might enable our enemies to question the charitableness of our motives. That is why the first draft is written in rather cagey terms.[58]

> — Oliver Smedley, co-founder of Britain's first neoliberal think tank, the Institute of Economic Affairs, on drafting the institute's Aims (1955).

In order to avoid undesirable criticism, how the organization is controlled and directed should not be widely advertised.[59]

> — Charles Koch, when founding the Center for Libertarian Studies, a neoliberal think tank (mid-1970s).

Think tanks exist to research and develop policy, and often to advocate for it—for which reason they often style themselves 'policy institutes'. Long established in the United States, these days even countries such as China, Bulgaria, Somalia and Iraq have think tanks.

A minority of these institutes are funded by governments, unions, non-profits or public subscription. A few exist inside publicly funded universities. But in the main, think tanks are *plutophile* institutions—funded by corporations, or their owners, or the owners' foundations—to develop policy that benefits the wealthy in general or the donor in particular.

As American investor Adam Townsend put it, 'Think tanks think about getting paid.'[60]

You could say that this type of work began a century ago, when Ludwig von Mises wrote his tracts on economics in the employ of the Vienna Chamber of Commerce.[61]

Think tanks would not exist if they had no effect on public opinion or official policy—to say nothing of regulation, election results, court nominations and legal judgments. So, as with campaign finance and the revolving door (above) and the media (Part Four), the question of undue influence naturally arises.

One of the best-known US think tanks is the American Legislative Exchange Council (ALEC), which promotes over 1,000 bills per year, about a fifth of which become law. ALEC is funded by tobacco, oil and drug companies and the Koch family. The results of its work include state bills that lowered the minimum wage, granted corporations immunity from prosecution, and outlawed the investigation of factory farming practices (the 'ag-gag' laws).

Such laws are often drafted inside ALEC. Legislators attend meetings at which the bill is explained to them, then take it back to their home state for ratification. Corporations lodge hefty fees to participate: drafting sessions are strictly pay-to-play.[62]

A more straightforward type of circularity is at work when the Australian Strategic Policy Institute is paid hundreds of thousands of dollars by Lockheed Martin to lobby for higher defence spending, and Lockheed Martin is awarded contracts by the Australian Government worth hundreds of millions of dollars.[63]

Think tanks may also be paid to go on the offensive against social movements. In 2019, the British think tank Policy Exchange was funded by energy companies to produce a paper condemning Extinction Rebellion—which it claimed was led by extremists. (XR was established by academics and schoolgirls.)

A researcher who offends a donor can cause funds to dry up: so researchers train themselves to stick to the script. ('It's the self-censorship that really affects us over time,' an anonymous scholar from the Brookings Institution told *The New York Times*.[64])

A think tank tends to work on public opinion via its 'research', and on politicians via personal links. In a surreptitiously recorded conversation, former British Labour minister Patricia Hewitt described one formula by which a corporation could make its case:

> Now the think tank and the seminar route I think is a very good one and will remain a good one... And saying ok, does that think tank already have a relationship with Minister X? Can we invite Minister X to give a seminar on this subject? Your client would then sponsor the seminar and you do it via the think tank. And that's very useful, because what you get for your sponsorship is basically you sit next to the Minister.[65]

The pattern didn't improve under Conservative rule. In 2019, the nation's original think tank, the Institute of Economic Affairs, announced that 14 of the appointees to Boris Johnson's cabinet were 'alumni of IEA initiatives'.[66]

Being a part of the system of favors also seems to help with visibility in the press. Of the 15 US think tanks most-quoted on the Ukraine War, 14 were funded by Pentagon contractors.[67]

Even small nations wanting to influence big ones go the think tank route. According to a 2012 document leaked from the Norwegian Ministry of Foreign Affairs:

> In Washington, it is difficult for a small country to gain access to powerful politicians, bureaucrats and experts. Funding powerful think tanks is one way to gain such access, and some think tanks in Washington are openly conveying that they can service only those foreign governments that provide funding.[68]

Indeed, in recent years more than a dozen Washington policy institutes have accepted millions of dollars to advocate policies for foreign governments. (The Brookings Institution has received $14 million from Qatar, for example. The Atlantic Council has taken funds from 25 countries.)

They are generally safe in doing so: the first task of undue influence is to undo constraints on undue influence. In a 2012 *New York Times* story headed *Foreign Powers Buy Influence at Think Tanks*, numerous apparent breaches of the Foreign Agents Registration Act were exposed. The Obama Administration declined to act.[69]

As with most forms of political contamination, this one sometimes reaches bizarre extremes. Philip Morris bankrolled a think tank to discredit the risks of second-hand cigarette smoke named the Advancement of Sound Science Coalition (TASSC). TASSC also campaigned against asbestos regulation, the Clean Air Act, and the 'dioxin scare'. One scholar at the Hudson Institute— which is funded by Monsanto and DuPont—wrote an op-ed titled *Organic Foods Can Make You Sick*, and another wrote a book titled *Saving the Planet with Pesticides and Plastic*.[70]

Astroturfing

That brings us fairly logically to astroturfing—an influence effort by special interests disguised as a grassroots campaign.

By other names, astroturfing goes back to at least the 1930s, when utility monopolies organized 250,000 telegrams to American legislators, purportedly from ordinary people, opposing their break-up under the New Deal. The utilities hid behind fronts like 'the American Liberty League' and the 'Farmers' Independence Council', which were funded by families such as the Rockefellers, the du Ponts, the Mellons and the Morgans.

To this day, American astroturf operations are named with much care:

Save Our Tips, supposedly representing waiters, was established by restaurant owners to prevent increases to the minimum wage. *The National Wetlands Coalition* is funded by real estate developers and oil companies. The *American Council on Science and Health* is funded by fracking interests and makers of soft drinks, chemicals and e-cigarettes.

Coca-Cola funds the *Global Energy Balance Network*, whose 'research' found that obesity is best countered with exercise rather than diet change. (Independent studies have found no such thing.[71])

Certain themes recur: A colloquial name suggests ordinary people; *coalition* suggests broad support (a diverse group of groups); *council* or *convention* suggest authority and believability.

And *citizens*, of course, suggests a groundswell of civic feeling

—although the citizens who united to fund Citizens United have names such as Rockefeller and Koch.

In 2015, the *Family Office Institute* helped persuade the Australian Government to reverse its decision to make corporations reveal how much tax they pay. The Institute—representing itself as a grassroots group—was in fact put together by a corporate lobbyist and a couple of lawyers. It has no members.[72]

In the US, as state governments acted against the pandemic in April 2020, Facebook ads began appearing: 'The people are rising up against these insane shutdowns', and: 'We're fighting back to demand that our elected officials reopen America.'

The ads were funded—as were some of the street demonstrations that followed—by the *Convention of States*, an ostensibly grassroots organization launched with funds from the billionaire Mercer family.

In astroturf outfits, pains are generally taken to keep donor identities secret. Rick Berman, a consultant behind many such groups in the US, was covertly recorded explaining how this is done:

> People always ask me one question all the time: how do I know that I won't be found out as a supporter of what you're doing? We run all our stuff through non-profit organizations that are insulated from having to disclose donors. There is total anonymity.[73]

Astroturfing is even easier on the Internet. The illusion of mass support can be generated via blizzards of bot-driven tweets and forum comments, multiple websites, Wikipedia edits and fake reviews.

Astroturfing even has its service industries. In New Orleans in 2017, a company named Entergy campaigned for permission to build a power plant by arranging for a crowd to appear at a public meeting, complete with placards and T-shirts. These 'supporters' were rounded up by a company named Crowds on Demand: they were actors. Each was issued with talking points, which they repeated, one after the other, at the microphone.

Corporate funding of education

> It would be necessary to use ambiguous and misleading names, obscure the true agenda, and conceal the means of control. This is the method that Charles Koch would soon practice in his charitable giving, and later in his political actions.[74]

> — Charles Coppin, official historian of Koch Industries, describing its strategy for influencing universities.

Academic study was once a bastion of disinterested information. Not in the era of the 'free market'.

Corporations such as Dow, Monsanto and DuPont now 'partner' universities via research, seminars, training, mentoring and the provision of equipment. Increasingly, this is in return for control over research, ownership of results, and the right to shape teaching curriculums.

As ever, the problem of secrecy compounds the problem of influence. In the US, little data is disclosed, or even kept, on the private funding of universities.

In 2010, the Center for American Progress, a progressive think tank (with admittedly murky funding of its own[75]) analyzed ten 'university-industry agreements' made over a decade, collectively worth $833 million.[76]

In nine, the university sacrificed majority control over the research. Seven of the agreements granted a 'high degree' of rights over results to the sponsor. Most sharply limited the institution's right to share results with the academic community.

These constraints on traditional academic freedom arose—in the words of Ivan Oransky from New York University—so corporations could pick questions and study designs 'that are likely to give them the answer they want'.[77]

The 'Googlefication' of schools

At primary and secondary level, tech giants are moving in to sign schools up to 'affiliate programs'—often unbeknownst to parents—to get the school to use the company's products. For example, in an 'Apple Distinguished School' in Australia, every teacher and student is compelled to use an Apple product as their primary teaching or learning device.

A school can likewise become a 'Microsoft Showcase School', or its teachers 'Adobe Education Leaders'.[78] Worldwide, 120 million students and teachers use Google's 'G Suite'. Australian investigative journalist Anna Krien describes this as 'a brand loyalty scheme presented as an education revolution'.

Taking their cue from drug companies, these corporates provide accommodation, air fares and meals for staff, to induce schools into these arrangements. As for parents, there's an 'opt-out' form they can sign—but it took Anna Krien six months to find one. None of the 60 parents she interviewed knew it existed.

Krien cites a former headmaster of Sydney Grammar School on the Australian Government's $AU2.4 billion, seven-year 'Digital Education Revolution':

> It didn't really do anything…except enrich Microsoft and Hewlett-Packard and Apple. They've got very powerful lobby influence in the educational community.[79]

Chapter 19
Remedies

We humans have a sixth sense of when we're being deceived, and that sense is now mobilized everywhere. We can't always identify the Minotaur lurking among us, but we sniff it on the breeze.

Had the corporate class brought only legislators under control, the independent institutions that remained—press, universities, think tanks, grassroots groups—could have unravelled the capture. So a comprehensive approach was needed—a 'chorus'— involving not just the purchase of legislation, but of public attitudes, of research, of educational content, of civil society, of expert opinion: the ancient guideposts of our law and knowledge.

All of society's cognitive and moral signage is skewed to reflect a dollar payment somewhere up the line.

The goal of Article I of the Bill of Change is not to continue the lopsided war against this takeover of our intellectual commons, but to replace the political architecture that makes it possible.

Remedies: Political contributions

Special interests must be eliminated.[1]

— One of the '15 core non-negotiable beliefs' at
teaparty.org

Plutocracy isn't wealth—a subject on which third draft democracy is neutral—but the control of our common institutions by the wealthy. Any aspect of plutocracy, and all of them, can be legally dissolved. All that would require is a scheme to match today's public mood—a set of mechanics—and 50% or so of us to vote for it in a referendum.

Perhaps the most infamous element in plutocracy is the morass of political money. There are already ideas afoot to reform it.[2] Seattle has introduced 'democracy vouchers' worth $25, funded by property taxes. A citizen can donate four of these to city council candidates she favors.

But the scheme didn't outlaw competing corporate funding—and the perils of a 'partial fix' soon became obvious. Seattle's vouchers inspired megadonors such as Amazon to respond with massive cash increases to their favored candidates.[3]

A system like Seattle's is bound to be gamed by corporations. We do need something like 'democracy vouchers': but any scheme that permits big donations will soon be dominated by them.

Contributing money to politics may be part of the popular 'buy-in' the system needs. But some people can't afford to contribute anything. Of those who can, we don't want the rich to have an outsized influence.

There's a simple formula that answers to these criteria:

(i) At election time, every citizen makes a small political pledge
(ii) There are no other sources of political funding
(iii) The pledges are funded by a financial transactions tax (FTT)

Beyond this pledge, the maximum legal value of a political

contribution—in cash, kind or loan: to a candidate, party, politician, regulator, judge, civil servant or their staffers and family—is zero dollars.

For simplicity, citizens could pledge to a party or candidate by ticking a box in their tax return, once per election cycle. Those who don't pay tax could do it via a government office, in person or online.

It won't hurt to simultaneously cut off the *demand* for funds. That can be done by reducing political advertising—usually the largest item of campaign spending—to something like 20% of its pre-Bill level. As with the FTT, we're talking about an already-popular measure. No less than 78% of Americans want less campaign advertising.[4]

In the US, the campaigning 'arms race' between parties has been accelerating from 1981: when the Democrats were still paying off debts from the 1968 election, and the only place to turn for money was corporate America. Thereafter, policies became more pro-corporate, and voter turnouts plummeted. The number of *neos* (first-time voters) fell: the young began opting out of the system. The quality of congressional committees also declined—because, in the words of one Congressman, today's 'top level committee assignments are generally given to top fund-raisers'.[5]

The amount of each 'pledge' would vary according to a society's wealth. In the US, each citizen might pledge $25 per four-year presidential election cycle. In 2020, 158,000,000 people voted[6]—so this would yield a 'civic endowment' of about four billion dollars. That's less than a third of the $14 billion that was spent on presidential and congressional races in 2020.[7] For mid-terms, you could probably halve these amounts.

Once politics is no longer a bidding war between competing monied interests, campaign spending can be much lower.

The pledge is distributed among parties and candidates, in the primary and general elections, as specified by the voter. Parallel schemes operate at the state and local levels.

Four billion dollars is about one thousandth of the 2018 US federal budget of $4.11 trillion. It compares well to the $100 billion spent annually by the American taxpayer on corporate welfare,[8] and the trillions lost to the War on Terror and the GFC.

The subtraction of organized money from politics should be a bedrock democratic principle.

The FTT

Presently, politics is controlled by large interests because individuals cannot bear the costs—time and money—of monitoring and directing politicians; nor are there any mechanics by which they can do so. Third draft democracy supplies not only the mechanics but the costs.

A financial transactions tax of, say, 0.1% on shares and 0.01% on derivatives, would have a minuscule effect on traders' profits. It would bring dramatic, outsized benefits to the society those traders live in. The European Union believes that taxing financial transactions (the exchange-traded ones—not our bank withdrawals or mortgages) at these rates is both 'progressive' and easy to implement.[9]

The thinking about an FTT goes back to John Maynard Keynes, who felt it would stabilize national economies by making more room for investors and less for speculators.[10]

The government of Peru introduced a 0.1% FTT in 2003, to raise money for education. The International Monetary Fund predicted disaster, as did the financial press: bank deposits would be withdrawn, and the supply of credit would shrink. In fact, bank deposits and credit grew significantly.

When FTTs were announced in Argentina, Brazil and Colombia, the same dire warnings were made, and the same results ensued.[11]

Banks have their own suite of dire warnings, to be issued whenever reform is broached. The commonest one is the threat of capital flight: the bank announces that if the reform goes through, it will relocate. In London, Barclays, HSBC and Lloyds made statements like this after 2008, in response to talk of re-regulation. The threat's credibility was not enhanced when Deutsche Bank issued a threat of its own—to quit Germany for London.[12]

Any such move would cost a bank immense disruption and hundreds of millions of euros, and is very unlikely.[13]

If the EU model for an FTT were applied in the United States, it would yield a civic endowment of $130 billion—funding the entire electoral system, federal, state and local—and leaving plenty aside to lift the nation's infrastructure, provide proper care for its injured veterans, or pay down the deficit.[14]

If such a surplus is seen as desirable, the spending priorities should be decided by voters as they make their pledges. (This would amount to a national exercise in 'participatory budgeting'—Part Five.) If a surplus is not wanted, voters could simply opt for a lower FTT rate.

Under existing schemes in some countries, the government supplies electoral funding. The pledge system is better:

- It builds participation: you vote with your pledge even before you vote with your pencil.

- Reaching a certain 'vote threshold' in the previous election is no longer required to secure funds. The pledge goes to the party you like now, not the one you liked three or four years ago.

- A pledge system is a *demotic institution* that's out of government hands permanently, and so free from manipulation.

- Presently, minor parties and independents are overlooked by corporate investors, and so are less likely to get a foot on the funding ladder. They have a better chance of this when funding comes straight from voters.

How 'politically possible' is all this? Would majorities support a small tax on financial trades, and a ban on large political donations—entrenched in the constitution, no less?

It would seem so.

Large bipartisan majorities of Americans would like a financial transactions tax of 0.1%.[15]

Likewise, big majorities in the UK, Japan, Canada, Australia and across Europe, support an FTT.[16]

Thirty-nine percent of Americans want 'fundamental changes' to the campaign funding system, and another 46% want a 'complete rebuild'—a total of 85%.[17]

Americans seem to grasp the need for upstream action. 'Ending the culture of corruption in Washington' is more important to them even than protecting Medicare or creating jobs.[18]

But how popular would putting campaign funding reform into the constitution be?

A survey by *World Public Opinion* found that a constitutional amendment allowing government to limit campaign funding is supported by 88% of Americans: 84% of Republicans and 92% of Democrats.[19]

Root-and-branch campaign finance reform is very popular. So is an FTT.

Fig. 3.5: John Maynard Keynes (right) with Assistant Secretary of the US Treasury, Harry Dexter White, in 1946. Keynes wrote: 'Speculators may do no harm as bubbles on a steady stream of enterprise. But the situation is serious when enterprise becomes the bubble on a whirlpool of speculation... The introduction of a substantial Government transfer tax on all transactions might prove the most serviceable reform available, with a view to mitigating the predominance of speculation over enterprise in the United States.'

Remedies: The revolving door

Wealth should be a democratic 'externality'—a factor lying outside the system. Presently, however, the shaping of policy by money is the key feature of modern governance. This lies at the root of large social, environmental and economic ills.

This influence is not limited to cash contributions. Exchanges of personnel are the grease in the wheels. For that reason, decontamination also means locking the revolving door between corporate and political employment.

Once again, this is what the public desires. A majority of Americans believe that when a company offers a regulator a job, it is 'bribery'.[20] Supermajorities of Democrats (77%) and Republicans (80%) want the revolving door severely curtailed.[21] In Illinois, the only state in which the question has been polled, a majority want it banned outright.[22]

For more than a century, the work background of three-quarters of the US cabinet has been the 'elite corporate sphere'. More recently, the rate is 82%.[23] In 2020, Americans elected a Congress dominated by businesspeople, lawyers and professional politicians. There were a dozen bankers—but no bank tellers; 89 former congressional staffers—but no former congressional drivers; and (representing two million Americans[24]) one artist.[25]

Locking the revolving door will encourage a new diversity of people into representative politics—will make it representative again.

How do you 'lock' the revolving door, exactly?

The core principle would be that achievement in one realm—government or corporate business—should be enough.

Thus there would be a lifetime ban on government employees taking jobs with corporations (lobbying, directorships and consultancies included)—and on corporate managers (though not lower-downs) moving to government.

As small businesses have not corrupted the political system, the rule might exclude those up to the size of a 'Small and Medium Enterprise' (SMEs). (Exactly where lines like this are drawn can be decided by the institutions described in Part Five.)

Finally, salaries and resources for regulators need to be increased.

In the years 2006-08, Britain's Financial Services Authority did only 504 checks on the nation's 29,000 financial firms—which helps to explain the country's 2008 bank crash. This laxity had much to do with the FSA's inability to attract staff: it paid much less than banks did. As a result, a third of FSA staff supervising investment banks were seconded from the financial industry they were supposed to be policing. This included many from the banks whose trading practices brought on the crash.[26]

The appropriate citizen assembly (Part Five) might contemplate indexing salaries at a regulator to those in the industry it is regulating.

Locking the revolving door will not only eliminate regulatory contamination—it should bring the ethic of public service back from the dead.

Remedies: Lobbying

> One of the other ones that aren't talked about is Senator Coons, who's from Delaware, who has a very close relationship with Biden. So we've been working with his office. As a matter of fact, our CEO is talking to him next Tuesday. Then you take it out a little bit more, and you say, 'OK, well, who's up for reelection in 2022?' That's Hassan. That's Kelly. And then, obviously, the Republicans. We have a great relationship with the senators where we have assets… The 2022 class is focused on reelection, so I know I have them. Those are the Marco Rubios. Those are the Senator Kennedys. Those are the Senator Daines. So, you can have those conversations with them because they're a captive audience. They know they need you.[27]
>
> — Keith McCoy, Capitol Hill lobbyist for ExxonMobil, on how the company uses 'assets' in Congress to reduce its tax. Interviewed by activists posing as corporate headhunters (2021).

Lobbying and campaign contributions usually go together—few people lobby without money in their hand[28]—so the two have got conflated. But technically they're different things. Lobbying in this section means what it originally meant: 'seeking to persuade public officials'.

Wealthy corporations should have the right to lobby. The goal should be to bring their influence to some kind of parity with that of small business, churches, non-profits and other groups in society.

The first task is to make lobbying transparent.

The registration of lobbyists is generally a requirement in democracies, but it's fudged or ignored in virtually all of them. So, first and foremost, groups or individuals who attempt—in a methodical or regular way—to persuade a politician of anything will need to be on the lobbyists' register.

(Enforcement of this, and all third draft reforms, is for the Democracy Commission—directly elected, independent of government, with constitutionally guaranteed funding: Part Eight.)

Once registered, a lobbyist needs to disclose details of her budget, activities and funding sources—including the *ultimate* source. Meetings need to be logged and the logs published. All this must happen without *delays*—which are currently a key strategy by government and corporations to evade public accountability.

Right now, modestly funded pro-social groups—religious, environmental, patriotic, recreational, sporting—are outspent hundreds to one by an army of coal, oil, finance, tobacco and drug lobbyists. So, after ensuring transparency, the second task is to create equal access to government.

Limiting the content of lobbying would be Orwellian. Indeed, it is a third draft principle to target funding—not content. So the approach here would be to reduce corporate lobbying expenditure to 20% of the level of the non-corporate sector's—all of it, put together—and to freeze it there, in real dollars, *in perpetuum*.

(Again, 'lobbying' here does not refer to campaign contributions handed over by lobbyists—which are banned outright—but to money used to pay lobbyists and their costs.)

Non-corporate lobbyists—small business, churches, non-profits—represent a much larger slice of the electorate than do corporations, so giving them greater representation is logical enough. Non-corporate lobbying needs to be monitored, however, for those who game the system. For example, if the Democracy

Commission judges that a corporation is funding a charity lobby to advantage itself financially, that would need to be penalized.

Lobbyists these days also act as 'virtual staff' to legislators—advising on legislation and regulation, and frequently writing it. That, too, should be banned. (Many legislators will then find themselves 'short-staffed', so parliamentary staffing budgets will probably need to be increased in the legislation enacted on the back of the third draft reforms.)

With graduation to life as a lobbyist no longer possible, public service can now be a lifetime commitment. In any sphere, this type of commitment tends to harvest the most knowledge and yield the deepest perspective.

Whilst the backbone of all this will be constitutional change, there will also be legislative and regulatory change. I suggest some principles for 'triaging' these in Parts Five and Eight.

Change of this kind also requires more detail than can fit in one book. Briefly, some rules to prevent shadow, indirect or back-door lobbying might include the following:

(i) Reduce the hours a legislator may engage with corporate lobby-ists. (US legislators spend so much time talking to donors and lobbyists that they have little left in which to do useful work.[29])
(ii) Restrict foreign lobbying.
(iii) Outlaw misleading names for lobby groups.
(iv) Establish a regime of voluntary reporting and random audits.
(v) Protect and encourage whistleblowers.
(vi) End large payments for expert court testimony.
(vii) End the power of public officials to issue waivers for any of the above.

'Overwhelming' majorities of Americans want restrictions on lobbying by former government officials.[30] A large majority of Australians think 'lobbyists have too much influence over politi-cians'.[31] The British perception of lobbyists is so poor that lobby-ists themselves are uncomfortable with it.[32] In the European Union, according to *Transparency International*, 'the practice of lobbying is widely associated with secrecy and unfair advantage'.[33]

Lobbying reform will not be a hard sell.

Remedies: Think tanks

> The more I saw the more I thought this was the product of the neocons, who didn't understand the region and were going to create havoc there. These were dilettantes from Washington think tanks who had never had an idea that worked on the ground.[34]
>
> — General Anthony Zinni, former Centcom Commander, on the Iraq invasion (2003).

Reforming the think tank landscape is a part of normalizing society's moral signage: the array of implicit and explicit messages from media, social media, education, astroturfing, et al, that wash over us daily, and shape our thinking.

A few think tanks are ideologically independent; a few were even established to benefit society. But most are essentially lobby organizations that exist to shape policy and opinion for their wealthy investors.

Supporting a corporate viewpoint falls well within the bounds of free speech. But think tanks should not have an unfair advantage, unless we believe a sponsored opinion is worth more than a freely given one.

The approach here is comparable to the approach to political donations. Citizens can contribute an amount that the pre-referendum process settles on—let's say $20 each per electoral cycle—to the think tank of their choosing: paid, again, from the financial transactions tax. Thinks tanks should receive zero funding from any other source.

When a citizen makes her pledge, there might be an option to lodge a vote for an issue she wants the think tank to study.

Funding for think tanks would now come from a large, diverse voter-base—and no longer from a tiny, wealthy section of the population. This would almost certainly create a think tank culture we could be proud of. Think tanks would do research and develop policy that citizens want.

The democratization of think tanks would also head off the alarming trend of foreign influence, which often uses think tanks as beachheads.

In the US, where 252 million people are of voting age,[35] $20 per citizen would raise $5 billion. If the scheme were voluntary—a healthy fraction of the population probably knows or cares little about think tanks—this might still yield $2 billion.

As with every element of the Bill of Change, the rules on think tanks need to be re-assessed once in a while. So, via direct and deliberative democracy (Part Five), that amount could be raised or lowered every ten years, depending on how the electorate views think tanks at the time.

Many government-funded policy institutes, such as the RAND Corporation, exist mostly to expand military spending. Unless the electorate wants to make exceptions, taxpayer funding for think tanks can be phased out over a year or two.

Instead of creating a thousand rules at the outset, and a monster bureaucracy to police them, 'mutable democracy'—made from institutions we'll look at in Part Five—allows the *demos* to make a mosaic of adaptations as hazards arise.

The importance of this is underlined by Dean Wells—once Attorney General of the Australian state of Queensland. In 2019, Wells reflected on the Criminal Justice Commission he'd ushered in 30 years earlier, in the wake of the landmark Fitzgerald Inquiry into official corruption:

> The Criminal Justice Commission did... have some success in cleaning up the police service for a period of time, but eventually the germs mutated to defeat the antibiotic. And the disease came back in a new form. Process corruption is still rife in Queensland.
> ...What we've got is a commission that over the years has been captured by the interest groups that it is supposed to be regulating. Of course it's not what [Fitzgerald] had in mind... We didn't go wrong. All law reform is a dynamic process. You're

building on the shifting sands of a social system that's constantly changing.

You need a Fitzgerald Inquiry every generation. You need a Fitzgerald Inquiry in every jurisdiction every 25 years. Society is dynamic. They change, they adapt. You need to change the antibiotic.[36]

This kind of 'mutability' is intrinsic to third draft democracy. Rules can be useful—but giving the public the power to make them is the main game. This allows governance to keep pace with social evolution, and indeed to become a part of it: something we've not really seen since the Greeks.

Remedies: Astroturfing

In addition to mutability, third draft democracy draws on the principle of *syzygy*—where reforms 'line up' to increase their collective gravity, and thus negate the pull of the old system. In other words: a set of mutually reinforcing tools is more powerful than one. As Aesop wrote:

This bundle of sticks you can't break.
Take them singly, and with ease
You may break them as you please.

Plutocracy is far-flung, strategic and multi-faceted. Attacking it with a single weapon won't slow it for long.

An example of 'single stick syndrome' would be to put an end to the campaign donor system—in isolation. You could be sure that revolving door employment, or universities, or astroturfing— or all three—will soon be awash with corporate cash, to compensate for the loss of influence. They'd also be used, over time, to roll back your reform.

Dealing with organized money requires holism. Only a suite of complementary tools can work against a foe that has implanted itself everywhere.

Astroturfing is one more strand to be pulled loose from this weave. Because it seeks to deceive us into believing that an idea has arisen organically from public opinion—when in fact it's been confected for corporate ends—astroturfing is an illegitimate form of influence: one more plutocratic thumb on the scales by which we balance our facts.

Putting an end to astroturfing pretty much begins and ends with transparency. Any group seeking to influence opinion needs to publicly disclose the source of its funding (including the original source).

Deceitful names need to be outlawed. *Working Families for Walmart*—which is sponsored by the Walmart and Edelman public relations departments—will have to find an honest name for itself.[37]

Then, once astroturfing is transparent, it's no longer astroturfing: you have ended it.

Remedies: Corporate funding of education

In developed countries, most educational funding *doesn't* come from the corporate sector. So the contamination of academia represents a case where we can arrest the parasite before it consumes the host.

Much good has come from some university-corporate collaborations. The goal should not be to end them, but to make them less one-sided, more transparent and better directed to the public good.

Some corporate leaders want to act pro-socially. Present rules encourage a race to the bottom. A few simple changes can redraw this picture:

- Any partnership agreement between an educational institution and a donor must be made public.
- A donor can't have 'majority control' over an academic project.
- All study results must be published; those inconvenient to a donor can't be 'bottom-drawered'.

- Researchers cannot be blocked from testifying in court about their results.
- Corporations can have no role in funding or influencing university curriculums.
- Ditto schools: no more 'affiliate programs'; no more corporate bribes in the form of accommodation and travel.

Remedies: International bodies

We are in an era of emerging left-right consensus on certain major issues. One of these issues is the unwholesome power of global bodies. Corporations now influence not only government, information, education and civil society—they also control the international organizations.

For decades, the left has wanted to reshape bodies like the International Monetary Fund, the World Bank and the World Trade Organization—to make them serve the interests of ordinary people. Now, the anti-globalist right wants this too.

Reform is needed not only in the larger bodies, but in the international 'policy boards' in which corporations have invested much money and personnel.

Executives from Shell, for example, have sat on the board of the UN Climate Technology Network. Meetings of the UN Climate Convention (UNFCC) have received corporate sponsorships—indeed Monsanto (of all companies) once chaired a UNFCC working group.[38] Naturally the result has been an increasing focus on 'market solutions' to climate change.

It's especially important to end the capacity of corporations to sue governments under the rules of the World Trade Organization. Astra Taylor explains these 'investor-state dispute settlements' (ISDS) in her book, *Democracy May Not Exist But We'll Miss It When It's Gone*:

> ISDS establish secret tribunals in which foreign investors have the right to sue governments for lost profits, including the loss of 'future expected profits'... Thus one dispute tribunal awarded

Houston-based Occidental Petroleum $1.8 billion after Ecuador canceled an oil exploration contract, a sum approximately equal to the country's annual health budget. Countless similar cases are currently playing out around the world: Transcanada is suing the United States for $15 billion in damages because the government, under overwhelming public pressure, declined to approve the company's plan to build the Keystone XL Pipeline; Lone Pine, an American company, is suing Quebec for passing a moratorium on fracking...

These suits are adjudicated in private arbitration panels rather than in public courts. There is no central registry of ISDS disputes and also no transparency, due process, or conflict of interest guidelines. The individuals who serve on the tribunals may play the role of a judge one day and lobbyist the next, yet they have the power to award corporations vast sums that must be paid by taxpayers. There is no right of appeal and losing governments must pay all legal costs. There is also no reciprocity: governments cannot sue corporations for damage they cause to public health, security, or if they violate a contract.[39]

Thus when COVID arrived, drug giant Pfizer was able to force countries worldwide to change laws to protect it from lawsuits: no changes, no vaccines. As we saw earlier, the indemnities Pfizer forced on governments included those for injuries arising from Pfizer's own negligence or fraud.[40]

These ethical absurdities can be ended both domestically and internationally. Domestic legislation could bar local corporations from funding or staffing international or multilateral bodies. And governments could vote within such bodies to end untoward corporate influence—or end this influence simply by withdrawing participation. Where a government won't act, it can be instructed to do so by the *national citizens' assemblies* discussed in Part Five.

The more sophisticated instrument, which should evolve over time, is to link these assemblies across borders: that is, demotic international law.

Chapter 19

Remedies: Foreign influence

Tactics without strategy is the noise before defeat.

— Sun Tzu

An authoritarian nation harms a democracy to advantage itself geopolitically—but also to damage the credibility of the democratic model. We saw several decades of this activity during the Cold War.

In 1983, KGB defector Yuri Bermezov explained that espionage was only incidental to the work of the Soviet Union's intelligence agencies.[41] Their real work was demoralization: undermining the faith of Western peoples in their institutions. Bermezov compared the KGB to a judo player throwing a stronger opponent off balance by using his own weight against him. The West, he believed, was undermining itself. The Soviets just accelerated the process where they could.

Our long era of spycraft and propaganda continues—these days with China as the leading anti-democratic nation. But the neoliberal period has yielded a new tool, to complement those traditionally used against us: our leaders have become purchasable.

China, in particular, now grasps that a democracy is more easily neutralized on home soil than on far-off battlefields. The result is a growing Chinese influence over policy in parts of the democratic world.

We hardly needed another hazard of plutocracy to emerge, but now one has. Because there are so few protections against political contamination—other than registers lobbyists don't use, and laws ministers don't enforce[42]—a foreign government can now influence the policies of one's own.

In 2017, Australia's national security agency, ASIO, announced that it was 'overwhelmed' by 'foreign powers clandestinely seeking to shape the opinions of members of the Australian public, media organisations and government officials'.[43] In 2019, ASIO's recently retired head warned that the Chinese Government was attempting to 'take over' the Australian political system, via espionage and interference.[44]

The Chinese Communist Party (CCP) has launched cyber attacks against Australia's parliament and its three main political parties.[45] It infiltrates Australian schools and universities via 'Confucius Institutes'.[46] Through an intermediary, the Chinese News Service (the CCP's 'armslength' propaganda outfit) secretly gained majority ownership of *The Pacific Times*, a leading Chinese language newspaper in Australia.

This buying up of Chinese language papers has occurred across Southeast Asia.[47] Those papers that refuse to publish CCP propaganda have had their advertisers in China threatened, forcing them to withdraw their ads.[48]

John Garnaut, an Australian writer on China, experienced the CCP's 'hidden world of inducements, threats and plausible deniability' at firsthand:

> I was offered red envelopes, neatly packed with US$100 bills. And sounded out for a lucrative 'consultancy' arrangement with a Hong Kong bank. In one encounter, I was offered air tickets, hotel accommodation, a five-star family holiday, a job, and a gift bag containing bottles of Bordeaux wine valued at up to US$2000 each. These were all reciprocity traps, to be avoided at all costs. Gradually, over time, the ratio of carrots to sticks was inverted...[49]

Numerous Australian universities, parliamentarians, public servants and regional councils have clouds hanging over them due to claims of Chinese influence.[50] China has been permitted to closely monitor its foreign students, insert spies into classes, and pay thugs to rough up dissidents. In 2020, an Australian student at the University of Queensland held an on-campus protest against China, and was beaten up publicly by Chinese thugs. The university, which depends heavily on Chinese funding, declined to act against the perpetrators, but suspended the student.[51]

In 2017, Australian academic Clive Hamilton wrote *Silent Invasion*—a book that detailed many such episodes, and the strategy guiding them. The book was 'pulled' by its publisher when the possibility of a 'vexatious defamation action' from Beijing became clear.[52]

John Garnaut writes:

> I had seriously underestimated the extent to which the CCP had inoculated itself against the values and institutions of the European Enlightenment that underpinned the development of capitalism in the West. The tools of coercion, co-option and deception that had proven so effective in revolution were still hardwired into the governing system.[53]

Russia has a somewhat different bag of tricks, and somewhat different goals. Its well-known 2016 cyber attacks on the United States were intended to influence the election in favor of Donald Trump, but equally—as per Bermezov's warning—to erode faith in the democratic system.[54]

In the same year, the Russians were running an espionage campaign to help to get Brexit across the line: a Western rift being in Russia's interests.[55]

Citizen legislation is well-suited to crafting a deterrent regime to all this. That way, foreign influencers, donors and propagandists are neutralized by a people rather than a government. This a stronger message to send.

As elites in authoritarian countries value visiting the West for business and holidays, one such deterrent would be to deport perpetrators and deny future visas. This is something governments are presently reluctant to do when the foreigner has money.

Moreover, defences against foreign interference will be more robust if the democratic nations team up.[56] That, too, can be led by citizens. This international aspect of third draft democracy is discussed in Part Five.

Perhaps most important of all, citizen legislation should craft laws to end the home government's own interference abroad. The United States, for example, engages in more of this activity than either China or Russia. This will reduce the incidence of retaliation-in-kind.

Our present defences against foreign meddling—speeches, spycraft and sanctions—are tactics without strategy. For the democracies, the real defence is democracy. We won't, in the end, ring-fence our institutions through expulsions and penalties, but by reinventing them for the present-day.

This means making them fluid enough to survive and attractive enough to emulate.

Remedies: Unions

Back in 1972, American historian Carroll Quigley noted that

> we now have a plutocratic system, and many politicians see it simply as a matter of buying elections. Here's why. As our economy is now structured, the big corporations—aerospace, oil, and so on—are able to pour out millions to support the candidates they favor...
>
> The second reason is that labor unions are now a part of the system. They too want to get on the gravy train, and are no longer concerned with defending the rights of ordinary men or making the political system more democratic. Their outlook is little different from that of the big corporations, because this in effect is what they are. They are enormously rich, they are not democratically run, and they have increasingly taken on the characteristics of great corporations: irresponsibility, anonymity, and undemocratic procedures.[57]

Labor unions were integral to the development of modern democracy, and still have a serious role in it. But if other sectors of society are expected to democratize, the same should be required of them.

One doesn't have to go far to find cases of contamination and corruption in the union movement. In 2020, the president of New York's construction union, James Cahill, was indicted for racketeering and fraud, along with ten colleagues. It was alleged he accepted more than $100,000 in bribes to help employers escape penalties for hiring non-union labor. The non-union labor consisted of workers who would replace the members of Cahill's own union.[58] In December 2022, he pled guilty to the charges, and now faces many years in prison.[59]

In 2019, the former chief executive of the United Auto Workers (UAW) union in the US was charged with embezzling '$1 million for extravagant meals, golf outings, cigars and apparel'.[60] Even before these claims came to light, the socialist magazine *Jacobin* had described the UAW as 'a corrupt and incompetent bureaucracy' and 'a labor movement tragedy'.[61]

Fig. 3.6: Charles 'Lucky' Luciano—considered the 'father' of organized crime in the United States, for his development of the National Crime Syndicate in the 1930s. Like many mobsters then & now, Luciano made much of his fortune from union corruption.

Today's union governance model, *Jacobin* notes, began with Teamsters boss Jimmy Hoffa—who essentially centralized the union's power in himself. This gave Hoffa the power to award salaries and pensions to union officials. *Jacobin* sees the Teamsters' decline as being rooted in 'patronage and unaccountable leadership'. [62] Thus the headline-grabbing corruption of unions such as the Teamsters often begins as contamination, which is typically a quiet affair.[63] For example, when the brother and sons of Joe Biden cited Biden's union connections to persuade unions to invest their pension funds with them, this was unremarkable, and perfectly legal

—though you wouldn't need a large imagination to spot the slippery slope.[64]

Centralizing power and rewards in the leadership, rather than members, makes a union weaker; conversely, fixing their internal democracy problem would make unions more effective and their message more persuasive.

A union might begin its 'third draft' era with a re-draft *by members* of its constitution—especially the rules governing elections and finances. Thereafter, major decisions of policy—on internal elections, finances, wage claims, industrial actions, political endorsements—should be made by the members alone, via direct and deliberative democracy (Part Five).

Remedies: Political parties

Of 15 million Australian voters, barely 30,000 have even a nominal involvement in political parties—an engagement of just 0.2 percent. The parties are small, closed, secretive, and oligarchic, and they prefer it that way.[65]

— Barry Jones, former President of the Australian Labor Party (2020)

The real issue in government is not 'how to do X much better'. In most areas we know. The real issue is big players in the system tend to be either uninterested in improving X or actively opposed. Almost everyone in Westminster is much happier with the existing system failing dismally than facing what it means to change seriously… The key institution blocking what the public wants is the broken old parties who are locked into mindsets that *aren't even rational for them.*[66]

— Dominic Cummings, former chief advisor to British PM Boris Johnson (2022)

Wealth sharpens its influence by causing power to concentrate at the top of a political organization.

In the US, it is party leaders, committee members and aspirants to the White House who receive the lion's share of corporate funding. It's little different across the pond. Boris Johnson received large donations from bankers, hedge funds and property developers during his 2019 campaign for the British Conservative Party leadership. (There were strenuous attempts to keep these quiet.)[67]

At the party level, this feedback loop makes for top-heaviness: squandering lots of lower-down talent, and ensuring limited scrutiny of a government or opposition from within.

The $2.5 trillion omnibus budget bill which passed Congress on December 21, 2020, was written entirely by congressional leaders and the White House. Congress was handed the bill—at 5,593 pages, the longest ever passed—at 1.46 pm. It was required to vote on it at 7.35 pm. Ordinary members, such as Republican Senator Rick Scott, objected:

> It is almost 5,600 pages long and we're expected to vote on it tonight. Who in their right mind thinks that this is a responsible way of governing?[68]

The top-heaviness of parties should diminish automatically once politics is decontaminated. The pledge system only funds candidates for public elections: zero dollars are permitted to candidates for intra-party races, such as leadership positions and committees. Candidates for these will now rise or fall on their merits.

Remedies: Non-profits

Certain environment groups are run dictatorially; others seek funding from the developer interests they're established to fight.[69] Quite a few non-profits are simply managed incompetently. So civil society groups might also want to democratize, where members see the need.

In non-profits, the results of contamination range from the banal to the calamitous. The administrators of USA Swimming knew for decades of the sexual abuse of child swimmers, and kept quiet about it. This was to prevent sponsor defections, and so to protect the group's $40 million in revenue.[70] In 2020, the Boy Scouts of America faced no less than 82,000 claims of sexual abuse.[71] How could democratically run civil society groups do worse than this?

After decontamination, how do non-profits replace their corporate funding?

As the financial transactions tax will yield much more revenue than is needed in the electoral system, citizens might be allowed to pledge extra funds to a non-profit. Joining this scheme might be conditional on an assembly of the non-profit's members effecting a transition to clean governance.

Chapter 20
Divorcing wealth from power

We've decided that kings and despots can no longer govern us—that whites should no longer rule non-whites, and that men should no longer rule women. So why are we still ruled by wealth? As we've seen, it can be as despotic as any king, as blind as any colonial settler, and as violent as any abusive husband. Like monarchs, dictators and colonial invaders, it rules by fiat, orders theft and massacre, and is accountable to no-one.

Perhaps the earliest recorded instance of political decontamination was the decision to pay jurors in Athens. This was introduced by Pericles to counter Cimon, a citizen rich enough buy himself favors in the courts. The principle soon became essential to classical democracy.

It was also essential to Britain's Great Reform Act of 1832, and the American Progressive Era, from the 1890s to the 1920s: which took down political machines, broke up monopolies, and established direct democracy. Americans have been through this cycle already, as have many cultures.

From the Stone Age to the Information Age, a test of any human group's survivability has been its ability to divorce wealth from power.

For that reason, Decontamination is the first Article of the Bill of Change.

Part Four

Isegoria

Chapter 21
Speech in the first democracy

Trace our ideas on public speech in a democracy to their Greek origins, and you find that the most important word relating to it was not *parrhesia*—'free speech', the freedom to say what you like—but *isegoria*: 'the equal right by all to speak and be heard by the public'.

The notion of *isegoria* (pronounced *ee*-see-*ghor*-ia) arrived by degrees from the time of Solon. It derives from *iso* (equal) and *agora*—the public space where Athenian public speech originated. In the *agora*, all had an equal right to be heard. By perhaps the 460s BC, the Athenians had coined this all-important word to describe it.[1]

With *isegoria,* there's a bit to unpack:

- It's the right to speak publicly.
- It's an *equal* right—every citizen has it in the same measure.
- Additionally, a citizen has *the right to be heard by society*.
- Finally, for the listener, *isegoria* is sometimes defined as 'the right to hear all views'.[2]

So, this wasn't merely the right to speak your mind: you had the right to be heard, just as your audience had the right to hear you. Where today's 'freedom of speech' gives us one right, *isegoria* conferred several.

In the Athenian Assembly, where the practice of *isegoria* was refined over some decades, it demonstrated that the Assembly's laws were the will of the people. *Isegoria* legitimized government.

It didn't end there. The word also served to describe the type of society Athens was. A travelling Athenian, asked what sort of regime he lived under, may have answered '*demokratia*'—but was just as likely to have said '*isegoria*'.

To Herodotus, the first 'scientific' historian, *isegoria* was the crowning achievement of the Athenian experiment.[3] He attributed Athens' greatness to it.[4] In the words of classical philologist Mogens Herman Hansen:

> When Herodotus describes the birth of Athenian democracy it is *isegoria* not *isonomia* [equal political rights] that he singles out as the principal form of democratic equality, and his account conforms with what we find in Athenian sources: the aspect of equality most cherished by Athenian democrats was *isegoria*.[5]

Herodotus depicts *isegoria* as the system of government that replaced tyranny. He notes that after introducing it, Athens defeated a three-pronged invasion led by the fearsome Spartans:

> The Athenians at this point became much stronger. So it is clear how worthy an object of attention is isegoria, not just in one respect but in every sense. Since they were ruled by tyrants, the Athenians did not stand out from their neighbors in military capability, but after deposing the tyrants, they became overwhelmingly superior.[6]

Historian Josiah Ober affirms that the 'political liberation' of *isegoria* resulted 'not in a cascade of free riding, but in the coherent collective military action that defeated the Spartan coalition'.[7] Athens became the benchmark for progress in Classical civilization, Ober believes, because *isegoria* enabled 'disseminated knowledge', 'institutional learning' and 'collective wisdom':

> Herodotus claims that the Athenian leap forward in state strength demonstrates the general value of 'equality of public speech'. This claim is initially puzzling. But if we attend to the reform of the deliberative Council, and the ways in which equality of speech could, under the right conditions, pay out in bold and innovative new policies, Herodotus' comment becomes perfectly comprehensible.[8]

Athens did not have a passive, voyeur culture like our own. To an Athenian, the one-way direction of our mass media, and its narrow spectrum of voices, would have seemed closer to slavery than citizenship.

The Athenian Assembly was not only 'the people' but also 'the legislature'—which more or less made it 'the state' as well. And, as it was where ideas were aired, and absorbed into society, it was also effectively 'the media'. The tasks we hive off to others the Athenians assumed for themselves.

Chapter 22
Speech today

Real shame we can't show it here.[1]

— CBS journalist Mike Wallace to John Pilger,
when Pilger showed him his documentary on low
morale among US troops in Vietnam (1970).

A modern citizen's right to say anything he wants is comparable to his right to stable his horse at an inn—present in law but of little practical use. His views have slender influence beyond his immediate circle. Print, TV and radio are one-way. Even where feedback is permitted, it is still *feedback*. The power of agenda-setting remains with the news organization.

The rise of social media has not improved this picture. Whilst its mass organizing power is prodigious, social media has not much enhanced the transmission of news. Most news posts are re-posts from mainstream media. Most tweets about current affairs are links to news from (most commonly) *The New York Times*, *The Hill*, CNN, *The Washington Post* and Fox News.[2]

BuzzFeed News was a leader in news distributed via social media—but it collapsed in 2023, and that whole trend is now seen to have declined or even ended.[3] Compounding all this, social media companies now 'partner' with the intelligence agencies to censor 'disinformation'.[4]

Large, legacy news outlets still do the vast majority of news reporting.[5] Only minuscule numbers of social media users have ever 'covered the news themselves, by posting photos or videos of news events'.[6]

'Social's' power to amplify, de-amplify and censor news would be slightly less disturbing if there were thousands of platforms. But, in the US, the vast majority of social media news content is purveyed by Facebook, YouTube, *X* and Instagram. Even the second-hand news market has been cornered.[7]

As with television, radio and print before it, news on the Internet is the province of a cartel.

Two *Chicago Tribune* journalists wrote in 2020—as their paper was about to be asset-stripped by a hedge fund:

> Facebook and other social media sites give the impression that they offer everything you need to know. But, in reality, most of Facebook's news is generated in traditional newsrooms. If we disappear, their news feed will consist of little more than news releases and opinion-based screeds.[8]

American media companies of the early 20th Century were more local and numerous than today's; this at least distributed the power to air news and views to a few thousand people. The march to monopoly began when the great crusading periodicals—*Harper's* and *The Atlantic*—were bought up by the financiers whose activities they'd exposed, John D Rockefeller and JP Morgan.[9]

By 1983, 90% of the US media was controlled by 50 companies, and by 2011 the number was six.[10] Things are similar in many developed countries—in France it's nine, in Australia it's three.

In Australia, News Corp controls most of the metropolitan daily newspapers, and the national daily. It has large holdings in free-to-air, cable and satellite TV; and in magazines, Internet, market research, and DVD and film production.[11]

At the behest of Mexico's media corporations, its government privatised the public TV stations. Now two companies administer 94% of the country's TV broadcasters.

In Italy, Mediaset—owned till his death by Silvio Berlusconi—is the only private TV broadcaster, the biggest publisher, and the biggest advertising company. Two of the country's national dailies are owned by Berlusconi's family. When he was prime minister, giving him authority over state outlets, Berlusconi directly or indirectly controlled nearly 90% of Italy's mass media.

Alexander Stille's 2006 book, *The Sack of Rome,* zeroes in on what happens when the politics-media feedback loop approaches extreme values:

> Once Berlusconi came to power, journalists on state television were required to adhere strictly to a news formula known as the sandwich, in which virtually every political story began by stating the government's (or Berlusconi's) point of view, followed by a sound bite or two from the opposition and concluded with a rebuttal from the government. Berlusconi himself occupied an incredible 50 percent of airtime on the state-owned newscasts, while the opposition accounted for barely 20 percent...
>
> When the Italian economy struggled through three straight years of recession and near-zero growth, Rai [the state broadcasting company] showed a world of happy prosperity.
>
> ...when Berlusconi won in 1994 and then again in 2001... social scientists found to their surprise that the strongest predictors of a voter's orientation were no longer class or church affiliation but what television stations a person watched and for how long...[12]

In our world, media is the place in which the few address the many. The arrangement is itself normalized via an elaborate media silence. The control of society's informational circulatory system by a handful of billionaire men is the subject of zero mainstream news stories per year.

As we saw earlier, the feedback loop—where *A* produces more of *B* which in turn produces more of *A*—tends to characterize a doomed system. In the loop's final phase, dysfunctions can arise that would normally only occur in dystopian fiction. In the United States, President Donald Trump watched so much Fox News—sometimes seven hours a day—that industries wanting government favors produced advertisements for him alone.[13]

In Russia, Vladimir Putin's political advisor, Gleb Pavlovsky, has observed:

> The main difference between propaganda in the USSR and the new Russia…is that in Soviet times the concept of truth was important. Even if they were lying they took care to prove what they were doing was 'the truth'. Now no one even tries proving 'the truth'. You can just say anything. Create realities.[14]

The architect of George W Bush's election victories, Karl Rove, outlined his own thinking to Ron Susskind of *The New York Times*. Rove told the journalist that people like him (Susskind) were 'in what we call the reality-based community'. These were people who

> believe that solutions emerge from your judicious study of discernible reality… That's not the way the world really works anymore. We're an empire now, and when we act, we create our own reality. And while you're studying that reality—judiciously, as you will—we'll act again, creating other new realities, which you can study too, and that's how things will sort out. We're history's actors…and you, all of you, will be left to just study what we do.[15]

In 2018, Rudolph Giuliani discussed the subject of 'truth' with CNN journalist Chris Cuomo:

> *Giuliani*: It's in the eye of the beholder.
> Cuomo: No, facts are not in the eye of the beholder.
> *Giuliani*: Yes they are. Nowadays they are.[16]

Communication is from the Latin *communicationem*—to 'unite' or 'participate in'. *Co* signifies 'together': the word denotes that *munia* (duties, public duties, functions) are conducted 'between', 'together', 'among'. *Communication* implies a two-way street, or more closely a busy intersection.

The Athenians would have viewed our societies as economically developed, like their neighbors in Egypt and Persia, but not as democratic. To them, democracy without *isegoria* would have been a contradiction in terms. A wit like Aristophanes might have compared our media regime to the confining of public speech to monarchs.

In the Stone Age, and for a long time thereafter, there was only face-to-face conversation—in which a rough equality prevailed. It only became possible to convince large numbers of people of nonsense when communication became one-way.

Chapter 23
Does the media shape our thinking?

Hermann Göring: Why, of course the people don't want war. Why would some poor slob on a farm want to risk his life in a war when the best he can get out of it is to come back to his farm in one piece? Naturally, the common people don't want war; neither in Russia, nor in England, nor in America, nor for that matter in Germany. That is understood. But, after all, it is the leaders of the country who determine the policy and it is always a simple matter to drag the people along, whether it is a democracy, or a fascist dictatorship, or a parliament, or a communist dictatorship.

    Gustave Gilbert: There is one difference. In a democracy the people have some say in the matter through their elected representatives, and in the United States only Congress can declare wars.

    Hermann Göring: Oh, that is all well and good, but, voice or no voice, the people can always be brought to the bidding of the leaders. That is easy. All you have to do is tell them they are being attacked, and denounce the pacifists for lack of patriotism and exposing the country to danger. It works the same way in any country.[1]

Chapter 23

— Interview with Hermann Göring by American
psychologist Gustave Gilbert, Nuremberg, 1945.

I n a 2006 poll of US troops in Iraq, 85% believed the
occupation was 'to retaliate for Saddam's role in the 9-11
attacks'.[2]

The Iraq War demonstrated that engineered opinion can, even
decades after 1945, bring destitution and death on a colossal scale.
The electorates of the United States, Britain and Australia walked
blindfolded into the largest foreign policy disaster since World
War Two. This is only possible when agenda-setting power is
concentrated in few hands.

This works the same anywhere. Journalist Milos Vasic describes
the effect of the state-controlled *Radio Television Serbia* during the
1990s:

> All it took was a few years of fierce, reckless, chauvinist, intoler-
> ant, expansionist, war-mongering propaganda to create enough
> hate to start the fighting among people who had lived together
> peacefully for 45 years.[3]

The first study of 'agenda-setting' (it coined the phrase) was in
the North Carolina town of Chapel Hill in 1968. Its finding was
radical for the time:

> Five issues dominated the media and public agendas during the
> 1968 US presidential campaign—foreign policy, law and order,
> economics, public welfare, and civil rights. There was a nearly
> perfect correspondence between the rankings of these issues by
> the Chapel Hill voters and their rankings based on their play in
> the news media during the previous twenty-five days.[4]

Thirty-five years later, in 2003, Maxwell McCombs, one of the
study's authors, wrote:

> Since that initial study during the 1968 US presidential election,
> more than 300 hundred published studies worldwide have docu-

mented this influence of the news media. It should be noted that this evidence encompasses a wide variety of research designs, including numerous panel studies, time-series analyses, and controlled laboratory experiments…

Subsequent studies have examined much longer periods of time—for example, a year-long, nine-wave panel study during the 1976 US presidential election—and found similar evidence of strong agenda-setting effects…

What we know about the world is largely based on what the media decide to tell us… Elements prominent on the media agenda become prominent in the public mind.[5]

In their book *News That Matters*, Shanto Iyengar and Donald Kinder describe numerous controlled experiments they ran on groups of TV news viewers, in which they repeatedly altered the order and emphasis of news stories. They found what McCombs and his colleagues did: what's important to news-creators becomes important to viewers. As one shifts priorities, so does the other.[6]

In a survey conducted in 2000, 9,000 towns newly connected to the Fox network were compared to towns that were not. The 'Fox' towns swung measurably to Republican candidates, and the 'Fox effect' likely shifted enough presidential votes to put George W Bush in the White House.[7]

News programming by the liberal media is a mirror image. This conversation with Charlie Chester, Technical Director of CNN, was secretly recorded in mid-2021:

Chester: Look what we did—we got Trump out…

When [Trump's] hand was shaking we brought in so many medical people, to all tell a story—that was all speculation—that he was neurologically damaged, that he was losing it… We were creating a story there that we didn't know anything about, you know? I think that's propaganda…

Our focus was to get Trump out of office, right? Without saying it, that's what it was, right? So our next thing is going to be for climate change awareness…

Journalist: Who decides that?

Chester: The head of the network.

Journalist: Is that [CNN president Jeff] Zucker?

Chester: Zucker, yeah…

Journalist: So that's, like, the next…

Chester: Pandemic-like story, yeah—that we'll beat to death. But that one's got longevity, you know what I mean? There's a definitive ending to the pandemic… Climate thing is going to take years. So they'll probably be able to milk that for quite a bit.[8]

Chapter 24
The blind sector

Fig. 4.1: Left: Nazi propaganda against the Soviets. Right: Soviet propaganda against the Nazis.

Traditional propaganda, like that practised in Nazi Germany, distributes information and misinformation proactively:

Chapter 24

Every morning the editors of the Berlin daily newspapers and the correspondents of those published elsewhere in the Reich gathered at the Propaganda Ministry to be told by Dr Goebbels or by one of his aides what news to print and suppress, how to write the news and headline it, what campaigns to call off or institute and what editorials were desired for the day.[1]

— William L Shirer (*The Rise and Fall of the Third Reich*)

The 'old model' was also employed in the Soviet Union. For example, when spy chief Lavrentiy Beria was purged in 1953, citizens who had purchased *The Great Soviet Encyclopedia* were mailed a letter instructing them to turn to its 'B' section, tear out the three pages on Beria, and replace them with pages—enclosed in the letter—on FW Bergholz, Bishop Berkeley and the Bering Sea.[2]

Where once it was authoritarian leaders who shaped public thought, today the media corporation is in the driver's seat—and new methods have proven superior to the clumsy brainwashing of old. The key one of these is agenda-setting: stipulating the topics that are permissible to discuss.

As there are usually more things off an agenda than on it, this results in a capacious *blind sector*.

In avionics, a 'blind sector' is a segment of a radar screen in which objects can't be seen (usually because of an obstruction near the antenna). Analogously, a long list of missing voices, issues and events makes up the blind sector in our media, and so in our field of knowledge. This hinterland of missing information shapes opinion as surely as the missing electron causes atomic events.

A blind sector item might be (i) a simple one-off story, (ii) a long-running event, or (iii) an entire political theme.

An example in the first category would be the media neglect of the 450,000 US service personnel who suffered traumatic brain injuries between 2000 and 2021—most commonly from 'longterm exposure to explosive weapons'.[3]

An example in the 'long-running event' category might be Norway's 'Government Pension Fund Global'—an 'inter-generational wealth-sharing fund' drawn from the country's surplus oil revenues. The fund is worth more than $1 trillion, or nearly $200,000 per Norwegian citizen. It won't invest in the tobacco, coal, oil, gas and nuclear industries. It owns 1.4% of all stocks worldwide.

The fund receives almost no media exposure. It's larger than the world's largest public companies, such as Apple. It's good for Norway's economy, and citizens, and also for the global environment. But for the media, even the business media, it appears to lack relevance.

The third category ('an entire political theme') might include America's overseas military bases—roughly 750 as of 2021, across 80 countries, according to academic David Vine.[4] (The Pentagon has lost count of its bases—and uses Professor Vine's lists in its studies.) There is a clear US strategy to encircle China with many of these bases.[5]

At their heights, the Roman and British empires had 37 and 36 foreign bases, respectively. China today has one.[6] In mainstream Western media, this world-shaping phenomenon—one which so contextualizes the War on Terror, the West's confrontation with China, the war in Ukraine, the Israel-Gaza war, and many other issues—will not generally draw a mention from one year to the next.

In his book *The Media Monopoly*, Ben Bagdikian cites a well-known historical example of this third kind of omission:

> The mainstream news media postponed for more than fifty years full public awareness of the hidden dangers of the medically known threat to public health from tobacco… They did [this] to protect a major advertiser.[7]

One building block of the 'bias against relevance' is the media's selection of interviewees.

A 1998 survey of 141 Washington bureau chiefs found that

> it is government officials and business representatives to whom journalists 'nearly always' turn when covering economic policy.

Labor representatives and consumer advocates were at the bottom of the list.[8]

During Year 1 of the Iraq War, US media chose doves to interview very rarely:

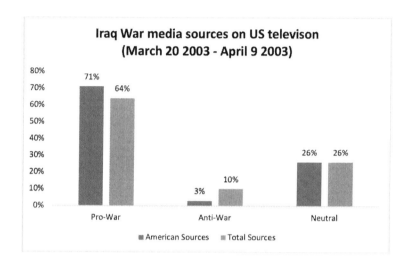

Fig. 4.2: *Media sources used for the Iraq War by US network news*

A result of this selectivity is that many subjects which impact every person every day are rarely discussed. One example is the meaninglessness of modern work. There's an almost universal media silence on the subject, despite only 32% of Americans being 'engaged' at work, and only 8% of Britons.[9]

Whilst epidemics of depression, divorce and fentanyl are aired in our media, one of their probable sources—the dissolving of our geographical communities: perhaps the largest cultural shift of modern history—seems to be of little interest.

The no-show of the long-awaited 'peace dividend' following the collapse of Soviet communism—the tax breaks and public infrastructure that failed to materialize: an absence that towers over the post-Cold War landscape—is also passed over in silence.

The 'preventable hospital mishaps' that kill 250,000 to 400,000 Americans annually[10]—the third leading cause of death in the US—likewise receive almost no coverage. (As one observer put it: 'We are burying a population the size of Miami every year from medical errors that can be prevented.'[11])

In the same vein, there's no media reporting on the harm Coca-Cola does to health—of some objective importance given that Coke is drunk 1.9 billion times daily.[12]

After it was revealed that its weedkiller, Roundup, causes cancer, there was similarly little mainstream reporting of Monsanto's 'multimillion dollar spying and disinformation campaign' against scientists and journalists.[13] Monsanto, like Coke, is a major media advertiser.

Finland's world class education system, and Switzerland's direct democracy, likewise languish together in the blind sector.

As government policy is significantly driven by corporations, and media outlets are owned by many of those same corporations, the blind sector tends to be a joint enterprise between corporations and government. Ralph Nader captured the spirit of the enterprise when he summarized President Biden's two-hour news conference on January 20, 2022, one year after taking office:

> The media never asked about climate disruption. They didn't ask about the military budget, where Congress gave Biden $24 billion more than the Pentagon even asked for. They didn't ask about the drain on the treasury from hundreds of billions of dollars of corporate welfare. They didn't ask about the corporate crime wave that is ripping off consumers and exploiting labor. And he didn't raise those questions either.[14]

A future historian might observe that a hallmark of our era was the gap between what occurred and what was publicly discussed.

Russia's invasion of Ukraine

> Putin certainly has authoritarian or thuggish tendencies—there's no question about that. But I actually think that what's going on here is that the West is leading Ukraine down the primrose path. And the end-result is that Ukraine is going to get wrecked…

Chapter 24

What we're doing is encouraging the Ukrainians to play tough with the Russians. We're encouraging the Ukrainians to think that they will ultimately become part of the West, because we will ultimately defeat Putin. And the Ukrainians are playing along with this. The Ukrainians are almost completely unwilling to compromise with the Russians—and instead want to pursue a hardline policy. As I said before, if they do that, the end-result is that their country is going to be wrecked.[15]

— Professor John Mearsheimer (2015)

Starting in the Obama administration, you see a shift in how America fights its wars—where the wars need to remain hidden. So you use proxies, you use contractors, you use drones, you use special operations troops… As long as you have other people doing your killing for you, the American public won't notice, and it won't have a political consequence.[16]

— Matthew Hoh—Marine company commander in Iraq; former Pentagon and State Department planner (2023).

The big military contractors want to add new countries to NATO all the time—why? Because then that country has to conform its military purchases to NATO weapons specifications. Which means certain companies—Northrup Grumman, Raytheon, General Dynamics, Boeing and Lockheed—get a trapped market.

In March of 2022, we committed $113 billion [to Ukraine]. Just to give you an example: we could have built a home for nearly every homeless person in this country for that… But the big, big expenses are going to come after the war, when we have to rebuild all the things we destroyed.[17]

— Robert F Kennedy Jr (2024)

Some topics receive good media coverage *per se*—but key elements are consigned to the blind sector. This was the case with the big geopolitical story of the early 2020s, Russia's invasion of Ukraine.

Russia's war crimes were indeed worth exposing. These began in February with the crime of aggression: 'the supreme international crime' at Nuremberg, for which the Nazi leadership was hanged. Missing, however, was most of the war's context.

The most significant omission was the invasion's backstory: the expansion of NATO to Poland, Hungary and the Czech Republic, and later to nearly a dozen other Russian neighbors, former allies and ex-Soviet states.[18]

As the Soviet Union neared its end through 1990-91, the US, British, German and French leaders—Bush, Thatcher, Major, Kohl, Mitterand—assured their Soviet counterparts that the West would not try to separate the Soviets from eastern Europe, that NATO would not be strengthened, that 'not an inch of NATO's present military jurisdiction will spread in an eastern direction'. ('Nothing of the sort will happen', British PM John Major emphasized.)

The West's goal, the Soviets were told, was a new European security architecture that both sides could join—and which would in time replace both NATO and the Warsaw Pact. The proposed vehicle was the Conference for Security and Co-operation in Europe. US Secretary of State James Baker told Soviet leader Gorbachev that the CSCE

> could create a role for both the Soviet Union and the eastern Europeans... I see it is as being a cornerstone over time in the development of a new Europe.[19]

Fig. 4.3: Presidents Bush & Gorbachev in Washington, June 1990. Through that year, the Soviets were promised a 'new Europe' that included them, & that NATO would not expand 'one inch' to the east. The breaking of these promises helped to lay the ground for the invasion of Ukraine in 2022.

In 1997, six years after the assurances were made, the Clinton administration embarked on enlarging NATO eastward. The move was condemned even by the 'architect of the Cold War', retired diplomat George Kennan. Kennan believed that the NATO enlargement

> would be the most fateful error of American policy in the entire post-cold-war era.
>
> Such a decision may be expected to inflame the nationalistic, anti-Western and militaristic tendencies in Russian opinion; to have an adverse effect on the development of Russian democracy; to restore the atmosphere of the cold war to East-West relations, and to impel Russian foreign policy in directions decidedly not to our liking.[20]

In May 1998, the US Senate debated, then ratified, the expansion—over bitter Russian objections. Kennan said:

I was particularly bothered by the references to Russia as a country dying to attack Western Europe. Don't people understand? Our differences in the cold war were with the Soviet Communist regime. And now we are turning our backs on the very people who mounted the greatest bloodless revolution in history to remove that Soviet regime... Of course there is going to be a bad reaction from Russia.[21]

Though many found the American decision mystifying, there was at least one plausible explanation. A month earlier, *The New York Times* had published the results of a long investigation:

ARMS CONTRACTORS SPEND TO PROMOTE AN EXPANDED NATO

American arms manufacturers, who stand to gain billions of dollars in sales of weapons, communication systems and other military equipment if the Senate approves NATO expansion, have made enormous investments in lobbyists and campaign contributions to promote their cause in Washington.

...[E]xpansion of the North Atlantic Treaty Organization— first to Poland, Hungary and the Czech Republic, then possibly to more than a dozen other countries—would offer arms makers a new and hugely lucrative market.[22]

In 2008, Gorbachev—now long out of office—observed:

We had 10 years after the Cold War to build a new world order and yet we squandered them. The United States cannot tolerate anyone acting independently. Every US president has to have a war...

The Americans promised that NATO wouldn't move beyond the boundaries of Germany after the Cold War but now half of central and eastern Europe are members, so what happened to their promises?[23]

Vladimir Putin often echoed Gorbachev's words in the years leading up to the Ukraine War. He was particularly displeased when, in 2014, the US participated in a coup to overthrow Ukraine's elected president—corrupt and unpopular, but Russia-leaning—then sent the country weapons systems to put near the Russian border.[24]

As Putin's invasion got underway, Western media mentioned little of this—generally depicting Moscow as motivated by lust for territory and regional domination.

From the start, there were those arguing for the unlikelihood of a Ukrainian victory:

> The narrative has never been based on reality in my view. I was arguing for at least six months before the war started that we should not have this war—that we should avoid it—because it cannot be won. There were many off-ramps available... I'm just thinking how many tens of thousands of men have died because we were unwilling to do that?
>
> Ukraine tried to have the big offensive in the Summer [of 2023]. Again, in the months before, I was arguing that it was not going to succeed, for very plain military reasons: insufficient air power, insufficient air defence, insufficiently trained troops, not an adequate equipment set—and they didn't have enough mine-clearing equipment.[25]
>
> — US Lt-Col Daniel Davis (2024)

But such voices were given little airtime. Instead, through the invasion's early months, TV and newspapers speculated that Putin's unpopularity in Russia would result in a coup. In fact, his approval was 71% in March 2022, and was still at 71% in December.[26]

The same Western outlets depicted a plucky, popular Ukrainian government and military. In fact, pre-invasion, President Zelensky's approval was at 27%, and the parliament's was at 11%. More than two-thirds of Ukrainians believed the country was headed in the wrong direction. Forty percent said they would not defend it if attacked.[27]

In 2021—a typical year—36 senior Pentagon officials joined

defense firms; conversely, the firms employing ex-Pentagon officials did business worth $89 billion with the Pentagon. When Russia's invasion began in early 2022, US arms corporations had hundreds of their people in government—including the Defense Secretary, a former Raytheon man. All this greased the wheels of the massive military support allocated to Ukraine by the end of 2023.[28]

Most of this would have been news to the average Western media consumer. The war was given saturation coverage, but most of its context was dispatched to the blind sector.

Coverage in the West was more or less a mirror image of Russian coverage: which avoided mention of Russian crimes and strategic errors, and painted Ukrainians as Nazis and child-killers.

Which might tell us that we will never get a two-sided view of an event till media is taken out of the hands of both governments and conglomerates.

The night the world did not end

The blind sector has a special attraction for events that portend the end of organized life. Soil loss and the decline of insect populations dwell there, as do the ever-increasing insecticides, herbicides, heavy metals, coolants and detergents that enter our food chain.

Perhaps the loudest silence of all, in our public discourse, is the risk of our extermination by nuclear weapons.

In 2007, long-term US Administration insider Robert Gates recounted an anecdote told to him by Zbigniew Brzezinski, who had been national security advisor to President Carter:

> Brzezinski was awakened at three in the morning [on November 9, 1979] by [his military assistant William] Odom, who told him that some 250 Soviet missiles had been launched against the United States. Brzezinski knew that the President's decision time to order retaliation was from three to seven minutes. Thus he told Odom he would stand by for a further call to confirm Soviet launch and the intended targets before calling the President. Brzezinski was convinced we had to hit back and told

Odom to confirm that the Strategic Air Command was launching its planes. When Odom called back, he reported that '2,200 missiles had been launched'—it was an all-out attack. One minute before Brzezinski intended to call the President, Odom called a third time to say that other warning systems were not reporting Soviet launches. Sitting alone in the middle of the night, Brzezinski had not awakened his wife, reckoning that everyone would be dead in half an hour. It had been a false alarm. Someone had mistakenly put military exercise tapes into the computer system.[29]

The event was confirmed when documents in the National Archive were declassified in 2012.[30] A year later, Brzezinski confirmed the story himself: his call to President Carter to recommend the nuclear annihilation of the Soviet Union had been averted by a minute.[31]

The event was not a standalone. Since the 1950s, an array of errors, machine and human, have led to dozens of 'nuclear near-misses'.[32] During the Cuban Missile Crisis in 1962, a Soviet submarine commander ordered a nuclear-armed torpedo to be fired at an American ship—which would have produced a nuclear response from the Americans: but was countermanded by another officer. Also during that crisis, US radar operators detected a nuclear attack underway on Tampa, Florida. After the scheduled explosion did not occur, the 'attack' was found to be the unexpected appearance of a satellite over the horizon, at the same time as 'a test tape simulating a missile launch from Cuba' was run.

American equipment has mistaken the rising moon for missiles. A bug in a routine NORAD report, stating that '000' Soviet missiles had been launched, replaced the first zero with a 2. A solar flare jammed US equipment, which the Americans took to be an act of war by the Soviets: nuclear-equipped bombers were prepared for launch.

When President Trump visited Beijing in 2017, a Chinese official stopped his military aide, walking behind the president, from carrying the nuclear 'football' into the Great Hall of the People.

Trump's chief of staff, John Kelly, intervened, and was grabbed by Chinese security. A scuffle broke out.[33]

Four years after Brzezinski's broken sleep, on September 26, 1983, Lieutenant-Colonel Stanislav Petrov was at his post in the Soviet missile early warning centre, when the alarms went off—telling him the United States had launched five intercontinental ballistic missiles at the USSR. It was at a tense time in the Cold War: the Soviets had just shot down a Korean Airlines jet, killing 269 people, including a US Congressman. Ronald Reagan was inveighing against the 'evil empire'. The computers told Petrov the information was at the 'highest level' of reliability.

Petrov was the man charged with notifying the military leadership of such an event. For five tense minutes, 200 pairs of eyes bored into him as he studied the data that was streaming in, and talked to colleagues near and far by intercom and phone, as alarms flashed all around him.

Like Brzezinski, Petrov had to act in well under the 25 minutes it would take for enemy missiles to reach his country. Had he gone by the book, he'd have called the top brass, told them of the attack, and triggered the world's final war.

But, he later recounted: 'I couldn't move.' Off his own bat, Petrov decided that five missiles was an unlikely number. If this was war, he reasoned, the US would surely launch more. He declined to act—conjecturing that the 'missile strike' was a system malfunction of some kind. He later described this as 'a 50-50 guess'. He'd made that guess, he said, because 'I had a funny feeling in my gut'.[34]

On such threads has the fate of humanity hung since the beginning of the nuclear age.

Although nuclear stockpiles are much lower than they were in the Cold War, they are still large enough to wipe out most of humanity—making the reduction somewhat academic.

Despite the long series of hair-raising 'near-misses' since 1962, nuclear proliferation was barely mentioned in the 2016, 2020 and 2024 US presidential campaigns—by candidates, parties or media.

Whilst the sense of urgency that surrounded the abolition of nuclear weapons a half-century ago has evaporated, the threat itself has not. William Perry, Defense Secretary under President Clinton (and another recipient of an erroneous late-night call about a Soviet nuclear attack) believes the risk of nuclear disaster is greater now than in the Cold War.

In the view of General George Lee Butler, head of the US Strategic Command during the George HW Bush administration:

> We escaped the Cold War without a nuclear holocaust by some combination of skill, luck, and divine intervention, and I suspect the latter in greatest proportion.[35]

This thinking was echoed by UN Secretary-General Antonio Guterres, as he opened a conference on the Nuclear Non-Proliferation Treaty, in August 2022:

> We have been extraordinarily lucky so far. But luck is not a strategy.[36]

When a scheme is…

1. a mortal hazard to society
2. so irrational that even experts are puzzled by it
3. never discussed in the mass media
4. a financial windfall for several large industries

…we are probably seeing the fingerprints of plutocracy.

In 1986, the multi-disciplinary report *Medical Implications of Nuclear War* was published—detailing an atomic war's sequelae: 'superfires', 'nuclear winter', 'atmospheric perturbations', 'toxic environments', 'casualties due to blast, heat and radioactive fallout', 'incidence of cancer'…[37]

When Carl Sagan read the report, he wrote:

> The immediate and especially the long-term consequences of nuclear war seem to hold an enormous number of surprises, almost all of which are unpleasant. It is as if we live in a field of stones that no-one has ever looked under… The population of

the planet has, by and large, been sleepwalking through the last 40 years.[38]

Back in 1920, Walter Lippmann explained this 'sleepwalking' era some years in advance:

> In a few generations it will seem ludicrous to historians that a people professing government by the will of the people should have made no serious effort to guarantee the news without which a governing opinion cannot exist. 'Is it possible,' they will ask, 'that at the beginning of the Twentieth Century nations calling themselves democracies were content to act on what happened to drift across their doorsteps; that apart from a few sporadic exposures and outcries they made no plans to bring these common carriers under social control?'[39]

A century later, Dominic Cummings' remark on the Western nuclear brinksmanship that the Russia-Ukraine war had unleashed went unreported by the media:

> If you care about 'preserving western values', I strongly advise that you focus on regime change in London and Washington, not in Moscow.[40]

Fig. 4.4: 1961, Russian Arctic Circle: Fireball of the 'Tsar Bomba' or 'king of bombs'—the largest nuclear device ever detonated. The fireball was visible nearly 1,000 kilometres away, & the mushroom cloud was seven times the height of Mount Everest. All buildings were destroyed in the nearest village, 55 kilometres away. Windows were broken in Norway & Finland. The blast's shockwave circled the world three times.

Chapter 25
Remedies

For those who stubbornly seek freedom, there can be no more urgent task than to come to understand the mechanisms and practices of indoctrination.[1]

— Noam Chomsky

All foundational democratic theories—including the first amendment itself—assume a functional press system. The fourth estate's current collapse is a profound social problem.[2]

— US media scholar Victor Pickard (2020)

We've survived without large media corporations for 25 of the 26 centuries since Solon. It is time to revert to the mean.

The words of Karl Rove and Rudolph Giuliani might suggest an Orwellian world is already upon us—that history has happened. But it's likely that our skeletal democracy retains the integrity to support flesh: and that a broad, diverse story, teeming with characters and ideas, is salvageable from today's lifeless media narrative.

The first need is to acknowledge that the present system has no capacity to deliver change. As with nearly all 'democratic reform' for decades, 'media reform' has so far elicited mere tinkering:

Australia's Finkelstein Inquiry (2011); Canada's Davey Commission (1970), Kent Commission (1981) and Senate Standing Committee study (2003); a European Commission working paper (2007); an EU directive; a British House of Lords Select Committee; Britain's Leveson Inquiry (2012); and the UK Government's 'consultation on media ownership and plurality'— variously 'expressed concern' at the growing concentration of media; 'raised questions' about the poor state of regulation which had led to this; asked legislators to 'consider the adoption of rules aimed at limiting the influence of a single person, company or group', proposed a 'three-step approach for advancing the debate on media pluralism', called for higher standards on the 'right to information and freedom of expression'; criticized the 'diminishing employment standards' for journalists that media concentration had led to—and provided 'recommendations', 'approaches' and 'suggestions' for all of the above.

All of those calls, concerns, questions, criticisms, proposals, recommendations and suggestions were ignored, and are now forgotten.[3]

None of these inquiries focused themselves on the capture of information by wealth, which made the failures they identified inevitable.

The Athenians began with a clear grasp of what democracy was for. They crafted *isegoria* precisely to dilute the influence of the plutocratic class on opinion and policy. They understood that information lay at the root of the constitution.

Article II of the Bill of Change ensures that disseminating information, and shaping public attitudes, are not the preserve of organized money. Policy can't reflect human diversity if news content doesn't; and news content can't be diverse unless media ownership is.

So, how to replace the media cartel?

The less disruptive way would be to retire it in stages, over three or four years; and in the same period to underwrite a multitude of new outlets, via a modest levy on the advertising turnover of the social media companies. (I'll describe and justify the levy below.)

From a business cycle point of view, the timing for this is good. Advertising revenue is fast migrating to social media—indeed the 'advertising model' by which mainstream news media has supported itself since the 19th Century is dying. As media analyst Robert McChesney writes:

> Advertising gave the illusion that journalism is a naturally, even supremely, commercial endeavor. But when advertising disappears, journalism's true nature comes into focus: it is a public good.[4]

Presently, two of the replacements in view for the advertising-supported news cartels are government broadcasters and private subscriptions. But the expansion of government broadcasting to fill the void has obvious risks. And the vast majority of media consumers are not prepared to part with the funds to get them beyond paywalls.[5]

A third scenario is playing out presently: media assets are owned purely to exert influence over politics and public opinion. News Corporation, for example, holds loss-making newspapers in the US, Britain and Australia in order to influence the political process.[6] Las Vegas casino magnate Sheldon Adelson bought that town's respected *Review-Journal*, and shut down its investigative stories into the casino industry. It now produces industry puff pieces.[7]

And, of all the troubled newspapers in the world, Jeff Bezos bought *The Washington Post*.

The field, finally, contains vulture capitalists—who buy up media outlets simply to strip their assets. For example, the vulture firm MNG Enterprises now controls 200 US publications including *The Denver Post* and *The Boston Herald*, and is selling off assets and retrenching journalists from all of them.[8]

Two thousand American newspapers have shut since 2004, creating many 'news deserts'—counties with no local news. The route to a 'news desert' is often marked out by a vulture firm.[9] Or sometimes a paper will cling to life. *The Mercury* in Pottsville, Pennsylvania, for example, was taken over by a hedge fund. The paper is down to one reporter, the editor, who has relocated his office to his attic.[10]

So our theoretical third and fourth alternatives—leaving the bones of our media to those seeking political advantage, or to be picked over by vulture firms—are no more viable than the first two: government broadcasters and private subscriptions.

Where Facebook's news content—indeed all news content— will come from after today's news producers have gone is not hard to guess. The wealthy will be the only sector with the capacity and the need to create news.

By this process of elimination, we arrive at the remaining plausible option by which media can be supported: a 'pledge' system similar to that for the electoral system.

It may be our last choice, but it's a sound one: as it resolves the age-old problem of media concentration, and the more recent death spiral of news, in one move.

The pledge system—which has been championed by Robert McChesney and others for some years—isn't complex. Each year, a citizen pledges (say) $200 to the media outlet(s) of his choice. An outlet begins life when it attracts a threshold amount in pledges—say $15,000. No outlet can receive more than 10% of the total.

In the US, if every voter did this, it would yield a 'civic endowment' of nearly $32 billion. (The present total revenue for US 'radio and television broadcasting establishments' is $20 billion.[11] Advertising revenue for newspapers is $14 billion.[12])

These are not astronomical sums by historical standards, especially as breaking up the Internet 'backbone' and other distribution monopolies (see below) will bring costs down dramatically.

Robert McChesney points out that public funding for newspapers began in the 19th Century, in the form of postal subsidies. This 'government subsidy of journalism as a percentage of GDP in the 1840s,' he writes, 'would be worth around $35 billion in today's economy'.[13]

The principle of breaking up monopolies

> The public airways belong to the people. We're the landlords.
> The television and radio stations are the tenants. They lease the
> space.[14]

— Ralph Nader

Before proceeding, we need to be clear about whether it's appropriate or ethical to break up monopolies at all.

History is certainly on our side. Opposition to monopoly has been integral to the philosophies of both left and right for generations.

As we've seen, the American Revolution itself has roots in the Boston Tea Party, which was aimed at a business monopoly. Jefferson believed the Bill of Rights should include 'restriction against monopolies'. Madison warned against 'arbitrary restrictions, exemptions and monopolies'. The Maryland constitution of 1776 stated, 'Monopolies are odious, contrary to the spirit of free government…and ought not to be suffered.'[15]

The US 'agrarian conservatives' of the 1930s were as opposed to monopoly as they were to socialism—as both centralized power in all-controlling monoliths. Conservatives in that era disliked both financial capitalism and corporate farming, and their results: 'wage slavery' (as they dubbed it) and the death of the small town.[16] Monopolies have likewise been the enemy of progressives from Woodrow Wilson to Bernie Sanders.

Monopolies are 'odious' because when competition vanishes, the new company can become the price-maker. As economist Denise Hearn puts it:

> If you're wondering why inequality is so high, it is because the
> wealthy control the toll roads of American life, and everyone else
> must pay to use them. Inequality is a symptom, not the disease.
> The true disease is industry concentration.[17]

In the US, the Sherman Act of 1890 empowered injured

parties to claim 'treble damages'—three times what the monopolistic behavior had cost them. As Republican Senator John Sherman explained it:

> If we will not endure a king as a political power, we should not endure a king over the production, transportation, and sale of any of the necessities of life. If we would not submit to an emperor, we should not submit to an autocrat of trade, with power to prevent competition and to fix the price of any commodity.[18]

In 1914, the Clayton Antitrust Act focused on stopping mergers and acquisitions that led to monopolies; and the Federal Trade Commission Act established the FTC to police competition law. All this resulted from pressure on government by an organized public.

Tim Wu backgrounds these developments in his 2018 book, *The Curse of Bigness*.[19] According to Wu, the modus operandi of the Gilded Age monopolist was 'lying to investors, bribing politicians, and paying off journalists and professors'[20]—which does sound familiar.

Many of these Gilded Age monopolies were too bloated to be efficient, and stayed alive only because they'd swallowed their competitors. So when monopolies were broken up there was often an economic explosion. The 34 companies that were Standard Oil doubled in value in a year. When the first film trust was broken up, the US movie industry was born.[21]

Theodore Roosevelt opined that it was necessary to break up a 'combination' or 'trust' not merely because it was big—that wasn't a valid reason—but when it 'has gained its position by unfair methods, and by interference with the rights of others, by demoralizing and corrupt practices, in short, by sheer baseness and wrong-doing'. The Republican president later wrote:

> It was imperative to teach the masters of the biggest corporations in the land that they were not, and would not be permitted to regard themselves as, above the law.

> Suits were brought...[and] it was only these suits that made
> the great masters of corporate capital in America fully realize
> that they were the servants and not the masters of the people.[22]

Roosevelt—in office from 1901 to 1909—acted against 45 of these trusts, and broke many of them up. His successor, William Howard Taft (1909-13), pursued 75 such cases. Woodrow Wilson took office in 1913, on a platform of 'regulated competition', and the next year Congress criminalized anti-competitive behavior.

By 1920, nearly every trust in the country had been impacted in some way, or broken up wholesale.

Public sentiment against monopolies did not end in the 1920s. During World War Two, Franklin Roosevelt drafted a 'Second Bill of Rights' for the industrial era, which included this one:

> The right of every businessman, large and small, to trade in an
> atmosphere of freedom from unfair competition and domina-
> tion by monopolies at home or abroad.[23]

Speaking at the pre-dawn of the post-War world, the American president grasped that new forces had come into play that were not to do with 'our rights to life and liberty'—those rights were already established—but with 'economic truths' arising from the expansion of 'our industrial economy'.

Tim Wu tells us that, in his last State of the Union address, President Eisenhower attributed the health of the US economy to his administration's 'vigorous enforcement of antitrust laws over the last eight years and a continuing effort to...enhance our economic liberties.'[24]

European countries were going down the same road. It was understood that World War Two had begun in part because of the power of monopolies in Italy and Germany. On both continents, Wu writes,

> breaking up monopolies and prohibiting cartels was essential to
> democratic governance, human thriving, and a prevention of a
> return to the despotism of the 1930s and 1940s.[25]

By the late 1950s, feeling was so high that leading antitrust attorney Lee Loevinger—soon to become President Kennedy's antitrust chief—told Congress:

> The problems with which the antitrust laws are concerned—the problems of distribution of power in a society—are second only to the questions of survival in the face of threats of nuclear weapons.[26]

Media was very much a part of this picture. In 1969, the Supreme Court—by an 8-0 vote—upheld the 'equal time' provision of the government's 'Fairness Doctrine' in these terms:

> A license permits broadcasting, but the licensee has no constitutional right to be the one who holds the license or to monopolize a radio frequency to the exclusion of his fellow citizens… It is the right of the viewers and listeners, not the right of the broadcasters, which is paramount.[27]

In the US, the trust-busting era lasted a century, only going to sleep in the 1990s after two final cases against IBM and Microsoft.[a] The free market suffered its most serious blow from the arrival of 'free market' economics.

Media cartels *can* be terminated easily enough. Bolivians outlawed theirs in a 2009 constitutional referendum.[28] Argentina broke up its largest media monopoly in 2013.[29] Venezuela, Ecuador and Uruguay have pioneered scores of community media outlets, and downsized the behemoths. In 2013, Mexicans voted for a constitutional amendment to hand the country's broadcast 'backbone' to government, and empowering it to break up media monopolies.

Had a diverse, independent and fact-based media existed in the US, Britain and Australia, could the calamity in Iraq have

---

a   There was a brief revival in 2020, when the government, under pressure from the mainstream media, sued to have Facebook divest two acquisitions. The suit was dismissed.

occurred? Would the corruption that characterized the pandemic have been swept under the carpet? Would taxpayers still be facing trillion-dollar bills for each?

You could probably retire an awful lot of socialism if you broke up media monopolies.

Remedies: The 'horizontal' dimension

Media monopoly needs to be addressed both 'horizontally' and 'vertically'.

The 'horizontal' plane is where a company owns different *kinds* of media—for example, a TV station, a radio station and a newspaper.

To wind up these pan media monopolies—of the kind we see in Italy, the US, Britain and Australia—Article II requires that no media company (or shareholder of any significance) should own stock in more than one medium. The media monoliths of the present would be replaced by non-profit outfits or employee-owned firms—most new, a few spun off from the originals, and each with a maximum capitalization of, say, $20 million.

Networks may still exist if they're actual *networks*: groups of independent radio and TV outlets sharing content, and teaming up for larger projects. Just no more centrally owned conglomerates with God-like powers.

In this non-profit counter-model, a media organization is controlled by its employees. As businesses, such 'co-ops' have a good track record. The largest of Spain's co-ops is *Mondragon*—the country's seventh-largest corporation, containing 257 separate organizations and employing 74,000 people—in finance, industry, retail and 'knowledge'.[30]

Spain's many co-ops are owned by their workers—who set wages and conditions, determine their own profit-share, and design their healthcare and pension plans. Executive salaries are modest.

These worker-owned firms tend to be pleasant to work for without sacrificing productivity. Even when closed by COVID, Spain's co-ops continued to pay staff, on the promise that staff would make up lost hours post-crisis. They reduced wages by 5%, but there were none of the mass firings seen in other COVID-affected businesses. Where for-profits went bankrupt in large numbers in 2020, the co-ops remained profitable. The Spanish co-ops have also established a common 'unemployment fund' to which they all contribute—sharing risk among the network.

Indeed, Mondragon saw almost no unemployment during the GFC, compared to a peak of 26% in Spain as a whole. During the pandemic, production at its factories fell 75%—but again there was virtually no unemployment.[31]

The best-known book on employee-owned companies is *Beyond the Corporation*. Its author, David Erdal, writes:

> Over the last twenty-five years and more, study after study has shown that companies with employee ownership—even quite low levels of employee ownership—out-perform the competition. They are more productive. They survive better in the bad times. They last longer. Employee turnover is low. Absenteeism is low. They also give good service—their customers tend to rate them more highly than their conventionally structured competition.
>
> Not surprisingly, at the human level as well as economically, employee-owned businesses do better. Employees tend to learn more participation skills. They are better trained. They contribute more innovative ideas. They implement change quicker. And they are wealthier, because they have one of the key rights of owners: to participate in the profits they help produce. Their communities benefit not only from the flow of that wealth into the local economy, but also because the skills of participation learned at work can be deployed in community activities.[32]

Third draft democracy does not argue for more employee-owned enterprises in the economy as a whole: the electorate can weigh such decisions if and when the time comes. It merely insists that wealth cannot control the information on which a society bases its decisions. Wealth cannot be where wealth does not belong.

Remedies: The 'vertical' dimension

Reform in the 'vertical' plane occurs when a corporation controls more than one level in a supply chain—for example a company that owns cable backbone, TV drama production and TV channels; or tree plantations, newsprint and newspapers.

As Ben Bagdikian wrote, in the past

> it was understood that corporations which have control of a total process, from raw material to fabrication to sales, also have few motives for genuine innovation and the power to seize out anyone else who tries to compete.[33]

So breaking up this vertical dimension makes economic sense. Article II, therefore, states that a media outlet can only operate on one tier.

It can't, for example, own both cables and software. It can own a print mill but not a newspaper, and vice-versa. It can own an ISP but not a web design company; or a web design company but not a Wi-Fi supplier; or a TV station but not bandwidth. (And so on.)

Remedies: Size

After the horizontal and vertical issues are addressed, individual companies within a former conglomerate will themselves at times be too large. Article II 'decaps' them—reduces their capitalization to a reasonable size.

One of these companies might manufacture Wi-Fi chipsets; another might broadcast commercial radio; a third may be a press agency. Where it has a capitalization of more than $20 million, it is downsized ('decapped') to that value or less.[b]

---

[b] There are various ways to assess the capitalization of a media outlet: for example, material assets + cash, or 'nett present value' (which brings in future cashflows). Choosing the best option is the kind of thing citizen assemblies are good at. The method chosen will of course dictate the way an organization is 'decapped'—and, later, if it grows larger than $20 million, how the excess in asset value is returned to the civic endowment. (All amounts should be indexed to the rate of inflation.)

After a three- or four-year de-monopolization process, no company will work in more than one medium, or will operate on more than one tier of the supply chain, or will be valued at more than $20 million.

News will be diverse, and eliminating the profit motive is likely to have restored its credibility. Thousands of new journalists will be employed—with better pay—and they will no longer fear to unearth the secrets of the wealthy.

Light will enter the blind sector.

Social media acquisitions and mergers

We can likely always just buy any competitive startups.[34]

> — Facebook internal memo from Mark
> Zuckerberg (2012)

Nationalizing social media, or turning its ownership over to users —as some have suggested[35]—are beyond the Bill's scope and intent. Nonetheless, a scheme that breaks up the mainstream media giants but leaves the social media cartels untouched would be an anomaly. It also leaves in place the risk that these cartels will expand to fill the news vacuum.

How we structure social media can be thrashed out by the community in the post-Bill landscape. In the meantime, this fine line might be walked by leaving the individual social media companies intact—but breaking up their cartels. That means making the social media giants divest their acquisitions.

There is no shortage of acquisitions to divest: Facebook has acquired more than 80 companies; Apple and Amazon more than 100 each; and Alphabet and Microsoft more than 200 each.[36]

Facebook's co-founder, Chris Hughes, feels that Facebook should be made to divest the companies it has bought up, such as WhatsApp and Instagram, and that future acquisitions should be outlawed. Hughes wrote about Facebook, and his friend Mark Zuckerberg, in 2019:

> Together, we founded Facebook in 2004. Now, 15 years later, I think Facebook has grown too big and too powerful. Every week brings new headlines about privacy violations, election interference or mental health concerns...
>
> Today, nearly three billion people use Facebook, Instagram, and WhatsApp, and they're all owned and controlled by the same company. Of every dollar spent buying ads on social media, $0.84 goes to Facebook. It's now worth over half a trillion dollars. That's roughly the size of the GDP of the bottom 65 countries in the world—combined.
>
> First, the Facebook empire needs to be broken up. America's regulated corporate empires before, and we can do it again. This isn't unprecedented and surprisingly, it often boosts the value of these companies in the long run.[37]

The United States would be ground zero for the divestment process, as so many IT cartels have their HQs there.

Divesting the giants of their acquisitions will not only be good for society broadly, but for tens of thousands of other businesses. New York University marketing professor Scott Galloway states:

> If one company becomes so powerful that it can deny the mother's milk of business, which is capital, you end up where we are —which is that new business formation has halved in 40 years, two-thirds of the stocks have gone away, and it's harder to build a middle class. The middle class is failing because of the consolidation of power among a few companies.[38]

Forcing the giants to hive off their acquisitions will go quite some way to restoring the free market in the social media sphere.

Chapter 25

Mechanics of decapping

- Decapitalization has no effect on audience size or content. (Ownership is our only problem.)
- Media decapping can progress at the rate of 20% per year, with all media companies down to $20 million in capitalization by the end of Year 5.
- Start-ups funded by the social media levy (next section) could start up at about the same rate—with about 20% of them up and running by the end of Year 1.
- Decapping only affects companies that generate news and current affairs. It wouldn't affect a cartoon channel, for example. If a media company wants to remain unaffected by the Bill, it needs to not be in the news business.
- Cartel shareholders are cashed out at fair (not inflated) market value of their investments, from the social media levy and the sale of assets.
- The question of national broadcasters (BBC, PBS, ABC, CBC), which tend to be very popular, is put to a referendum.
- Foreign and local websites that flout the rules are blocked. (India shut down TikTok in 2020, by ordering ISPs to block access, and then to supply compliance reports.[39] TikTok lost nearly a third of its global market overnight.[40])
- Tricky, borderline or contentious issues are put to citizen assemblies (which are fleshed out in Part Five). For instance: can market players who mass produce hardware (cable, chipsets) be realistically contained to a size of $20 million? Or will exceptions or workarounds be required? Citizen assemblies have a long track record of solving knotty challenges like these.
- Using the same mechanics, it's important to de-monopolize:

- Science and medical journals (which habitually distort information in the interests of advertisers).[41]

- Press agencies—some of which are global media monoliths in their own right.

- Internet service providers—some of the world's most stultifying monopolies, famed for poor service and high prices.

- Internet-related services such as Wi-Fi chipset manufacturers (also often monopolies).

- Public relations firms—responsible (depending on study) for between 30 and 80 percent of all media content.[42]

The way to terminate a monopoly hasn't changed since the days of Standard Oil. You break up its horizontal and vertical holdings, and reduce the size of what remains.

The social media levy

> I do think that sometimes you have to treat truth as a public good. And you have to decide that you will pay for it—not at the price that the market will bear, but at a higher price, because it is in the longterm interests of your society's survival.[43]
>
> — Eric Weinstein, mathematician and CEO of
> Thiel Capital

There are at least 10 equitable grounds for asking social media companies to pay for a revived, democratic media landscape:

1. Social networks possess some of the legal elements of a commons. Facebook, for example, shares the resource of knowl-

edge under specific rules (some of them designed by users) among billions of people. Facebook itself refers to its platform as an 'environment'[44] and its users as a 'community'.[45]

2. Citizens generate virtually all social media content. In the process, we are psychologically profiled daily for the benefit of advertisers and political parties.[46] The data mined from us (usually without our involvement or knowledge) generates the revenue of the social media corporations. The value in Facebook's share price lies mostly in your data and mine. We are the product it sells to advertisers.

3. The social networks publish vast amounts of news gathered by journalists without paying for it.

4. The social networks derived most of the resources they generate their profits from—hardware, software, algorithms—from taxpayers. The American taxpayer funded the invention of the Internet—at about ten times the cost of the Manhattan Project.[47] Google's search engine was developed on a National Science Foundation grant.[48] The taxpayer likewise funded the development of GPS, the touchscreen and all the key technologies of the iPhone and iPad.

5. The tech giants are not paying their taxes. They achieve this by 'booking' profits to offshore subsidiaries. Thus—for example—in the UK in 2014, Facebook paid £4,327 in tax. In 2021, Facebook Australia paid $AU24 million in tax, after sending most of its revenue—$AU949 million—offshore. It describes the practice as 'resale of advertising inventory'.[49]

6. Public opinion favors reform. More than two-thirds of Australians believe Big Tech does not pay enough tax, and only 16% think it can be trusted to regulate itself.[50] Most Americans believe technology companies privilege the views of some sections of society over others—for example 85% of conservatives believe they're politically biased. Only 24% of Americans believe the companies protect users' data well enough, and 72% believe social media companies have too much influence in politics.[51] A majority of Americans[52] and Britons[53] believe government should regulate these companies.

7. After hundreds of acquisitions, Facebook dominates social media, Amazon dominates commerce, Google controls search, and Apple gets 79% of global smartphone profits.[54] The Internet giants are *monopolies*—and as such quash competition and hold back innovation by sheer market power. Historically, well-functioning capitalist societies regulate and break up monopolies. These companies, however, have immobilized that capacity, via political contamination—enabling large increases in value.

8. This market domination has also come about through the breaking of competition law. In July 2020, the US Congress subpoenaed texts and emails from the tech giants, which revealed that:

- Facebook used the aggressive cloning of features to force companies to sell out to it.
- Amazon lost money by selling goods below cost to drive competitors into the ground—then bought them.
- Google bought out YouTube purely to remove a competitor.

Tim Wu commented:

The Big Tech companies insist that their rise to power has been…a saga of ingenuity and courage, and that their market dominance is a byproduct of continued excellence…

The subpoenaed documents destroy that narrative. No one can deny that these are well-run companies, loaded with talent, and that each at some point offered something great. But it appears that without illegal maneuvers—without, above all, the anticompetitive buying of potential rivals—there might be no Big Tech, but rather a much wider array of smaller, better, more specialized tech companies.[55]

9. Many observers, including tech experts and intelligence officials, believe Facebook is in 'way over its head' in trying to deal with—or even understand—the kinds of social polarization its platform is making possible.[56] Yael Eisenstat, who was Facebook's political advertising overseer, resigned after six months when the company declined to heed her recommendations for reform. She later said:

As long as the company continues to merely tinker around the margins of content policy and moderation, as opposed to considering how the entire machine is designed and monetized, they will never truly address how the platform is contributing to hatred, division and radicalization.[57]

10. Social media harms human brains, health and functioning. The companies know this, and cover it up.

There were internal studies at Facebook through 2019 and 2020, into the effects of Instagram—the company's photo-sharing app—on teen mental health. Excerpts included:

We make body image issues worse for one in three teen girls.

Teens blame Instagram for increases in the rate of anxiety and depression. This reaction was unprompted and consistent across all groups.

Thirty-two percent of teen girls said that when they felt bad about their bodies, Instagram made them feel worse.[58]

In March 2021—a few months before these excerpts were leaked—Mark Zuckerberg had told Congress:

The research that we've seen is that using social apps to connect with other people can have positive mental health benefits.[59]

There are dozens of studies supporting claim number 10. Many of the worst issues—such as mental health problems, body disorders and online harassment—were laid out in an April 2024 UNESCO report.[60] However, it may be enlightening to see what the inventors of social media themselves say:

• Aza Raskin, who in 2006 designed 'infinite scroll'—the ability to scroll down a page without having to click—says of social media: 'It's as if they're taking behavioral cocaine and just sprinkling it all over your interface and that's the thing that keeps you coming back and back and back.'[61]

• In 2007-8, Justin Rosenstein headed the team that created the Facebook *Like* button. In recent years, he's weaned himself off Reddit and Snapchat, and programmed his iPhone so he can no longer download apps. He's now concerned enough about the *Like* button—which he describes as 'bright dings of pseudo pleasure'— to limit his own Facebook use. Rosenstein believes the world he helped to create brings about 'continual partial attention', which breaks up the ability to concentrate.

• A member of Rosenstein's team, Leah Pearlman, also became hooked on Facebook—noting with alarm that she has based her self-worth on the quantity of *Likes* she received. 'When I need validation—I go to check Facebook. I'm feeling lonely, "Let me check my phone." I'm feeling insecure, "Let me check my phone.'"[62]

• Loren Brichter, who designed Twitter's 'pull-to-refresh' mechanism, says: 'I have two kids now and I regret every minute that I'm not paying attention to them because my smartphone has sucked me in.' As for Twitter, he says, 'I still waste time on it, just reading stupid news I already know about.'

• In 2009, Chris Wetherell invented *X's* retweet button. He regretted doing so as soon as he'd witnessed the first Twitter mob. He likens his creation to 'handing a four-year-old a loaded weapon'.[63]

• James Williams, who helped build Google's search engine, wonders whether democracy can survive the 'attentional control' of the tech age. He quit Google when he realized he could no longer focus on the things he wanted to—his concentration had deteriorated. Now that he grasps what technology has done to his own brain, he wonders why this issue is not 'on the front page of every newspaper every day':

> The dynamics of the attention economy are structurally set up to undermine the human will. If politics is an expression of our human will, on individual and collective levels, then the attention economy is directly undermining the assumptions that democracy rests on.[64]

Asked if there'll come a point when democracy no longer functions, Williams replied: 'Will we be able to recognize it, if and when it happens? And if we can't, then how do we know it hasn't happened already?'[65]

To these 10 reasons for the social media levy, as of 2023 we could add an 11th: social media companies censor free speech for the government.

Journalist Emma-Jo Morris' testimony before the House of Representatives in 2023—on Hunter Biden's 'laptop from Hell'—covers some of the bases:

> My reporting showed that despite then-candidate Joe Biden's repeated and furious denials, he was apparently involved in the foreign business deals of his family… The [*New York*] *Post* published exactly how the material was obtained, even identifying our sources, as well as a federal subpoena showing that the FBI was in possession of the material the story was based on, and had been since 2019.
>
> But when the stories appeared on social media that morning…within hours the reporting was censored on all major platforms, on the basis of being called 'hacked' or 'Russian disinformation'. Twitter refused to allow users to share the link to the stories, banned the links from being shared in private messages—a policy typically used to clamp down on child porn distribution—and locked the *Post* out of its verified account. Facebook said it would curb distribution and reach of the links on its platform.
>
> On October 19 [2020], five days after the *Post* began publishing, *Politico* ran a story headlined 'Hunter Biden story is Russian disinfo, dozens of former intel officials say' [laughs]—God, I can't even say that with a straight face…
>
> Just last Spring, House investigators revealed it was a call by now Secretary of State Anthony Blinken to acting CIA Director Anthony Morell that prompted the spy letter published by *Politico*.[66]

It's obviously time for society to rethink its arrangement with the social media companies.

Making them pay for the extraordinary privileges we grant them, in order to fund a new media landscape, is also a creative way to reduce the society-distorting effects of monopoly, to bring back a level playing field for start-ups, to restore fairness to the tax code, and to repay us citizens for the R&D we sponsor, and the content we create.

The social media levy is raised on advertising turnover—because profit is easy to hide and turnover is not. It's raised on *real domestic* turnover, to sidestep offshoring.

As with the campaign funding pledges discussed in Part Three, each taxpayer could assign his pledge to the media outlet(s) of his choice in his annual return. Non-taxpayers could, again, pledge online or via a government office.

The system of media pledges would be 'preferential': if your first choice has hit its funding ceiling, your pledge goes to your second (and so on).

Let's say that 20% of the 95,000 voters in the Australian city of Bendigo divert $200 each, per year, to the city's local media. (The other 80% might pledge to media further afield.) That amounts to $3.8 million a year. Bendigo's newspaper and TV station could hire new journalists, and cover hundreds of local issues that are presently ignored. Its community radio station could add news segments, and run on a professional basis. There may be two or three news website start-ups.

Scores of local journalists would have well-paying jobs, and an autonomy their present-day counterparts can only dream about. For the first time in the city's history, the primary loyalty of its media would be to residents and not advertisers.

Democratizing information

In Australia at least, thanks to the inaction or even collusion of the present Government, the potential for news manipulation is such that it makes George Orwell sound like an optimist. But what we've proved with *The Echo* is that if you give people a local, human-scale, independent alternative, they will desert the monopolies.[67]

— Nick Shand, co-founder of Australia's *Byron Shire Echo* (1988)

Under Isegoria, media start-ups will include newspapers and magazines (online and print), television (broadcast, cable, satellite), radio, podcasts—and any new form of media that comes along. All of which could be local, regional or national.

The status of these outlets as ad-free non-profits will, of course, cause a downturn in the advertising industry. This will bring roughly as much societal harm as a downturn in the tobacco industry. However, we may want to direct some levy funds to retraining advertising workers, in many cases as journalists. This may be welcomed by advertising workers themselves, who have extremely low job satisfaction.[68]

The advertising-free model liberates media executives from the degrading process of raising money from advertisers; journalists from distorting stories to keep advertisers happy; and the public from having to thumb past what results.[c] It is likely to give us our long-sought 'viewpoint diversity'. Views conservative and progressive, libertarian and authoritarian, will get their chance at currency.

Moreover, those who believe climate change is exaggerated—or that there was no moon landing—will have a better chance of proving their case (if true) in an environment where information is not sponsored. The war over 'disinformation' should gradually resolve. Conspiracy theories are likely, over time, to be proven true or to sink into obscurity.

Both the 'corporate monopoly' and 'state-owned' models of media entail a tiny group determining what the rest of us may and may not learn about the world. By crafting the information environment, but not the information, Isegoria steers us away from both.

If democracy's out-breath is the ballot box, its in-breath is information.

---

[c]   In mid-2023, US presidential candidate Robert F Kennedy Jr was airing negative media reports *on himself* as part of his campaign advertising—judging, presumably, that the mainstream media was in such bad odor that this could only help him.

Chapter 25

Democracy's in-breath

In 2013, Australia's prime minister Julia Gillard publicly floated the idea of minor media reforms. Rupert Murdoch summoned his Australian editors, and told them he wanted her removed.[69] After a campaign of vilification in the Murdoch media, Gillard fell in a party room coup.

Gillard's predecessor, Kevin Rudd—another critic of Murdoch's influence—had endured years of News Corporation attacks, including cartoons caricaturing him as a Nazi and a bank robber, and epithets from columnists such as 'foul-mouthed back-stabber' and 'psychopath'.[70]

Murdoch has been overthrowing Australian prime ministers since his campaigns against the conservative William McMahon in 1972 and the progressive Gough Whitlam in 1975.

Four decades on, in 2018, the moderate-conservative prime minister Malcolm Turnbull was discarded by his party at Murdoch's behest.[71] 'I wasn't going to run my government in part-nership with Rupert or Lachlan Murdoch or their editors, and I knew [News Corp would] resent that,' Turnbull later wrote.[72] He believes the Murdochs disliked him not because he was 'too liberal' but because of his lack of deference to them, and because his personal wealth made him uncontrollable.[73]

The sequence in these falls tends to be the same. The first step is a warning—as described by John Hewson, Australia's conserva-tive party leader in the 1990s:

> I most vividly remember an early meeting with Paul Kelly, then editor of *The Australian*. Kelly stated quite emphatically that The Oz had a specific policy agenda, and if I said the right things, consistent with that agenda, I would 'get a run'. If I erred, I could expect to get a drubbing.[74]

A leader who falls out of line is mercilessly punished. The attacks on Whitlam in 1975 were so unbalanced that Murdoch's own journalists went on strike—describing the deliberate and careless slanting of headlines, seemingly blatant imbalance in news presentation, political censorship and, more occasionally, distortion of copy from senior specialist journalists, the political management of news and features, the stifling of dissident and even palatably impartial opinion in the papers' columns…[75]

What often follows is a series of Murdoch lunches with the opposition leader, or the emerging challenger in the ruling party. Finally, *coup* speculation in the Murdoch media reaches fever pitch, and the prophecy self-fulfils.

Prime minister Tony Abbott (2013-15) was not subject to any of this. Abbott gave Murdoch's editors access to cabinet decisions before they were confirmed,[76] and agreed to discuss legislation with them before introducing it to the parliament.[77]

Abbott was succeeded by Scott Morrison, who, Turnbull later wrote, was 'determined not to suffer the same fate I did…so Morrison is cleaving very closely to the Murdoch press and they are backing him up'.

Murdoch learned his approach from his press baron father, Sir Keith, who had famously said of Australian prime minister Joseph Lyons in the 1930s: 'I put him there. And I'll put him out.'

When journalist Anthony Hilton asked him why he opposed the European Union, Rupert Murdoch showed that the apple doesn't fall far from the tree:

That's easy. When I go into Downing Street they do what I say; when I go to Brussels they take no notice.[78]

Politicians begin this game believing they can retain their autonomy—that it's a 'deal' that both sides benefit from. The truth gradually dawns. In the words of George W Bush speechwriter David Frum:

Republicans originally thought that Fox worked for us. Now we're discovering that we work for Fox.[79]

But this is not, finally, a Murdoch problem: it's a plutocracy problem. And its costs go well beyond the unseating of national leaders. If organized wealth controls society's information, it can create a reality that kills millions of people, makes tens of millions of refugees, loses trillions of dollars from public revenue, and delivers inequality so steep that it destabilizes society.

When money can buy not only government policy but the sphere of public information, society walks blindfolded into traps that cost it much blood and treasure.

Share of global wealth 2010-2015

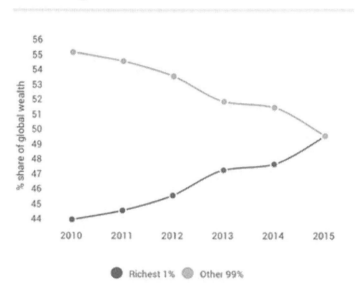

Fig. 4.5: Five-year snapshot of rapidly advancing global wealth inequality

The words of Cold War geopolitical strategist George Kennan, in the midst of Ronald Reagan's nuclear build-up, could not have been written of a public that governed its own affairs, or understood how they are managed.

We have gone on piling weapon upon weapon, missile upon missile, helplessly, almost involuntarily, like the victims of some kind of hypnosis, like men in a dream, like lemmings headed for the sea.[80]

The way out of this has been available to us since the Stone Age. A successful society begins with institutions that restrain 'upstarts'—those who try to monopolize power, information or resources. Back then, these were 'soft' institutions such as shaming and ridicule, expulsion and mutiny. We moderns still employ these: but we've also devised 'hard' institutions. A key one of these is the free press.

This 'free press' is now in a state of dishonor and disrepair. In restoring to society its informational circulatory system, Article II achieves with formal architecture what pre-modern societies did organically.

Part Five

Renovating the democratic machinery

Written in 1787, ratified in 1788, and in operation since 1789, the United States Constitution is the world's longest surviving written charter of government. Its first three words—'We the People'—affirm that the government of the United States exists to serve its citizens.[1]

— Website of the United States Senate

USAID would not grant unconditional funding to a country whose democratic design looked like ours.[2]

— Article by six US constitutional law and political science professors in *The Boston Review*

Chapter 26
Consensual government

In many nations, the growing alienation from politics, media and other institutions makes consensus, and political mandates, hard to secure.

Much of this is down to political contamination and the capture of information. But it's also the result of antiquated political technology. Second draft democracy was assembled in the Steam Age; and we may need to upgrade the political technology from that era, just as we've upgraded the transport and the lighting.

This is the subject matter of Article III of the Bill of Change.

Arend Lijphart (pronounced *Lipe*-hart) is one of the most influential political scientists of the last half-century: specializing in vast comparative analyses of different kinds of democratic regime. In his 2012 magnum opus, *Patterns of Democracy*, Lijphart concludes that the great variety of rules and institutions in the world's democracies can be reduced to a contrast between 'majoritarian' and 'consensual' styles of government. (No nation is perfectly one or the other.)

Each model is an answer to the question, 'Who decides?'

The majoritarian answer is, 'The majority of the people'.

The consensual answer is, 'As many people as possible.'[1] That is, consensualism accepts majority rule only as a minimum requirement: its real goal is to expand the majority.

Lijphart's 'majoritarian' governments have features such as a presidency, cabinets made up from a single party, two main parties competing for power, a 'winner-takes-all' electoral system, and centralized government.

His 'consensual'-style governments have such features as a parliamentary system, a cabinet made from a coalition, the sharing of power between executive and legislature, a multiparty (not two-party) system, voting via proportional representation, and a decentralized, federal state.

Lijphart's data, gleaned from 36 countries around the world, tells us that consensual democracies tend to be more democratic than majoritarian ones. They share power among more people.[2] They have higher voter turnouts. And they have better civil liberties—for example less gender inequality, and many more women in parliament.

The benefits of all this flow downstream to every sector of society. Consensual systems have healthier economies (less unemployment, lower inflation),[3] and less violence from instability, conflict and terrorism. They have better 'government effectiveness', 'regulatory quality' and 'rule of law'—and less corruption.[4]

They also produce less income inequality—with 'a Gini index,' Lijphart writes, 'more than 9 points lower than the average majoritarian democracy'.[5]

Satisfyingly, he finds there are no unpleasant sacrifices to be made for all these gains:

> Contrary to the conventional wisdom, there is no trade-off at all between governing effectiveness and high-quality democracy—and hence no difficult decisions to be made on giving priority to one or the other objective: almost too good to be true.[6]

So—why do…

- a parliamentary system
- executive-legislature power-sharing

- decentralized government
- proportional representation
- multiparty coalitions
- and a federal structure

…produce such good results?

In Lijphart's words, it's mostly because they 'divide and disperse' power.

Majoritarian systems, on the other hand, tend to concentrate it: from people to congress, from congress to executive, from executive to leader.

When it comes to the 'dividing and dispersing' of power, Lijphart attributes special importance to proportional representation and a parliamentary style of government—both of which perform dramatically better than (respectively) the winner-takes-all and presidential systems.

You see a real-world example of the consensual-majoritarian divide when you compare one of the most 'consensual' nations, Switzerland, with the United States, which is more majoritarian. Pretty much everything goes Switzerland's way: it is less politically divided. It produces higher standards of living, health, education and infrastructure. It's much less violent.

Perhaps the United States has mediocre politicians and a disgruntled public because its political design produces them.

That can always change. Lijphart points out that nations have evolved into consensual governance out of the most unpromising histories:

> Consensus democracies like Switzerland and Austria may have consensual cultures today, but they have not always been so consensual: the Swiss fought five civil wars from the sixteenth to the middle of the nineteenth century, and the Austrians fought a brief but bloody civil war as recently as 1934.[7]

Switzerland's 'cleavages' along ethnic, religious and language lines are much larger than those of the United States. Thanks to a 'consensual' political design, it has largely overcome them.

Chapter 27
Mutable democracy

Laws and institutions must go hand in hand with the progress of the human mind.[1]

— Thomas Jefferson

Over the centuries, as the Greeks progressively chiselled their laws onto white marble, democracy was set in stone—but only literally. In fact, this new way of organizing society mutated constantly. For the first time, government was drawing on the organic character of crowds.

The Athenian experiment emerged piecemeal over generations, via advances, reversals, tweaks and amendments. This strikes a contrast with the despotisms, old and new—monarchism, communism, fascism—which don't evolve much, and tend to gain (limited) public involvement only after large propaganda efforts.

Democracy is not an *ism*: it's more an arena in which *isms* can compete. It does contain some core principles, most falling under the rubric of 'liberty'. Otherwise, it's more about how decisions are reached than what those decisions should be.

This gives it a unique flexibility. Whilst political *isms* have come and gone, the notion of democracy has survived since there were pharaohs in Egypt and emperors in China. It seems to understand something the *isms* don't.

Lao Tzu wrote in the *Tao Te Ching*:

Names emerge when institutions begin. When names emerge, know likewise when to stop. To know when to stop is to be free of danger.[2]

Which RL Wing, in her commentary, takes to mean:

Leaders who insist on exacting systems and roles in their organizations cannot create a natural, effortless atmosphere for the completion of tasks, because the structure they conceive of is suited for machines, not humans. When people are forced into roles, and every aspect of their work defined, their possibilities become limited, and they no longer create, and they do not evolve. When leaders systematize every detail in their organization, they close it off from the possibility of evolution.[3]

In his book *The Fix*, Jonathan Tepperman gives ten case studies of leaders who fixed a particularly vexing problem—for instance how Lee Kwan Yew rid Singapore of corruption, and Pierre Trudeau neutralized Québécois separatism. There was no ideology that proved successful in all cases. The 'fix' varied with the situation. Tepperman suggests that we forget ideology, and embrace what works.

This is a possibility that democracy will allow. A successful political system requires a full picture of human nature. And whilst you'll never get that picture at the design stage, you can create a system that allows it to constellate over time.

Mathematician Eric Weinstein says:

Think about any of the major schools of thought that have failed to carry the day—It could be Austrian economics, it could be market socialism, it could be mercantilism, it could be hard core capitalism… The reason that none of these schools has prevailed totally is that none of these ways of thinking work under all circumstances.

People have fantasies—like 'the market always knows the true value of everything'. Well, even a free marketeer should know that markets fail for various reasons, like in the case of public goods. So you have to hybridize all of these extreme positions in order to get anything that functions.[4]

Of the two great 20th Century forces to escape obsolescence in the 21st, it's the corporation that has come to dominate democracy, and not the reverse. This is probably because one has been allowed to evolve and the other has not.

How, exactly, do we let democracy evolve?

Eric Weinstein's brother Bret, an evolutionary biologist, was asked whether we could 'design a sustainable, fair, antifragile future that liberates our descendants to live meaningful lives'. He thought not:

> However, what we can do is *navigate* to such a world...
>
> If you make a prototype of some machine, that prototype is likely to be clumsy, it's liable to not be intuitive, it's liable to be inefficient...
>
> But that's not really the purpose of the prototype. A prototype is designed to teach you what you don't know...
>
> We should nowhere have in our minds the idea that we know so much about how human beings function, or how systems are going to interact with human psychology, that we can design a system that works really well...
>
> It's actually surprisingly easy to figure out what values we would share, and what a successful civilization would have to do in order for us to regard it as such. Once we name those values, and we figure out some prioritization mechanism...we can begin to prototype a mechanism that returns on those values. It is a navigation problem more than it is a design problem.[5]

This humbler and more gradual approach gains credence when you contemplate projects the most influential minds of their time believed to be viable—collectivizing agriculture, invading Russia—and events that other such minds (Winston Churchill, for one) believed could never occur: such as a female prime ministership, or democracy coming to undeveloped India.

Others better understood the limits of human wisdom. The United States, according to Abraham Lincoln, was 'dedicated to the proposition that all men are created equal'. According to the scholar George Will, Lincoln's choice of the term 'proposition' denotes that American democracy is an experiment—with all the fluidity, blind corners and serendipities that that implies.

David Hume, who was much admired by the American founders, wrote:

> To balance a large state or society, whether monarchical or republican, on general laws, is a work of so great difficulty, that no human genius, however comprehensive, is able, by the mere dint of reason and reflection, to effect it. The judgments of many must unite in this work: Experience must guide their labour: Time must bring it to perfection: And the feeling of inconveniences must correct the mistakes, which they inevitably fall into, in their first trials and experiments.[6]

For the sake of brevity, you might call the teaching effect of experience, time and mistakes *mutability*. Mutability happens to be one of several 'themes' running through third draft democracy.

In a new scenario—where uncertainty and risk are higher—this principle institutionalizes a slow, investigatory approach to change. It hedges against risk by limiting downside. Typically, an experiment begins on a small scale, with a conservative prototype, and proceeds via regular testing. As in biological evolution, there's a built-in failure rate.

The machinery of third draft democracy (Bill of Change, Articles I-IV) does enable the prompt picking of low-hanging fruit—in remedying political contamination, for instance. (Clear-cut problem; known solution with strong public backing.)

Mutable democracy allows for the testing of a change where

the ethics aren't quite so clear, or potential effects are less predictable.

We'll look at how reforms are 'triaged', for one approach or the other, in the next section.

The goal of 'mutable democracy' is not to always be right but to be incrementally less wrong. Failure in a marriage, a large investment, or the invasion of Russia, is a disaster. Not so here. With downside kept on a short leash—no billion-dollar, million-person trials of untested ideas—mutable democracy starts small, mimics evolution, and is nourished by good ideas and bad alike. In that way it domesticates experience.

'Sturdy' and 'hairy' reforms

If you accept the premises of third draft democracy, the way to set a rational system in motion is to:

(i) delete money from politics
(ii) decentralize information
(iii) democratize decision-making
(iv) broaden civic engagement

Because these broad categories of reform are (i) needed, (ii) perceived to be needed, and (iii) devoid of large risks, you could call them 'sturdy' reforms.

For example, in our badly skewed information sphere, democratizing media ownership is an obvious step. No apparent 'bear traps' await us. The public is ready for change. ('Sturdy'.)

On the other hand, bits of the detail are unclear. Whilst enacting Article II, how do we provide for the arrival of new media we can barely imagine yet? And once Isegoria is in place, how do we deal with unintended consequences, such as unemployment in a sector nobody thought about? What do we do with an unexpected surplus from the social media levy?

Reforms that invoke mutable democracy, as these do, I call 'hairy'. (*Hairy* in mathematics means 'difficult to deal with or comprehend'.) Because they deal with the world's open-ended, evolving, unpredictable aspect—its mutability—hairy reforms are incremental and cautious. They're generally implemented in a smallish geographical area, for a finite period, on a limited scale. When the trial period is up, the reform is rigorously assessed— then amended, expanded or tossed out.

In sturdy design, you largely know what works. In hairy design you discover what works.

The precondition of sturdy reform is experience. In Nassim Nicholas Taleb's words:

> In a complex domain, only time—a long time—is evidence.[7]

The credo of hairy reform might be these words of Elinor Ostrom:

> We have never had to deal with problems of the scale facing today's globally interconnected society. No one knows for sure what will work, so it is important to build a system that can evolve and adapt rapidly.[8]

You could say a reform becomes 'hairy' when its risks require it to be started carefully and modestly. You could say it is 'sturdy' when its risks are outweighed by the risks of delay.

Chapter 28
Demotic institutions

To the Greek way of thinking, it was the political institutions that shaped the democratic man and the democratic life, and not vice-versa: the institutions of the polis educated and moulded the lives of the citizens, and to have the best life you must have the best institutions.[1]

— Mogens Herman Hansen, doyen of the
scholars of Classical Greece

In democracy's role as 'host' and honest broker for competing ideas, some of those ideas have inevitably been about democracy itself. It's this ability to evolve itself that allowed democracy to outlive the totalitarian alternatives. It also positions it to make better sense of the future than could an *ism*. Democracy makes room for new knowledge and new viewpoints as they arise. It cherry-picks the best bits of an ideology without becoming shackled to the whole.

On the other hand, ideologies such as the CCP's model, and Western market pantheism, tend to be impossible 'global' explanations for things. Both tend to take us backwards—to steep hierarchies, and unaccountable power: in the general direction of buccaneer capitalists, absolute monarchs, feudalism and warlords:

> Xi said he wanted to work with Trump for six more years, and Trump replied that people were saying that the two-term constitutional limit on presidents should be repealed for him. Xi said the US had too many elections, because he didn't want to switch away from Trump, who nodded approvingly.[2]

> — John Bolton, *The Room Where It Happened* (2020)

Whilst our future has not yet arrived, the future of our ancestors has—and we live with both the successes and the failures of their constitutional schemes. Thomas Paine appears to have sensed the dangers as early as the late 18th Century:

> Every age and generation must be as free to act for itself... The vanity and presumption of governing beyond the grave is the most ridiculous and insolent of all tyrannies.[3]

We can free ourselves from the grip of the dead not by crafting a tech utopia—or a socialist, statist or free market one—but by constructing *demotic institutions*.

These are the machinery of third draft democracy: the devices by which political power is liberated from its plutocratic constraints. By making the citizen the agent of selection, demotic institutions restore to government a capacity for faithful responsiveness.

Chapter 29
The machinery of third draft democracy

1. Deliberative democracy

> My encounters as a reporter with ordinary citizens have led to optimism about the potential for democratic renewal... Even in the most benighted corners of this country, in burned-out slums or on desolate Indian reservations, I have always met some whose forceful intelligence shone through the barriers of language and education and class. I frequently came away thinking to myself: Those people would be running things if they had been born with a bit more luck.[1]
>
> — William Greider, US journalist and author

In the 18th Century, Edmund Burke advanced the idea that democracy should be confined to elections—and that between times the public should stay out of politics.

Modern publics beg to differ. In 2008, *World Public Opinion* polled that question across 17 nations:

> On average 74 percent endorse the view that the public should have ongoing influence and 22 percent hold the 'Burkian' view

that elections are the only time the public should have a say in the government's decisions.[2]

The catch with this aspiration has always been: how, exactly, do large numbers of people exert ongoing influence? The intrinsic problem in a modern democracy is *dispersion*. We're numerous, and geographically spread out. How do you get five thousand—let alone ten million—people to come together on an issue, discuss it intelligently, and agree on a solution?

The demos, in short, is *unorganized*. It has ceded its decision-making to middlemen. And these 'representative' bodies soon develop a life of their own—an identity, a set of needs that differs from ours, and a collective self-preservation instinct. Dispersion shunts power upwards.

Time, too, works in favor of consolidated authority. People gather to vote only briefly—but a government develops organizational continuity. Its power has time to coalesce.

By such products of space and time is the power of the demos harvested by an elected elite. When power centralizes like this, there's a shrinking of citizen buy-in, of civic knowledge, and of the range of permissible viewpoints. Public disengagement evolves into public ignorance.

An opposite approach would be a legislative process that brings together a diverse group of participants who are statistically representative of the population, that allows them to study an issue at length, and that empowers them to reach a decision on behalf of the whole.

Such an approach would look much like *deliberative democracy*.

All else aside, deliberative democracy is an intensive education. It confronts the participant with full-spectrum reality—the complexities of a decision, its cost, the compromises it demands, its potential side effects, and how it will be received by different sections of society.

Because its participants are randomly chosen from the voter roll, deliberative democracy is counter-intuitive: the randomness of selection suggests a randomness in outcome. But in practice random selection guarantees not chaos but representativeness:

generally, such a group closely represents the spectrum of views in the community.

In most parliaments, legislators are selected via various 'filters'—the party filter, the money filter, the 'telegenic' filter… Thus few MPs are mechanics or teachers, and an unseemly number are lawyers and political professionals. The result is a kind of soul-lessness in the centres of power. As one former advisor to the British Labour Party leadership put it:

> Joining the Labour Party in 2009 felt a lot like signing up to a glorified market research agency. Rather than feeling like I was a part of a movement that gave me a voice, it instead resembled doing unpaid work for an increasingly detached political elite.[3]

John Adams, second president of the United States, wrote that the legislature 'should be an exact portrait, in miniature, of the people at large'. For all the reasons we've looked at so far, it did not work out that way. Nonetheless, our 'exact portrait in miniature' may be in reach.

Deliberative democracy has a 2,500-year pedigree. In the modern era, it has been successfully employed in dozens of countries—at levels ranging up to national constitution-making. Participants are near-unanimous in their enthusiasm for it. It tends to produce outcomes the public likes.

At a time when representative democracy is in trouble, an experiment with deliberative democracy is a logical move. Anyone who has seen a dozen not-especially-promising people morph into a hard-working and collaborative trial jury knows what ordinary people are capable of when given an important community task.

A survey conducted in 2010 by the Program for Public Consultation gave 2,000 randomly selected Americans the chance to say how they'd reduce the budget deficit. On average, respondents cut the deficit by 70% over five years; and made spending cuts of $145 billion—most of them from the defence budget, which they wanted reduced by $109 billion. Next on the list were 'the wars in Iraq and Afghanistan' and 'intelligence agencies', which they de-funded by $13 billion each.

Deep cuts were made by independents, Democrats, Republicans and those 'very sympathetic to the Tea Party'. The researchers noted that 'there was remarkable agreement on which areas should be increased or decreased'.

'It is striking,' they wrote, 'that no group—Republican, Democrat, or independents—acted on average in ways that fit their respective media stereotypes.'[4]

Had this poll been an actual, citizen-run budgeting process, the name for its selection method would be *sortition* or *selection by lot*. The group empowered to make decisions would be a *citizen assembly* or *deliberation, deliberative assembly, citizen jury, deliberative poll* or (more colloquially) *mini-public*. Its members would be known as *participants* or *jurors*. All of this, of course, adds up to *deliberative democracy*—with this particular variant called *participatory budgeting*.

With today's large populations, representative democracy makes few inroads into the dispersion problem. Even the reforms described in Parts Three and Four—Decontamination and Isegoria —don't do a lot. We can have decontaminated politics and diverse information, but we remain numerous and scattered. That has necessitated representative government: centralized, closed and capturable. That in turn yields voter disengagement and (downstream again) self-selected pressure groups—noisy minorities— that don't necessarily represent the populace.

Representative government also takes the *nuance* out of politics. You may not like 49% of your party's policies (or more), but you vote for it anyway to keep an even worse party out of power.

Dominic Cummings' account of his pre-Brexit polling gives an idea of how particularized voters' preferences are, and how poorly they're captured by the platforms of the political parties:

> Swing voters who decide elections…support much tougher policies on violent crime than most Tory MPs AND much higher taxes on the rich than [Labour's] Blair, Brown, and Miliband. They support much tougher anti-terrorism laws than most Tory MPs AND they support much tougher action on white collar criminals and executive pay than Blair, Brown, and Miliband.

One of the key delusions that 'the centre ground' caused in SW1 [the postcode for Westminster] concerned immigration. Most people convinced themselves that 'swing voters' must have a 'moderate' and 'centre ground' view between Farage [UKIP] and Corbyn [Labour]. Wrong. About 80% of the country including almost all swing voters agreed with UKIP that immigration was out of control and something like an Australian points system was a good idea. This was true across party lines.[5]

Polling has found 'mosaic' patterns like these worldwide, and not just among swing voters. Representative democracy does not and cannot capture them. All too often, it requires us to elect people we don't like, from a political class that's remote from us, to legislatures that don't do what we want them to.

This is a significant set of deficits. In something of a design *coup*, deliberative democracy resolves all of them.

Because it statistically represents the citizenry with some accuracy, deliberative democracy closely reflects its will. It achieves this without needing to do the impossible—to involve every citizen in every decision.

As it generally tackles one issue at a time, there's no 'platform' a participant is obliged to vote for. And as she doesn't have to worry about re-election, she can contribute to decisions without fear of career consequences. This mimics the decision-making model humans followed for hundreds of thousands of years, where leaders were 'situational, temporary and nonbinding'.[6]

As a way of locating public opinion, deliberations easily trump opinion polling. According to political scientist James Fishkin of Stanford University, deliberative democracy's guiding spirit, there's a simple reason for this:

> Normally public opinion represents what people think when they don't have a lot of time to think about an issue and they are talking to people like themselves.[7]

Deliberative democracy puts you in a room with people who

are mostly unlike yourself, thereby capitalizing on the fact that *diversity trumps ability*.

Professor Scott Page, who researches complexity in the social sciences, has studied organizational diversity—both in the field and via mathematical modelling. He found that 'cognitive diversity' produces better decisions than groups of experts:

> People from different backgrounds have varying ways of looking at problems, what I call 'tools'. The sum of these tools is far more powerful in organizations with diversity than in ones where everyone has gone to the same schools, been trained in the same mold and thinks in almost identical ways.
>
> The problems we face in the world are very complicated. Any one of us can get stuck. If we're in an organization where everyone thinks in the same way, everyone will get stuck in the same place.
>
> But if we have people with diverse tools, they'll get stuck in different places. One person can do their best, and then someone else can come in and improve on it. There's a lot of empirical data to show that diverse cities are more productive, diverse boards of directors make better decisions, and the most innovative companies are diverse.[8]

Deliberative democracy translates this 'organizational diversity' into the political realm. In the words of Canadian political scientist Tom Malleson:

> If we combine the modern mathematical notion of a representative mini-public with the new insights about the democratic potential of deliberation, what we get is a political epiphany: a novel kind of democratic mechanism that provides us with something that elections never can—a clear indication of what the considered judgement of the entire adult population would be if they were able to deliberate on issues thoroughly, freely, and in an informed manner.[9]

Deliberative democracy is, finally, an engine of *mutability*.

Chapter 29

With its capacity to explore complex problems and locate the public mood—and its independence from governments and special interests—it has the fine-tuned responsiveness required to evolve society in safe directions.

Athens

> The democrats themselves seem to have preferred sortition not because of its being the obvious method of selection when all are alike, but because it safeguarded the powers of the people, prevented conflict and counteracted corruption.[10]
>
> — Mogens Herman Hansen

Deliberative democracy was no peripheral feature of the first democracy. It just about defined it.

Isegoria (the equal right of all to speak and be heard) was the democracy's key principle, with *isonomia* (equality before the law) perhaps its second—but sortition was central to the implementation of both.[a]

Athens' primary deliberative bodies were its courts, which had no judges or lawyers—only juries. On each of 200 days per year, jury duty occupied about 2,000 citizens. Everything was chosen by lot: the jury 'pool' of 6,000 men, the individual juries, and the duties within each—three levels of sortition.

The lot was administered via the *kleroterion*, a machine into which Athenians inserted their bronze citizen IDs—which then

---

[a] Sortition is also employed by hunter-gatherers. The *Ju/'hoan* people in southern Africa gave distribution rights on meat not to the hunter who killed the animal, but (a more or less random thing) to the one who owned the arrow that hit it. This was to prevent power and status accruing to the good hunters. Plus 'the elderly, the short-sighted, the clubfooted and the lazy got a chance to be the centre of attention once in a while'. (James Suzman, *Work, A Deep History, From the Stone Age to the Age of Robots* (New York: Penguin, 2022).)

randomly dispensed black or white balls. If you drew a white ball, you'd been chosen as a juror.

Fig. 5.1: Remains of a *kleroterion* in the Agora Museum, Athens

Most of the city's 1200 administrators were also chosen by lot, again via the *kleroterion*.[11] The administrators worked in 'boards', each of which administered a department of the 'civil service'—finances, mint, markets, courts, dockyard, public workers, and so on.

The Council of 500—a kind of super-board, responsible for setting the Assembly's agenda, and a key player in state finances—was likewise selected by lot.

Members of a board were equals, and decisions were usually reached collegially—a system that diluted damage from the odd incompetent or power junkie that sortition threw up.

A basic principle of the democracy was 'to rule and be ruled in turn'.[12] To achieve this, its courts and public administration were about as randomized as the Athenians could make them. Sortition, and regular rotation, eliminated the possibility of administrators and courts becoming weapons of power.

Through Athens' second democratic century, the *polis* gave

increasing power to the juries and boards, and less to the Assembly. Deliberative democracy was regarded as even safer than direct.

To certify that he was qualified to serve on a jury, each Athenian citizen received a small bronze plaque known as a *pinakion*. This 'jury token' often displayed an owl, the emblem of Athens. Many an Athenian was buried with his *pinakion*.

Fig. 5.2: Bronze *pinakion* of a citizen named Archilochos of Phaleron, c. 370 BC

Deliberative democracy in the modern world

You talk about freedom a lot, in the company—right? Let me give you the best definition of freedom I've ever heard. It's 2100 years old—Marcus Cicero: 'Freedom is participation in power.' When you talk about freedom in your literature, are you talking about participation in power? By the masses? That's what freedom is. By that measure, citizens don't have that much freedom. They have personal freedom—buy what they want, marry who they want, eat what they want… You've got that in a lot of dictatorships. The key is civic freedom—to shape the future. How much voice do we have on foreign and military policy, or the federal budget? Or something as simple as labelling food products when they're genetically engineered? Ninety percent want it, Monsanto doesn't. Monsanto wins. Is that democracy?[13]

— Ralph Nader, to an audience of Google
employees (2008)

Today, sortition-based democracy is proving as useful for drafting constitutional amendments, and setting municipal water rates, as it once was for maintaining Athens' currency and sacred statuary.

According to a book-length study of constitutional deliberations in British Colombia, Ontario and the Netherlands, participants were observed to 'dedicate themselves to the task' and became 'interested, engaged and knowledgeable'. Their preferences 'did not fluctuate haphazardly, [but] emerged as knowledge accumulated'. They were not unduly swayed by the better-educated.[14] In British Colombia, one witness commented:

> Observing the assemblies, it was hard not to be impressed with the capacity of citizens to learn, absorb, and understand the intricacies of a subject to which most had given little, if any, prior thought.[15]

It was also noticed that participants' decisions were *not influenced by partisan leanings*. If that proves to be generally true, we may be in possession of a tool that lifts the curse of tribalism.

All this resembles the education and engagement that flowed from Athens' sortition system 2,500 years ago. Perhaps every second Athenian citizen had at some time been involved in a jury or board, and one in three had served on the Council of 500. As a result, historian Josiah Ober notes, 'knowledge of the day-to-day workings of government was very widely distributed across the Athenian population'.[16]

Modern sortition, of course, is not limited to one race or gender—a large improvement on the Athenian democracy—or to a narrow group of professions: a large improvement on our own. Teachers, farmers, nurses, laborers, clerks, shop workers and small businesspeople will gain a voice. Women and minorities will be represented according to their numbers in the community, not their ability to win a political rat race. All this can be achieved without quotas and affirmative action (giving us one less thing to argue about).

Deliberative assemblies could get started in numerous ways:

- The electorate could initiate an assembly on a particular issue, via the collection of signatures (for example, 4% of those on the voter roll).

- A referendum might mandate a series of assemblies on a broad subject area (such as 'the economy').

- The government might also be able to designate an assembly.

Random selection will bring a lot of people under 40 into the political sphere. In many countries, the young now vote in low numbers—frequently deciding an election by their absence. This makes for older parliaments, which legislate for their own generations. Who knows what we're missing out on? Jefferson was 33, a 'Millennial' in our terms, when he penned the Declaration of Independence.

There are also the questions of character and mental balance. In the words of former Australian foreign minister Gareth Evans:

> Anyone who gets to senior levels in politics, and particularly leadership levels, as I've often said, you've got to be a deeply flawed personality... You've got to be a bit psychologically strange to ever fight your way to the top and stay there for any period of time.[17]

Donald Trump's 2024 running mate, JD Vance, seems to concur:

> We don't have that many non-insane people in Washington.[18]

Where today's political system selects for those who long for power, the very act of sortition favors those who don't (a.k.a. normal people). Random selection equalizes the quiet with the outspoken, the observers with the campaigners—the unaligned with the true believers.

Finally, deliberative democracy—low on 'them-and-us', insulated from media alarums, and closely representative of regular people—deprives demagogues of their native habitat.

Professor James Fishkin sums up the case:

> I've got colleagues who make a good living demonstrating how stupid the public is. In fact the public is potentially very smart. You just have to create social conditions and a design where they have a reason to pay attention, and make it easy for them to engage with competing arguments. Then they are consistently brilliant.[19]

Professor Fishkin has, so far, organized 109 deliberations in 28 nations.[20] His team even reintroduced deliberative democracy to Athens.[21] These experiences left him optimistic:

> If people think their voice actually matters, they'll do the hard work, really study their briefing books, ask the experts smart questions and then make tough decisions. When they hear the experts disagreeing, they're forced to think for themselves. About 70% change their minds in the process.[22]

The problem, it turns out, was not 'the people' but how you organize them.

Potential uses under third draft democracy

> Our ancestors evolved to suppress self-serving behaviors that are destructive for the group, at least for the most part, so that the main way to succeed was as a group. Teamwork became the signature adaptation of our species.[23]
>
> — Evolutionary biologists David Sloan Wilson and Dag Olav Hessen

There is no limit to the applications of deliberative assemblies in a third draft environment. These are some examples:

> Constitutional

>> Bill of Change assemblies will play the key role in the lead-up to the Bill referendum. They'll draft the articles of the Bill, and their supporting laws, and the referendum questions (Part Eight).

These assemblies are not government institutions, but demotic ones. Given that 'diversity trumps ability', they're likely to be fairer and better at updating constitutions than are politicians, lawyers and other experts with interests to protect.

After the Bill is enacted, it will need periodic updating in further referendums. Assemblies are the obvious way to guide that work too.

Fig. 5.3: 669 Mongolian citizens gather at the parliament building in 2017 to draft amendments to the national constitution. Each was randomly selected from a family & region that were also randomly selected. Stanford University's Center for Deliberative Democracy provided technical assistance.

> Legislation, regulation, administration, oversight

For the chief of state under modern conditions, a limiting factor is too many subjects and problems in too many areas of govern-ment to allow solid understanding of any of them, and too little time to think between fifteen-minute appointments and thirty-page briefs. This leaves the field open to protective stupidity. Meanwhile bureaucracy, safely repeating today what it did yesterday, rolls on as ineluctably as some vast computer, which, once penetrated by error, duplicates it forever.[24]

— Barbara Tuchman (*The March of Folly*)

Four decades on from Barbara Tuchman's observation, a look at how well our policy-makers are making policy suggests that citizens could hardly do worse.

In 2021, Dominic Cummings was asked what it was like to be the prime minister's senior advisor the previous year, as he began to realize how serious COVID could get:

It was obviously extremely frightening—and pretty surreal as well… You're looking around the room at different people who are in key positions, and thinking, 'They're not the people that should be in charge of this kind of thing.'[25]

In 2020, in the US, the Former Members of Congress organization interviewed congresspersons from both parties who'd left politics in the previous two years. The consensus view of these former representatives was that

Congress has largely become a dysfunctional institution unable to meet the critical needs of our country.[26]

As we saw in Part Three, the American people are in full agreement with them.

It's testimony to the grip that money has on the system that both public and politicians believe it has failed—yet it remains standing.

It's likely that the best way to replace a failing hierarchy is with a network.

Unlike a hierarchy—a small group that governs a large group —a network is 'distributed'. That tends to maximize human talent, which makes it more robust.

A citizen assembly is a good approximation of a network. It has a flat, non-competitive structure—a design that promotes openness. Members are constantly in communication with each other and modifying each other's views. When required, the assembly can break down into smaller groups for specialized tasks. Or it can join up with a larger network—for example a national or international one. An assembly mirrors the fluidity and serendipity of human society—and it recreates society's nesting of groups within groups—as legislatures and executives cannot.

Greek-American sociologist Nicholas Christakis, who studies the information, habits and norms that 'ripple and flow' through human networks, notes that a network—which he calls a 'super-organism'—can be much greater than the sum of its parts:

> Like for example…a flock of birds that's able to pool their wisdom and navigate and find a tiny speck of an island in the middle of the Pacific. Or a pack of wolves that's able to bring down larger prey.[27]

As Latin American politics has long illustrated, and the Capitol invasion of 2021 confirmed, purely representative government and winner-takes-all electoral systems tend to bring civil strife by design.

Citizen deliberations (assemblies) routinely surpass political hierarchies at sorting out political issues—especially curly, difficult, divisive issues.

Such deliberations could manage elections. They could audit government. They could 'shadow' departments, as select committees are supposed to do. They could unravel long-standing 'wicked' problems in the regulatory sphere—e.g. issues mired in red tape, like planning permits and ethics approvals. They could take on a decent slice of local government.

Under certain conditions (Part Eight), they could legislate on our behalf. That would enable them to reform domains that government has largely ignored—such as the housing crisis.

Internationally, linked assemblies (described below) might enable multi-centre studies of issues that are of no interest to corporate-sponsored science, such as falling global sperm counts and testosterone levels, and the rise in autism.

Fig. 5.4: In 2019, Professors James Fishkin & Larry Diamond organized America's largest-ever deliberative assembly. 523 'citizen delegates' discussed five polarizing issues—alternating between small, moderated groups & large plenary sessions. A 55-page briefing book was provided, including 'for' & 'against' arguments. A bipartisan panel of experts answered questions—as did no less than five presidential candidates. Most participants moved toward the centre on nearly all issues: more extreme policies lost support on both the right & left. Those who thought the other side had 'good reasons' for their views grew from 34% to 54% throughout. Most of the changed attitudes had 'stuck' one year later.

>> Shaping emerging technologies

>>> **Biomed**: Radical medical innovations such as gene editing, brain chip implants to raise cognition, and synthetic blood to heighten physical performance, are in our near-term future.[28] We can be sure that if citizens don't shape the ways these technologies are used, corporations will.[29]

>>> **Lethal autonomous weapons systems** (LAWS) are said to be 'years, not decades' away—and will take various forms,

including swarms of flying robots programmed to 'select and engage targets without human intervention'.

LAWS are sometimes seen as the third revolution in warfare after gunpowder and nuclear weapons.[30] They're increasingly easy and cheap to make, and are presently subject to no public supervision. Their leading developers—the US, the UK and Israel—reject the idea of an international treaty to limit them.

If we don't believe it is a good idea to develop fleets of tens of thousands of tiny, armed rotorcraft that can 'manoeuvre unaided at high speed in urban areas and inside buildings'—craft that are autonomous—we might consider deliberative assemblies to restrain them.

Further along, we'll look at ways that cross-border deliberative democracy can contain threats like this regionally and globally.

>> Bureaucratization

> One of the things I feel about the age we live in is the predominance of the administrative or bureaucratic mind over almost every aspect of our lives. I think this is deeply damaging, and is an exhibition of the left hemisphere's way of trying to understand—but *mis*understanding—what it's dealing with: and above all of trying to control it.[31]
>
> — Neuroscientist Iain McGilchrist, on his book
> *The Master and His Emissary: The Divided Brain
> and the Making of the Western World.*

Today, the most elementary transaction with government or corporation—seeking a permit, applying for a refund, asking a question—can entail form-filling, ID checks, privacy statements, surveys, warnings, disclaimers and above all delays. On the phone to any large institution, the norm is an automated voice menu—then a sub-menu, and another—and then mood music that plays, and plays... Periodically, 'Your call is important to us' provides a nice Orwellian flourish.

In hospitals and universities, procedures and protocols—

reporting, quality assurance and other middle management impedances—get between doctors and their patients, and academics and their students, on a daily basis.

As the elderly whale moves through the ocean blanketed in barnacles and lice, ordinary citizens and professionals alike now move through life blanketed in bureaucracy.

Third draft democracy yields what is useful to all people, not just to social engineers and rule-writers. Deliberations view society from the citizen's viewpoint, and act accordingly. They miniaturize the 'hive mind'—seeking to see a decision's full social implications, not just an immediate departmental need.

They are well-placed to dissolve the plague of hyper-bureaucracy.

>> Economic policy

Deliberative democracy is close to society's diverse, less predictable 'people' tier, and far from its tiny, homogenous 'elite' tier. The former is where complexity tends to manifest, in ways that are often opaque to governments.

An assembly—informed by economists but comprised of citizens—might inquire into who benefits, and loses, from the monetary inflation of recent decades. Politicians often lack the political capital (or the motivation) to explore tricky questions like this.

Another assembly might inquire into corporate welfare—to see whether spending decisions are being made in the public interest.

Assemblies might look into the origins of our 'boom and bust' cycles—and what structural changes can be made to moderate them—or seek ways to level the macro-economic playing field so small businesses (shops, contractors, tradespeople, start-ups) are less disadvantaged against large ones. (They might begin by asking why nearly all government contracting goes to big players—and how much can be redirected to smaller ones.)

The above are mostly major, national issues. So, once assemblies studied them and came up with options, they could refer those options to the referendum system—so the public can consider enacting the appropriate laws or (more rarely) constitutional amendments.

The smaller and more local an issue is, the more likely that an assembly will be given the latitude to decree the solution itself. For example, assemblies might look at the 'bodies corporate' that manage apartment blocks in a given city, and whether they do so competently and non-exploitatively—and make rule-changes if needed.

In Part Eight we'll look at the ways that deliberative assemblies can interact with direct democracy—perhaps the most potent of the third draft *syzygies*. That combination should serve to put on the map the multitude of issues that worry ordinary people—but not governments—and to bring them under popular control.

>> Growth

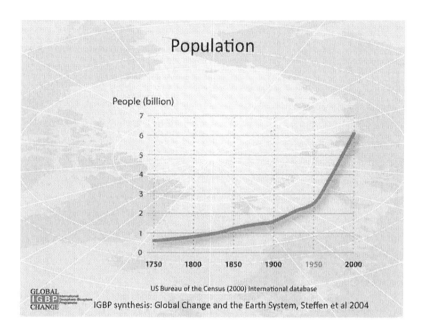

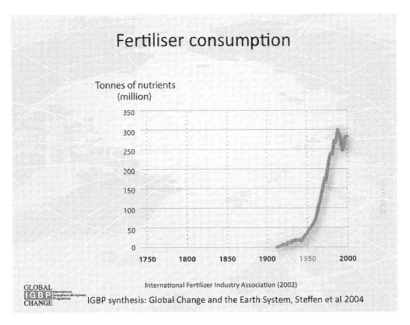

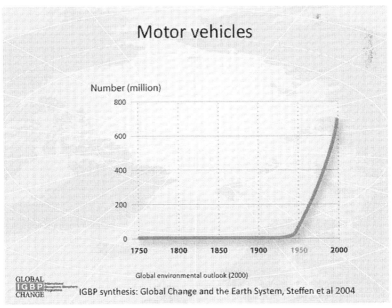

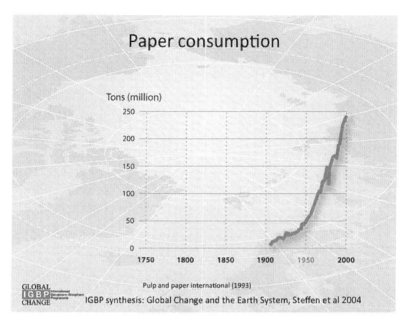

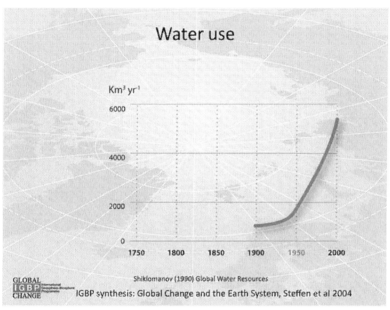

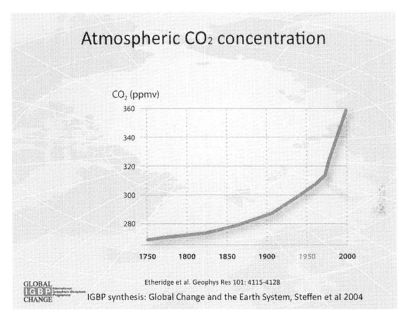

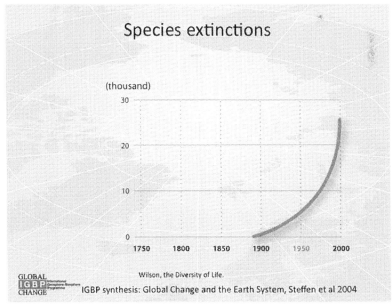

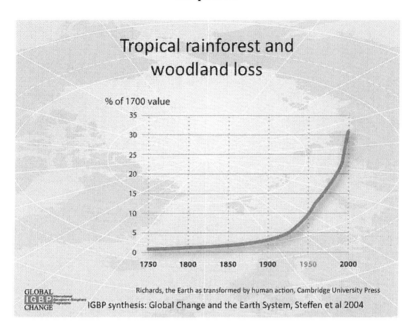

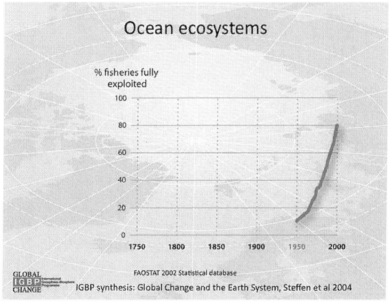

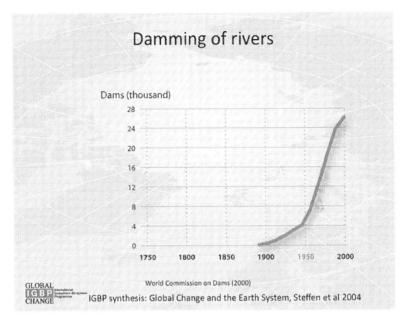

Fig. 5.5: Graphs depicting increasing human population, fertilizer & paper consumption, motor vehicles, water use, atmospheric carbon, fully exploited oceans, river-damming, & losses of species, rainforests & woodlands. There was an especially sharp increase in these since about 1950: sometimes known as 'The Great Acceleration'.

As recently as 1946, one of growth theory's founders, Evsey Domar, said that growth was 'a concept which has been little used in economic theory'.[32]

That soon changed. And as growth went geometric, so did its effects on our cities, natural environment, families and psychology.

Neither human societies nor ecosystems can expand forever. At what point do we wish to shift our focus from 'more' to 'better'?

>> The war on the banes

A broad project, for separate but linked assemblies, would be to bring order to *the war on the banes*: the series of official 'wars'—such as those on drugs, street crime, terror and cancer—that divert billions of taxpayer dollars to legislators' corporate patrons, and often bring slender returns to the public.

>> Censorship

In the years since about 2015, a problem that had been put to bed in the 1970s re-emerged in a new, more virulent form.

On government instructions—often arising from corporate requests—thinkers, scientists, journalists, videographers, political candidates and others were demonetized, de-amplified or de-platformed from social media after claims—frequently spurious—of anti-Semitism, hate speech, pseudo-science, disinformation, misinformation, 'malinformation', and so on.

The American leftist anti-war comedian Lee Camp has been banned partly or wholly by Facebook, YouTube, Wikipedia, Twitter, Spotify and Instagram. His RT television show was terminated when Russian sanctions began, and his emails to his mailing list were marked as 'phishing attempts'—apparently so no-one would open them.[33]

GoFundMe froze money donated to antiwar journalists, and PayPal shut down their accounts.[34] Elon Musk's *X* was threatened with massive fines by the EU for permitting what it deemed 'misinformation' on the Israel-Hamas war.[35]

In Britain, activist Russell Brand was hit with sexual harassment allegations that showed remarkably close co-operation between his most common targets—Britain's Government and its legacy media. On the strength of the anonymous claims, Brand was demonetized, at government request, by YouTube.

The campaign ranges up to full-scale intimidation. A British journalist who'd exposed misdeeds by the security services was detained for eight hours by counter-terror police.[36] In Australia, whistleblowers who'd revealed crimes by the intelligence agencies were put on trial in a closed courtroom.[37] And, of course, for bringing news of government crimes to those who paid for them, Julian Assange was jailed and Edward Snowden exiled to Russia.

Under the Biden administration, anti-war conservatives are perhaps the key targets—just as anti-war progressives were the key targets of the Nixon administration.

Former Republican State Department official Mike Benz believes the present methods descend from the Defense Advanced Research Projects Agency's history in countering ISIS recruiting online:

> What DARPA was doing for counterinsurgency and counterter-rorism in 2014-2015 is what the National Science Foundation is doing for conservative sentiment or COVID skepticism now.[38]

As a result of the crackdown on speech occurring in the US, Germany[39], Brazil[40], Ireland,[41] Scotland,[42] the UK,[43] India,[44] Turkey,[45] Australia and beyond, in October 2023 hundreds of the world's journalists and scholars signed the 'Westminster Declaration' to call for an end to it.

A deliberative assembly at national level might tackle this problem in the spirit of the Westminster Declaration.

>> Organized crime

In Australia, Vietnamese, Chinese, Japanese, Russian, Italian, Serbian and other ethnic mafias are a growing presence—adding to motorcycle gangs that arose in the 1950s, and Anglo-Irish criminal groups that have been active since the 19th Century.[46] Organized crime costs the country more than $30 billion annually,[47] well above the federal expenditure on schools.[48] According to the Australian Criminal Intelligence Commission:

> Organised crime in Australia is proficient and enduring. It is transnational in nature, technology enabled and increasingly functions as a business: employing professionals; outsourcing key activities such as money laundering; diversifying into multiple criminal markets; and developing strong, consistent

revenue streams through involvement in comparatively low-risk activities.[49]

Thus, in addition to such interests as drugs, extortion, fraud and human trafficking, these groups accumulate real estate[50] and restaurant chains.[51] Foreign members gain visas, residency or citizenship; convicted foreign criminals are not automatically deported on release.[52]

During the long sleep of second draft democracy, organized crime has been mainstreamed.

Deliberative assemblies—using the crime and intelligence agencies as resources—would be able to design robust measures to undo this activity. Attacking organized crime is unlikely to be politically contentious: it's something conservatives and progressives can agree on.

Because so much organized crime takes place in regional areas —for example, bribing officials to approve developments[53]— there's an obvious role for local assemblies. At the other end of the scale, organized crime is worth $2.2 trillion globally, and the various players are deeply enmeshed: so it's also an issue that can be dealt with on the international tier.[54]

>> Chronic illness

Beginning in around the 1950s, and partly due to antibiotics, society's disease burden started to shift from acute illnesses to chronic ones.[55] Today, in the developed world, perhaps half or more of citizens have one, two or more chronic illnesses.[56] Prevalence probably increases by something like .5 to 1% of the population per year in developed countries.[57] It's unclear whether this rate of increase will continue. If it does, we're heading to a cliff-edge. In time, we'll run out of people to treat and care for the sick.

This is one of many 'cliff-edge' issues that second draft democracy has been unable to tackle. Whilst an individual disease will at times gain much attention from media and government, the gradual expansion of the chronic illness epidemic does not. Nor is there a proposed solution. As with nuclear armories and dissolving communities—and numerous other slow-moving, low-visibility crises—it ticks away beyond the fringes of official awareness: a more or less existential issue that resides in the media/legislative blind sector.

The only debate is between those who want to increase health spending to deal with it, and those who say we can't afford to. This is well downstream of causes.

A political class that thinks in three- or four-year terms of office, and a media focused on the political 'horse race', will not think 30 years ahead. The myopia is just as serious among experts. Partly due to contamination of medical research and practice by drug companies, cures for chronic diseases are virtually non-existent outside of natural healing circles. Most drug treatments address symptoms only, and some are worse than the disease.[58]

A core third draft principle is that profit does not trump human welfare. This applies not only to governing a society, but to training a doctor or teaching a child. How to apply that practically?

With chronic illness, citizen assemblies might seek to identify root causes (soil depletion? education? sedentism? pesticides? the loss of our ancient gut biome?), to start work on the study of treatments, and most importantly to devise policy change aimed at prevention.

An assembly might not be able to change national law off its own bat—it would work with the referendum system for that—but it might (for example) decree that a controlled study of a non-patentable medical agent (such as vitamin D for viral illness) is funded from state revenue.

Various assemblies might address potential causes like food quality, water treatment, the contamination of scholarship, and so on—as well as specific diseases such as depression, autoimmune and allergy. Each of those might pick delegates to a 'next-level' assembly, which deals with the multiple and overlapping causes of chronic illness—and weaves together as many upstream solutions as possible.

It's become apparent that elites have few incentives to provide for a society's future. For that, we need *disintermediation*: to dissolve the power of political middlemen.

>> The climate schism

None of the political issues I've used to illustrate my arguments is beyond question. Take climate change: to avoid constant qualifications, and a plethora of footnotes, I've worked from the assumption that it's roughly as real, and as serious, as the scientific consensus says.

That's only my assumption though—and an uneducated one at that. The problems are obvious. Some readers will believe that the scientific consensus is wrong. This book itself has explored how science can be contaminated.

Between 30 and 40 percent of Americans (depending on poll) believe there's no solid evidence for climate change, or that it is occurring but largely from natural causes. Such doubters crop up in every society, though outside of the US they are fewer.

Skeptics say their views rest on suspicion of 'overblown crisis rhetoric', on doubts over the 'financial motivations' of climate scientists, and most of all on a complete distrust of politicians and media. [59] [60] [61] [62] [63]

Here we have an *epistemological* problem—a problem of how knowledge is arrived at. Many think the sources of our information on climate are tainted by ideology and money.

As a result, skeptics live under policies they think are pointless or harmful, and believers live in a world where climate action is hindered by skeptics.

Compromise is usually a good idea. But here the cost of being wrong is high for believers, and astronomical for skeptics. We need to discover what is true, and then to try to have it better accepted.

Under our present systems, the climate schism is likely to go on indefinitely. For one thing, it can be monetized—turned into both financial and political capital. For another, trust in institutions has evaporated: there are no longer generally accepted sources of truth.

A government could fund another expert panel to write another long report to be spruiked by media outlets. But given the general cynicism toward governments, experts and media, such a report is no longer likely to move the needle.

Our emotions tell us that because climate change is so obviously real—or unreal—we should not be wasting our time on our opponents. However we can't proceed without them. Until the truth is determined in an incorruptible or 'ground-up' way, the climate schism will persist.

For this, we need new ways to generate information, to weigh it, and to act on it. A new tier of professionals to perform this task —a new group of specialists—won't be enough.

Early in the piece, third draft democracy decontaminates politics, media and science. Human error will continue to occur, but the massive biases built into these systems today will no longer exist. Journalists will be free to use truth as their criterion, and politicians to govern to benefit the community.

The third draft also puts more proactive mechanisms in play. Deliberative assemblies can receive public submissions, call witnesses from all sides, and convene for as long as it takes to agree on facts. Where big decisions are required, they can design referendum questions.

The process begins by taking the arguments of both sides seriously.

Whichever climate crisis you subscribe to—an artificially warming world, or a fishy transfer of resources to the usual culprits —this is the way in which it can be explored, understood and undone.

Deliberative democracy is in a good position to dismantle our epistemological deadlocks.

>> Biosecurity

The *Bulletin of the Atomic Scientists* warned in 2019:

> Mammal-transmissible bird flu research poses a real danger of a worldwide pandemic that could kill human beings on a vast scale.[64]

Accidental releases of pathogens, it added, 'are fairly likely over time, as there are at least 14 labs (mostly in Asia) now carrying out this research'. The *Bulletin* did not accept that these labs were safeguarded against human error—always the largest factor in lab accidents.[65]

And, almost immediately, the pandemic reminded us that biosecurity in pathogen research is a global risk.

Biosecurity is in a bad state largely because of poor peer monitoring among nations. This stems from mutually suspicious governments. So, whilst a national deliberation could mandate stronger biosecurity for labs, and establish better early warning systems, it could also link with deliberations in other countries— so methods are standardized, and risks are monitored across borders.

The network might also contemplate a global ban of the gain-of-function research that may have brought us the pandemic.[66] [67] [68]

This brings us, logically enough, to the role of cross-border deliberative assemblies.

> The international tier

We're in an era of growing equality between women and men, gays and heterosexuals, children and adults, students and teachers, patients and doctors, parishioners and priests… Government is the holdout. It entrenches secrecy, celebrity and pecking orders. It concentrates power instead of dispersing it. It's swimming against the societal tide. This final bastion of hierarchy must topple at some point.

Deliberative democracy is a good way to ensure a soft landing. In lieu of hierarchies, it enlists the dynamics of networks. In a third draft scenario, these networks of deliberations may occur across local, state and national borders.

Our era of geopolitical tension is also (a bit paradoxically) an era of xenophilia: as the world's governments continue to quarrel, and even go to war, the world's cultures are increasingly entranced by one another. Linked deliberations are well-placed to create solidarity between populaces.

On transnational issues such as pandemics, boundary disputes, wars, tax and trade, people around the world want better co-operation.[69] Most believe, for example, that such co-operation could have blunted the damage from COVID.[70] This aspiration for greater global co-operation can be realized via linked assemblies, working to develop cross-border policies and agreements—to legislate, regulate and administer.

Third draft democracy means that not only can governments meet to bring about some common end—but societies can as well. This is not 'globalization': such assemblies could just as easily meet to preserve local culture, protect national sovereignty, or wind back the power of the WHO.

There is, finally, a large class of issues that could *only* be dealt with by the people, directly—the issues in which governments have a vested interest in ongoing mischief. One example is the 'Pegasus' spyware made by Israel's NSO Group: used by governments worldwide to spy on opposition politicians, journalists, activists, and foreign leaders, via their mobile phones.[71] It's hard to see anything but citizen bodies undoing this transborder menace.

Chapter 29

>> Reform of international institutions

There can be no democratic choice against the European treaties.

> — Jean-Claude Juncker, President of the
> European Commission, reminding Greeks that
> the anti-austerity government they'd elected
> would not be allowed to over-ride EU financial
> directives. (2015)

Sri Lanka—like so many other countries struggling for solvency —remains a colony with administration outsourced to the International Monetary Fund. The country is still divided and conquered by local elites, while real economic control is held abroad.[72]

> — Sri Lankan writer Indrajit Samarajiva, on the
> country's worst economic crisis in 74 years (2022)

Key scientists advising the World Health Organization on planning for an influenza pandemic had done paid work for pharmaceutical firms that stood to gain from the guidance they were preparing. These conflicts of interest have never been publicly disclosed by WHO, and WHO has dismissed inquiries into its handling of the A/H1N1 pandemic as 'conspiracy theories'.[73]

> — *British Medical Journal*, June 4, 2010

Greece's then-finance minister Yanis Varoufakis became an advocate of democratizing the EU after his experience with the Greek debt crisis of 2015. Varoufakis recounts a conversation, about the 'austerity' the eurozone was demanding of Greece, with its representative, the German finance minister:

Wolfgang Schäuble admitted to me, 'Of course we are not going to get our money back from Greece.' He even admitted that it was cruel and unusual punishment that was being inflicted upon the majority of our people. At that point I couldn't believe my ears, and I said to him: 'So why are you doing it?' He said to me, 'Don't you understand? I'm sending a message to Paris. They cannot…conduct their own fiscal policy.'

So deep down, for them it [debt] is just a chess game. And they use that, strategically, to divide countries, and to divide populations within countries. For them, it is simply war by other means.[74]

The first solution here is for people's assemblies in the 'target' nation to put an end to the kind of plutocratic corruption that led Greece into bankruptcy.

But there's another, further-reaching answer. That kind of action on the home front could be complemented by assemblies from the EU's member nations—triggering referendums where needed—that link up to democratize the EU's 'constitution', the Lisbon Treaty.

This is dealing with causes, not effects.

Such assemblies might also de-fang the unelected 'Eurogroup'—which not only exercises despotic economic power (it deepened Greece's depression in 2015) but is unnecessarily secretive (allowing no minutes to be made of its meetings).[75]

Other such linked assemblies might address the oligarchic weapon of debt.

Others again might even look at ways to implement the plan, discussed by Soviet and Western leaders in 1990, to sideline both the NATO and Soviet/Russian military blocs, in favor of a political architecture that absorbed both: a 'common European home', as Mikhail Gorbachev termed it.[76]

There is, finally, no reason such linked assemblies shouldn't convene to undo the Security Council's monopoly over major decisions at the UN; to decontaminate the international body; and to reshape it in line with the emerging multipolar world.

Once again, such cross-border networks could be used to undo globalization's injurious aspects, or to advance its beneficial aspects —either or both.

The powers of the global institutions were conferred by the

governments of member nations—whose own authority derives solely from their people.

Fig. 5.6: French component of a global citizen assembly on climate & energy, 2015—the 'World Wide Views'. WWVs often serve as adjuncts to international conferences, such as COP. Though the assemblies have no legislative power (they make 'recommendations'), they involve thousands of people from dozens of countries. The WWVs could be thought of as a dry run for a global citizen legislation process.

> Stasis

Change for the worse generally occurs when we fail to make change for the better. Neglect of structural reform leads not to stability but stasis.

This stasis is showing its face the world over. In Australia, according to political scientist John Dryzek, the federal parliament is

> composed almost entirely of people who are good at justification but terrible at reflection. It is…a theatre of expression where politicians from different sides talk past each other in mostly ritual performance. Party politicians do not listen, do not reflect and do not change their minds.[77]

As for the Australian electorate, in the words of economist Nicholas Gruen it resembles a punch drunk boxer lurching from one dimly comprehended drama to the next.[78]

On average, 63% of people across the world think their country is 'on the wrong track'. This includes majorities in Australia, Japan, Britain, Israel, Germany Belgium, Poland, Spain, Sweden, Italy, Brazil, South Korea, France and Mexico.[79] In the US, large majorities believe the same[80]—with polls, long before the mayhem of 2021 and 2024, eliciting such descriptors as 'disarray,' 'turmoil,' 'polarized,' 'shambles' and 'declining'.[81]

There's a lot of ground to be captured by something new.

John Dryzek believes 'there are no issues that are off-limits for deliberation'. When they are given time, resources and expert testimony, and get to hear both sides of a case,

> it's really quite remarkable seeing the degree to which ordinary people can handle complex issues.

Sortition-based assemblies proved valuable adjuncts to an array of systems—direct, representative, even monarchical—in some of history's most civilized cultures: northern Italy from the 12th to the 18th centuries (including Florence from the 14th to the 15th), and Switzerland from the 17th to the 19th.[82]

In Athens, deliberative juries were on a par with the Assembly itself, and eventually overshadowed it. We don't know that this couldn't be true for us too.

At first glance, deliberative democracy can look a little ramshackle. And there will indeed be wrong turns and retreats. That is natural to the experimental, stepwise evolution of democracy. But in an age of scripted elites, eternally on-message—and their corollary: a disgruntled, lethargic public—a dose of the ramshackle Athenian ethos might be what we need.

At brief moments in history—Athens in the Classical era, the early American Republic, and very few others—a citizenry becomes enamored not of a cultural hero or military leader but of its system of government. These rare epochs are sustained by a common spirit, to be sure—but they equally ride on the legal instruments that liberate it.

On the evidence to date, deliberative democracy is likely to be one of those instruments.

2. Parliamentarism

How would a parliamentary system handle a shutdown? It wouldn't have one. In Canada a few years ago, around the same time Washington was gripped in yet another debt-ceiling crisis, a budget impasse in Ottawa led to new elections, where the parties fought to win over voters to their fiscal plan. One side won, then enacted its plan—problem solved.[83]

— Alex Seitz-Wald in *The Atlantic*

We basically run a coalition government, without the efficiency of a parliamentary system.[84]

— US House of Representatives Speaker Paul Ryan (2017)

On the strength of the evidence, the world's presidential regimes, including the United States, would reap great rewards from a transition to a parliamentary system.

Not one study comparing the two systems shows that a presidential system works better than a parliamentary one. The vast majority tell us the reverse.[85]

Globally, there's 'a strong relationship between parliamentarism and good governance'.[86] The 'parliamentary' nations experience much better human and economic development than the 'presidential' ones.

In a parliamentary system, the prime minister is elected by her party, rules 'collegially' with her ministerial colleagues, is a member of the legislature, and is responsible to it. In a presidential system, the president is elected directly by the people, can't normally be removed by the legislature, and works almost as a one-person executive. Many of her decisions don't require legislative approval.[87]

Parliamentarism prevails in Australasia, most of Western Europe, and Canada. Presidentialism prevails in the US and Latin America, the former USSR, and other spots such as the Philippines and South Korea.

Arend Lijphart—who systematically compared the two systems across 36 nations—found that parliamentarism produces stabler societies mostly because the executive and the legislative majority must belong to the same party. Presidentialism, which doesn't require this, is always in danger of 'dual democratic legitimacy'.

The phrase actually comes from political scientist Juan Linz, who established himself as the leading critic of presidentialism in the essay collection, *The Failure of Presidential Democracy*. When president and congressional majority are from different parties, Linz asks:

> Who, on the basis of democratic principles, is better legitimated
> to speak in the name of the people: the president, or the
> congressional majority that opposes his policies?[88]

As no democratic principle exists to resolve such a conflict, he notes, the military often steps in to do so. In the US, the face-offs have been less dramatic—though dramatic enough. In recent years, government shutdowns, fights over judicial nominations, and the attempt on Donald Trump's life in 2024, increasingly resemble events in South American countries en route to *putsch* and revolution.

Parliamentarism experiences few such confrontations—and is free of Richard Nixon-style constitutional crises. Had he been a prime minister, Nixon would likely have been deposed fairly early by his own side, and a successor elected in the party room.

The Yale political scientist Oona Hathaway has canvassed the work of hundreds of political scientists who'd compared the presidential system with the parliamentary, especially in terms of each system's survival. The presidential systems, she found, 'are significantly more likely to collapse'. For example:

> A study of fifty-three democratic countries conducted in the early 1990s found that democracy survived sixty-one percent of the time in parliamentary systems and twenty percent of the time in presidential systems. In other words, a parliamentary democracy was roughly three times more likely to survive.[89]

Hathaway cites a second study, of 135 modern nations, in which the expected lifespan of a parliamentary democracy was 74 years, and a presidential one 24 years:

> The authors also concluded that the difference in durability was not due to the political conditions under which the countries were formed. Presidential democracies are 'simply more brittle under all economic and political conditions'.

Hathaway also looked at studies of systems that mimicked the American one specifically:

> All of these countries have experienced constitutional crises, with presidents disbanding intransigent congresses.

For example, one of the studies, by the constitutional scholars Alfred Stephan and Cindy Skach,

> showed that during a ten-year period between 1980 and 1989, not one of the fifty-two countries that chose a non-parliamentary model evolved into a continuous democracy—that is, a stable and surviving democracy.[90]

Arend Lijphart laments that, despite this copious, lopsided data, the inferior presidential system is still being introduced:

> In the 1980s and 1990s, for instance, all of the new democracies in Latin America and Asia chose presidentialism, [as did] about

three-fourths of the approximately 25 countries in Eastern Europe and the area of the former Soviet Union.[91]

Fig. 5.7: Russia's legislative building in September 1993, after President Yeltsin ordered it to be shelled over a conflict with the parliament. The attack killed at least 147 people.

The notion of a single person being the head of all branches of government is inimical to democracy itself. Democracy is about sharing power, not concentrating it.

How, exactly, could the presidential states achieve a transition to a parliamentary system?

As reforms go, this is undeniably 'sturdy'—you can't half-do it. But if a more cautious approach were desired, a nation could trial it in one state. For example, a state referendum in the US could make a change from directly elected governor to indirectly elected premier, on a trial basis for an electoral cycle or two.

But is such an experiment needed, when the evidence is already in, from scores of real-world cases, across the planet and across modern history?

3. Proportional representation (PR)

> Politics need not, indeed must not, be a zero-sum game. The idea that 'winner takes all' has no place in a democracy, because if losers lose all they will opt out of the democratic game.[92]
>
> — Margaret Stimmann Branson, Center for Civic Education

The goal of proportional representation is for the proportion of seats a party gains in a legislature to be as close as possible to the proportion of votes it gains from the electorate. If it wins, say, 33% of the votes, it should win about 33% of the seats.

Here again, the ultra-competitive US system provides our anti-model. Millions of Americans are not represented in the House of Representatives by someone from their party. This is because House districts elect only one member—and up to 49.9% of electors (occasionally more) don't vote for her. Their votes don't elect anyone.

At the macro level, that can mean a party having a big majority of seats, all won by a narrow margin.

A real-world example is Massachusetts, where Republicans make up a third of the electorate: yet none of the state's nine electoral districts has sent a Republican to the House since 1994. That's a large distortion of the principle of one vote, one value.[93]

Britain is another winner-takes-all system. In 2005, a negative vote of nearly 65% was not enough to dislodge the Labour government.[94] In 2020, the Conservatives won 56.2% of the seats on 43.6% of the votes. 2024 saw the largest gap between vote-share and seat-share in British history.[95]

The unfairness that abounds under 'winner-takes-all' chips away at the system's legitimacy. So, if representative democracy is to remain feasible, an obvious way forward is to:

(i) have fewer districts
(ii) make each of them much larger
(iii) elect several members from a district, not just one

That's proportional representation.

Let's say a fictitious state of the US has nine electoral districts —each containing 66% Democrat voters and 33% Republican voters. Presently, it would return nine Democrats to the House, and zero Republicans.

A 'proportional' system might reduce the number of districts to three. Each of the three districts would return three members. Under this arrangement, two of those members would be Democrats, and one Republican.[96] For the state, that adds up to six Democrats and three Republicans.

The state still has nine members overall—but now the Republican third of its voters is represented.

Countrywide, the introduction of PR to the United States would ensure that few electorates were single-party—most would have a mix.[97] Urban Republicans, and rural Democrats, would regain their voice.

Zero-sum electoral systems accumulate frustrated groups of unrepresented people.

In PR legislatures, there tend to be numerous parties—not just two—which often results in multiparty ruling coalitions in the centre of the political spectrum. Arend Lijphart found that that produces less 'whipsawing' from left to right, from one election to the next. That increases policy coherence.

Indeed, proportional representation is associated with a long list of benefits:

- policies that are closer to the wishes of the 'median voter'
- greater citizen satisfaction with democratic institutions
- more civil liberties
- more women representatives
- lower income inequality
- more fiscal surpluses
- more politically knowledgeable citizens [98]
- much lower military expenditures
- much less involvement in war
- less carbon emissions

- greater use of renewables[99]

PR nations ratified the Kyoto Protocol faster.[100]

And all this without more elections.

Experts often recommend six to eight members per district as the happiest medium.[101] But there are numerous PR formulas. One of the best-known is Tasmania's 'Hare-Clark' system.

For Arend Lijphart, proportional representation epitomizes the 'power-sharing' that typifies 'consensual' systems:

> When I was a graduate student in the 1960s, I was an admirer of the British electoral system—first past the post or FPTP. But I have gradually come to the conclusion that proportional representation, or PR, is the better option. This has also been the trend among political scientists generally. And the empirical evidence is now overwhelmingly strong in support of this conclusion.

As we democratize of our societies, proportional representation will play an essential part. Smaller groupings of voters will find representation; smaller parties will get a chance to prove their mettle; and people of great value, who would otherwise have remained unknown, are likely to take the political stage.

Preferential voting

Proportionality is usually enhanced by a *preferential* voting system.

Under a 'first past the post' (FPTP) system, the candidate who wins the most votes wins the election—even if it's under 50% of the total. The nuance of voter preference is lost.

Because of this, 12 American presidential elections have likely been won by candidates who were not the unambiguous choice of the electorate.

For example, in 1992, Bill Clinton (43%) beat George HW

Bush (37.4%) because the candidacy of Ross Perot (18.9%) bled away conservative votes from Bush.

In 2000, George W Bush won against Al Gore because, in Florida, 97,000 probable Gore voters opted for third party candidate Ralph Nader—giving Bush a hairs-breadth lead in that key state.[102]

Under a preferential system. Ross Perot's votes, and Ralph Nader's, would have gone to their voters' second preferences. It's likely George HW Bush would have won the presidency in 1992, and Al Gore in 2000.

'Preferential' systems have several variations. Under one of them, 'ranked-choice voting', when a voter's first choice is not elected, her vote goes to her second, then her third, and so on, till it helps one candidate reach the *quota* needed to win the seat. The quota is usually 50% of votes + 1 vote.

The big advantage of preferential voting—in the words of Harvard University's Danielle Allen—is that 'people have the opportunity to fully express their preferences, so the information value is much higher'.[103] This in turn creates friendlier, less negative campaigns: as parties have to appeal to a broader swathe of voters.[104]

Most of all, preferential voting dilutes the diabolical 'lesser of two evils' choice that voters often face. If your first preference is balloted out, your vote generally goes to someone you find desirable, or at least tolerable.

4. Direct democracy

My colleagues in Parliament include, in my new intake, family doctors, businesspeople, professors, distinguished economists, historians, writers, and army officers ranging from colonels down to regimental sergeant majors. All of them however, including myself, as we walk underneath those strange stone gargoyles just down the road, feel that we've become less than the sum of our parts—feel as though we have become profoundly diminished.[105]

Chapter 29

The 20th Century's best-known theorist of representative democracy, Hanna Pitkin, pointed out that in order to be represented you have to be absent.

Pitkin explained that representation arose, in England, not from a wish to have ordinary people represented before the king, but from the royal practice of summoning knights and burgesses as a matter of 'convenience and need':

> Representation has a problematic relationship with democracy, with which it is often thoughtlessly equated. The two ideas have different, even conflicting, origins. Democracy came from ancient Greece and was won through struggle from below. Greek democracy was participatory and bore no relationship to representation. Representation dates—at least as a political concept and practice—from the late medieval period, when it was imposed as a duty by the monarch. Only in the English Civil War and then in the eighteenth-century democratic revolutions did the two concepts become linked.
>
> Democrats saw representation—with an extended suffrage—as making possible large-scale democracy. Conservatives instead saw it as a tool for staving off democracy.[106]

In America, the notion of Greek-style direct democracy moved James Madison to all-caps. He wanted 'THE TOTAL EXCLUSION OF THE PEOPLE, IN THEIR COLLECTIVE CAPACITY, from any share' in the government.[107] Madison believed the value of representation was

> to refine and enlarge the public views, by passing them through the medium of a chosen body of citizens, whose wisdom may best discern the true interest of their country, and whose patriotism and love of justice will be least likely to sacrifice it to temporary or partial considerations.[108]

A long book could be written on what the Founders got wrong; this idea would merit a chapter.

Today, but a small fraction of Americans trust to the 'wisdom and patriotism' of their leaders. Public approval of Congress has been as low as 9% in the last decade. In 2015, the last time Gallup asked the question, the majority of Americans thought that 'most members' of Congress were 'corrupt'.[109]

It's sometimes held that the exclusion of the ordinary person from government is inescapable. In *The Iron Law of Oligarchy*, published in 1911, the German scholar Robert Michels states that centralization of power is inevitable in any system—including representative democracy. The people's 'delegates' soon learn how to control the government's information flow, to shape its bureaucracy, and to reward loyalty. This is made easier by the indifference of ordinary people. Representative democracy is a façade, to legitimise rule by the few.

'Who says organization,' Michels wrote, 'says oligarchy.'

Fig. 5.8: Robert Michels

With his usual prescience, Alvin Toffler, in his 1980 book *The Third Wave,* predicted that representative democracy would gradually lose its vitality.

Toffler described the transition then beginning from the industrial era to a more decentralized information age. He drew an analogy between machinery and political systems. Engineers (he wrote) distinguish between two fundamentally different classes of machine—'batch processors' and 'continuous flow'. (A punch press is in the first-class, an oil refinery in the second.[110]) In our political arrangements, he believed, 'a continuous flow of influence' from lobbyists and pressure groups shapes policy every day of the year: whereas the public's input is limited to the 'punch press' of intermittent voting:

> The public is allowed to choose between candidates at specific times, after which the formal 'democracy machine' is switched off again.[111]

This dynamic arose, Toffler wrote, because the people's 'representatives'—in governments, unions and elsewhere—were enlisted by the economic elite:

> In theory, the need to stand for re-election guaranteed that representatives would stay honest and would continue to speak for those they represented. Nowhere, however, did this prevent the absorption of representatives into the architecture of power. Everywhere the gap widened between the representative and the represented.
>
> Representative government—what we have been taught to call democracy—was, in short, an industrial technology for assuring inequality. Representative government was pseudorepresentative.[112]

It certainly seems so now. All of our era's large popular movements have arisen outside of representative politics.

When *The Third Wave* was published, the world was about to emerge from a half-century struggle between two titanic institutional forces—Soviet communism and the capitalist West. When communism went down, representative democracy stood unmolested. But instead of the democracies now becoming more democratic, the project of relocating power to the corporation was accelerated.

The machinery of third draft democracy

Today, the countervailing force to Western political power is not Soviet communism, or any single ideology—it is grassroots networks, and networks of networks, in which power is distributed. There's no leader or central committee. Three of the most impactful political movements of the last 15 years—the Tea Party, Occupy and France's *gilets jaunes*—had very different ideologies, but all fit this pattern of leaderlessness.

More than any dogma or policy, a 'flat' organizational structure is the political trend of the 21st Century. Whilst its elite wants society to become more vertical, society itself wants to become more horizontal.

These two opposed forces have brought our *stasis*—a sense of no forward movement—as the tectonic plates of elite and popular will grind up against each other. Such impasses don't tend to go on forever. People become disgruntled with stasis:

[SOVIET PRESIDENT GORBACHEV'S] POPULARITY IS IN SHARP DECLINE…AND HE HIMSELF APPEARS ON THE DEFENSIVE. HIS POSITION IS IMPERILLED NOT BY CONSERVATIVE APPARATCHIKS OR MEN ON WHITE HORSES, BUT RATHER BY THE POWERFUL SOCIAL FORCES HIS REFORMS HAVE UNLEASHED…

GORBACHEV HAS YET TO FASHION A COHERENT SYSTEM OF LEGITIMATE POWER AROUND NEW STATE INSTITUTIONS TO REPLACE THE OLD PARTY-DOMINATED, STALINIST ONE HE HAS EXTENSIVELY DISMANTLED…

MANY SOVIETS, INCLUDING EMBASSY CONTACTS ACROSS THE POLITICAL SPECTRUM, WONDER WHETHER HE HAS A CLEAR SENSE OF WHERE HE WANTS TO TAKE THE COUNTRY AND HOW TO GET THERE.[113]

— Cable from the US Embassy in Moscow to the
State Department, May 11, 1990.

As we now know, the result of Gorbachev's inability to fashion a new system was the return of authoritarianism.

As with *perestroika*, so too with the Western anti-war movement, the Tiananmen uprising, Occupy, the Arab Spring—and countless local revolts such as the 2013 protests across Turkey. All had the capacity to transform society. Due to limited decision-making mechanics, a focus on fixing policy instead of politics, and the absence of a comprehensive, long-range plan, all dissipated after achieving few, if any, of their goals. These movements involved hundreds of millions of people, so this is one of the tragedies of the modern era.

Fig. 5.9: Rally in Gezi Park, Istanbul: one of 5,000 protests across Turkey in 2013, involving 3.5 million people.

More than three decades after the Soviet empire left the stage, the free world faces a comparable void—and representative democracy has no plan to fill it. Fascism in the Thirties, and neoliberalism in the Seventies, stepped into just such vacuums.

But so did *demokratia* in anarchic 6th Century Athens. In confusing times, people are attracted to clarity. The side that prevails usually has a plan.

Thanks to the labors of many, there are democratic tools at our disposal by which to make the sprawling Earth governable.

One of these tools is direct democracy. Just as deliberation cuts the Gordian knot of dispersion, so does direct democracy undo the iron law of oligarchy.

The Swiss

In most countries, direct democracy forms an occasional adjunct to the representative system: in Switzerland it's the jewel in the democratic crown.

In the *cantons*—the mini-states that make up the Swiss Confederation—direct democracy has functioned for 150 years. It's entrenched at the federal tier as well—and in the municipalities, right down to towns and villages.[114] No country has a record comparing to this. So, if we want to know how direct democracy works in practice, we need to study Switzerland.

Switzerland's federal republic was founded in 1848, but by the 1860s the public had soured on its representative system—which it saw as being under the thumb of large financial and business interests. In the words of Karl Bürkli, one of the era's reformers:

> The upwardly striving plutocracy can now be held in check only by shifting the centre of gravity of the legislative process further out, to encompass the entire people; for a few hundred cantonal councillors, i.e. representative democracy, are not powerful enough to resist corruption.[115]

As popular pressure reached critical mass, large assemblies spontaneously formed around the country, demanding what citizens called 'pure democracy'. Before the decade was out, patrician cantonal governments across Switzerland had caved in.

Chapter 29

Article 1 of the constitution of the canton of Zurich had previously read:

> Sovereignty resides in the people as a whole. It is exercised in accordance with the constitution by the Great Council as the representative of the people.

In Zurich's new constitution, proclaimed on April 18, 1869, Article 1 read:

> The power of the state resides in the people as a whole. It is exercised directly by those citizens who are entitled to vote, and indirectly by the authorities and the officials.[116]

Today, the Swiss may amend or enact a federal or cantonal law via a citizens' *initiative*—a referendum triggered when a threshold of signatures is reached.[117] Most cantons also have the *finance referendum*—where voters can (and sometimes must) approve a large expenditure.

The *Landsgemeinde*, where citizens meet in the open and vote with a show of hands, dates back to the 13th Century. In two cantons, it remains the highest legislative authority.

Fig. 5.10: A 2009 *Landsgemeinde* in Glarus canton, Switzerland

Referendums for all three tiers of government—municipal, cantonal, federal—tend to occur together on 'voting days'. These are held on a Sunday, several times a year.

For example, on Sunday, May 18, 2003, citizens of the municipality of Freienbach voted on nine national referendum questions —two of them constitutional—as well as three cantonal issues, three municipal issues, and eight applications for citizenship: a total of 23 matters.

In the weeks before a referendum, citizens receive their voting forms in the mail, along with a 'referendum booklet' in which the case for each side is presented. The booklets are widely read, and they're central to the public's buy-in to direct democracy.[118] Political advertising on TV is banned. Debates occur widely in the media and public forums.

The result, according to the European *Guidebook to Direct Democracy*, is that

> the average Swiss voter is better and more comprehensively informed when he or she comes to vote on an issue than the average German member of parliament.[119]

Direct democracy has not produced a legislative free-for-all. Of every ten initiatives for a new law, nine fail. Neither have the Swiss used their direct voice in government to award themselves a flood of social services, pay rises and tax breaks. In fact they generally vote down measures to increase public spending.

Direct democracy has yielded some notable victories. In 1918, a referendum brought in proportional representation for the lower house. Via this syzygy—one sound institution (direct democracy) giving rise to another (PR)—the gravity of the overall system was strengthened.

Successful referendums in 1921, 1977 and 2003 progressively expanded the role of citizens in foreign policy decisions. The Swiss have been involved in no wars since direct democracy took its place at the heart of the system. One reason for Switzerland's prosperity is that it has not spent large amounts on the architecture of repair.

Switzerland's direct democracy also acts to monitor its representative democracy—preventing the latter from becoming isolated and corrupt. The phrase 'threat of a referendum' features regularly in media discussion of politics.[120]

As a result—and bafflingly to outsiders—most referendums sponsored by the government *succeed*. Apparently you can trust a small dog on a short leash.

The majority of government-sponsored *constitutional* referendums also succeed—140 out of 188 to date. That suggests that regularly updating a nation's constitution may nudge it in the direction of stability. (Switzerland is so stable it's the subject of jokes from its neighbors.[121])

In France, the anti-government *gilets jaunes* (Yellow Jackets) sparked parallel movements in countries as far away as Taiwan and Canada. No *gilets jaunes* movement arose in next-door Switzerland.

Whilst plutocracy means nearly everyone is miserable, genuine democracy means that no-one is entirely happy. The value of Swiss direct democracy lies not in granting every citizen's every wish, but in assuring the citizen that, even if she disagrees with it, the collective will Is being realized.

The machinery of third draft democracy

Every Swiss voter has been on the losing end of a referendum many times. The Swiss find it much easier to accept a veto by a majority of their peers than by a remote elite. Indeed, they sometimes characterize their country as 'the land of contented losers'.

An antidote to democratic decline

A tool like direct democracy begins as a rather dull technical matter, but downstream (so a lot of data tells us) it manifests as prosperity and health; as less war and inequality; as happier societies and stronger families.

Switzerland is not only an example of the blessings a better-designed system can bring, but a counter-example to the gathering disorder elsewhere. It suggests that the democratic *stasis* worldwide stems, in the main, not from economic factors, or outside interference, or the personalities of leaders, or the ideologies of ruling parties, but from the design of the political system.

This *stasis* is present not only in the world's older democracies, but in the more recent democracies that copied the old methods. In 2019, the *Journal of Democracy* published the first comprehensive analysis of how these post-1974 ('third wave') democratic transitions had fared:

> The findings are sobering: Among the 91 new democracies that (by our count) emerged from 1974 to 2012, 34 experienced breakdowns, often in short order. In 28 cases, democracy stagnated after transition, usually at a fairly low level, and in two more it eroded. Democracy advanced relative to the starting point in only 23 cases. Few countries have succeeded in creating robust liberal democracies.[122]

Thus the *Journal* these days is sprinkled with headlines such as *Cambodia's Transition to Hegemonic Authoritarianism*, *Bolsonaro and Brazil's Illiberal Backlash*, and *Zimbabwe: An Opportunity Lost*. The largest of these democratic collapses has occurred in India

—once the world's largest democracy. Here, what's been described as 'an intolerant Hindu supremacist majoritarianism' has sidelined the old pluralism. The ruling party uses disinformation, deploys angry mobs, and co-opts press and courts. Journalists are arrested; Muslims are persecuted routinely.

As usual, the causes lie upstream: weak institutions, overly centralized government, internally undemocratic political parties, and no rules against the corporate control of politics. The latter has led to neoliberal economic policies, and a permanently impoverished class of hundreds of millions. In 2019, 72 years after independence, 706,000 Indian children died of malnutrition.

India, with 1.3 billion people, has been demoted to an 'electoral autocracy' by Sweden's V-Dem Institute. According to Freedom House, its democratic downturn leaves less than 20% of the world living in societies that are deemed 'free'.[123]

The hush emanating from media, political establishments and think tanks on the subject of democratic reform might suggest that all this is 'the arc of history' or 'the human condition'. But societal decline isn't pre-ordained. Thoughtfully made reform generates well-accepted laws, political stability and public commitment.

The Swiss are not where they are by a streak of good luck. The country has multiple ethnicities and religions that have often, in the past, been at each other's throats. Through the 1830s and 1840s, cantonal governments fell repeatedly, and there were regular assassinations. In Zurich, this was the era in which the German word *putsch* gained its modern meaning. There was a civil war in 1847, between conservatives and liberals.

On the back of the power-sharing constitution of 1848, Switzerland's racial and religious differences were gradually reconciled.

A late instance of this came via the French-speaking, Catholic minority of the Jura region, who had long protested—sometimes violently—at being lumped in with Bern canton's German-speaking Protestant majority. In 1974, these French-speaking municipalities voted to create a canton of their own. The matter was put to a national referendum.

The machinery of third draft democracy

Every canton in Switzerland voted Yes. In a country with a history of communal strife, a dangerous, Yugoslavia-style ethnic conflict had been avoided—a dog that didn't bark. Such 'dogs' have lain silent in Switzerland since the mid-19th Century. The nation's responsive political system, with direct democracy its centrepiece, has shown how to manage a multi-ethnic society.

Swiss direct democracy suffered from a century of attacks from vested interests—notably big business groups. Economics professors and other experts chimed in: prophesying that, in time, direct democracy would 'ruin the Swiss economy'. The 'citizen incompetence' argument was also deployed.

The latter put cause and effect in the wrong order. In Switzerland, it turned out, participation *builds* competence. Sixty percent of Swiss regard themselves as politically 'well-informed'. In next-door Austria the figure is 30%.[124] Swiss cantons with more participatory budgeting have 15% higher GDPs. Those with the 'finance referendum' have 30% less tax avoidance, and so lower debt.

Municipalities with the finance referendum have lower spending *and* much cheaper public services.[125]

It is not citizens but elected politicians who tend to over-spend and over-borrow—a downstream effect of bureaucracies, special interests and disengaged electorates. In recent years, Swiss citizens increased their fuel tax to balance the budget. They created a VAT to fund pensions. And they reduced the size of the army by one-third.[126]

Switzerland's direct democracy does not favor progressives or conservatives, but the 'median voter'. In perhaps the world's most tight-fisted *demos*, there has been no questioning of its cost.[127]

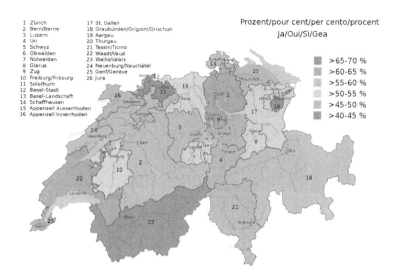

Fig. 5.11: In 2004, the Swiss Government passed a law legalizing same-sex partnerships. In 2005, its opponents gathered enough signatures to trigger a referendum on the law. Fifty-eight percent of citizens voted to uphold it. In 2021, a new referendum expanded the right to full marriage. The map shows the demographics of the 2005 vote.

Is there public support for direct democracy?

Yes—everywhere it's been surveyed.

Table 5.1 shows the results of various opinion polls over the last generation.[128]

Country	Direct democracy, % popular support
Germany	55
USA	76
Britain	77
Europe	70
Denmark	53
Belgium	82
Portugal	80
Ireland	79
Greece	76
Austria	73
Spain	72
Britain (again)	72
Finland	66
Italy	66
Luxembourg	63
Netherlands	61
New Zealand	71

Table 5.1: Percentage of public support for direct democracy by country

Additionally, a 2017 poll across 38 nations found that, on average, support for direct democracy was 66%. (This dwarfed support for rule by 'a strong leader'.[129])

Chapter 29

How direct democracy could be used

The first task, as ever, is to design out manipulation.

In California, insurance companies have put millions of dollars behind an initiative to permit a new (and well-disguised) method of raising premiums. Oil companies funded an initiative to repeal the state's clean air legislation. Paid signature-gathering proliferates —with signature-gathering firms pitching initiatives to industry sectors, then getting a contract to raise the signatures.[130]

Billions of corporate dollars are spent each decade in the state to promote initiatives. In the 2022 election cycle, corporations spent $769 million on only seven measures.[131] Most of this largesse aims to reduce regulation or tax on an industry. As a result, Californian journalist John Diaz has observed: 'No initiative resulting purely from a volunteer drive has reached the ballot in three decades.'[132]

This is a dismal way to practise direct democracy—as Californians appear to know. The state's Republicans and Democrats both overwhelmingly support the initiative system, but (equally overwhelmingly) dislike the role money plays in it.

Direct democracy, ancient and modern, was created to counter plutocracy. The corporate funding of referendums doesn't fit that picture. Large-dollar donations to initiative campaigns should be outlawed, along with paid signature-gathering.

Again, corporate money can be replaced by the pledge system. Pledges for initiatives might be limited to, say, $20 per voter per referendum cycle, and provided from the financial transactions tax.

In California, large majorities of Republicans, Democrats and independents want an 'independent citizens' initiative commission' that holds public hearings on an initiative, and issues guidelines to the public. A citizen deliberation would be ideal for the task. A second one could oversee the actual referendum.[133]

Nevadans have a nice innovation called 'statute affirmation', where they vote to 'affirm' or protect an existing law—whereupon the legislature is not allowed to touch it. One wonders why Americans—reputed for their suspicion of government—have not laced their entire system with provisions like this.

In the same spirit, Article III of the Bill of Change would spell out that citizen legislation is *sovereign*. Neither president nor legislature nor court nor transnational authority has the power to tamper with a law passed by the people. Never again could a legal ruling like Citizens United stay in place, in the teeth of opposition from three-fourths of Americans.

And never again could a European economic supremo announce to national finance ministers:

Elections cannot be allowed to change an economic programme of a member state![134]

(The supremo was, once again, the Eurogroup's Wolfgang Schäuble—speaking in 2015. The finance ministers were those of Greece and France. The 'economic programme' Schäuble referred to was the austerity regime imposed by the EU and the European Central Bank. The elections were those in which Greeks had recently rejected that regime—or thought they had.)

The British philosopher AC Grayling makes a strong case for compulsory voting in elections—and the same logic might apply to referendums. Grayling argues that if 30% of the electorate does not vote, their non-votes amplify the value of those that do. Voting, Grayling says, is a civic duty like paying taxes and obeying laws.[135]

In the Swiss cantons, the signature threshold to trigger a referendum ranges from .9% to 5.7% of electors. In California, it's 5% for a statute and 8% for a constitutional amendment. California's numbers might be a reasonable ballpark.[136]

In referendums in 2018, large majorities in Michigan, Missouri and Ohio—and a slim one in Utah—supported gerrymandering reform. Majorities introduced same-day voter registration in Michigan, ranked-choice voting in Maine and campaign finance restrictions in Missouri; banned foreign political contributions in North Dakota; and restored ex-felon voting rights in Florida.[137] (All these states were won by Donald Trump in 2016.)

Typically, the referendum system does not yield a discernible left-right pattern. Outside of the polarizing representative system, citizens become more individualistic, and their voting patterns more a *mosaic*. For example, Swiss referendums in 2014:

- limited immigration from the EU
- rejected a cap on overall immigration
- endorsed choice in abortion
- vetoed the purchase of a jet fighter
- rejected a minimum wage
- and federalized rail infrastructure.

Our legislative chambers epitomise modern democracy's conceptual exhaustion. Many years on from Alvin Toffler's forecast, people continue to disengage from representative politics.

Establishing the initiative system in the constitution puts it at the heart of the democratic enterprise. Crucially, it allows direct democracy to evolve itself. The Swiss system is dynamic—it gets better all the time—because it can auto-fine-tune.

The Swiss call this 'the democratization of democracy'.

5. Abolishing the dismal art

Political egalitarianism among nomadic foragers is not an effortless or static state in which all members accept the egalitarian ethos; it is accompanied by repeated attempts by individuals who test the limits of group norms.[138]

— From a multi-disciplinary study of human egalitarianism during the last Glacial period (2009)

We have three major voter suppression operations under way.[139]

— Anonymous Trump official in 2016, on the campaign's efforts to dissuade 'idealistic white liberals', young women and African-Americans from voting.

Wherever a system of government enhances equality and fairness, vested interests have tried to game, distort, bypass and corrupt it. This dismal art goes back to the 6th Century BC:

> Cleomenes' friend Isagoras held the leading position in Athens after the withdrawal of the Spartan troops, but he was not unopposed. Cleisthenes, of the restored Alemaeonid clan was his chief rival. Isagoras tried to restore a version of the pre-Solonian aristocratic state by purifying the citizen lists.[140]

Isagoras' ploy backfired: It helped to spark Cleisthenes' democratic revolution. But two and a half millennia later, his game is still going.

In the 'Jim Crow' era in the United States, black would-be voters in Alabama were asked questions such as, 'Name Alabama's 67 county judges' and 'How many bubbles are there in a bar of soap?' With the Voting Rights Act of 1965, and its five subsequent expansions, problems like this diminished for a time.

But today the American epidemic of voter suppression has revived in new forms—some of which are being emulated by other procedural democracies. ID laws hinder minorities from voting. Dubious electronic voting machines, supplied by Republican donors to Republican administrations, return dubious results. New Jersey Democratic legislators tried to ensure that Republicans could never again win a legislative majority, by virtually entrenching a gerrymander in the state constitution.[141]

For an electoral reformer, the American system is a target-rich environment. Probably for that reason, the United States also where the most creative antidotes are found.

Once again, the key to success against a bad system with multiple parts is a package—a suite of interlocking reforms.

We'll begin by looking at Universal Vote By Mail (UVBM) and Automatic Voter Registration (AVR). These two reforms come first because (in an example of syzygy) they much-fortify each other, and (in demonstrating the value of an *upstream focus*) they render so many other reforms unnecessary.

(i) Universal Vote By Mail (UVBM)

UVBM was pioneered by Oregon's secretary of state in the 1990s, Phil Keisling. As a result of this experience, Keisling now believes that the most effectual voter suppression method is *the existence of polling places.*

With UVBM, needless to say, there are none.

The usefulness of mail voting became clearer to Americans in 2020, when it was ramped up under pandemic conditions.[142] But even in normal times UVBM would top the list of ways to neutralize the dismal art. It appears to boost voter participation more than any other single measure.

Where there are qualms about the safety of mail voting (this was the case among some Trump supporters in 2024), it can be bullet-proofed with stronger ID protections, tougher audits, random 'address checks', and other measures. Indeed automatic voter registration (AVR—next section) satisfies most ID concerns by itself. Third draft 'technologies' like UVBM and AVR are designed (in deliberations) by ordinary citizens from both sides—and cannot become law (via referendums) till majorities are happy with their fairness and safety.

Keisling was once attached to the 'democratic ritual' of the polling place—what he calls the 'crunch of autumn leaves' mythology. His early experience with vote-by-mail changed his thinking:

> Once I grasped the dramatic cost savings from no longer having to operate and staff thousands of traditional polling stations, and realized how much voter turnout had soared in local and special elections—by a factor of three or even five—I saw that I'd been confusing a particular ritual of democracy with its essence, which is participation.[143]

Oregon introduced UVBM in 1995 for a special Senate election. That vote, and the preceding primary, Keisling says, 'shattered all previous national records for a special Senate election'.

UVBM was put to a citizens' initiative in 1998. Oregonians

voted for it by 69 to 31%—winning in all counties, Republican and Democrat.

Back in the polling station era, Oregon's percentage turnout was typically in the 50s. These days it's in the 70s.

Since UVBM was introduced, Oregonians have mailed in about 100 million ballots—in 50 local, state and national elections. There have been 12 cases of ballot fraud—a rate of .0000001%.

Fig. 5.12: Oregonians post their vote via the mail system, or drop it in one of the return boxes placed around the electorate prior to election day.

Being paper-based, UVBM won't easily malfunction or break down. There are no voting machines to make errors, cease working or make fraud easier.

UVBM saves Oregon $3 million per election cycle.

In San Diego's mayoral election in 2013, the mail-in portion of the vote—which was two-thirds of it—cost the county $84,000. Managing polling places for the other third cost $360,000.[144]

Voting machines are still used in 30 US states.[145] But there's an impending crisis: they tend to become obsolete in about a decade. Countrywide, this will cost $1 billion to remediate.[146]

Many of the present approaches to voting reform revolve around polling places. But UVBM brings out way more voters than polling place-centred reforms such as 'early voting' and 'same-day registration'.[147]

Moreover, polling places often mean electronic voting machines and proprietary software—and therefore errors, obsolescence and higher costs. UVBM is unplugged from the Net, with audits occurring via paper trail. An alarmingly high proportion of voting machines can be hacked (for example 'to record voting data or inject malicious data'). UVBM is pretty much hack-proof.[148]

Phil Keisling writes:

> Mail-based voting systems today are far less risky than most polling place elections… To have any reasonable chance of success, an organized effort to defraud a mail-based system and its safeguards must involve hundreds (if not thousands) of separate acts, all of them individual felonies…
>
> Contrast that to the risks inherent in polling place elections… A single successful software hack potentially could affect thousands of votes. It's the difference between 'retail' fraud and 'wholesale' fraud.[149]

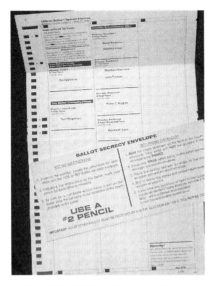

Fig. 5.13: Mail-in ballot paper, Oregon

Vote-by-mail puts an end to election day schedule-juggling, driving, parking and queueing. Rain, heat, fractious children and wheelchair ramps are no longer issues. In the US elections of 2020, there were often long queues and crowded polling places: some voters and poll workers were infected with COVID.[150] UVBM would have prevented this as well.

A writer in *Vox* describes gathering at the dining table with his family, and their mail ballots, in Washington State:

> We went through the ballot vote by vote—president, governor, on down to ballot initiatives on carbon taxes and public transit —discussing the opposing arguments, allowing the boys (11 and 13) to ask questions. Overall, it took about an hour. When we were done, we put our ballots in a special envelope, affixed stamps, and dropped them in the mailbox. That's it.[151]

To allay qualms in the US in the wake of 2020, UVBM would be established by non-government, non-partisan demotic institutions such as referendums and deliberative assemblies—and managed by the bodies they establish.

Mail ballots are historically popular among Republicans, and have been introduced by Republican state administrations such as Arizona's. The Trump campaign team in 2020 calculated that mail-ins would benefit Trump, and Trump himself acknowledged that in a clean electoral system mail voting is secure. Sixty-one court challenges to the 2020 election result were rejected, often by Trump-appointed judges. Trump's own Attorney General advised him that the result—mail-ins and all—was above board.[152] [153] [154] Trump's lawyers including Sidney Powell and Rudy Giuliani made numerous claims to the media of fraudulent mail-in ballots. But those lawyers disavowed such claims in court, where professional ethics rules apply, and evidence is required.[155]

Voting by mail is the safest form of voting.

Phil Keisling estimates that if the method he introduced in Oregon were used nationwide, 20 to 50 million extra votes would be cast per two-year election cycle.[156]

> Why not online voting?

Why don't we put the whole thing online? Voting would be easier, and votes faster to tally. Absentees could vote from anywhere. Vote-casting errors could be instantly flagged to the voter.

This is probably all true. Nevertheless, the shortcomings of Internet voting have not been overcome at this stage.

When he was California's secretary of state, US Senator Alex Padilla, a former software programmer, put it this way:

> My background is in engineering. I love technology. There's a lot of room for technology to improve the voter experience…everything from registration to information…to tabulation and reporting of results… But that central point—where someone is casting their vote—a piece of paper that you can go back to count, and re-count, and audit—is going to continue to be paramount.[157]

British tech blogger Tom Scott believes that online voting offers the opportunity for a 'man-in-the-middle' attack at any point in the vote's 'chain of custody'.[158] He points out that 'it takes about the same effort to change one vote as it takes to change a million'.

Of the 32 US states offering e-voting for overseas citizens, 28 require those citizens to waive their constitutional right to a secret ballot.[159] When put to the test in 2019, Russia's blockchain-encrypted cyber voting system was hacked in 20 minutes.[160]

As for **voting machines**, Tom Scott pairs a couple of salient facts:

1. Most of them run on software from large corporations.
2. Trillions of dollars can ride on who wins an election.

(ii) Automatic voter registration (AVR)

With AVR, when you register a car, marry, enter university, get a passport, go on welfare, enrol at a university, buy or sell property, lodge a tax return—and so on—you're automatically added to the voter roll.

AVR is used in 16 US states and territories.[161] But in other democratic nations it's standard—mainly because voluntary registration misses so many people. In the United States, via one misadventure or another, perhaps a quarter of citizens don't make it onto the voter roll even when they register[162]—although 1.8 million dead people *are* on the rolls.[163] Further registrations are lost via the 11% of the population that changes address each year.[164]

AVR cleans all this up automatically—as vehicle registrations, mortgages and probate certificates roll into the system. US states with AVR have 38% more new voter registrations.[165] They have dramatically higher youth voting and registrations by people of color.[166]

Like vote-by-mail, AVR saves money. In Maricopa County,

Arizona, where processing a registration lodged by a voter costs 83 cents, an AVR registration costs three.[167]

As with many of the Article III reforms, AVR should be entrenched constitutionally. If it is unable to begin that way, legislation, or even an executive order, will get the ball rolling.

It's been estimated that introducing AVR across the US would result in 22 million new registered voters in the first year.[168]

Reforms that UVBM and AVR make redundant

The field of electoral reform is crowded with ideas to mend the abuses now in play. Enacting UVBM and AVR together means many of these reforms will no longer be needed.

A hint of their combined power is seen in Colorado, where AVR was introduced in 2017 and UVBM in 2020. In 2020, against a 2010 baseline, the state's youth voter turnout had risen 42%.[169]

Here's a summary of reforms that AVR and UVBM make redundant:

Reforms of polling station ploys:
Siting stations far from poor or black areas
Early closing
Polling place advertising
Polling place interference and harassment
Hacking of voting machines
Queues (delays, engineered or unintended)

Other reforms:
Voter ID reform
Early in-person voting
'Ballot harvesting'
Expanded absentee voting
Election day registration
Registration portability
Election day holiday
Voter roll purges

Fair weather elections

That's 15 reforms that no longer need to be campaigned for or implemented—but whose benefits will be harvested as if they had been.

US studies on some of these reforms suggest the kinds of numbers AVR and UVBM will add to national registration and turnout:[170,171,172,173,174,175]

Reform	Est. registration or turnout gain
Election day registration	+5-7%, or +4.8 million
Online registration	+500,000
Early voting	+800,000
'Vote-at-home'	+2-5%
No-excuse absentee voting	+3%
More reasonable voter ID requirements	+2-3%
Portable registration	+2%
Eliminating polling queues (deterred from showing up)	+730,000
Eliminating polling queues (give up and go home)	+3%

Table 5.2: Estimated registration or turnout gain for electoral reforms in the United States

Even allowing for the overlap between some items, it would be surprising if AVR and UVBM on their own did not cause a revolution in civic participation.

(iii) Further reforms of the dismal art

> Felon disenfranchisement

In the US presidential election in 2000, which George W Bush famously won by virtue of 537 votes in Florida, 12,000 felons—and *people wrongly identified as felons*—had been purged from the state's electoral rolls. Had a decent fraction of those

12,000 voted, it's likely there would have been no Bush presidency (and no Iraq War).

Today, this ploy disenfranchises 6.1 million Americans overall, including one in 13 African Americans.[176] In Florida's Orange County, in the 2018 mid-terms, there were neighborhoods that politicians didn't bother to canvass because no-one in them could vote.[177]

Happily, at those same elections, Floridians overwhelmingly passed Amendment 4 to the state's constitution, which re-enfranchised most ex-felons.[178]

During the Amendment 4 campaign, focus groups were asked how far citizens would go in re-enfranchising felons. The groups drew the line at murderers and sex offenders.[179] This experience will be relevant when drafting Article III of the Bill of Change in any given jurisdiction. Where citizens make such caveats, the amendment should probably be tailored accordingly.

> Gerrymandering

In mid-20th Century Australia, residents of the state of South Australia lived under the 'Playmander'—in which conservative premier Thomas Playford created rural electorates from as few as 4,200 voters, and urban ones from as many as 42,000. Playford also abolished the multi-member electorates that had been in place since 1857. He managed thereby to hold power for 28 years.[180] The opposition Labor Party won the popular majority—but not government—in 1944, 1953, 1962 and 1968.

In our era, gerrymandering remains rife. Hungary's prime minister Viktor Orban has redistricted the entire country to ensure his party cannot lose office in the foreseeable future.[181] In the US and across the world, this blight on democracy stems from the power of the ruling party to redraw electoral boundaries.[182]

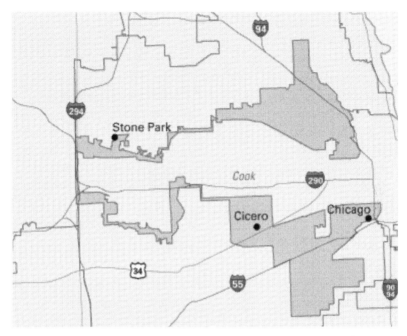

Fig. 5.14: One of America's best-known modern gerrymanders: the 4ᵗʰ
Congressional district of Illinois—less than 50 metres wide in parts—in
2004. The district, created by a Democrat majority in the state assembly,
was nicknamed 'earmuffs'. It inspired the 'Ugly Gerry' typeface. In the
terminology of gerrymandering, it had lots of 'packing', a 'hairline
contiguity' along Interstate 294, & two 'necks'.

Independent redistricting is therefore the key.

Here, a common 'solution' is a bipartisan commission.
However, these tend to produce 'incumbent protection plans'—
dividing the electoral spoils between the two parties that dominate
the commission.[183] A *New York Times* investigation in 2020
described some results of this approach:

> The official who oversees voter registration in New York City is
> the 80-year-old mother of a former congressman. The director of
> Election Day operations is a close friend of Manhattan's Repub-
> lican chairwoman. The head of ballot management is the son of
> a former Brooklyn Democratic district leader. And the adminis-
> trative manager is the wife of a City Council member.[184]

The story's header was *Inside Decades of Nepotism and Bungling at the NYC Elections Board.*

A better idea is to choose, by sortition, a group of citizens to draw boundaries—a deliberative assembly. This eliminates partisan influence *and* is transparent. Districting is complicated and time-consuming: it's not an ideal referendum item. Deliberation creates the time for participants to dive deep.

The Bill of Change should spell out principles for redistricting, to guide these assemblies. The California Citizens Redistricting Commission has several criteria that might help: population equality, non-penalising of minorities, geographical contiguity (parts of the electorate must connect to each other), geographical integrity (not carving up localities), and compactness.[185]

Majorities of Americans from all sides of politics want independent citizen commissions to draw electoral boundaries.[186] As with most third draft reforms, public support is already there.

> Merging voter rolls

Like all forms of hyper-bureaucracy, separate local, state and national voting rolls disadvantage the already disadvantaged. Merging these rolls would mean that multiple registrations across states can be eliminated, along with mountains of local-state-national bureaucratic duplication. Here, the idea is that once you register at one tier, you're automatically registered in the others.

In the US, this will assist with a situation where 24 million registrations are inaccurate or invalid, and 2.75 million people are registered in more than one state.[187]

> Cyber vote-shifting

In the US, the old-style dismal arts are often Republican specialties—but the most innovative form is practised by Democrats.

Professor Robert Epstein is the former editor-in-chief of *Psychology Today*, and a self-described 'left-leaning' Democrat. For many years Epstein and his team at the American Institute for

Behavioral Research and Technology have quantified what he calls the *Search Engine Manipulation Effect*—how Google skews its search results to help its preferred political candidates:

> Our research shows that just by manipulating search suggestions, you can shift a 50-50 split among undecided voters into more than a 90-10 split—with no-one aware that they are being manipulated.
>
> In 2016 before the presidential election, if you typed in 'Hillary Clinton is...' on Bing or Yahoo, you would get all the things that people were actually searching for... If you typed that in on Google, you would get 'Hillary Clinton is awesome' and 'Hillary Clinton is winning'—neither of which anyone was searching for.
>
> In 2016, we recruited 95 field agents in 24 states. We developed special software that we installed on their computers. That allowed us to look over their shoulders as they were doing politically related searches. We preserved 13,000 searches and 100,000 webpages.... We found pro-Hillary Clinton bias in all ten search positions on the first page of Google search results... We calculated that that level of bias, if it had been seen nationwide, would have shifted between 2.6 and 10.4 million votes to Hillary Clinton, without anyone knowing that that had occurred.

Epstein found that Google's public messaging is used to the same end:

> Before elections, Google says on their homepage: 'Register to vote—here's a link'. 'Mail in your ballot—here's a link'. And on election day they say, 'Go vote'... In Florida, 100% of liberals got those 'Go vote' reminders over and over again during the day. Fifty-nine percent of conservatives did.[188]

Epstein's team has built an elaborate online system for monitoring and exposing these abuses. (Twice, it even forced Google to briefly abandon them.)

These practices are already against US law. A national deliberative assembly could study them, and (if necessary) design referendum legislation aimed at ensuring the law is enforced. A second assembly might decide on whether outlawing the practices at constitutional level is desirable.

(iv) Omnibus approaches to the dismal art

There are certain ways of blocking voter turnout that are sly, impromptu, not foreseeable, or not immediately visible.

In Texas in 2016, for example, a judge ruled that photo ID was not required to vote—but polling officers left the 'Photo ID required' signs in place.[189]

In 2018, North Dakota's election auditor, Barbara Hettich, ruled that a vote cast in black ink on a voting form was invalid;[190] and Georgia's secretary of state, Brian Kemp, ordered criminal proceedings against non-profits that registered citizens from minorities.[191]

Who could foresee every such tactic? As reformers undo one, their opponents will field another. This undermines a democracy by giving it the sense that it will never be able to contain its bad actors.

One approach to such activities is eternal whack-a-mole. Another is to create a legal environment that is inhospitable to them.

These approaches are technical—but in brief:

- The constitution should give citizens the 'right to vote'. A 'right to vote' amendment would stymie many of the existing stratagems (and many that wait in Otzar) by putting them in breach of the constitution automatically.

- Sections of the Bill should begin with a 'declaration of intent'—to explain the framers' motives and intentions to future legislatures and courts. That way the spirit of the article becomes clear and unambiguous.

- The wording of the Bill should encourage a 'teleological interpretation'—should make the *purpose* of the Bill overall the guide to the interpretation of each part.

- Citizens should have 'standing to sue' (a right severely restricted in the US), in order to force a government to cease breaking the law.[192]

6. Subsidiarity

The village or township is the only association which is so perfectly natural that, wherever a number of men are collected, it seems to constitute itself.[193]

— Alexis de Tocqueville

My friend in Delphi for the fortnight I was there was Yannis—a waiter at the beautiful café, sitting under a plane tree, in the middle of the Y intersection that marks the town entrance. It was through talking to Yannis that I began to make the connection between the ancient Greek character and the modern one—a connection I'd missed before.

Whilst Greece no longer has the institutions that made it the envy of the Classical world, to me the Greeks themselves didn't seem to have changed much. Like their ancestors who live on the pages of classical literature, they are doughty, self-confident (though never haughty), averse to 'light' or frivolous humor, family-centric, child-friendly, fond of the (moderate) good life, logical and organized, quick to judge, and not especially materialistic.

Delphi, the religious centre of the ancient world, is now a small tourist village. It had a mayor until the global economic crisis. After that, the powers-that-be in Athens caught the global bug of local government amalgamation.

'We are now a part of a larger government district,' said

Yannis. 'And these regional government people don't take much interest in small towns.'

The irony of that, in the navel of ancient Greece, is that the Greeks of that era were that world's great decentralizers. Each of the several hundred *poleis,* or city-states, tried to maintain a fierce independence from the other.

Nonetheless, these small political units were perfectly able to deal with large collective problems. They did so simply by combining *ad hoc,* for as long as the need was there. In four famous battles—Thermopylae, Artemisium, Salamis and Plataea—dozens of city-states, large and small, allied to confront the Persian menace, and eventually to repel it.

Those who believe decentralization leads to weakness or unco-ordination might ponder the Battle of Marathon, in 490 BC. Here about 10,000 combined Greeks defeated Darius I of Persia, the world's first great political centralizer. Darius fielded tens, perhaps hundreds, of thousands of troops.[194]

Around the modern world, small entities like Delphi are being stripped of their political autonomy: handing power to a large, anonymous and geographically distant authority. You see this phenomenon (decried by locals, applauded by efficiency-obsessed governments) everywhere from peri-urban Australia to rural France.

In the former, it has increased the incentive for corruption—because the economic value of zoning decisions has increased. In the latter, it has brought an epidemic of resignations by village mayors—who are expected to fix and manage everything, as they have for centuries, but have had their powers and budgets taken away.[195]

A rough universal rule is: *The smaller, the more democratic.*

There's a link, for example, between small states and the longevity of democracy—the small Caribbean and Pacific states being examples.[196] Small states also appear to act more adroitly when crises strike. During the 2008 bank crash, nations such as Denmark, Ireland and Switzerland responded promptly and coher-ently—emerging from the crisis faster than large nations such as the US.[197]

The local level is where life's *detail* exists—and all that teeming detail can't easily be dealt with, or even understood, by a remote authority that has no physical contact with it.

It isn't necessary to make large nations smaller, or to divide up provinces. What's required is to shift some power down—to the political units that are better at exercising it. When localities in the UK were put in charge of COVID tracing in 2020, for example, they traced eight times more contacts than did the national body, at a fraction the cost.[198]

Devolving some responsibilities down to smaller jurisdictions —from national to provincial, from provincial to local—is a way to dilute overly concentrated power, and to restore some of our long-vanished political engagement.

The word for this—coined by the Catholic Church in 1891— is *subsidiarity:* the idea being that a central authority should have only a 'subsidiary' role.

In 1931, Pope Pius XI lamented that

> things have come to such a pass through the evil of what we have termed 'individualism' that, following upon the overthrow and near extinction of that rich social life which was once highly developed through associations of various kinds, there remain virtually only individuals and the State. This is to the great harm of the State itself; for, with the taking over of all the burdens which the wrecked associations once bore, the State has been overwhelmed and crushed by almost infinite tasks and duties.[199]

The rationale for subsidiarity is simple enough: the more local an issue is to people, the more engaged and knowledgeable they are.[200] As our physical proximity to each other increases empathy, and breaks down differences,[201] devolving power down makes for consensuality.

Having powerful cantons doesn't seem to have harmed the Swiss. They have the world's second-highest per capita GDP, are placed second in the Human Development Index, top the Heritage Foundation's Index of Economic Freedom, and have very low tax rates. They enjoy broad public services, low unemployment and one of the world's largest current account balances. They've kept their population down to eight million.

Whilst Switzerland's central government has power over defence, currency, telecommunications and foreign policy, the 26 cantons control healthcare, welfare and public education. They have their own courts, police, hospitals and schools. Cantons can even conclude treaties with other nations.[202]

Each cantonal constitution delegates power down to the next tier—the municipalities—which can likewise pass local laws and raise local taxes.

The Swiss motto is that government should be 'as centralized as necessary—and as decentralized as possible'.

Nicholas Nassim Taleb, an admirer of the Swiss system, writes:

> The top-down nation-state…is a very modern system and cannot handle complexity. The system that's been most successful in history is the bottom-up city-state system. The quality of the government when small is much higher than when it's big—people are penalized for their mistakes. Mayors—New York City, other cities—are doing a vastly better job than governments. It's not because they're more intelligent—It's because of scale.[203]

Thomas Jefferson made an uncanny forecast in 1822:

> If ever this vast country is brought under a single government, it will be one of the most extensive corruption, indifferent and incapable of a wholesome care over so wide a spread of surface.[204]

The philosopher Isaiah Berlin whimsically divided thinkers into 'hedgehogs'—who see the world in the light of one defining idea—and 'foxes', who draw on disparate experiences, and for whom the world has no overarching theme.

You might say that government is our hedgehog and the people are the foxes. The 'big picture' of the hedgehog is essential for the cohesion of the overall scheme—the nation—but the foxes deal with the endless, diverse detail of life to which the hedgehog is blind.

As James Scott points out in his modern classic *Seeing Like a State*, the Greeks distinguished this kind of practical knowledge by the term *metis*.

Presently, we're all hedgehog and no fox. The state intrudes on everything (increasingly ham-fistedly), yet there are a million small and informal practices, day-by-day evolutions and exceptions that it can't see. Ignore or mishandle those, and governance becomes a vast over-simplification—and a richly-hued society can become a monochrome, a production line, or a cult.

The idea of third draft democracy, and particularly of subsidiarity, is to give the fox her due. Whilst preserving some of the uniformity and conformity of the modern state—which are useful up to a point—subsidiarity limits their reach, by diffusing power and responsibilities down through the tiers.

No distant authority is able to see the third- and fourth-order effects of its blueprint. By restoring power to the regions, the municipalities, the towns, the neighborhoods, and the individual, subsidiarity brings back our capacity to deal with particularity and individuality: the applied, the unique, the unpredictable, the open-ended, the local.

Knowledge that is local in place and time is the way to grapple with complexity.

7. The amendment amendment

The plan now to be formed will certainly be defective, as the Confederation has been found on trial to be. Amendments will therefore be necessary.[205]

— George Mason, opening the 'amendment' session of the Philadelphia convention (1787)

The warmest friends to and the best supporters of the Constitution, do not contend that it is free from imperfections... And as there is a Constitutional door open for it, I think the people...

can decide with as much propriety on the alterations and amendments which shall be found necessary, as ourselves; for I do not conceive that we are more inspired—have more wisdom —or possess more virtue than those who will come after us.[206]

— George Washington (1787)

Our political system has become difficult to use because it is difficult to change.

Our constitutions need not only to be amended, but to be made more amendable.

With the ticking clocks of population, climate and inequality in our ears, our obdurate constitutions are providing too few options. Even when popular opinion favors action, we can't act.

Only about 40% of the world's constitutions may be amended by the people. In many nations, an amendment requires a three-fifths, two-thirds or even three-fourths parliamentary majority.[207]

A constitution *should* be harder to change than ordinary legislation; but it should also evolve with its host culture. Many Western constitutions were penned five to ten generations ago, and have become as brittle as the parchment they're written on.

Rigidity works in opposition to stability. As change accelerates, a constitution's increasingly poor integration with society puts pressure on both. Constitutions last longer when they're fluid.

This would have remained an intuition had it not been for the work of Tom Ginsberg, James Melton and Zachary Elkins, of the University of Chicago Law School—who studied the constitutions of every independent state from 1789 to 2005. This was, they write, '935 different constitutional systems for more than 200 nation-states, both past and present'.[208] (This is 'the complete universe of cases, not just a reasonable sample', they add.)

The three scholars found that, when it comes to the longevity of constitutions, historical circumstances have been over-emphasized, and the design of the document under-rated. Constitutions *do* collapse through war and revolution—but also because they're poorly constructed.

The authors isolated three features that help a constitution to endure: its *inclusiveness*, its *specificity* and its *flexibility*.

Inclusiveness means 'the degree to which the constitution includes relevant social and political actors', and seems quite close to Arend Lijphart's 'consensuality'.

They explain *specificity* as 'the level of detail and scope'—finding that:

> Detailed documents may be more enduring than general framework documents so celebrated in American constitutional thought.[209]

The final factor that helps a constitution to endure is *flexibility*. This is 'the constitution's ability to adjust to changing circumstances': in other words, 'the ease of formal and informal amendment'.

In short: constitutions that last a long time are not only inclusive and specific—they are more easily revised.

There's a view in political science that less amendable, more rigid constitutions lead to stabler nations. According to the best analysis we have to date, that is not so.

The authors, of course, spot the extreme outlier in this data. The United States Constitution contains many elements that normally spell an early death—but it's still with us. Because it so defies expectations, the authors call it 'the Jeanne Calment of higher law'—Jeanne Calment being the French woman who smoked cigarettes, drank port wine and ate two pounds of chocolate a week, till she died at the age of 122: the longest-lived person on record.

An absentee from the convention of 1787, Thomas Jefferson—he was in Paris as Minister to France—believed that every new generation should have the right to 'choose for itself the form of government it believes most promotive of its own happiness' and that 'a solemn opportunity of doing this every nineteen or twenty years, should be provided by the constitution'.[210]

Much later, in his retirement in Virginia, Jefferson wrote that, of those alive when that state's constitution was enacted 40 years earlier, two-thirds were now dead. Did the remaining third—a minority of the current population—have the right to hold the majority 'in obedience to their will'?

> Some men look at constitutions with sanctimonious reverence, and deem them like the ark of the covenant, too sacred to be touched. They ascribe to the men of the preceding age a wisdom more than human, and suppose what they did to be beyond amendment. I knew that age well... It was very like the present, but without the experience of the present; and forty years of experience in government is worth a century of book-reading; and this they would say themselves, were they to rise from the dead.[211]

> Mechanics

There's little doubt among constitutional lawyers that a constitution's amendment procedure can be used to amend itself.[212]

Still, the way forward isn't straight. In many nations, an amendment requires passage through both legislative houses (sometimes in two succeeding parliaments), often requiring onerous supermajorities. In some, additional constitutional councils and conventions are called for. There's sometimes a popular referendum after that. Even then, 'final approval' is often required from the executive branch, a constitutional court or the provincial governments.[213]

Austria is one of the nations where the only body that can amend the constitution is the legislature. This has resulted in hundreds of laws that are known locally as 'constitutional garbage'.

Britain's parliament, too, has the right to make and unmake parts of the nation's uncodified constitution simply by legislating: a poor state of affairs given that the ruling party sometimes holds power on as little as 35% of the vote.

In some nations, an amendment to the amendment procedure will be achievable under existing rules.

In others—where the rules are too onerous or the government is intransigent—logjams will only be broken by citizen assemblies constituting themselves and designing popular Bill of Change referendums (Part Nine). The 'amendment amendment' would not normally be enacted alone, but as a part of the Bill as a whole.

What should the 'amendment amendment' contain?

Most importantly, if we think the word 'democracy' has any meaning, it should stipulate that amendment of the constitution will require popular approval alone.

The amendment also needs to specify how a constitutional referendum is triggered—probably via the gathering of a certain number of signatures in a specified time. (Say, 8% of registered voters within three months.)

The amendment procedure—verifying signature thresholds, managing the vote, declaring the result—could be supervised by citizen assemblies, with an assist from the (popularly elected, non-government) Democracy Commission. Government would provide support services, such as security and printing.

Chapter 30
Transparency and whistleblower protection

The third draft reforms and institutions float on a sea of transparency. Without transparency, it will not be a third draft reform or institution. Every amendment, law or regulation—and the institutions and practices they establish—needs to reflect this.

When it wishes, the public should be able to gain prompt, cheap information on the workings of its government. The roadblocks to transparency in use by governments—such as long delays, groundless redactions and high freedom of information fees—will now be unconstitutional.[a]

---

[a] In 1975, Australia's prime minister, Gough Whitlam, was removed from office by the Queen's representative, Sir John Kerr. The official rationale was thin, so there began a long series of public clamors, and lawsuits, to establish what had happened that day. This process concluded when a court ordered Australia's National Archives to release the files—45 years after the event.

Kerr (it was revealed) had discussed Whitlam's dismissal with Queen Elizabeth and her son Prince Charles—now King Charles III—for some weeks in advance. All three had received legal advice that there were no grounds for removing an elected prime minister, but Kerr did so anyway, with no objection from the Palace.

When I heard the news of Whitlam's dismissal, I was in a restaurant celebrating my 24th birthday. When I learned how he was dismissed, and who was involved, I was a grandfather.

Transparency and whistleblower protection

The protection of whistleblowers is integral to the transparency principle. This should feature in every third draft reform.

Similarly, Americans have been waiting for more than 60 years for the release of documents clarifying the role of the CIA in the assassination of John F Kennedy.

Chapter 31
How much power should each institution have?

O nce government assumes its proper place in the world, as the epitome and the language of public intention, the question of *interoperability* will arise—as it did with the early American Republic (and for that matter the early Internet two centuries later). Which of its elements—deliberations, executives, courts, parliaments, referendums—are responsible for which tasks, and how do they interact?

We don't yet fully know. But lines of demarcation should draw themselves fairly organically. Political money will no longer be exerting an artificial pressure on institutions. And more power to the people, and less to parties, should resolve the problem John Adams recognized in 1813:

> Parties and Factions will not Suffer, or permit Improvements to be made. As Soon as one Man hints at an improvement his Rival opposes it. No sooner has one Party discovered or invented an Amelioration of the condition of Man or the order of Society, than the opposite Party, belies it, misconstrues it, misrepresents it, ridicules it, insults it, and persecutes it.[1]

Under the third draft, if point-scoring conflicts in legislatures persisted, the *demos* is likely to transfer decision-making to the deliberation and referendum systems—at least to the extent needed to end the problem. Branches of government today have many constituencies to which they owe loyalty, but the third draft institutions have only one.

In accepting our present ignorance of where the demarcation lines will fall, we sidestep monolithic blueprints and give social evolution its due. In this way, demotic institutions cater for the future without claiming to know what it contains.

Chapter 32
Awakening the democratic instinct

I n the 19th Century, the German chief of staff, Helmuth Von
Moltke said, 'No plan survives contact with the enemy.'[1]
In the 20th, Mike Tyson pursued the same notion:

Everybody has a plan till they get punched in the mouth.

In the 21st, evolutionary biologist Bret Weinstein lends the
idea a little refinement:

The founders of the United States did not know anything
about evolution. Those who constructed our markets did not
know anything about evolution. What they have done repeatedly is accidentally set up an evolutionary system in which
adaptation begins to take place without anybody's awareness.
That tends to result in dangerous patterns like regulatory
capture...
   I believe the answers we are looking for are not on the map
of possibilities that we are familiar with. We are effectively living
in flatland and what we have to do is detect the Z axis, so that
we can seek solutions of a type that will at first be unfamiliar
to us.[2]

The Z axis is a third axis in graphing, which represents a less-often-used variable. By introducing the extra factor, the Z axis allows you to see what's being graphed more comprehensively. To length and width, for example, it might add depth.

It may be that the 'Z axis' we've been neglecting relates not to one aspect of policy or another—nor to a 'conservative' or 'progressive' orientation—but to the way our decisions are made.

It's well-substantiated that direct and deliberative democracy, proportional representation, parliamentarism, clean electoral mechanics, and a more amendable constitution, tend to maximize welfare, unite societies, and increase happiness. Yet none of them represent a victory for 'the right', 'the left', or even 'the centre'.

To date, the instruments we've devised to crack the nut of governance are sledgehammers with names like nationalism, socialism, capitalism, neoliberalism, fascism, communism. Each of these *isms* presupposes that its doctrine captures the present reality, diagnoses it accurately, and will even be able to deal with situations that don't yet exist.

But a terrain bears little resemblance even to the best-drawn map; and the directions society will go in are not that knowable. The world's complexity does not need another monumental *ism*, but governance that can *evolve into* it.

Whilst the third draft begins with certain scaffolding, it's essentially a *process*: an ever-moving flywheel running on sovereignty, participation, information and sound mechanics.

In 2016, the Program for Public Consultation in Maryland did an in-depth study in the midst of that year's general election, finding that:

> Trump's victory was buoyed by a broad-based, nearly universal crisis of confidence in how the federal government makes decisions.
>
> The central critique voters express is not about policy or ideology: it is that government ignores the people—both their interests and their views—in favor of special interests, campaign donors, and their parties...
>
> A remarkable nine-in-ten voters agreed that 'Elected officials

think more about the interests of their campaign donors than the common good of the people…'

Asked whether government 'is run for the benefit of all the people' or is 'pretty much run by a few big interests looking out for themselves' in the 1960s only a minority said that it was run by big interests. In recent years this number has risen to eight-in-ten. In the current study this leapt to an unprecedented 92 percent. Among angry Trump supporters, 99 percent said the government is run for big interests, rather than the people…

85 percent of voters said that the people should have more influence… Asked how much influence the people should have on a scale of 0 to 10 the mean response was 8.0.[3] [4]

The world's most influential constitutions were laid down when society was a tight hierarchy rooted in gender, wealth and ethnicity, and life moved slowly. We're in a new landscape with old maps.

The Article III reforms are a response to the collapse in democratic legitimacy that confronts us everywhere.

Self-government was innate to human societies for hundreds of millennia. It's the human norm. We now have the tools to do it at scale.

Democratic reform should top the list of every reformer, activist and idealist, as it carries within it the seed of all reform.

Part Six

Teaching the democratic arts

I say that democracy can never prove itself beyond cavil, until it founds and luxuriantly grows its own forms of art, poems, schools, theology, displacing all that exists, or that has been produced anywhere in the past, under opposite influences.[1]

— Walt Whitman

Chapter 33
The two-way street

Most of this book is about what rational governance might give us. This part—Part Six—is about the skin that we, the people, have in the game. We shouldn't allow an expansion of democratic rights to occur without an expansion of democratic obligations.

The central one of these is participation. The insight of the Greeks was that without popular involvement in government, the political class takes on a life of its own. So involved were Athenians in their democracy that they called those who didn't participate in it *idiotai.*[1] (I don't need to tell you which English word comes from that one.)

John Stuart Mill depicted political participation as what we'd now call a two-way street. People give their time and skill to the community—and in return, he wrote, that made them into

> very different beings, in range of ideas and development of faculties, from those who have done nothing in their lives but drive a quill, or sell goods over a counter.[2]

In Part Five, we saw that deliberative assemblies bring out something remarkably like civic virtue; that politicians behave better, and the people are happier, under proportional systems; that direct democracy allows voters to lose with grace. For wisdom and responsibility to flower *en masse*, a specific environment is required. The more proportional, parliamentary, direct, deliberative and mutable a democracy is, the more its citizens self-educate, vote, follow rules and respect outcomes. The better the democratic tools, the less we sort into mindless tribes.

The US National Center for Constitutional Studies believes it's for citizens to take on 'the task of seeing that order, justice and freedom are maintained'.[3] And yet there is only a Bill of Rights. There's no Bill of Responsibilities.

There probably should be. It might include items like these:

- To understand the political system by which we're governed.
- To vote.
- To support the political institutions, or work to improve them.
- To become acquainted with both sides of a political argument.
- To confront one's own biases.
- To actively oppose political contamination and corruption.
- To ensure one's children are civically educated.
- To respect (not necessarily agree with) every genuinely democratic decision.
- To serve as a legislator or deliberator when chosen.

Right now, the world seems to have abandoned civic education. Of all academic priorities, it's among the lowest.

Things were different in the Greek city-state or *polis*—which was understood to be not just a political entity but an educational one. *Politiká* (politics) went hand-in-hand with *paideia*: personal excellence, moral, mental and physical refinement, civic education. Athens was a school for democracy—via its citizen juries, boards and administrators, its bulletin boards, *symposia* and salons, its Assembly and *agora*.

Similarly, the post-revolutionary United States swarmed like an ant heap with democratic ideas, civic meetings, 'election day picnics', and poetry, novels and even clothing that celebrated democracy. Thomas Paine's *Common Sense,* published in 1776, sold more copies in proportion to population than any book in American history.

Our own democracies won't be out of danger till we become like this.

To that end, Article IV of the Bill of Change constitutionalizes the teaching of the Democratic Arts.

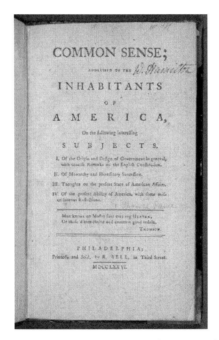

Fig. 6.1: *Common Sense,* Thomas Paine's 47-page pamphlet—
published in 1776—rallied sentiment for an
American revolution.

Chapter 34
The worship of jackals by jackasses

Politics has always abounded in distrust of the people's ability to govern themselves. The essential objection has been the same for 2,500 years: the populace is too ignorant to make wise decisions, and too self-interested to make objective ones.

The grumbling began in democracy's first century, when Aristophanes opined that to shape popular opinion, all a demagogue needed was 'unbridled audacity, untiring chatter and a shameless voice'.[1] In his play *The Knights*, he has an *arriviste* sausage-seller displace the city's populist leader by virtue of being louder, more vulgar, and readier with a promise of lower prices. The sausage-seller bribes the Council to accept his leadership—with a handful of leeks—and persuades the *demos* to do so with dodgy oracles and religious mumbo-jumbo. He inspires himself with such exhortations as:

To my aid, my beloved lies!

In *The Knights*, democracy is one demagogue being succeeded by another with 'better tricks in his sack'.

The anonymous Athenian writer now known as the 'Old Oligarch' wrote that

> everywhere on Earth the best element is opposed to democracy. For among the best people there is minimal wantonness and injustice but a maximum of scrupulous care for what is good; whereas among the people there is a maximum of ignorance, disorder, and wickedness.[2]

Plato thought democracy 'a pleasing, lawless, various sort of government, distributing equality to equals and unequals alike'.

In the Roman era that succeeded the Greek, Cicero believed that *some* democracy was useful—if it was guided by the wise and the good—but that full democracy

> can never be maintained; for the people themselves, so dissolute and so unbridled, are always inclined to flatter a number of demagogues.[3]

Cicero lived at the beginning of the long age in which democracy fell into disuse. For centuries it survived only in writing: Greek Classical era manuscripts were carted from one library to another, as one empire gave way to the next. Once a live experiment, it existed now only in dusty codices and papyrus bookrolls, to be stumbled on by the occasional scholar. Indeed, thanks to Plato, Aristotle and other Greek writers, it was Sparta's 'political stability' that was remembered by posterity. For the most part, the Athenian democratic period was written off as 'mob rule', 'rule by the poor' or 'collective tyranny'.[4]

These attitudes were still going strong in the 16th Century. One scholar who studied the Greek experiment was the French political philosopher Jean Bodin, who in 1576 commented in his *Six Bookes of a Commonwealth*:

> How can a multitude, that it to say, a Beast with many heads, without judgement, or reason, give any good councel?... To ask councel of a Multitude... is to seek for wisdom of a mad man.[5]

In his *Pseudodoxia Epidemica* in 1646—an enquiry into the 'commonly presumed truths' or 'vulgar errors' of ordinary folk—Sir Thomas Browne wrote that

> Democratical enemies of the truth live and die in their absurdities; passing their days in perverted apprehensions, and conceptions of the World...[6]

In the next century, to *some* of the American Founders, democracy was 'government of the worst' (George Cabot), or 'the confusion of the multitude' (James Madison) who 'are constantly liable to be misled' (Roger Sherman).[7]

In the 19th Century, the British historian Thomas Babington Macaulay believed power should not be accorded 'to the poorest and most ignorant part of society':

> I have long been convinced that institutions purely democratic must, sooner or later, destroy liberty, or civilization, or both.[8]

For the 20th Century American writer HL Mencken, democracy—'the worship of jackals by jackasses'—

> is based upon propositions that are palpably not true and what is not true, as everyone knows, is always immensely more fascinating and satisfying to the vast majority of men than what is true. Truth has a harshness that alarms them, and an air of finality that collides with their incurable romanticism. They turn, in all the great emergencies of life, to the ancient promises, transparently false but immensely comforting, and of all those ancient promises there is none more comforting than the one to the effect that the lowly shall inherit the earth. It is at the bottom of the dominant religious system of the modern world, and it is at the bottom of the dominant political system.[9]

In the present era, Christopher Hitchens defined the essence of American politics as 'the manipulation of populism by elitism',[10] and legal scholar Richard Posner has argued that Americans are so ignorant about politics that democracy can never be anything but a way to rotate elites.[11]

Evidence for these propositions isn't exactly hard to find: Since the 1960s, both party membership and voter turnouts have dropped sharply in most established democracies.[12] In the Brexit referendum, about three-quarters of young people wanted Britain to remain in the EU—but only a third of them voted.[13]

In 2018, Steven Pinker wrote in *Enlightenment Now*:

> Most voters are ignorant not just of current policy options but of basic facts, such as what the major branches of government are, who the United States fought in World War II, and which countries have used nuclear weapons. Their opinions flip depending on how a question is worded: they say that the government spends too much on 'welfare' but too little on 'assistance to the poor', and that it should 'use military force' but not 'go to war'. When they do formulate a preference, they commonly vote for a candidate with the opposite one.[14]

A poster in *The Guardian* rounds out the 2,500-year consensus:

> At present we have a situation where the corporations are more powerful than they were in Weimar Germany, and the masses, thanks to the rise of tabloid newspapers and celebrity culture, if anything, are more stupid and apathetic. With these two criteria, a plutocracy ruling over an idiocracy, the joke is on us.

Chapter 35
'A mode of associated living'

I t's at this grim juncture that the analysis generally goes wrong: the dismal facts are paired with a flawed conclusion.

The flawed conclusion is that the populace *must* be ignorant—is ignorant by nature.

We know this is wrong. Firstly, there have been several deeply engaged, well-informed democratic populaces. These include the first one in Athens (regardless of what Aristophanes thought), the early American republic, and the modern-day Swiss. Secondly, as we saw in Part Five, there is a suite of well-tested democratic tools that bring civic engagement to life in the real world.

Rule by the ignorant is not prevented by depriving the people of power, but by depriving them of ignorance. We may, most of us, be civically illiterate and disengaged: but a large upside awaits us.

'A democracy is more than a form of government,' wrote the American educator John Dewey. 'It is primarily a mode of associated living, of conjoint communicated experience.'[1]

An unusual, twenty-year study in the Italian regions—published in book form in 1993, under the title, *Making Democracy Work*[2]—discovered the same thing: sound political institutions do not develop in the absence of a civic community. The

344

study found that 'associationism, trust, and cooperation' lead to 'good governance and economic prosperity'. Indeed, the study's authors say, you can't separate the two. 'Civic experience' is the soft power that makes institutions work.

Our constitutional ship must be set afloat on a sea of civilization—culture, comity, education, reconciliation, self-knowledge. If we think that can't be done, we need to get comfortable with oligarchy.

But if we think 'the people' may be redeemable, there's need for a plan. How do the *idiotai* become the engaged? Can 'we' educate 'us'?

The end of slavery, and the fact that there are women voters, suggest that the answer is yes. Both were 'bootstraps efforts'— created by activists who began with almost no knowledge base, educated themselves, and then educated society at large—within cultures that were hostile at worst and apathetic at best.

If organized human life survives, we'll by definition look back on our present arrangements—a specialist political class, a disaffected *demos* lingering at the margins—with the grim smile we now produce for the divine right of kings.

Chapter 36
What to teach

1. History of democracy

> For true blissed-out and vacant servitude... you need an other-wise sophisticated society where no serious history is taught.[1]
>
> — Christopher Hitchens

The new civics should probably begin with a healthy dose of the old. Our 2,500-year democratic history—in Greece, North America, Europe and the developing world—is the obvious foundation for the democratic arts.

John Keane's encyclopedic *Life and Death of Democracy* traces democracy from its pre-Greek roots to every region of the modern world, including Latin America, Eastern Europe and South Asia. It should probably be a basic text.

The spread of democracy in the developing world may have been spotty and imperfect, but it has shaken the idea in traditional societies that a certain class, family or gender has been born to rule. Often this occurs as a cultural transformation inside an institutional failure. Burma, Cambodia and Thailand, for example, have slid back into authoritarianism over the past decade or so.

But their citizens at least now know what democracy is—and that it's possible. After a thousand years of feudalism, it's on the mental map.

Students in every country should learn of the blood sacrifices that were made so people like them could one day vote:

> One sunny day I was carrying a child in a long white dress to its baptism. The way to the church led up a steep hill. But I was holding it firmly and safely in my arms. Suddenly a crevasse appeared in front of me. I had just enough time to place the child safely on the other side, before I fell into the depths.[2]

This is 21-year-old German anti-Nazi activist Sophie Scholl, on February 21, 1943, hours before her execution. Scholl was describing to her cellmate a dream she'd had the night before. 'The child in the white dress,' she explained,

> is our idea and it will win through despite all obstacles. We have got to pave the way, but we must die for it first.

Describing democracy's progress through history via a series of biographies—biographies like Sophie Scholl's—will prove more successful than lessons about institutions and reform bills. Indeed, the dates and facts about institutions and reform bills are more likely to stick if they're subsumed in the biographies—rather than the reverse.

Democratic history, from Cleisthenes to Rosa Parks, contains thousands of such individual stories, many of them captivating. And there's no need to put all the focus on the 'stars'. For every Emmeline Pankhurst, there were a thousand women who painted banners, showed up at marches or went to jail for the cause. Quite a lot is known about some of them.

Millions of us, moreover, are descended from such people—so school projects could identify these forebears via ancestry sites.

If students are to learn from history, there's also the need to understand that democracy arose from a very cribbed, selective version of itself: that equality and progress can have almost unrecognizable beginnings. Greek democracy included only the male, the free and the locally born. Modern democracy, too, was launched on a tiny franchise; among those excluded were the poor, non-property owners, and (again) the female half of the population.

In recent decades, democracy's successes are less to do with formal democratization—there's been more backsliding than anything—than with the movements that brought rights and opportunities to the once-marginalized. The incremental removal of barriers for women, ethnic minorities and gay people has affected billions of people worldwide. Taken together, this may constitute the largest civilizing trend of the *Myriade*.

Fig. 6.2: Left: Annie Kenney & Christabel Pankhurst, Suffragette leaders, 1908. Right: Sanna Marin & Kaja Kallas, prime ministers of Finland and Estonia, 2021.

While these mega-movements (you could call them the 'three liberations') took root in democratic soil, they also spread to places where democratization *per se* went backwards. In 2010, I taught at a school for kids living on and around Phnom Penh's garbage dump. The girls from that class have now (thanks to that school) become part of the first generation of Cambodian women to win jobs in companies and government. Where their grand-mothers might never have seen another province, some of them have travelled the world. Every nation, including the authoritarian ones, has benefitted from the changes the Suffragettes began.

The study of democratic history might also shed light on the *fresh war fallacy*. This is the message—vigorously promoted whenever a new war looms—that whilst the last war was a strategic or moral error, the impending one is key to the defence of democracy, the preservation of civilized values, or somesuch.

Thus, by 2003, whilst the falsehoods on which the wars in Indochina were launched had long since become known, those underlying the new war—against Iraq—could be suppressed for the time being. This permitted the fresh war fallacy to take hold among the public. A generation later, the Iraq adventure was discredited—but the fresh war fallacy could be mobilized in the defence of Ukraine.

Finally, no student should be left unaware of the *democratic arc*: democracy's dynamism has sometimes translated into economic and military power, and thus into war, exploitation and decline. (Part Nine.) Democracy has proven the pre-eminent system not only for rights and participation, but for business and the economy. However the temptation to exploit its advantages for harmful ends—*hubris*—goes back to Greece.

Athens' long Peloponnesian War, against Sparta and its allies, was a result of Athenian empire-building that inspired fear and resentment in the region. The war's eventual price for Athens was the collapse of its power. The cost to all of Greece—including the Spartan 'victor'—was a large fall in prosperity.

2. Information literacy

The conscious and intelligent manipulation of the organized habits and opinions of the masses is an important element in democratic society. Those who manipulate this unseen mechanism of society constitute an invisible government which is the true ruling power of our country... In almost every act of our daily lives, whether in the sphere of politics or business, in our social conduct or our ethical thinking, we are dominated by the relatively small number of persons...who understand the mental processes and social patterns of the masses. It is they who pull the wires which control the public mind.[3]

— Edward Bernays, co-founder of the public relations industry, in his book, *Propaganda.*

At school and university we're taught how to read information, and sometimes how to analyze and interpret it—but rarely to study the motive of its provider. This knowledge adds another layer of meaning to what we read, see and hear—whether it be a newspaper story or a scientific paper.

For instance, some of the stories on the TV network RT (formerly Russia Today) are accurate, and a lot of its analysis is plausible; but readers need to be aware that its content exists, ultimately, not to provide balanced information but to further the interests of its controlling entity, the Russian state. (You'd be lucky to find an RT story that reflected poorly on President Putin.) Similarly, because mainstream Western outlets have wealthy owners, audiences in the millions, and run on corporate advertising, they can be expected to screen out most stories adverse to the interests of corporations, with *feints* in the direction of populism. (And they don't disappoint.)

The precepts of information literacy should also be taught to tertiary students. A medical student should learn how to distinguish a science journal from a 'predator' (fake) journal, and to assess scientific data and results on the basis not only of their methods and accuracy, but of who is paying for the study.

To grasp how money affects information is to know the rationale for Isegoria.

Kaleidoscopy

The public's ever-present sense of being deceived is probably driven by this dimly perceived relationship between money and content.

The deceptions began, in the modern West, with the 'conscious and intelligent manipulation of organized habits and opinions' in Ed Bernays' day. The most recent iteration is the bewildering 'kaleidoscopy' of our era: where a stream of contradictory memes and images keeps media and public debating the spectacle, as policy change proceeds in the background.

Kaleidocopy's best-known American exponent is probably Steve Bannon. In 2018, Bannon disclosed that the way the Trump administration dealt with media criticism was to 'flood the zone with shit'.[4]

Thus Trump would sometimes dispatch more than 100 tweets in a morning—including sensational provocations, blatant contradictions and schoolboy lies—then allow a global babel of commentary and outrage to distract the public from what he was wanting to achieve that day. In his book on the Trump administration, John Bolton wrote that, in 2018, Trump strongly defended Saudi crown prince Mohammed bin Salman over the murder of journalist Jamal Khashoggi—to distract from some hot water his daughter was in for using private email servers for government business:

> This will divert from Ivanka. If I read the statement in person, that will take over the Ivanka thing.[5]

Journalist Mike Mariani reported that, in the early days of the Trump administration,

> as controversial Cabinet picks like Jeff Sessions, Scott Pruitt, and Rex Tillerson went through the confirmation process, Trump continued sucking up media attention, picking fights on Twitter, doubling down on long-discredited lies, and sparking biweekly conflagrations. The effect is a permanent state of disorder: a de-stabilized media, an exasperated citizenry, and a fractured opposition, divided and pulled into mudslinging sideshows.[6]

Across the Atlantic, when Boris Johnson's reign as British prime minister came to an end in 2022, the *New Statesman* satirized his long run of falsehoods and logical somersaults by depicting him as an unusually talented circus clown:

> For he alone would gloss and counter-gloss his own appearances. He would write his own previews, for example, saying that his coming show was both 'the only way to go' and 'the wrong way to go'. He would vehemently assert one and then the opposite and then both—trumpet his ability to do so—only to debunk himself by denying he had made any such statements at all.[7]

The approach has its roots in Soviet *dezinformatsiya* (disinformation), which goes back to the era of Lenin. *Dezinformatsiya* was refined for modern times in the 1990s by Russia's early 'political technologists'. Journalist Peter Pomerantsev describes the first of these, Boris Berezovsky—who in 1996

> managed to win then-President Boris Yeltsin a seemingly lost election by persuading the nation that he was the only man who could save it from a return to revanchist Communism and new fascism. They produced TV scare-stories of looming pogroms and conjured fake Far Right parties, insinuating that the other candidate was a Stalinist (he was actually more a socialist democrat), to help create the mirage of a looming 'red-brown' menace.[8]

A more expanded version emerged under the key Russian political technologist of the modern era, Vladislav Surkov. In Pomerantsev's words:

> In the 21st century, the techniques of the political technologists have become centralized and systematized, coordinated out of the office of the presidential administration, where Surkov would sit behind a desk with phones bearing the names of all the 'independent' party leaders, calling and directing them at any moment, day or night. The brilliance of this new type of authoritarianism is that instead of simply oppressing opposition, as had been the case with 20th-century strains, it climbs inside

all ideologies and movements, exploiting and rendering them absurd. One moment Surkov would fund civic forums and human-rights NGOs, the next he would quietly support nationalist movements that accuse the NGOs of being tools of the West. With a flourish he sponsored lavish arts festivals for the most provocative modern artists in Moscow, then supported Orthodox fundamentalists, dressed all in black and carrying crosses, who in turn attacked the modern-art exhibitions. The Kremlin's idea is to own all forms of political discourse, to not let any independent movements develop outside of its walls.[9]

In 2013, as street protests were mounting against rigged elections and Kremlin corruption, a law was passed prohibiting the spread of 'gay propaganda' to minors. The idea, apparently, was to stir up public opinion about the new law—for or against didn't matter much—and to attract Western condemnation. A local squabble over homosexuality, or denunciations from the West, were better than domestic opposition to Putin.[10]

Thus kaleidoscopy contains not only *dezinformatsiya* and 'controlled opposition' (which go back to the 1920s) but a newer idea: a campaign of rapidfire alarms, wild claims and confected conflicts. The latter seems to be to divert attention from the leadership's misdeeds, by occupying the media with rebuttals and fact-checking: to overwhelm it. The approach has its parallels in the opposing messages or 'strategic confusion' generated inside cults— messages designed to short-circuit thought and monopolize time.[11]

In 2020, Surkov resigned, or was fired, or dropped out of view but remains as influential as ever—appropriately enough, no-one quite knows. Before his disappearance, he asserted that the ideology he champions—'Putinism'—will be copied worldwide.[12] He believes it will triumph over modern democracy (which only gives the 'illusion of choice') as it faces the reality that there is no possibility of human freedom.

Because Surkov regards Western media content as mere propaganda, he sees Western criticism of his 'informational counterattack against the West' as hypocrisy. He rejects the West's neoliberal economics and its globalism. He believes that Western governments are a façade hiding a 'deep state' that is 'absolutely undemocratic'. This, he argues, is 'the real power' behind the West's so-called 'democratic institutions'.[13]

Surkov, in short, mobilizes all the glaring deficits of second draft democracy in a very effectual propaganda war against it.

3. Activism

In the 1960s, American social scientist Mancur Olson observed that the small and organized will always dominate the large and disorganized.

As there is little chance that our elites will become disorganized, the only way things will change is for the majority to become organized.

Historically, it does this through activism—one of modern history's key drivers. The history of activism should be familiar to every public that wishes to understand how it came to have the rights it does.

In 2018, Yoni Appelbaum wrote in *The Atlantic* that, in its early years, American democracy was rooted in thousands of small organizations:

> To almost every challenge in their lives, Americans applied a common solution. They voluntarily bound themselves together, adopting written rules, electing officers, and making decisions by majority vote.[14]

Indeed, civic participation was a hallmark of the United States for its first two centuries. Shareholders controlled boards; trade unions were often directed by their members; mutual insurers, churches, fraternities, women's auxiliaries and volunteer fire brigades were managed by committees elected by the members.

In 1892, Appelbaum writes, the president of the University of Georgia studied a small town in the state as a test case, and discovered that nearly every person over the age of ten held an office of some kind:

Democracy had become the shared civic religion of a people who otherwise had little in common.[15]

All of this was governed by thousands of constitutions. In 1876, an American best-seller was the *Pocket Manual of Rules of Order for Deliberative Assemblies.*

In 1944, historian Arthur Schlesinger Snr wrote that Americans

> have been trained from youth to take common counsel, choose leaders, harmonize differences, and obey the expressed will of the majority. In mastering the associative way they have mastered the democratic way.[16]

Today, involvement in civic groups has collapsed. Only about one in ten Americans serves on the committee of an association—with white, educated liberals being the worst offenders. In 2020, political scientist Eitan Hersch called this group

> the news bingers, online debaters and kitchen-table exasperators who are emotionally invested but do not participate in organized political life… In a 2018 survey, for instance, I found that college-educated whites reported spending much more time on political consumption than did blacks and Hispanics, but significantly less time volunteering in political organizations.[17]

'If liberals shy away from face-to-face political communities,' Hersch writes, 'choosing to spend their free hours as at-home hobbyists rather than participating in weekly political meetings and canvasses, they should expect to reap as little as they sow.'

Students of the democratic arts should be encouraged to volunteer for activist groups, political parties and independent candidates. They should learn the strategies of their predecessor generations, recent and ancient. Political activism embodies the millennia-old struggle for rights and freedoms. Understanding its timeline—which is as old as civilization—restores it to democracy's heart.

4. System design

To be able to plan or even to dream about social change from a young age should help to restore the sense of agency that citizens now lack. Students can be encouraged into games and exercises that critique and improve the democratic system. They might be primed with simulations, based on real-world data, showing—for example—the ways in which a particular voting system can affect a society's economy, foreign policy and social relations; or the economic and social differences between democracies and non-democracies.

5. Democratic capture

> War is a racket. It always has been.
>
> It is possibly the oldest, easily the most profitable, surely the most vicious. It is the only one international in scope. It is the only one in which the profits are reckoned in dollars and the losses in lives.[18]
>
> — US Marine Corps Major General Smedley Butler (1933)

> Thousands of businesses around the globe are positioning themselves for a possible multibillion-dollar gold rush: the reconstruction of Ukraine once the war is over...
>
> The profound human tragedy is unavoidably also a huge economic opportunity... Early cost estimates of rebuilding the physical infrastructure range from $138 billion to $750 billion.[19]
>
> — *New York Times* (2023)

Learning how democracies are captured by special interests is central to comprehending the environmental, economic and political crises that today's students will inherit.

In an attempt to avoid long lectures and long lists, one way of teaching this topic would be graphically. For example, political contamination is easy to depict through network diagrams.

6. Defragging

Computer 'fragmentation' occurs when a file is broken up and saved in bits, all over the hard disk—slowing the machine down. Defragmentation (defrag) software fixes the problem by unifying each file in one location.

Communities get fragmented too—this is often referred to as 'polarization'—especially when change is too big, or too fast, or economic security declines. A nation can also fragment when its leadership becomes venal or incompetent—causing people to transfer their group identity to a smaller 'tribe'.

The data tells us that our voting blocs are increasingly 'sorted' into demographic groups based on race, age, religious attendance and education; and that, in time, these groups tend to coalesce geographically.

Among societies that aren't enduring actual civil war, this fragmentation is today most identified with the United States. A 2019 analysis in the American journal *Governing* concluded that

> most voters now are loyal partisans. Pollsters and political scientists have shown that individuals will change their positions on climate science, trade, immigration and the economy to jibe with their party's positions. Recent studies have found that people are shifting their religious or secular affiliations to comport with their party.[20]

In the words of Bill Bishop, author of a book on this subject, *The Big Sort*: 'Parties are about identity now, not about policy.'

Thus the two sides now share less in the way of demographics: for example, blacks have largely migrated to the Democrats, and Christians to the Republicans. Republicans and Democrats tend to eat at different restaurants these days. And each side has its preferred media outlets, where partisans are less likely to find things that are culturally offensive, or to gain knowledge inconsistent with their views.[21]

As a result of this mutual 'drift', 49% of Republicans say the Democratic Party makes them afraid, and 55% of Democrats say the same of the Republican Party.[22]

In fact neither of the warring parties is as dangerous to the nation's future as the divide itself. And, remarkably, given the scale of the sorting, the grounds for the polarization are quite thin. Stripping away political labels and identities (we do this exercise in Part Seven) reveals that conservatives and progressives, to a surprising extent, believe in the same things.

The power to delude and fragment will diminish when we've decentralized politics and information—but it won't vanish. We'll also need *defrag* skills to break up polarization from within. A citizen versed in these will be much harder to turn against some 'other'—whether it be immigrants, colored minorities or white conservatives.

(a) Scientific method

Science is now sometimes construed as an ideological camp like 'neoliberals' or 'socialists'. This is the kind of belief you'd expect to take root in a civilization soon before it disappeared.

In fact, science (when uncontaminated) is an approach to truth-finding made up of elements such as accurate observation, analysis of evidence, and forming a theory based on repeated, successful testing. Aristotle, a product of the Athenian golden age, is seen as the first great contributor to the scientific method.

The 'method' works well in biology and atmospheric science, but it can also be a good way to examine a political claim, by providing a framework in which to test it.

> **Statistics**, a science in itself, is used for forecasting and modeling, and for determining the strength of study results. (Statistical *significance*, a measurable value, reveals how strong a statistical finding is.) Statistical science tells us what the immigration rate is, or whether there's a correlation between a lower income and poor health—and which might cause the other.

In a third draft environment, where more people are journalists, and many are legislators, a grasp of statistics will help citizens to analyze claims, understand patterns and build models.

(b) Critical thinking and logic

> The point of modern propaganda isn't only to misinform or push an agenda. It is to exhaust your critical thinking.[23]
>
> — Gary Kasparov

Reality is a mosaic to which ideological loyalty blinds us. Thus did the 1920s Left insist on the good intentions of Soviet communism, and the 1960s Right on the nobility of the Vietnam War.

Along with the first glimmerings of philosophy—our early attempts at self-knowledge—came the understanding that we shouldn't leave our thinking to its own devices. Without some 'meta-cognition'—some thinking about thinking—our thoughts can manifest flaws such as over-generalization and groupthink.

Critical thinking, as a practice, rests on the premise that much of our thinking is 'biased, distorted, partial, uninformed or downright prejudiced'. (It gets worse: much of this is due to 'our native egocentrism'.)[24] Critical thinking skills undo these errors by showing us the ways in which we fall prey to cognitive illusions.

John Dewey was one of many educationalists who recognized that a curriculum including critical thinking skills will greatly benefit a democracy.

(c) Cognitive bias

In 1969, the Beatles released their final album, *Abbey Road*. On the cover, John Lennon wore white, Ringo Starr black, and George Harrison denim. Paul McCartney was barefoot.

A group of students in Iowa, prepped by several years of media and government deception over the Vietnam War, saw these as clues. One of them duly announced in a student newspaper that the figures represented (respectively) a deity, an undertaker, a gravedigger and a corpse. The number plate of a Volkswagen in the photo—LMW281F—was said to stand for 'Linda McCartney Weeps', and to connote that Paul would have been 28, *if* he had lived.

Thus began the worldwide 'Paul is dead' meme. Hundreds of further clues were inferred from Beatle lyrics and album art. Even old material was re-examined. At the end of *Strawberry Fields Forever,* recorded three years earlier, John Lennon was now heard to utter, 'I buried Paul'. (His actual words were 'cranberry sauce'.)[25]

'Paul is dead' is seen as a textbook example of cognitive bias— a worldview that recreates reality in its own image.

We're good at this. For example, we make judgments on an issue after gaining very limited information (as the Iowa students did). We're more likely to think something is true if it's easily understood. We value an idea less when it comes from an adversary.

We tend to obsess on an initiative—such as economic growth —and lose sight of the broader goal it's meant to advance. We overrate the usefulness of innovations, and underestimate their harms. We see 'phantom patterns' in data. We believe we're less biased than other people: whose biases, of course, we think we can unfailingly spot.[26]

The good news is that cognitive biases generally fall apart under challenge. The more we're required to explain the factual basis of our beliefs, the less solid they become.[27]

Teaching about cognitive biases, and exploding them in class-rooms—via videos, slideshows, exercises and games—might do wonders for civic life. One effectual method (championed by Steven Pinker) is to ask a person who has a strong opinion on, say, the Ukraine war or NAFTA, to explain the basic facts of the Ukraine war or NAFTA. Often the person has only the vaguest idea of these, and more humility results.[28]

(d) Null Corner Analysis

Null Corner is the figurative abode of the 'absences that define reality'. Few have mapped it better than Sir Arthur Conan Doyle:

> *Inspector Gregory* (Scotland Yard): Is there any other point to which you would wish to draw my attention?
> *Sherlock Holmes*: To the curious incident of the dog in the night-time.
> *Gregory*: The dog did nothing in the night-time.
> *Holmes*: That was the curious incident.[29]

Had the dog barked—as a famous racehorse was stolen, in *The Adventure of Silver Blaze*—it would mean the horse had been stolen by a stranger. That it didn't bark was therefore most informative.

Similarly informative are the silences in our public debate on subjects such as plutocracy, hyper-bureaucracy and limitless economic growth: realities that grind up against us everywhere but in the media space.

Null Corner Analysis seeks to identify such voids in media, history, government and everyday thought—to add flesh to the missing subjects, and to give students a more accurate picture of the world. Another case study might be the trillions of dollars in infrastructure, public services and debt reduction that American taxpayers lost to the War on Terror.

Null Corner contains not only current affairs issues (the 'blind sector'), but history's lost content.

In Britain (to cite one example) students are not taught of the estimated $45 trillion that their country extracted from colonized India: roughly half of 2022's world GDP.[30]

How could a student understand the Industrial Revolution, or the development of Canada and Australia, without learning that all of these were underwritten by super-profits from the occupation of India? To scratch this from the historical record—none of it rates a mention in *The Cambridge Economic History of India*, for example—is to write a rather patchy account of the British Raj.[31]

Chapter 36

Similarly, China's 19th and 20th Century occupation by various Western powers and Japan—known locally as the 'century of humiliation'—sheds much light on China's present-day distrust of the West: or would do if Western students were to learn about it.

Fig. 6.3: French political cartoon (1898) showing the Chinese 'pie' being divided by Britain's Queen Victoria, Germany's Willem II, Russia's Nicholas II, the French 'Marianne', & a Japanese samurai. A Chinese official gestures helplessly behind them.

362

In the same spirit, *Life in the United Kingdom*, a government handbook for would-be British citizens, discusses slavery—but not the role of slaves in ending it. The number of slaves Britain transported—three million—is also relegated to Null Corner. The handbook does mention colonization, but not the decades of uprisings and massacres that brought it to an end.

Although Australia's Aboriginals fought back against state-sanctioned eradication, and tens of thousands of Kenyan rebels were killed in the name of 'counter-insurgency', the colonial resistance movements are likewise passed over in silence.[32]

The goal of Null Corner Analysis is to show how our worldview is formed both from what is taught and from what is not.

(e) Projection

In the process of deporting me in November 1993, the chief of East Timor's immigration service, Mr Triswoyo, explained that he was doing so for my own safety. The locals—whom I'd found to be friendly and peaceable—were in fact 'violent people' who were 'planning riots'. He literally trembled with outrage at the idea.

Then, out of the blue, Mr Triswoyo gestured to the soldiers that surrounded him: 'And if you attack me, they will stop you!'

I exchanged a look with my fellow deportee, Hugh O'Shaughnessy of *The Irish Times*. It had no more occurred to us to attack Mr Triswoyo than to fly to the moon. But this is the nature of projection.

Mr Triswoyo had been sent to East Timor in the wake of Indonesia's invasion 18 years earlier. By the time of my visit, he and his colleagues had exterminated about one third of the population. This was perhaps the most violent occupation in the world at that time.

A more famous example of projection is Adolf Hitler's depiction of Winston Churchill to the Reichstag, in 1941:

For over five years this man has been chasing around Europe like a madman in search of something he could set on fire. Unfortunately he again and again finds hirelings who open the gates of their country to this international incendiary.[33]

Projection is where something 'inside'—dishonesty, cruelty, greed—is believed to be coming from 'outside'. Good qualities—honesty, kindness, even greatness of spirit—can equally be projected, for example onto a guru or political leader.

Thus, in the United States, it is common for Trump or Biden supporters to regard their man as the defender of the Constitution, and his opponent as bent on 'destroying the country'.

Projection seems to intensify when the objective quality of the candidates is low. (Trump promised to 'drain the swamp' in 2016 —as did Biden in 2020.[34] Both presided over administrations awash with corporate lobbyists.[35]) It's as if the voter refuses to face that both his options are bad, and projection is his way of doing so. He thereby fails to spot a hallmark of late stage plutocracy —*plural iniquity*. Because politics has been made inhospitable to the public-spirited, there are few good candidates on either side. Choosing a team where there is *plural iniquity* is very human—but perverse.

We also project meanings onto large social patterns. Recent times have seen plutocratic gains, and civic losses, from the subjugation of the state to corporations and the international bodies they control. These changes have been blamed on *both* rising fascism and rising Marxism—on the Koch brothers on the right and George Soros on the left. They've also been attributed to a centralized plan by (variously) the World Economic Forum, the Council on Foreign Relations, the Club of Rome, the Bilderberg Group, the Trilateral Commission, the United Nations, the Illuminati, 'the Jews', the Antichrist, and interstellar reptiles.

Projection—in all its forms—is a key driver of modern politics, and citizens can only benefit from studying it.

(f) Reverse debates

> If only there were evil people somewhere, insidiously commit-
> ting evil deeds, and it were necessary only to separate them from
> the rest of us and destroy them. But the line dividing good and
> evil cuts through the heart of every human being.[36]
>
> — Alexander Solzhenitsyn, *The Gulag Archipelago*

A common plotline in the movies is the confrontation of a belief system with reality: a bigot becomes a victim of bigotry; a white racist falls in love with a black girl... The character gets to experience someone else's reality—and it's no longer possible for him to maintain his limited view of the world.

Such expansions of perception are rare outside of the movies. One way to bring them into the actual world is to have a student argue another person's case—to take a position in a debate opposite to his own. Students who want less immigration, for example, would be required to make the case for more. Those who want more must make the case for less.

The same principle can be applied in essay-writing. The teacher identifies a student's belief on a subject (conscription, free healthcare, harsh penalties for crime) and gets him to write an essay putting the opposite case—mustering all the evidence he can find. The better the case, the higher the grade.

Of CG Jung's many contributions to the lexicon, the most overlooked may be his critique of 'the one-sided view': the biased, partial and often self-serving take on a subject to which we're prone. 'Reverse debates' dissolve the one-sided view by activating meta-cognition.

(g) Learned Optimism

Optimism is a strategy for making a better future. Because

unless you believe that the future can be better, it's unlikely you will step up and take responsibility for making it so.[37]

— Noam Chomsky

After the setbacks of recent decades—the planet-wide capture of government, a growing likelihood of environmental breakdown—our mental processes, our subliminal selves, need to be reminded that history is not a force but a record, and that there's nothing inevitable about any of it.

Thus any curriculum on democracy should probably contain a unit on dismantling pessimism.

From the early 1960s, Martin Seligman and colleagues have experimented to discover what ends depression, pessimism and helplessness. Out of their hundreds of clinical studies have come a suite of techniques that can be easily learned. The crux of Seligman's approach is to dispute negative thoughts and beliefs. Hundreds of thousands of people have ended depression by applying Learned Optimism.

The Bill of Change decontaminates governance, ends information monopoly and makes electoral politics rational. But once freed of our civic constraints we don't want to be like the goldfish dropped into the lake who continued to swim in small circles.

Like most units in the *Defrag* curriculum, Learned Optimism will serve as a psychological tool for the student's lifetime.

(h) Travel

Views that develop in cities and on coasts often differ from those in the regions.

Defragging needs a geographical component—such as student exchanges between regions and cities. Middle England should come to London, Middle Europe to Berlin and Paris, and Middle America to New York and LA—and vice-versa.

Students might also take study trips to places where an element of third draft democracy is already in place. For example:

- Armenia, Austria, Belgium, Brazil, Denmark, Estonia, Ireland (and dozens more)—proportional representation.
- Switzerland—direct democracy, subsidiarity.
- Mongolia, and parts of Australia, China, Taiwan, US —deliberative democracy.
- Oregon, USA—home of UVBM.
- New Zealand—high-quality, impartial election management.

Despatching students to all points of the compass is indisputably 'hairy'. This scheme would need to be started small, scaled up gradually, and refined along the way.

(i) Virtue

> The Revolution was effected before the war commenced… This radical change in the principles, opinions, sentiments, and affections of the people was the real American Revolution.[38]
>
> — John Adams (1818)

'Virtue' is a common translation of the Greek *aretê*—which also translates as 'excellence'. Its meaning evolved during the Classical period to embrace the qualities of justice and self-control.

Virtue is an old-fashioned concept that's due for a revival. Institutions aren't enough: a citizen body is not sustainable without *aretê*.

In the years before the culture wars, schools did teach virtue— qualities such as telling the truth; taking responsibility for your actions; respecting the opinions of others; restraining your impulses… What could we teach now, in an age of moral relativism?

Well, whilst the world has worsened in many ways in the last half-century, in that same span we've learned a lot more about who we are, and how to overcome our less desirable traits.

Martin Seligman's work on reducing depression is helpful here too. Depression fans the flames of a slew of civic vices, including social withdrawal, low self-control, social media addiction, and political extremism.

But Seligman has also turned his attention to making functional people more functional. In 2005, he and two colleagues published the paper *Shared Virtue: The Convergence of Valued Human Strengths Across Culture and History*.[39] On examining the philosophical and religious traditions of China, South Asia and the West, the authors 'found that 6 core virtues recurred in these writings: *courage*, *justice*, *humanity*, *temperance*, *wisdom*, and *transcendence*'. (The last refers to the human impulse to serve some greater purpose than the needs of self.)

In other words, Seligman and colleagues found there are universal virtues: not 'exact semantic and cultural equivalences', but 'broad family resemblances'.

To underpin a democracy, this conception of virtue might be incorporated into training for the professions. For example, programmers and algorithm-writers, whose work affects the way people behave, might study it as they learn to code.

(j) Civility

Athena was not only the patron goddess of Athens, but the goddess of civility. She governed reason and self-control. Thus Solon forbade speaking ill of anyone in Athens' public spaces— reasoning that 'it shows a violent and uncultivated nature not to be able to restrain one's passion in certain places and at certain times'.[40]

Today, nearly every American believes that incivility is a

national problem.[41] In politics—or political commentary—these days, one's opponent is rarely just wrong: he is a *liar*, a *grifter* or a *moron*. The average Thanksgiving meal got shorter after the 2016 election.[42]

And incivility breeds incivility. The Congressman who shouted 'You lie!' at Barack Obama in 2009 is now showered with the phrase when he speaks at town hall meetings.[43] When Michael Flynn appeared on the steps of a courthouse after his fall from grace, he was met with chants of 'Lock him up!'

If Solon's rule were enforced now, we'd lose half our public and seven-eighths of our politicians.

The fight-or-flight system is a good way to duck a flying baseball or corral a dangerous dog, but it's not the way to reckon with migration numbers.

Strong emotions tend to go hand-in-hand with political ignorance. Studies by the cognitive scientists Steven Sloman and Philip Fernbach found that the less Americans know about a subject, the more strongly they feel about it. In a study in 2014, for example, the less able people were to identify Ukraine on a map, the more they believed the US military should intervene there.[44]

Fig. 6.4: Statue of Athena outside the Austrian parliament

Chapter 37
How to teach

Were I to compare democracy to life-giving radiation, I would say that while from the political point of view it is the only hope for humanity, it can only have a beneficial impact on us if it resonates with our deepest inner nature.

The effective expansion of democracy therefore presupposes a critical self-examination, a process that will lead to its internalization. [1]

— Vaclav Havel

Actual space

We evolved as a species, and grew as children, in a world defined by space and time. The virtual world is not that world, and cyberspace is not that space.

The citizens of a Greek *polis* were united for numerous reasons —but first and foremost because they were united physically. They fought together in the *phalanx*, socialized together in the *agora*, and legislated together in the Assembly. As a result, their political extremes were closer together than ours, and fanaticisms were

371

blunted. They were successful enough that, 25 centuries later, Merriam-Webster defines *polis* as:

> a Greek city-state
>> *broadly*: a state or society especially when characterized by a sense of community[2]

The things that make a society work begin with shared physical space—a bit of common sense that's been confirmed by scholarship. According to various studies, it's in each other's company that we reach our best empathy, and our best levels of concentration. When we're physically together (in contrast to being in indirect communication), we broach the more difficult issues, and are more likely to resolve them. The place we most readily admit fault, and apologize for it, is in the flesh, where we can read the subtleties of each other's body language and eyes.[3]

More than 100 social science experiments confirm that co-operation increases markedly when we are face-to-face. When people with different political views are brought physically together to deliberate a decision, everyone feels better about the outcome—whatever it is—because they understand it, and had a role in forming it.[4]

Athenian citizens didn't stay in their homes and exchange political letters; nor did they write down their votes and send them in to a meeting. There were no 5th Century equivalents of flaming strangers online, or trolling. Protagonists eyeballed each other. The Council, Assembly and juries may have been all-male —as was all public life in the ancient world—but the three bodies did at least contain a mix of aristocrats and the middle class, farmers and city folk, young and old, philosophers and laborers.

This mixing of social types and worldviews makes for quite a contrast to today's societies—where law-makers are a small, separate elite, and citizens are sharply divided by party.

Nothing breaks down barriers like shared space. What works in campaigning—where door-knocking has a large effect, and electronic outreach has none—will work in civic education.

This represents a step back from the digital age. That step back is long overdue on many grounds.

Finland

If you look around at the world's secondary education systems to see what you can learn from them, you'll find most of it in one country. After revolutionizing school education in the 1970s, Finland now has the world's highest-ranked school system.[5]

Finland leads the world not because it put education online, or increased workloads—or doubled down on specialization, or testing, or school discipline: none of those things. It succeeded because it has:

* Smaller schools
* Smaller class sizes
* Shorter lessons
* Lessons that integrate several subjects
* No testing till high school, and then not much
* Less 'teacher talk time'
* Little homework
* Lessons rooted in real-world situations, not blackboard abstractions
* Less written words, more spoken words, and more visuals
* A three-month Summer vacation

The humanities, finally, are woven into every subject: students get *life context*.[6]

This has quite a few parallels with the longest-established system of education on Earth—that of hunter-gatherers. Here, boys typically learn the habits of two or three hundred species of game, and girls where to find hundreds of varieties of roots, nuts, seeds and fruits, and how to process them.[7] This is all done via observation, play and exploration. Kids observe adults as they make tools, build huts, prepare food and nurse babies—and mimic these activities in play. As they gain in years, the play gradually morphs into the real thing.

Finnish education is, likewise, hands-on, small-scale, fun, and light on theory. It's often meshed with real life, and the learning it delivers has context—ethical, social, emotional. The Finns often describe their education system as 'democratic', as it smooths away the competitiveness encouraged by other systems.

The Finnish system's foundation is high teaching standards. Trainees do a three-year bachelor's degree and a two-year master's —the goals of which are to 'teach teachers how to think'. Because teachers learn how to think, schools are mostly able to develop their own curriculums.

The downstream results are impressive. Finland is among the world's top five countries for innovation, global competitiveness and entrepreneurship; it is number one in the UN rankings for 'technological achievement'; and *Newsweek* ranks it as world Number 1 in education, citizenship and quality of society. To 2023, it had ranked as the world's happiest country six years in a row.[8]

Any fears about the cost of teaching the Democratic Arts— which should likewise have small classes, quality materials and well-paid teachers—might be calmed by looking at these economic and social gains. If that isn't enough, a cost comparison reveals that although Finland ranks first in the world for secondary education, it spends less per student than Britain (20th), the United States (32nd) and Australia (39th).[9]

Chapter 38
Who to teach

Compelling a whole population to undergo civic education is pretty onerous. There's a less intrusive and more targeted method: teaching the captive audience.

Because society already contains groups that are undergoing education or training, this would require less new educational infrastructure, and no more compulsion than exists now.

Such groups include:

- Primary students
- Secondary students
- University students
- Trade and technical trainees
- Civil servants and applicants
- Applicants for professional accreditation (real estate, quantity surveying, etc)
- Police candidates
- Military enlistees
- Would-be immigrants
- Residency and citizenship applicants
- Prisoners
- Parolees and probationers

- Judges and court officials
- Welfare applicants
- Royal family members and their staffs
- Political candidates
- Legislative staffers and interns
- Political party staffs
- Registered lobbyists

It would not be hard to include the Democratic Arts in the education, training and professional development curriculums for these groups. Thereby, within a decade or so, the new civics may have reached about half the population.

The course might be taught 60 to 90 hours per year from primary school to year 12, with perhaps 100 hours for the various other groups. (Refreshers could be incorporated into professional development courses thereafter.) How he is governed—and how he can plug into government—would be something every biologist and mechanic learns as part of his training: every plumber and meteorologist, plasterer and literature major, carpenter and agricultural scientist.

The course can be taught standalone, or absorbed into subjects such as social studies (schools), political science (universities) and public engagement training (police).

Would-be migrants would take a course in their home country, as a precondition of entry; citizenship might be conditional on completing a higher level.

The reason to weave the new civics throughout regular study and work is simple: without a grasp of how society's large decisions are made, we learn our professions in a civic vacuum.

Foreign students

Every year, millions of students come from undemocratic nations to democratic ones for their education. Pre-COVID, Australia alone took in nearly 700,000 international students annually. Thirty percent of these were from China, with others from Vietnam, Thailand and other non-democracies.[1] Globally, 6.4 million students annually are educated outside their home country—the vast majority in developed countries.[2]

Australia educates many of the children of China's elite. Teaching these kids democratic values, in a third draft environment, can only benefit the China of the future. Even children of strongmen such as Muammar Gaddafi (Libya), Hun Sen (Cambodia) and Kim Jong-Il (North Korea) tend to return home from their Western educations a little more democratically inclined.

As for the children of the developing world's emerging middle class: nearly all of these have grown up observing the corruption hoops their parents had to jump through to get anything done. An overseas education tends to deepen their discomfort with their own country's despotism.

On studying a set of the more recent democratic success stories, Romanian political scientist Alina Mungiu-Pippidi found that the international anti-corruption movement—UN agencies, intergovernmental organizations, et al—played no role in their transitions to good governance. One thing did have an effect, where it happened, was emulation. Estonia emulated Scandinavia and the United States, Georgia emulated Estonia, South Korea emulated Japan, and Uruguay (with a pan-European population) emulated Europe as a whole. What helped to set this 'emulation' in motion was members of the Estonian and Georgian elites studying in the US, South Koreans studying in Japan, and Uruguayans studying in Europe.[3]

Chapter 39
The hidden superpower

Because democracy is rooted in instinct, the democratic arts should—via a kind of shuttle diplomacy between conscious and unconscious—instil knowledge and practices that, over time, become automatic and natural: 'bone learning'.

The new civics teaches that we exercise our ownership of government first and foremost by understanding it. An ignorant majority is a disaster-in-waiting: at exactly the wrong moment it will side with Neville Chamberlain against war, and with George W Bush for it.

Conservatives and progressives have lived through a kind of slow-moving coup, in which much political power has shifted to a handful of corporations that are unconcerned with the values of either. In this bloodless upheaval, the two sides have been most profitably pitted against each other.

Without each other's buy-in, any 'victory' by conservatives, or progressives, will be temporary. Thus, instead of using our skills of co-operation to mobilize against the other team, we can, with some civic and psychological knowledge, use them to expand the tribe. History shows that societies win remarkable achievements when citizens organize around a transcendent goal. The prospect of a revived democracy has the potential to be such a goal.

In 1925, in *The Phantom Public,*[1] Walter Lippmann argued for the negative in the age-old debate over whether citizens are capable of exerting a responsible influence on government. He wrote that the 'the sovereign and omnicompetent citizen' is a myth: people know little about their nation's politics, and have virtually no influence on it. The sheer volume of things he needs to learn leaves the citizen 'as bewildered as a puppy trying to lick three bones at once'. There is no 'public', Lippmann wrote: just a small minority of 'insiders' and a large majority of 'outsiders'—he called them 'agents' and 'bystanders'. All a citizen can realistically do is choose between elites.

In a riposte to Lippmann, in 1927 John Dewey wrote *The Public and Its Problems*. Dewey argued that the public did exist, and could exert influence—but was presently 'in eclipse'.

Paradoxically, a further century's experience has yielded us a Lippmannesque landscape, but may have resolved the argument in Dewey's favor. The public is indeed quiescent, disconnected and uninformed. But there's now a mountain of evidence that it can, given the right tools, be active, engaged and knowledgeable.

The people are the hidden superpower. We possess a weave of demotic instruments that show us with some precision how dispersion can be overcome, and the citizen can govern. One of those instruments is the democratic arts. Ultimately, only a democratic culture—not democratic rules—can withstand the pull of despotism.

Building the democratic arts curriculum will require the input of thousands. So the object of this Part (for all its specificity) is to offer themes, examples and beginnings—a starter culture for time and mutability.

Our world is different from Walter Lippmann's. Demographies are more complex; and media—in his day quite diverse—is now a purely plutocratic instrument. The electoral machinery, cleaned up in the Progressive Era, is now rotten again.

But the world is also different in a way that Article IV can capitalize on. While all this has been going on, thousands have been tinkering in the background to refine the components of a democratic restoration.

Part Seven
The invisible consensus

Both parties are using this as a wedge issue, because, if they solve it, they've got nothing to talk about to rile you up... We are all, here in this room, the hired help. And they are pitting us against one another.[1]

— Houston police chief Art Acevedo, addressing a deliberative assembly on immigration (2019).

Chapter 40
Why do we have political differences?

The premise of this part (Part Seven) is that whilst the 'progressive' and 'conservative' labels are of great use to those who shape our world, they have less explanatory power than we think they do.

The evidence we look at in the next few chapters suggests that conservative and progressive citizens are much less opposed to each other than they are to the modern governance package: privatization, corporate deregulation, tax evasion, corruption, monopoly, bureaucracy, surveillance and the centralization of political power.

But let's begin by acknowledging the obvious—that we do have *some* political differences—and by asking where they come from, and why they are there.

Firstly, attitudes are influenced by our genetics. More exactly, genes seem to influence the extent to which we respond to certain environmental cues, if those cues arise.

On average, genes may account for around 40% of people's stances toward school prayer, property tax, capitalism and the draft, for example; with a contribution of more than 30% to attitudes to socialism, foreign aid, immigration, women's liberation and the death penalty.[1]

Of course, beliefs also percolate into you from your environment. If you had authoritarian parents, you're more likely to be a conservative.[2] If your parents separated when you were young, you're more likely to be leftwing.[3] These influences can, in turn, be nullified by an adult environment—as when you marry someone with different views, or move to a town where the politics are different.[4]

Attitudes can even be manipulated in the short term. Conservatism increases with time pressure, blood-alcohol[5] and cognitive load.[6] George W Bush's approval rating rose from 51% to 90% overnight after 9/11.[7] Indeed, it rose whenever the government updated a terror alert.[8]

Why is there *any* such diversity? Wouldn't society work better if all its members thought much the same?

Evolution didn't seem to think so.

One way of looking at our spectrum of differences is as a *polymorphism*—like the two complementary sexes, or the several blood types. According to this view—advanced from the 1990s by political scientists in the US,[9] and elaborated in 2012 by Australian philosopher Tim Dean—such differences aid our collective survival. Dean believes this 'moral diversity' exists

> because the very nature of the problems of social living meant that evolution was not able to settle upon a single psychological type that reliably produces adaptive behaviour in every social environment. Instead, a diversity—or 'polymorphism'—of psychological types working together tended to be more evolutionarily stable.[10]

A simple analogy can be seen in Darwin's Finches in the Galapagos—another polymorphic species. These birds have a short-billed and a long-billed *morph* (or sub-type), which enables them to get at different food sources. This increases the survivability of the species.

Humans (the theory goes) developed in ecosystems in which no specific approach—for example 'cautious' or 'adventurous'— worked under all circumstances. There was too much nuance in both our threats and our opportunities to make a standard response reliable. There was no single behavioral 'type' to evolve towards. Having a capacity for 'cautious' and 'adventurous' responses—and the judgement to choose between them based on circumstance—proved more adaptive than for human evolution to settle on one or the other.

Losing the 'conservative' capability, or the 'progressive' one, would cut our options—would halve our ability to deal with the situations the world throws at us: which are often quite novel and often quite ambiguous.

If this theory is right, the human group is an organism that transforms the dialectic among individuals—even disagreements— into something useful to the whole.

Chapter 41
How meaningful are 'left' and 'right'?

I f our ancestors lasted the entire Stone Age with a set of modestly different viewpoints that worked, via a group dialectic, to bring their small forager bands to sound decisions, how did we get to the extreme left-right polarization of today? Can this be 'natural'?

A scan of our recorded history offers some clues.

There has been no historically stable left and right—no political spectrum that contained the same spread of elements from one era to the next.

Athenian citizens, for instance, practised war and open male homosexuality with equal enthusiasm. Their legal system included both citizen juries and the death penalty. They thought wealth rather gauche—and kept women out of politics. Every citizen had the right to be heard by the multitude, to initiate legislation—and to own slaves. Progressives or conservatives?

In Renaissance Florence, Friar Girolamo Savonarola (1452-98) gained great influence, via his electrifying sermons, over the city-state and its government. Savonarola had new laws passed against sodomy, and sent out religious police to enforce modesty of dress. He organized public bonfires for 'vanity items' such as cosmetics, mirrors and fine dresses, along with 'immoral books'. But

Savonarola also orchestrated the exiling of the Medici princes, and inspired a democratic republic in Florence. He harshly denounced priestly corruption, and the exploitation of the poor: indeed, he took on the Pope himself in their cause. Paleo-conservative or Leninist?

Half a millennium after Savonarola was burned at the stake (the Medicis won), the Australian Labor Party's first national manifesto, in 1908, called for 'the cultivation of an Australian sentiment, based on the maintenance of racial purity' and 'the collective ownership of monopolies, and the extension of the industrial and economic functions of the state'.[1]

Our present notions of 'left' and 'right' cease to be meaningful when we step back from the historical canvas.

Chapter 42
How real is our famous polarization?

You fight for your area. As dumb as that sounds to most people, for us out here it's something to die for.[1]

> — Gang member explaining Sydney's 'postcode wars', in which members fight and kill those in rival gangs for the honor of their zipcode.

Our frozen, cantankerous politics suggest that we no longer have a matrix—a set of fluid institutions—that permits play between diverse viewpoints. Such a matrix existed in the simpler world of the hunter-gatherer: an ethic of consensus, mediated by daily deliberation and small numbers.

In our world, consensus has been broken down by one modern *deconstraint* after another. The design goal of third draft democracy is to reassemble it.

In many of the 'democracies', the public mood is sour. That derives from many sources—environmental breakdown, rising costs, falling real incomes… Increasingly, 'solutions' imposed from above are rejected.

We're nearing the point where only answers enacted by the community are likely to garner community buy-in. Making that kind of politics possible means dissolving monopoly rights over power and information (Parts Three to Six).

All this sounds too idealistic inside our present worldview, in which political division reigns supreme. (The dystopian movie *Civil War* topped the US box office in April 2024.) But that division is mostly an illusion. There's much more agreement on the issues than we believe—even in the United States, the most infamously divided populace in the West.

In his seminal study in 1964, *The Nature of Belief Systems in Mass Publics*, political scientist Philip Converse showed that when ordinary Americans thought about issues, they did not think in 'ideological wholes': that is, in abstractly 'conservative' or 'liberal' ways. Only political elites tended to do that. The positions of ordinary people, he found, were 'fragmentary' and 'diverse', and lacked 'overarching ideological frames of reference'.[2]

This has been confirmed numerous times since. In 1984, the political scientist Pamela Conover wrote that 'the inescapable conclusion' of the studies of American belief systems was that

> relatively few Americans think 'ideologically' in the sense that they order their political beliefs according to certain basic ideological principles.[3]

In 2012, the political scientists Iyengar, Sood and Lelkes addressed the question of American political polarization from a different angle. In the 60 years from 1959 to 2009, they found, polarization had grown greatly. By one measure, it had multiplied by six. In fact, political partisanship was well outstripping the old racial and religious divisions.

But—the three emphasized—it is 'affect' (feeling or emotion) driving the two sides apart, not issues. Or, as they put it, 'a primordial sense of partisan identity', not 'policy preferences'.

In her 2018 study, *Ideologues Without Issues*,[4] the American political scientist Lilliana Mason analyzed two US voter datasets for the year 2016—separating out 'tribal, emotional, affective' ideology from voters' positions on the issues.

Mason measured each subject's willingness to marry, befriend, live next door to, or spend time with, an ideological opposite. These markers of tribal identity were carefully separated from views on specific political issues. Then the two—tribal identity and issue stances—were compared to see which of them drove polarization.

The answer was: mostly tribal identity. Its effect was more than twice as strong as that of disagreements on issues. And the two were not even strongly correlated.

'American identities,' Mason concluded, 'are better than American opinions at explaining conflict.'

> Americans are dividing themselves socially on the basis of whether they call themselves liberal or conservative, independent of their actual policy differences.

This takes us back to anthropology, where it's long been understood—in the words of the American writer on evolution, Joseph Carroll—that 'the identity of the social group is integral to individual identity':

> Individual humans share in the collective imagination of their social groups, and within those groups, they construct narratives about their own individual lives.[5]

The *diploid* character of the modern citizen—host to an 'emotional' domain of tribal feeling, alongside a more 'mental' domain of policy opinions—sheds light on the bizarre contradictions of our politics.

It also makes today's social division more understandable. When Lilliana Mason analyzed the data on voter attitudes for the entire three decades to 2004, she found that Americans are in

> a new electorate that generally agrees on most issues but is nevertheless increasingly biased, active, and angry.[6]

In 2016, these contradictions incarnated in the figure of

Donald Trump, an avowed conservative—whose voters seemed not to notice that many of his policies were leftwing. Indeed, candidate Trump's progressive positions were supported as zealously by the Republican base as were his conservative ones—presumably because the leader of the conservative 'tribe' had uttered them.

If we put aside what he really believed, and also what he did after taking office—and look only at the policy statements that helped to get him elected—we find that candidate Trump promised to make health insurance premiums tax-deductible,[7] leave social security untouched,[8] cut the big banks down to size,[9] bring troops home, make medical marijuana widely available,[10] and end space exploration till America's potholes were fixed. He attacked the distorted reality purveyed by the corporate media. He pledged to expand Veterans Affairs, increase job creation in an 'unprecedented' way, raise the income tax threshold, eliminate corporate tax loopholes, increase funds for drug addiction treatment,[11] ban foreign lobbyists from raising money for US elections,[12] end permanent war, clean up the election system, rebuild the country's infrastructure, raise corporate taxes, and terminate corporate influence in Washington.[13] Trump criticized 'hedge fund guys that are making a lot of money that aren't paying anything [in tax]'.[14] He promised to renegotiate or withdraw from NAFTA[15]—and to stop mergers such as that of AT&T and Time Warner, saying: 'It's not just the political system that's rigged, it's the whole economy.'[16]

That Trump was elected on the back of so many classically progressive policies—tens of millions of conservatives voted for him—raises a question: Are these policies actually 'progressive'? If they're held by both sides, aren't they simply 'public opinion'?

The Left of 30 years ago was anti-deep state, anti-corporate, anti-globalization, anti-war, anti-pharma, anti-censorship, anti-surveillance, and partial to natural medicine and chemical-free food. This much resembles large portions of today's Right.

Humans evolved to forage in small bands—bands that formed larger 'ethnolinguistic networks', with distinctive moral codes, body paint, clothes, music and other identifiers. So you'd expect that the tendency to tribalize runs deep in us.

In that context, some early 1970s experiments in Bristol, UK, were not as surprising as they first seemed.

The experiments were run by the psychologist Henri Tajfel (pronounced *Tai*-fel), a Polish Jew who'd experienced Nazism at first hand in the 1930s. Tajfel had observed that anti-Semitism was practised by large numbers of Germans, not just a few pathological personalities, and he wanted to understand what drove such 'identitarian' extremes.

In Tajfel's first experiment, a display covered in a few hundred dots was shown to high school boys, one boy at a time. Each was asked to estimate how many dots there were. Naturally some guessed high, and some low.

The students were then divided into two groups—the 'over-estimators' and the 'under-estimators'. Such groupings could only exist in a laboratory. They were designed to be meaningless and arbitrary—as weak a tribal identity as Tajfel could think of. Moreover, no physical group ever met: each boy was dealt with in isolation.

The student was then involved in a series of games, where he got to award points (with a monetary value) to other students.

The under-estimators consistently awarded significantly more points to each other. The over-estimators did the same. Students quickly bonded to their group: even though its identity was inconsequential, it would exist for less than a day, and it never gathered in the same room.

Fig. 7.1: Henri Tajfel

Tajfel did parallel experiments involving paintings (some allegedly by 'Klee' and some by 'Kandinsky'), and with coin-tosses. Again, students favored 'their' group, even when it had a nondescript name like 'Group X'.[17]

Tajfel wrote that

> as soon as the notion of 'group' was introduced into the situation, the subjects discriminated against those assigned to another random category.[18]

The subjects awarded points to a member of their own group even when this penalized the larger group—containing both. Participants rewarded their fellow over-estimators, Klee-likers, heads-tossers and Group X members, even if it meant the original, larger group lost out.

Henri Tajfel concluded that groups give us not only *identity* (they tell us who we are) but *self-esteem* (they make us feel good about ourselves)—and that stigmatizing other groups assists the process by giving better definition to our own.[19]

So, in another instance of deconstraint, an impulse that was useful in the Stone Age now appears to be deranging perception and distorting politics. This results in a strange *diploidism*, where a voter has two distinct mental 'compartments'. One compartment might predispose her to certain policies, and the other to a politician espousing the opposite policies—but who displays the right tribal cues.

More often than not, the latter trumps the former.

The week before the 2016 US election, 61% of Democrats believed the economy was getting better; the week after it—once Donald Trump had been elected—46% did. The Republican figures were 16% (before) and 49% (after).[20] The same pattern was on display once Joe Biden had defeated Trump in late 2020. The number of Democrats expecting a continuous economic expansion 'over the next five years' doubled. The number of Republicans expecting it halved.

The partisan cognitive split is growing more pronounced over time.[21] We are bitterly divided on identity—'emotional attachments that transcend thinking', as Lilliana Mason calls them—and these divisions are not only psychological and emotional. 'We are,' Mason ventures, 'starting to feel culturally different from each other'.

This anachronistic tribal *affect* will play out till we adopt a system that sidelines it—one that ushers forward our better angels.

There are strong grounds for believing this can be achieved. As our emotional polarization widened over recent years, polling repeatedly found that most people are close enough on most issues to get things done.

In the US (for instance), majorities on both sides of politics want government to invest in infrastructure, to enforce environmental regulations, to transition to alternative energies like solar and wind, to set tougher standards on fracking, and to prioritize the environment over economic growth.

Likewise, majorities of both Republicans and Democrats support:

- Cutting the budget deficit[22]
- Reducing defence spending[23]

- Taxing wealthy Americans on their net worth[24]
- Tighter border security to stop illegal entry
- Single payer universal healthcare[25]
- Programs like Medicare and Medicaid for seniors and the poor[26]
- A woman's legal right to an abortion[27]
- Legalizing marijuana[28]
- Increased education spending[29]

Those who oppose marriage equality, rights for minorities, and a woman occupying the White House, are numerically fading away.[30]

Overwhelming majorities on both sides support a Green New Deal.[31]

Ninety-six percent of Americans (including 96% of Republicans) believe that money in politics is responsible for the nation's dysfunctional political system.[32]

Both sides think the news media is 'having a negative effect on the nation'.[33]

Clearly, the Republicans and Democrats in power are not acting on the wishes of Republicans and Democrats in the electorate.

Even toward the political extremes, there's agreement in unexpected quarters. Supporters of the Tea Party and the socialist left agree on eliminating special interests from government, outlawing taxpayer bailouts, opening up politics to ordinary citizens, weakening the professional governing class, and reining in civil rights infringements—such as the illegal government surveillance exposed by Edward Snowden and Julian Assange.[34]

So—how real is our famous polarization?

When we focus on issues: not that real. The 'ideological divide' isn't much of a divide at all.

In summing up his classic studies of decision-making power in the US, Princeton scholar Martin Gilens unearthed something closer to a true divide:

Policy outcomes strongly reflect the preferences of the most affluent but bear virtually no relationship to the preferences of poor or middle income Americans.[35]

The real gulf is not between left and right, but between the ruling elite and everyone else—making it necessary to divide 'everyone else' into warring camps.

Fig. 7.2: Western Front, December 25, 1914: Some of the 100,000 German & British troops who put down their guns & got together for Christmas. Through the year, the rival armies regularly shouted out greetings, passed on football news, & sang for each other's entertainment. Then on Christmas Day men met on No Man's Land to exchange gifts, give each other haircuts, hold joint Christmas services, & play football. Soldiers on both sides expressed mystification as to why they were fighting each other. News of the gatherings was suppressed by the newspapers—& they were soon banned by the high commands. However they broke out spontaneously, even under penalty of court martial, for the rest of the war.

Chapter 43
Divide et impera

The public is not to see where power lies, how it shapes policy, and for what ends. Rather, people are to hate and fear one another.[1]

— Noam Chomsky

There is a potentially all-powerful mass of voters who occupy the middle two-thirds of opinion (the 'omnipotent middle'), but who are sidelined by unrepresentative electoral mechanics—and also by a method that probably goes back to the Neolithic.

From ancient times, a key strategy by a tyrant or emperor who wished to hold together his domain has been *divide et impera*—divide-and-rule. Once the opposition has been divided, the new groupings are not only smaller but are now fighting each other. Divide-and-rule is required where a population left to its own devices would be broadly able to agree on things.

The strategy was central to the success of some of history's best-known conquerors, including Phillip of Macedon, Julius Caesar and Napoleon. It was also instrumental to the expansion of the British Empire. Whenever India's Muslims and Hindus united against British rule in the 19th and 20th centuries, it became necessary to create strife between them:

> The British collector would secretly call the Hindu Pandit, pay him money, and tell him to speak against Muslims, and similarly he would secretly call the Maulvi, pay him money, and tell him to speak against Hindus. This communal poison was injected into our body politic year after year and decade after decade.[2]

In world history, a divide-and-rule strategy is characteristic of amoral leaders who care much about their own control of a society, and less about its welfare. In family and workplace psychology, it's chiefly seen in narcissists and psychopaths.[3] In politics, it's the domain of party strategists and the mass media.

Divide-and-rule works in tiny groups and in entire world regions—in geopolitical space and cyberspace. The goal of Vladimir Putin's campaigns against Western institutions is less to influence policy than to turn the elements of Western society against each other. The staff of Russia's Internet Research Agency (IRA) work in teams where members take opposite sides in an argument in a Western chatroom.[4] In one campaign, for example, 'competing' IRA teams spread emotional pro- and anti-vaccine viewpoints simultaneously.[5]

From British India to modern America, divide-and-rule works because its victims do not perceive the strategy, and oblige the manipulator by turning on each other.

Divide-and-rule has worked especially well against modern-day progressives and conservatives. Progressives have been persuaded that society's problems are caused by 'rightwing market fundamentalists', and conservatives that they're the work of 'liberal elites'. The right has been told that 'government' is the problem, the left that 'corporations' are.

This brings to mind the Kray twins, Reggie and Ronnie—co-heads of the crime syndicate that terrorized London in the 1960s. A conservative is one who believes she's under threat from Reggie, and a liberal one who thinks she's under threat from Ronnie.

Divide et impera

Fig. 7.3: The Kray twins (1965)

Divide-and-rule may split populations—but it stems from a very pragmatic unity at the top. As discussed in Part Three (Decontamination), big business and politics tend to have the same investors, and to be staffed by the same people at different stages of their careers. They've become a functional unity—a Dyad.

The notion of business and government converging into a *complex* goes back to Dwight Eisenhower. Though his 'military-industrial complex' has broadened out—'military' is now 'most of government', and 'industrial' now embraces finance and IT—the principle is unchanged. Democratic governments have largely morphed into the special interests they were invented to contain. In gazing at this inkblot, conservatives see an old lady in a hat, and liberals see a young girl with a mirror.

The recipe that brought us our present era—which you might call the *Precarian*—had ingredients like privatization, financialization, fiscal austerity and war. It was crafted by an elite comprised of conservatives and progressives: businessmen and politicians.

The American economist John Perkins, one of the early implementers of 'structural adjustment', provides a snapshot of the dyadic arrangement:

> My job was to convince heads of state of countries with resources our corporations covet, like oil, to accept huge loans

from the World Bank and its sister organizations. The stipulation was that these loans would be used to hire our engineering and construction companies, such as Bechtel, Halliburton, and Stone and Webster, to build electric power systems, ports, airports, highways and other infrastructure projects that would bring large profits to those companies and also benefit a few wealthy families in the country, the ones that owned the industries and commercial establishments. Everyone else in the country would suffer because funds were diverted from education, healthcare and other social services to pay interest on the debt. In the end, when the country could not buy down the principal, we would go back and, with the help of the International Monetary Fund, 'restructure' the loans. This included demands that the country sell its resources cheap to our corporations with minimal environmental and social regulations and that it privatize its utility companies and other public service businesses and offer them to our companies at cut-rate prices.[6]

Now third world 'structural adjustment' has become 'fiscal austerity' in the first world, and many publics in the global north are experiencing the kind of straitening visited a generation ago on Chile and Argentina.

According to a RAND Corporation study published in 2020, if the fairer policy settings of the immediate post-War period had been retained, each American income-earner outside the top 10% would today earn an extra $1,144 per month. The study found that only at the 99th and 100th percentiles do incomes grow faster than economic growth. This minority aside, everyone—from conservative, white businessmen to black, female socialists—became relatively poorer.[7]

Market pantheism is not conservative or 'rightwing' any more than it is 'pro-business'. It's the enemy not only of leftists and liberals, but of conservatives—whose values it is disintegrating—and of traditional, local and regional capitalism, which it has devoured.

Even the wealthy class has been 'restructured'—with wealth

being transferred from makers of goods and services to accruers of interest, rent and capital gains.

The end to which all this proceeds is monopoly—as explained by Facebook co-founder Chris Hughes:

> Starting in the 1970s, a small but dedicated group of economists, lawyers and policymakers sowed the seeds of our cynicism. Over the next 40 years, they financed a network of think tanks, journals, social clubs, academic centers and media outlets to teach an emerging generation that private interests should take precedence over public ones… By the mid-1980s, they had largely managed to relegate energetic antitrust enforcement to the history books.
>
> This shift, combined with business-friendly tax and regulatory policy, ushered in a period of mergers and acquisitions that created megacorporations. In the past 20 years, more than 75 percent of American industries, from airlines to pharmaceuticals, have experienced increased concentration, and the average size of public companies has tripled. The results are a decline in entrepreneurship, stalled productivity growth, and higher prices and fewer choices for consumers.[8]

The exchange of monetary favors between corporations and governments that drives all this has become so blatant that, in Canada in the 2010s, twelve-year-old Victoria Grant lectured adult audiences on how it is done.[9]

In the media sphere, an outlet's goal is no longer a balance of views, but to cater to a leftwing or a rightwing audience. Both left and right, who instinctively oppose the new order, are trained to believe the other is responsible for it.

Beyond this, the dominant media strategy is silence. Discussion of the reigning economic model, or of democratization, lingers in the blind sector. That ensures the neoliberal project the evolutionary advantage of invisibility. Even the name 'neoliberalism' has vanished from the public debate.

Thus neoliberalism is no longer a mere system. Like 15th Century Catholicism, it's the lens through which all possible systems are viewed, and the language in which all possible systems are described.

The hazy air of unrealism that results has spawned exaggerated mass psychologies. As the murderous Thirty Years' War brought the witch frenzy to a head, so has the neoliberal epoch coincided with the rise of conspiracy theories and political correctness—ways to fill gaps in information, to offer the illusion of influence, and to flag loyalty in a fragmented society.

Divide-and-rule is why the invisible consensus remains invisible.

Chapter 44
Common ground

As far as I can tell, nobody on either the left or the right has any serious meaningful vision for where humanity will be in 2050. Most of what you get is nostalgic fantasies about the past.[1]

— Yuval Noah Harari

Each citizen tends to hold a range of views that are not consistent ideologically. That is, there's no rational reason for today's extreme partisanship.

The third draft argument is that a happy society originates not in less or more public debt, or more liberal or conservative values, or a new foreign policy—but in citizens' access to decision-making. Switzerland reminds us that people want a say in the system much more than they want to get their own way on every issue.

There are ways to speed the process of left-right consensus-building—such as the 'parsing session' (see Glossary). But consensus sometimes grows organically. In his book *Unstoppable*, Ralph Nader documents numerous victories for the public interest by liberal-conservative coalitions. The $8.8 billion Clinch Breeder Reactor in Tennessee, for instance, was halted in 1983 by an alliance of the Friends of the Earth, the National Taxpayers Union, the Council for a Competitive Economy, and the Union of Concerned Scientists.[2]

In France in 2018 and 2019, the consensus cast aside its cloak of invisibility to manifest the *gilets jaunes* (or 'yellow vests'): a movement that pragmatically combined left and right, in a protest against neoliberalism, that shook the French establishment.

According to an analysis of 56,000 petition comments and millions of social media posts, the movement is focused on such issues as economic unfairness, lack of rural infrastructure, the need for an 'ecological transition', and the drop in purchasing power.[3] Its supporters are both working and middle class. A study of the group's wish list found ideas from both the left and right—all of them 'very far removed' from the neoliberal policies of the French government.

(The meld was personified by a pair of friends interviewed by the BBC at the Paris protests of 2018. One stated, 'She's far left, and I'm far right—and we're here together for the *gilets jaunes*.'[4])

Vast demonstrations in major cities—290,000 turned out on the first weekend—wrung large policy reversals out of President Macron.

The group has no 'representatives'; it reaches decisions via deliberative democracy; it agitates to have the citizen's initiative entrenched in the constitution.

Despite a massive media campaign against them, the *gilets jaunes* won immediate public sympathy. In a poll taken in November 2018, their approval was 84%. This included support from:

The far left	(90%)
The traditional left	(90%)
The far right	(96%)
The traditional right	(75%)

In the same poll, a recent speech by President Macron was deemed 'unconvincing' by 78% of respondents.[5]

Fig. 7.4: A protest at Vesoul blocking National Route 19, on the first day of *gilets jaunes* actions, November 17, 2018.

Had you proposed to political observers, in 2017, that large sections of the French right and left would join forces, you'd have invited disbelief. But an existential threat degrades tribal allegiances. Progressives and conservatives learn they share opinions they thought they'd had to themselves.

The hallmark division in modern society is probably not 'left-right', but the gap between what the public wants from government and what it gets.

If you stylized the political science findings of recent years, the result may look something like this:

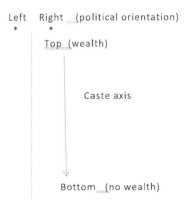

The horizontal axis depicts a left and right that are closer on most policy issues than is usually believed. The vertical axis depicts the real gulf—that between the actions of plutocratic government and the public interest.

The conservatives and liberals at the top design the economy—rentierism, tax breaks, offshoring, bailouts and so on—and the conservatives and liberals below them (the 99%) bear the consequences.

These days, the 'political spectrum' has diminished information value. The 'caste axis' might be a more useful way to capture our social divide.

The new dispensation does not, indeed, care much about your politics. Modern policy-making has resulted in stagnant incomes and less certain futures for artists and farmers, minimum wage workers and business owners, liberals and conservatives.[6]

And the 1% treats dissidents from the left and right much the same:

> We saw the first hints in communications between Twitter executives before the 2020 election—when we read things like 'Flagged by DHS' or 'Please see attached report from FBI for potential misinformation'. This would be attached to an Excel spreadsheet with a long list of names—whose accounts were often suspended shortly after.
>
> The evidence of the Twitter-Government relationship includes tens of thousands of names on both the left and right. The people affected include Trump supporters—but also left-leaning sites such as Consortium and TruthOut, the leftist South American channel Telesur, the Yellow Vest movement. That in fact is a key point of the Twitter files—that it's neither a left nor right issue.[7]
>
> — Congressional testimony of journalist Matt Taibbi on the government effort to limit information on the Internet

Over the last half-century, as the revolutions for women,

ethnic minorities and gay people reshaped the world, market fundamentalism absorbed these changes without itself changing. As a result, a dozen existential crises knock at the door of the present generation, and at least one of them is likely to blow down the house of the next.

Extremists are rising because, as yet, there is no counter-narrative: no mechanism by which a *natural consensus* can manifest.

By such signs is second draft democracy telling us it's nearing the end of its useful life.

Part Eight
The Bill of Change

Democracy in its present Western form arouses skepticism and mistrust in many parts of the world.

I admit that I, too, am not entirely satisfied with this recipe for saving the world, at least not in the form offered today. Not because it is bad, or because I would give preference to other values. It does not satisfy me because it is hopelessly half-baked.[1]

— Vaclav Havel

Freedom…is threatened from many directions, and these threats are of many different kinds—demographic, social, political, psychological. Our disease has a multiplicity of cooperating causes and is not to be cured except by a multiplicity of cooperating remedies. In coping with any complex human situation, we must take account of all the relevant factors, not merely of a single factor. Nothing short of everything is ever really enough.[2]

— Aldous Huxley (*Brave New World Revisited,* 1958)

Chapter 45
The scheme so far

Because this Part is about the mechanics of implementation, it may be opportune to recap third draft democracy's key features, and why it is likely to work:

I argue that political contamination, information capture, biased electoral mechanics and an excluded public are the architectural flaws that supply most of the defects in our democratic 'house'. And that these four issues, therefore, are ripe for *constitutionalization*. That is, because they're our 'wellspring inequities'—those that give rise to most others—they're innately constitutional matters.

Because isolated reforms are fragile, third draft democracy has four elements. Each of these elements not only adds to the weight of the others, but helps to protect the others from harm: they have what I call *syzygy*. To illustrate:

- There's no point in eradicating money from politics if big media can campaign to restore it.

- There's no point in legislation to restructure the media if legislators can be paid off to repeal it.

- The fairest, most perfectly engineered electoral system will be captured if civic consciousness is not raised.

- Conversely, the new civics will be meaningless if the content is a broken system.

To leave any of the four 'wellspring' items unaddressed would leave plutocracy in possession of a loaded gun.

The Bill of Change relocates power across the civic map, to ensure the constitution cannot be captured by one set of interests. Remote elites will no longer be required for governance.

The third draft reforms are coherent with democratic tradition. (Part of the democratic tradition, after all, is democratic expansion.) They dilute none of the hard-won freedoms in existing constitutions—such as citizens' rights, the separation of powers and regular elections—and will strengthen most of them.

The Bill establishes *mutability* in governance, allowing a society to gradually assimilate experience, and to navigate new scenarios as they arrive. This kind of incremental progress is likely to prevent sudden reversals or violent revolutions.

To enact change of this order, a written design needs to be in place well before the heat of battle: to make the goal concrete and to provide a rallying point.

In the 'democracies', this *Bill of Change* will work its way through society to a referendum. In authoritarian states, the old regime will usually have to be toppled in the process. Both will require a people's movement that reconciles left and right.

Chapter 46
The deliberation stage

Once public support for the Bill reaches a certain threshold, citizen bodies would come together to reach agreement on the Bill's articles, and then write them down.

The Irish Republic uses such assemblies to prepare the way for constitutional referendums.[1]

Sensibly, the Irish reduce the task for each assembly to a bite-sized chunk.

Likewise, a single Bill of Change assembly wouldn't deal with (say) all of Article III. It would deliberate one section of it—say, direct democracy—and write both the amendment and the referendum question. Another assembly takes on deliberative democracy, a third proportional representation, and so on.

When that's done: one level up, an assembly made of delegates elected from the earlier ones weaves the sections into Article III.

Each of the articles—including a fifth one to establish the Democracy Commission—comes together in this way.

Fig. 8.1: The Grand Hotel on the Dublin seaside—where an Irish citizens' assembly met from 2016 to 2018, to deliberate issues such as population ageing, abortion, climate change, gender equality, a revamped referendum system, & fixed-term parliaments. The assembly had 99 members (with 99 substitutes), two-thirds of whom were randomly selected. It made 18 recommendations to government on constitutional change, & 20 on laws & standing orders—some of which were implemented via referendums & policy change. The assembly was staffed by a secretariat from the civil service, & cost €2,355,557. It was one of several such assemblies since 2012 which have brought major change to Irish society.

Each assembly might contain 50 to 100 randomly chosen citizens. As they see fit, they'd break down into smaller groups to tackle sub-issues—then reconvene in a 'plenary' session for the big picture. Depending on the complexity of the issue, a deliberation might last anything from a few days to several months.

The final one of these assemblies is selected from members of the 'second tier' assemblies that composed each of the articles. This 'third-tier' assembly puts the five articles into a single document: the Bill of Change. Altering content is not permitted at this point, so this assembly's main task is to organize a preamble—which lays out the document's broad intent—in particular sketching out the constitution's shift in emphasis to demotic power. It would also oversee formatting, printing and distribution, and trigger the creation of an assembly to manage the referendum.

Pending the establishment of our civic endowment, funding for all this might be raised from public donations, large and small; sources of donations over $1,000 may need to remain anonymous to prevent undue influence.

Where change is deemed too large for a political system to digest at once, the 'third-tier' assembly might stretch timelines a little. For example, deliberative and direct democracy, proportional representation and the measures against voter suppression might come in immediately—with parliamentarism beginning in Year Two, and subsidiarity in Year Three.

Since the Glorious Revolution of 1689, the *constitutional convention* has been the standard 'instrument of transition' from one system of government to another. With an eye to history, we might give our final gathering that name.

Chapter 47
The referendum

When the campaign (which is covered in the next Part) is over, the Bill is voted on in a referendum.

Citizens should vote on each article separately. The sections in Article III should also be voted on individually: you can't lump big issues like proportional representation, vote-by-mail and direct democracy together.

High turnouts always add legitimacy to the result. Australia's gay marriage plebiscite attracted a 79.5% turnout (partly thanks to all-mail voting) and a 61.6% Yes vote.[1] Debate over marriage equality, which had been going on for many years, ceased the day after the vote, and seems unlikely to revive.

One way to ensure you *don't* get high turnout—or that a referendum question is voted down—is to muddy the wording. Another is to lump several changes together in the same question. The Italian government achieved this double in 2016:

> Do you approve the text of the Constitutional Law concerning 'Provisions for overcoming equal bicameralism, reducing the number of Members of Parliament, limiting the operating costs of the institutions, the suppression of the CNEL and the revision of Title V of Part II of the Constitution' approved by Parlia-

ment and published in the Official Gazette no. 88 of 15 April 2016?

(People don't vote for word salad. The *No* side won.)

A referendum proposal should generally be a single, simple sentence in the form of a question. Australia's marriage equality plebiscite was a model of clarity:

Should the law be changed to allow same-sex couples to marry?

The choice of answer was *Yes* or *No*.

On the minus side, the Australian Government had not prepared legislation by the day of the vote, so citizens didn't know what they were voting for in any detail. The best idea is to have the question linked to a much-circulated written amendment. For example:

Should the Australian Constitution be changed to include Article I of the Bill of Change, which abolishes large political donations and 'revolving door' jobs between government and corporations?

Leaving the amendment unwritten by referendum day allows middlemen—politicians, committees, draftsmen—to specify the content *after* the vote.

Fig. 8.2: Another model of simplicity: the Scottish
government's proposed ballot for a future independence
referendum

Management of the referendum

The third draft movement should insist that the referendum
process is managed by one or more citizen assemblies—not by
government.

New Zealand's experience in 1992 shows why this is so. Here,
New Zealanders decided by a very large majority (70.5%) that the
nation should switch from 'first past the post' voting to 'mixed-
member proportional' (MMP).

But the government had decided that a second referendum was
needed to 'confirm' the result—in a year's time.

Parliamentarians elected under proportional systems are harder
for business to control: corporate interests now had one year to
organize a scare campaign. They raised a colossal war chest, and
New Zealand was saturated with ads, and warnings from political
and business leaders: MMP would bring 'chaos' and 'economic
ruin'; it would be 'a catastrophic disaster for democracy'.[2]

The second referendum won with a 53.9% majority. In one year, organized money had shifted the opinions of 16.6% of the electorate—normally enough to swing the result.

In 2023, New Zealand celebrated 30 years (and ten elections) with MMP—most of them under stable, multiparty and minority governments. MMP has resulted in less extreme policies. The old gender and racial imbalances in parliament have gone. So has the electoral inequity of the past, where a vote in the low-40s could deliver government to a single party.[3]

Today, New Zealand has one of the world's most responsive electoral systems. The number of parties in parliament has increased from two or three to seven or eight. Politics is less divisive.

Neither chaos, catastrophe nor economic ruin resulted from MMP—though had New Zealanders been able to manage their own referendum process, it would have been achieved earlier, cheaper and less divisively.

Chapter 48
Dealing with anti-democratic roadblocks

One reason people insist you use the proper channels to change things is because they have control of the proper channels and they're confident it won't work.[1]

— British Journalist Jon Stone

As we saw in Part Five, most nations don't let the people amend the constitution. This includes 'democratic' ones that require congressional majorities as high as three-fourths.[2]

In the United States, under Article V of the Constitution, an amendment must be *proposed* by two-thirds of both houses—or two-thirds of states (via their legislatures, not the people). Thereafter, it must be *passed* by an even larger super-majority—three-quarters of states. (Again, legislatures only.)

Provisions this undemocratic will sometimes make amendment all but impossible. They should be quashable by a majority of voters via an *assertion of authority* (below).

Section 21 (3) of the Universal Declaration of Human Rights reads:

The will of the people shall be the basis of the authority of government; this will shall be expressed in periodic and genuine elections...[3]

The Declaration has been translated into 530 languages—the most of any document in history. Since it was adopted by the nations of the UN General Assembly in 1948, it has been incorporated into laws and treaties around the world. At least 90 national constitutions are inspired by it, or reproduce elements of it.

Fig. 8.3: Eleanor Roosevelt, chair of its drafting committee, holds a copy of the Universal Declaration of Human Rights, 1949.

Another landmark document, the International Covenant on Civil and Political Rights of 1976, has been joined by the majority of nations (167). The Covenant is seen as more legally binding than the Declaration, as it commits its state parties to civil and political rights for individuals, including electoral rights.[4]

The Covenant's Article 25 (b) gives each citizen 'the right and opportunity'

To vote and to be elected at genuine periodic elections which shall be by universal and equal suffrage and shall be held by secret ballot, guaranteeing the free expression of the will of the electors.

The *assertion of authority* encapsulates several of the rights spelled out in the Declaration and the Covenant—including this one. Like them, it arises from *natural law*: law based on intrinsic human values and the age-old *mōres* of society. (There are few *mōres* that are more age-old than equality, which goes back hundreds of millennia.)

Natural law was invoked in abolishing the divine right of kings. It underpins the Declaration of Independence. In the words of the US National Center for Constitutional Studies, it is 'the ultimate source of constitutional law'.[5]

In 1950, Professor Edward Corwin, Constitutional advisor to the US Attorney General, wrote:

Natural Law is entitled by its intrinsic excellence to prevail over any law which rests solely on human authority.[6]

The *assertion* is a legal concept that undergirds specific acts to undo the capture of governance. The principal such acts would be forming citizen assemblies, and holding referendums, in pursuit of democratization. Thus, where irrational roadblocks stand between a populace and its freedom, that populace should constitute itself as an electorate and do both.

This is consistent with much legal thinking, modern and ancient. Scholars have argued, for example, that Article V in the US Constitution is merely the means for *government* to alter the Constitution—and that the Declaration of Independence establishes 'the Right of the People to alter or to abolish' their government as they see fit. Indeed, the Declaration describes this right as 'unalienable'.

In his revolutionary writings, Alexander Hamilton repeatedly cites the people's right to throw off an unjust regime under 'the laws of nature'.[7] James Wilson, chief designer of the executive branch—who signed both the Declaration and the Constitution—believed that 'the people may change [their] constitutions whenever and however they please' because 'in our governments, the supreme, absolute, and uncontrollable power remains with the people'.[8]

Under New Hampshire's Bill of Rights,

> whenever the ends of government are perverted, and public liberty manifestly endangered, and all other means of redress are ineffectual, the people may, and of right ought to reform the old, or establish a new government. The doctrine of nonresistance against arbitrary power, and oppression, is absurd, slavish, and destructive of the good and happiness of mankind.[9]

In his article *The Consent of the Governed: Constitutional Amendment Outside Article V*, Professor Akhil Reed Amar of Yale University argues that the US Constitution begins with the words *We the People of the United States...do ordain and establish this Constitution*—and that these words say it all.[10]

Fig. 8.4: First three words of the US Constitution

Democracy was founded on this premise. The Greek Classical era began when the people banded together, expelled a tyrant, and formed an Assembly. Thereafter, the citizen body could alter its law-making methods, and its own powers, at will.

When significant power shifted from Assembly to courts in the 4th Century, it was the citizens who made the change. The need to shape their institutions—and not merely to work within them—was keenly appreciated by the first democrats.

The *assertion* protects against coups and anarchy by specifying a fairly conducted vote, and a clear majority, before change can occur.

423

A government or high court that attempted to veto the result might expect widescale protest—perhaps civil service strikes, military desertions, boycotts and demonstrations.

In proclaiming the Declaration of Independence, the American colonists repealed—off their own bat—the British law that had governed them to that moment. The same right was exercised by the English parliament itself in the previous century, when it issued a Declaration of Rights to depose James II.[11]

If these minority declarations are still viewed as legitimate, majorities of the entire people should be unassailable.

Fig. 8.5: 'The unanimous Declaration of the 13 united States of America'— the Declaration of Independence—is presented to the Continental Congress by its drafting committee in July 1776. In the eyes of the British king & government, the Congress was illegal, & its members were a 'desperate conspiracy'. The 'united States' were colonies that remained 'subordinate' to Britain. Their people were British subjects. The rebellion's leaders had committed 'treason'. 'Independency' was null & void. None of this prevented the birth of the new nation.

Chapter 49
The Democracy Commission

Third draft democracy is implemented, and the provisions of the Bill of Change overseen, by the Democracy Commission—established in the Bill's Article V.

The Commission is neither government nor private. Legally, it's a little like a *commons*. Its establishment does not rely on founding fathers, nor its existence on parliaments. It's a *demotic institution*:

- Established by the people
- Directly elected by the people
- Responsible only to the people

Like South Korea's National Election Commission (NEC), it is established in the constitution as 'equal in status' with the government, the legislature and the high court.[1]

(South Korea's NEC manages referendums, along with parliamentary, presidential, intra-party, recall and even school elections. It offers civic education to everyone from serving politicians to schoolchildren. Its mission is 'to actively lead democratization'.)

The Democracy Commission forms a kind of 'watchdog' government: though in the sphere of governance only—not in spheres such as foreign policy or budgeting. This concept of a 'watchdog' goes back to Sparta, where administrators, the *ephors*, were appointed to monitor kings. The Commission's budget—say, 0.1% of national expenditure—is constitutionally mandated.

The Commission enforces the decisions of the Article III institutions, such as deliberations and referendums. It co-ordinates media de-capping, Decontamination and the development of the new civics curriculum—most often by farming out the work to citizen deliberations.

On occasions, the Commission will help a jurisdiction get up to speed on a third draft reform—for example, by designing a vote-by-mail system for it, or advising on how to phase out voting machines.

The Commission is the repository of the third draft knowledge base.

Each component of third draft democracy is effectively a field experiment, so another part of the Commission's job will be to monitor and evaluate how well these components are succeeding.

Whilst this may sound like another large bureaucracy, much of the load will be shouldered by the deliberations.

Keeping a lid on Commission bureaucracy should be a crucial goal. Conservatives, deficit hawks, libertarians and others will abandon the third draft project if it turns into a byzantine mess. (A long section on keeping the Commission's bureaucracy under control was omitted here for space reasons; I'll put it on the book's website.)

The Commission exists because, without *the means to implement*, the best paper reforms would come to nothing. This was illustrated in 2010, when Kenyans enthusiastically enacted a new constitution—ushering in the nation's 'second republic'.

Despite the dramatic on-paper changes, the second republic soon developed an uncanny resemblance to the first:

- The new constitution did indeed devolve power down to the nation's counties—but the resources needed to implement their decisions remained with the national government.

- The people were indeed given the right to recall poorly performing MPs—but the MPs themselves chose when that right could be exercised.

The new constitution contained many other pleasing reforms. The political class retained the power to ensure that they were never put into effect.

To the dismay of Kenyans, those politicians who'd avidly supported reform in opposition dropped it on entering government—including two consecutive presidents.[2]

It's for such reasons that, under the third draft, certain vital powers are not in the hands of government—for example the powers

- to implement or manage the third draft reforms
- to manage elections, or appoint the people who do
- to amend the constitution

A directly elected, popularly monitored Commission should put society on the path to restoring trust in institutions. This is inescapable if democracy is not to disappear. Francis Fukuyama wrote:

> The inability to agree on the most basic facts is the direct product of an across-the-board assault on democratic institutions—in the US, in Britain, and around the world. And this is where the democracies are headed for trouble…
>
> The belief in the corruptibility of all institutions leads to a dead end of universal distrust. American democracy, all democracy, will not survive a lack of belief in the possibility of impartial institutions.[3]

Chapter 50
Cost savings from the Bill of Change

The costs associated with amateurs spending part of their productive energies on the business of governance (loss of productivity in the nongovernment sector, steep learning curves) were more than made up for by the benefits that arose from the assurance that the incentives of decision-making bodies were aligned with those of the citizen population.[1]

— Historian Josiah Ober, on the Greek democratic city-states

The Bill should reduce public spending significantly.

As some of the legislative burden shifts to deliberations, we should see less of some things: late-night sittings in near-empty chambers; acrimonious point-scoring debates; bills vetoed to score a win over the opposition; back-scratching deals between parties over government jobs…

But the costs of running a government are only the tip if the iceberg. The big savings will be downstream.

Firstly, government will become transparent—and when something becomes transparent, costs melt away. More importantly again, the public will be in control of how its money is spent.

Presently, the incentives for government overlap the public interest at times—and at times they don't. When they don't—as when governments order hundreds of billions of dollars in faulty jet fighters (the United States[2]), or incur billions of pounds in cost over-runs for aircraft carriers (Britain[3])—the public can pay through the nose. Such problems will end only when the public itself defines the public interest, and monitors it.

A system obligated to wealth has large structural inefficiencies —a rigged economy that significantly lowers the income of the average citizen. (We look at the data behind that claim in the final part, Part Ten.) Ordinary people are much poorer because so much of the economy's 'cream' is diverted to the cronies of the major parties.

With politics decontaminated, and information untethered from corporate earnings targets, the costs of third draft democracy are likely to be recouped many times over. The savings will mostly be Null Corner items—'things that no longer occur'. Some events that reshaped our world over the last generation may give us an idea of their magnitude:

- The War on Terror has probably cost the world public $6 trillion.

- It also displaced between 37 and 59 million people, many of whom subsequently swarmed across borders —including Western borders.[4]

- During the Global Financial Crisis, US household net worth fell by $19 trillion.[5] In the US alone, GDP dropped by an estimated $2.6 trillion, and 'programs and bailouts' cost $23 trillion.[6]

- Sixty-four countries went into recession in the wake of the GFC.

- From 2000 to 2018, US corporations received $1.8

trillion in taxpayer funding ('contracts, grants, loans, direct payments and farm subsidies').[7]

- During the pandemic, the wealth of the world's billionaires increased by $5.5 trillion (or 68%) to July 2021.[8]

- S&P 500 companies spent $2 trillion on stock buybacks in the three years before the pandemic—about the value of their subsequent bailouts. The airlines, for example, spent $44 billion on buybacks, and then required a bailout of $50 billion.[9]

- The world's largest companies have caused environmental damage that would cost them $2 trillion, were they required to pay for it.

- Fossil fuel subsidies worldwide are worth $4.9 trillion.

- Parked in the world's tax havens is another $21 to $36 trillion.[10]

The total of these taxpayer losses and plutocratic gains is unknowable, though it would probably exceed 2023's Gross World Product of $105 trillion.[11]

Chapter 51
How much time will third draft democracy cost us?

M aking all kinds of things mandatory is a way to ensure people will not want to do them. Participation needs to come from the heart. For most, it's likely to kick in when the system bears its first fruit. In the meantime:

Article I (Decontamination) requires making a financial pledge each election cycle.

With **Article II** (Isegoria), it's an annual pledge to the media outlet of your choice.

Each of these probably requires less time than completing a crossword.

Article III might require voting on initiatives (say) two to five times a year. On the other hand, it returns the time it once took to:

organize ID
register
travel to and from a polling station
queue
vote

For a small minority of citizens annually, there will be a

compensated gig in a deliberative assembly that may take a day, several days, or (for big issues) some weeks.

Learning the democratic arts—**Article IV**—forms part of existing curriculums, and so makes for little extra time or inconvenience. In any given year, the majority of the population is not enrolled.

For the transformation of society, these are not large sacrifices.

Chapter 52
Homeostasis

T he purpose of a fresh draft of the democratic experiment is not just to improve democracy, but to make sure it continues. According to *The Economist*:

The 2013 Pew Survey of Global Attitudes showed that 85% of Chinese were 'very satisfied' with their country's direction, compared with 31% of Americans...

And why should developing countries regard democracy as the ideal form of government when the American government cannot even pass a budget, let alone plan for the future? Why should autocrats listen to lectures on democracy from Europe, when the euro-elite sacks elected leaders who get in the way of fiscal orthodoxy?[1]

Critics of democracy, from Plato to Nietzsche, target either its 'inevitable' capture by sectional interests, or the incapacity of the masses to rule themselves.

If these things were ever true, they are not true now. We possess the tools to translate the wishes of vast numbers into coherent policy: and to transform people from passive economic units into informed citizens who shape their society.

A more fluid, horizontal and 'connected' model of human organization is taking root in activism, journalism, entrepreneurship, social media, science, sport—even book publishing and organized religion. A final bastion of the bad old ways is politics: still governed by rigid hierarchies, guided from the shadows by vested interests, and not subject to the creative destruction of the free market in ideas.

That bastion will have to fall sooner or later, as did the monarchies, theocracies and command economies of the past. The choice is whether to shape the change, or have it shaped for us by corporations and alienated mobs.

There are many environmental, economic and political reforms on offer that are desirable in themselves. But they tend to beget *ad hoc* campaigns, which atomize protest by their variety. A petition, demonstration or website—an activist group or movement—a protest against a tax, polluter or war—addresses one wrong at a time.

A suite of constitutional reforms is more efficient:

Firstly, being upstream of these issues, it won't so much cure problems as prevent them.

Secondly, it's a *type* of change and a *vehicle* for change in one. The Bill is not only a proposal, but the mechanism by which the proposal is realized.

Thirdly, the Bill is proactive and positive, rather than reactive and negative. It doesn't denounce the evil at hand—it replaces it.

Fourthly, in place of the protests and patch-ups now occurring all over the map, the third draft is one campaign. Where single-issue movements attract thousands, it may—when its potential is understood—attract millions.

There is a single Bill and a single referendum day. All being well, this yields a political system that is capable of responding to our crises—not to one, two or three, but the entire series.

Constitutional reform may appear dull compared to chaining yourself to a tree or dumping tea outside the Capitol. But this single exercise will produce a wider array of benefits than any number of individual campaigns. It much enhances your chance of saving that tree.

Homeostasis

Our body politic doesn't require radical medicine—it requires homeostasis. Democracy was invented, and reinvented, to remove the distortions of state capture by the few—to allow a society to accurately self-correct. All its sub-items—universal franchise, human rights, rule of law—proceed outward from that core. Democracy is the subtraction of special interests from governance.

Part Nine

Strategy

Chapter 53
Society is ready for wholesale change

In 1768, the Massachusetts assembly formally renounced 'the most distant thought' of independence—stating that the colonies

would refuse it if offered to them, and would even deem it the greatest misfortune to be obliged to accept it.[1]

Within five years, Massachusetts had experienced the Boston Massacre and the Boston Tea Party—two triggers of the American Revolution—and became the most radical of the colonial assemblies.

We appear to be well past our 1768 moment. A change of political system is no longer the province of conspiracists and extremists; of utopians and the young; of late nights and altered states.

Political tribalization is making societies harder to manage. Confidence in institutions—including organized religion, newspapers and banks—is in seemingly unstoppable decline.[2] This has brought a new openness to the idea of structural reform—of changing the game.

Below are eleven reasons I believe society is ready for a fresh draft of the democratic ideal.

1. Democracy naturally expands

Democracy has never been static. From the first, growth has been integral to it. In Athens, the people's institutions expanded right through the 6th and 5th Centuries—through the eras of Solon, Cleisthenes, Ephialtes and Pericles. A new set of innovations arrived in the 4th Century, as direct democracy ceded ground to deliberative.

The US Constitution written in 1787 was, in the words of constitutional law professor Noah Feldman, 'a complex political compromise grounded in perceived practical necessity, not moral clarity'.[3] For the nation to survive, he states, the rules of the game had to evolve.

This occurred via such reforms as the Bill of Rights (1791), the abolition of slavery (1865), the expansion of voting (1870), the direct election of senators (1913), the women's franchise (1920) and the Voting Rights Act (1965).

Britain's uncodified constitution similarly advances, one piece of legislation at a time, in a slow enlargement of democracy: from Magna Carta in 1215 through to the Habeas Corpus Act of 1679, the Bill of Rights of 1689, the Great Reform Act of 1832 (extending the men's franchise) and the arrival of full women's suffrage in 1928.

For democracy to expand now would simply continue its age-old pattern.

2. Democracy is probably not in an historic reversal

Steven Pinker's 2018 book *Enlightenment Now* described in exacting detail the ways in which the world has improved in recent centuries. As the *New Statesman* summarized it:

> In the last 250 years, average global life expectancy has increased from 29 years to 71, wealth has risen 200-fold, the rate of

extreme poverty has fallen from 90 per cent to 10 per cent (with half the decline in the past 35 years) and the number of people living in democracies has increased from 1 per cent to nearly two-thirds.[4]

Pinker has been challenged on numerous points, but it would be churlish to argue that his broad view is wrong. Few today would exchange what we have for 15th Century governance, 14th Century mortality rates, or 13th Century dentistry.

That's our 'long cycle'. But the fifty-year cycle—the medium-term—yields some disquiet. Whilst the global birth rate continues to fall, and smallpox is gone, environmental stability, family cohesion and the average worker's share of productivity, are all going in the wrong direction. Inequality is rising steadily.[5] In 2022-24, there were several veiled threats, from both sides, to use nuclear weapons over Ukraine.[6] Trust in political institutions—in most institutions—is dead in the water.

If this were the technical analysis of markets, this latter pattern might be called a 'medium-term retracement', and the first a 'secular uptrend'.

Things are objectively dismal in the democratic realm—and in many realms downstream. But stepping back from the medium-term does reveal the longer-term timescale, in which democratization—and such factors as literacy, health and longevity—have expanded for two centuries.

This leaves us room for some *secular optimism.*

Political scientist Samuel Huntington wrote that we have seen three global waves of democratization since the 19th Century—with a third wave beginning in 1974, and still in train when Huntington was writing in the early 1990s.[7] Each of the first two waves was followed by a reversal—but then the upward trend resumed.

In 1999, another political scientist, Larry Diamond, predicted that the third wave, too, would see its reversal.[8] As we now know, Diamond was right.

But we also know to keep our eye on those resuming uptrends. Whilst today's democratic downturn threatens democracy's survival, it is also provoking the kind of universal discontent that usually precedes reform.

3. Practical necessity

The present-day government of the United States is in some ways comparable to the frozen-up administration of the 1780s, when the Continental Congress was bound by the restrictive Articles of Confederation.[9] Struggling to raise funds, Congress was unable to pay off its revolutionary war debt, deal with civil unrest, manage trade, or even defend against enemies. Leaders such as Washington and Madison realized that this was an existential crisis. Under these arrangements, the union wouldn't continue.

The new constitution of 1787 was the result.

Now, once again, the old rules have been overtaken by social evolution, to create dysfunction and stasis. Citizens and leaders, from left and right, perceive that competent governance will remain very hard to achieve under the present formula.

4. In polarized times, comprehensive change offers stability

Sometimes, root-and-branch reform appears to be too much for the public to support: only smaller reforms seem politically possible. We don't appear to be in those times.

As the research outfit *More In Common* discovered:

> America's political landscape is much more complicated than the binary split between liberals and conservatives often depicted in the national conversation.[10]

Only very small numbers (they report) are deeply committed to the liberal or conservative cause. The public is fatigued by polarization—is ready to be flexible. Moreover, the researchers identified what they call the 'Exhausted Majority'—diverse in policy views, but in full agreement on one thing:

They overwhelmingly believe that the American government is rigged to serve the rich and influential, and they want things to change.[11]

Surveys by *More in Common* identified similar trends in France, Germany, the Netherlands, Italy and Greece.[12]

In times like our own, broadscale change becomes possible via its capacity to animate jaded electorates.

5. People want an end to extremism

> When I first met him, he was like a tired stray dog looking for a master.
>
> — Karl Mayr, Adolf Hitler's superior in the Great War

Extremism has its taproot in disempowerment—and the causes of disempowerment have now become plain enough.

The alternative to any form of totalism is the expansion of democracy. Inclusion and fairness confine the Trotskys and Hitlers to the corners of public parks.

6. Third draft democracy is proactive, concrete and simple

Proactive

The lawgiver who put us on the road to democracy may also have been the world's first protestor. When, after three decades, his constitution was overthrown by a tyrant, the elderly Solon went to the *agora*, and begged everyone he found to resist. People were frightened, and no-one listened. According to Plutarch, Solon went home, armed himself, and 'took his post in the street outside his door'.[13]

We owe a great deal to protest. It's a bit like democracy's 'twin'.

Its only deficit is that it is reactive: it's always shaped by what someone else is doing. To translate demonstrations and campaigns into a better world, the other 'twin' must manifest. The Bill of Change spells out what its proponents are for, not what they're against.

Concrete

Countless uprisings, such as the Egyptian Spring of 2011, lacked an agreed, written program, and went down in history as noble failures. Like many of their predecessors, Egypt's revolutionaries did not lack in courage or commitment—but they were vague about what they wanted, apart from the departure of President Mubarak. Once he was gone, the Islamists—who were very clear about what they wanted—stepped in to fill the vacuum.

This 'agendalessness' is a hallmark of the 21st Century's failed revolutions.

So, as well as being proactive, a draft constitution is an antidote to the imprecision of mere principles. It specifies what change will occur, and when, and how. It can be read, copied, uploaded and cited. It exists to be enacted.

Simple

Third draft democracy doesn't fix potholes, save farmers, stop foreign wars or cut government debt. It's the cornucopia, not the fruit. It sets aside downstream problems—but provides institutions by which they can be solved. It's a simple device for wrangling complexity.

7. Radical change is occurring anyway

They call it 'the whole-of-society counter-disinformation framework'. The 'whole-of-society' refers to four categories of institutions that are joined in a co-operative censorship network. Those are government institutions, private sector institutions, civil society institutions, and media and fact-checking organizations. They have all this stuff drawn up on charts…

Basically, every federal agency does its part—whether that's through censorship funding, censorship policy coordination, censorship outsourcing, or censorship direct pressure like the FBI was doing…

They organized a 'whole-of-society framework' to onboard the bluechip companies, to onboard for-profit censorship mercenary firms, to onboard US universities to do 'misinformation research' and mass flagging campaigns. They fund the fact-checking orgs. Poynter, the largest fact-checking group in the entire Universe, got something like 25 State Department grants in the last year.[14]

— Mike Benz, former State Department official
specializing in information technology (2023)

In many democracies, most pointedly the United States, the constitution is being bypassed by executive decree, sidelined by congressional gridlock, undermined by censorship arrangements like the above, and radically reinterpreted via judicial activism.

This upsets the argument that constitutional change is risky. Extensive constitutional change is occurring already.

8. Crises yield reform

It's axiomatic that wars, pandemics, depressions and other crises make for social and political change. The Great Depression, which ushered in the New Deal, might serve as the archetype.

These days, crises that disrupt everyday life seem to be landing fairly regularly.

During the COVID Recession, the Canadian unemployment rate hit 13.7%,[15] and 600,000 Brazilian small businesses went broke—with nine million people laid off.[16] In the US, unemployment reached an historical high.[17]

Most countries and sectors saw large downturns: Ethiopia's flower trade,[18] Argentina's agro-exports,[19] Bangladesh's garment industry,[20] Singapore's aviation sector,[21] Britain's banks…[22]

The pandemic also gave people the chance to reflect on the lives they'd been living, and the society they lived them in. Few liked what they saw.

In 2020, the global average for those who were 'engaged' at work came in at 20%.[23] Almost no-one in Britain wanted to 'return to normal' post-COVID,[24] and forty-three percent of employed Americans re-evaluated their career paths.[25]

In a 2020 global poll of 21,000 people, 86% said that, when the pandemic ended, they 'would prefer to see the world change significantly—and become more sustainable and equitable—rather than revert to the status quo ante'.[26]

COVID was one of several global crises in a single generation. Historically, crises—especially in multiples—cause societies to make sea changes.

9. Public opinion is behind change

Just as anxiety is best beaten when you are anxious, depression when you are depressed, and temptation when you are tempted, plutocracy is most easily countered when its symptoms are all over the body politic.

Because plutocratic rule has never been more obvious, for ordinary people the case for wholesale reform has never been stronger.

In a survey of all the democracies in 2020, Pew polling found: 'Globally, people are more dissatisfied than satisfied with the way democracy is working.'[27] In 2020, researchers at Cambridge University found that 55.5% globally were dissatisfied with democracy—a rise of 19 points in 15 years:

As a result, many large democracies are at their highest-ever recorded level for democratic dissatisfaction.[28]

In Australia, satisfaction with 'how democracy works' halved in the eleven years from 2007 to 2018.[29] Americans remain democrats, but two-thirds are ready for 'significant change' to the 'design and structure' of government.[30] A European survey found that

> while Europeans across the continent share a powerful faith in democracy, they think their countries are lacking some of its most fundamental components.[31]

The pattern, in the procedural democracies, is trust in the democratic ideal and disappointment in the democratic reality. There is immense dissatisfaction—but no coherent plan for change. In the disorderly, reactive interregnum we are in, people everywhere are electing candidates because they have never before been in politics, or have promised to blow up the system.

10. The elements of third draft democracy have public support

There is not only a general readiness for change. People tend to favor the specific components of third draft democracy.

Article I: Decontamination:

Vast majorities in the United States think money has too much influence on politics, and want root-and-branch reform of the campaign finance system.[32] The public overwhelmingly rejects the logic of the Supreme Court 'Citizens United' ruling that political contributions are free speech.[33]

In a survey of complaints about Washington's elected officials, top of the list was: 'Influenced by special interest money'.[34]

In October 2021, Britons overwhelmingly supported democracy—but agreed that in its present form 'British democracy is rigged to serve the rich and influential'.[35]

Article II: Isegoria:

Most Americans, Republican and Democrat, have lost trust in the media.[36] In one recent study, only six percent had 'a great deal of trust in the press'.[37] In another, trust had fallen to an 'historical low'.[38] In a third, it had taken 'its deepest dive yet'.[39]

Worldwide, trust in media has likewise been declining steadily.[40] According to the 2021 Edelman Trust Barometer, 59% globally believed that 'most news organizations are more concerned with supporting an ideology or political position than with informing the public'.[41]

'Trust in all information sources,' Edelman noted—traditional media, social media, even search engines—is 'at record lows.'

Article III: Renovating the democratic machinery:

Surveys suggest there would be major support for reforming the entire political structure—and for direct and deliberative democracy specifically:

Across 34 countries, nearly two-thirds of people believe elected elites 'do not care what people like them think', and over half are dissatisfied with the way democracy is working.[42]

Most Americans—conservative and liberal—believe 'ordinary Americans would do a better job solving the country's problems than elected officials'.

The public believes elected officials in Washington are not much different from typical Americans in terms of their intelligence and work ethic—but are less honest, less patriotic, and more selfish.

Under the present electoral system, both sides of US politics see their side as 'losing'.

Fifty-nine percent of Americans say government needs 'very major reform'.[43]

Percentage-wise, support for **direct democracy** is in the 70s in the US and Britain; in some European nations it's in the 80s. Germans much prefer it to representative government.[44]

Over several years, **proportional representation** has found support from about 70% of Canadians.[45] New Zealanders voted twice to introduce it, and once more to retain it.[46] The majority of Americans would like Congress to be elected via ranked choice voting, a form of **preferential voting**.[47]

Universal Vote By Mail is popular in every US state that has introduced it, as seen in the large increases in turnout. British voter turnout also increased markedly when mail voting was trialled.[48]

And to pick the most well-known **voter suppression** reform: solid majorities of Americans want ex-felons to be re-enfranchised.[49]

Article IV: Teaching the democratic arts:

There's not much polling on civics, but the US Civics Education Initiative—a measure to teach civics to high school students—has the support of 84% of Republicans, 68% of Democrats, and large majorities in all ethnic groups.[50]

Ninety-three percent of Americans support citizenship education in schools. However they don't think present efforts are at all useful: 'The public gave an average grade of B-/C to their own civics instruction and an F to their perception of the job the nation's schools are doing in educating the next generation of citizens.'[51]

Overall:

In 2019, just before COVID, the Edelman Trust Barometer surveyed 28 major nations, to find that

> the world is united on one front—all share an urgent desire for change. Only one in five feels that the system is working for them, with nearly half of the mass population believing that the system is failing them.[52]

Its president, Richard Edelman, commented:

The past two decades have seen a progressive destruction of trust in societal institutions... Traditional power elite figures, such as CEOs and heads of state, have been discredited. The growth of social media platforms fully shifted people's trust from a top-down orientation to a horizontal one in favor of peers or experts.[53]

Two years later, in 2021, the Barometer revealed

an epidemic of misinformation and widespread mistrust of societal institutions and leaders around the world. Adding to this is a failing trust ecosystem unable to confront the rampant infodemic, leaving the four institutions [that it sought people's opinions on]—business, government, NGOs and media—in an environment of information bankruptcy and a mandate to rebuild trust and chart a new path forward.[54]

In short: Wherever the measures that make up Articles I, II, III and IV have been surveyed, they've drawn strong public support. Bad governance and bad information loom large in people's minds across the planet.

If ever there were a vacuum waiting to be filled, it is this.

11. Plutocratic confidence is waning

Their prerogative being thus reduced within reasonable bounds, the Spartan kings were at once freed from all further jealousies and consequent danger, and never experienced the calamities of their neighbors at Messene and Argos, who, by maintaining their prerogative too strictly for want of yielding a little to the populace, lost it all.[55]

— Plutarch's *Life of Lycurgus*

Plutocracy rests on a morality that's been denounced by religions and social codes since the beginnings of written history. It is unsurprising that the roots of plutocratic self-doubt run deep.

This is especially so in industries that most easily get their way with government—where advancement flows not from merit but nefarious influence.

There's an epidemic of drug and alcohol abuse among Wall Street traders—often brought on by the depression and dissociation caused by long work hours.[56] Silicon Valley is replete with people whose attention spans, and family lives, have fallen victim to their own killer apps (Part Four).

In 2011, the late anthropologist David Graeber observed that the information desk at the Occupy protest in New York's financial district saw a steady stream of 'young Wall Street types' on six-figure incomes, confessing that they felt trapped in careers that were 'not doing the world any good'. Graeber noted that most of the corporate lawyers and lobbyists he knew did not believe their industry needed to exist.[57]

Looked at through the morals of any previous human era—Paleolithic, Neolithic, Classical, Medieval—today's market fundamentalism is legitimized *avaritia,* or greed.

These are three of the observations made by journalist Deborah Copaken when she attended the 30-year reunion of her Harvard class:

- Every classmate who became a teacher or doctor seemed happy with the choice of career.

- Many lawyers seemed either unhappy or itching for a change (with the exception of those who became law professors).

- Nearly every banker or fund manager wanted to find a way to use their accrued wealth to give back, and many seemed to want to leave Wall Street as soon as possible to take up some sort of art.[58]

The doubt harbored by plutocrats about plutocracy goes beyond the fear of spiritual insolvency. Many are uneasy about the deep inequality that their annexation of government has wrought.

Multi-billionaire Nick Hanauer is no bad forecaster of social trends. (He once invested a large sum with an acquaintance, Jeff Bezos, to found a 'tiny start-up bookseller'.) In a 2014 magazine article, Hanauer addressed his 'fellow .01%ers':

> What sets me apart, I think, is a tolerance for risk and an intuition about what will happen in the future. Seeing where things are headed is the essence of entrepreneurship. And what do I see in our future now?
>
> I see pitchforks.
>
> What everyone wants to believe is that when things reach a tipping point and go from being merely crappy for the masses to dangerous and socially destabilizing, that we're somehow going to know about that shift ahead of time. Any student of history knows that's not the way it happens. Revolutions, like bankruptcies, come gradually, and then suddenly. One day, somebody sets himself on fire, then thousands of people are in the streets, and before you know it, the country is burning. And then there's no time for us to get to the airport and jump on our Gulfstream Vs and fly to New Zealand. That's the way it always happens. If inequality keeps rising as it has been, eventually it will happen. We will not be able to predict when, and it will be terrible—for everybody. But especially for us.[59]

Just as patriarchy is bad for men and racism is bad for racists, it may be that plutocracy bad for plutocrats.

The political life may also be bad for politicians. It often leads to worry, strain, fatigue and sleep difficulty.[60] Representatives can find the formalistic grind a high price to pay for having an impact. 'Parliament,' Bob Hawke told me in 1982—the year before he became Australia's prime minister—'is a pain in the arse.'

It's no exaggeration to say that all three of America's 'Indochina War' presidents—Kennedy, Johnson and Nixon—were tortured by doubts over their prosecution of that war. Riding roughshod over these doubts (rather than seeing where they took them) led them, variously, to moodiness, tantrums, sleepless nights, and the terror of triggering a nuclear war.[61]

For most ex-politicians interviewed in a 2017 British study, *leaving* office had also been dislocating. Many described life after politics with words like 'bleakness' and 'depression'.[62]

In *Adults in the Room*, his memoir of the Greek crisis of 2015, the country's then-finance minister Yanis Varoufakis vividly conveys not only the facts and figures of the crisis—but the spell under which Greece's plutocratic enemies had been cast. In imposing austerity on Greece, Europe's leaders and technocrats simply did what a poorly designed union, and the bankers who ultimately controlled it, compelled them to. They didn't especially like it: some even confessed it wasn't right. But they lacked individual agency.

Some members of the global elite do appear to grasp that our present political-economic arrangement, and its media spruikers, create a feedback loop that, in time, collapses the human and social 'externalities' on which that system depends.

Tucker Carlson—conservative news host and self-described patriot, whose father was the director of Voice of America and a US ambassador—said in 2022:

> You can have a system with some lying in it. All systems do. We all lie if we're pushed—I get it. I try not to be too judgmental about it. But you can't have a system *based on* lying. If a system is based on lying, that's a foundation of sand. It will not continue much longer. That's how I feel about our system. And by 'our system' I mean our political system, our financial system, and our foreign policy assumptions. They are not rooted in reality. They're not wise. And no-one can defend them in clear, non-hysterical language.[63]

Some epic studies of social stability across the millennia find that a key element in successful revolutions is a splintering of the elite.[64]

Such a split occurred in Finland during the 1930s, when an armed blackshirt movement, which had the sympathy of the president and prime minister, was blocked from a takeover by army officers. Judges dealt harshly with the insurrectionaries.

Likewise, in Columbia in 2010, Alvaro Uribe's attempts to secure himself a life presidency were blocked by the constitutional court. In Sri Lanka in 2015, the kleptocratic Rajapaksa regime was stopped from reversing an election result by army and police commanders, and the attorney general.

These reversals were a result of ministers, judges, electoral officials, and senior police and military figures being able to turn against the regime for one reason: they had strong public support.[65]

One tactic in the Bill campaign is likely to be the families of regime insiders persuading those insiders to undermine attacks on the emerging democracy—for example through whistleblowing. Such regime turncoats might include ministers, bureaucrats, intelligence agents, military officers, journalists and think tank analysts.

Intra-regime dissent has a long history. In Cambodia, teams that today locate American UXO—unexploded ordnance—report that about every third bomb had been disabled in the factory. The forest around Prey Trolach, a Cambodian village where I worked in the 2010s,[66] has dozens of craters from American bombs which *did* explode. The village would have been as easy target—but the bombs, older villagers recall, were dropped all around it: not on it.

Intra-establishment dissent at a high level was evident in 2021, when former US officials divulged secret discussions on abducting Julian Assange from London's Ecuadorian Embassy—and on assassinating him—to Yahoo News. One scenario involved a gun battle on the streets of London with the Russian agents that the CIA believed would appear to rescue Assange.

The actions against Assange were launched under Barack Obama and scaled up under Donald Trump. They escalated after 2017's *Vault 7* data leak to WikiLeaks, which contained the CIA's code for 500 malware apps. These apps gave the Agency the capability to surveil most users of operating systems, web browsers and smart phones worldwide—nearly all of us.[67]

The code was leaked by a CIA employee apparently incensed by US foreign policy.[68]

The disclosures on the government's war on Assange came from more than 30 former national security officials: men and women from the CIA, the National Security Agency, and the Obama and Trump White Houses.

This is not a picture of a unified national security structure.[69]

One of the most famous elite splits occurred in 1986 when Filipinos removed the Marcos dictatorship. The conservative Catholic archbishop, Jaime Sin, backed Marcos' challenger, Corazon Aquino—contrary to instructions from the Vatican.[70] Disobeying the orders of military HQ, the 15th Strike Wing refused to fire on protestors—and instead joined them. Army defectors captured a TV station and broadcast 'people power' messages. A rebellious supreme court judge swore in Aquino as president, even before Marcos had resigned. All these actions were made possible by the presence on the streets of crowds of one and two million.

Fig. 9.1: Corazon Aquino is sworn in as President of the Philippines, February 1986

Today's 1%, and their loyalists, are better exposed to the thoughts of ordinary people than were the courts of Xerxes or King John. It may be sinking in that devastating the Earth will destroy their future as well—that they're the first-class passengers on the *Titanic*. Reformers might get more support from them than they expect.

Chapter 54
The campaign

The conceit that the United States can be saved by Washington insiders and the Constitution is part of a common narrative about the origins of American institutions. According to this narrative, Americans owe their democracy and freedoms to founders' brilliant, foresighted design of a system with the right types of checks and balances, separation of powers, and other safeguards.

As we explain in our book, this is not how democratic institutions and freedoms come about. Rather, they emerge and are protected by society's mobilization, its assertiveness, and its willingness to use the ballot box when it can and the streets when it cannot.[1]

> — Daren Acemoglu and James A Robinson,
> authors of *The Narrow Corridor*

Work on all political tiers

Local

Where authorities won't play ball, local assemblies might start off on their own—like the 18th Century Americans and the 19th Century Swiss. At the least, that will create publicity, carry moral weight, and bring pressure to bear on mayors and councils. Over time, these assemblies can lay the ground for a change of system.

And where local authorities acquiesce: Assemblies could meet to (say) develop skate parks and fire roads, adjudicate on forest burn-offs, or make planning regulations people-friendly. They could refer major structural decisions—say, on election methodology—to local referendums. All this might get rolling well before the Bill of Change reaches the localities.

State

States and provinces tend to be more homogenous than the nation. They're generally more creative politically. For example, since 1787 there has never been a national constitutional convention in the US—but there have been 233 state ones.[2]

For those reasons, the Bill of Change may often make faster progress at the state level. If a state's populace is adventurous, as in the Australian state of Tasmania—or politically active, as in Minnesota, USA—it's likely to be early off the mark with a Bill of Change referendum. That will make it a proving ground for other states and the nation.

National

The national jurisdiction usually sees the most consequential political action.

It also much-affects the jurisdictions below it, and the international tier above. It won't necessarily be the first domino to fall, but it is probably the centre of attention in the third draft picture (at least till the public decides how far it wishes to go with subsidiarity).

International

Third draft democracy is not likely to properly internationalize till it's established at the national tier. In some cases, however, the international tier could come first.

For example, because the EU Parliament is elected via various forms of proportional voting (which better mirrors public opinion), a Bill of Change bloc might be elected to it even before the member nation democratizes. As the third draft should never be a political party (it's the system in which parties compete), the 'bloc' might be comprised of two or more parties and/or independents. They wouldn't necessarily have policies in common—just a commitment to democratize the EU.

Over time, regional organizations such as the Association of Southeast Asian Nations (ASEAN) and the Organization of American States, and international ones such as the UN, the OECD and the World Economic Forum, could adopt the Bill's principles, either as 'aspirations' for member states, or (in due course) as a requirement for membership.

As groups of neighboring nations democratize, linked third draft assemblies extending across their borders could (for instance) decontaminate regional organizations, and break up cross-border media monopolies.

International change tends to occur via *organic conquest*: the spreading of ideas through social media, trade, family links and travel. Protests against authoritarian rule in Gdansk in the 1980s, for example, spread throughout Poland, and eventually the entire communist bloc. No organization co-ordinated it.

Likewise, the Tunisian Revolution of 2011 spontaneously

diffused, in the form of the Arab Spring, to Libya, Egypt, Yemen, Syria and Iraq (as a revolution or major uprising), and to Morocco, Bahrain, Algeria, Iran, Lebanon, Jordan, Kuwait, Oman and Sudan (as large street protests).[3] Even the Occupy movement on the US east coast was partly inspired by the Arab Spring.

Occupy itself spread to 82 countries—as diverse as Armenia, Australia, Brazil, Britain, Colombia, Denmark, Germany, Hong Kong, Israel, Malaysia, Nepal and Nigeria.[4]

Both movements played a large role in putting inequality and the 'democratic deficit' on the global agenda. It is time to capitalize on that.

Chapter 55
Bringing the third draft to a non-democracy

The Arab Spring uprisings of 2011 were revolutions unprepared for power.

In Tunisia—the closest thing to an exception—some of the revolutionaries had been working on a new constitution since 2001. When the moment came—when the large crowds gathered—the factions buried their differences, and knuckled down to consultation and design. They established a popular assembly, with proportional representation.

Fatally, however, they chose a presidential system, and left too much power in the hands of the army. When a crisis came in 2021 —in the form of COVID, and a declining economy—most power was concentrated in the president. That allowed him to mount a *coup*, suspend parliament and arrest political opponents.

The exact chain of causation is noteworthy:

- *2014*: Tunisia chooses a presidential system.
- *Early 2021*: President refuses to ratify a law creating a constitutional court.
- *Later in 2021*: President's coup, dissolving parliament. No independent body exists to declare it illegal.[1]

The other Arab Spring countries did worse again. In Egypt, the military was allowed to steer the transition. At its insistence, half the legislature's seats were winner-takes-all. This shut out many women and secularists, and greatly exaggerated the Islamist vote.[2] And the Egyptians, too, stuck with a presidential system.

All this reduced the new constitution's survivability. An Islamist government was elected, and brought in a quasi-Islamist constitution which promoted the role of Shariah law.[3] The new president soon issued a declaration concentrating power in his own hands.[4] By 2013, this had brought enough discontent to allow the army to overthrow democracy.

The Egyptians did everything wrong: an army-brokered transition, an unproportional electoral system, a presidential regime.

A forerunner of these bungled transitions had occurred in Russia after the Iron Curtain fell. The Western powers delivered Russia a 'package' that contained not only presidential democracy but economic shock therapy. The imposition of privatization gave us the Russian oligarchs of today. The neoliberal package overall drove years of 'hyperinflation, austerity, depression, unemployment, corruption, and then ultranationalist reaction'.[5]

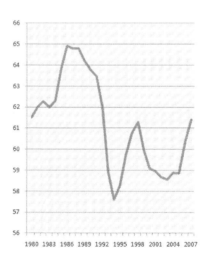

Fig. 9.2: Russian male life expectancy after the neoliberal 'reforms' of the late 1980s

Approval of the US among Russians went from 80% in 1990 to 32% in 1999. Thereafter, under Vladimir Putin, Russia neutered its democratic institutions, and began to actively undermine democracy in the West.

This list of mega-blunders suggests that when a sovereign people wishes to democratize, it should do so not via a foreign-imposed hybrid of economics and politics, but via existing, well-honed democratic tools (Parts Three to Six).

In *Twitter and Tear Gas*—her 2017 study of world protest movements over the previous decade—Zeynep Tufekci suggests that, whilst the 'horizontality' of modern movements is a strength during their protest phase, it can be a limitation later, when it comes to translating popular energies into policy decisions. A common pattern is a 'tactical freeze'—organizational paralysis—as the movement's ground troops confront those who have emerged as its 'leaders'.

'These others may challenge the de facto spokespersons,' Tufekci writes, 'but the movements have few means to resolve their issues or make decisions.'[6]

Thus, a movement is advantaged not only if it begins with a written constitutional goal, but if it uses the third draft decision-making machinery itself. That way, by referendum day, both a culture and an infrastructure of mass decision-making have taken shape.

'Cold democracy'—bringing democratic institutions to a society with little history of them—is undeniably uphill work. Burma, for example, has never had a Magna Carta, a Renaissance, an Enlightenment, an Industrial Revolution, a Scientific Revolution, or a women's revolution. Nonetheless, the yen for democracy is strong among ordinary Burmese. After the latest military coup, in 2021, much of the country joined its expanding civil war: pitting its despots against an increasingly broad and confident democratic resistance.

Even in the world's 'great authoritarian success story', a democratic transition is not unthinkable. A large portion of the Chinese intelligentsia embraced the democratic creed up till the Beijing Massacre of 1989. In that year, a million pro-democracy demonstrators took to the streets of the capital—not just students and intellectuals, but party cadres, soldiers and police.[7]

Fig. 9.3: Goddess of Democracy, Tiananmen Square, June 1989—made of plaster & foam by students from the Central Academy of Fine Arts. Soldiers sent to prevent its arrival in the square were blocked by Beijing residents. The statue attracted a crowd of 300,000, & stood for five days. It has been reproduced in bronze, epoxy, marble & fibreglass in cities around the world.

Critically, however, the reformists were disorganized. They split into squabbling factions; they differed on how to elect their leaders; they hadn't agreed on a reform program.[8] That weakened their ability to resist the might of the state.

Otherwise, the 1989 rebellion had most of the ingredients of success. It did not miscarry, for example, from lack of courage:

hundreds of protestors put their bodies in front of tanks, and hails of frangible bullets. Seeing the student carnage around Tiananmen Square, ordinary citizens poured onto the streets to attack the army with sticks and rocks.

Nor did it fail from a lack of discipline: when the crew of a personnel carrier that had run over student tents was captured, the crew was protected from those who wanted to beat them, and escorted away. Students who captured weapons in skirmishes with the army had them confiscated by their leaders.[9]

Neither did the 1989 rebellion lack in scale. Through April, May and early June, there were pro-democracy protests in 400 cities, across every region in China. Crowds were often in the tens of thousands.[10] Such crowds attacked soldiers across Beijing,[11] and in one suburb a convoy of 100 military vehicles was torched.[12]

Most promising of all, there was an elite split, of the kind that had finished off Marcos three years earlier. Some media outlets sided with the democratic revolt, and some against. There were firefights between pro- and anti-democracy army units around Beijing. The Politburo itself was divided.[13]

China's landscape today is very different—on the surface.

In a February 2020 essay, Chinese legal scholar Xu Zhangrun described the ramping up of purges and social surveillance, and the party's abandonment of the people in favor of its own interests.[14] When COVID ravaged the population of Hubei, and there was a failed cover-up, Xu stated that because the Chinese Communist Party had not allowed China to evolve beyond clumsy authoritarianism, its one-party rule was ripe for collapse:

> The time to establish a meaningful constitutional order is upon us.

Xu promptly disappeared. Whilst his abduction suggests a still-all-powerful CCP, it equally suggests a party that knows it is sitting on a powder keg—one projecting fear in equal measure with strength.

China's security agencies track citizens with an estimated 540 million surveillance cameras.[15] Facial recognition cameras scan crowds at pop concerts: those who are 'wanted' are arrested.[16] The citizen's inner life is tracked via the apps, messages, photos, posts, emails and contacts on her phone. This is augmented by the iris scans, voiceprints and DNA samples that are proactively collected.

In some cities, microphones with a 300-foot radius are mounted on security cameras—so police can listen in on street conversations and match them to pre-collected voiceprints.[17]

Will the Chinese population tolerate all this indefinitely?

Fig. 9.4: Detainees listen to propaganda in a Xinjiang re-education camp. Xinjiang Muslims are incarcerated for reasons such as 'links to sensitive countries', 'studying the Koran without state permission', 'switching off a phone repeatedly', & 'having extremist thoughts'. Classified Chinese Government documents, leaked to the International Consortium of Investigative Journalists, revealed that, in 2017, 15,000 Xinjiang residents were arrested in one week when data collected on them triggered an algorithm. A passage in John Bolton's book on his time in the Trump White House evokes the indifference of elites in *both* systems toward common people. In the 2019 summit between Donald Trump & Xi Jinping, 'Trump said that Xi should go ahead with building the camps, which Trump thought was exactly the right thing to do.'

Commentators have drawn few parallels between Asia's two big demotic rebellions of the 1980s—those of the Philippines and China—apparently because one system was 'capitalist' and the other 'communist'. The distinction is secondary: both rebellions (like nearly all in history) were rooted in revulsion at plutocracy.

After his fall, Marcos took enough cash, gold bricks and jewelry with him to the US to fill two C-141 transport planes (approximately 1/650th of his overall wealth).[18] Similarly, in the weeks leading up to the Beijing Massacre, every senior member of China's Politburo confidentially approached the Swiss ambassador about 'transferring very significant amounts of money to Swiss bank accounts'.[19]

The families of leaders dating back to Deng Xiaoping have offshored vast sums.[20] Bloomberg has tracked hundreds of millions of dollars in assets held by Xi Jinping's extended family alone.[21] Ordinary Chinese dislike this kind of looting intensely; and China is now in the 'middle level' of economic development: the stage at which authoritarian regimes most often break down.[22]

Threats hover over China, such as the fall of its over-leveraged super-corporations, and a widening wealth gap. Its role in sparking the pandemic, then covering it up, have darkened attitudes toward China worldwide.[23]

In 2005, the last year such statistics were reported, there were 87,000 public protests in China.[24] In the first half of 2021, no less than 178,431 personnel were punished in a purge of the politico-legal system.[25] Spending on domestic security now exceeds that on defence.[26] This would not appear to be a regime that's sure of its internal support.

What was possible in 1989 remains possible in the 2020s.

Democracy—even the 'cold' variety—could arise anywhere. But an authoritarian nation contemplating the transition needs strong exemplars. Without democratic nations to look to, its people see themselves as adrift on a sea of despotisms. The best thing the West could do for democracy in the developing world is to reverse its disintegration at home.

Chapter 56
Leaders

It made me realize that no matter how much hope you have, it can be taken away in a second.[1]

— Juan Romero, the busboy shaking Robert F Kennedy's hand as he was shot.

I t's important for the movement not to become too closely associated with one leader. A powerful individual at the top furnishes a multitude of potential problems: she might be a great campaigner, but turn out to be an incompetent politician; she can run out of steam; she can be corrupted by power; or she can be felled by scandal, sickness, mental illness or death. A movement that risks collapse on the eclipse of a leader is *fragile*.

At the same time, democracy is a means for elevating talent, not levelling it. When savants like Thomas Jefferson or Annie Kenney appear, it makes sense to pay close attention to them.

Money does not act as the agent of selection in democratic revolutions, so they have often brought genius to the fore.

Fig. 9.5: Suffragette strategist Annie Kenney. The first of Kenney's 13 prison sentences was in 1905, for disrupting a public appearance by politicians Edward Grey & Winston Churchill. The act is credited with inaugurating a new, more militant phase of Suffragette activism. Kenney was also an activist for labor rights & prison reform. Weak from a prison hunger strike, she was brought to one Suffragette meeting by horse-drawn ambulance, & carried onstage on a stretcher.

Chapter 57
Numbers

The political scientists Maria Stephan and Erica Chenoweth, in their well-known study of social movements between 1900 and 2006, found that *all* such movements reached their goals when popular involvement exceeded 3.5% of the population.[1] The active involvement of most of the populace wasn't required—just a healthy fraction.

American author Paul Hawken, who spent a decade researching social and environmental movements, found that there were about a million of them worldwide.[2] There are also millions of local religious and community groups worldwide, many of which have concerns about the direction that human society is heading in.

Taking these findings together: if even a decent fraction of these groups and movements turned their attention to democratization, a lot could happen quite quickly.

Chapter 58
Collaboration

The moment constitutional reform becomes a 'conservative project' or a 'progressive project', it will mobilize the other side against it.

Humanity's age-old governance problem does not stem from progressive elites or conservative elites—it stems from elites. Most of the corruption and incompetence in our system come not from the 'leftwing agenda' or the 'rightwing agenda'—but from small groups making decisions for large groups that can neither control them nor monitor them.

Given how diverse we are in ethnicity, income and age—and given the political labels we're still so attached to—success will by definition mean coalitions.

Modern history's most recurrently successful coalition is the middle and working classes. Change is irresistible when they combine. When the two split in Germany's democratic revolution of 1848, the aristocracy was able to defeat them. When they formed an alliance of convenience in the Philippines in 1986, President Marcos was ejected from office.

Conservatism and progressivism—the other two 'mega-blocs'—are equally capable of combining.

As we've seen, a lot of the differences between these two blocs are stage-managed or emotion-driven. But even real differences on some issues do not preclude joint action on others. A conservative and a liberal could agree to disagree on the death penalty, for instance, whilst working together to cut military spending or roll back pork barreling.

Change can succeed even if conservatives and progressives want it for *different reasons*. For example, conservatives may want to end corporate welfare because it damages small business and distorts the free market, and progressives because it harms the environment and threatens food quality.

There are already many such unions. Global Trade Watch, which opposes civically harmful trade agreements, is a coalition of civic, labor and business groups. The American Civil Liberties Union and the Tea Party have joined forces to end the surveillance provisions in the Patriot Act,[1] and to reject a national ID law.[2]

Lock the Gate, an Australian alliance between farmers and environmentalists, fights coal mining on both environmentally sensitive land and family farms.

In his 2015 book *Unstoppable*, Ralph Nader cites many coalitions of convenience—such as the *Left/Right Alliance Against Government Reading Your Email Without a Warrant*. He describes alliances that arose in several US states after neighborhoods were razed to make way for factories for General Motors and Pfizer.[3] These left-right alliances brought about state laws to prohibit the use of the government's 'eminent domain' power to benefit corporations.

There are similar left-right interests at stake in opposing opaque government procurement, unconstitutional wars, and the commercialization of childhood. Ralph Nader also believes there is common cause in introducing a financial transactions duty which taxes the 'takers', not the 'makers'.

It was an alliance between Nader himself—a progressive—and the arch-conservative chief of the General Services Administration that saw the introduction of airbags to American cars.

One reader-reviewer of Nader's book, Robert Krebsbach, wrote:

Corporatism is the enemy that lovers of democracy, freedom, and justice must unite against. The right/left, conservative/liberal labels are petty distractions that keep us from uniting to stop corporate tyranny. I thought I was progressive until reading this book, but I resonated so completely with the thoughts of the Greats of conservatism that Nader quotes, that I could just as easily regard myself as conservative. That's how little it matters in the face of corporate economic globalization.[4]

To carry each of these shared tasks forward, the progressive wing of the coalition did not have to become more conservative, nor the conservative wing more progressive. The two groups had merely to agree on one thing.

Chapter 59
Planning

The Sanders campaign in 2016 nearly defeated the Democratic Party machine because it dangled 'big target universes' before voters—ambitious plans that would transform society. That, its planners discovered, is what animates people these days.[1]

The Tea Party had discovered the same principle ten years earlier. Its vision differed markedly from Sanders'—but both campaigns were ambitiously 'big picture'. Neither achieved system change, but both gave the establishment a fright, and didn't fail by large margins.

The British Suffragettes had found the same thing: a large idea will outcompete large funding. Their national success began when Annie Kenney—a mill worker from the age of 10, and a regular church-goer—boarded a train from Manchester to London, to start the movement there, with two pounds in her pocket.[2]

Because there is no incentive for those within the political system to change it, and every incentive to keep it as it is, the third draft campaign will necessarily be planned and executed by ordinary people.

Once in campaign mode, the immediate task is to get decision-making running smoothly. This both moves things along toward the referendum, and provides a capacity to repel attacks.

Popular uprisings are handy vehicles for outside groups to hijack—especially groups from the far left and far right. Trotskyists call this tactic *entryism*. In Australia in 1985, when the Nuclear Disarmament Party was taken over by Trotskyists, key members resigned and the party collapsed.[3] Today, Australian climate rallies are distinguished by large minority contingents waving the hammer and sickle. In Ukraine, key elements of 2014's Maidan Revolution were taken over by an extremist minority.

A campaign to democratize a nation begins with a frank assessment of the lay of the land, and then the crafting of a long-term strategy that identifies the main obstacles, and how they can be overcome. Organizers would seek to discover:

- potential allies
- where plutocracy is most vulnerable
- what kind of symbolism will mobilise the population
- which institutions might be brought behind democratization (the civil service? the corporate work force?)
- and what kind of training activists will need [4]

This list is adapted from chapters 7, 8 and 9 of Gene Sharp's classic on political defiance, *From Dictatorship to Democracy*. Sharp's book focuses on dictatorships—but most of his principles will equally apply to the procedural democracies of the West.

Sharp's strategic approach to change helped numerous uprisings around the world.[5] He was a complex man: strongly opposed to dissident groups taking money from the CIA, though not without foreign policy connections of his own. [a]

---

[a] Sharp, who died in 2018, worked with Cold Warriors during the Cold War, and it's a little curious that his ideas were not much applied against US client states. His early research was funded by the Defense Department; Burmese activists he trained received funding from the US National Endowment for Democracy. The 'color revolutions' he contributed to tended to replace communism with neoliberalism—frying pan to fire—though this wasn't his doing. Sharp lived in a modest row house

Planning

His writing focuses repeatedly on the importance of a coherent plan devised by locals:

> Some exponents of freedom in various parts of the world do not bring their full capacities to bear on the problem of how to achieve liberation. Only rarely do these advocates fully recognize the extreme importance of careful strategic planning before they act. Consequently, this is almost never done.[6]

To stay on track, a revolution needs a North Star. The campaign begins with both a draft Bill and a written strategy.

---

crammed with books and papers (not suggestive of a deep state payroll). He has been defended against claims of neoliberal and neoconservative sympathies by some of the most implacable opponents of US foreign policy: Daniel Ellsberg, Noam Chomsky and Howard Zinn. None of his books display such sympathies. Sharp was a conscientious objector when drafted to Korea, so went to jail. Gandhi was a large influence, and Coretta Scott King wrote the foreword to one of his books. Sharp was sympathetic to the aims of Occupy Wall Street (though he thought its strategies inept).

Unsurprisingly, Gene Sharp has been both criticized and praised by people on the left and the right. Wherever you believe his sympathies lay, his ideas for overthrowing illegitimate governments are among the best we have.

Chapter 60
Symbols

Any human power can be resisted and changed by human beings. Resistance and change often begin in art.[1]

— Ursula LeGuin

The symbolism of the third draft will be important. A revolution needs names and slogans, signs and symbols, and maybe a color.

There are many potential symbols for third draft democracy. For example, an anchor suggests the stability it's likely to bring:

Fig. 9.6

Athena's owl (the original 'wise owl') recalls democracy's origins:

Fig. 9.7: Athenian coin, 2nd Century BC

477

The stylized columns of a Greek temple do that too:

Fig. 9.8

A network diagram suggests a non-hierarchical way of governing:

Fig. 9.9

And an Earthrise conjures the universality of the democratic idea:

Fig. 9.10

A candidate for the *color* of third draft democracy might be a 'gleaming silvery-blue-grey'—by many accounts the color of Athena's eyes.[2] The patron deity of Athens brought the olive tree (wood, oil, food), the justice system, the plough, the loom, the flute. Since the Renaissance, she has served as an international symbol of wisdom, democracy and freedom. She helped to inspire the Statue of Liberty.[3]

Fig. 9.11: Coin of Athena found in the ruins of Troy

Chapter 61
Keep the reforms focused

Once it senses its power, a third draft campaign might be tempted to go further: to seek to abolish farm debt, or surveillance, or plastic bags...

Firstly, these issues are not usually in the province of constitutions. More importantly, this is *adhocracy*—issue-by-issue reform that distracts from the main game and makes referendum majorities harder to obtain.

The reforms desired by a well-informed majority will follow—can only but follow—on the arrival of clean democracy. Our immediate need is not to abolish plastic bags—it's to create a system capable of abolishing plastic bags.

Chapter 62
Don't expand government power

When you watch the apex of power you feel like, 'If this were broadcast, everyone would sell everything and head for the bunker in the hills'. It's impossible to describe how horrific decision-making is at the apex of power and how few people watching it have any clue how bad it is.[1]

— Dominic Cummings, former advisor to British
prime minister Boris Johnson

One thing that stands out from Australia's century of referendums is that nearly every proposal to expand the federal government's power failed, including all 17 proposals to expand its economic power.[2] Proposals on social issues had a much higher success rate.

Americans' strong libertarian streak, and the British dislike of domestic and European bureaucracy, suggest that aversion to big or intrusive government is not limited to Australia.

Third draft democracy is a revolution for the *demos*, not the administrative state.

Chapter 63
Non-violence

Gene Sharp believed that violence is strategically inept—as it chooses 'the very type of struggle with which the oppressors nearly always have superiority'. Opposition violence, he wrote:

- Makes a regime more violent
- Weakens the opposition through death, injury and imprisonment
- Can lead to a new government more dictatorial than the old [1]

Here, the researchers Maria Stephan and Erica Chenoweth again help us out. In a multi-country study of civil resistance over recent years, they found that non-violent movements were twice as successful as violent ones.

This was because they tended to:

- Attract broader support
- Invite international pressure
- Deter violence by the regime

They were also more likely to induce the regime to negotiate.[2]

Stephan and Chenoweth found that non-violent campaigns were on average four times larger than violent ones, and that they tended to be more representative of gender, age, race, political parties and class.

Separately, Erica Chenoweth collected data on every violent and non-violent movement to liberate a territory, or overthrow a government, from 1900 to 2006—several hundred cases. She found that non-violent campaigns were more than twice as likely to usher in democratic institutions as violent ones.[3]

Instead of attacking a regime where it is strongest, Gene Sharp believed, you should attack it where it's most vulnerable. He found 'political defiance' to be the best approach—using 'psychological, social, economic, and political weapons': deployed by the people, and any institutions they control.

Sharp listed about 200 such 'weapons'. He categorized them under 'protest and persuasion' (parades, marches, vigils), 'noncooperation' (boycotts, tax strikes, general strikes, military desertions) and 'interventions' (fasts, occupations, a parallel government).[4]

One further tactic, in the face of criminal activity by government (more do-able in Britain or France than in, say, Burma) would be for the populace to start scaling up demotic institutions, and to incrementally begin practising third draft democracy. The stratagem—basically, to declare the old system defunct—has a well-known precedent:

Well before the British had been beaten, in each of the thirteen American colonies the patriots drove away their officials and shut down their courts. Outside of any pre-existing legal framework, they held conventions that drew up constitutions and convoked legislatures.

Chapter 64
Keep political parties armslength

Whilst bipartisan parliamentary endorsement would be useful,[1] having parties directly involved in the third draft campaign is problematic. This is especially so where a proposal is supported by only one major party. That can cause the other to oppose it, to inflict a loss on the first.

Parties find it hard to resist this kind of thing. In Australia in 1974, the conservative opposition opposed a government-sponsored constitutional amendment for simultaneous elections for the upper and lower houses. In 1977, the conservatives—now in power—introduced the very reform they'd opposed three years earlier. It didn't pass—but when the conservatives were again in opposition, in 1984, the reform was reintroduced, and they opposed it.[2]

In a saga we look at in the next chapter, the Progressive Party backed Iceland's 2012 referendum for constitutional change—then changed sides mid-campaign.[3] In Greece's 2015 'austerity' referendum, the governing Syriza party pressed the *No* case before the referendum, then signed up for austerity three days after the *No* case had won.[4]

Political parties are not widely respected. Being associated with one is of doubtful value.

Chapter 65
Expect major opposition

You'll recall from Part One that, when forced to sign Magna Carta, King John

gnashed his teeth, rolled his eyes, grabbed sticks and straws and gnawed them like a madman.

The Bill of Change can expect a similar reception.

Initially, it is likely to be relegated to the blind sector. Journalists, politicians and experts will tend not to understand it.

(Egon Bundy, a leader in the Czech anti-Soviet underground, observed that the opposition's reform agenda was 'incomprehensible' and 'unknown' to the Establishment—off their mental map.[1])

When pressure for reform builds, the Bill will have to be acknowledged, and explicitly countered.

By this point, the campaign should have identified every conceivable form of attack, and have set down a plan to counter it.

After the American Revolution, the British government and press engaged in a worldwide campaign of libel against the young republic, claiming it was in 'anarchy'. The effort was so successful, Jefferson observed, that even Americans believed it, despite the evidence of their eyes.

Expect major opposition

If the campaign survives the early assaults—ridicule, defamation, et al—we can be sure that the plutocracy will dig in for its Battle of Stalingrad.

There would be little advantage in watering down the Bill's articles: the noise of reaction will reach saturation levels regardless.

A second level of resistance will be institutional resistance.

Iceland's attempt to rewrite its badly dated constitution, in the wake of its 2008 bank crash, was opposed by some of the major political parties, and was largely ignored by the media. No opinion polls were run.

Despite the media blackout, so corrupt was Iceland's elite perceived to be that, in 2010—in the wake of the nation's 'Kitchenware Revolution'—the government allowed a popular assembly of 950 randomly selected Icelanders to meet to propose a new constitution. The assembly decided that the document's keystones would be electoral reform and the common ownership of fish exports—Iceland's major industry.

Fig. 9.12: A November 2008 protest during Iceland's Kitchenware Revolution

So an assembly of 25 people from all walks of life was elected by popular vote, to formally rewrite the document.

But the nation's supreme court—mostly appointed by an anti-reform party—was petitioned, by three people connected to that party, with 'technical complaints'.

The court declared the election invalid. Two of its grounds were that voting booths had been separated by cardboard dividers rather than full enclosures, and that some ballots had not been folded before being cast.

Now a constitutional council of the same 25 people was appointed by the government, and—after four months of work—voted for a draft constitution in line with the ideas of the original assembly. The draft constitution provided for direct democracy, for Iceland's natural resources to become public property, and for an end to gerrymandering.

(The council's vote was 25-0—an example of the consensus that tends to arise when a group of ordinary people is led by facts rather than party platforms.)

The major parties and their sponsors now grasped what they stood to lose. Iceland's leaders reach office via heavily gerrymandered electorates, and fishing licences are granted almost free to wealthy interests. Billions of dollars were at stake.[2]

The referendum on the new constitution was planned to coincide with the presidential election of June 2012, to ensure good turnout. But the major parties mounted a long filibuster to prevent that.

When the referendum was eventually held, in October, 83% of Icelanders approved national ownership of natural resources, 67% approved an end to the gerrymander, and 67% approved the bill as a whole.

That should have been the end of it. But now a 'committee of lawyers' was handed the changes, and began watering down the natural resources clause. When this interference was over-ruled by a parliamentary committee, the bill was passed on to a committee of the Council of Europe. This committee suggested alterations, which the government duly made. After this, the bill was supposed to be voted on by parliament.

Another well-orchestrated filibuster ensured that that never occurred.

The parliamentary session expired. Thereafter, the major parties dropped the bill as an issue. The media followed suit.

That was the last anyone heard of Iceland's new constitution.

As the Bill of Change travels toward realization, it can expect this kind of institutional resistance. House committees and special inquiries will look into the proposals, refer them on to each other, and farm them out to consultants, for as long as it takes for the campaign to lose steam. Where unavoidable, minor reforms may be allowed, amid fanfare about 'breakthroughs' and 'historic concessions'.

The campaign must make clear that it won't tolerate any of this —and it must be prepared to mount its own referendum if official channels are closed to it, or in the face of government foot-dragging.

The mindset of waiting for government to provide practical support, or give its blessing, should be avoided. Third draft democracy is not a bargain to be struck with government: it's a withdrawal of the consent of the governed.

Corporations generally view the loss of their right to control policy as an existential threat—so a third type of response may be physical violence from governments looking after their donors' interests. In the 1950s, the US overthrew the democratically elected—and highly popular—governments of Iran and Guatemala. This was at the behest of (respectively) the Anglo Iranian Oil Company (now BP) and the United Fruit Company: companies whose market domination was under threat from those governments.[3]

Fourthly—in addition to media attacks, institutional resistance and possible government violence—we're likely to see 'co-optation'.

Emmeline Pankhurst described how, in the 1880s, Britain's Liberal prime minister, William Gladstone, succeeded in dissolving the early female suffrage movement by enlisting politically active women in the 'Women's Liberal Federation'. This group made good use of the women's energies for the benefit of the

Liberal Party, on vague promises of reform—none of which were ever honored.[4]

If things have gone badly for elites, another type of co-optation may be to allow the Bill to pass in one jurisdiction, then to sow chaos in that society—and thereafter to point to this as an example of what third draft democracy leads to. (This may sound melodramatic—but the Central Intelligence Agency has staged numerous interventions more far-fetched than this.)

An 'interim Bill of Change' (Chapter 68) would short-circuit many of these problems—a *blitzkrieg* that stymies plutocratic tactics early. Once in place, the interim Bill deprives elites of the tools that come with ownership of the system: campaign funds, political office, media power, and the ability to rig the rules.

One final peril is external. In the West, it's likely that China, Russia and possibly other nations, will seek to hack, infiltrate and mimic a third draft movement.[5]

Campaigns against the democracies are now a feature, not a bug, of the Russian modus operandi. This new war began at 10pm on April 26, 2007, when Russia shut down most of Estonia's Internet—banks, parliament, ministries, businesses, citizens—and paralyzed the country. Another branch of the Russian onslaught stirred up street protests.[6]

Russian attacks caused much damage in Georgia in 2008, and Crimea in 2014—and are not unknown in the West. In 2016, a group named *BlackMattersUS* paid American activists to run Facebook ads, organize rallies, and conduct self-defence training for black people concerned about police violence. Their sponsor, the activists later discovered, was Russia's Internet Research Agency.[7]

No influential nation is likely to take kindly to a geopolitical trend to democratization. The United States, for example, may seek to subvert, divert or co-opt any third draft campaign that gains traction, or any third draft regime that is established. According to one study, the US was complicit in covert attempts to change the regimes of 64 nations during the Cold War. According to another, it surreptitiously interfered in the elections of 81 nations between World War Two and the end of the 20th Century.[8]

Expect major opposition

Thus, enacting the third draft reforms early on in China, Russia, and especially the United States, would have outsized effects globally. If that can't be done, third draft campaigns will need plans in place to monitor and divert the expected interference.

Chapter 66
Use the next crisis

In 'doldrum' eras, proposing root-and-branch change attracts little attention. But in 'quickening' eras like our own, wholesale reform is a strategic advantage. Small changes seem inadequate.

Things are often brought to a head by a crisis. Thomas Paine said of the American Revolution: 'Independency was a doctrine scarce and rare, even towards the conclusion of the year 1775'.[1] It was Britain increasing its punitive laws and taxes and escalating its tyranny—an acute crisis on top of a slow-moving one—that pushed colonial leaders to make the final break.

Tunisia in 2011 experienced such a crisis when the street vendor Mohamed Bouazizi, who'd been robbed and humiliated by local officials, self-immolated outside the provincial government headquarters in the city of Sidi Bouzid.

The background conditions to the Tunisian Revolution had existed for a long time: unemployment, poor living conditions, official corruption, a lack of political freedoms. But Bouazizi's suicide brought things to the crunch. There were street protests and strikes, which spread through the country. Lawyers and teachers stopped work; prisons were raided to free political prisoners. Finally, the army turned.

Use the next crisis

We never quite know when the *zeitgeist* of change is going to strike, so we need to be ready with new institutions when it does.

Kristinn Mar Arsaelsson, who was involved in drafting the new Icelandic constitution, afterwards wrote:

> People will not call for things they don't know about or turn to unfamiliar ideas. And that is our greatest regret—that there was no Plan B when the financial crisis hit in 2008.[2]

A crisis is the language in which the logic of change declares itself. As our present governmental design will generate crises till it is reformed, our Plan B needs to be ready for the next one.

Chapter 67
Escalating entrenchment

The Bill of Change is third draft democracy's centrepiece. But third draft reforms will arrive not only via constitutional change, but via regular legislation, and what's called 'secondary legislation': regulations, orders, directives, etc. Most of this will occur on the national, provincial and local tiers of government.

That's three levels of legislation and three tiers of government: it could get complicated. We need an orderly way to introduce these changes.

The *most* orderly way is referendums that put the Bill's five articles in the national and the state constitutions as a package—with supporting legislation to follow, and regulation after that.

Change that is more gradual, or more partial, will be less stable. Individual reforms will have no 'bodyguard' of complementary reforms—will lack syzygy. Pitched against a recalcitrant system that is only half-democratized, singular reforms, or slow-to-arrive reforms, may also consume a lot of time, energy and goodwill.

Thus, only when the chances of the entire Bill succeeding are judged to be about zero should *escalating entrenchment* be fallen back on.

Under escalating entrenchment, a measure begins where it can, and 'migrates' to where it should optimally be. It is established at gradually higher levels of law—and gradually higher tiers of government—till it reaches its *native domain*. At this point it's at its most useful: it is 'entrenched'.

For example, voter suppression—a key electoral malpractice —should be addressed in the constitution. But if that's impossible for political reasons, the antidotes might begin with regulation. When the way is clear, legislation might follow. Perhaps after three or four years the entire Bill—including the clause outlawing voter suppression—will make its way into the constitution.

Equally (in this very abstract example), the voter suppression measure might begin at the local tier, and migrate up to the state or provincial, then finally the national.

Defining a measure's 'native domain' keeps a campaign focused on the ultimate goal, rather than a single legislative victory: strategy, not tactics.

In another example: Vote-by-mail might be introduced by administrative order. Later, when conditions favor it, parliament passes a Universal Vote By Mail Act. In time, there's a constitutional referendum to entrench the entire Bill—including UVBM.

There's another example in the Article II realm. As the United States democratizes, the cartel holdings of behemoths like Google (YouTube, DeepMind, Boston Dynamics, et al) and Microsoft (Skype, LinkedIn, Mojang, et al) are divested via existing antitrust legislation. Later, when it becomes possible, the full Bill of Change is entrenched in the Constitution.

In one final hypothetical: The adoption of the New Civics is stymied at the national level, so state and local governments incorporate it into their education and training programs, pending a change in the wider political climate.

Escalating entrenchment allows for the setting of good examples by one jurisdiction to another.

The central goal is to establish the main reform package in the constitution. Where politics prevents this—and when the *pros* of partial reform are judged to outweigh the *cons*—escalating entrenchment is the roadmap. It's the *realpolitik* of getting reform done in an adverse political environment.

Chapter 68
Interim Bill option

When there's some urgency for change, and the way is open, an off-the-shelf version of the Bill could be put to a referendum early in the piece: perhaps after a large, single deliberation of, say, two or three months.

This 'interim Bill of Change' would enact the five articles. It would establish the main third draft institutions, such as the Democracy Commission and citizen assemblies. And it would set a date—say, three years thence—for a second referendum, to enact the more polished and well-debated version of the Bill.

Over those three years, assemblies are tasked with refining and improving the Bill: moving it toward its more settled state. There's extensive discussion, among the assemblies and among the public.

The 'boilerplate' or transitional Bill would establish all the basics—decontamination, information diversity, electoral reform, the new civics. It would not claim to be perfect—merely perfect enough to get us through the transition.

Why an interim Bill?

The main advantage is that the transition can occur sooner. This in turn will forestall much plutocratic opposition.

A second advantage is that the 'confirming' referendum, three years down the track, will be held in an atmosphere of information freedom and money-free politics—of clean elections and a raised civic IQ. Instead of three years of debate under a degenerated system—designed to narrow debate and marginalize the voter—the electorate faces the second referendum with three years of practical experience of third draft democracy under its belt: and three years of public discussion that is not controlled by special interests.

Another advantage of the interim Bill—for campaigners at least—is that it reduces conflict fatigue. In long, bitter campaigns, activists can become not merely exhausted but traumatized. Many Greek campaigners from 2015 are in this unhappy state: they want their country freed from the reign of the international banks, but their nervous systems can't take another fight.[1]

Plutocrats have an endless supply of hired guns to throw against reformers; the reformers have only themselves. So it's important to choose fights carefully, and (Tea Party-style) to have lots of social events where activists can get together and recharge batteries.

Best of all, however, is what the interim Bill offers: a short campaign.

Chapter 69
Bedding down
a post-Bill society

Preventing capture

We didn't love freedom enough... We spent ourselves in one unrestrained outburst in 1917, and then we hurried to submit... We purely and simply deserved everything that happened after.[1]

— Alexander Solzhenitsyn, *The Gulag Archipelago*,
vol. 1

There seems to be a *democratic arc,* along which mixed blessings are distributed. With the advent of democracy, tremendous dynamism arrives, as the talents of hidden sectors of society are unleashed. Excluded classes—slaves, the poor, women, the middle class, small businesspeople—are made citizens, which gives them rights: and are educated and empowered, which gives them capacities.

In modern democratic design, which is poorly defended against capture, what tends to follow is a single sector—the old elite or a new one—gradually gaining control of the rules, so as to corner power and resources. Activities that bring super-profits often come next: wars, forced 'alliances', lopsided trade treaties, exploitation of poor countries via debt… At home, there's first an increase, then a slow collapse, of living standards.

As the Greek states found near the end of the Peloponnesian War, and the United States from about 1970, war abroad and inequality at home breed unrest, poverty and international disdain. You lose your social cohesion, your wealth and your reputation.

The largest free democratic election in history, to that time, was the post-revolutionary vote for the Russian Constituent Assembly, in November-December 1917. The Bolshevik party gained less than a quarter of the vote. However they swiftly purged other socialists from government—as well as liberals and democrats—then began rounding them up in their hundreds for execution. Locally run factory councils, which were supposed to control 'the means of production'—the very definition of socialism—were now subjugated to the leadership in Moscow. Independent-minded factory workers were executed *en masse*. To keep a lid on discontent, Lenin resurrected the tsarist system of oppression—the secret police.[2]

Within two or three years, all was lost, and the scene was set for Stalinism. For lack of a sound democratic design, Russia's revolution had succumbed to an internal coup. Years of preparation had gone into ideology and strategy, and none into governance.

Fig. 9.13: Russian soldiers beside a banner reading *Death to the bourgeoisie and their helpers. Long live the Red Terror.* Lenin's Red Terror was aimed at eliminating all dissent to Bolshevik rule & 'exterminating the bourgeoisie as a class'. Within weeks, the Terror had achieved at least twice the number of executions that the tsarist empire had in the previous 92 years. By one estimate, it murdered 28,000 people per year between 1917 & 1922.

A system change throws up two perils: either a fallen autocrat will try to get back into power, or a new despot will rise from the ferment of revolution. Leon Trotsky had warned of the latter as far back as 1904. Lenin's methods, he wrote, would lead to a situation where

> the organisation of the party substitutes itself for the party as a whole; then the Central Committee substitutes itself for the organisation; and finally the dictator substitutes himself for the Central Committee.[3]

As Russia scholar Neil Ascherson wrote, 'Few prophecies have been fulfilled with such ghastly precision.'

Twenty years on, a spot in the senior leadership had changed the way Trotsky saw the world:

> Clearly, the Party is always right ... We can only be right with

and by the Party, for history has provided no other way of being in the right.[4]

The lesson here is not about Russian communism, which is not much relevant to us now, but an archetypal pattern in politics. Leaders of revolutions—regardless of ideology—often morph into the tyrants they replace. A regime transition is a time when dangerous chancers can take control. These people are often hard to spot till it's too late, as they internalize the message of 'change'—convincing even themselves that they are idealists.

For that reason, from the moment of its birth, third draft democracy is constantly critiqued by its owners.

Harvesting talent

The Obama administration of early 2009 offered a good lesson on wasting talent. Obama's presidential campaign had 800,000 users on its social network platform, and 13 million email addresses. Of the 550,000 Obama activists polled in a post-election survey, 86% wanted to help pass legislation via grassroots organizing. Fifty thousand wanted to run for elected office.[5] On the day after the election, campaign HQ was deluged by calls and emails—typified by this one from Pennsylvania:

> ALL the leader volunteers are getting bombarded by calls from volunteers essentially asking: Nowwhatnowwhatnowwhat?

Obama's answer, apparently, was: Now nothing.

He folded his massive campaign organization into the Democratic National Committee, essentially extinguishing it. His Republican opponents quickly became the masters of grassroots organizing, which they used against him to great effect over the next eight years.[6]

Meanwhile, Thomas Ferguson, the economist who had studied candidate Obama's donor list, saw his predictions come true: Obama appointed Goldman Sachs executives to manage the economy, bailed out the banks, ramped up military spending, and doubled down on nuclear weaponry.

For these reasons, once the Bill referendum is won, the third draft activist base shouldn't 'go back to farming'—the mistake many Athenians made after Solon's reforms. It should mount assemblies to draft the follow-up law and regulation, begin crafting the new institutions, and start the process of internationalizing third draft democracy.

Chapter 70
Possible trajectories

Historically, revolutions have followed all kinds of trajectories—none of them binding on the present. Gene Sharp's advice was to plan for a long struggle but be prepared for a short one.[1]

A painfully long campaign is indeed one possibility. Third draft democracy is, like women's suffrage, a global issue based on a universal principle—and it took more than half a century of campaigning in the US for women's suffrage to reach the statute books. Internationally, progress was slower again:[2]

Decade	No. of nations granting women the vote
1890s	1
1900s	2
1910s	19
1920s	13
1930s	10
1940s	41
1950s	43
1960s	32
1970s	16
1980s	3
1990s	2
2000s	2

Sometimes we may see a 'paradigm lag': where a movement establishes a powerful new mass psychology (a *tableau*) but formal change comes later. British women, after all, got full suffrage only after the suffrage movement had died down. The campaigners had established a new way of thinking, and over time that thinking—reinforced by the role women played in the first war—made the legislation inevitable. So it's possible that third draft democracy will become popular—but Establishment tacticians, or the campaign's poor organization, will keep it from being enacted for some time.

The steady diffusion of third draft democracy through a region or bloc is a further scenario.

Organic conquest—the victory of an idea via 'contagion'—is common with constitutional issues. The themes in constitutional preambles, for example, spread between neighboring countries over time.[3] Sometimes whole regions move together. For instance, women in *all* Scandinavian and Baltic states gained the franchise between 1900 and 1920.

A short, sharp struggle is equally possible—especially given the rising ecological and economic stakes.

If pandemics, heatwaves, cyclones and wars oblige—and continue to deliver supply chain crashes and recessions in their wake—our political leaders, even our corporations, may decide that survival trumps profit: that system change is required. If social conditions are grim enough, and with good planning, the serious work might be done across a whole region in a decade or so.

As for a trigger: some might describe a *non-existential* crisis as our best-case scenario. For instance, an economic crash worse than the Great Depression—one that puts millions on the streets—might make change irresistible, even before we're desolated by environmental overshoot or nuclear miscalculation.

There is no reason to take long struggles as a given. If a violent Tunisian dictator, with a full state apparatus behind him, can be thrown out in weeks, under good conditions a peaceful revolution could take months.

Remnant scenario: A final possibility is that we'll not muster the will to renovate democracy before much of the Earth is laid to waste by one of our existential threats. If this occurs (assuming anyone survives), third draft societies will at least be preferable to the kind of life depicted in Cormac McCarthy's novel *The Road*. Life would be miserable, but at least the human remnant may be able to start again on a footing that made evolutionary sense.

Chapter 71
The sharpest weapon

The Constitution aids the plutocracy in many ways. It is like an old, rambling mansion, which cannot be lighted, and in the dark places of which our enemies secrete themselves. The plutocracy benefits by the sharp limitations which the Constitution places upon national and state efforts for reform.[1]

— Walter Weyl, *The New Democracy* (1912)

Whilst the arrow of time moves exclusively forward, the arrow of civilization does so only on average. We tend to progress toward better governance back and forth, stepwise, over multiple generations. And because a human lifetime is well under a century, a fifty-year setback—most of a human adulthood—can give the impression that the civilizing process is in long-term decline.

Dissent in such an interlude seems an exercise in eternal frustration. New ideas are ignored by the media, and bank up at the doors of congress. There's no way the dispersed public can get things done. In these 'doldrum' eras, nothing seems to move.

It is likely that the present period of *stasis* has turned up because democracy—which history, political science and common sense tell us is the most successful form of government—is reaching the end of its current incarnation.

This endgame is evident in both old democracies and new. Across the world, polling finds people enthusiastic about democratic principles and depressed about democratic practices.

In 1991, when democracy arrived in the former Soviet nations, enthusiasm was high. These days, their people still favor democratic institutions, such as free media and an independent judiciary, but they don't believe 'democracy' has delivered them.[2]

The new democracies are experiencing the same disenchantment as their Western counterparts because the model they imported contains all the flaws of the original.

Our crises—social, environmental, economic, military—are crises of over-concentrated power and information. Democracies old and new will either respond to this reality or submit to the fate of any organism that loses survival value in a changed environment.

Of all possible weapons we could raise against this fate, the much-neglected constitution is the sharpest. Plutocrats know instinctively that a dated, rigid constitution is their best asset. It ensures that reforms can only be few and limited, and will tie up their advocates in battles that go on for years. To an elite, an obdurate constitution signifies ongoing revenue and influence: to an electorate it is an enduring lesson in learned helplessness.

Compared to the Greeks, we haven't been very imaginative. Via an ever-evolving constitution, the Athenians gradually redistributed all political power from elite to citizenry. The modern citizen, by contrast, commits hundreds of hours a year to studying the political battles *de jour*, and none to the battleground. For all our political savvy, our analysis of politics is a tier too low.

With third draft democracy, the content is the strategy. A renovated constitution gives proponents of change something concrete around which to coalesce, and concentrates presently diverse energies in one place. It lays a potent weapon in the hands of the ordinary citizen. When it succeeds, it entrenches the elements of our sovereignty where they are very hard to tamper with.

Part Ten
Striking at the root

Chapter 72

Inferior binaries

A polity that deteriorates in all its major domains—government probity, information freedom, political machinery, civic engagement—tends to lose faith in itself.

Thus, by 2015, belief in the major US institutions—Supreme Court, presidency, Congress, newspapers, big business and others—had fallen to record lows.

And by 2021 those records seemed quaint. (The Gallup headline read, 'Record-Low Confidence Across All Institutions'.[1])

Gallup also measures what it calls 'global unhappiness'. This has been rising at a near-45-degree angle worldwide since 2008. When it hit a record in 2022, this time the headline was, 'Anger, stress, sadness, physical pain and worry reach a new global high.'[2]

Old words like *declinism* were gaining new currency. In 2022, the Zurich Insurance Group—discussing the global risk landscape—noted that the term *polycrisis* had become popular. *Permacrisis* was Collins Dictionary's word of the year:

> It is a sign of the chaos and uncertainty of recent times that people have been searching for new words to describe them.[3]

Whilst there was, in 2015, a mild general unease about the world's direction and future, by 2024 this had—in my subjective view—ripened into a deep disquiet.

All this tended to confirm the book's premise: change cannot occur within the present framework. The meaningful choice—the choice that will designate our fate—is that between continuing with government by small, secretive minorities and replacing it. The shocks to which Iraq, the GFC and COVID are prelude will not require troubleshooting but architecture.

Presently—in place of the needed 'metapolitics'—we're stuck in *inferior binaries*: Trump v. Biden; conservative v. liberal; Chinese authoritarianism v. Western 'democracy'. An inferior binary serves as a displacement activity: a secondary choice to distract from the meaningful one.

Our transnational elite knows it has to sideline its internal differences over conservative and liberal values in the interests of control. To date, the global *demos* has had no such insight. Thus one rules the world and the other does not.

The human nadirs of the last two centuries were caused by regimes that were British colonialist, German fascist, Soviet communist, Chinese Maoist, and American 'democratic'. Death arrived in many *personae*—ideology, patriotism, xenophobia, greed —but the vessel they all sailed in was unaccountable power.

Chapter 73
Fateful complexity

Had third draft democracy been in place in the West in the 1980s, it would presumably have been the model Russia turned to when communism collapsed. If that were the case, in this alternative universe, would Russia have slid into oligarchy? Would Chechnya today be dotted with mass graves?[1] Would Ukraine have been invaded?

Had democracy been on offer to China in 1989—not our Potemkin version, but clean, transparent governance rooted in community—would China have put its entire population under surveillance, or incarcerated a million Muslims in Xinjiang?[2]

Had the West been governed by people power in recent decades, would global democratic backsliding be today's norm? (And would it be happening at double the rate among US allies?[3]) Would the Iraq War have occurred, or the destruction of Yemen? Had both sides replaced their corrupt leaderships, and democratized, would the crisis between Israel and Palestine still be with us?

Democracy lost its geopolitical clout because its environmental threats evolved and it did not—like an animal species that remains static as those around it develop longer claws and faster speeds. Failure to adapt, in a moving world, spells not stability but decline.

The human horizon has expanded since 1789 via intellectual discoveries such as Darwinism and quantum physics, but our societies are still governed as if they were early Victorian machines running on Newtonian clockwork—linear, static, homogenous, predictable.

What finished off state communism has also brought the Western system to its knees: the inability of the whole to exchange information with the parts, and for the parts to affect the direction of the whole.

This democratic *stasis* has allowed the authoritarian model, till recently in disgrace, to re-emerge as an alternative centre of gravity. The model's shining light is China, which expounds the message of its superior form of government with increasing confidence. Its president, Xi Jinping, calls for his nation to 'lead the reform of the global governance system'.[4]

'The chaotic 2016 presidential election has highlighted the defects in the US election system and the dysfunction of democracy', *The China Daily* stated in that year. The election had 'made one thing clear,' it added: 'The US needs political reform.'[5]

2020 was another bumper year for such stories in the Chinese official media. One of them was headed *Time to wake up to the Western system superstition*:

> Western democracy is short-sighted, political parties fragmented, and money politics are on the rise. The form of democracy is greater than the content.[6]

The Chinese media made much of the January 2021 invasion of the US Capitol. One article was headed: *A landmark night in US history: Capitol riots nation's Waterloo, destroy global image*:

> Chinese experts said this unprecedented incident will mark the fall of 'the beacon of democracy,' and the beautiful rhetoric of 'City upon a Hill' will perish…
>
> A tweet written in Portuguese by a Brazilian web user said 'this is the first coup attempt in the continent of America without the participation of the US embassy'.[7]

The Russian foreign ministry was also quick to make hay from January 6:

> The electoral system in the United States is archaic, it does not meet modern democratic standards, creating opportunities for numerous violations, and the American media have become an instrument of political struggle.[8]

To which Vladimir Putin added:

> This certainly gives no one the right to point the finger at the flaws in other political systems.[9]

The authoritarian model will not be beaten by democracy in its present condition. Since the Greeks defeated Xerxes, the only thing that has out-competed an efficient oligarchy is an efficient democracy.

The problems of our species don't end with Xi Jinping's emerging masterplan. As China prepares to eclipse the democratic West, the planet is preparing to eclipse both. On this planetary level, we're dealing with a collection of threats, not just one: over-population in the developing world and over-consumption in the developed, disappearing insects and soil, river and ocean pollution, rising atmospheric carbon, bioweapons, artificial intelligence, nuclear armories...

From the 12th Century BC, when drought, famine, earth-quakes, rebellions and invaders together wiped out the Bronze Age Mediterranean cultures—all eight of them, more or less at once—this kind of 'fateful complexity' has generally been lethal.[10]

We've just witnessed a half-century experiment on whether our existing forms of government can deal with this assemblage of risks. After countless laws, conferences, negotiations, treaties and UN programs, all have increased.

Jared Diamond writes, in his book *Collapse*, that, in past societies that went out of existence, leaders often refused to face up to environmental threats, such as over-population and the degradation of farmland, because they were personally in a position to escape them.

That recipe for eclipse—environmental overshoot driven by indifferent elites—looks much like our own.

All this has not come about from a run of bad luck. Our 'delta' of problems diffuses down from the great river of the constitution —whose institutions time has gradually optimized for the interests of the few. Within this framework, there is no reversing our predicament. A hundred Level 2 solutions won't solve a Level 1 problem.

By the 2020s, Westerners were turning away from their governments and media as decisively as Russians, Romanians and Poles had done four decades earlier. The democratic West was nearing its 1989 moment.

Chapter 74
Third draft efficiency

T he solution, when you have multiple problems with a single cause, is to address that cause. We're not good at this. As Henry David Thoreau put it:

> There are a thousand hacking at the branches of evil, to one who is striking at the root.[1]

Let's briefly recap how to achieve the latter via the four articles of the Bill of Change.

Article I (Decontamination)

Underlying most of our social and economic troubles is the problem of economic game-rigging.

How bad is this? Can you quantify it?

Apparently, yes. In their book *Game of Mates* (now in a second edition as *Rigged*), research economists Cameron Murray and Paul Frijters dug out large amounts of data on the flow of benefits between Australia's politicians and their corporate 'mates'.

They compared the windfall corporate gains this yields to a 'benchmark world' of best practice. Their 'best practice' world is not abstract—it is real jurisdictions: Norway (for mining taxation), Denmark (for superannuation), New Zealand (for healthcare), and so on.

Murray and Frijters ran a series of comparisons between the Australian practices and these international benchmarks. They found that, each year, the corporate benefactors of Australian politicians achieve the following gains—above and beyond what a free market would yield them:

- For **miners**: About $20 billion per year (48% of their profits)—plus another $36 billion in publicly subsidized infrastructure, and future environmental damage they won't be required to pay for.[a]

- **Real estate developers**: Re-zonings worth $11 billion.

- The **superannuation industry** skims 27% off ordinary Australians' superannuation, via exorbitant fees, and control of default funds—and by investing in projects owned by their own 'mates'.

- **Bankers**: $15 billion via regulatory capture.

- The **pharmaceutical industry**: $10 billion via sales of needlessly expensive medicines.

- **Corporate control of universities** bring higher staff costs, and exorbitant salaries for senior managers—doubling what a student pays for his education.

When the authors focused the picture down on the individual —adding the citizen's lost income to his increased costs—they found that the average Australian works 30 minutes out of every hour for the corporate 'mates' of politicians. As Cameron Murray

---

[a]   These Australian examples use Australian dollars.

phrases it: 'If it wasn't for these "mates", we'd all be twice as well-off.'

Murray and Frijters dug a little further:

> You might think that if you were in a similar position, you'd act differently. But you'd be wrong. In experimental tests, we've been able to demonstrate that given the opportunity to game the system to benefit our mates, 84% of us do. This isn't a conspiracy. Human beings are just wired to co-operate in these ways.[2]

If these are the figures in Australia, what would they be in the United States—whose citizens fear 'corrupt government officials' more than any other thing, including 'people I love becoming seriously ill' and 'nuclear weapons attack'?[3]

Mathematician Carter Price and his colleague, the economist Kathryn Edwards, give us an idea. In 2020, the two published a study of US incomes from 1975 to 2018. Taking a worker on the 2018 median income—about $50,000—they found that, had economic growth been shared in the way it was in the three decades to 1975, he would instead be earning $92,000 to $102,000.[4]

Once again, the average worker yields about half his income to a contaminated political economy.

Anyone who thinks that a redesign of democracy is too revolutionary might consider that the political donor network has already achieved it.

Given the institutional vastness of this game, what political leader could take it on? It's the very system that brings leaders to office. An array of industries—mining, banking, pharma, war-making and more—divert huge sums from taxpayer to corporation, swelling the size of government *en route*.

This is why Article I constitutionalizes the problem of political contamination—cutting off the game at source. Decontamination breaks the nexus between politics and wealth—relocating each to its separate domain.

Article II (Isegoria)

An information system controlled by a few wealthy men is going to be narrow and partial, virtually by definition. As we're now seeing, its narrowness will in time give birth to an epidemic of mistrust. This in turn yields an 'arms race' of disinformation, counter-disinformation, counter-counter-disinformation, and so on.

When the numbers controlling information are tiny, society no longer acts from a grasp of its own best interests, but from a cascade of commercially underwritten deceits. Reality lives behind a veil, and billions of dollars will be spent, and good people persecuted, to keep the veil in place.

Article II breaks up the advertiser-driven media giants, and replaces them with news driven solely by audience demand. It sets the stage for human survival by returning us to the world of fact—and also a world in which no opinions are off the table.

Article III (Renovating the democratic machinery)

Women comprise 49.6% of the world's population and occupy 24% of the world's legislative seats.[5] To put more women in legislatures, you could stage a march, or picket parliament. Or organize a letter-writing campaign to demand female quotas.

Fair enough.

But there's a better route to putting more women in power. You could work to establish a proportional electoral system—which does the trick as a matter of course.

This strategy also:

(i) Enables women to take their seat at the table 'organically', without invoking complaints of bias.
(ii) Brings other benefits simultaneously: less polarization, stabler governments, more civil liberties, bigger fiscal surpluses…

Perhaps you want more representation for minorities—such as a conservative minority in a progressive state, or an Asian minority in a largely Caucasian state. Under PR, that will occur automatically.

In times like these, citizens—especially in the less steady 'presidential' nations—long for sound government, and a stable society. Here, there are a thousand social, political and economic 'branches' they could hack at. But merely switching to a parliamentary system—which ends presidentialism's 'split mandate'—results in much greater human and economic development, and a political system three times less likely to collapse.

Deliberative democracy bestows a similar weave of benefits—less adversarial politics and knee-jerk partisanship, more civic awareness, more youth participation—all without the need for individual campaigns for these things.

Maybe you want less public debt and tax avoidance. You could agitate for these reforms individually—then pass the task on to your children. Alternatively, you could campaign for direct democracy, which typically produces both, along with a multitude of other boons.

Finally, rather than an array of campaigns to eliminate polling station queues, low turnouts, election day interference, and the hacking of voting systems—more *adhocracy*—you could support UVBM, which eliminates all of them at once.[6]

Article III takes its lead from our democratic forebears: whose reforms were targeted upstream, where change tends to stick.

Article IV (The democratic arts)

Those concerned by how dumbed down we've become, or how disengaged from civic life—or by our growing tribalization—could lobby government and media to do something about it all. But they'd hit a wall—not because government and media are unaware of these problems, but because they're beneficiaries.

By establishing participation as a constitutional imperative—a civic responsibility to complement civic rights—Article IV comprehends what today's constitutions do not: that cultivating communal energies and the capacity to think go to a nation's survival.

Chapter 75
Syzygy

Life did not take over the world by combat, but by networking.[1]

— Biologist Lynn Margulis

The Bill's firepower lies in it being both comprehensive and specific—an interlocking framework of black letter laws that are individually powerful but (more importantly) add strength to each other. This is not only synergy (to do with functioning) but syzygy (to do with survival). The system as a whole exerts enough gravity to keep its parts in place.

Thus each article shares the work of the other three. How a third draft constitution deals with political contamination provides an example:

The standard formula for contamination was outlined to a business audience in 1896, by US Senator Boies Penrose:

> I believe in the division of labor. You send us to Congress; we pass laws under which you make money...and out of your profits, you further contribute to our campaign funds to send us back again to pass more laws to enable you to make more money.[2]

Syzygy

As little has changed since 1896, you could say that the chances of persuading government to crack down on campaign finance are in the region of zero.

Outlawing political money at constitutional level is more feasible, and more final. But **Article I** (Decontamination) is only part of the solution. **Article II** helps too. It constructs an information environment shaped by ordinary people, not the super-rich. Organized money will no longer create the narrative by which we live our lives. And it will become subject to the same scrutiny as other sectors.

The **Article III** reforms of direct and deliberative democracy also do their part, by bringing in the finance referendum and participatory budgeting. These mean more people analyzing more money flows for signs of unfair influence—and less ability to exert that influence in the first place.

All this is backstopped (**Article IV**) by a more vigilant and politically savvy public—equipped now with knowledge of how systems can be gamed, and outfitted with the tools of political engagement.

In such ways, Articles I, II, III and IV *each* contributes to the rollback of the bribes, deals and boondoggles that distinguish contemporary politics.

Syzygy brings the precautionary principle into play—minimizing risk by making the entire system contamination-proof, not just part of it: closing all doors to government capture, not just one.

Fig. 10.1: Planetary syzygy

Chapter 76
Giant-killing

M uch of this book was written in public settings—in various bits of Australia, Cambodia and Greece—so I had many comments from random strangers I met along the road.

When they learned the book's subject was democracy, my companions' reactions had a certain uniformity: 'Democracy is dead.' 'It must be a fantasy novel.' 'You can't save democracy.'

For them, our governance was now separate from ordinary life, just as, say, organized crime and religious cults are. ('Leave the politicians to their games. I don't want anything to do with them.')

I understood what these people were saying. Even had they taken an interest in government, what kind of entity would they be dealing with?

In the United States, it would be one whose policies have 'zero' statistical relationship to the wishes of working and middle class people, but correlate in a 'straight line' fashion with those of corporations. In Britain, it would be one bankrolled by tech, mining and banking corporations, and staffed by their former and future employees. In Australia, it would be one dominated by 'ten large companies'.

Yet all these comments were made in a place—a café, an *agora*, an airport—and in a 'condition'—sickness, health, employment, marriage, parenthood—that were directly affected by the state democracy was in that day.

That is to say: wholesale rejection of the political class offers no escape.

Board an airplane, and you'll lack legroom. Watch the in-flight sports, to learn that your childhood football team has been bought by a beer company. Arrive at your Thai island, to find the beaches awash in plastic. Return home, to learn that the local fruit shop is gone. Build a home extension, and find yourself in a blizzard of red tape. Turn on the TV news, to behold the bias against relevance.

Because of the sheer scale of the task ahead, the Bill of Change becomes operational not at the level of everyday politics, but at the level where giants are killed: the constitution.

The Bill has several of these giant-killing aspects. It's not only *constitutional* (addressing government by wealth at the top of the causal chain), but *mutable* (allowing it to evolve into places where new problems emerge), *comprehensive* (broad enough to counter our era's many existential risks), *syzygistic* (each article makes the others more robust), '*evolutionary*' (a fit with human nature), and a *mosaic* (locating consensus, one issue at a time).

By these virtues, it proposes to resolve the conundrum posed by Adams to Jefferson in 1813:

> While all other Sciences have advanced, that of Government is at a Stand; little better understood; little better practiced now than 3 or 4 thousand years ago.[1]

What was true in the early 19th Century remains true today. As we've seen, Occupy and the Arab Spring, which spanned entire world regions and drew in tens of millions, led to few concrete improvements. The Chinese uprising of 1989 was crushed. The 'color revolutions' brought civic gains in a few countries, made things worse in others—and resulted in little nett improvement in the majority.[2]

A cardinal feature of post-Cold War societies is vast popular mobilizations that achieve little. Our era replaces its fashions, social norms and technologies with cold-blooded efficiency, but has proven inept at replacing bad governance.

By adding to our social evolution some formidable instruments of popular control—and by subtracting artificial selection by a small, self-interested group—the Bill intends to reverse the age-old demographical absurdity in which the many are sidelined by the few.

Evolving policy along popular lines, and simultaneously evolving democracy, may prove to be the Ariadne's thread through the maze of modernity.

For most of the human timeline, our political arrangements allowed us to change the mix between careful and bold—selfish and 'groupish': autonomous and dependent—as circumstances demanded. It was this fluidity, not opting for a rightwing or left-wing bias, that saw *Homo sapiens* through 300,000 years of ice ages and genetic bottlenecks.

Since civilization got underway, we have rarely mastered fair government because we have rarely prevented the capture of institutions. This is at least self-limiting: present-day plutocracy is not only destructive but self-destructive. We now have social schisms, a collapse of trust, and the appearance of baffling 'liminal' figures on the political stage, to force an uncomfortable rethink. So far, this rethink comprises *ad hoc*, disparate efforts without an overarching theme. This is a poor match for our societies, which are deeply networked, and for our crises, which display an alarming synergy.

Single crises might be dealt with in single campaigns, but the terrain on which we fight a web of crises is the system—the constitutional environment. A one-off reform—even one as vast as abolishing nuclear weapons—will lack the synergies needed to reshape the system as a whole. Only doing that can prevent the next calamity from stepping into the shoes of the last.

Fig. 10.2: The author at the Pnyx, Athens

To review or buy this book: https://books2read.com/thirddraft

Glossary

Adhocracy: The 'divided up' character of the activist landscape—in which individual problems are targeted but not the problem-generating institutions. The atomization of reform campaigns into myriad downstream issues.

The architecture of repair: The trillions of dollars spent reconstructing societies destroyed by war, bank deregulation, environmental overshoot, and other 'preventables'. Money and time for remediation that need not have been spent. The eternal troubleshooting necessitated by our present political paradigm.

The architecture of repair is a signature of modern governance. Its retirement is a by-product of third draft democracy.

Assertion of authority: A universal civil right, rooted in natural law and international legal instruments, that may be invoked when no procedure exists to amend a constitution, or the procedure is onerous or denies natural justice. In *asserting authority*, the populace unilaterally constitutes itself as an electorate. If a simple majority votes to amend the constitution in a fairly conducted referendum, it is deemed to be so amended.

The resulting amendment shall prevail over the constitution's previous wording, and over any law or directive by a government or finding by a court.

The *assertion* makes concrete the principle of the people's sovereignty.

Blind sector: A subset of Null Corner (below). The objectively significant issues that are not on the public agenda of either media or government. For example, Turkey's treatment of the Kurds— with its systematic executions of civilians, torture and destroyed villages—is not covered in the Turkish media.

Such absences shape public knowledge as surely as the daily news. When one set of facts is absent, another is permitted to emerge.

Very occasionally, an issue will transit from wall-to-wall coverage to the blind sector overnight. For instance, the 2001 anthrax attacks in the United States, which terrified the country and helped mobilize opinion against Saddam Hussein, vanished from the headlines once it was discovered that the anthrax came from a US Army laboratory.[1] [2] [3] [4]

The blind sector may undergird much voter irrationality. Voters intuit that they're being hoodwinked, but can't locate the facts—so default to a state of emotionality.

> At the most basic level, the news you consume is a lie—a lie of the stealthiest and most and insidious kind. Facts have been withheld on purpose, along with proportion and perspective. You are being manipulated… The best you can hope for in the news business at this point is the freedom to tell the fullest truth that you can. But there are always limits. And you know that if you bump up against those limits often enough, you will be fired for it. That's not a guess—it's guaranteed. Every person who works in English language media understands that.
>
> The rule of what you can't say defines everything.[5]
>
> — Tucker Carlson (2023)

(From avionics: that part of the landscape occluded from a radar screen.)

Bone learning: Knowledge and practices that over time become reflexive and natural. As it is based in human instinct, third draft democracy may be expected to transition from the rehearsed and the unfamiliar to 'bone learning'.

A **bootstraps effort** (as in 'pulling ourselves up by our bootstraps') breaks the circularity of modern governance—by which rigid, centralizing structures block their own reform—and achieves the 'impossible' via a suite of reforms that disable most of plutocracy's offensive capabilities at once.

Caste axis: A vertical axis superimposed on the horizontal progressive-conservative axis (the 'political spectrum') to model the social divide that distinguishes the present era. Progressives and conservatives at the top of the caste axis enact significant redistribution of wealth and power (to their caste). Progressives and conservatives below them (the '99%') mostly oppose this but cannot affect it. The end appears to be a permanent underclass and a permanent aristocracy.

The vertical axis (wealth) is long and the horizontal axis (political spectrum) narrow—to stylize the pre-eminence of the wealth-and-power divide over the less consequential ideological divide. This yields a model more apposite to the 2020s:

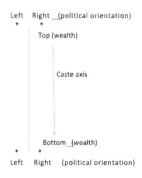

Chorus effect: The establishment, via financial inducements, of a homogenous viewpoint among disparate institutions—business, political, non-profit, media—to persuade the public that 'every credible source' supports it. E.g. a drug company will sponsor trial scientists, trial committees, journalists, regulators, doctors, professional associations and patient groups to endorse a vaccine.

Via the chorus effect, a minority belief is transformed into 'received wisdom' or 'common knowledge', and its dissenters into 'cranks'.

The chorus effect arises from the finding that individuals tend to conform to the majority opinion even when they think it may be wrong. In 1951, the original scientist in this field, Solomon Asch, called this the 'distortion of perception under the stress of group pressure'.[6]

Circularity: The most visible feature of modern democracy's positive feedback loops. Money and personnel circulate from government to corporation and back, accumulating value along the way. As time passes, more outputs from each system—corporate and government—go to the other, rather than to society at large.

As with a Ponzi scheme, circularity can create a compelling illusion—of talent rising to the top, market forces at work, or a just war. This is often allowed to evaporate once profits have been taken.

Clean democracy: Democracy shaped by equitable mechanics, and a politically literate public, in an information environment undistorted by wealth. (Colloquial term for third draft democracy.)

Cold democracy: Democracy introduced to a country with no democratic culture.

Contamination: The influence on politics, in second draft democracies, of organized money.

Decapping: Reducing a media corporation's capitalization to a certain maximum value. (Part Four.)

Deconstraint: The erasure by modern life of an environmental constraint on an instinctive behavior. The harm caused by this. For example:

(i) In the Stone Age, carbohydrate foods contained good nutrition but were harder to obtain than now, which prevented over-consumption. *Homo sapiens'* innate desire to eat them, therefore, wasn't especially dangerous. Today it has become dangerous, as carbohydrates are universally available, and obtaining them expends little energy.
(ii) The power urge was likewise once constrained by the environment: Stone Age bands were small and mobile, with strong egalitarian norms. Individuals could be rebuked up-close, and marginalized, when they threatened to become dominant. As a result, resources and power were hard to corner—rendering the power urge almost harmless. In modern societies, such constraints can be evaded via mass media, the second draft political design, etc (deconstraint).

Defragging: The 'new civics' methods, outlined in Part Six, to inoculate against mind viruses, emotion-clouded judgements and blind spots, and to broaden thinking. *Defragging* is designed to reduce society's political fragmentation. (Borrowed from IT.)

The democratic arc: The trajectory of a democratic state, where the initial social dynamism, prosperity and cultural florescence can transmute into military power, war and conquest, which ultimately bring decline. Third draft democracy is designed to break the feedback loop between wealth and political power, and so to contain the democratic arc to dynamism and prosperity.

Democratic ally: A regime servant who, when rebellion arrives, sides with the democratic transition. This may involve a refusal to obey orders: e.g., a police officer refusing to arrest democrats, a judge to fine them, or a soldier to fire on them. A corporate journalist may refuse to write propaganda.

A regime servant will often be won to the status of 'democratic ally' by family, friends or colleagues. Sergei Popović—a leader of the Serbian resistance movement in the 1990s—describes how the movement brought in allies from the 'pillars' of the regime—police, army, courts, civil servants, et al:

> We were telling the police that we are both victims of the same system. They are pushed to do things they don't like to do. We are pushed to the streets instead of sitting in the classrooms. There is no reason to have war between victims and victims. Some victims are in blue uniforms, other victims are in blue jeans...
>
> This is the way you do it—you go and co-opt from the 'pillars'. You don't throw stones at the police.[7]

The democratic instinct: The ancient tendencies in human nature to co-operation, sharing and equality, based in a series of cultural, and probably biological, adaptations. Democracy arises out of this long-existing human capacity for egalitarianism, and aversion to hierarchy.

Demotic institution: An institution, 'hard' or 'soft', controlled directly by the people. A demotic institution could be a cultural norm such as civic participation; a practice such as deliberative democracy; a legally constituted body such as the Democracy Commission; or a product of third draft democracy such as a science journal supported by readers.

The 'hard' demotic institutions established directly by the Bill of Change form a fourth branch of government, distinguishable from legislature, executive and judiciary.

Diploidism: Condition of the modern voter, in whom two discrete mental 'chambers' tend to exist side-by-side—one emotional and tribal, the other rational and policy-oriented. Diploidism can cause a voter to support a candidate whose policies she opposes; or to support policies she once opposed because they're advocated by a candidate she identifies with.

(From *diploid* = 'twofold'.)

Disintermediation: Replacement of the power of political middlemen (politicians, political investors) with that exercised directly by the people.

(Borrowed from marketing, where disintermediation describes retail stores ceding market share to wholesalers that sell direct to the public.)

The dismal art: The suite of underhanded methods by which voting blocs such as the black, the poor and the young—and more recently conservatives—are prevented from voting. Examples include onerous ID requirements, the purging of voter rolls, and the broadscale skewing of Google searches. The dismal art began in Athens in the 6th Century BC. In the modern era it has been highly developed in the United States.

A scheme to abolish the dismal art is outlined in Part Five.

The Dyad: The capture of government by the corporation, and the merging of the purposes of the two, creating an entity that is functionally single.

Encapsulated by Naomi Klein's remark: 'It's hard to tell where the Australian Government ends and the coal industry begins.'

End-to-end containment: A kind of full spectrum narrative control, which manufactures a 'general view' or 'accepted truth', usually via the *chorus effect*.

End-to-end narrative containment is a standard protocol in any major industry sector.

Escalating entrenchment: The orderly establishment of a reform at gradually higher legal levels, or higher tiers of government, or both. For example, Universal Vote By Mail (Part Five) may begin as a regulation, progress to legislation, and finally be entrenched in the constitution. Decontamination (Part Three) might begin life in a municipality, then 'migrate' to the state level—then finally the national.

Establishing the entire Bill at once is optimal—and much safer. Escalating entrenchment is a gradualist compromise when that route isn't open.

A reform begins in the domain where it's immediately enactable. It moves 'up' where further entrenchment will make it more robust. It stops where it finds its 'native domain'—where it's at its most effectual, and least fragile.

Not all reforms will 'escalate'. One might only apply locally, and find its 'native domain' there. Another might be innately constitutional, and begin and end in the constitution.

Eternal protest ('Letters to the Sphinx'): The practice of protesting downstream effects but not institutional causes, producing campaigns that go on for years or decades without result, and at times outlive their founders. 'Eternal protest' serves as a displacement activity—akin to tidying a house when there is a cyclone bearing down on it.

Externality (or constitutional externality): An issue that is not innately constitutional, such as residential zonings or traffic rules. Issues such as political contributions and the control of information *are* innate to the constitution—due to their wide effects on political decisions, public opinion, individual rights, etc—but tend to be classed by experts as externalities.

The remedy for this sidelining of innately constitutional matters is *constitutionalization*.

(Adapted from economics.)

The 'free market': Rough opposite of the free market, or *laissez-faire*, and thus an instance of Orwellian *doublethink*. (Placed in inverted commas to contradistinguish the two.)

The 'free market' results from proactive policy settings that tend to reward those who extract from the economy, often at the expense of those who add value. The 'free market' is brought about by media owned by 'free market' beneficiaries, by payment for political favors, by the deregulation of the finance industry, and by a political system that can no longer respond to the popular will. It leads to planned debt for the middle class, the shift of economic power from producer to rentier, unpoliced insider trading and highly policed everyday crime (a two-tier rule of law), an offshore money-hiding regime to transfer wealth from the middle class to the rich (a two-tier tax regime), tax incentives that redirect investment from productivity to mergers and acquisitions (a two-tier capitalist system), international investors' rights agreements that are termed free trade agreements, higher prices, stagnant wages and the decline of the natural world.

The 'free market' favors monopoly over competition.

Fresh war fallacy: Popular tendency to trust a government and media narrative that, whilst past wars were strategic or moral mistakes, the new war is justified.

Thus, by 2003, whilst the Vietnam War was acknowledged to have been a grave error, the invasion of Iraq was promoted for its strong ethical rationale. By 2022, with the Iraq War now acknowledged as an error, the war against Russia in Ukraine was sold as legitimate, essential, based on noble principles, etc.

Hairy reform: A reform invoking mutable democracy. A 'hairy' reform addresses an evolving or less-well-understood issue, with a less certain outcome (higher risk). There are degrees of 'hairiness'; but an archetypal 'hairy' reform is begun on a small scale in a limited jurisdiction for a finite time. It expands only as benefits materialize; if they don't, the reform is redesigned or abandoned.

Homeostasis: Condition by which the right democratic instruments allow a society to promptly and accurately self-correct. The present democratic machinery, white-anted by special interests, fails to bring homeostasis; third draft democracy is designed to do so.

(Borrowed from biology.)

Inferior binary: A false or less important choice that distracts from a more fertile one. Where the actual present-day choice is people power v. elite rule, government, media and experts keep the populace focused on binaries such as Trump v. Biden, conservative v. liberal, and China v. the United States.

Information capture: The control of public information by conglomerates or governments, leading to an information environment that has been narrowed to advance their interests.

Isegoria (pronounced 'ee-see-*ghor*-ia'): In Classical Greece, this was the equal right of all to speak and be heard. The components *iso* (equal) and *agora* (marketplace or square) mean that, in the public space, citizens share these rights equally. The word is distinct from *parrhesia*, which has the narrower meaning of 'freedom of speech'.

Third draft democracy applies the ideal of *isegoria* to modern societies, to enable a diverse information environment, unskewed by organized money or government strictures. Isegoria (Article II) outlines a public information 'circulatory' system that is not controlled by narrow interests, state or private.

Kaleidoscopy: A political strategy to deploy constant, high-volume memes and messages—often flamboyant, contradictory or obviously false—to keep the public debate focused on noise, not signal.

Kaleidoscopy was developed by the Russian 'political technologists'—most notably Vladislav Surkov—but is now deployed in the United States, Britain, Brazil, and to a lesser extent elsewhere. It aims to create strategic confusion by preventing a coherent picture forming in the public mind, and by numbing public responsiveness. The Russians have not given this practice a name, so far as I can discover.

Parts Four (on liberating information) and Six (on the democratic arts) describe how kaleidoscopy may be neutralized.

Market pantheism: (i) Ubiquity of the market; tendency of the market to condition every aspect of life. (ii) Superstition that the market is immanent in all things.

Metacompassion: Compassion for those in the future who—unless they're provided with a fork in the road to yield them a better world—are destined for selfish or unethical lives. Compassion for those deprived of sensibility by the environment they are born to. The view that 'bad' people born to the right conditions would not be bad.

> **Higgins**: Have you no morals, man?
> **Doolittle**: Can't afford them, Governor. Neither could you if you was as poor as me.[8]
>
> — From *Pygmalion*, by George Bernard Shaw

Mary Wollstonecraft was onto the same idea in *A Vindication of the Rights of Woman* (1792), where she argued that women were not inferior, but only appeared so because they'd been trained from childhood to focus on their looks, and had been given no education.

From the Greek *meta*, meaning in this sense 'beyond'.

Metapolitics: Politics grounded in the insight that system, not ideology, is the true genesis of policy.

Politics that transcends the inferior binary of left v. right. The leopard, not the spots.

The concern of metapolitics is not the victory of one viewpoint, but to bring an end to political decision-making by small groups.

(Literally: 'beyond politics' as presently understood.)

'Migration': The progress of a reform from its beginning point to its 'native domain': say, from an executive order to legislation to the constitution; or from local to state to national tiers.

Moral signage: The array of signals, signs, symbols, suggestions—and absences—deployed by society's rulers and agenda-setters to guide the individual in making choices. Whereas the 15th Century's moral signage stemmed from the Church, today's stems from institutions underwritten by wealth.

The corporate-slanted premises that underlie our social direction. Sponsored thinking.[9]

Economy to recover strongly, but wages and jobs will not

Shane Wright
July 6, 2020 — 12.01am

Headline, Sydney Morning Herald

Mosaic: The fine mesh of 'left' and 'right' attitudes that characterized hunter-gatherer societies, and later ones such as the Athenian democracy and the medieval Italian city-states. The non-ideological weave of policies that results.

The third draft encourages a *mosaic* style of governance by tending to legislate issues singly, rather than via monolithic party platforms. Policies are thereby likely to be more diverse and moderate. Presently, when a party wins an election, *all* of its policies become government policy. Under the third draft, direct and deliberative democracy make for political power that is better distributed. In this landscape, winners win less and losers lose less.

Mutability: Principle governing a slow, investigatory approach to democratic reform in less-understood areas, to limit downside. With mutable democracy, an experiment begins small, with a conservative prototype, and proceeds via rigorous testing. As with biological evolution, it has a certain built-in failure rate.

The mutability principle ('mutable democracy') is balanced against time constraints. For example, progress against an ecological crisis such as over-fishing can't be *too* slow, as time is short.

Glossary

The Myriade: Human culture since the dawn of agriculture. More exactly, the tens of thousands of cultures existing through the roughly 11,650 years since the beginning of agriculture and human settlement.[a]

The *Myriade* overlaps the geological, climatic, cultural and ecological epoch known as the Holocene—but its criteria are solely cultural. It began earlier and has broader qualities than 'civilization' (centralization, division of labor, the wheel, writing, mathematics: beginning 3,000 to 6,500 years ago).

The *Myriade* describes the commonalities among post-Stone Age cultures, such as fixed settlement, secrecy, privacy, accumulation of surpluses, diverse and 'chaotic' forms of movement being replaced by repetitive tasks, social hierarchies, larger populations, and (as time went on) inequality in the ownership of resources.

From *myriad* ('ten thousand') and *–ade* ('process of' or 'product of').

Native domain: The tier of government (local, state, national) and level of enactment (regulatory, legislative, constitutional) at which a reform is most effectual and least fragile.

Natural consensus: The broad, rough agreement on most issues that studies tell us lies beneath our more emotional, 'tribal' polarization. Third draft democracy is designed to capture the natural consensus.

Neo: One who has never voted or participated in politics.

The new civics (or New Civics): Informal name for the Democratic Arts (Part Six). A set of modules on topics such as information literacy and voting; on 'defragging' skills such as statistics and cognitive bias; and on third draft democracy itself.

---

[a] The work of Bruce Pascoe and others establishes that agriculture, fish-trapping and other attributes of 'settlement' go back tens of thousands of years on the Australian continent—though details are still sparse, and some are contentious. This work confirms what has been observed on other continents: there is usually no sharp line dividing the chronologies of hunter-gathering and agriculture.

Glossary

Null Corner: Figurative abode of the absences that define what is present. Analogous to the missing electron, or the dog that didn't bark. For example:

- *Bacteriophages*—natural viruses that kill bacteria—have been known about for a century, but are difficult to monetize. Their neglect leaves the field of infection control largely to antibiotics and those who make them.
- The absence of laws against buying government policy silently moulds legislative output and civic norms.
- The absence of a post-Cold War peace dividend (less military spending, lower taxes, better public services) has shaped several decades of life in the West.

More favorably, Null Corner contains once-contentious issues that are now settled ('non-issues'). For example, the near-absence of war in Western Europe since 1945 made possible decades of security and prosperity.

In its largest sense, Null Corner is all we do not know—the 'unknown unknowns'.

> Thirty spokes converge on one hub.
> What is not there makes the wheel useful.
> Clay is shaped to form a vessel.
> What is not there makes the vessel useful.
>
> — Tao Te Ching

Obduracy, constitutional: The fixed and difficult-to-change nature of constitutions—in an era when crises and fast social change call for both structural reform and fluidity.

An obdurate constitution ensures that reforms can only be attempted in limited domains, tie up their advocates in long battles, and make the larger task of system reform appear to be unthinkable.

If our adversaries come to govern, they'll be forced to take actions that are not so different from the ones we'd want.[10]

— Jaime Guzmán, drafter of the Chilean
constitution under General Pinochet

Omnipotent middle: The potentially all-powerful mass of voters who occupy the middle two-thirds of opinion—but who are presently sidelined by an unrepresentative system, and by the strategy of divide-and-rule.

Organic conquest: The spread of democracy, or one of its elements, via imitation. This diffusion commonly occurs within a continent or geographical region, and even more commonly via a shared culture (e.g., Spanish language or Islamic religion).[11] It can also happen worldwide, as with the women's franchise through the 20th Century, and second draft democracy after World War Two.

Otzar: Metaphorical dwelling place of a political factor that did not exist when the nation's constitution was written, and to which the constitution is therefore blind. Examples include mass media monopolies and corporate campaign finance, which were 'unborn' when most modern nations were founded.

From the Hebrew *Otzar*—the 'treasury of souls', where the unborn await their incarnation.[12]

Paradigm lag: The upshot of a *tableau* (below). Where a new social norm is established—usually by activists—but awaits propitious political conditions to be formalized in law and institutions.

The clock of communism has stopped striking. But its concrete building has not yet come crashing down.[13]

— Alexander Solzhenitsyn in 1990

Parsing session: Meeting of two or more politically disparate groups—e.g., progressive and conservative, or low- and middle-income—to sift through a set of issues one at a time: quickly eliminating those on which they believe they can't for now reach agreement. The process is designed to yield issues that the opposed groups *can* agree on, as a basis for campaigning on them together.

In a parsing session, each issue is given a limited timeframe—say 20 minutes—in which agreement must be reached. Otherwise, it is shelved. The session is not for arguing an issue's merits (this is avoided by mutual agreement). Its focus is rigorously pragmatic: to locate areas of agreement for an *ad hoc* coalition.

Plural iniquity: A system with perverse incentives tends to attract politicians of poor calibre, regardless of their politics. ('No good guys.') Because of the human tendency to tribalism, voters often identify with one side—whose flaws become invisible to them, and whose virtues they overstate—and denounce the other.

Plutophile: A 'useful idiot' for the plutocracy—generally a journalist or think tank expert. Mainstream media, think tanks, and increasingly universities, tend to be *plutophile institutions*.

Precarian (era): The period, roughly since 1980, in which standards of living fell in line with the diminishing political impact of citizens. The era that gave rise to the *precariat*.

Second draft democracy: The debilitated form of governance presently understood as 'democracy'. A.k.a. procedural democracy, Potemkin democracy.

Secular optimism: The sense of illumination gained by stepping back from a negative short-term trend to observe civilization's net upward direction.

For example, in terms of health, living standards and political rights, the West has been in a secular upswing since about 1215. Secular optimism means staying conscious of the long-term picture amid the more recent social, economic and democratic downturns.

(In disciplines such as astronomy and the study of financial markets, long-term or historical trends are dubbed *secular*.)

Single stick syndrome: The fragility of a single reform enacted in a system whose remaining elements are loaded against it.

For example, in an environment of skewed information, astro-turfing, corporatized education and voter roll purges, a reform of campaign finance would have a short life expectancy.

The antidote to single stick syndrome is *syzygy* (below)—where the gravity of multiple reforms overwhelms the pull of the old system.

(From a fable by Aesop, which taught that one stick, lacking the strength of several, will easily be broken. The same analogy is attributed to the warlord Mori Motonari in 16th Century Japan, who gave each of his three sons an arrow and instructed them to break it. He then gave each three arrows—which they were unable to break.[14])

Spending cascade: A windfall event that employs the routine principles of corporate welfare via a series of connected projects.

A spending cascade may be manufactured (say, a war) or be a natural event that is opportunistically repurposed for profit (say, a pandemic). Its hallmarks are its *special* character—it doesn't occur routinely—and that each of its elements (e.g. excessive military spending) precipitates the next (e.g. launching a war), which mandates the next (e.g. reconstruction).

Sturdy reform: A reform that is straightforward, overdue and desired by most people. Decontaminating legislatures and reno-vating the electoral system fit these criteria, for example.

Sturdy reforms have low downside: they're unlikely to go seri-ously wrong, or if they do the costs will be modest. Their upside is generally high.

The advantage of implementing sturdy reforms is immediacy. They get elementary improvements on the books early, which enables society to begin to grapple with its crises.

Syzygy: Reforms that 'line up' for increased 'gravity'—i.e. aggregate for greater survivability. The syzygy of a suite of inter-locking reforms creates sufficient 'gravitational force' to counter the weight of the old, degenerating system.

Limited third draft-style syzygies already exist. E.g.: (i) In California, *deliberative democracy* is used to improve *direct democracy*. (ii) A *referendum* was used to make Switzerland's electoral system *proportional*. (iii) Because Oregonians are able to launch *citizen initiatives*, they were able to bring in *Universal Vote By Mail*.

'Synergy' denotes a system's parts enhancing each other—and *syzygy* emphasizes the effect of this on the system's survivability.

(From astronomy: 'Three or more celestial bodies lining up together in a gravitational system.'[15] Syzygy has various adjectives, though I prefer *syzygistic*.)

Tableau: A change in public attitudes effected by a reform movement, pending its realization in law. The establishment of a new general understanding, which has later legislative effect. The writing on the wall.

Examples: (i) Whilst World War One and the reforms following it spelled the end of monarchy, it took about a century for the ceremonial monarchies that remained to disappear or sputter into irrelevance. (ii) Australia's Eureka Rebellion, though crushed, led to a raft of democratic reforms in the years that followed. Mark Twain called Eureka 'a victory won by a lost battle'. This is often true of a *tableau*.

(In solitaire, a *tableau* is an initial deal of cards from which, across the course of the game, better combinations are made.)

Third draft democracy: Fair, efficient demotic machinery of several kinds (Parts Three to Six) to replace plutocracy as the mode of government.

(From a scheme in which democracy's first 'draft' was the two- or three-century experiment in Classical Greece, and its second the Euro-American model now reaching senescence.)

The three liberations: The most recent, half-century phase of the campaigns to advance rights and opportunities for women, ethnic minorities and gay people.

Upstream principle (or rule): The imperative to deal with a problem high in the chain of causation. Applying the upstream rule tends to prevent rather than cure. Moreover, as societal problems tend to be 'siblings', intervening higher in their 'family tree' heals more of them.

Thus, third draft democracy addresses ailments such as environmental overshoot and war by reforming their common causes in governance.

The wars on the banes: Official 'wars', such as those on drugs, crime, cancer and terror, whose *raison d'être* is not to be won, but to indefinitely divert taxpayer funds to the patrons of those who enact them. The 'war on the banes' has the secondary advantage of making second draft governments appear to be useful.

Wellspring inequities: The foundational modern inequities—misinformation, civic disengagement, bought government, broken electoral machinery—from which most others arise.

Worldwork: Activity intended to reshape the world as a whole, rather than a family, locality or nation. Worldwork arises from the growing sense that we are not just of race or place, but of the Earth —that identification with the home planet confers meaning.

Sources for Figures

Fig. 1.1: Photograph by Robert Stewart Burrett, August 2009. Licensed under CC BY-SA 4.0.

Fig. 1.2: Photograph by Beytullah Ele, March 2019. Licensed under CC BY-SA 4.0.

Fig. 1.3: Photograph by Zdenek Kratochvil, April 2014. Licensed under CC BY-SA 4.0.

Fig. 1.4: Bust by Anna Christoforidis, March 2004. Copyright Ohio Statehouse.

Fig. 1.5: Photograph by the author. Licensed under CC0.

Fig. 1.6: Roman copy after Greek original c. 430 BC, collection of Vatican Museums. Photograph by Marie-Lan Nguyen, January 2009. Licensed under CC BY 3.0.

Fig. 1.7: Photograph by the author. Licensed under CC0.

Fig. 1.8: British Library, Cotton MS Augustus II 106. Public domain.

Fig. 1.9: Artwork by Edward Burne-Jones. Public domain.

Fig. 1.10: Photograph by William Edward Kilburn, Wikimedia. Public domain.

Fig. 1.11: Collection of King Family and Ballarat Fine Art Gallery. Public domain.

Fig. 1.12: Photograph by International News Service, May 1914. Public domain.

Fig. 2.1: Photograph by Master Sgt. Jim Varhegyi, USAF. Public domain.

Fig. 2.2: From video published by WikiLeaks, April 2010.[1]

Fig. 2.3: Collection of Marine Corps Archives and Special Collections. Licensed under CC BY 2.0.

Fig. 2.4: Collection of OpenTheBooks.

Fig. 2.5: Transparency International.

Fig. 2.6: Photograph by Simon Rutherford. Licensed under CC BY 2.0.[2]

Fig. 2.7: Copyright Sennett Devermont.[3]

Fig. 3.1: Artwork by Edward Burne-Jones, 1861. Wikimedia, public domain.

Fig. 3.2: Image by Wikipedia user AndreasJS, January 2021. Licensed under CC BY-SA 3.0.

Fig. 3.3: Image by Wikipedia user GliderMaven, September 2014. Licensed under CC0 1.0.

Fig. 3.4: Photograph by Helene C. Stikkel, May 2001. Collection of the US Department of Defense. Public domain.[4,5]

Fig. 3.5: Collection of the International Monetary Fund. Public domain.[6]

Fig. 3.6: Collection of New York Police Department. Public domain.[7]

Fig. 4.1: Left: Collection of German Propaganda Archive, Calvin University. Right: Collection of The National Archives, UK, INF 3/327. Both public domain.

Fig. 4.2: Data sourced from Steve Rendall, "Amplifying Officials, Squelching Dissent," *FAIR*, May 1, 2003. Public domain.

Fig. 4.3: Wikimedia. Public domain.[8]

Fig. 4.4: Copyright Minatom.[9]

Fig. 4.5: Copyright Oxfam.

Fig. 5.1: Wikipedia user Marsyas, December 22, 2005. Licensed under CC BY-SA 2.5.

Fig. 5.2: Wikipedia user Drono1, April 2010. Licensed under CC BY-SA 3.0.

Fig. 5.3: Parliament Secretariat of Mongolia.[10]

Fig. 5.4: Helena Foundation, September 20, 2019. Licensed under CC BY-SA 2.0.[11]

Fig. 5.5: International Geosphere-Biosphere Programme, 2004.

Fig. 5.6: Lamiot, June 7, 2015. Licensed under CC BY-SA 4.0.[12]

Fig. 5.7: Chris LaTondresse. Public domain.

Fig. 5.8: Collection of Sociólogos blog. Licensed under CC BY 3.0.

Fig. 5.9: Photograph by Keremcan Büyüktaşkın, November 2015. Public domain.

Fig. 5.10: Photograph by Max Schlumpf, May 2009. Licensed under CC BY-SA 3.0.

Fig. 5.11: Jedi Friend, November 2016. CC BY-SA 4.0.[13]

Fig. 5.12: Photograph by Chris Phan, October 2006. Licensed under CC BY-SA 3.0.

Fig. 5.13: Scan by Wikipedia user Owen, May 2005. Public domain.[14]

Fig. 5.14: National Atlas of the United States, 1970. Public domain.[15]

Fig. 6.1: Scan by Indiana University. Public domain.

Fig. 6.2: Left: Collection of Wikimedia Commons. Public domain. Right: Photograph by Fanni Uusitalo, October 4, 2021. Collection of Finnish Government. Licensed under CC BY 2.0.

Fig. 6.3: Henri Meyer, 16 January 1898. Public domain.

Fig. 6.4: Photograph by Berthold Werner, April 1, 2006. Public domain.

Fig. 7.1: Collection of *Age of the Sage*. Licensed under: CC BY-SA 4.0.

Fig. 7.2: Photograph by Harold Burge Robson, December 25,

1914. Collection of the Imperial War Museums, London, Q 70719. Wikimedia, public domain.[16]

Fig. 7.3: Copyright David Bailey. Wikimedia Commons.

Fig. 7.4: Photograph by Wikipedia user Obier, 17 November 2018. Licensed under CC BY-SA 4.0.

Fig. 8.1: Photograph by Harold Strong, August 2007. Licensed under CC BY-SA 2.0.[17]

Fig. 8.2: Screenshot of proposed Scottish Independence Referendum Bill. Collection of Scottish Government. Licensed under Open Government Licence.

Fig. 8.3: Collection of FDR Presidential Library and Museum, 64-165. Licensed under CC BY 2.0.

Fig. 8.4: Collection of US National Archives and Records Administration, Washington D.C., 595951. Public domain.

Fig. 8.5: Painting by John Trumbull, 1818. Collection of US Capitol, NPG D1357. Public domain.[18]

Fig. 9.1: Collection of Malacañang Palace archives. Licensed under CC0 1.0.

Fig. 9.2: Data source: HSE University, Moscow. Graphic by Wikipedia user Cold Light. Licensed under CC BY 3.0.

Fig. 9.3: Copyright Uncle of Shelley Zhang.[19]

Fig. 9.4: Image and copyright 牙生.[20,21]

Fig. 9.5: Photograph by Bain News Service, 1909. Collection of Library of Congress Prints and Photographs Division, Washington, D.C., LC-B2- 562-15. Public Domain.[22]

Fig. 9.7: Photograph by Matthias Kabel, Glyptothek, Munich, January 2006. Licensed under CC BY-SA 3.0.

Fig. 9.9: Titz B, Rajagopala SV, Goll J, Hauser R, McKevitt MT, et al. (2008) The Binary Protein Interactome of Treponema pallidum. PLoS ONE 3(5): e2292. Licensed under CC A 1.0 Generic.

Fig. 9.10: NASA, Goddard Space Flight Center, Arizona State University, October 2015. Public domain.

Fig. 9.11: Classical Numismatic Group, Inc. Licensed under CC BY-SA 3.0.

Fig. 9.12: Photograph by Oddur Benediktsson, November 2008. Licensed under CC BY-SA 3.0.

Fig. 9.13: Photograph by unknown, September 1918. Scan from Scherbakowa Knigge, *GULAG - Spuren und Zeugnisse 1929-1956*, p. 16. Collection of US Holocaust Memorial Museum, Washington D.C. Public domain.

Fig. 10.1: Image by NASA. Public domain.

Fig. 10.2: Licensed under CC0.

Citations

Introduction

1. "Polarization and the Pandemic: How COVID-19 Is Changing Us" (More in Common, April 3, 2020). https://www.moreincommon.com/media/3iwfb5aq/hidden-tribes_covid-19-polarization-and-the-pandemic-as-released-4-3-20.pdf
2. Saif Khalid, "Q&A: 'India Is Heading towards a Full Ethnic Democracy,'" *Al Jazeera*, May 3, 2019. https://www.aljazeera.com/news/2019/5/3/qa-india-is-heading-towards-a-full-ethnic-democracy
3. "75% in U.S. See Widespread Government Corruption," *Gallup*, September 19, 2015. https://news.gallup.com/poll/185759/widespread-government-corruption.aspx
4. Jim Clifton, "Explaining Trump: Widespread Government Corruption," *Gallup*, January 6, 2016. https://news.gallup.com/opinion/chairman/188000/explaining-trump-widespread-government-corruption.aspx
5. "75% in U.S. See Widespread Government Corruption."
6. Peter Mair, *Ruling the Void: The Hollowing of Western Democracy*, 2nd ed. (London; New York: Verso, 2023). Glenn Greenwald, "Lessons for the West From Jair Bolsonaro's Victory in Brazil," *The Intercept*, October 29, 2018. https://theintercept.com/2018/10/29/the-lessons-for-western-democracies-from-the-stunning-victory-of-brazils-jair-bolsonaro/

1. Human egalitarianism

1. Jean-Jacques Hublin et al., "New Fossils from Jebel Irhoud, Morocco and the Pan-African Origin of Homo Sapiens," *Nature* 546, no. 7657 (June 7, 2017): 289–92. https://doi.org/10.1038/nature22336 Ewen Callaway, "Oldest Homo Sapiens Fossil Claim Rewrites Our Species' History," *Nature*, June 7, 2017. https://doi.org/10.1038/nature.2017.22114
2. Fiona M. Jordan et al., "Cultural Evolution of the Structure of Human Groups," in *Cultural Evolution: Society, Technology, Language, and Religion*, ed. Peter J. Richerson and Morton H. Christiansen (Cambridge, MA: The MIT Press, 2013), 88–116.
3. Eiluned Pearce and Theodora Moutsiou, "Using Obsidian Transfer Distances to Explore Social Network Maintenance in Late Pleistocene Hunter-Gatherers," *Journal of Anthropological Archaeology* 36 (December 1, 2014): 12–20. https://doi.org/10.1016/j.jaa.2014.07.002
4. Mary C. Stiner and Steven L. Kuhn, "Changes in the 'Connectedness' and Resilience of Paleolithic Societies in Mediterranean Ecosystems," *Human Ecology* 34, no. 5 (October 1, 2006): 693–712. https://doi.org/10.1007/s10745-006-9041-1
5. Doron Shultziner et al., "The Causes and Scope of Political Egalitarianism during the Last Glacial: A Multi-Disciplinary Perspective," *Biology & Philos-*

ophy 25, no. 3 (June 2010): 319–46. https://doi.org/10.1007/s10539-010-9196-4

6. David Erdal et al., "On Human Egalitarianism: An Evolutionary Product of Machiavellian Status Escalation?," *Current Anthropology* 35, no. 2 (April 1994): 175–83. https://doi.org/10.1086/204255

7. Christopher Boehm, *Hierarchy in the Forest: The Evolution of Egalitarian Behavior*, 1st ed. (Cambridge, Massachusetts: Harvard University Press, 2001), chap. 5.

8. Mark Dyble et al., "Sex Equality Can Explain the Unique Social Structure of Hunter-Gatherer Bands," *Science* 348, no. 6236 (May 15, 2015): 796–98. https://doi.org/10.1126/science.aaa5139

9. Boehm, *Hierarchy in the Forest*, chap. 5.

10. Richard Joyce, review of *A Natural History of Human Morality*, by Michael Tomasello, *Utilitas* 31, no. 2 (June 2019): 207–11. https://doi.org/10.1017/S0953820818000274

11. Keith Jensen, Amrisha Vaish, and Marco F. H. Schmidt, "The Emergence of Human Prosociality: Aligning with Others through Feelings, Concerns, and Norms," *Frontiers in Psychology* 5 (2014). https://www.frontiersin.org/articles/10.3389/fpsyg.2014.00822

12. Eric Alden Smith et al., "Wealth Transmission and Inequality Among Hunter-Gatherers," *Current Anthropology* 51, no. 1 (February 2010): 19–34. https://doi.org/10.1086/648530

13. Shultziner et al., "The Causes and Scope of Political Egalitarianism during the Last Glacial."

14. Erdal et al., "On Human Egalitarianism."

15. Tim Ingold, "On the Social Relations of the Hunter-Gatherer Band," in *The Cambridge Encyclopedia of Hunters and Gatherers*, ed. Richard B. Lee and Richard Daly (Cambridge: Cambridge University Press, 1999), 399–410.

16. Erdal et al., "On Human Egalitarianism."

17. Boehm, *Hierarchy in the Forest*, chap. 1.

18. Christopher Boehm et al., "Egalitarian Behavior and Reverse Dominance Hierarchy [and Comments and Reply]," *Current Anthropology* 34, no. 3 (June 1993): 227–54. https://doi.org/10.1086/204166

19. Boehm et al.

20. Boehm, *Hierarchy in the Forest*, chap. 5.

21. Boehm et al., "Egalitarian Behavior and Reverse Dominance Hierarchy [and Comments and Reply]."

22. Marshall Sahlins, The Western Illusion of Human Nature: With Reflections on the Long History of Hierarchy, Equality and the Sublimation of Anarchy in the West, and Comparative Notes on Other Conceptions of the Human Condition (Chicago, Illinois: Prickly Paradigm Press, 2008), 51.

23. Kevin B. Smith et al., "Evolutionary Theory and Political Leadership: Why Certain People Do Not Trust Decision Makers," *The Journal of Politics* 69, no. 2 (May 2007): 285–99. https://doi.org/10.1111/j.1468-2508.2007.00532.x

24. Boehm, *Hierarchy in the Forest*, chap. 5.

25. Jordan et al., "Cultural Evolution of the Structure of Human Groups."

26. José María Gómez et al., "The Phylogenetic Roots of Human Lethal Violence," *Nature* 538, no. 7624 (October 2016): 233–37. https://doi.org/10.1038/nature19758

27. Douglas P. Fry, ed., *War, Peace, and Human Nature: The Convergence of Evolutionary and Cultural Views* (New York: Oxford University Press, 2013).

2. The long march

1. David Wengrow, "Everything We Think We Know About Early Human History Is Wrong," interview by Aaron Bastani, *Downstream*, Novara Media, December 4, 2022. https://www.youtube.com/watch?v=UR-EN0YIBIg

2. "Which Came First, Monumental Building Projects or Farming?," *Archaeo News*, December 14, 2008. https://www.stonepages.com/news/archives/003061.html

3. Ian Hodder, "Entangled: An Archaeology of the Relationship Between Humans and Things," Author Talks at Google, May 4, 2015. https://www.youtube.com/watch?v=zKwSg7OyvoE

4. Origins of Settled Life | Ian Hodder | Talks at Google (YouTube). https://www.youtube.com/watch?v=zKwSg7OyvoE&ab_channel=TalksatGoogle

5. "Çatalhöyük Excavations Reveal Gender Equality in Ancient Settled Life," *Hürriyet Daily News*, October 2, 2014. https://www.hurriyetdailynews.com/catalhoyuk-excavations-reveal-gender-equality-in-ancient-settled-life-72411

6. Nemanja Batrićević and Levente Littvay, "A Genetic Basis of Economic Egalitarianism," *Social Justice Research* 30, no. 4 (December 1, 2017): 408–37. https://doi.org/10.1007/s11211-017-0297-y

7. Harald Haarmann, *Roots of Ancient Greek Civilization: The Influence of Old Europe* (Jefferson, North Carolina: McFarland & Company, Inc, 2014), 188.

8. John Keane, *The Life and Death of Democracy*, 1st American ed. (New York: W.W. Norton & Co, 2009), xi.

9. Haarmann, *Roots of Ancient Greek Civilization.*

10. Yulia Ustinova, "Consciousness Alteration Practices in the West from Prehistory to Late Antiquity," in *Altering Consciousness: Multidisciplinary Perspectives*, ed. Etzel Cardeña and Michael Winkelman (Santa Barbara, California: Praeger, 2011).

11. Plutarch, "The Life of Lycurgus," in *Plutarch's Lives. 1: Theseus and Romulus. Lycurgus and Numa. Solon and Publicola*, trans. Bernadotte Perrin (Harvard, Massachusetts: Harvard Univ. Press, 2007).

12. Mary Fragkaki, "The Great Rhetra," *Rosetta*, no. 17 (2015): 33–51.

13. Plutarch, *Plutarch: Lives of the Noble Grecians and Romans*, ed. Arthur Hugh Clough (Urbana, Illinois: Project Gutenberg, 1996). https://www.gutenberg.org/ebooks/674

14. Boris Johnson, "Athenian Civilisation: The Glory That Endures," Legatum Institute, September 4, 2014. https://www.youtube.com/watch?v=qeSjF2nNEHw

15. Percy Bysshe Shelley, *A Defence of Poetry and Other Essays* (Urbana, Illinois: Project Gutenberg, 2013). https://www.gutenberg.org/ebooks/5428

16. Frederic William Henry Myers, *Essays--Classical* (London: Macmillan, 1911).

17. Yulia Ustinova, *Caves and the Ancient Greek Mind: Descending Underground in the Search for Ultimate Truth* (Oxford: Oxford University Press, 2009). Nassos Papalexandrou, "Boiotian Tripods: The Tenacity of a Panhellenic Symbol in a Regional Context," *Hesperia* 77, no. 2 (June 23, 2008): 251–82. https://doi.org/10.2972/hesp.77.2.251

Citations

18. Michael Scott, *Delphi: A History of the Center of the Ancient World* (Princeton, New Jersey: Princeton University Press, 2014).
19. Plutarch, *Plutarch's Lives, Volume 1 (of 4)*, trans. George Long and Aubrey Stewart (Urbana, Illinois: Project Gutenberg, 2004). https://www.gutenberg.org/ebooks/14033
20. Aristotle, *The Athenian Constitution*, trans. Frederic G. Kenyon (Urbana, Illinois: Project Gutenberg, 2008). https://www.gutenberg.org/ebooks/26095
21. Plutarch, *The Rise and Fall of Athens: Nine Greek Lives* (London: Penguin, 1973).
22. Plutarch, *Plutarch's Lives, Volume 1 (of 4)*.
23. Plutarch, *Lives. Solon*, trans. Bernadotte Perrin (Boston: Harvard University Press, 1914). https://doi.org/10.4159/DLCL.plutarch-lives_solon.1914
24. Mogens Herman Hansen, *The Athenian Democracy in the Age of Demosthenes*: Structure, Principles, and Ideology (Norman: University of Oklahoma Press, 1999), 29–33.
25. Aristotle, *The Athenian Constitution*.
26. Aristotle.
27. Hansen, *The Athenian Democracy in the Age of Demosthenes*, 34–36.
28. Hansen, 109.
29. Luc Brisson, "Women in Plato's Republic," trans. Michael Chase, *Études Platoniciennes*, no. 9 (December 15, 2012): 129–36. https://doi.org/10.4000/etudesplatoniciennes.277
30. Josiah Ober, *The Rise and Fall of Classical Greece*, The Princeton History of the Ancient World (Princeton: Princeton University Press, 2015), chap. 1.
31. "Athens: The Truth about Democracy," *The Ancient Worlds* (Channel 4, 2007).
32. Hansen, *The Athenian Democracy in the Age of Demosthenes*, 70.
33. Aristotle, *The Athenian Constitution*, trans. Frederic G. Kenyon (Urbana, Illinois: Project Gutenberg, 2008). https://www.gutenberg.org/ebooks/26095
34. Thucydides, *The History of the Peloponnesian War*, trans. Richard Crawley (Urbana, Illinois: Project Gutenberg, 2004). https://www.gutenberg.org/ebooks/7142
35. Thucydides.
36. Aristotle, *The Athenian Constitution*.
37. Was Athens in the Age of Pericles Aristocratic? LaRue Van Hook. *The Classical Journal*, Vol. 14, No. 8 (May, 1919), pp. 472-497.
38. Hansen, *The Athenian Democracy in the Age of Demosthenes*, 87.
39. Hansen, 38.
40. Joseph Henrich and Francisco J Gil-White, "The Evolution of Prestige: Freely Conferred Deference as a Mechanism for Enhancing the Benefits of Cultural Transmission," *Evolution and Human Behavior* 22, no. 3 (May 2001): 165–96. https://doi.org/10.1016/S1090-5138(00)00071-4
41. Kurt A. Raaflaub, Josiah Ober, and Robert W. Wallace, *Origins of Democracy in Ancient Greece*, Joan Palevsky Imprint in Classical Literature (Berkeley: University of California Press, 2007), 78.
42. Boris Johnson and Mary Beard, "Greece vs Rome," debate hosted by Intelligence Squared, November 19, 2015. https://www.youtube.com/watch?v=2k448JqQyj8
43. Lantern Jack, "Democracy and Demagogues w/ Josiah Ober," *Ancient Greece Declassified*, January 9, 2017. https://www.greecepodcast.com/democracy-and-demagogues-in-ancient-athens-w-josiah-ober/

44. Raaflaub, Ober, and Wallace, *Origins of Democracy in Ancient Greece*, 18.
45. Hansen, *The Athenian Democracy in the Age of Demosthenes*, 350.
46. Donald Kagan, *Pericles of Athens and the Birth of Democracy*, 1st Touchstone ed. (New York: Simon & Schuster, 1991).
47. Hansen, *The Athenian Democracy in the Age of Demosthenes*, 335.
48. Hansen, 336.
49. Josiah Obier, "Ancient Glory Explained," *Greece Is*, October 9, 2015. https://www.greece-is.com/ancient-glory-explained/
50. Jacob Spon et al., *Voyage d'Italie, de Dalmatie, de Grece, et du Levant: fait aux années 1675. & 1676.* (Amsterdam: Chez Henry & Thedore Boom, 1679). http://archive.org/details/voyageditalieded02spon

3. The long sleep

1. John Macgregor, "Gnostics, the Sacred Feminine, & Constantine's Corporate Takeover of Christianty," *The Age*, December 19, 1988. https://john-macgregor.com/entryPage.php?entid=84 "Third Draft Democracy," *Third Draft Democracy*, accessed June 14, 2023. https://thirddraftdemocracy.com/
2. Keane, *The Life and Death of Democracy*, 135–53.

4. Scattered reappearance of democratic practices

1. Edward Burne-Jones, "1888 Illustration," in *A Dream of John Ball and A King's Lesson*, by William Morris (London: Longmans, Green and Co., 1920), iv.
2. Hansen, *The Athenian Democracy in the Age of Demosthenes*, 2.
3. Dan Jones, *Realm Divided: A Year in the Life of Plantagenet England* (London: Head of Zeus, 2015).
4. Mark Cartwright, "Peasants' Revolt," in *World History Encyclopedia*, January 23, 2020, https://www.worldhistory.org/Peasants'_Revolt/
5. "List of Peasant Revolts," in *Wikipedia*, May 28, 2023. https://en.wikipedia.org/w/index.php?title=List_of_peasant_revolts
6. Puritanism and Liberty, being the Army Debates (1647-9) from the Clarke Manuscripts with Supplementary Documents. University of Chicago Press, 1951. https://oll.libertyfund.org/titles/lindsay-puritanism-and-liberty-being-the-army-debates-1647-9
7. Gilbert Burnet, *History of His Own Time* (London: Olms, 1838), p. 406. https://books.google.co.uk/books?id=9S6jvd9yX80C&dq
8. Thomas Jefferson to Roger Weightman, Letter, June 24, 1826, Thomas Jefferson Exhibition. Library of Congress. https://www.loc.gov/exhibits/jefferson/214.html

5. Why democracy was reinvented (the second draft)

1. Adam Smith, *An Inquiry into the Nature and Causes of the Wealth of Nations* (Urbanik, Illinois: Gutenberg Press, 2002), chap. 11. https://www.gutenberg.org/ebooks/3300

2. Dorothy Thompson, *The Chartists: Popular Politics in the Industrial Revolution*, 1st ed. (New York: Pantheon Books, 1984)
3. Dawn of a Democracy; The Age, November 27, 2004.
4. https://www.theage.com.au/national/dawn-of-a-democracy-20041127-gdz2jh.html Mark Twain, *Following the Equator: A Journey Around the World* (Urbana, Illinois: Project Gutenberg, 2004). https://www.gutenberg.org/ebooks/2895
5. Emmeline Pankhurst, *My Own Story* (London: Eveleigh Nash, 1914), 1.
6. Estelle Sylvia Pankhurst, *The Suffragette: The History of the Women's Militant Suffrage Movement 1905-1910* (New York: Sturgis & Walton Company, 1911). https://www.gutenberg.org/ebooks/54955

6. The two thousand-year counter-revolution

1. Simcha Paull Raphael, *Jewish Views of the Afterlife*, 2nd ed. (Lanham: Rowman & Littlefield, 2009).
2. "Old European Culture: Yin and Yang," *Old European Culture*, February 5, 2018. https://oldeuropeanculture.blogspot.com/2018/02/yin-and-yang.html

II. The upstream principle

1. Thomas Paine, *Common Sense* (Urbana, Illinois: Project Gutenberg, 1994). https://www.gutenberg.org/ebooks/147

7. A problem has a family tree

1. Meatpacking has become less safe: Now it threatens our meat supply. Chris Deutsch, Washington Post; May 1, 2020. https://www.washingtonpost.com/outlook/2020/05/01/meatpacking-work-has-gotten-less-safe-now-it-threatens-our-meat-supply/
2. Meatpacking More Dangerous Today Than A Generation Ago; Food and Power, May 7, 2020. https://www.foodandpower.net/latest/2020/05/07/meatpacking-more-dangerous-today-than-a-generation-ago-amplifying-covid-19-crisis
3. Stephen R. Greenwald and Robert L. Herbst, "Campaign Finance and State Constitutions" (Hugh L. Carey Institute for Government Reform, October 24, 2017). https://wagner.edu/carey-institute/files/2008/04/Campaign-Finance-and-State-Constitutions-SG-RH.pdf.pdf
4. US Department of Treasury, The State of Labor Market Competition; Mar 7, 2022. https://home.treasury.gov/system/files/136/State-of-Labor-Market-Competition-2022.pdf
5. "Divided Decade: How the Housing Market Changed in the Last 10 Years," *APM Research Lab*, February 12, 2019. https://www.apmresearchlab.org/housingcost
6. C. G. Jung, *Memories, Dreams, Reflections*, ed. Aniela Jaffé (London: Fontana Press, 1995).

8. The war on terror

1. "Forces in Iraq and Syria Discovers 72 Mass Graves in Areas Freed from ISIS," *Iraqi News*, August 30, 2016. https://www.iraqinews.com/iraq-war/forces-in-iraq-and-syria-discovers-72-mass-graves-areas-freed-from-isis/

2. Ellen Nakashima, Mark Berman, and William Wan, "Ahmad Rahami, Suspected New York Bomber, Cited al-Qaeda and ISIS, Officials Say," *The Washington Post*, September 21, 2016. https://www.washingtonpost.com/news/post-nation/wp/2016/09/20/new-york-bombing-suspect-charged-with-using-weapons-of-mass-destruction/

3. Alan Blinder, Frances Robles, and Richard Pérez-Peña, "Omar Mateen Posted to Facebook Amid Orlando Attack, Lawmaker Says," *The New York Times*, June 16, 2016, sec. U.S. https://www.nytimes.com/2016/06/17/us/orlando-shooting.html

4. "Islamic State (ISIS) Releases Pamphlet On Female Slaves," *MEMRI*, December 3, 2014. https://www.memri.org/jttm/islamic-state-isis-releases-pamphlet-female-slaves

5. Amelia Smith, "ISIS Publish Pamphlet on How to Treat Female Slaves," *Newsweek*, December 9, 2014. https://www.newsweek.com/isis-release-questions-and-answers-pamphlet-how-treat-female-slaves-290511

6. Stephanie Savell, "How Death Outlives War: The Reverberating Impact of the Post-9/11 Wars on Human Health," Costs of War (Providence, Rhode Island: Watson Institute for International & Public Affairs, May 15, 2023). https://watson.brown.edu/costsofwar/files/cow/imce/papers/2023/Indirect%20Deaths.pdf

7. UN High Commissioner for Refugees (UNHCR), "UNHCR Monitoring Visit to the Republic of Nauru" (Lyons: UNHCR, November 26, 2013). https://www.refworld.org/docid/5294a6534.html

8. Ben Doherty and Christopher Knaus, "Liberal Party Donor's Revenue from Uncontested Contracts for Offshore Processing Rises to $1.5bn," *The Guardian*, July 20, 2021, sec. Australia news. https://www.theguardian.com/australia-news/2021/jul/21/liberal-party-donors-revenue-from-uncontested-contracts-for-offshore-processing-rises-to-15bn

9. "Syrian Cities Damage Atlas" (Geneva: REACH, March 16, 2019). https://reliefweb.int/sites/reliefweb.int/files/resources/reach_thematic_assessment_syrian_cities_damage_atlas_march_2019_reduced_file_size_1.pdf

10. "Syria Emergency," UNHCR, accessed August 22, 2023. https://www.unhcr.org/emergencies/syria-emergency

11. "UNHCR Iraq Country Portfolio Evaluation," UNHCR Australia, accessed June 22, 2023. https://www.unhcr.org/au/media/unhcr-iraq-country-portfolio-evaluation

12. David Vine et al., "Creating Refugees: Displacement Caused by the United States' Post-9/11 Wars," Costs of War (Providence, Rhode Island: Watson Institute for International & Public Affairs, September 21, 2020). https://watson.brown.edu/costsofwar/files/cow/imce/papers/2020/Displacement_Vine%20et%20al_Costs%20of%20War%202020%2009%2008.pdf

13. Iraq Family Health Survey Study Group, "Violence-Related Mortality in Iraq from 2002 to 2006," *New England Journal of Medicine* 358, no. 5 (January 31, 2008): 484–93. https://doi.org/10.1056/NEJMsa0707782

14. "Iraq Body Count," Iraq Body Count, accessed August 23, 2023. https://www.iraqbodycount.org/database/

15. Gilbert Burnham et al., "Mortality after the 2003 Invasion of Iraq: A Cross-Sectional Cluster Sample Survey," *The Lancet* 368, no. 9545 (October 2006): 1421–28. https://doi.org/10.1016/S0140-6736(06)69491-9 Gilbert Burnham et al., "The Human Cost of the War in Iraq: A Mortality Study 2002-2006" (Cambridge, Massachusetts: Center for International Studies, Massachusetts Institute of Technology, October 11, 2006). https://web.mit.edu/humancostiraq/reports/human-cost-war-101106.pdf

16. "Iraqi Deaths Survey 'Was Robust,'" *BBC News*, March 26, 2007. http://news.bbc.co.uk/1/hi/uk_politics/6495753.stm

17. IPPNW, Physicians for Social Responsibility, and Physicians for Global Survival, *Body Count: Casualty Figures after 10 Years of the "War on Terror,"* trans. Ali Fathollah-Nejad (Berlin: Internationale Ärzte für die Verhütung des Atomkrieges, 2015). https://stacks.stanford.edu/file/druid:rs154fr6978/body-count.pdf

18. IPPNW, Physicians for Social Responsibility, and Physicians for Global Survival.

19. Amy Belasco, "The Cost of Iraq, Afghanistan, and Other Global War on Terror Operations Since 9/11" (Congressional Research Service, December 8, 2014).

20. Aida Edemariam, "The True Cost of War," *The Guardian*, February 28, 2008, sec. World news. https://www.theguardian.com/world/2008/feb/28/iraq.afghanistan

21. Edemariam.

22. Neta C. Crawford, "United States Budgetary Costs of the Post-9/11 Wars Through FY2019: $5.9 Trillion Spent and Obligated," Costs of War (Providence, Rhode Island: Watson Institute for International & Public Affairs, November 14, 2018).

23. Stephen Daggett, "Costs of Major U.S. Wars" (Congressional Research Service, June 29, 2010).

24. Tucker: DC insiders push for war with Iran, Fox News; Jan 7, 2020. https://video.foxnews.com/v/6120207776001#sp=show-clips

25. Patrick Cockburn, "After IS," *London Review of Books*, February 4, 2021. https://www.lrb.co.uk/the-paper/v43/n03/patrick-cockburn/after-is

26. Lawrence Wilkerson, "'I Am Willing to Testify' If Dick Cheney Is Put on Trial," interview by Amy Goodman, *Democracy Now!*, August 30, 2011. http://www.democracynow.org/2011/8/30/ex_bush_official_col_lawrence_wilkerson

27. Jon Schwarz, "15 Years Ago, Colin Powell Lied to the United Nations," *The Intercept*, February 6, 2018. https://theintercept.com/2018/02/06/lie-after-lie-what-colin-powell-knew-about-iraq-fifteen-years-ago-and-what-he-told-the-un/

28. Bureau of Public Affairs Department of State. The Office of Electronic Information, "Remarks to the United Nations Security Council" (Department of State. The Office of Electronic Information, Bureau of Public Affairs., February 5, 2003). https://2001-2009-state.gov/secretary/former/powell/remarks/2003/17300.htm

29. Lawrence Wilkerson, "Pre-War Intelligence," interview by David Brancaccio, *NOW*, PBS, February 3, 2006. https://web.archive.org/web/20120226093037/https://www.pbs.org/now/politics/wilkerson.html

30. Seymour M. Hersh, "Selective Intelligence," *The New Yorker*, May 4, 2003. https://www.newyorker.com/magazine/2003/05/12/selective-intelligence

31. "John M. Olin Foundation," Militarist Monitor, accessed June 22, 2023. https://militarist-monitor.org/profile/john_m_olin_foundation/

32. "Bradley Foundation," Militarist Monitor, accessed June 22, 2023. https://militarist-monitor.org/profile/bradley_foundation/

33. "Scaife Foundations," Militarist Monitor, accessed June 22, 2023. https://militarist-monitor.org/profile/scaife_foundations/ "Scaife Foundations";. "Project for the New American Century," Militarist Monitor, accessed June 22, 2023. https://militarist-monitor.org/profile/project_for_the_new_american_century/ "Project for the New American Century," in *SourceWatch*, accessed June 22, 2023. https://www.sourcewatch.org/index.php?title=Project_for_the_New_American_Century

34. William J. Bennett et al. to William J. Clinton, Letter, Project for the New American Century, January 26, 1998. https://web.archive.org/web/20110217020049/http://www.newamericancentury.org/iraqclintonletter.htm

35. Nafeez Ahmed, "Iraq Invasion Was about Oil," *The Guardian*, March 20, 2014, sec. Environment. https://www.theguardian.com/environment/earth-insight/2014/mar/20/iraq-war-oil-resources-energy-peak-scarcity-economy Neil Mackay, "Bush Planned Iraq 'regime Change' before Becoming President," *Sunday Herald*, September 15, 2002.

36. "Project for the New American Century."

37. Hersh, "Selective Intelligence."

38. George Kenney, "General Condemnation," *In These Times*, March 8, 2006. https://inthesetimes.com/article/general-condemnation

39. Grant Smith, "Does AIPAC Have Only Two Major Donors?," *Antiwar*, August 10, 2011. https://original.antiwar.com/smith-grant/2011/08/09/does-aipac-have-only-two-major-donors/

40. "Donald H. Rumsfeld," *SourceWatch*, accessed June 22, 2023. https://www.sourcewatch.org/index.php/Donald_H._Rumsfeld

41. Seymour M. Hersh, "Lunch With the Chairman," *The New Yorker*, March 9, 2003. https://www.newyorker.com/magazine/2003/03/17/lunch-with-the-chairman "Trireme Partners LP," *SourceWatch*, accessed June 22, 2023. https://www.sourcewatch.org/index.php?title=Trireme_Partners_LP

42. David E. Rosenbaum, "A Closer Look at Cheney and Halliburton," *The New York Times*, September 28, 2004, sec. U.S. https://www.nytimes.com/2004/09/28/us/a-closer-look-at-cheney-and-halliburton.html

43. Maud Beelman et al., "U.S. Contractors Reap the Windfalls of Post-War Reconstruction," *ICIJ*, May 7, 2012. https://www.icij.org/investigations/windfalls-war/us-contractors-reap-windfalls-post-war-reconstruction-0/

44. Rosenbaum, "A Closer Look at Cheney and Halliburton"; "Winning Contractors," *Center for Public Integrity*, October 30, 2003. http://publicintegrity.org/national-security/winning-contractors/

45. Wesley Clark, "The US Will Attack 7 Countries in 5 Years," clip from talk at Commonwealth Club of California, October 3, 2007. https://www.youtube.com/watch?v=nUCwCgthp_E

46. FAIR, "Iraq and the Media: A Critical Timeline," *FAIR*, March 19, 2007. https://fair.org/take-action/media-advisories/iraq-and-the-media/

47. Steve Rendall, "Amplifying Officials, Squelching Dissent," *FAIR*, May 1, 2003. https://fair.org/extra/amplifying-officials-squelching-dissent/

48. Nafeez Mosaddeq Ahmed, "More Pontification, More Propaganda on Iraq: Notes on John Ware's BBC Iraq Fiasco: Dissecting the Disinformation on Western Secret Strategy in the New Middle East Wars," *Media Monitors Network (MMN)*, November 4, 2007. https://mediamonitors.net/more-pontification-more-propaganda-on-iraq-notes-on-john-wares-bbc-iraq-fiasco-dissecting-the-disinformation-on-western-secret-strategy-in-the-new-middle-east-wars/

49. Greg Palast, "The Economic Conquest of Iraq," *Global Research*, October 29, 2004. https://www.globalresearch.ca/the-economic-conquest-of-iraq/551

50. Antonia Juhasz, "Whose Oil Is It, Anyway?," *The New York Times*, March 13, 2007, sec. Opinion. https://www.nytimes.com/2007/03/13/opinion/13juhasz.html

51. Greg Muttitt, "Whatever Happened to Iraqi Oil," A Day in Iraq Conference, April 5, 2013. https://www.youtube.com/watch?v=3kQeFOwCdqU

52. Smedley D. Butler, *War Is a Racket* (Los Angeles, California: Feral House, 2003).

53. Barbara W. Tuchman, *The March of Folly: From Troy to Vietnam* (London: Abacus, 1985).

54. Neil Sheehan, "Vietnam Archive: Pentagon Study Traces 3 Decades of Growing U.S. Involvement," *The New York Times*, June 13, 1971. https://archive.nytimes.com/www.nytimes.com/books/97/04/13/reviews/papers-overview.html

55. Craig Whitlock, "U.S. Officials Misled the Public about the War in Afghanistan, Confidential Documents Reveal," *The Washington Post*, December 9, 2019, sec. The Afghanistan Papers. https://www.washingtonpost.com/graphics/2019/investigations/afghanistan-papers/afghanistan-war-confidential-documents/

9. The global financial crisis

1. Tom Coburn, "Wall Street and The Financial Crisis: Anatomy of a Financial Collapse," Majority and Minority Staff Report (Washington, D.C.: HSGAC, April 13, 2011)

2. "Finance/Insurance/Real Estate," *OpenSecrets*, accessed June 27, 2023. https://www.opensecrets.org/industries/indus.php?Ind=F

3. Kenneth Peres, "Joe Biden Serves Wall Street, Not Main Street," *Common Dreams*, February 23, 2020. https://www.commondreams.org/views/2020/02/23/joe-biden-serves-wall-street-not-main-street

4. Eamon Javers, "Rubin: 'We All Bear Responsibility,'" *POLITICO*, April 8, 2010. https://www.politico.com/story/2010/04/rubin-we-all-bear-responsibility-035547 Henry Kaufman, "Preventing the Next Global Financial Crisis," *Washington Post*, January 28, 1998. https://www.washingtonpost.com/archive/opinions/1998/01/28/preventing-the-next-global-financial-crisis/935b3f79-dfc3-446a-8bb9-f9d092681e57/ Stephen Gandel, "Here's Why a Special Commission Thought Robert Rubin May Have Broken the Law during the Financial Crisis," *Fortune*, March 13, 2016. https://fortune.com/2016/03/13/robert-rubin-financial-crisis-commission-justice-department/ J. Crotty, "Structural Causes of the Global Financial Crisis: A Critical Assessment of the 'New Financial Architecture,'" *Cambridge Journal of Economics* 33, no. 4 (July 1, 2009): 563–80. https://doi.org/10.1093/cje/bep023 Sameer Dossani and

Emily Schwartz Greco, "Chomsky: Understanding the Crisis Markets, the State and Hypocrisy," *Foreign Policy In Focus*, February 9, 2009. https://fpif.org/chomsky_understanding_the_crisis_markets_the_state_and_hypocrisy/ Michael Hirsh, "The Comprehensive Case Against Larry Summers," *The Atlantic*, September 13, 2013. https://www.theatlantic.com/business/archive/2013/09/the-comprehensive-case-against-larry-summers/279651/

5. United States, ed., "Conclusions of the Financial Crisis Inquiry Commission," in The Financial Crisis Inquiry Report: Final Report of the National Commission on the Causes of the Financial and Economic Crisis in the United States, Official government ed. (Washington, D.C.: Financial Crisis Inquiry Commission, 2011), xv–xxviii.

6. "Corporate Governance in the Wake of the Financial Crisis" (UN, n.d.).

7. Simon Johnson, "The Quiet Coup," *The Atlantic*, May 1, 2009. https://www.theatlantic.com/magazine/archive/2009/05/the-quiet-coup/307364/

8. Johnson.

9. Lynn Parramore, "Money and the Midterms: Are the Parties Over? Interview With Thomas Ferguson," *Huffington Post*, November 12, 2010, sec. Politics. https://www.huffpost.com/entry/money-and-the-midterms-ar_b_782660

10. "Financial Crisis Losses and Potential Impacts of the Dodd-Frank Act," Report to Congressional Requesters (United States Government Accountability Office, January 2013). https://www.gao.gov/assets/gao-13-180.pdf

11. "Chart Book: The Legacy of the Great Recession," Center on Budget and Policy Priorities, June 6, 2019. https://www.cbpp.org/research/economy/the-legacy-of-the-great-recession

12. Condé Nast, "'The Politics of Hiring Wall Street People Is Bad': Biden Has Kept the Bankers and Traders at Bay, but Will It Last?," *Vanity Fair*, December 3, 2020. https://www.vanityfair.com/news/2020/12/biden-has-kept-the-bankers-and-traders-at-bay-but-will-it-last

13. Theodoric Meyer and Alex Thompson, "Goldman Sachs Vets Quietly Added to Biden Transition," *POLITICO*, June 21, 2023. https://www.politico.com/newsletters/transition-playbook/2020/12/14/goldman-sachs-vets-quietly-added-to-biden-transition-491143

10. The COVID pandemic

1. Frank Snowden, "How Will COVID-19 Change the World? Historian Frank Snowden on Epidemics from the Black Death to Now," interview by Amy Goodman, *Democracy Now!*, May 18, 2020. https://www.democracynow.org/2020/5/18/frank_snowden_covid_19_epidemics_history

2. Kavya Sekar, "Domestic Funding for COVID-19 Vaccines: An Overview," Insight (Congressional Research Service, March 29, 2021). https://crsreports.congress.gov/product/pdf/IN/IN11556 "COVID-19: Urgent Actions Needed to Better Ensure an Effective Federal Response," *U.S. Government Accountability Office*, November 30, 2020. https://www.gao.gov/products/gao-21-191 Chad P. Bown and Thomas J. Bollyky, "Here's How to Get Billions of COVID-19 Vaccine Doses to the World," *PIIE*, March 18, 2021. https://www.piie.com/blogs/trade-and-investment-policy-watch/heres-how-get-billions-covid-19-vaccine-doses-world Lisa Cornish, "Interactive: Who's Funding the COVID-19 Response and What Are the Priorities?," *Devex*,

Citations

February 13, 2023 https://www.devex.com/news/sponsored/interactive-who-s-funding-the-covid-19-response-and-what-are-the-priorities-96833

3. Hussain S. Lalani, Jerry Avorn, and Aaron S. Kesselheim, "US Taxpayers Heavily Funded the Discovery of COVID-19 Vaccines," *Clinical Pharmacology and Therapeutics* 111, no. 3 (March 2022): 542–44. https://doi.org/10.1002/cpt.2344 Katalin Karikó et al., "Suppression of RNA Recognition by Toll-like Receptors: The Impact of Nucleoside Modification and the Evolutionary Origin of RNA," *Immunity* 23, no. 2 (August 1, 2005): 165–75. https://doi.org/10.1016/j.immuni.2005.06.008 Samuel Cross et al., "Who Funded the Research behind the Oxford–AstraZeneca COVID-19 Vaccine?," *British Medical Journal Global Health* 6, no. 12 (December 1, 2021): e007321. https://doi.org/10.1136/bmjgh-2021-007321

4. Sydney Lupkin, "A Federal Coronavirus Vaccine Contract Released At Last, But Redactions Obscure Terms," *NPR*, October 24, 2020. https://www.npr.org/sections/health-shots/2020/10/24/927474041/a-federal-coronavirus-vaccine-contract-released-at-last-but-redactions-obscure-t

5. "For Whose Benefit? Transparency in the Development and Procurement of COVID-19 Vaccines." (Transparency International, May 2021). https://ti-health.org/wp-content/uploads/2021/05/For-Whose-Benefit-Transparency-International.pdf

6. Kevin J. Hickey, "The PREP Act and COVID-19, Part 1: Statutory Authority to Limit Liability for Medical Countermeasures," CRS Legal Sidebar (Congressional Research Service, April 13, 2022). https://crsreports.congress.gov/product/pdf/LSB/LSB10443

7. Ariel Gorodensky and Jillian C. Kohler, "State Capture through Indemnification Demands? Effects on Equity in the Global Distribution of COVID-19 Vaccines," *Journal of Pharmaceutical Policy and Practice* 15, no. 1 (August 19, 2022): 50. https://doi.org/10.1186/s40545-022-00442-y

8. Kathryn Ardizzone, "Letter to BARDA on Enforcing Moderna Disclosure Requirements," *Public Citizen*, August 3, 2020. https://www.citizen.org/article/letter-to-barda-on-enforcing-moderna-disclosure-requirements/

9. "Another Shot at Vaccine Transparency," *Transparency*, October 25, 2021. https://www.transparency.org/en/blog/shot-at-vaccine-transparency-pfizer-covax "For Whose Benefit? Transparency in the Development and Procurement of COVID-19 Vaccines"; Transparency International, May 25, 2021. https://ti-health.org/content/for-whose-benefit-transparency-in-the-development-and-procurement-of-covid-19-vaccines/#:~:text=Transparency%20here%20is%20paramount%3B%20publicly,into%20the%20global%20vaccination%20process.

10. Madlen Davies et al., "'Held to Ransom': Pfizer Demands Governments Gamble with State Assets to Secure Vaccine Deal," *The Bureau of Investigative Journalism*, February 23, 2021. https://www.thebureauinvestigates.com/stories/2021-02-23/held-to-ransom-pfizer-demands-governments-gamble-with-state-assets-to-secure-vaccine-deal

11. Francesco Guarascio, "EU's von Der Leyen Can't Find Texts with Pfizer Chief on Vaccine Deal -Letter," *Reuters*, June 29, 2022, sec. Europe. https://www.reuters.com/world/europe/eus-von-der-leyen-cant-find-texts-with-pfizer-chief-vaccine-deal-letter-2022-06-29/

12. Carlo Martuscelli, "MEPs Want to Grill von Der Leyen over Pfizer Vaccine

Citations

Contract," *POLITICO*, January 11, 2023. https://www.politico.eu/article/mep-european-parliament-ursula-von-der-leyen-pfizer-vaccine-contract/

13. Carlo Martuscelli, "EU Stonewalls over von Der Leyen's Role in Multibillion-Euro Pfizer Vaccine Deal," *POLITICO*, September 12, 2022. https://www.politico.eu/article/eu-stonewalls-over-von-der-leyens-role-in-multi-billion-euro-pfizer-jab-deal/

14. Carlo Martuscelli, "EU Prosecutor's Office Opens Investigation into COVID Vaccine Purchases," *POLITICO*, October 15, 2022. https://www.politico.eu/article/ursula-von-der-leyen-pfizer-eu-prosecutors-office-opens-investigation-into-covid-vaccine-purchases/

15. "EU Watchdog Raps Commission over von Der Leyen's Texts with Pfizer Boss," *POLITICO*, January 28, 2022. https://www.politico.eu/article/eu-watchdog-ursula-von-der-leyen-pfizer-messaging-maladministration/

16. Maxence Peigné, "EU Unable to Cap COVID-19 Vaccine Prices in Secret Deals," *Investigate Europe*, September 23, 2021. https://www.investigate-europe.eu/en/2021/eu-negotiators-covid-19-vaccine-price-moderna-pfizer/

17. Julia Kollewe, "Pfizer Accused of Pandemic Profiteering as Profits Double," *The Guardian*, February 8, 2022, sec. Business. https://www.theguardian.com/business/2022/feb/08/pfizer-covid-vaccine-pill-profits-sales

18. "Another Shot at Vaccine Transparency," *Transparency*, October 25, 2021. https://www.transparency.org/en/blog/shot-at-vaccine-transparency-pfizer-covax "For Whose Benefit? Transparency in the Development and Procurement of COVID-19 Vaccines".

19. Peter Doshi, Fiona Godlee, and Kamran Abbasi, "Covid-19 Vaccines and Treatments: We Must Have Raw Data, Now," *British Medical Journal* 376 (January 19, 2022): o102. https://doi.org/10.1136/bmj.o102

20. Florence T. Bourgeois, Srinivas Murthy, and Kenneth D. Mandl, "Outcome Reporting Among Drug Trials Registered in ClinicalTrials.Gov," *Annals of Internal Medicine* 153, no. 3 (August 3, 2010): 158–66. https://doi.org/10.1059/0003-4819-153-3-201008030-00006

21. Peter Whoriskey, "As Drug Industry's Influence over Research Grows, so Does the Potential for Bias," *Washington Post*, November 24, 2012. https://www.washingtonpost.com/business/economy/as-drug-industrys-influence-over-research-grows-so-does-the-potential-for-bias/2012/11/24/bb64d596-1264-11e2-be82-c3411b7680a9_story.html

22. Sameer S. Chopra, "Industry Funding of Clinical Trials: Benefit or Bias?," *JAMA* 290, no. 1 (July 2, 2003): 113–14. https://doi.org/10.1001/jama.290.1.113

23. British Medical Journal Publishing Group, "Collaboration between Academics and Industry in Clinical Trials: Cross Sectional Study of Publications and Survey of Lead Academic Authors," *British Medical Journal* 363 (October 11, 2018): k4298. https://doi.org/10.1136/bmj.k4298 Clare Watson, "Undisclosed Industry Payments Rampant in Drug-Trial Papers," *Nature*, March 24, 2022. https://doi.org/10.1038/d41586-022-00835-8

24. Ben Goldacre, "Trial sans Error: How Pharma-Funded Research Cherry-Picks Positive Results [Excerpt]," *Scientific American*, February 13, 2013. https://www.scientificamerican.com/article/trial-sans-error-how-pharma-funded-research-cherry-picks-positive-results/ Lisa Bero et al., "Factors Associated with Findings of Published Trials of Drug–Drug Comparisons: Why Some Statins Appear More Efficacious than Others," *Public Library of Science Medicine* 4,

no. 6 (June 2007): e184. https://doi.org/10.1371/journal.pmed.0040184 Joel
Lexchin et al., "Pharmaceutical Industry Sponsorship and Research Outcome
and Quality: Systematic Review," *British Medical Journal (Clinical Research
Ed.)* 326, no. 7400 (May 31, 2003): 1167–70. https://doi.org/10.1136/bmj.
326.7400.1167

25. Schmeling et al, Batch-dependent safety of the BNT162b2 mRNA COVID-
    19. Eur J Clin Invest. 2023;53:e13998. DOI: 10.1111/eci.13998 https://
    pubmed.ncbi.nlm.nih.gov/36997290/

26. Viral vaccine paper, Dr John Campbell, YouTube. July 6, 2023. https://www.
    youtube.com/watch?v=KgldG9r-i9M&ab_channel=Dr.JohnCampbell

27. Richard Smith, "Medical Journals Are an Extension of the Marketing Arm of
    Pharmaceutical Companies". PLOS, May 17, 2005.

28. Jennifer E. Miller, Joseph S Ross, and Michelle M. Mello, "Far More Trans-
    parency Is Needed for Covid-19 Vaccine Trials," *STAT*, November 5, 2020.
    https://www.statnews.com/2020/11/05/transparency-is-needed-for-covid-19-
    vaccine-trials/

29. Harvey Gavin, "Poor Transparency in Vaccine Trials and Secretive Contracts
    Risk Success of Global COVID-19 Response, Report Finds," *University of
    Toronto, Leslie Dan Faculty of Pharmacy*, May 25, 2021. https://www.phar
    macy.utoronto.ca/news-announcements/poor-transparency-vaccine-trials-and-
    secretive-contracts-risk-success-global-covid-19-response-report-finds

30. "For Whose Benefit? Transparency in the Development and Procurement of
    COVID-19 Vaccines."

31. Doshi, Godlee, and Abbasi, "Covid-19 Vaccines and Treatments."

32. Phillip Broadwith, "Clinical Trial Data Release Blocked by Companies,"
    Chemistry World, May 8, 2013. https://www.chemistryworld.com/news/clini
    cal-trial-data-release-blocked-by-companies/6151.article

33. David G. Nathan and David J. Weatherall, "Academic Freedom in Clinical
    Research," *New England Journal of Medicine* 347, no. 17 (October 24, 2002):
    1368–71. https://doi.org/10.1056/NEJMsb020394

34. Dani Thompson, "Challenges with Large CROs," *Vial*, March 9, 2023.
    https://vial.com/blog/articles/challenges-with-large-cros-misaligned-incentives-
    and-unnecessary-burden/ "The Global Contract Research Organization
    (CRO) Services Market Is Projected to Grow from $82.60 Billion in 2023 to
    $188.52 Billion by 2030" (Contract Research Organization, June 2023).
    https://www.fortunebusinessinsights.com/industry-reports/contract-research-
    organization-cro-services-market-100864

35. J. Lenzer, "Truly Independent Research?," *British Medical Journal* 337, no.
    7670 (August 21, 2008): a1332. https://doi.org/10.1136/bmj.a1332

36. Paul D. Thacker, "Covid-19: Researcher Blows the Whistle on Data Integrity
    Issues in Pfizer's Vaccine Trial: Video 1," *British Medical Journal* 375, no. 83`3
    (November 2, 2021): n2635. https://doi.org/10.1136/bmj.n2635

37. Shein-Chung Chow, Susan S. Chow, and Annpey Pong, "Review of Current
    Controversial Issues in Clinical Trials," *General Psychiatry* 34, no. 5 (October
    1, 2021): e100540. https://doi.org/10.1136/gpsych-2021-100540

38. "Committee for Medicinal Products for Human Use (CHMP) Guideline on
    Data Monitoring Committees," *Statistics in Medicine* 25, no. 10 (May 30,
    2006): 1639–45. https://doi.org/10.1002/sim.2585

39. Steven Salzberg, "Highly Profitable Medical Journal Says Open Access
    Publishing Has Failed. Right.," *Forbes*, April 1, 2019. https://www.forbes.com/

sites/stevensalzberg/2019/04/01/nejm-says-open-access-publishing-has-failed-right/

40. RELX PLC, MarketScreener. https://www.marketscreener.com/quote/stock/RELX-PLC-14302/company/

41. Informa website: What we do. https://www.informa.com/about-us/what-we-do/

42. John Wiley & Sons, Inc. CNN Business website. https://money.cnn.com/quote/shareholders/shareholders.html?symb=WLY&subView=institutional

43. "The Lancet: Revenue, Competitors, Alternatives," Growjo, accessed July 4, 2023. https://growjo.com/company/The_Lancet

44. Richard Smith, "Medical Journals and Pharmaceutical Companies: Uneasy Bedfellows," *British Medical Journal* 326, no. 7400 (May 31, 2003): 1202–5. "Sources of Revenue," *The BMJ*, accessed July 4, 2023. https://www.bmj.com/about-bmj/sources-of-revenue Adriane Fugh-Berman, Karen Alladin, and Jarva Chow, "Advertising in Medical Journals: Should Current Practices Change?," *Public Library of Science Medicine* 3, no. 6 (June 2006): e130. https://doi.org/10.1371/journal.pmed.0030130

45. O. Dyer, "Journal Rejects Article after Objections from Marketing Department," *British Medical Journal* 328, no. 7434 (January 31, 2004): 244-b-244. https://doi.org/10.1136/bmj.328.7434.244-b

46. Fugh-Berman, Alladin, and Chow, "Advertising in Medical Journals."

47. Ben Goldacre, *Bad Pharma: How Drug Companies Mislead Doctors and Harm Patients*, 1st ed. (New York: Faber and Faber, Inc., 2013).

48. Bob Grant, Merck published fake journal, The Scientist; Apr 29, 2009. https://www.the-scientist.com/the-nutshell/merck-published-fake-journal-44190

49. David T. Healy, "Transparency and Trust: Figure for Ghost Written Articles Was Misquoted," *British Medical Journal* 329, no. 7478 (December 12, 2004): 1345. https://doi.org/10.1136/bmj.329.7478.1345 A. Flanagin et al., "Prevalence of Articles with Honorary Authors and Ghost Authors in Peer-Reviewed Medical Journals," *JAMA* 280, no. 3 (July 15, 1998): 222–24. https://doi.org/10.1001/jama.280.3.222 Sankalp Yadav and Gautam Rawal, "Ghostwriters in the Scientific World," *The Pan African Medical Journal* 30 (2018). https://doi.org/10.11604/pamj.2018.30.217.16312 Peter C. Gøtzsche et al., "Ghost Authorship in Industry-Initiated Randomised Trials," *Public Library of Science Medicine* 4, no. 1 (January 2007): e19. https://doi.org/10.1371/journal.pmed.0040019 Lisa M. DeTora et al., "Ghostwriting in Biomedicine: A Review of the Published Literature," *Current Medical Research and Opinion* 35, no. 9 (September 2, 2019): 1643–51. https://doi.org/10.1080/03007995.2019.1608101

50. Doshi, Godlee, and Abbasi, "Covid-19 Vaccines and Treatments."

51. Antony Barnett, "Revealed: How Drug Firms 'hoodwink' Medical Journals," *The Observer*, December 7, 2003, sec. Society. https://www.theguardian.com/society/2003/dec/07/health.businessofresearch

52. Ben Goldacre, "Medical Ghostwriters Who Build a Brand," *The Guardian*, September 18, 2010, sec. Opinion. https://www.theguardian.com/commentisfree/2010/sep/18/bad-science-medical-ghostwriters Barnett, "Revealed".

53. Richard Smith, "The optimal peer review system?" BMJ, November 8, 2016.

54. https://blogs.bmj.com/bmj/2016/11/08/richard-smith-the-optimal-peer-review-system/ Jefferson, et al, "Effects of editorial peer review: a systematic

review". JAMA, June 5, 2002;287(21):2784-6. doi: 10.1001/jama.287.21.2784.

55. V Demicheli, et al. "Peer review for improving the quality of grant applications". Cochrane Database Syst Rev, April 18, 2007; 2007(2):MR000003. doi: 10.1002/14651858.MR000003.pub2.

56. Jessica J Liu et al., "Payments by US Pharmaceutical and Medical Device Manufacturers to US Medical Journal Editors: Retrospective Observational Study," *British Medical Journal*, October 26, 2017, j4619. https://doi.org/10.1136/bmj.j4619

57. Dr Jason Fung, "The Corruption of Evidence Based Medicine — Killing for Profit," *Medium*, April 10, 2018. https://drjasonfung.medium.com/the-corruption-of-evidence-based-medicine-killing-for-profit-41f2812b8704 Jessica J. Liu et al., "Payments by US Pharmaceutical and Medical Device Manufacturers to US Medical Journal Editors: Retrospective Observational Study," *British Medical Journal* 359 (October 26, 2017): j4619. https://doi.org/10.1136/bmj.j4619

58. Jon Jureidini and Leemon B. McHenry, "The Illusion of Evidence Based Medicine," *British Medical Journal* 376 (March 16, 2022): o702. https://doi.org/10.1136/bmj.o702

59. Maryanne Demasi, "From FDA to MHRA: Are Drug Regulators for Hire?," *British Medical Journal* 377 (June 29, 2022): o1538. https://doi.org/10.1136/bmj.o1538

60. Demasi.

61. MHRA Customer Service Centre, "Freedom of Information Request on Whether the MHRA Receives Funding from the Bill and Melinda Gates Foundation (FOI 21-624)," June 21, 2021. https://www.gov.uk/government/publications/freedom-of-information-responses-from-the-mhra-week-commencing-21-june-2021/freedom-of-information-request-on-whether-the-mhra-receives-funding-from-the-bill-and-melinda-gates-foundation-foi-21-624 Jamie Grant, "Triennial Review of the Commission on Human Medicines: Review Report" (London: Department of Health, March 26, 2015); "One Post Available for the Paediatric Medicines Expert Advisory Group," Commission on Human Medicines, 2023. https://assets.publishing.service.gov.uk/government/uploads/system/uploads/attachment_data/file/1141795/PM23-1_Advert_-_CHM_Paediatric_Medicines_Expert_Advisory_Group.pdf

62. Charles Piller, "FDA's Revolving Door: Companies Often Hire Agency Staffers Who Managed Their Successful Drug Reviews," *Science*, July 5, 2018. https://www.science.org/content/article/fda-s-revolving-door-companies-often-hire-agency-staffers-who-managed-their-successful Jeffrey Bien and Vinay Prasad, "Future Jobs of FDA's Haematology-Oncology Reviewers," *British Medical Journal* 354 (September 27, 2016): i5055. https://doi.org/10.1136/bmj.i5055 Sheila Kaplan, "From FDA Expert to Biotech Insider: The Drug Industry Thrives on the Revolving Door," *STAT*, September 27, 2016. https://www.statnews.com/2016/09/27/fda-biopharma-revolving-door-study/

63. Hussain S. Lalani et al., "US Public Investment in Development of mRNA Covid-19 Vaccines: Retrospective Cohort Study," *British Medical Journal* 380 (March 1, 2023): e073747. https://doi.org/10.1136/bmj-2022-073747 Jenna Greene, "We'll All Be Dead before FDA Releases Full COVID Vaccine Record, Plaintiffs Say," *Reuters*, December 14, 2021, sec. Government. https://

www.reuters.com/legal/government/well-all-be-dead-before-fda-releases-full-covid-vaccine-record-plaintiffs-say-2021-12-13/

64. Adam Andrzejewski, "Anthony Fauci Defended NIH Culture Of Secrecy: The $325M Third-Party Royalty Complex". OpenTheBooks Substack, August 10, 2023. https://www.openthebooks.com/substack-anthony-fauci-defended-nih-culture-of-secrecy--the-325m-third-party-royalty-complex-now-we-know-more-details/

65. Adam Andrzejewski, "Substack Investigation: Faucis Royalties and the $350 Million Royalty Payment Stream HIDDEN By NIH," *Open The Books*, May 16, 2022. https://www.openthebooks.com/substack-investigation-faucis-royalties-and-the-350-million-royalty-payment-stream-hidden-by-nih/

66. Andrzejewski.

67. Jon Ungoed-Thomas, "Top Tory MPs Ask for £10,000 a Day to Work for Fake Korean Company," *The Observer*, March 25, 2023, sec. Politics. https://www.theguardian.com/politics/2023/mar/25/top-tory-mps-ask-for-10000-a-day-to-work-for-fake-korean-company

68. Jennifer Block, "Covid-19: Researchers Face Wait for Patient Level Data from Pfizer and Moderna Vaccine Trials," *British Medical Journal* 378 (July 12, 2022): o1731. https://doi.org/10.1136/bmj.o1731 Katie Thomas, "Vaccine Makers Keep Safety Details Quiet, Alarming Scientists," *The New York Times*, September 13, 2020, sec. Science. https://www.nytimes.com/2020/09/13/science/coronavirus-vaccine-trials.html

69. Adele Ferguson and Eric Johnston, "The Other Drug War - the Politics of Big Business," *The Sydney Morning Herald*, February 26, 2010, sec. Business. https://www.smh.com.au/business/the-other-drug-war--the-politics-of-big-business-20100226-p8zi.html Danielle Wood, Kate Griffiths, and Carmela Chivers, "Who's in the Room? Access and Influence in Australian Politics" (Grattan Institute, September 2018). https://grattan.edu.au/wp-content/uploads/2018/09/908-Who-s-in-the-room-Access-and-influence-in-Australian-politics.pdf "Weighted Average Monthly Treatment Cost (WAMTC)" (Pharmaceutical Benefits Pricing Authority, April 2009). https://www.pbs.gov.au/industry/pricing/pbs-items/wamtc/wamtc-manual-april-2009.pdf

70. Tom Jefferson, "The UK Turns to Witty, Vallance, and Van Tam for Leadership: Revolving Doors?," *The BMJ*, December 6, 2017. https://blogs.bmj.com/bmj/2017/12/06/tom-jefferson-the-uk-turns-to-witty-vallance-and-van-tam-for-leadership-revolving-doors/

71. Karen Hobert Flynn, "For Big Pharma, the Revolving Door Keeps Spinning," *The Hill*, July 11, 2019. https://thehill.com/blogs/congress-blog/politics/452654-for-big-pharma-the-revolving-door-keeps-spinning/

72. Timi Iwayemi and Fatou Ndiaye, "The Industry Agenda: Big Pharma," *Revolving Door Project*, July 22, 2021. https://therevolvingdoorproject.org/the-industry-agenda-big-pharma/

73. Sydney Lupkin, "Big Pharma Greets Hundreds of Ex-Federal Workers at the 'Revolving Door,'" *Kaiser Health News*, January 25, 2018. https://www.fiercepharma.com/pharma/big-pharma-greets-hundreds-ex-federal-workers-at-revolving-door

74. "Services," *Commonwealth Informatics*, accessed July 18, 2023. https://commoninf.com/services/ "Commonwealth Informatics Customers," *CB*

Citations

Insights, accessed July 18, 2023. https://www.cbinsights.com/company/commonwealth-informatics/customers

75. George Fradley, "Stanley Capital-Backed Portfolio Company Qinecsa Acquires Commonwealth Informatics," *Qinecsa*, December 15, 2022. https://qinecsa.com/resources/stanley-capital-backed-portfolio-company-qinecsa-acquires-commonwealth-informatics/ "Qinecsa Solutions Company Overview" (Qinecsa Solutions, 2022). https://qinecsa.com/wp-content/uploads/2022/09/Qinecsa_company-overview_July-2022.pdf Michelle Tully, "Commonwealth Informatics Helps Life Science Companies and Regulatory Agencies Improve Drug Safety," *Bloomberg*, March 22, 2021. https://www.bloomberg.com/press-releases/2021-03-22/commonwealth-informatics-helps-life-science-companies-and-regulatory-agencies-improve-drug-safety Commonwealth Informatics, "The UK Medicines and Healthcare Products Regulatory Agency (MHRA) Selects Commonwealth Informatics Inc to Explore the Use of AI and Machine Learning across Safety Surveillance," *PRNewswire*, September 13, 2021. https://www.prnewswire.com/news-releases/the-uk-medicines-and-healthcare-products-regulatory-agency-mhra-selects-commonwealth-informatics-inc-to-explore-the-use-of-ai-and-machine-learning-across-safety-surveillance-301373640.html

76. "Mr Andrew Bridgen MP", Dr John Campbell, April 29, 2023. https://web.archive.org/web/20230429154613/https://www.youtube.com/watch?v=N3WzCZbprJo

77. Dr John Campbell interview with Dr Angus Dalgleish, YouTube, Jan 11, 2024. https://www.youtube.com/watch?v=rxBz8sAfUQk&ab_channel=Dr.JohnCampbell

78. Pharma and healthcare industry advertising in the U.S. - statistics & facts; Statista, Aug 21, 2023. https://www.statista.com/topics/8415/pharma-and-healthcare-industry-advertising-in-the-us/#topicOverview

79. Michele Majidi, "Pharmaceutical industry TV advertising spending in the United States from 2016 to 2020". Statista, May 11, 2023. https://www.statista.com/statistics/953104/pharma-industry-tv-ad-spend-us/

80. Chris Pandolfo, The federal government paid media companies to advertise the COVID-19 vaccines while those same outlets provided positive coverage of the vaccines; Blaze Media, Mar 3, 2022. https://www.theblaze.com/news/review-the-federal-government-paid-media-companies-to-advertise-for-the-vaccines

81. Ray Arora, Federal government paid media outlets to promote COVID vaccine, The Illusion of Consensus, Nov 29, 1913. https://www.illusionconsensus.com/p/the-federal-government-paid-media

82. Kim Ivsersen, Tucker reveals why he was fired, Rumble video, Dec 4, 2023. https://rumble.com/v3zmuzp-tucker-reveals-why-he-was-fired-israel-warns-who-theyre-going-to-bomb-them.html

83. Missouri v. Biden, (Case no. 3:22-CV-01213.) July 4, 2023. https://storage.courtlistener.com/recap/gov.uscourts.lawd.189520/gov.uscourts.lawd.189520.293.0_1.pdf

84. Missouri v. Biden.

85. Gabriel Hays, "Zuckerberg says 'establishment' asked Facebook to censor COVID misinfo that ended up true: 'Undermines trust'". Fox News, June 9, 2023. https://www.foxnews.com/media/zuckerberg-says-establishment-asked-facebook-censor-covid-misinfo-ended-true-undermines-trust

Citations

86. Nitasha Tiku, "Facebook has a prescription: more pharmaceutical ads". Washington Post, March 4, 2020. https://www.washingtonpost.com/technology/2020/03/03/facebook-pharma-ads/

87. Robert Hart, "Here's Why Big Pharma Spends More On Ads Pushing Lower Benefit Drugs, Study Suggests". Forbes, February 7, 2023. https://www.forbes.com/sites/roberthart/2023/02/07/heres-why-big-pharma-spends-more-on-ads-pushing-lower-benefit-drugs-study-suggests/?sh=44ed74b7711b

88. Pharma and Healthcare Social Media Marketing Market Snapshot (2022 to 2032). 2024. https://www.futuremarketinsights.com/reports/pharma-and-healthcare-social-media-marketing-market

89. Wouters, O, Lobbying Expenditures and Campaign Contributions by the Pharmaceutical and Health Product Industry in the United States, 1999-2018. JAMA Intern Med. 2020 May; 180(5): 1–10. Published online 2020 Mar 3. doi: 10.1001/jamainternmed.2020.0146 https://www.ncbi.nlm.nih.gov/pmc/articles/PMC7054854/

90. Levy Facher, More than two-thirds of Congress cashed a pharma campaign check in 2020; STAT, June 9, 2021. https://www.statnews.com/feature/prescription-politics/federal-full-data-set/

91. Pharmaceuticals / Health Products Background, OpenSecrets. https://www.opensecrets.org/industries/background?cycle=2024&ind=H04

92. Lev Facher, Pharma funded more than 2,400 state lawmaker campaigns in 2020, new STAT analysis finds. Prescription Politics, June 9, 2021. https://www.statnews.com/feature/prescription-politics/state-full-data-set/

93. Julia Kollowe, Former Covid medical officer Van-Tam takes role at vaccine maker Moderna. The Guardian, Aug 19, 2023. https://www.theguardian.com/business/2023/aug/18/former-covid-medical-officer-van-tam-takes-role-at-vaccine-maker-moderna

94. Lee Fang and Jack Poulsen, Moderna is Spying on You. Lee Fang website, Nov 29, 2024. https://www.leefang.com/p/moderna-is-spying-on-you

95. Lee Fang, Moderna Surveillance Operation Targeted Independent Media Voices; Lee Fang website, Jan 17, 2024. https://www.leefang.com/p/moderna-surveillance-operation-targeted

96. The Twitter blacklisting of Jay Bhattacharya, Wall Street Journal, Mar 14, 2023. https://www.congress.gov/118/meeting/house/115286/documents/HHRG-118-GO00-20230208-SD011.pdf

97. Matt Taibbi, Not a Nothingburger: My Statement to Congress on Censorship. Racket News, Dec 2, 2023. https://www.racket.news/p/not-a-nothingburger-my-statement?utm_source=post-email-title&publication_id=1042&post_id=139363850&utm_campaign=email-post-title&isFreemail=true&r=bburx&utm_medium=email

98. Tweet by Bari Weiss, Dec 9. 2022. https://twitter.com/bariweiss/status/1601011428579717121?lang=en

99. Charles Ornstein Jones, Tracy Weber, and Ryann Grochowski, "We Found Over 700 Doctors Who Were Paid More Than a Million Dollars by Drug and Medical Device Companies," *ProPublica*, October 17, 2019. https://www.propublica.org/article/we-found-over-700-doctors-who-were-paid-more-than-a-million-dollars-by-drug-and-medical-device-companies

100. Goldacre, *Bad Pharma*.

101. Iwayemi and Ndiaye, "The Industry Agenda."

Citations

102. Eric G. Campbell et al., "Physician Professionalism and Changes in Physician-Industry Relationships From 2004 to 2009," *Archives of Internal Medicine* 170, no. 20 (November 8, 2010). https://doi.org/10.1001/archinternmed.2010.383

103. Elaine Silvestrini, "Drug and Device Companies Gave Billions to Doctors in 2016," *Drugwatch*, July 3, 2017. https://www.drugwatch.com/news/2017/07/03/big-pharma-influence-doctors-2016/

104. Health Committee, "The Influence of the Pharmaceutical Industry" (London: The House of Commons, April 5, 2005). https://publications.parliament.uk/pa/cm200405/cmselect/cmhealth/42/42.pdf

105. Ashley Wazana, "Physicians and the Pharmaceutical Industry Is a Gift Ever Just a Gift?," *JAMA* 283 (January 19, 2000): 373–80. https://doi.org/10.1001/jama.283.3.373 Kevin Connolly, "How Big Pharma Influences Doctors," *Drugwatch*, January 18, 2012. https://www.drugwatch.com/news/2012/01/18/pharmaceutical-companies-bribing-doctors/

106. Joel Lexchin, "Statistics in Drug Advertising: What They Reveal Is Suggestive What They Hide Is Vital," *International Journal of Clinical Practice* 64 (July 1, 2010): 1015–18. https://doi.org/10.1111/j.1742-1241.2010.02398.x

107. Laura Hensley, "Big Pharma Pours Millions into Medical Schools — Here's How It Can Impact Education," *Global News*, August 12, 2019. https://globalnews.ca/news/5738386/canadian-medical-school-funding/

108. Alice Fabbri et al., "Industry Funding of Patient and Health Consumer Organisations: Systematic Review with Meta-Analysis," *British Medical Journal* 368 (January 22, 2020): l6925. https://doi.org/10.1136/bmj.l6925

109. "Funding from Pharmaceutical and Biotech Companies and Device Manufacturers," *American Heart Association,* 2021-2022. https://www.heart.org/-/media/Files/Finance/21_22_Pharma_Funding_Disclosure_0323.pdf

110. "Pre$cription For Power: The Patient Advocacy Database," *KFF Health News*, April 6, 2018. https://kffhealthnews.org/patient-advocacy/ Emily Lucas, Kopp, Sydney, and Lupkin, Elizabeth, "Patient Advocacy Groups Take in Millions from Drugmakers. Is There A Payback?," *KFF Health News*, April 6, 2018. https://kffhealthnews.org/news/patient-advocacy-groups-take-in-millions-from-drugmakers-is-there-a-payback/

111. Parker et al, 'Lines in the sand': an Australian qualitative study of patient group practices to promote independence from pharmaceutical industry funders. BMJ Open. 2021; 11(2): e045140. Feb 9, 2021. doi: 10.1136/bmjopen-2020-045140. https://www.ncbi.nlm.nih.gov/pmc/articles/PMC7875302/

112. Kopp et al, KHN launches "Pre$cription for Power," a groundbreaking database to expose Big Pharma's ties to patient groups. KFF Health News, APRIL 6, 2018. https://kffhealthnews.org/news/patient-advocacy-groups-take-in-millions-from-drugmakers-is-there-a-payback/

113. Rachel Bluth and Emily Kopp, "Nonprofit Linked to PhRMA Rolls Out Campaign to Block Drug Imports," *KFF Health News*, April 19, 2017. https://kffhealthnews.org/news/non-profit-linked-to-phrma-rolls-out-campaign-to-block-drug-imports/

114. Goldacre, *Bad Pharma*; Neil J. Stone et al., "2013 ACC/AHA Guideline on the Treatment of Blood Cholesterol to Reduce Atherosclerotic Cardiovascular Risk in Adults," *Circulation* 129, no. 25_suppl_2 (June 24, 2014): S1–45. https://doi.org/10.1161/01.cir.0000437738.63853.7a

115. Sarah Boseley, "The Selling of a Wonder Drug," *The Guardian*, March 29, 2006, sec. Science. https://www.theguardian.com/science/2006/mar/29/medicineandhealth.health

116. Shai Mulinari et al., "Five Years of Pharmaceutical Industry Funding of Patient Organisations in Sweden: Cross-Sectional Study of Companies, Patient Organisations and Drugs," *Public Library of Science One* 15, no. 6 (June 24, 2020): e0235021. https://doi.org/10.1371/journal.pone.0235021 Shai Mulinari, Dylan Pashley, and Piotr Ozieranski, "Advancing International Comparison of Pharmaceutical Industry Funding of Patient Advocacy: Focus on Denmark," *Health Policy* 126, no. 12 (December 1, 2022): 1256–62. https://doi.org/10.1016/j.healthpol.2022.11.003 Christopher Knaus, "Pharmaceutical Companies Spent $34m on Patient Advocacy Groups, Research Finds," *The Guardian*, January 16, 2019, sec. Australia news. https://www.theguardian.com/australia-news/2019/jan/16/pharmaceutical-companies-spent-34m-on-patient-advocacy-groups-research-finds Piotr Ozieranski, Emily Rickard, and Shai Mulinari, "Exposing Drug Industry Funding of UK Patient Organisations," *British Medical Journal* 365 (May 22, 2019): l1806. https://doi.org/10.1136/bmj.l1806 Alex Ruoff, "AbbVie, Bristol-Myers Among Patient Advocacy Groups' Big Backers," *Bloomberg Government*, October 8, 2019. https://about.bgov.com/news/abbvie-bristol-myers-among-patient-advocacy-groups-big-backers/

117. Karl Evers-Hillstrom, Pharma lobby poured millions into 'dark money' groups influencing 2020 election. OpenSecrets, Dec 8, 2020. https://www.opensecrets.org/news/2020/12/pharma-lobby-poured-millions-into-darkmoney-groups/

118. Lee Fang, "Pfizer Quietly Financed Groups Lobbying for COVID Vaccine Mandates". Lee Fang website, April 25, 2023. https://www.leefang.com/p/pfizer-quietly-financed-groups-lobbying

119. Hristio Boytchev, "Medical royal colleges receive millions from drug and medical devices companies". *BMJ*, July 26, 2023. https://www.bmj.com/company/newsroom/21851-2/

120. Das et al, "Revealed: pharma giants pour millions of pounds into NHS to boost drug sales". *The Guardian*, July 9, 2023. https://www.bmj.com/company/newsroom/21851-2/

121. Ryan Grim, "Key scientist in COVID origin controversy misled Congress on status of $8.9m NIH grant". The Intercept, July 21, 2023. https://theintercept.com/2023/07/21/covid-origin-nih-lab-leak/

122. David Walker, "No evidence to support COVID lockdowns in Scotland during pandemic says new report". Scottish Daily Express, July 14, 2023. https://www.scottishdailyexpress.co.uk/news/scottish-news/no-evidence-support-covid-lockdowns-30470038

123. Matt Ridley & Alina Chan, "The Covid Lab-leak Deception". *Wall St Journal*, July 26, 2023. https://www.wsj.com/articles/the-covid-lab-leak-deception-andersen-nih-research-paper-private-message-52fc0c16

124. Western Australian Vaccine Safety Surveillance – Annual Report 2021. https://www.health.wa.gov.au/~/media/Corp/Documents/Health-for/Immunisation/Western-Australia-Vaccine-Safety-Surveillance-Annual-Report-2021.pdf

125. Qui, Y, et al, "Covid-19 vaccination can induce multiple sclerosis via cross-reactive CD4+ T cells recognizing SARS-CoV-2 spike protein and myelin peptides". Multiple Sclerosis Journal ; 28(3 Supplement):776, 2022. https://

pesquisa.bvsalud.org/global-literature-on-novel-coronavirus-2019-ncov/resource/pt/covidwho-2138820?lang=en

126. Neil, M, et al, "Latest statistics on England mortality data suggest systematic mis-categorisation of vaccine status and uncertain effectiveness of Covid-19 vaccination" (preprint). DOI:10.13140/RG.2.2.14176.20483

127. Prof Martin Neil, Thread Reader. https://threadreaderapp.com/thread/1633450719519842304.html

128. Martin Neil & Norman Fenton, "The very best of cheap trick". July 30, 2023. https://wherearethenumbers.substack.com/t/vaccine-safety

129. Dr John Campbell, Excess deaths, no debate allowed. Rumble video, 2023. https://rumble.com/v31tndq-excess-deahs-no-debate-allowed.html

130. Buergin et al, "Sex-specific differences in myocardial injury incidence after COVID-19 mRNA-1273 booster vaccination". European Journal of Heart Failure (2023) doi:10.1002/ejhf.297. https://onlinelibrary.wiley.com/doi/full/10.1002/ejhf.2978

131. Hoeg et al, "'Potential "Healthy Vaccinee Bias' in a Study of BNT162b2 Vaccine against Covid-19". NEJM, July 20, 2023. DOI: 10.1056/NEJMc2306683 https://www.nejm.org/doi/full/10.1056/NEJMc2306683

132. Global excess deaths associated with COVID-19, January 2020 - December 2021". WHO, May 2022. https://www.who.int/data/stories/global-excess-deaths-associated-with-covid-19-january-2020-december-2021

133. Former CIA Agent John Stockwell Talks about How the CIA Worked in Vietnam and Elsewhere, Witness to War YouTube channel, Sep 30, 2017. https://www.youtube.com/watch?v=NK1tfkESPVY&ab_channel=WitnesstoWar

134. CRUSHING DISSENT: GoFundMe Freezes Funds to Anti-War Outlet 'The Grayzone'; Glenn Greenwald Rumble channel, Aug 31, 2024. https://www.youtube.com/watch?v=K59Xb7gktIk&ab_channel=GlennGreenwald

135. C. Glenn Begley and Lee M. Ellis, "Raise Standards for Preclinical Cancer Research," *Nature* 483, no. 7391 (March 29, 2012): 531–33. https://doi.org/10.1038/483531a

136. Peter Doshi, "Covid-19 Vaccine Trial Protocols Released," *British Medical Journal* 371 (October 21, 2020): m4058. https://doi.org/10.1136/bmj.m4058

137. Goldacre, *Bad Pharma*.

138. Ben Goldacre, "What Doctors Don't Know about the Drugs They Prescribe," TEDMED, June 2012. https://www.ted.com/talks/ben_goldacre_what_doctors_don_t_know_about_the_drugs_they_prescribe

139. Erick H. Turner et al., "Selective Publication of Antidepressant Trials and Its Influence on Apparent Efficacy," *New England Journal of Medicine* 358, no. 3 (January 17, 2008): 252–60. https://doi.org/10.1056/NEJMsa065779

140. John PA Ioannidis, "Effectiveness of Antidepressants: An Evidence Myth Constructed from a Thousand Randomized Trials?," *Philosophy, Ethics, and Humanities in Medicine* 3 (May 27, 2008): 14. https://doi.org/10.1186/1747-5341-3-14

141. Irving Kirsch et al., "Initial Severity and Antidepressant Benefits: A Meta-Analysis of Data Submitted to the Food and Drug Administration," *Public Library of Science Medicine* 5, no. 2 (February 2008): e45. https://doi.org/10.1371/journal.pmed.0050045

142. Florian Prinz, Thomas Schlange, and Khusru Asadullah, "Believe It or Not: How Much Can We Rely on Published Data on Potential Drug Targets?,"

Nature Reviews Drug Discovery 10, no. 9 (September 2011): 712–712. https://doi.org/10.1038/nrd3439-c1 Begley and Ellis, "Raise Standards for Preclinical Cancer Research"

143. Monya Baker, "1,500 Scientists Lift the Lid on Reproducibility," *Nature* 533, no. 7604 (May 1, 2016): 452–54, https://doi.org/10.1038/533452a; Marta Serra-Garcia and Uri Gneezy, "Nonreplicable Publications Are Cited More than Replicable Ones," *Science Advances* 7, no. 21 (May 21, 2021): eabd1705. https://doi.org/10.1126/sciadv.abd1705

144. Jon Jureidini and Robyn Clothier, "Elsevier Should Divest Itself of Either Its Medical Publishing or Pharmaceutical Services Division," *The Lancet* 374, no. 9687 (August 1, 2009): 375. https://doi.org/10.1016/S0140-6736(09)61404-5 Peter Dockrill, "A Neuroscientist Just Tricked 4 Dodgy Journals Into Accepting a Fake Paper on 'Midi-Chlorians,'" *ScienceAlert*, July 24, 2017. https://www.sciencealert.com/a-neuroscientist-just-tricked-4-journals-into-accepting-a-fake-paper-on-midi-chlorians

145. Marcia Angell, "Drug Companies & Doctors: A Story of Corruption," *The New York Review*, January 15, 2009. https://www.nybooks.com/articles/2009/01/15/drug-companies-doctorsa-story-of-corruption/

146. Richard Smith, "Editors' Conflicts of Interest," *The BMJ*, November 2, 2010. https://blogs.bmj.com/bmj/2010/11/02/richard-smith-on-editors-conflicts-of-interest/

147. Geoffrey Spurling, Peter Mansfield, and Joel Lexchin, "Pharmaceutical Company Advertising in The Lancet," *The Lancet* 378, no. 9785 (July 2, 2011): 30. https://doi.org/10.1016/S0140-6736(11)61019-2 Fung, "The Corruption of Evidence Based Medicine — Killing for Profit." https://whitecedarclinic.com/wp-content/uploads/2021/05/Corruption-of-Evidence-based-medicine.pdf

148. Dr Peter Gøtzsche exposes big pharma as organized crime; Dr McDougall Medical Center video, Apr 2, 2015. https://www.youtube.com/watch?v=dozpAshvtsA&ab_channel=Dr.McDougallHealth%26MedicalCenter

149. Goldacre, *Bad Pharma*.

150. John P. A. Ioannidis, "Why Most Published Research Findings Are False," *Public Library of Science Medicine* 19, no. 8 (August 25, 2022): e1004085. https://doi.org/10.1371/journal.pmed.1004085

151. John P. A. Ioannidis, "Evidence-Based Medicine Has Been Hijacked: A Report to David Sackett," *Journal of Clinical Epidemiology* 73 (May 2016): 82–86. https://doi.org/10.1016/j.jclinepi.2016.02.012

11. Throwing away our advantages

1. Ukraine, Taiwan and The True Cause of War; Interview of John Mearsheimer by John Anderson. YouTube, Dec 8, 2023. https://www.youtube.com/watch?v=huDriv7IAa0&ab_channel=JohnAnderson

2. Evelyn Cheng, "China: We Can Lead World beyond 'crisis' of Western Democracy and Capitalism," *CNBC*, January 23, 2017. https://www.cnbc.com/2017/01/23/china-we-can-lead-world-after-crisis-in-western-democracy-capitalism.html "US Election Undermines Democracy, China Says as It Watches Trump-Clinton Battle," *CNBC*, October 12, 2016. https://www.cnbc.com/2016/10/11/us-election-undermines-democracy-china-says-as-it-watches-trump-clinton-battle.html Charlie Merton, "Really Interesting," Face-

book, March 27, 2020. https://www.facebook.com/charlie.trumpet/videos/
10163325883405080/ Frances Martel, "China: Trump Victory Shows
'Fragility of Western Democracy,'" *Breitbart*, January 23, 2017. https://www.
breitbart.com/national-security/2017/01/23/one-china/

12. The spending cascade

1. Tyler Clifford, "Jim Cramer: The Pandemic Led to 'One of the Greatest
   Wealth Transfers in History,'" *CNBC*, June 4, 2020. https://www.cnbc.com/
   2020/06/04/cramer-the-pandemic-led-to-a-great-wealth-transfer.html
2. Juliette Garside & Joseph Smith, Tory-linked firm involved in testing failure
   given new £347m Covid contract. The Guardian, Nov 5, 2020. https://www.
   theguardian.com/world/2020/nov/04/tory-linked-firm-involved-in-testing-fail
   ure-awarded-new-347m-covid-contract
3. Ed Conway, Coronavirus: Test and Trace consultants paid equivalent of £1.5m
   salary. Sky News, Oct 15, 2020. https://news.sky.com/story/coronavirus-test-
   and-trace-consultants-paid-equivalent-of-15m-salary-12104028
4. Jasper Jolly & Rajeev Sayal, Consultants' fees 'up to £6,250 a day' for work on
   Covid test system. The Guardian, Oct 15, 2020. https://www.theguardian.
   com/world/2020/oct/14/consultants-fees-up-to-6250-a-day-for-work-on-
   covid-test-system
5. "Summary of the Effectiveness and Harms of Different Non-Pharmaceutical
   Interventions," September 21, 2020. https://assets.publishing.service.gov.uk/
   government/uploads/system/uploads/attachment_data/file/925854/
   S0769_Summary_of_effectiveness_and_harms_of_NPIs.pdf
6. Conway, "Coronavirus."

13. Eternal protest

1. Jared M. Diamond, "Why Societies Collapse," TED, February 2003. https://
   www.youtube.com/watch?v=IESYMFtLIis Jared M. Diamond, *Collapse: How
   Societies Choose to Fail or Succeed* (Harmondsworth: Penguin Books, 2006).
2. Diamond, "Why Societies Collapse."
3. George Monbiot, "The Obsession with the Birthrates of the Poor Has a Grim
   History, and Is Used by the Rich to Transfer Blame.," *The Guardian*, August
   26, 2020. https://www.monbiot.com/2020/08/31/population-panic/ Intergovernmental Panel on Climate Change, Climate Change 2014: Mitigation of
   Climate Change: Working Group III Contribution to the Fifth Assessment
   Report of the Intergovernmental Panel on Climate Change, ed, Ottmar Eden-
   hofer et al. (New York: Cambridge University Press, 2014).

14. Grapes from brambles

1. Matthew 7:16 (NASB).

III. Decontamination

1. Smith, *An Inquiry into the Nature and Causes of the Wealth of Nations*, chap. 24.
2. Jeff Jefferson Looney, ed., "Thomas Jefferson to George Logan, 12 November 1816," in *The Papers of Thomas Jefferson, Retirement Series, Vol. 10, May 1816 to 18 January 1817*, vol. 10, Retirement (Princeton: Princeton University Press, 2013), 521–22.
   https://founders.archives.gov/documents/Jefferson/03-06-02-0230
3. Arnaud Imatz, "Democracy: The Failure of a System Become Religion," *The Postil Magazine*, June 1, 2022.
   https://www.thepostil.com/democracy-the-failure-of-a-system-become-religion/
4. Theodore Roosevelt, *Progressive Covenant with the People*, Theodore Roosevelt: His Life and Times on Film, 1912, Library of Congress.
   https://www.loc.gov/collections/theodore-roosevelt-films/articles-and-essays/sound-recordings-of-theodore-roosevelts-voice/
5. F. D. Roosevelt, *F.D.R.: His Personal Letters: 1928-1945*, ed. Elliott Roosevelt (New York: Duell, Sloan and Pearce, 1947), 372.
6. Jon Schwarz, "'Yes, We're Corrupt': A List of Politicians Admitting That Money Controls Politics," *The Intercept*, July 30, 2015.
   https://theintercept.com/2015/07/30/politicians-admitting-obvious-fact-money-affects-vote/
7. Schwarz.
8. E. Scott Reckard, "Charles Keating Jr. Dies at 90; Key Figure in S&L Collapse," *Los Angeles Times*, April 2, 2014, sec. Business.
   https://www.latimes.com/business/la-me-charles-keating-20140402-story.html
9. Wilkerson, "Pre-war Intelligence."
10. Kevin Baker, "Thanks, Trump!," *The New Republic*, November 14, 2016.
    https://newrepublic.com/article/138020/what-donald-trump-got-right-american-democracy
11. Ezra Klein, "Jack Abramoff's Guide to Buying Congressmen," *Washington Post*, November 7, 2011.
    https://www.washingtonpost.com/blogs/ezra-klein/post/jack-abramoffs-guide-to-buying-congressmen/2011/08/25/gIQAoXKLvM_blog.html
12. Matt Taibbi, "Why Isn't Wall Street in Jail?," *Rolling Stone*, February 16, 2011.
    https://www.rollingstone.com/politics/politics-news/why-isnt-wall-street-in-jail-179414/
13. Michiko Kakutani, "Up Ahead: The World According to Gore," *The New York Times*, January 23, 2013, sec. Books.
    https://www.nytimes.com/2013/01/24/books/the-future-by-al-gore.html
14. Schwarz, "'Yes, We're Corrupt.'"
15. John Kerry, "Senator John Kerry Delivers Senate Farewell Floor Address," *Foreign Relations Committee*, January 30, 2013.
    https://www.foreign.senate.gov/press/rep/release/senator-john-kerry-delivers-senate-farewell-floor-address
16. Lawrence Wilkerson, "Who Makes US Foreign Policy?," *Reality Asserts Itself*, The Real News Network, May 10, 2019.
    https://www.youtube.com/watch?v=0eCJdbSi2cY

17. Jon Schwarz, "Jimmy Carter: The U.S. Is an 'Oligarchy With Unlimited Political Bribery,'" *The Intercept*, July 30, 2015.
    https://theintercept.com/2015/07/30/jimmy-carter-u-s-oligarchy-unlimited-political-bribery/

18. Jill Ornitz and Ryan Struyk, "Donald Trump's Surprisingly Honest Lessons About Big Money in Politics," *ABC News*, August 11, 2015.
    https://abcnews.go.com/Politics/donald-trumps-surprisingly-honest-lessons-big-money-politics/story?id=32993736

19. Thomas Ferguson, Paul Jorgensen, and Jie Chen, "How Money Drives US Congressional Elections: Linear Models of Money and Outcomes," *Structural Change and Economic Dynamics* 61 (June 2022): 527–45.
    https://doi.org/10.1016/j.strueco.2019.09.005

20. Ryan Grim, "Dick Durbin: Banks 'Frankly Own The Place,'" *Huffington Post*, May 30, 2009, sec. Politics.
    https://www.huffpost.com/entry/dick-durbin-banks-frankly_n_193010

21. "Senate Majority Leader Mitch McConnell and Labor Secretary Thomas Perez," *This Week* (ABC News, June 26, 2016).
    https://abcnews.go.com/Politics/week-transcript-senate-majority-leader-mitch-mcconnell-labor/story?id=40131578

22. Nancy MacLean, "Democracy in Chains", Harvard Law School, October 16, 2017.
    https://www.youtube.com/watch?v=eowEmcS75JM

23. Eric Lipton, "Special Interests Mobilize to Get Piece of Next Virus Relief Package," *The New York Times*, July 19, 2020, sec. U.S.
    https://www.nytimes.com/2020/07/19/us/politics/coronavirus-relief-lobbyists-special-interests.html

24. Nassim Nicholas Taleb, "Inequality and Skin in the Game," *INCERTO*, October 21, 2018.
    https://medium.com/incerto/inequality-and-skin-in-the-game-d8f00bc0cb46

25. Peter Walker, "Boris Johnson given £1m Donation by Former Brexit Party Backer," *The Guardian*, January 12, 2023, sec. Politics.
    https://www.theguardian.com/politics/2023/jan/12/boris-johnson-given-1m-donation-by-former-brexit-party-backer

15. Ariadne's thread

1. Joseph Campbell, *The Hero with a Thousand Faces*, Bollingen Series (New York: Pantheon, 1949).

16. An inter-tribal issue

1. Hansen, *The Athenian Democracy in the Age of Demosthenes*, chap. 11.

2. Tucker Carlson, "Mitt Romney Supports the Status Quo. But for Everyone Else, It's Infuriating," *Fox News*, January 3, 2019. https://www.foxnews.com/opinion/tucker-carlson-mitt-romney-supports-the-status-quo-but-for-everyone-else-its-infuriating

3. George Monbiot, "The European Union Is the Worst Choice – Apart from the Alternative," *The Guardian*, June 15, 2016, sec. Opinion. https://www.

theguardian.com/commentisfree/2016/jun/15/european-union-eu-britain-sovereignty

4. Lawrence Lessig, "The Left and Right Share a Common Enemy: Capitalists Who Corrupt Capitalism," *Evonomics*, January 13, 2016. https://evonomics.com/how-capitalists-corrupt-capitalism/

5. George Monbiot, "Dark Arts," *The Guardian*, February 3, 2017. https://www.monbiot.com/2017/02/04/dark-arts/

6. Thomas Bassetti and Filippo Pavesi, "Electoral Contributions and the Cost of Unpopularity," *Economic Inquiry* 55, no. 4 (October 2017): 1771–91. https://doi.org/10.1111/ecin.12461

7. Sharangan Maheswaran, "Lifting the Shroud: Government, Investment Banks and Power in Post Financial Crisis United Kingdom" (Sydney, University of Sydney, 2011), https://ses.library.usyd.edu.au/bitstream/handle/2123/8284/Sharangan%20Maheswaran.pdf?sequence=1&isAllowed=y

8. Bob Graham et al., "Deep Water: The Gulf Oil Disaster and the Future of Offshore Drilling: Report to the President" (Washington, D.C.: National Commission on the BP Deepwater Horizon Oil Spill and Offshore Drilling, 2011).

9. Thomas Ferguson, Paul Jorgensen, and Jie Chen, "Revealed: Why the Pundits Are Wrong About Big Money and the 2012 Elections," *Alternet*, December 20, 2012, sec. News and Politics. https://web.archive.org/web/20170226202912/http://www.alternet.org/news-amp-politics/revealed-why-pundits-are-wrong-about-big-money-and-2012-elections/

10. "The Top 10 Things Every Voter Should Know About Money-in-Politics," *OpenSecrets*, accessed August 3, 2023. https://web.archive.org/web/20230427094423/https://www.opensecrets.org/resources/dollarocracy/

11. Warwick Smith, "Political Donations Corrupt Democracy in Ways You Might Not Realise," *The Guardian*, September 11, 2014, sec. Opinion. https://www.theguardian.com/commentisfree/2014/sep/11/political-donations-corrupt-democracy-in-ways-you-might-not-realise

12. George Monbiot, "The Corporate Begging Bowl," *The Guardian*, December 13, 2005. https://www.monbiot.com/2005/12/13/the-corporate-begging-bowl/

13. Liam McLoughlin, "The Canadian Plan That Could Help Australia Beat Neoliberalism," *New Matilda*, April 27, 2016. https://newmatilda.com/2016/04/27/the-canadian-plan-that-could-help-australia-beat-neoliberalism/

14. Adam Andrzejewski and Thomas W Smith, "Federal Funding of Fortune 100 Companies," Oversight Report (Burr Ridge, Illinois: OpenTheBooks, May 2019). https://www.openthebooks.com/assets/1/6/Oversight_Report_-_Fortune_100_FINAL.pdf

15. Toni Dixon, "Tax Lobbying Provides 22,000 Percent Return to Firms, KU Researchers Find," *The University of Kansas News*, April 9, 2009. https://web.archive.org/web/20210223150329/http://archive.news.ku.edu/2009/april/9/taxlobbying.shtml

16. Johan Norberg, "The Real Adam Smith: Ideas That Changed The World," Free to Choose Network, March 28, 2016. https://www.youtube.com/watch?v=8ruiUOQERnw

17. Larry Lessig, "Our Democracy No Longer Represents the People. Here's How We Fix It," TEDxMidAtlantic, October 20, 2015. https://www.youtube.com/watch?v=PJy8vTu66tE

18. Lawrence Lessig, "How Money Corrupts Congress and a Plan to Stop It". The Long Now Foundation, Jan 2012. https://longnow.org/seminars/02012/jan/17/how-money-corrupts-congress-and-plan-stop-it/

19. Richard Wike, "With 41% of Global Wealth in the Hands of Less than 1%, Elites and Citizens Agree Inequality Is a Top Priority," *Pew Research Center*, November 8, 2014. https://www.pewresearch.org/short-reads/2014/11/08/with-41-of-global-wealth-in-the-hands-of-less-than-1-elites-and-citizens-agree-inequality-is-a-top-priority/

20. Zaid Jilani, "Backed by Airline Dollars, Congress Rejects Effort to Address Shrinking Legroom," *The Intercept*, February 21, 2016. https://theintercept.com/2016/02/21/backed-by-airline-dollars-congress-rejects-effort-to-address-shrinking-legroom/

21. Tom Hickey, "William K. Black — The Myth That Obama's Taking Huge Contributions from Wall Street Was Fine," *Mike Norman Economics*, April 8, 2016. http://mikenormaneconomics.blogspot.com/2016/04/william-k-black-myth-that-obamas-taking.html

22. Janet Hook, "The Burden of a 40-Year Career: Some of Joe Biden's Record Doesn't Age Well," *Los Angeles Times*, March 18, 2019, sec. Politics. https://www.latimes.com/politics/la-na-pol-biden-senate-record-controversies-20190318-story.html

23. Matt Taibbi, "Obama's Big Sellout: The President Has Packed His Economic Team with Wall Street Insiders," December 13, 2009. https://www.commondreams.org/news/2009/12/13/obamas-big-sellout-president-has-packed-his-economic-team-wall-street-insiders

24. Martin Gilens, "Inequality and Democratic Responsiveness," *Public Opinion Quarterly* 69, no. 5 (January 1, 2005): 778–96. https://doi.org/10.1093/poq/nfi058

25. Martin Gilens and Benjamin I. Page, "Testing Theories of American Politics: Elites, Interest Groups, and Average Citizens," *Perspectives on Politics* 12, no. 3 (September 2014): 564–81. https://doi.org/10.1017/S1537592714001595

26. Jean-Louis Huot, "Xerxes I," in *Encyclopedia Britannica*, May 17, 2023. https://www.britannica.com/biography/Xerxes-I

27. Henry M. Paulson, "When It Comes to Trump, a Republican Treasury Secretary Says: Choose Country over Party," *Washington Post*, June 24, 2016, sec. Opinion. https://www.washingtonpost.com/opinions/when-it-comes-to-trump-a-republican-treasury-secretary-says-choose-country-over-party/2016/06/24/c7bdba34-3942-11e6-8f7c-d4c723a2becb_story.html

17. A feedback loop

1. Lee Fang, "Where Have All the Lobbyists Gone?," *The Nation*, February 19, 2014. https://www.thenation.com/article/archive/shadow-lobbying-complex/

2. "Trump's Corporate Cabinet," *Public Citizen*, September 18, 2019. https://www.citizen.org/article/corporatecabinet/

3. Andrew Prokop, "Joe Biden's Controversial Comments about Segregationists and Wealthy Donors, Explained," *Vox*, June 19, 2019. https://www.vox.com/policy-and-politics/2019/6/19/18690910/biden-fundraiser-controversy-segregationists-donors

4. "Summary Data for Joe Biden, 2020 Cycle," *OpenSecrets*, accessed August 21,

2023. https://www.opensecrets.org/2020-presidential-race/joe-biden/candi date?id=N00001669

5. Deborah D'Souza, "Top Donors to Biden 2020 Campaign," in *Investopedia*, January 7, 2021. https://www.investopedia.com/top-donors-to-biden-2020-campaign-5080324

6. Karl Evers-Hillstrom, "K Street Sees Record Revenues amid Biden Lobbying Boom," *The Hill*, July 20, 2021. https://thehill.com/business-a-lobbying/lobby ing-revenue/563965-k-street-sees-record-revenues-amid-biden-lobbying-boom/

7. Karl Evers-Hillstrom, "Lobbyists with Biden Ties Enjoy Surge in Revenue, Clients," *The Hill*, July 21, 2021. https://thehill.com/business-a-lobbying/busi ness-a-lobbying/564086-lobbyists-with-biden-ties-enjoy-surge-in-revenue/

8. On US Military Budgets (Noam Chomsky interviewed by Ira Shorr), Chomsky website, Feb 11, 1996. https://chomsky.info/19960211/

9. "Positive Feedback," in *Wikipedia*, August 6, 2023. https://en.wikipedia.org/w/index.php?title=Positive_feedback

10. Fang, "Where Have All the Lobbyists Gone?"

11. Gareth Hutchens, "Labor Senator Sam Dastyari Claims 10 Companies Have Taken Control of Australian Politics," The Sydney Morning Herald, February 5, 201. https://www.smh.com.au/politics/federal/labor-senator-sam-dastyari-claims-10-companies-have-taken-complete-control-of-australias-political-process-20160205-gmmy30.html

12. James S. Henry, "The Price of Offshore Revisited" (Tax Justice Network, July 2012). https://tjn-usa.org/storage/documents/The_Price_of_Offshore_Revisit ed_-_22-07-2012.pdf James S. Henry, "Taxing Tax Havens," *Foreign Affairs*, April 12, 2016. https://www.foreignaffairs.com/articles/belize/2016-04-12/taxing-tax-havens

13. John Lanchester, "After the Fall," *London Review of Books*, July 5, 2018. https://www.lrb.co.uk/the-paper/v40/n13/john-lanchester/after-the-fall

14. "Large Majorities Oppose Trump Administration Move to Allow More Offshore Drilling, Ease Inspection Requirements," *World Public Opinion*, May 9, 2018. https://worldpublicopinion.net/large-majorities-oppose-trump-admin istration-move-to-allow-more-offshore-drilling-ease-inspection-requirements/

15. "Overwhelming Bipartisan Public Opposition to Repealing Net Neutrality Persists," *World Public Opinion*, April 18, 2018. https://worldpublicopinion. net/overwhelming-bipartisan-public-opposition-to-repealing-net-neutrality-persists/

16. "Two-Thirds Oppose US Withdrawal from Intermediate Nuclear Forces Treaty, New Survey Finds," *World Public Opinion*, February 6, 2019. https:// worldpublicopinion.net/two-thirds-oppose-us-withdrawal-from-intermediate-nuclear-forces-treaty-new-survey-finds/

17. "Public Supports Reforming How Members of Congress Are Elected," *World Public Opinion*, April 12, 2018. https://worldpublicopinion.net/public-supports-reforming-how-members-of-congress-are-elected/

18. The plutocratic armory

1. Paul Krugman, "Why Petulant Oligarchs Rule Our World," *The New York Times*, December 19, 2022. https://www.nytimes.com/2022/12/19/opinion/columnists/elon-musk-twitter-oligarchs.html

Citations

2. Kenneth P. Vogel, Michael LaForgia, and Hailey Fuchs, "Trump Vowed to 'Drain the Swamp,' but Lobbyists Are Helping Run His Campaign," *The New York Times*, July 6, 2020, sec. U.S. https://www.nytimes.com/2020/07/06/us/politics/trump-lobbyists-swamp-campaign.html

3. Jonathan Guyer, "How Biden's Foreign-Policy Team Got Rich," *The American Prospect*, July 6, 2020. https://prospect.org/api/content/a128af92-bcaa-11ea-aa6b-1244d5f7c7c6/

4. "Corporate Capture Report Card: Day 100" (Washington, D.C.: The Revolving Door Project, April 2021), 100. https://therevolvingdoorproject.org/wp-content/uploads/2021/04/Corporate-Capture-Report-Card.pdf

5. Guyer, "How Biden's Foreign-Policy Team Got Rich."

6. Sydney P. Freedberg et al., "How Uber Won Access to World Leaders, Deceived Investigators and Exploited Violence against Its Drivers in Battle for Global Dominance," *The International Consortium of Investigative Journalists*, July 10, 2022. https://www.icij.org/investigations/uber-files/uber-global-rise-lobbying-violence-technology/

7. "Ministers Attack 'MPs for Hire,'" *BBC News*, March 21, 2010, sec. Politics. http://news.bbc.co.uk/1/hi/uk_politics/8578597.stm

8. Jill Treanor, "The RBS Crisis: A Timeline of Events," *The Guardian*, May 22, 2017, sec. Business. https://www.theguardian.com/business/2017/may/21/royal-bank-of-scotland-a-timeline-of-events

9. Douglas Keenan, "My Thwarted Attempt to Tell of Libor Shenanigans," *Financial Times*, July 27, 2012. "Libor Scandal: RBS Fined £390m," *BBC News*, February 6, 2013, sec. Business. https://www.bbc.com/news/business-21348719 Jason Fernando, "What Was the LIBOR Scandal? What Happened and Impacted Companies," in *Investopedia*, June 12, 2022. https://www.investopedia.com/terms/l/libor-scandal.asp

10. Jill Treanor, "RBS Fined £390m for 'widespread Misconduct' in Libor-Rigging Scandal," *The Guardian*, February 6, 2013, sec. Business. https://www.theguardian.com/business/2013/feb/06/rbs-fined-libor-rigging-scandal

11. "Eagle Fried," *The Economist*, June 30, 2012. https://www.economist.com/finance-and-economics/2012/06/30/eagle-fried

12. Stephen Mangan, "Home Owners File Class Action Suit versus Banks over Libor: FT," *Reuters*, October 15, 2012, sec. Banks. https://www.reuters.com/article/us-banking-libor-lawsuit-idUSBRE89E01G20121015

13. Clea Benson, "Fannie Mae, Freddie Mac Libor Loss Tops $3 Billion in Audit," *Bloomberg*, December 19, 2012. https://www.bloomberg.com/news/articles/2012-12-19/fannie-mae-freddie-mac-libor-loss-tops-3-billion-auditor-says

14. Andrea Tan, Gavin Finch, and Liam Vaughan, "RBS Instant Messages Show Libor Rates Skewed With Traders," *Bloomberg*, September 25, 2012. https://www.bloomberg.com/news/articles/2012-09-25/rbs-instant-messages-show-libor-rates-skewed-for-traders

15. Will Martin, "Britain Was Hours from Breakdown of Law and Order during GFC: Ex-Chancellor," *Stuff*, May 29, 2018/ https://www.stuff.co.nz/business/world/104295018/britain-was-hours-from-breakdown-of-law-and-order-during-gfc-exchancellor

16. Andrew Rawnsley, "The Weekend Gordon Brown Saved the Banks from the Abyss," *The Observer*, February 21, 2010, sec. Politics. https://www.theguardian.com/politics/2010/feb/21/gordon-brown-saved-banks

17. "RBS Stake May Be Sold at a Loss, Chancellor Admits," *BBC News*, April 18, 2017, sec. Business. https://www.bbc.com/news/business-39636449 "Equity Ownership Statistics," accessed August 25, 2023. https://investors.natwest group.com/share-data/equity-ownership-statistics.aspx Rob Davies, "RBS Pays Its First Dividend since £45.5bn Bailout 10 Years Ago," *The Guardian*, October 12, 2018, sec. Business. https://www.theguardian.com/business/ 2018/oct/12/rbs-pays-its-first-dividend-since-bailout-10-years-ago   Eshe Nelson, "No Matter How You Look at It, the British Government Has Lost Billions Selling RBS Shares," *Quartz*, June 5, 2018. https://qz.com/1297178/ how-much-has-the-british-government-lost-by-selling-rbs-shares "Office for Budget Responsibility: Economic and Fiscal Outlook" (Office for Budget Responsibility, March 2018). https://web.archive.org/web/20190323212146/ https://cdn.obr.uk/EFO-MaRch_2018.pdf David Crow, "Treasury Puts Back Deadline for Divestiture of RBS Shares by One Year," *Financial Times*, March 11, 2020. https://www.ft.com/content/0a3b3c1e-63b1-11ea-a6cd-df28cc3c6a68

18. Jill Treanor, "Losses of £58bn since the 2008 Bailout – How Did RBS Get Here?," *The Guardian*, February 24, 2017, sec. Business, https://www. theguardian.com/business/2017/feb/24/90bn-in-bills-since-2008-how-did-rbs-get-here-financial-crisis-

19. Jill Treanor and Simon Bowers, "RBS Failure Caused by 'Multiple Poor Decisions,'" *The Guardian*, December 12, 2011, sec. Business. https://www. theguardian.com/global/2011/dec/12/royal-bank-of-scotland-fsa-report

20. Maheswaran, "Lifting the Shroud: Government, Investment Banks and Power in Post Financial Crisis United Kingdom."

21. The Jefferson Monticello, Thomas Jefferson Foundation. https://www.monti cello.org/research-education/thomas-jefferson-encyclopedia/private-banks-spurious-quotation/

22. Zachary D. Carter, "Obama's $400,000 Wall Street Speech Is Completely In Character," *Huffington Post*, April 27, 2017, sec. Politics. https://www.huffpost. com/entry/obama-wall-street-speech-400k_n_5900bf16e4b0af6d718ab7b9

23. Ed Davey, "Enough to Educate 17 million Children: The True Cost of Brazil's Car Wash Scandal," *New Statesman*, March 23, 2018. https://www.newstates man.com/world/americas/south-america/2018/03/enough-educate-17-million-children-true-cost-brazil-s-car-wash-scandal "Petrobras Scandal," in *Britannica*, August 23, 2023. https://www.britannica.com/event/Petrobras-scandal

24. Paul Kiernan, "Brazil's Petrobras Reports Nearly $17 Billion in Asset and Corruption Charges," *Wall Street Journal*, April 22, 2015, sec. Business. http:// www.wsj.com/articles/brazils-petrobras-reports-nearly-17-billion-impairment-on-assets-corruption-1429744336

25. "'The Largest Foreign Bribery Case in History,'" *BBC News*, April 21, 2018, sec. Business. https://www.bbc.com/news/business-43825294

26. OCCRP Staff, Jair Bolsonaro: 2020 PERSON OF THE YEAR IN ORGANIZED CRIME AND CORRUPTION, OCCRP website, 2020. https:// www.occrp.org/en/poy/2020/

27. Sharon Tan and Austin Ramzy, "Najib Razak, Malaysian Leader Toppled in 1MDB Scandal, Faces First Graft Trial," *The New York Times*, April 3, 2019, sec. World. https://www.nytimes.com/2019/04/03/world/asia/najib-case-malaysia.html Hannah Ellis-Petersen, "1MDB Scandal Explained: A Tale of

Malaysia's Missing Billions," *The Guardian*, July 28, 2020, sec. World news. https://www.theguardian.com/world/2018/oct/25/1mdb-scandal-explained-a-tale-of-malaysias-missing-billions

28. Nancy Bélanger, "Lobbying Commissioner Releases 2018-19 Annual Report" (Ottawa: Office of the Commissioner of Lobbying of Canada, June 18, 2019). https://web.archive.org/web/20200206211505/https://lobbycanada.gc.ca/eic/site/012.nsf/eng/01490.html

29. "A Giant Problem," *The Economist*, September 17, 2016. https://www.economist.com/leaders/2016/09/17/a-giant-problem

30. Fang, "Where Have All the Lobbyists Gone?"

31. ACCESS ALL AREAS When EU politicians become lobbyists; Transparency International (report), 2017. https://transparency.eu/wp-content/uploads/2017/01/Access-all-areas.pdf

32. Tariq Ali, "The Rise of ISIS and the Origins of the New Middle East War," *CounterPunch.Org*, September 29, 2014. https://www.counterpunch.org/2014/09/29/the-rise-of-isis-and-the-origins-of-the-new-middle-east-war/

33. Belinda M. Edwards, "Dark Money: The Hidden Millions in Australia's Political Finance System" (GetUp!, 2016). http://cdn.getup.org.au/1969-Dark_Money.pdf Readfearn, "Get to Know Your Lobby Groups," *ABC News*, March 22, 2012. https://www.abc.net.au/news/2012-03-22/readfearn-get-to-know-your-lobby-groups/3906036 Christopher Knaus, "Australian Government Powerless against Lobbyists with Hidden Interests, Audit Finds," *The Guardian*, June 29, 2020, sec. Australia news. https://www.theguardian.com/australia-news/2020/jun/29/australian-government-powerless-against-lobbyists-with-hidden-interests-audit-finds Becky Freeman and Christina Watts, "We Worked out How Many Tobacco Lobbyists End up in Government, and Vice Versa. It's a Lot," *The Conversation*, May 11, 2023. http://theconversation.com/we-worked-out-how-many-tobacco-lobbyists-end-up-in-government-and-vice-versa-its-a-lot-205382

34. "In Defence of Lobbyists," *ABC Listen* (ABC News, March 27, 2019). https://www.abc.net.au/listen/programs/abc-news-daily/in-defence-of-lobbyists/10945982

35. Zuzana Bednarik and Jirina Jilkova, "Why Is the Agricultural Lobby in the European Union Member States so Effective?," *Ekonomie a Management* 15 (April 1, 2012): 26–37. https://www.researchgate.net/publication/271039732_Why_is_the_agricultural_lobby_in_the_European_Union_member_states_so_effective

36. George Monbiot, "Leave Well Alone," *The Guardian*, June 21, 2016. https://www.monbiot.com/2016/06/21/leave-well-alone/

37. Arthur Neslen, "Revealed: Majority of Politicians on Key EU Farming Panel Have Industry Links," *The Guardian*, May 24, 2018, sec. Environment. https://www.theguardian.com/environment/2018/may/24/revealed-majority-politicians-key-eu-farming-panel-industry-links

38. Bruce Drake, "Majority of Americans Say Banks, Large Corporations Benefitted Most from U.S. Economic Policies," *Pew Research Center*, September 20, 2013. https://www.pewresearch.org/short-reads/2013/09/20/majority-of-americans-say-banks-large-corporations-benefitted-most-from-u-s-economic-policies/

39. "Beyond Distrust: How Americans View Their Government" (Pew Research

Center, November 23, 2015). https://www.pewresearch.org/politics/2015/11/23/6-perceptions-of-elected-officials-and-the-role-of-money-in-politics/

40. Hailey Fuchs, "Drain the Swamp? This Guy's Trying to Fill It.," *POLITICO*, October 15, 2021. https://www.politico.com/news/2021/10/15/lobbyist-hunter-ivan-adler-516069

41. Alan Zibel, "Revolving Congress: The Revolving Door Class of 2019 Flocks to K Street" (Public Citizen, May 30, 2019). https://www.citizen.org/article/revolving-congress/

42. Marcus Stanley, "Government Sachs and the Trump Administration," *Common Dreams*, October 15, 2017. https://www.commondreams.org/views/2017/10/15/government-sachs-and-trump-administration

43. "List of Former Employees of Goldman Sachs," in *Wikipedia*, July 11, 2023. https://en.wikipedia.org/w/index.php?title=List_of_former_employees_of_Goldman_Sachs

44. Stanley, "Government Sachs and the Trump Administration."

45. Jake Johnson, "Biden Quietly Adds Goldman Sachs Veterans to Transition Team," *Salon*, December 18, 2020, sec. News & Politics. https://www.salon.com/2020/12/18/biden-quietly-adds-goldman-sachs-veterans-to-transition-team_partner/

46. Dealbook, "The People From 'Government Sachs,'" *The New York Times*, March 16, 2017, sec. Business. https://www.nytimes.com/2017/03/16/business/dealbook/goldman-sachs-goverment-jobs.html

47. James Kwak, "America's Top Prosecutors Used to Go After Top Executives. What Changed?," *The New York Times*, July 5, 2017, sec. Books. https://www.nytimes.com/2017/07/05/books/review/the-chickenshit-club-jesse-eisinger-.html

48. Kwak.

49. Jamie Doward, "Google: New Concerns Raised about Political Influence by Senior 'Revolving Door' Jobs," *The Observer*, June 4, 2016, sec. Technology. https://www.theguardian.com/technology/2016/jun/04/google-influence-hiring-government-officials

50. Alan Macleod, "The Federal Bureau of Tweets: Twitter Is Hiring an Alarming Number of FBI Agents," *MintPress News*, June 21, 2022, sec. Daily Digest. https://www.mintpressnews.com/twitter-hiring-alarming-number-spooks-secret-agents/281114/

51. Alex Kotch, "Dozens of Facebook Lobbyists Tied to Members of Congress, Investigation Shows," *The Guardian*, November 20, 2019, sec. Technology. https://www.theguardian.com/technology/2019/nov/20/dozens-of-facebook-lobbyists-tied-to-members-of-congress-investigation-shows

52. David Corn and Dan Spinelli, "Amazon Has Become a Prime Revolving-Door Destination in Washington," *Mother Jones*, March 2, 2021 https://www.motherjones.com/politics/2021/03/amazon-has-become-a-prime-revolving-door-destination-in-washington/

53. "LIVE: House Weaponization of the Federal Government Subcommittee Holds Hearing on 'Twitter Files,'" NDA, March 9, 2023. https://www.youtube.com/watch?v=DISvG-VhcJ4

54. Elon Musk and Joe Rogan Interview Episode 2054; Nov 3, 2023. https://www.youtube.com/watch?v=Deh4cpOpIB4&list=PLT0ZvHigLj-VFbYdTkpCsP0zY_HrUrocV&ab_channel=JoeRoganExperienceClips

55. Demasi, "From FDA to MHRA."

Citations

56. Readfearn, "Get to Know Your Lobby Groups."

57. Russell Berman, "An Exodus From Congress Tests the Lure of Lobbying," *The Atlantic*, May 1, 2018. https://www.theatlantic.com/politics/archive/2018/05/lobbying-the-job-of-choice-for-retired-members-of-congress/558851/ "Is Lobbying Good or Bad?," *RepresentUs*, accessed August 25, 2023. https://represent.us/action/is-lobbying-good-or-bad/

58. Adam Curtis, "The Curse of Tina," *The Meaning and the Message*, September 13, 2011. https://www.bbc.co.uk/blogs/adamcurtis/entries/fdb484c8-99a1-32a3-83be-20108374b985

59. Bill McKibben, review of *The Koch Brothers' New Brand*, by Jane Mayer, *The New York Review of Books*, March 10, 2016. https://www.nybooks.com/articles/2016/03/10/koch-brothers-new-brand/

60. Adam Townsend, "Polls. How to Create Opinions with No Information Assembly Required," *Adam Townsend*, November 1, 2019. https://www.adamtownsend.me/polls-how-to-create-opinions/

61. John Bellamy Foster, "Capitalism Has Failed—What Next?," *Monthly Review*, February 1, 2019, https://monthlyreview.org/2019/02/01/capitalism-has-failed-what-next/

62. "What Is ALEC?," *ALEC Exposed*, accessed August 25, 2023. https://www.alecexposed.org/wiki/What_is_ALEC%3F

63. Marcus Reubenstein, "'Independent' Think-Tank ASPI behind Push for More Defence Spending Rakes in Advisory Fees," *Pearls and Irritations*, July 4, 2020. https://johnmenadue.com/independent-think-tank-aspi-behind-push-for-more-defence-spending-rakes-in-advisory-fees/

64. Eric Lipton, Brooke Williams, and Nicholas Confessore, "Foreign Powers Buy Influence at Think Tanks," *The New York Times*, September 7, 2014, sec. U.S. https://www.nytimes.com/2014/09/07/us/politics/foreign-powers-buy-influence-at-think-tanks.html

65. Patricia Hewitt, "Politicians for Hire", interviewed by Antony Barnett, *Dispatches* (Channel 4, 22 March 2010).

66. Felicity Lawrence et al., "How the Right's Radical Thinktanks Reshaped the Conservative Party," *The Guardian*, November 29, 2019, sec. Politics. https://www.theguardian.com/politics/2019/nov/29/rightwing-thinktank-conservative-boris-johnson-brexit-atlas-network

67. Bryce Greene, "Report Shows How Military Industrial Complex Sets Media Narrative on Ukraine". FAIR, June 30, 2023. https://fair.org/home/report-shows-how-military-industrial-complex-sets-media-narrative-on-ukraine/

68. Lipton, Williams, and Confessore, "Foreign Powers Buy Influence at Think Tanks."

69. Lipton, Williams, and Confessore.

70. Sheldon Rampton, John Stauber, and Steven Milloy, "Industry Hacks Turn Fear on Its Head," *PR Watch* 7, no. 3 (2000). https://www.prwatch.org/files/pdfs/prwatch/prwv7n3.pdf

71. Anahad O'Connor, "Coca-Cola Funds Scientists Who Shift Blame for Obesity Away From Bad Diets," *The New York Times*, August 9, 2015, sec. Fitness. https://archive.nytimes.com/well.blogs.nytimes.com/2015/08/09/coca-cola-funds-scientists-who-shift-blame-for-obesity-away-from-bad-diets/ Marcus Strom, "Coke's Cash: 14 Health Experts Who've Taken the Soft-Drink Giant's Money," *The Sydney Morning Herald*, March 11, 2016, sec. Consumer affairs.

https://www.smh.com.au/business/consumer-affairs/cokes-cash-14-health-experts-whove-taken-the-softdrink-giants-money-20160311-gngi7j.html

72. Heath Aston, "The 'institute' with No Members Embarrasses Senate Committee," *The Sydney Morning Herald*, November 8, 2015, sec. Federal. https://www.smh.com.au/politics/federal/the-institute-with-no-members-embarrasses-senate-committee-20151029-gkm71n.html

73. "Astroturfing", *Last Week Tonight with John Oliver* (HBO, August 13, 2018). https://www.youtube.com/watch?v=Fmh4RdIwswE

74. Jane Mayer, "The Secrets of Charles Koch's Political Ascent," *POLITICO*, January 18, 2016. https://www.politico.com/magazine/story/2016/01/charles-koch-political-ascent-jane-mayer-213541

75. Chris Frates and Ben Smith, "Where's Transparency of Podesta Group?," *POLITICO*, December 8, 2008. https://www.politico.com/story/2008/12/wheres-transparency-of-podesta-group-016318

76. Jennifer Washburn, "Big Oil Goes to College" (Washington, D.C.: Center for American Progress, October 14, 2010). https://www.americanprogress.org/article/big-oil-goes-to-college/

77. Molly McCluskey, "Public Universities Get an Education in Private Industry," *The Atlantic*, April 3, 2017. https://www.theatlantic.com/education/archive/2017/04/public-universities-get-an-education-in-private-industry/521379/

78. Anna Krien, "The screens that ate school," *The Monthly*, June 1, 2020. https://www.themonthly.com.au/issue/2020/june/1590933600/anna-krien/screens-ate-school

79. Krien.

19. Remedies

1. "About Tea Party," *Tea Party*, 2023. https://teaparty.org/about-us/

2. Lawrence Lessig, "We the People, and the Republic We Must Reclaim," TED, April 3, 2013. https://www.youtube.com/watch?v=mw2z9lV3W1g

3. Mike Baker, "Amazon Tests 'Soul of Seattle' With Deluge of Election Cash," *The New York Times*, October 30, 2019, sec. U.S. https://www.nytimes.com/2019/10/30/us/seattle-council-amazon-democracy-vouchers.html

4. "Americans' Views on Money in Politics," *The New York Times*, June 2, 2015, sec. U.S. https://www.nytimes.com/interactive/2015/06/02/us/politics/money-in-politics-poll.html

5. Mike Gallagher, "How to Salvage Congress," *The Atlantic*, November 13, 2018. https://www.theatlantic.com/ideas/archive/2018/11/gallagher-congress/575689/

6. David Wasserman et al., "2020 Popular Vote Tracker," *Cook Political Report*, accessed August 24, 2023. https://www.cookpolitical.com/2020-national-popular-vote-tracker

7. "2020 Election to Cost $14 Billion, Blowing Away Spending Records," *Open-Secrets*, October 28, 2020. https://www.opensecrets.org/news/2020/10/cost-of-2020-election-14billion-update/

8. Tad DeHaven, "Corporate Welfare in the Federal Budget," *Cato Institute Policy Analysis* 703 (July 25, 2012). https://papers.ssrn.com/abstract=2224142

9. "Financial Transaction Tax under Enhanced Cooperation: Commission Sets out the Details," Press Release, European Commission - European Commis-

sion, February 14, 2013. https://ec.europa.eu/commission/presscorner/detail/en/IP_13_115

10. John Maynard Keynes, *The General Theory of Employment, Interest, and Money* (London: Palgrave Macmillan, 1936).

11. Stephen Spratt, "A Sterling Solution: Implementing a Stamp Duty on Sterling to Finance International Development" (Stamp Out Poverty, September 2006). https://www.stampoutpoverty.org/wp-content/uploads/2012/10/A-Sterling-Solution.pdf

12. "Scottish Independence: RBS Confirms London HQ Move If Scotland Votes 'Yes,'" *BBC News*, September 10, 2014, sec. Scotland politics. https://www.bbc.com/news/business-29151798

13. Maheswaran, "Lifting the Shroud: Government, Investment Banks and Power in Post Financial Crisis United Kingdom."

14. Dean Baker, "Bernie Sanders Takes It to Wall Street With Financial Transactions Tax," *Huffington Post*, May 26, 2015, sec. Business. https://www.huffpost.com/entry/bernie-sanders-takes-it-t_b_7438808

15. "Majorities of Republican and Democratic Voters Agree on $128 Billion in Deficit Reduction, Raising Revenue and Cutting Spending," *Program for Public Consultation*, July 31, 2018. https://publicconsultation.org/federal-budget/majorities-of-republican-and-democratic-voters-agree-on-128-billion-in-deficit-reduction-raising-revenue-and-cutting-spending/

16. Gemma Swart, "ITUC Global Poll 2012 - How Banks Can Contribute To Society: Very Strong Popular Support For Financial Transactions Tax" (ITUC, 2012). https://www.ituc-csi.org/IMG/pdf/en_ftt_global_poll.pdf

17. "Americans' Views on Money in Politics," *The New York Times*, June 2, 2015, sec. U.S. https://www.nytimes.com/interactive/2015/06/02/us/politics/money-in-politics-poll.html

18. Greenberg Quinlan Rosner Research, "First Agenda Item for Congressional Majority: Ending the Culture of Corruption in Washington," November 19, 2018. https://endcitizensunited.org/wp-content/uploads/2019/01/ECU-Post-Elect-Public-Memo-FINAL-112018.pdf

19. "Very Large Majorities Support Congressional Bills to Reduce Influence of Big Campaign Donors," *World Public Opinion*, May 10, 2018. https://worldpublicopinion.net/very-large-majorities-support-congressional-bills-to-reduce-influence-of-big-campaign-donors/

20. "51% Think It's Bribery When A Company Offers A Government Regulator A Job," May 23, 2011, sec. Business. https://www.rasmussenreports.com/public_content/business/general_business/may_2011/51_think_it_s_bribery_when_a_company_offers_a_government_regulator_a_job

21. "Overwhelming Bipartisan Majorities Favor Greater Restrictions on Lobbying By Former Government Officials," *World Public Opinion*, December 12, 2017. https://worldpublicopinion.net/overwhelming-bipartisan-majorities-favor-greater-restrictions-on-lobbying-by-former-government-officials/

22. Tina Sfondeles, "Simon Poll: Voters Favor Graduated Income Tax, Lobbying Reforms," *Chicago Sun-Times*, March 4, 2020, sec. Politics. https://chicago.suntimes.com/politics/2020/3/3/21163495/poll-graduated-income-tax-lobbying-reform-pritzker-constitutional-amendment

23. Timothy M. Gill, "The Persistence of the Power Elite: Presidential Cabinets

and Corporate Interlocks, 1968–2018," *Social Currents* 5, no. 6 (December 1, 2018): 501–11. https://doi.org/10.1177/2329496518797857

24. "Artists and Arts Workers in the United States" (National Endowment for the Arts, October 2011). https://www.arts.gov/sites/default/files/105.pdf

25. Jennifer E. Manning, "Membership of the 116th Congress: A Profile" (Congressional Research Service, December 17, 2020). https://sgp.fas.org/crs/misc/R45583.pdf

26. Maheswaran, "Lifting the Shroud: Government, Investment Banks and Power in Post Financial Crisis United Kingdom."

27. Charlie Kronick, "Exxon Exposed: Greenpeace Tricks Top Lobbyists into Naming Senators They Use to Block Climate Action," interview by Amy Goodman, *Democracy Now!*, July 6, 2021. https://www.democracynow.org/2021/7/6/exxon_blocks_congressional_action_climate

28. Sharyl Attkisson, "Behind the Closed Doors of Washington Lobbyists," *CBS News*, October 7, 2012. https://www.cbsnews.com/news/behind-the-closed-doors-of-washington-lobbyists/

29. Gallagher, "How to Salvage Congress."

30. "Overwhelming Bipartisan Majorities Favor Greater Restrictions on Lobbying By Former Government Officials."

31. Travers McLeod, "What Do Australians Want? Active and Effective Government Fit for the Ages," Discussion Paper (Centre for Policy Development, 2017). https://cpd.org.au/wp-content/uploads/2017/12/Discussion-Paper-Final-December.pdf

32. Philip Parvin, *Friend or Foe?: Lobbying in British Democracy: A Discussion Paper* (London: Hansard Society, 2007).

33. Suzanne Mulcahy, "Lobbying In Europe: Hidden Influence, Privileged Access" (Transparency International, April 15, 2015). https://www.transparency.org/en/publications/lobbying-in-europe

34. Quoted in Ralph Nader, *Unstoppable: The Emerging Left-Right Alliance to Dismantle the Corporate State* (New York: Nation Books, 2014), 178.

35. Wilbur Ross, "Estimates of the Voting Age Population for 2017," *Federal Register* 83, no. 34 (February 20, 2018): 7142–43.

36. Ben Smee, "Thirty Years after the Fitzgerald Inquiry, 'Corruption Remains Rife' in Queensland," *The Guardian*, July 2, 2019, sec. Australia news. https://www.theguardian.com/australia-news/2019/jul/03/thirty-years-after-the-fitzgerald-inquiry-corruption-remains-rife-in-queensland

37. PR firm admits it's behind WalMart blogs; CNN Money, October 20 2006. https://money.cnn.com/2006/10/20/news/companies/walmart_blogs/?postversion=2006102011

38. Michael Slezak, "Fossil Fuel Companies Undermining Paris Agreement Negotiations – Report," *The Guardian*, November 1, 2017, sec. Environment. https://www.theguardian.com/environment/2017/nov/01/fossil-fuel-companies-undermining-paris-agreement-negotiations-report

39. Astra Taylor, *Democracy May Not Exist, but We'll Miss It When It's Gone*, 1st ed. (New York: Metropolitan Books, 2019), chap. 9.

40. Allie Nawrat, "Pfizer Accused of 'Bullying' Latin America during Vaccine Negotiations," *Pharmaceutical Technology*, February 23, 2021. https://www.pharmaceutical-technology.com/news/company-news/pfizer-latin-american-vaccine/ David Pilling, Hannah Kuchler, and Donato Paolo Mancini, "The inside Story of the Pfizer Vaccine: 'A Once-in-an-Epoch Windfall,'" *Financial*

Citations

Times, November 30, 2021, sec. The Big Read. https://www.ft.com/content/0cea5e3f-d4c4-4ee2-961a-3aa150f388ec

41. *Soviet Subversion of the Free Press: A Conversation with Yuri Bezmenov*, interview by G. Edward Griffin (American Media, 1984). https://youtu.be/s2b-I0Yqisc

42. Peter Hartcher, "Power and Paranoia: Why the Chinese Government Aggressively Pushes beyond Its Borders," *The Sydney Morning Herald*, November 22, 2019, sec. National. https://www.smh.com.au/national/peter-hartcher-on-china-s-infiltration-of-australia-20191118-p53bly.html Alexander Zaitchik, "How Big Pharma Was Captured by the One Percent," *The New Republic*, June 28, 2018. https://newrepublic.com/article/149438/big-pharma-captured-one-percent

43. Shaun Ratcliff and Zoe Meers, "Australians Concerned about Growing Chinese Power," United States Studies Centre, October 3, 2019. https://www.ussc.edu.au/analysis/australians-concerned-about-growing-chinese-power

44. Australian Associated Press, "China Is Seeking to 'take over' Australia's Political System, Former Asio Chief Claims," *The Guardian*, November 21, 2019, sec. Australia news. https://www.theguardian.com/australia-news/2019/nov/22/china-is-seeking-to-take-over-australias-political-system-former-asio-chief-claims

45. "China Reportedly behind Cyber-Attack on Australian Parliament and Political Parties," *SBS News*, September 16, 2019. https://www.sbs.com.au/news/article/china-reportedly-behind-cyber-attack-on-australian-parliament-and-political-parties/igem664fp

46. Hartcher, "Power and Paranoia."

47. "China SOEs Snap Up Overseas Chinese Media," *Asia Sentinel*, March 9, 2016. https://www.asiasentinel.com/p/china-soe-snap-up-overseas-media

48. Nick McKenzie, Sashka Baker, and Chris Uhlmann, "The Chinese Communist Party's Power and Influence in Australia," *ABC News*, June 3, 2017. https://www.abc.net.au/news/2017-06-04/the-chinese-communist-partys-power-and-influence-in-australia/8584270

49. Hartcher, "Power and Paranoia."

50. Townsville Residents & Ratepayers Association, "The Great Betrayal," CIR Now, December 9, 2019. https://cirnow.com.au/the-great-betrayal/

51. "Enemy of the State: Update", *60 Minutes Australia* (Channel 9, July 26, 2020). https://www.facebook.com/watch/?v=286131232662471

52. Nick McKenzie and Richard Baker, "Free Speech Fears after Book Critical of China Is Pulled from Publication," *The Sydney Morning Herald*, November 12, 2017, sec. National. https://www.smh.com.au/national/free-speech-fears-after-book-critical-of-china-is-pulled-from-publication-20171112-gzjiyr.html

53. John Garnaut, "Australia's China reset," *The Monthly*, August 1, 2018. https://www.themonthly.com.au/issue/2018/august/1533045600/john-garnaut/australia-s-china-reset

54. Andrew Westrope, "Cybersecurity and Democracy Collide: Locking Down Elections," *Governing*, October 4, 2019. https://www.governing.com/news/headlines/GT-Cybersecurity-and-Democracy-Collide-Locking-Down-Elections.html

55. Luke Harding, "Dominic Raab Belatedly Acknowledges Russian Threat – but Why Now?," *The Guardian*, July 16, 2020, sec. Politics. https://www.theguardian.com/politics/2020/jul/16/dominic-raab-belatedly-acknowledges-

russian-threat-but-why-now Sean O'Neill, "Lubov Chernukhin: Quiet Russian's £1.7m Makes Her Top Female Tory Donor," July 18, 2020, sec. news. https://www.thetimes.co.uk/article/lubov-chernukhin-quiet-russians-1-7m-makes-her-top-female-tory-donor-z2c00bcxl Adam Bienkov, "The Wife of a Former Putin Ally Has Paid £90,000 for a Game of Tennis with Boris Johnson as He Continues to Sit on a Report Detailing His Party's Links to Russia," *Business Insider*, February 27, 2020. https://www.businessinsider.com/putin-ally-lubov-chernukhin-russia-report-auction-tennis-boris-johnson-2020-2

56. Mercy A. Kuo, "China's Challenges to Global Democracy: Insights from Kevin Sheives," *The Diplomat*, December 21, 2020. https://thediplomat.com/2020/12/chinas-challenges-to-global-democracy/

57. Carroll Quigley, "The Mythology of American Democracy" (Industrial College of the Armed Forces, Washington, D.C., August 17, 1972). http://www.carrollquigley.net/Lectures/The_Mythology_of_American_Democracy.htm

58. Benjamin Weiser and Jesse McKinley, "Politically Connected N.Y. Union Boss Is Accused of 'Shocking' Corruption," *The New York Times*, October 1, 2020, sec. New York. https://www.nytimes.com/2020/10/01/nyregion/union-boss-racketeering.html

59. Steven Dilakian, "Ex-Construction Boss Cahill Pleads Guilty to Bribery, Fraud," *The Real Deal*, December 15, 2022. https://therealdeal.com/new-york/2022/12/15/ex-construction-union-boss-pleads-guilty-to-bribery-fraud/

60. Noam Scheiber and Neal E. Boudette, "U.A.W. Corruption Case Widens as Former Chief Is Charged," *The New York Times*, March 5, 2020, sec. Business. https://www.nytimes.com/2020/03/05/business/uaw-indictment.html

61. Chris Brooks, "Democratizing the UAW: An Interview With Justin Mayhugh," *Jacobin*, December 23, 2019. https://jacobin.com/2019/12/united-automobile-workers-uaw-general-motors

62. Barry Eidlin, "We Shouldn't Be Nostalgic for Jimmy Hoffa," *Jacobin*, February 1, 2020. https://jacobin.com/2020/01/jimmy-hoffa-teamsters-the-irishman-union-corruption

63. Eidlin.

64. Ben Schreckinger, "Biden, Inc.: How 'Middle Class' Joe's Family Cashed in on the Family Name," *POLITICO Magazine*, August 2, 2019. https://politi.co/2KcoKUf

65. Barry Jones, *What Is to Be Done: Political Engagement and Saving the Planet* (Melbourne: Scribe, 2021), chap. 13.

66. Dominic Cummings, "Snippets 5: No10 Farce, UKR, Tory 'Strategy', AGI Ruin, Daycare, Direct Instruction, Do Shares Only Go up at Night?!, NSN, Abortion/US...," Substack newsletter, *Dominic Cummings Blog*, July 4, 2022. https://dominiccummings.substack.com/p/snippets-5-no10-farce-ukr-tory-strategy?utm_medium=email

67. Nick Sommerlad, "Boris Johnson Campaign Is Funded by Billionaires behind Development He Approved," *The Mirror*, July 4, 2019, sec. Politics. https://www.mirror.co.uk/news/politics/boris-johnsons-billionaire-backers-social-17428672 Thomas Colson and Adam Bienkov, "Bankers, Climate Change Sceptics, and Brexiteers: The Donors Funding Boris Johnson's Campaign for Prime Minister," *Business Insider*, July 1, 2019. https://www.businessinsider.com/who-is-funding-boris-johnson-conservative-leadership-prime-minister-campaign-2019-6

68. Matt Ford, "Congress Is the Problem Child of American Democracy," *The New Republic*, December 23, 2020. https://newrepublic.com/article/160750/congress-covid-relief-dysfunction

69. George Monbiot, "Road to Perdition," *The Guardian*, June 24, 2020. https://www.monbiot.com/2020/06/26/road-to-perdition/

70. Scott M. Reid, "100s of USA Swimmers Were Sexually Abused for Decades and the People in Charge Knew and Ignored It, Investigation Finds," *Orange County Register*, February 16, 2018. https://www.ocregister.com/2018/02/16/investigation-usa-swimming-ignored-sexual-abuse-for-decades/

71. Mike Baker, "Sex-Abuse Claims Against Boy Scouts Now Surpass 82,000," *The New York Times*, November 15, 2020, sec. U.S. https://www.nytimes.com/2020/11/15/us/boy-scouts-abuse-claims-bankruptcy.html

21. Speech in the first democracy

1. J. D. Lewis, "Isegoria at Athens: When Did It Begin?," *Historia: Zeitschrift Für Alte Geschichte* 20 (1971): 129–40. https://www.jstor.org/stable/4435186

2. Michael E. Newton, *The Path to Tyranny: A History of Free Society's Descent into Tyranny*, 2nd ed. (Scottsdale, AZ: Eleftheria, 2010), 24.

3. Donald Kagan, "Lecture 13 - The Athenian Empire" (Lecture, Introduction to Ancient Greek History - CLCV 205, Yale University, 2007). https://oyc.yale.edu/classics/clcv-205/lecture-13?width=800px&height=600px&inline=true#colorbox-inline-205288026

4. Paul Barry Clarke and Joe Foweraker, eds., *Encyclopedia of Democratic Thought*, 1st ed. (London: Routledge, 2003), 201. https://www.taylorfrancis.com/books/9781136908569

5. Hansen, *The Athenian Democracy in the Age of Demosthenes*, 83.

6. Ober, *The Rise and Fall of Classical Greece*, chap. 7.

7. Ober, chap. 7.

8. Ober, chap. 7.

22. Speech today

1. John Pilger, "The Revolution Will Not Be Televised: John Pilger on TV and Truth," *New Statesman*, September 11, 2006. https://johnpilger.com/articles/the-revolution-will-not-be-televised

2. Galen Stocking, Michael Barthel, and Elizabeth Grieco, "Sources Shared on Twitter: A Case Study on Immigration," *Pew Research Center's Journalism Project*, January 29, 2018. https://www.pewresearch.org/journalism/2018/01/29/sources-shared-on-twitter-a-case-study-on-immigration/

3. Mathew Ingram, "Does the End of BuzzFeed News Mean the Death of Social Journalism?," *Columbia Journalism Review*, May 11, 2023. https://www.cjr.org/the_media_today/buzzfeed_news_closure_social_news.php

4. "LIVE: House Weaponization of the Federal Government Subcommittee Holds Hearing on 'Twitter Files.'" Mar 10, 2023. https://www.youtube.com/watch?v=DISvG-VhcJ4&ab_channel=NTD

5. Amy Mitchell et al., "Local News in a Digital Age" (Pew Research Center, March 5, 2015). https://www.pewresearch.org/journalism/2015/03/05/legacy-outlets-drive-the-news-agenda-but-specialty-providers-diversify-the-ecosystem/

6. Monica Anderson and Andrea Caumont, "How Social Media Is Reshaping News," *Pew Research Center*, September 24, 2014. https://www.pewresearch.org/short-reads/2014/09/24/how-social-media-is-reshaping-news/

7. Manuel Castells (ed), The Network Society: A Cross-Cultural Perspective; EE Elgar Online, 2019. DOI: https://doi.org/10.4337/9781845421663 Paul Krugman, "Barons of Broadband," *The New York Times*, February 17, 2014, sec. Opinion. https://www.nytimes.com/2014/02/17/opinion/krugman-barons-of-broadband.html

8. David Jackson and Gary Marx, "Will The Chicago Tribune Be the Next Newspaper Picked to the Bone?," *The New York Times*, January 19, 2020, sec. Opinion. https://www.nytimes.com/2020/01/19/opinion/chicago-tribune-alden-capital.html

9. Ben H. Bagdikian, *The New Media Monopoly*, 3rd ed. (Boston: Beacon Press, 1990), 412.

10. Ashley Lutz, "These 6 Corporations Control 90% Of The Media In America," *Business Insider*, June 14, 2012. https://www.businessinsider.com/these-6-corporations-control-90-of-the-media-in-america-2012-6 Delian Peevski, "Media Oligarchs Go Shopping" (Paris: Reporters Without Borders, 2016). https://rsf.org/sites/default/files/2016-rsf-report-media-oligarchs-gpo-shopping.pdf

11. How large is Rupert Murdoch's reach through News Corp in Australian media, old and new?; ABC News, 14 Apr 2021. https://www.abc.net.au/news/2021-04-14/fact-file-rupert-murdoch-media-reach-in-australia/100056660

12. Alexander Stille, *The Sack of Rome: How a Beautiful European Country with a Fabled History and a Storied Culture Was Taken over by a Man Named Silvio Berlusconi* (New York: Penguin Press, 2006).

13. Deborah Friedell, "Short Cuts: Fox News," *London Review of Books*, November 5, 2020. https://www.lrb.co.uk/the-paper/v42/n21/deborah-friedell/short-cuts

14. Mark Lipovetsky, "A Culture of Zero Gravity," review of *Nothing Is True and Everything Is Possible: The Surreal Heart of the New Russia* by Peter Pomerantsev, *Boundary 2*, August 15, 2018. https://www.boundary2.org/2018/08/mark-lipovetsky-a-culture-of-zero-gravity/

15. Ron Suskind, "Faith, Certainty and the Presidency of George W. Bush," *The New York Times*, October 17, 2004, sec. U.S. https://www.nytimes.com/2004/10/17/magazine/faith-certainty-and-the-presidency-of-george-w-bush.html

16. "'Truth Isn't Truth,' Giuliani Says on Mueller Probe," *KCCI*, August 19, 2018. https://www.kcci.com/article/truth-isnt-truth-giuliani-says-on-mueller-probe/22768099

23. Does the media shape our thinking?

1. G. M. Gilbert, *Nuremberg Diary*, 1st ed. (New York: Da Capo Press, 1995).

2. "US Troops in Iraq," *Zogby International*, February 28, 2006. https://archive.globalpolicy.org/security/issues/iraq/justify/2006/0228zogby.htm

3. Peter Maass, "Fox News Is Poisoning America. Rupert Murdoch and His Heirs Should Be Shunned.," *The Intercept*, November 4, 2018. https://theintercept.com/2018/11/04/fox-news-is-poisoning-america-shun-rupert-murdoch/

4. Maxwell McCombs, *Setting the Agenda: The Mass Media and Public Opinion* (Cambridge: John Wiley & Sons, 2013).

5. McCombs.

Citations

6. Shanto Iyengar and Donald R. Kinder, *News That Matters: Television and American Opinion, Updated Edition* (Chicago, Illinois: University of Chicago Press, 2010); Annelise Russell, Maraam Dwidar, and Bryan D. Jones, "The Mass Media and the Policy Process," in *Oxford Research Encyclopedia of Politics*, ed. Annelise Russell, Maraam Dwidar, and Bryan D. Jones (Oxford University Press, 2016). https://doi.org/10.1093/acrefore/9780190228637.013.240
7. Stefano DellaVigna and Ethan Kaplan, "The Fox News Effect: Media Bias and Voting," Working Paper (Cambridge, Massachusetts: NBER, April 2006). https://www.nber.org/system/files/working_papers/w12169/w12169.pdf
8. "PART 1: CNN Director ADMITS Network Engaged in 'Propaganda' to Remove Trump from Presidency ... 'Our Focus Was to Get Trump Out of Office' ... 'I Came to CNN Because I Wanted to Be a Part of That,'" *Project Veritas*, April 13, 2021. https://www.projectveritas.com/video/part-1-cnn-director-admits-network-engaged-in-propaganda-to-remove-trump/

24. The blind sector

1. William L. Shirer, *The Rise and Fall of the Third Reich* (New York: RosettaBooks, 2011).
2. Scholarly Community Encyclopedia: Great Soviet Encyclopedia, Oct 31, 2022. https://encyclopedia.pub/entry/32049
3. Thomas R. Frieden and Francis S. Collins, "Report to Congress on Traumatic Brain Injury in the United States: Understanding the Public Health Problem among Current and Former Military Personnel" (Centers for Disease Control and Prevention, June 2013). https://www.cdc.gov/traumaticbraininjury/pdf/Report_to_Congress_on_Traumatic_Brain_Injury_2013-a.pdf Ling-Zhuo Kong et al., "Military Traumatic Brain Injury: A Challenge Straddling Neurology and Psychiatry," *Military Medical Research* 9, no. 1 (December 2022): 2. https://doi.org/10.1186/s40779-021-00363-y S Kim et al, "Association of Traumatic Brain Injury Severity and Self-Reported Neuropsychiatric Symptoms in Wounded Military Service Members". Neurotrauma Reports; 4(1): 14–24. Jan 2023. https://www.ncbi.nlm.nih.gov/pmc/articles/PMC9886188/#:~:text=According%20to%20the%20Department%20of,moderate%2C%20and%201.0%25%20severe
4. David Vine, "Lists of U.S. Military Bases Abroad, 1776-2021," Microsoft Excel (American University Library, July 7, 2021). https://doi.org/10.17606/7EM4-HB13 Buddy Blouin, "These Are the Largest U.S. Military Bases in the World," My Base Guide, accessed August 27, 2023. https://mybaseguide.com/largest-us-military-bases
5. John Reed, "Surrounded: How the U.S. Is Encircling China with Military Bases," *Foreign Policy*, August 20, 2013. https://foreignpolicy.com/2013/08/20/surrounded-how-the-u-s-is-encircling-china-with-military-bases/
6. Celia Perry, "My Bases Are Bigger Than Your Country," *Mother Jones*, August 21, 2008. https://www.motherjones.com/politics/2008/08/my-bases-are-bigger-your-country/ Nick Turse, "Empire of Bases 2.0," *TomDispatch*, January 9, 2011. https://tomdispatch.com/nick-turse-the-pentagon-s-planet-of-bases/
   "China Wants to Increase Its Military Presence Abroad," *The Economist*, May 5, 2022.
   https://www.economist.com/china/2022/05/05/china-wants-to-increase-its-military-presence-abroad

Citations

7. Bagdikian, *The New Media Monopoly*.
8. David Croteau, "Examining the 'Liberal Media' Claim," *FAIR*, June 1, 1998. https://fair.org/press-release/examining-the-quotliberal-mediaquot-claim/
9. "Increasing Employee Engagement Strategies," USC MAPP Online, November 14, 2016. https://appliedpsychologydegree.usc.edu/blog/lack-of-engagement-in-the-workplace/ Steve Crabtree, "Weak Workplace Cultures Help Explain UK's Productivity Woes," *Gallup*, October 6, 2017. https://news.gallup.com/opinion/gallup/219947/weak-workplace-cultures-help-explain-productivity-woes.aspx
10. John T. James, "A New, Evidence-Based Estimate of Patient Harms Associated with Hospital Care," *Journal of Patient Safety* 9, no. 3 (September 2013): 122–28. https://doi.org/10.1097/PTS.0b013e3182948a69 Vanessa McMains and Lauren Nelson, "Study Suggests Medical Errors Now Third Leading Cause of Death in the U.S.," *John Hopkins Medicine*, May 3, 2016. https://www.hopkinsmedicine.org/news/media/releases/study_suggests_medical_errors_now_third_leading_cause_of_death_in_the_us
11. "Hospital Errors Are the Third Leading Cause of Death in U.S., and New Hospital Safety Scores Show Improvements Are Too Slow," accessed July 18, 2023. https://www.hospitalsafetygrade.org/about-our-movement/newsroom/display/hospitalerrors-thirdleading-causeofdeathinus-improvementstooslow
12. Niraj Naik, "What Happens One Hour After Drinking A Can Of Coke," *The Renegade Pharmacist*, May 3, 2015. https://therenegadepharmacist.com/what-happens-one-hour-after-drinking-a-can-of-coke/ "How Many Drinks Does The Coca-Cola Company Sell Worldwide Each Day?," Coca-Cola, accessed August 27, 2023.
    https://web.archive.org/web/20200303014852/
    https://www.coca-cola.co.uk/faq/how-many-cans-of-coca-cola-are-sold-worldwide-in-a-day
    Cordelia Hebblethwaite, "Who, What, Why: In Which Countries Is Coca-Cola Not Sold?," *BBC News*, September 11, 2012.
    https://www.bbc.co.uk/news/magazine-19550067
13. Paul Rosenberg, "In Case You Missed It," *The American Prospect*, November 26, 2020. https://prospect.org/api/content/78f9463c-2f58-11eb-84a7-1244d5f7c7c6/ Mickey Huff and Andrew Lee Roth, eds., *Project Censored's State of the Free Press: The Top Censored Stories and Media Analytics of 2019-20. 2021* (New York; Oakland: Seven Stories Press, 2020).
14. Ralph Nader, "Biden's First Year Proves He Is Still a 'Corporate Socialist' Beholden to Big Business," interview by Amy Goodman and Nermeen Shaikh, *Democracy Now!*, January 20, 2022. https://www.youtube.com/watch?v=2jTIUtjkDss
15. John J. Mearsheimer, "The Causes and Consequences of the Ukraine Crisis," The University of Chicago, June 4, 2015. https://news.uchicago.edu/videos/uncommon-core-causes-and-consequences-ukraine-crisis-0
16. Iraq War: Twenty Years Later - Ralph Nader Radio Hour Ep 471 (YouTube channel); Mar 19, 2023. https://www.youtube.com/watch?v=ehb_PoWoHvo
17. Video tweet by Robert F Kennedy Jr, Feb 11, 2024. https://twitter.com/RobertKennedyJr/status/1756561127557718286
18. Svetlana Savranskaya and Tom Blanton, "NATO Expansion: What Gorbachev Heard," *National Security Archive*, December 12, 2017. https://nsarchive.gwu.

edu/briefing-book/russia-programs/2017-12-12/nato-expansion-what-gorbachev-heard-western-leaders-early

19. U.S. Department of State, "Memorandum of Conversation, Secretary Baker and Mikhail Gorbachev, Kremlin [with Cover Note and Underlining in President Bush's Handwriting]" (National Security Archive, May 18, 1990), George H.W. Bush Presidential Library. https://nsarchive.gwu.edu/document/20369-national-security-archive-doc-07-u-s-department

20. George F. Kennan, "A Fateful Error," *The New York Times*, February 5, 1997, sec. Opinion. https://www.nytimes.com/1997/02/05/opinion/a-fateful-error.html

21. Thomas L. Friedman, "Foreign Affairs; Now a Word From X," *The New York Times*, May 2, 1998, sec. Opinion. https://www.nytimes.com/1998/05/02/opinion/foreign-affairs-now-a-word-from-x.html

22. Katharine Q. Seelye, "Arms Contractors Spend to Promote an Expanded NATO," *The New York Times*, March 30, 1998, sec. World. https://www.nytimes.com/1998/03/30/world/arms-contractors-spend-to-promote-an-expanded-nato.html

23. Adrian Blomfield and Mike Smith, "Gorbachev: US Could Start New Cold War," *The Telegraph*, May 6, 2008. https://www.telegraph.co.uk/news/world news/europe/russia/1933223/Gorbachev-US-could-start-new-Cold-War.html

24. David R. Cameron, "Frustrated by Refusals to Give Russia Security Guarantees and Implement Minsk 2, Putin Recognizes Pseudo-States in Donbas and Invades Ukraine," *The MacMillan Center*, February 24, 2022. https://macmil lan.yale.edu/news/frustrated-refusals-give-russia-security-guarantees-imple ment-minsk-2-putin-recognizes-pseudo

25. Deceiving the public about our wars - Lt. Col. Daniel Davis, The Duran (Rumble video), Feb 6, 2024. https://rumble.com/v4br6lf-deceiving-the-public-about-our-wars-lt.-col.-daniel-davis-alexander-mercour.html

26. "Indicators," Yuri Levada Analytical Center, accessed August 28, 2023. https://www.levada.ru/en/ratings/

27. Nick Reynolds and Jack Watling, "Ukraine Through Russia's Eyes," RUSI, August 25, 2023. https://www.rusi.org "Public Opinion Survey of Residents of Ukraine" (Center for Insights in Survey Research (CISR), November 6, 2021). https://www.iri.org/wp-content/uploads/2022/02/FOR-RELEASE-2021-November-Survey-of-Residents-of-Ukraine_ENG.pdf

28. "The past, present and future of US aid to Ukraine", Center for Strategic and International Studies, Sep 26, 2023. https://www.csis.org/analysis/past-present-and-future-us-assistance-ukraine-deep-dive-data "How much aid the US has sent to Ukraine, in 6 charts"; PBS Newshour, Oct 1, 2023. https://www.pbs.org/newshour/world/how-much-aid-the-u-s-has-sent-to-ukraine-in-6-charts Ryan Summers, "The Pentagon's Revolving Door Keeps Spinning: 2021 in Review," *Project On Government Oversight*, January 20, 2022. https://www.pogo.org/analysis/2022/01/the-pentagons-revolving-door-keeps-spin ning-2021-in-review Michael Crowley, "Russian Invasion of Ukraine: U.S. Hits Russian Oligarchs and Companies With New Sanctions," *The New York Times*, August 2, 2022, sec. World. https://www.nytimes.com/live/2022/08/02/world/ukraine-russia-news-war Mark F. Cancian, "Aid to Ukraine Explained in Six Charts," November 18, 2022. https://www.csis.org/analysis/aid-ukraine-explained-six-charts "How Much Aid Has the U.S. Sent Ukraine? Here Are Six Charts," *Council on Foreign Relations*, accessed August 29, 2023.

https://www.cfr.org/article/how-much-aid-has-us-sent-ukraine-here-are-six-charts

29. Robert Michael Gates, *From the Shadows: The Ultimate Insider's Story of Five Presidents and How They Won the Cold War*, 1st ed. (New York: Simon & Schuster, 2006).

30. William Burr, "The 3 A.M. Phone Call: False Missile Attack Warning Incidents 1979–80," National Security Archive, March 1, 2012. https://nsarchive2.gwu.edu/nukevault/ebb371/

31. Charles Gati, "The World According to Zbig," *POLITICO Magazine*, November 27, 2013. https://www.politico.com/magazine/story/2013/11/the-world-according-to-zbigniew-brzezinski-100354

32. Lewis et al, Too Close for Comfort (Chatham House report); April 2014. https://www.chathamhouse.org/sites/default/files/field/field_document/20140428TooCloseforComfortNuclearUseLewisWilliamsPelopidasAghlani.pdf Close calls with nuclear weapons, Union of Concerned Scientists (fact sheet); https://www.ucsusa.org/sites/default/files/attach/2015/04/Close%20Calls%20with%20Nuclear%20Weapons.pdf

33. "Chinese Officials Tried to Get between Donald Trump and His Nuclear Codes," *ABC News*, February 19, 2018. https://www.abc.net.au/news/2018-02-20/scuffle-broke-out-over-nuclear-football-during-trumps-china-trip/9463976

34. Sewell Chan, "Stanislav Petrov, Soviet Officer Who Helped Avert Nuclear War, Is Dead at 77," *The New York Times*, September 18, 2017, sec. World. https://www.nytimes.com/2017/09/18/world/europe/stanislav-petrov-nuclear-war-dead.html

35. Eric Schlosser, "World War Three, by Mistake," *The New Yorker*, December 23, 2016. https://www.newyorker.com/news/news-desk/world-war-three-by-mistake

36. Amy Goodman, "Top U.S. and World Headlines," *Democracy Now!*, August 2, 2022. https://www.youtube.com/watch?v=mMcCgPvIZbQ

37. Fredric Solomon and Robert Q. Marston, *The Medical Implications of Nuclear War* (Washington D.C.: National Academies Press, 1986); Alan Robock, Luke Oman, and Georgiy L. Stenchikov, "Nuclear Winter Revisited with a Modern Climate Model and Current Nuclear Arsenals: Still Catastrophic Consequences," *Journal of Geophysical Research: Atmospheres* 112, no. D13 (July 16, 2007): 2006JD008235. https://doi.org/10.1029/2006JD008235

38. Carl Sagan, The medical implications of nuclear war; National Library of Medicine, 1986. https://www.ncbi.nlm.nih.gov/books/NBK219164/

39. Walter Lippmann, *Liberty and the News* (North Chelmsford: Courier Corporation, 2012).

40. Dominic Cummings, "'People, Ideas, Machines' II: Catastrophic Thinking on Nuclear Weapons," Substack newsletter, *Dominic Cummings Blog*, March 18, 2022. https://dominiccummings.substack.com/p/people-ideas-machines-ii-catastrophic

25. Remedies

1. "Propaganda, American-style" in Propaganda Review (1987).

2. Victor Pickard, "American Journalism Is Dying. Its Survival Requires Public Funds," *The Guardian*, February 19, 2020, sec. Opinion. https://www.

theguardian.com/commentisfree/2020/feb/19/american-journalism-press-publishing-mcclatchy

3. David Allen Green, "A Note on the Leveson Report, Ten Years On," *The Law and Policy Blog*, November 22, 2021. https://davidallengreen.com/2021/11/a-note-on-the-leveson-report-ten-years-on/ Freedman et al, Strategies for Media Reform: International Perspectives: Donald McGannon Communication Research Center's Everett C. Parker Book Series; Fordham university Press, 2016. https://doi.org/10.2307/j.ctt1ctxqc9

4. Robert W. McChesney, "Sharp Left Turn for the Media Reform Movement," *Monthly Review*, February 1, 2014. https://monthlyreview.org/2014/02/01/sharp-left-turn-media-reform-movement/

5. Richard Fletcher et al., "Reuters Institute Digital News Report 2019" (Oxford: Reuters Institute for the Study of Journalism, 2019). https://reutersinstitute.politics.ox.ac.uk/sites/default/files/inline-files/DNR_2019_FINAL.pdf

6. David McKnight, "Murdoch and His Influence on Australian Political Life," *The Conversation*, August 7, 2013. http://theconversation.com/murdoch-and-his-influence-on-australian-political-life-16752

7. Jennifer Szalai, "Yes, Fake News Is a Problem. But There's a Real News Problem, Too.," *The New York Times*, July 26, 2020, sec. Books. https://www.nytimes.com/2020/07/26/books/review-ghosting-news-local-journalism-democracy-crisis-margaret-sullivan.html

8. Dan Barry and Haruka Sakaguchi, "The Last Reporter in Town Had One Big Question for His Rich Boss," *The New York Times*, July 10, 2020, sec. U.S. https://www.nytimes.com/2020/07/10/us/alden-global-capital-pottstown-mercury.html

9. Szalai, "Yes, Fake News Is a Problem. But There's a Real News Problem, Too."

10. Barry and Sakaguchi, "The Last Reporter in Town Had One Big Question for His Rich Boss."

11. "Total Revenue for Radio and Television Broadcasting, Establishments Subject to Federal Income Tax," FRED, Federal Reserve Bank of St. Louis (FRED, Federal Reserve Bank of St. Louis, August 18, 2023). https://fred.stlouisfed.org/series/REV5151TAXABL144QNSA

12. "Newspapers Fact Sheet," *Pew Research Center's Journalism Project*, June 29, 2021. https://www.pewresearch.org/journalism/fact-sheet/newspapers/

13. Robert McChesney, "Between Cambridge and Palo Alto," *Catalyst* 2, no. 1 (2008). https://catalyst-journal.com/2018/06/between-cambridge-and-palo-alto

14. Ralph Nader, "The Central Contention of Politics Should Be the Distribution of Power, Campaign 2000, Los Angeles Press Club Press Conference," March 1, 2000. https://ratical.org/co-globalize/RalphNader/030100.html

15. Jonathan Tepper, "The Conservative Case for Antitrust," *The American Conservative*, January 28, 2019. https://www.theamericanconservative.com/the-conservative-case-for-antitrust-jonathan-tepper/

16. Nader, *Unstoppable*, 140–41.

17. Denise Hearn, "Capitalism and the American Dream Are a Myth," *NowThis News*, January 8, 2019. https://www.youtube.com/watch?v=fM6Nx0qNEW0

18. John Sherman, *Congressional Record* 21, Part 3 (March 21, 1890), 2457. https://www.congress.gov/bound-congressional-record/1890/03/21/21/senate-section/article/2454-2474

19. Tim Wu, *The Curse of Bigness: Antitrust in the New Gilded Age* (New York: Columbia Global Reports, 2018), chap. 1.
20. Wu, chap. 2.
21. Wu, chap. 3.
22. Theodore Roosevelt, "XV. The Peace of Righteousness. Appendix A: The Trusts, the People, and the Square Deal," in *An Autobiography* (New York: Bartleby, 1999). https://www.bartleby.com/lit-hub/theodore-roosevelt-an-autobiography/
23. Franklin D. Roosevelt, *The Public Papers and Addresses of Franklin D. Roosevelt*, ed. Samuel I. Rosenman (New York: Harper, 1950), 41.
24. Tepper, "The Conservative Case for Antitrust."
25. Wu, *The Curse of Bigness*.
26. *Hearings Before a Subcommittee, 85th Congress, 2nd Session, on the Extent to which Private Enforcement of the Antitrust Laws Offers a Practical Form of Protection to Small-business, Victims of Predatory Pricing Practices and Other Antitrust Wrongdoing. March 3-4, 1958* (Washington D.C: U.S. Government Printing Office, 1958), 6.
27. Red Lion Broadcasting v. FCC (1969), 395 u.s. 367, (Constitutional law for a changing America); Sage Publications. https://edge.sagepub.com/epsteinright s11e/student-resources/chapter-6-modern-day-approaches-to-free-expression/ red-lion
28. Alexandra Hall, "South America: A Panorama of Media Democratization," *NACLA*, October 26, 2012. https://nacla.org/article/south-america-panorama-media-democratization
29. Taos Turner and Ken Parks, "Argentina's Top Court Upholds Media Law," *Wall Street Journal*, October 29, 2013, sec. World. http://online.wsj.com/arti cle/SB10001424052702304470504579165601176901802.html
30. Mondragon Corporation website. https://www.mondragon-corporation.com/
31. Peter S. Goodman, "Co-Ops in Spain's Basque Region Soften Capitalism's Rough Edges," *The New York Times*, December 29, 2020, sec. Business. https://www.nytimes.com/2020/12/29/business/cooperatives-basque-spain-economy.html
32. David Erdal, *Beyond the Corporation: Humanity Working* (London: Bodley Head, 2011).
33. Bagdikian, *The New Media Monopoly*.
34. Mark Zuckerberg, "RE: Confidential Announcement," April 9, 2012. https:// judiciary.house.gov/uploadedfiles/0006760000067601.pdf
35. Blayne Haggart, "Why Not Nationalize Facebook?," *The Conversation*, March 29, 2018. http://theconversation.com/why-not-nationalize-facebook-93816 Vasant Dhar, "'Nationalize' Facebook and Twitter as Public Goods," *The Hill*, January 15, 2021, sec. Opinion. https://thehill.com/opinion/technology/ 534458-nationalize-facebook-and-twitter-as-public-goods/ Kevin Roose, "Can Social Media Be Saved?," *The New York Times*, March 28, 2018, sec. Technology. https://www.nytimes.com/2018/03/28/technology/social-media-privacy.html
36. "List of Mergers and Acquisitions by Meta Platforms," in *Wikipedia*, July 22, 2023. https://en.wikipedia.org/w/index.php?title=List_of_mergers_and_acqui sitions_by_Meta_Platforms "List of Mergers and Acquisitions by Apple," in *Wikipedia*, July 27, 2023. https://en.wikipedia.org/w/index.php?title= List_of_mergers_and_acquisitions_by_Apple "List of Mergers and Acquisi-

tions by Amazon," in *Wikipedia*, July 26, 2023. https://en.wikipedia.org/w/index.php?title=List_of_mergers_and_acquisitions_by_Amazon "List of Mergers and Acquisitions by Alphabet," in *Wikipedia*, June 10, 2023. https://en.wikipedia.org/w/index.php?title=List_of_mergers_and_acquisitions_by_Alphabet "List of Mergers and Acquisitions by Microsoft," in *Wikipedia*, June 27, 2023. https://en.wikipedia.org/w/index.php?title=List_of_mergers_and_acquisitions_by_Microsoft

37. Chris Hughes, "It's Time to Break Up Facebook," *The New York Times*, May 9, 2019, sec. Opinion. https://www.nytimes.com/2019/05/09/opinion/sunday/chris-hughes-facebook-zuckerberg.html

38. Scott Galloway, "Markets Are No Longer Competitive," *CNBC*, February 15, 2018. https://www.youtube.com/watch?v=A9qMLJlntLk

39. Devina Sengupta, "DoT Orders Telcos, ISPs to Block 59 Chinese Apps with Immediate Effect," *ET Telecom*, June 30, 2020. https://telecom.economictimes.indiatimes.com/news/telcos-isps-await-dots-instructions-on-blocking-59-chinese-apps/76706019

40. Maria Abi-Habib, "India Bans Nearly 60 Chinese Apps, Including TikTok and WeChat," *The New York Times*, June 29, 2020, sec. World. https://www.nytimes.com/2020/06/29/world/asia/tik-tok-banned-india-china.html

41. Goldacre, *Bad Pharma*.

42. https://publicrelationssydney.com.au/up-to-80-of-media-content-is-from-prs/#:~:text=His%20analy-sis%20showed%20the%20oft,40%2D75%20per%20cent%20common.

43. Eric Weinstein, "Inside the Intellectual Dark Web," *Rebel Wisdom*, December 12, 2018. https://www.youtube.com/watch?v=QOBa9sRn2zE

44. Lauren Gerber, "Why Did Mark Zuckerberg Create Facebook?," *Zimbio*, April 21, 2011. https://web.archive.org/web/20171016053554/http://www.zimbio.com/Why+Did+Mark+Zuckerberg+Create+Facebook/articles/irW6fWzojv2/Mark+Zuckerberg+Create+Facebook

45. John Naughton, "Biden's Path to the White House Could Hit a Dead End on Facebook," *The Observer*, July 26, 2020, sec. Technology. https://www.theguardian.com/technology/2020/jul/26/bidens-path-to-the-white-house-could-hit-a-dead-end-on-facebook

46. Timothy Summers, "Facebook Is Killing Democracy with Its Personality Profiling Data," *The Conversation*, March 21, 2018. http://theconversation.com/facebook-is-killing-democracy-with-its-personality-profiling-data-93611

47. Foster, "Capitalism Has Failed—What Next?"

48. David Hart, "On the Origins of Google," *National Science Foundation*, August 17, 2004. https://new.nsf.gov/news/origins-google

49. Zoe Samios, "Facebook's Australian Tax Bill Just $24 Million as Profits Double," *The Sydney Morning Herald*, May 24, 2022, sec. Companies. https://www.smh.com.au/business/companies/facebook-s-australian-tax-bill-just-24-million-as-profits-double-20220524-p5ao0i.html

50. Zoe Samios and David Crowe, "Voters Back Tougher Rules on Social Media, Survey Shows," *The Sydney Morning Herald*, November 28, 2021, sec. Federal. https://www.smh.com.au/politics/federal/voters-back-tougher-rules-on-social-media-survey-shows-20211128-p59cur.html

51. Monica Anderson, "Most Americans Say Social Media Companies Have Too Much Power, Influence in Politics," *Pew Research Center*, July 22, 2020.

https://www.pewresearch.org/short-reads/2020/07/22/most-americans-say-social-media-companies-have-too-much-power-influence-in-politics/

52. Ina Fried, "Americans Want Tighter Government Regulation of Social Media," *Axios*, December 15, 2021. https://www.axios.com/2021/12/15/social-media-regulation-poll

53. "Majority of British Public Would Support Governmental Regulation of Social Media Companies," *Redfield and Wilton Strategies*, July 31, 2020. https://redfieldandwiltonstrategies.com/majority-of-british-public-would-support-governmental-regulation-of-social-media-companies/

54. Wu, *The Curse of Bigness*, chap. 7. KH디지털2, "Apple Captures 79% of Global Smartphone Profits Last Year," *The Korea Herald*, March 8, 2017, sec. Technology. https://www.koreaherald.com/view.php?ud=20170308000345

55. Tim Wu, "What Years of Emails and Texts Reveal About Your Friendly Tech Companies," *The New York Times*, August 4, 2020, sec. Opinion. https://www.nytimes.com/2020/08/04/opinion/amazon-facebook-congressional-hearings.html

56. "The Facebook Dilemma Part 1," *Frontline* (PBS, October 29, 2018), 1. https://www.pbs.org/wgbh/frontline/documentary/facebook-dilemma/

57. Yael Eisenstat, "Dear Facebook, This Is How You're Breaking Democracy," *TED*, September 24, 2020. https://www.youtube.com/watch?v=plmL343TOy4

58. Georgia Wells, Jeff Horwitz, and Deepa Seetharaman, "Facebook Knows Instagram Is Toxic for Teen Girls, Company Documents Show," *Wall Street Journal*, September 14, 2021, sec. Tech. https://www.wsj.com/articles/facebook-knows-instagram-is-toxic-for-teen-girls-company-documents-show-11631620739

59. Wells, Horwitz, and Seetharaman.

60. Shannon et al, Problematic Social Media Use in Adolescents and Young Adults: Systematic Review and Meta-analysis; JMIR Publications, 14.4.2022 in vol 9, no. 4, Apr 14, 2022. https://mental.jmir.org/2022/4/e33450 Chassiakos et al, Children and Adolescents and Digital Media; Pediatrics, Vol 138, issue 5, Nov 2016. https://www.sciencedirect.com/science/article/pii/S2666920X22000662?via%3Dihub E Pohorskiy and J Beckman, From procrastination to engagement? An experimental exploration of the effects of an adaptive virtual assistant on self-regulation in online learning; Computers and Education: Artificial Intelligence, vol 4, 2023. https://doi.org/10.1016/j.caeai.2022.100111 Hunt, et al, No More FOMO: Limiting Social Media Decreases Loneliness and Depression. Journal of Social and Clinical Psychology. 37 (10): 751–768. Dec 2018. doi:10.1521/jscp.2018.37.10.751 Miller, et al, How the World Changed Social Media. University College London, 2016. doi:10.14324/111.9781910634493

61. "Social Media Apps Are 'deliberately' Addictive to Users," *BBC News*, July 3, 2018, sec. Technology. https://www.bbc.com/news/technology-44640959

62. "Social Media Apps Are 'deliberately' Addictive to Users."

63. Alex Kantrowitz, "Man Who Built The Retweet: 'We Handed A Loaded Weapon To 4-Year-Olds,'" *BuzzFeed News*, July 23, 2019, sec. Tech. https://www.buzzfeednews.com/article/alexkantrowitz/how-the-retweet-ruined-the-internet

64. Paul Lewis, "'Our Minds Can Be Hijacked': The Tech Insiders Who Fear a Smartphone Dystopia," *The Guardian*, October 6, 2017, sec. Technology.

Citations

https://www.theguardian.com/technology/2017/oct/05/smartphone-addiction-silicon-valley-dystopia

65. Lewis.

66. Emma-Jo Morris testimony to House Judiciary Committee, Jul 21, 2023. Transcript: https://judiciary.house.gov/sites/evo-subsites/republicans-judiciary.house.gov/files/evo-media-document/morris-testimony.pdf Video: https://www.youtube.com/watch?v=M28tXX0cvvI&ab_channel=ForbesBreakingNews

67. John Macgregor, "The Byron Echo - Bastion of Media Independence," *The Age*, May 26, 1988. https://john-macgregor.com/entryPage.php?entid=127

68. "Top Ten Lists: Highest Job Satisfaction," *MyPlan*, 2019. https://www.myplan.com/careers/top-ten/highest-job-satisfaction.php

69. McKnight, "Murdoch and His Influence on Australian Political Life."

70. Robert Manne, "Why Rupert Murdoch Can't Be Stopped," *The Monthly*, November 1, 2013. https://www.themonthly.com.au/issue/2013/november/1383224400/robert-manne/why-rupert-murdoch-can-t-be-stopped

71. Pamela Williams, "The War on Malcolm: Behind the Scenes of an Overthrow," *The Monthly*, February 2019. https://www.themonthly.com.au/issue/2019/february/pamela-williams/war-malcolm

72. Amanda Meade, "Malcolm Turnbull: News Corp Is like a Political Party with the Murdochs Encouraging Intolerance," *The Guardian*, April 16, 2020, sec. Australia news. https://www.theguardian.com/australia-news/2020/apr/16/malcolm-turnbull-news-corp-is-like-a-political-party-with-the-murdochs-encouraging-intolerance

73. Meade.

74. John Hewson, "Fourth Estate Corrupting the Political System," *ABC News*, July 8, 2010. https://www.abc.net.au/news/2010-07-08/36452

75. Joan Evatt, "The Day The Australian's Reporters Stopped Writing Lies," *Independent Australia*, March 15, 2013. https://independentaustralia.net/politics/politics-display/the-day-the-australians-reporters-stopped-writing-lies,5107

76. Ian Cunliffe, "Not Only Governments Exert Foreign Influence. What about Rupert Murdoch?," *Pearls and Irritations*, November 30, 2020. https://johnmenadue.com/not-only-governments-exert-foreign-influence-what-about-rupert-murdoch/

77. Jonathan Mahler and Jim Rutenberg, "Part 2: Inside the Succession Battle for the Murdoch Empire," *The New York Times*, April 3, 2019, sec. Magazine. https://www.nytimes.com/interactive/2019/04/03/magazine/james-murdoch-lachlan-succession.html

78. Anthony Hilton, "Stay or Go - the Lack of Solid Facts Means It's All a Leap of Faith," *Evening Standard*, February 25, 2016, sec. Comment. https://www.standard.co.uk/comment/comment/anthony-hilton-stay-or-go-the-lack-of-solid-facts-means-it-s-all-a-leap-of-faith-a3189151.html

79. David Frum, *Nightline* (ABC, March 22, 2010). https://archive.org/details/WMAR_20100323_033500_Nightline/

80. Tom Wicker, "In the Nation; A Collision Course," *The New York Times*, May 26, 1981, sec. Opinion. https://www.nytimes.com/1981/05/26/opinion/in-the-nation-a-collision-course.html

V. Renovating the democratic machinery

1. "Constitution Day," United States Senate, accessed September 5, 2023. https://web.archive.org/web/20210301145257/https://www.senate.gov/artand history/history/common/generic/ConstitutionDay.htm
2. Pamela S. Karlan et al., "Six Ways to Reform Democracy," *Boston Review*, September 6, 2006. https://www.bostonreview.net/articles/six-ways-to-reform-democracy-voting/

26. Consensual government

1. Arend Lijphart, *Democracy in the Twenty-First Century: Can We Be Optimistic?*, Uhlenbeck Lectures (Wassenaar: NIAS, 2000), chap. Introduction.
2. Lijphart, chap. 1.
3. "Constitution Day," United States Senate, accessed September 5, 2023. https://web.archive.org/web/20210301145257/https://www.senate.gov/artand history/history/common/generic/ConstitutionDay.htm
4. Lijphart, *Democracy in the Twenty-First Century*, chap. 15.
5. Vicki Birchfield and Markus M.L. Crepaz, "The Impact of Constitutional Structures and Collective and Competitive Veto Points on Income Inequality in Industrialized Democracies," *European Journal of Political Research* 34, no. 2 (October 1, 1998): 175–200. https://doi.org/10.1023/A:1006960528737
6. Lijphart, *Democracy in the Twenty-First Century*, chap. 17.
7. Arend Lijphart, *Patterns of Democracy: Government Forms and Performance in Thirty-six Countries* (New Haven: Yale University Press, 1999), 307.

27. Mutable democracy

1. Thomas Jefferson to Samuel Kercheval, Letter, 12 July, 1816, *Teaching American History*. https://teachingamericanhistory.org/document/letter-to-samuel-kercheval/
2. Lao Tzu and R. L. Wing, *The Tao of Power: A Translation of the Tao Te Ching by Lao Tzu*, 1st ed. (Garden City, N.Y: Doubleday, 1986).
3. Lao Tzu and R. L. Wing, *The Tao of Power*, chap. 32.
4. Eric Weinstein, "Inside the Intellectual Dark Web."
5. Bret Weinstein, "The Path to an Excellent World", March 30, 2018. https://www.youtube.com/watch?v=CLHdY5Cyf58
6. David Hume, Essays, Moral, Political, and Literary; Part I: The rise of arts and sciences, p. 117; Bell and Bradfute, 1825.
7. Nassim Nicholas Taleb, *Antifragile: Things That Gain from Disorder* (London: Penguin, 2012), 337.
8. "Nobel Prize Laureates and Other Experts Issue Urgent Call for Action After 'Our Planet, Our Future' Summit," *Future Earth*, May 7, 2021. https://futureearth.org/2021/05/07/nobel-prize-laureates-and-other-experts-issue-urgent-call-for-action-after-our-planet-our-future-summit/

28. Demotic institutions

1. Hansen, *The Athenian Democracy in the Age of Demosthenes*, 320.
2. Max Benwell, "John Bolton's Bombshell Trump Book: Eight of Its Most Stunning Claims," *The Guardian*, June 17, 2020, sec. US news. https://www. theguardian.com/us-news/2020/jun/17/john-bolton-book-trump-china-dicta tors-saudi-arabia
3. Thomas Paine, *The Writings of Thomas Paine (1779-1792): The Rights of Man*, vol. 2 (Urbana, Illinois: Project Gutenberg, 2003). https://www.gutenberg.org/ ebooks/3742

29. The machinery of third draft democracy

1. William Greider, *Who Will Tell the People: The Betrayal of American Democracy*, 1st ed. (New York: Simon & Schuster, 1993).
2. "World Publics Say Governments Should Be More Responsive to the Will of the People," *World Public Opinion*, May 12, 2008. https://worldpublicopinion. net/world-publics-say-governments-should-be-more-responsive-to-the-will-of- the-people/
3. Matt Zarb-Cousin, "We Need Mandatory Reselection," *Jacobin*, September 15, 2018. https://jacobin.com/2018/09/mandatory-reselection-labour-party- mps-democracy
4. "Majorities of Republican and Democratic Voters Agree on $128 Billion in Deficit Reduction, Raising Revenue and Cutting Spending."
5. Dominic Cummings, "On the Referendum #21: Branching Histories of the 2016 Referendum and 'the Frogs before the Storm,'" *Dominic Cummings Blog*, January 9, 2017. https://dominiccummings.com/2017/01/09/on-the-referen dum-21-branching-histories-of-the-2016-referendum-and-the-frogs-before- the-storm-2/
6. Boehm et al., "Egalitarian Behavior and Reverse Dominance Hierarchy [and Comments and Reply]."
7. Masha Gessen, "What Happens When a Group of Strangers Spends a Day Debating Immigration?," *The New Yorker*, July 23, 2019. https://www. newyorker.com/news/dispatch/what-happens-when-a-group-of-strangers- spends-a-day-debating-immigration
8. Scott E. Page, "In Professor's Model, Diversity Equals Productivity," *The New York Times*, January 8, 2008, sec. Science. https://www.nytimes.com/2008/01/ 08/science/08conv.html
9. Tom Malleson, "Beyond Electoral Democracy," *Jacobin*, May 29, 2018. https://jacobin.com/2018/05/legislature-lot-electoral-democracy-real-utopias
10. Hansen, *The Athenian Democracy in the Age of Demosthenes*, 84.
11. Hansen, chap. 9.
12. Humphrey Davy Findley Kitto, *The Greeks* (Harmondsworth: Penguin Books, 1951), 127.
13. Ralph Nader, "Talks at Google", *Policy Talks*, Google, Mountain View, California, May 12, 2008. https://www.youtube.com/watch?v=KR-V6bl41zU
14. Patrick Fournier, *When Citizens Decide: Lessons from Citizen Assemblies on Electoral Reform* (Oxford: Oxford University Press, 2011).
15. Fournier, 39.

Citations

16. Ober, *The Rise and Fall of Classical Greece*, chap. 7.
17. Derek Rielly and Bob Hawke, *Wednesdays with Bob* (Sydney: Pan Macmillan Australia, 2017).
18. Micah Meadowcroft, "'The World That We Will Live and Die In,'" *The American Conservative*, March 15, 2023. https://www.theamericanconservative.com/the-world-that-we-will-live-and-die-in/
19. James Fishkin, "Making Deliberative Democracy Real," Center for Deliberative Democracy, Stanford University, April 26, 2013. https://www.youtube.com/watch?v=Hr1MqokjqRQ James Fishkin, "Democracy When the People Are Thinking," *Crises of Democracy*, Hannah Arendt Center for Politics and Humanities, Bard College, October 12, 2017. https://www.youtube.com/watch?v=swsSnATcpqs
20. James Fishkin, "Democracy When the People Are Thinking," TEDxDesignTechHighSchool, June 11, 2018. https://www.youtube.com/watch?v=27tVMj6YUNM
21. James S. Fishkin et al., "Returning Deliberative Democracy to Athens: Deliberative Polling for Candidate Selection," Research Paper (Boston: American Political Science Association, August 28, 2008). https://deliberation.stanford.edu/news/returning-deliberative-democracy-athens-deliberative-pollingr-candidate-selection
22. Joe Klein, "How Can a Democracy Solve Tough Problems?," *Time*, February 9, 2010. https://content.time.com/time/magazine/article/0,9171,2015790,00.html
23. David Sloan Wilson and Dag Olav Hessen, "Blueprint For The Global Village. Norway Explained.," *Evolution Institute*, May 5, 2014. https://evolution-institute.org/blueprint-for-the-global-village/
24. Tuchman, *The March of Folly: From Troy to Vietnam*.
25. *Dominic Cummings: The Interview* (BBC Two, July 20, 2021). https://www.youtube.com/watch?v=ddHN2qmvCG0&ab_channel=PoliticalTV
26. Leonard Steinhorn and Mark Sobol, "Congress at a Crossroads," *FMC*, accessed: September 16, 2023. https://web.archive.org/web/20201113094210/https://www.usafmc.org/congressxroads
27. Nicholas Christakis, "The Hidden Influence of Social Networks," TED, May 10, 2010. https://www.youtube.com/watch?v=2U-tOghblfE
28. Cary Funk, Brian Kennedy, and Elizabeth Sciupac, "U.S. Public Wary of Biomedical Technologies to 'Enhance' Human Abilities" (Pew Research Center, July 2016). https://www.pewresearch.org/science/2016/07/26/u-s-public-wary-of-biomedical-technologies-to-enhance-human-abilities/
29. Nicholas Thompson, "When Tech Knows You Better Than You Know Yourself," *Wired*, October 4, 2010. https://www.wired.com/story/artificial-intelligence-yuval-noah-harari-tristan-harris/
30. Stuart Russell et al., "Robotics: Ethics of Artificial Intelligence," *Nature* 521, no. 7553 (May 28, 2015); 415–18. https://doi.org/10.1038/521415a
31. Iain McGilchrist, Rupert Sheldrake and Alex Gomez-Marin, "In Conversation," *Channel McGilchrist*, February 27, 2023. https://www.youtube.com/watch?v=4O3ITKAG4_8
32. Geoff Mann, review of *Reversing the Freight Train*, by Per Espen Stoknes et al., *London Review of Books*, August 18, 2022. https://www.lrb.co.uk/the-paper/v44/n16/geoff-mann/reversing-the-freight-train

Citations

33. Tweet by Lee Camp (Redacted)l Sep 25, 2023. https://twitter.com/LeeCamp/status/1702354697896571104

34. Max Blumenthal, Gofundme freezes Grayzone fundraiser 'due to some external concerns'; The Grayzone, Aug 28, 2024. https://thegrayzone.com/2023/08/28/gofundme-freezes-grayzone-fundraiser/#:~:text=The%20Silicon%20Valley%2Dbased%20crowdfunding,Rubinstein%20with%20long%2Dterm%20positions.

35. Graham Starr, EU threatens Musk with fines over Israel-Hamas disinformation on X; Australian Financial Review, Oct 11,2023. https://www.afr.com/technology/eu-threatens-musk-with-fines-over-israel-hamas-disinformation-on-x-20231011-p5ebbe

36. Matt Taibbi and Max Blumenthal on Neoliberal Censorship, usefulidiots (Rumble channel); Sep 2023. https://rumble.com/v3e43qr-matt-taibbi-and-max-blumenthal-on-neoliberal-censorship.html

37. Anthony Whealy, Secret whistleblower trial will only add to Australia's shame over spying cover-up; Sydney Morning Herald, Aug 29, 2019. https://www.smh.com.au/national/secret-whistleblower-trial-will-only-add-to-australia-s-shame-over-spying-cover-up-20190827-p52ldh.html

38. UNRAVELING THE WEB OF INTERNET FREEDOM; Federal Newswire, Apr 18, 2023 https://thefederalnewswire.com/stories/641707686-unraveling-the-web-of-internet-freedom-a-candid-conversation-with-mike-benz-former-diplomat-turned-digital-freedom-advocate

39. Hänel, Lisa. 'Germany criminalizes denying war crimes, genocide.' *Deutsche Welle*, 25 Nov. 2022. https://www.dw.com/en/germany-criminalizes-denying-war-crimes-genocide/a-63834791

40. Savarese, Mauricio, and Joshua Goodman. 'Crusading Judge Tests Boundaries of Free Speech in Brazil.' AP News, 26 Jan. 2023. apnews.com/article/jair-bolsonaro-brazil-government-af5987e833a681e6f056fe63789ca375

41. Nanu, Maighna. 'Irish People Could Be Jailed for "Hate Speech", Critics of Proposed Law Warn.' *The Telegraph*, 17 June 2023. www.telegraph.co.uk/world-news/2023/06/1   7/irish-people-jailed-hate-speech-new-law/?WT.mc_id=tmgoff_psc_ppc_us_news_dsa_generalnews

42. The Economist. (n.d.). Scotland's new hate crime act will have a chilling effect on free speech. The Economist. Nov 8, 2021. https://www.economist.com/the-world-ahead/2021/11/08/scotlands-new-hate-crime-act-will-have-a-chilling-effect-on-free-speech

43. Lomas, Natasha. 'Security Researchers Latest to Blast UK's Online Safety Bill as Encryption Risk.' TechCrunch, 5 July 2023. techcrunch.com/2023/07/05/uk-online-safety-bill-risks-e2ee/

44. Pahwa, Nitish. 'Twitter Blocked a Country.' *Slate Magazine*, 1 Apr. 2023. slate.com/technology/2023/04/twitter-blocked-pakistan-india-modi-musk-khalistan-gandhi.html

45. Stein, Perry. 'Twitter Says It Will Restrict Access to Some Tweets before Turkey's Election.' *The Washington Post*, 15 May 2023. www.washingtonpost.com/technology/2023/05/13/turkey-twitter-musk-erdogan/

46. "Asian Organised Crime in Australia," Discussion Paper (Canberra: Commonwealth of Australia, February 1995). https://www.aph.gov.au/Parliamentary_Business/Committees/Joint/Former_Committees/acc/completed_inquiries/pre1996/ncaaoc/report/index

47. "Organised Crime," Australian Taxation Office, accessed August 24, 2023. https://www.ato.gov.au/General/The-fight-against-tax-crime/Our-focus/Organ ised-crime/

48. "Budget 2021-22: Securing Australia's Recovery Guaranteeing the Essential Services" (Commonwealth of Australia, 2021). https://archive.budget.gov.au/2021-22/download/glossy_ges.pdf

49. "Organised Crime in Australia 2017" (Australian Criminal Intelligence Commission, 2017). https://www.studocu.com/en-us/document/mclennan-community-college/forensic-science-ii/organised-crime-in-australia/21322667

50. "Asian Organised Crime in Australia."

51. Natalie O'Brien, "Russian Dons Set up in Australia," *Nationwide News*, May 22, 2004. https://freerepublic.com/focus/news/1140290/posts. Nick McKenzie and Richard Baker, "Mafia Link to Melbourne Pizza Wars," *The Age*, March 7, 2014, sec. Victoria. https://www.theage.com.au/national/victo ria/mafia-link-to-melbourne-pizza-wars-20140307-34cyp.html

52. Paul Anderson, "Russian Gang in Tatters," *Herald Sun*, April 15, 2007, sec. True Crime Scene. https://www.heraldsun.com.au/news/law-order/true-crime-scene/russian-gang-in-tatters/news-story/f621fa53c077e09c086eef2756a96988

53. Tom Forbes, "Corruption Watchdog Won't Charge Gold Coast Councillors, but Mayor Faces Further Probe," *ABC News*, December 10, 2019. https://www.abc.net.au/news/2019-12-10/corruption-watchdog-not-charging-gold-coast-councillors/11786414

54. "Transnational Crime and the Developing World" (Washington, D.C.: Global Financial Integrity, March 27, 2017). https://gfintegrity.org/report/transna tional-crime-and-the-developing-world/

55. Halsted R. Holman, "The Relation of the Chronic Disease Epidemic to the Health Care Crisis," *ACR Open Rheumatology* 2, no. 3 (February 19, 2020): 167–73. https://doi.org/10.1002/acr2.11114

56. Partnership for Solutions National Program Office, "Chronic Conditions: Making the Case for Ongoing Care" (Johns Hopkins University, September 2004). https://web.archive.org/web/20120423222310/http:/www.rwjf.org/qualityequality/product.jsp?id=14685 Christine Buttorff, Teague Ruder, and Melissa Bauman, *Multiple Chronic Conditions in the United States* (Santa Monica, CA: RAND Corporation, 2017). https://doi.org/10.7249/TL221

57. Sandra H van Oostrom et al., "Time Trends in Prevalence of Chronic Diseases and Multimorbidity Not Only Due to Aging: Data from General Practices and Health Surveys," *Public Library of Science ONE* 11, no. 8 (August 2, 2016): e0160264. https://doi.org/10.1371/journal.pone.0160264 "Chronic Condi tions, 2017-18 Financial Year," Australian Bureau of Statistics, December 12, 2018. https://www.abs.gov.au/statistics/health/health-conditions-and-risks/chronic-conditions/latest-release "Chronic Conditions: Making the Case for Ongoing Care," (Washington, D. C.: The School of Medicine and Health Sciences, February 2010).
https://web.archive.org/web/20230421165227/https://smhs.gwu.edu/sites/default/files/ChronicCareChartbook.pdf

58. Peter C Gøtzsche, "Prescription Drugs Are the Third Leading Cause of Death," *The BMJ*, June 16, 2016. https://blogs.bmj.com/bmj/2016/06/16/peter-c-gotzsche-prescription-drugs-are-the-third-leading-cause-of-death/

59. Alec Tyson, What the data says about Americans' views of climate change; Pew

Citations

Research Center, Aug 9, 2023. https://www.pewresearch.org/short-reads/2023/08/09/what-the-data-says-about-americans-views-of-climate-change/

60. Alec Tyson, Americans Largely Favor U.S. Taking Steps To Become Carbon Neutral by 2050; Pew Research Center, Mar 1, 2022. https://www.pewresearch.org/science/2022/03/01/americans-largely-favor-u-s-taking-steps-to-become-carbon-neutral-by-2050/

61. James Bell, In Response to Climate Change, Citizens in Advanced Economies Are Willing To Alter How They Live and Work; Pew Research Center, Aug 14, 2021. https://www.pewresearch.org/global/2021/09/14/in-response-to-climate-change-citizens-in-advanced-economies-are-willing-to-alter-how-they-live-and-work/

62. Giancarlo Pasquini, Why Some Americans Do Not See Urgency on Climate Change; Pew Research Center, Aug 9, 2023. https://www.pewresearch.org/science/2023/08/09/why-some-americans-do-not-see-urgency-on-climate-change/

63. Jacob Poushter, Climate Change Remains Top Global Threat Across 19-Country Survey; Pew Research Center, Aug 31, 2022. https://www.pewresearch.org/global/2022/08/31/climate-change-remains-top-global-threat-across-19-country-survey/

64. Lynn Klotz, "Human Error in High-Biocontainment Labs: A Likely Pandemic Threat," *Bulletin of the Atomic Scientists*, February 25, 2019. https://thebulletin.org/2019/02/human-error-in-high-biocontainment-labs-a-likely-pandemic-threat/

65. Klotz.

66. COVID Origins Wrap Up: Facts, Science, Evidence, Point to a Wuhan Lab Leak (press release); Committee on Government Oversight, Mar 8, 2023. https://oversight.house.gov/release/covid-origins-hearing-wrap-up-facts-science-evidence-point-to-a-wuhan-lab-leak%EF%BF%BC/

67. Gain-of-function and origin of Covid19; Patrick Berche, Presse Med. 2023 Mar; 52(1): 104167. Jun 2, 2022. doi: 10.1016/j.lpm.2023.104167 https://www.ncbi.nlm.nih.gov/pmc/articles/PMC10234839/

68. Dave Wessner, Gain-Of-Function Research And Covid-19: Could Too Much Oversight Slow Progress? Forbes magazine, Mar 9, 2023. https://www.forbes.com/sites/davewessner/2023/03/09/gain-of-function-research-and-covid-19-could-too-much-oversight-slow-progress/?sh=5ce59be61f7f

69. James Bell et al., "International Cooperation Welcomed Across 14 Advanced Economies" (Washington, D.C.: Pew Research Center, September 21, 2020). https://www.pewresearch.org/global/2020/09/21/international-cooperation-welcomed-across-14-advanced-economies/

70. Bell et al.

71. Arundhati Roy, "This Is No Ordinary Spying. Our Most Intimate Selves Are Now Exposed," *The Guardian*, July 26, 2021, sec. Opinion. https://www.theguardian.com/commentisfree/2021/jul/27/spying-pegasus-project-states-arundhati-roy

72. Indrajit Samarajiva, "Sri Lanka Collapsed First, but It Won't Be the Last, Columns," *The Business Times*, August 16, 2022. https://www.businesstimes.com.sg/opinion-features/columns/sri-lanka-collapsed-first-it-wont-be-last

73. D. Cohen and P. Carter, "WHO and the Pandemic Flu 'Conspiracies,'" *British Medical Journal* 340 (June 6, 2010): c2912–c2912. https://doi.org/10.1136/bmj.c2912

74. Yanis Varoufakis, Astra Taylor, Jayati Ghosh and Frank Barat, "LTIO#5 Debt as Power," Let's Talk it Over, June 15, 2021. https://www.youtube.com/watch?v=Rygn4Fp8K9E

75. Yanis Varoufakis, Why we must save the EU; The Guardian, Apr 5, 2016. https://www.theguardian.com/world/2016/apr/05/yanis-varoufakis-why-we-must-save-the-eu

76. Svetlana Savranskaya and Thomas Blanton, "The Washington/Camp David Summit 30 Years Ago," *National Security Archive*, June 2, 2020. https://nsarchive.gwu.edu/briefing-book/russia-programs/2020-06-02/washington-camp-david-summit-30-years-ago

77. John Dryzek, "The Proposed Senate Voting Change Will Hurt Australian Democracy," *The Conversation*, February 24, 2016. http://theconversation.com/the-proposed-senate-voting-change-will-hurt-australian-democracy-55297

78. Nicholas Gruen, "Detox Democracy through Representation by Random Selection," *The Mandarin*, February 13, 2017, sec. Features. https://www.themandarin.com.au/75323-nicholas-gruen-detoxing-democracy/

79. "What Worries the World" (Ipsos Public Affairs, November 2016). https://www.ipsos.com/sites/default/files/migrations/en-uk/files/Assets/Docs/Polls/What-Worries-the-World-Nov-2016-Great%20Britain-charts.pdf

80. "Satisfaction With the United States," *Gallup*, October 12, 2007. https://news.gallup.com/poll/1669/General-Mood-Country.aspx "Direction of Country," Polling Report, 2022. https://www.pollingreport.com/right.htm http://www.rasmussenreports.com/public_content/politics/top_stories/right_direction_wrong_track_mar25

81. Ros Krasny, "Poll: Majority of Americans Say the U.S. Is Headed in the Wrong Direction Under President Trump," *Time*, January 27, 2019. https://time.com/5514235/americans-united-states-wrong-direction-poll/

82. Yves Sintomer, Random Selection, Republican Self-Government, and Deliberative Democracy; *Constellations,* Vol 17, No 3, 2010. https://newdemocracy.com.au/docs/researchpapers/20101103_Sintomer_random_selection.pdf   *A Chollet and A Dupois,* Kübellos in the canton of Glarus: A unique experience of sortition in politics; Participations 2019, pps 263 to 281, 2019. *https://www.cairn-int.info/article-E_PARTI_HS01_0263--kubellos-in-the-canton-of-glarus-a.htm*

83. Alex Seitz-Wald, "The U.S. Needs a New Constitution - Here's How to Write It," *The Atlantic*, November 2, 2013. https://www.theatlantic.com/politics/archive/2013/11/the-us-needs-a-new-constitution-heres-how-to-write-it/281090/

84. Tim Alberta, "The Tragedy of Paul Ryan," *POLITICO Magazine*, April 12, 2018. https://politi.co/2HdjHlA

85. Arend Lijphart, "Constitutional Design for Divided Societies," *Journal of Democracy* 15, no. 2 (April 2004): 96–109; Lijphart, *Democracy in the Twenty-First Century*. https://www.journalofdemocracy.org/articles/constitutional-design-for-divided-societies/

86. John Gerring, Strom C. Thacker, and Carola Moreno, "Are Parliamentary Systems Better?," *Comparative Political Studies* 42, no. 3 (March 1, 2009): 327–59. https://doi.org/10.1177/0010414008325573

87. Lijphart, *Democracy in the Twenty-First Century*.

Citations

88. Juan J. Linz and Arturo Valenzuela, eds., *The Failure of Presidential Democracy* (Baltimore: JHU Press, 1994).

89. Oona A Hathaway, "The Case for Promoting Democracy Through Export Control," *Harvard Journal of Law & Public Policy* 33, no. 1 (January 1, 2010), 19. https://core.ac.uk/display/72826977

90. Hathaway, "The Case for Promoting Democracy Through Export Control"; Alfred Stepan and Cindy Skach, "Constitutional Frameworks and Democratic Consolidation: Parliamentarianism versus Presidentialism," *World Politics* 46, no. 1 (October 1993): 1–22. https://doi.org/10.2307/2950664 Adam Przeworski, "Democracy and Economic Development," in *Democracy, Autonomy, and Conflict in Comparative and International Politics*, ed. Edward D. Mansfield and Richard Sisson, 1. ed, The Evolution of Political Knowledge / Edward D. Mansfield and Richard Sisson, Eds 2 (Columbus: Ohio State University Press, 2004), 300–324. Adam Przeworski et al., *Democracy and Development: Political Institutions and Well-Being in the World, 1950–1990*, 1st ed. (Cambridge University Press, 2000). https://doi.org/10.1017/CBO9780511804946 Linz and Valenzuela, *The Failure of Presidential Democracy*. Giovanni Sartori, "Neither Presidentialism nor Parliamentarism," in *The Failure of Presidential Democracy*, ed. Juan J. Linz and Arturo Valenzuela (Baltimore: JHU Press, 1994), 106–7. Alfred Stepan and Cindy Skach, "Presidentialism and Parliamentarism in Comparative Perspective," in *The Failure of Presidential Democracy*, ed. Juan J. Linz and Arturo Valenzuela (Baltimore: JHU Press, 1994), 119, 124–26.

91. Lijphart, *Democracy in the Twenty-First Century*.

92. Margaret Stimmann Branson, "Project Citizen: An Introduction," Center for Civic Education, February 1999. https://www.civiced.org/papers/articles_branson99.html

93. Reihan Salam and Rob Richie, "How to Make Congress Bipartisan," *The New York Times*, July 8, 2017, sec. Opinion. https://www.nytimes.com/2017/07/07/opinion/how-to-make-congress-bipartisan.html

94. RESEARCH PAPER 05/33, General Election 2005; House of Commons, MAY 18, 2005. https://researchbriefings.files.parliament.uk/documents/RP05-33/RP05-33.pdf Arend Lijphart, *Patterns of Democracy: Government Forms and Performance in Thirty-Six Countries*, 2nd ed. (New Haven: Yale University Press, 2012), chaps. 2, 16.

95. "Results of the 2019 General Election," *BBC News*, 2019. https://www.bbc.co.uk/news/election/2019/results

96. The Editorial Board, "A Congress for Every American," *The New York Times*, November 10, 2018, sec. Opinion. https://www.nytimes.com/interactive/2018/11/10/opinion/house-representatives-size-multi-member.html

97. Salam and Richie, "How to Make Congress Bipartisan."

98. European Consortium for Political Research (ECPR) website. https://ecpr.eu/Filestore/PaperProposal/5ca0166b-7466-4e37-9b1c-9dc11ed42d7f.pdf

99. "A Look at the Evidence for Proportional Representation," *Fair Vote Canada*, accessed September 7, 2023. https://www.fairvote.ca/a-look-at-the-evidence/

100. Darcie Roschen Cohen, "Do Political Preconditions Affect Environmental Outcomes? Exploring the Linkages between Proportional Representation, Green Parties and the Kyoto Protocol" (Simon Fraser University, 2010). http://summit.sfu.ca/item/10084

Citations

101. "Hare-Clark Explained," *ABC News Online*, February 2, 2006. https://web.archive.org/web/20200128123128/http://www.abc.net.au:80/elections/tas/2006/guide/hareclark.htm

102. Michel Balinski, "How Majority Voting Betrayed Voters Again in 2016," *The Conversation*, December 2, 2016. http://theconversation.com/how-majority-voting-betrayed-voters-again-in-2016-69206

103. Danielle Allen et al., "What's in a Vote?: Electoral Politics in an Ailing Democracy," *Harper's Magazine*, November 2020. https://harpers.org/archive/2020/11/whats-in-a-vote-electoral-politics-in-an-ailing-democracy/

104. "Research and Data on RCV in Practice," FairVote, accessed September 7, 2023. https://fairvote.org/resources/data-on-rcv/

105. Rory Stewart, "Is Democracy the Only Way?," TEDx, 30 July, 2012. https://www.youtube.com/watch?v=ydzNAuqUAnc

106. Hanna Fenichel Pitkin, "Representation and Democracy: Uneasy Alliance," *Scandinavian Political Studies* 27, no. 3 (September 2004): 335–42. https://doi.org/10.1111/j.1467-9477.2004.00109.x

107. James Madison, "The Same Subject Continued: The Union as a Safeguard Against Domestic Faction and Insurrection," *The Federalist*, November 23, 1787, 10 edition. https://guides.loc.gov/federalist-papers/text-1-10#s-lg-box-wrapper-25493273

108. James Madison, "The Utility of the Union as a Safeguard Against Domestic Faction and Insurrection (Continued)," *The Federalist*, November 22, 1787, 10 ed. https://web.archive.org/web/20200219080201/https://www.constitution.org/fed/federa10.htm

109. "Congress and the Public," *Gallup*, October 12, 2007. https://news.gallup.com/poll/1600/Congress-Public.aspx

110. Alvin Toffler, *The Third Wave* (New York: William Morrow and Company, 1980). http://archive.org/details/TheThirdWave-Toffler

111. Toffler, 95.

112. Toffler, 93-4.

113. US Embassy in Moscow to State Department, "Gorbachev Confronts Crisis of Power," Telegram, May 11, 1990. https://nsarchive2.gwu.edu/NSAEBB/NSAEBB320/01.pdf

114. Bruno Kaufmann, Rolf Büchi, and Nadja Brauneisen, *Guidebook to Direct Democracy in Switzerland and Beyond*, 3rd ed. (Bern: Initiative and Referendum Inst. Europe, 2008).

115. Kaufmann, Büchi, and Brauneisen.

116. Kaufmann, Büchi, and Brauneisen, chap. 3.

117. Kaufmann, Büchi, and Brauneisen.

118. Alexander Thoele, "Direct Democracy Also Has Its User Guide," *SWI Swissinfo*, February 9, 2016. https://www.swissinfo.ch/eng/business/handy-booklet_direct-democracy-also-has-its-user-guide/41773098

119. Bruno Kaufmann, Rolf Büchi, and Nadja Brauneisen, *Guidebook to Direct Democracy: In Switzerland and Beyond*, 4th ed. (Marburg: Initiative and Referendum Institute Europe, 2010).

120. "Referendums in Switzerland's System of Direct Democracy," Direct-Democracy Geschichte-Schweiz, 2005. http://direct-democracy.geschichte-schweiz.ch/switzerlands-system-referendums.html

121. "We're Glad to Be Boring in Era of Brexit and Trump, Swiss President Jokes,"

Reuters, November 5, 2018, sec. everythingNews. https://www.reuters.com/arti
cle/us-swiss-boring-idUSKCN1NA214

122. Scott Mainwaring and Fernando Bizzarro, "The Fates of Third-Wave Democracies," *Journal of Democracy* 30, no. 1 (January 2019). https://www.jour
nalofdemocracy.org/articles/the-fates-of-third-wave-democracies/

123. Bhanu Dhamija, "In Democratic India, Why Do We Still Have Autocratic
Parties?," *TheQuint*, April 21, 2017. https://www.thequint.com/voices/blogs/
no-inner-party-democracy-internal-elections-in-india Nazifa Alizada et al.,
"Autocratization Turns Viral," Democracy Report (Gothenburg: V-Dem Institute, March 2021). https://www.v-dem.net/static/website/files/dr/dr_2021.pdf
Sarah Repucci and Amy Slipowitz, "Democracy under Siege," Freedom in the
World (Washington, D.C.: Freedom House, 2021). https://freedomhouse.org/
report/freedom-world/2021/democracy-under-siege Debasish Roy Chowd-
hury, "Modi's India Is Where Global Democracy Dies," *The New York Times*,
August 24, 2022, sec. Opinion. https://www.nytimes.com/2022/08/24/opin
ion/india-modi-democracy.html Banjot Kaur, "2 of 3 Child Deaths in India
Due to Malnutrition: Report," September 18, 2019, sec. Health. https://www.
downtoearth.org.in/news/health/2-of-3-child-deaths-in-india-due-to-malnutri
tion-report-66792

124. Kaufmann, Büchi, and Brauneisen, *Guidebook to Direct Democracy in Switzerland and Beyond*.

125. Lars P. Feld et al., "The Political Economy of Direct Legislation: Direct
Democracy and Local Decision-Making," *Economic Policy* 16, no. 33 (2001):
331–67. https://www.eucken.de/en/employee/prof-dr-lars-p-feld/

126. Kaufmann, Büchi, and Brauneisen, *Guidebook to Direct Democracy in Switzerland and Beyond*; "Swiss Split on Compulsory Military Service," *SWI Swissin-
fo.Ch*, May 15, 2005. https://www.swissinfo.ch/eng/swiss-split-on-
compulsory-military-service/4509394

127. Kaufmann, Büchi, and Brauneisen, *Guidebook to Direct Democracy in Switzerland and Beyond*.

128. Russell J. Dalton, Wilhelm P. Burklin, and Andrew Drummond, "Public
Opinion and Direct Democracy," Journal of Democracy 12, no. 4 (2001):
141–53. https://doi.org/10.1353/jod.2001.0066 Katie Simmons, Laura Silver,
and Courtney Johnson, "Transatlantic Dialogues: In Europe and North America, Publics More Supportive Than Experts of Direct Democracy" (Washington, D.C.: Pew Research Center, November 7, 2017). https://www.
pewresearch.org/global/2017/11/07/europe-north-america-publics-more-
supportive-than-experts-of-direct-democracy/ "State of the Nation Survey
1995," Ipsos, March 31, 1995. https://www.ipsos.com/en-uk/state-nation-
survey-1995 Lara M. Greaves, Luke D. Oldfield, and Barry J. Milne, "Let the
People Decide? Support for Referenda since the New Zealand Flag Change
Referendums," Kōtuitui: New Zealand Journal of Social Sciences Online 16,
no. 1 (January 2, 2021): 133–47. https://doi.org/10.1080/1177083X.2020.
1786413

129. Richard Wike et al., "Globally, Broad Support for Representative and Direct
Democracy" (Washington, D.C.: Pew Research Center, October 16, 2017).
https://www.pewresearch.org/global/2017/10/16/globally-broad-support-for-
representative-and-direct-democracy/

130. Meghan McCarty Carino, "How California Initiatives Went from 'Power to
the People' to a Big Money Game," *LAist - NPR News for Southern California -*

89.3 FM, November 1, 2018. https://www.kpcc.org/2018-11-01/how-califor
nia-initiatives-went-from-power-to-the

131. Dustin Gardiner, "Corporations poured big money into California measures
on gambling, electric cars. They came up empty." San Francisco Chronicle,
Nov 9, 2022. https://www.sfchronicle.com/politics/article/Corporations-
poured-big-money-into-California-17572798.php

132. John Diaz, "California Initiative Process Is out of Control," *San Francisco
Chronicle*, September 7, 2018, sec. John Diaz. https://www.sfchronicle.com/
opinion/diaz/article/California-initiative-process-is-out-of-control-
13213651.php

133. Diaz; Mark Baldassare, "Reforming California's Initiative Process" (San Francisco: Public Policy Institute of California, October 2013). https://www.ppic.
org/publication/reforming-californias-initiative-process/

134. Yanis Varoufakis, Why we must save the EU; The Guardian, Apr 5, 2016.
https://www.theguardian.com/world/2016/apr/05/yanis-varoufakis-why-we-
must-save-the-eu

135. A. C. Grayling, *Democracy and Its Crisis* (London: Oneworld Publications,
2018), 161–62.

136. "Statewide Initiative Guide 2024" (Sacramento: California Secretary of State,
February 2023). https://elections.cdn.sos.ca.gov/ballot-measures/pdf/
statewide-initiative-guide.pdf

137. Laura Tyson and Lenny Mendonca, "America's New Democracy Movement,"
Project Syndicate, January 3, 2019. https://www.project-syndicate.org/commen
tary/america-new-democracy-movement-political-reforms-by-laura-tyson-and-
lenny-mendonca-2019-01

138. Shultziner et al., "The Causes and Scope of Political Egalitarianism during the
Last Glacial."

139. Joshua Green and Sasha Issenberg, "Why the Trump Machine Is Built to Last
Beyond the Election," *Bloomberg.Com*, October 27, 2016. https://www.
bloomberg.com/news/articles/2016-10-27/inside-the-trump-bunker-with-12-
days-to-go

140. Steven Kreis, "Lecture 6: The Athenian Origins of Direct Democracy," The
History Guide, August 3, 2009. https://web.archive.org/web/
20230218043942/https://www.historyguide.org/ancient/lecture6b.html

141. Nick Corasaniti, "Democrats in New Jersey Have a Firm Grip on Power. They
Want Even More.," *The New York Times*, December 13, 2018, sec. New York.
https://www.nytimes.com/2018/12/13/nyregion/redistricting-new-jersey-
democrats-republicans.html

142. Alexa Corse, "In Colorado, Voting by Mail Was Practiced Well Before Coronavirus," *Wall Street Journal*, October 28, 2020, sec. Politics. https://www.wsj.
com/articles/in-colorado-voting-by-mail-was-practiced-well-before-coron
avirus-11603900816

143. Phil Keisling, "Vote from Home, Save Your Country," *Washington Monthly*,
January 10, 2016. http://washingtonmonthly.com/2016/01/10/vote-from-
home-save-your-country/

144. Keisling.

145. "Voting Methods and Equipment by State," in *Ballotpedia*, accessed September
5, 2023. https://ballotpedia.org/Voting_methods_and_equipment_by_state

146. Frank Bajak, "Election Security: Expert Panel Calls for Sweeping Measures,"
Chicago Sun-Times, September 6, 2018, sec. Elections. https://chicago.

suntimes.com/2018/9/6/18392434/expert-panel-calls-for-sweeping-election-security-measures

147. Phil Keisling, "The Most Effective Voter Suppression Strategy: Requiring Polling Places," *Washington Monthly*, October 25, 2012. http://washington monthly.com/2012/10/25/the-most-effective-voter-suppression-strategy-requir ing-polling-places/ Phil Keisling, "Why Vote by Mail Is Better Than Early Voting," *Washington Monthly*, January 10, 2016. http://washingtonmonthly. com/2016/01/10/why-vote-by-mail-is-better-than-early-voting/

148. Lawrence Norden and Christopher Famighetti, "America's Voting Machines at Risk" (New York: The Brennan Center for Justice, September 15, 2014). https://www.brennancenter.org/our-work/research-reports/americas-voting-machines-risk

149. Keisling, "Vote from Home, Save Your Country."

150. Rachel M. Cohen, "Local Governments Lead the Charge on Safe Voting by Mail," *The Intercept*, April 20, 2020. https://theintercept.com/2020/04/20/vote-by-mail-wisconsin-pennsylvania-elections/ Akela Lacy, "Milwaukee Documents Seven Coronavirus Cases Linked to In-Person Voting," *The Intercept*, April 20, 2020. https://theintercept.com/2020/04/20/milwaukee-coron avirus-voting-election/ Chad D. Cotti et al., "The Relationship Between In-Person Voting And Covid-19: Evidence From The Wisconsin Primary," Working Paper (Cambridge: National Bureau of Economic Research, May 2020). https://www.nber.org/system/files/working_papers/w27187/ w27187.pdf

151. David Roberts, "Voting by Mail Is Fair, Safe, and Easy. Why Don't More States Use It?," *Vox*, May 27, 2017. https://www.vox.com/policy-and-politics/2017/5/27/15701708/voting-by-mail

152. Eric Cortellessa, Trump's Attacks on Mail Voting Bolstered 'Big Lie,' Jan. 6 Panel Says; TIME, Jun 13, 2022. https://time.com/6187273/jan-6-hearing-mail-voting-trump/

153. Russell Berman, The Republicans Telling Their Voters to Ignore Trump; The Atlantic, Jun 5, 2020. https://www.theatlantic.com/politics/archive/2020/06/trump-republicans-vote-mail-arizona-florida/612625/

154. Caitlin Oprysko, Trump backtracks on mail-in voting, says it's OK to do in Florida; Politico, Aug 4, 2020. https://www.politico.com/news/2020/08/04/trump-backtracks-mail-voting-florida-391373

155. Tessa Berenson, Donald Trump And His Lawyers Are Making Sweeping Allegations of Voter Fraud In Public. In Court, They Say No Such Thing; TIME, Nov 20, 2020. https://time.com/5914377/donald-trump-no-evidence-fraud/

156. Keisling, "The Most Effective Voter Suppression Strategy."

157. Jacob Leibenluft and Alex Padilla, "Election Cyber Security and Voting in an Era of Misinformation," Center for American Progress, November 15, 2018. https://www.youtube.com/watch?v=ofofkCiDVLo

158. Tom Scott, "Why Electronic Voting Is a BAD Idea," Computerphile, December 18, 2014. https://www.youtube.com/watch?v=w3_0x6oaDmI

159. Caitriona Fitzgerald, Pamela Smith, and Susannah Goodman, "The Secret Ballot at Risk: Recommendations for Protecting Democracy" (Washington, D.C.: Electronic Privacy Information Center, 2016). https://www.secretballotatrisk.org/

160. Catalin Cimpanu, "Moscow's Blockchain Voting System Cracked a Month

before Election," *ZDNET*, August 20, 2019. https://www.zdnet.com/article/moscows-blockchain-voting-system-cracked-a-month-before-election/

161. "History of AVR & Implementation Dates," *Brennan Center for Justice*, June 19, 2019. https://www.brennancenter.org/our-work/research-reports/history-avr-implementation-dates

162. "Evidence That America's Voter Registration System Needs an Upgrade," Issue Brief (Washington, D.C.: Pew Center on the States, 2012). https://www.pewtrusts.org/~/media/legacy/uploadedfiles/pcs_assets/2012/PewUpgradingVoterRegistrationpdf.pdf

163. Heather K. Gerken, "Make It Easy: The Case for Automatic Registration," *Democracy Journal*, no. 28 (March 12, 2013). https://democracyjournal.org/magazine/28/make-it-easy-the-case-for-automatic-registration/

164. Derick Moore, "Overall Mover Rate Remains at an All-Time Low," *Census*, December 21, 2017. https://www.census.gov/library/stories/2017/12/lower-moving-rate.html

165. Kevin Morris and Peter Dunphy, "AVR Impact on State Voter Registration" (New York: Brennan Center for Justice, April 11, 2019). https://www.brennancenter.org/our-work/research-reports/avr-impact-state-voter-registration

166. Henry Kraemer, "FACT SHEET: Automatic Voter Registration Transforms Oregon Youth Registration & Turnout Rates," *Alliance for Youth Organizing*, April 21, 2017. https://allianceforyouthorganizing.org/fact-sheet-automatic-voter-registration-transforms-oregon-youth-registration-turnout-rates/

167. Morris and Dunphy, "AVR Impact on State Voter Registration."

168. Robert Griffin et al., "Who Votes with Automatic Voter Registration?" (Washington, D.C.: Center for American Progress, June 2017). https://www.americanprogress.org/article/votes-automatic-voter-registration/

169. Adam Bonica et al., "All-Mail Voting in Colorado Increases Turnout and Reduces Turnout Inequality," Working Paper (Washington, D.C.: Vote at Home, May 4, 2020). https://voteathome.org/portfolio/all-mail-voting-in-colorado-increases-turnout-and-reduces-turnout-inequality/

170. Wendy Weiser, "Automatic Voter Registration Boosts Political Participation," 2016. https://doi.org/10.48558/50XT-Z714

171. Danielle Root and Liz Kennedy, "Increasing Voter Participation in America" (Washington, D.C.: The Center for American Progress, July 11, 2018). https://www.americanprogress.org/article/increasing-voter-participation-america/

172. Danielle Root and Aadam Barclay, "Voter Suppression During the 2018 Midterm Elections" (Washington, D.C.: The Center for American Progress, November 20, 2018). https://www.americanprogress.org/article/voter-suppression-2018-midterm-elections/

173. Michael P. McDonald, "Portable Voter Registration," Political Behavior 30, no. 4 (2008): 491–501.

174. Root and Kennedy, "Increasing Voter Participation in America."

175. Root and Kennedy.

176. Root and Kennedy.

177. Alice Speri, "Florida's Amendment 4 Would Restore Voting Rights to 1.4 Million People," *The Intercept*, November 3, 2018. https://theintercept.com/2018/11/03/florida-felon-voting-rights-amendment-4/

178. Maryam Saleh, "How Some Florida Prosecutors Are Pushing Back Against GOP Voter Suppression Efforts," *The Intercept*, July 15, 2019. https://theinter

cept.com/2019/07/15/florida-voting-rights-amendment-4/ Voting Rights Restoration Efforts in Florida, Brennan Center for Justice, May 31, 2019. https://www.brennancenter.org/our-work/research-reports/voting-rights-restoration-efforts-florida

179. Speri, "Florida's Amendment 4 Would Restore Voting Rights to 1.4 Million People."
180. Jenny Stock, The Playmander Revisited; Australian Journal of Political Science, Volume 26, 1991 - Issue 2. Sep 21, 2007. https://doi.org/10.1080/00323269108402153
181. Paul Krugman, "Hungary, An Election in Question, Part 2," *The New York Times*, February 28, 2014, sec. Opinion. https://archive.nytimes.com/krugman.blogs.nytimes.com/2014/02/28/hungary-an-election-in-question-part-2/
182. The Editorial Board, "Do-It-Yourself Legislative Redistricting," *The New York Times*, July 21, 2018, sec. Opinion. https://www.nytimes.com/2018/07/21/opinion/redistricting-gerrymandering-citizens-michigan.html
183. Karlan et al., "Six Ways to Reform Democracy"; Alan Ehrenhalt, "Will We Ever Slay the Evil Gerrymander?," *Governing*, November 4, 2020. https://www.governing.com/assessments/Will-We-Ever-Slay-the-Evil-Gerrymander.html
184. Brian M. Rosenthal and Michael Rothfeld, "Inside Decades of Nepotism and Bungling at the N.Y.C. Elections Board," *The New York Times*, October 26, 2020, sec. New York. https://www.nytimes.com/2020/10/26/nyregion/nyc-voting-election-board.html
185. Baldassare, "Reforming California's Initiative Process."
186. "Public Supports Reforming How Members of Congress Are Elected."
187. "Inaccurate, Costly, and Inefficient: Evidence That America's Voter Registration System Needs an Upgrade," Issue Brief (Washington, D.C.: The Pew Center on the States, February 2012).
188. Google Is Threatening Our Democracy And Threatening His Life For Exposing It | A Conversation With Dr. Robert Epstein; The Kim Iversen Show, Sep 1, 2023. (Rumble video.) https://rumble.com/v3dzcrq-september-1-2023.html
189. David Leonhardt, "The Real Voter Fraud," *The New York Times*, November 8, 2016, sec. Opinion. https://www.nytimes.com/2016/11/08/opinion/the-real-voter-fraud.html
190. German Lopez, "North Dakota's New Voting Restrictions Seem Aimed at Native Americans Who Vote Democrat," *Vox*, October 31, 2018. https://www.vox.com/policy-and-politics/2018/10/31/18047922/north-dakota-voter-id-suppression-heitkamp
191. Carol Anderson, "A Threat to Democracy: Republicans' War on Minority Voters," *The Guardian*, October 31, 2018, sec. World news. https://www.theguardian.com/world/2018/oct/31/a-threat-to-democracy-republicans-war-on-minority-voters Carol Anderson, "Voting While Black: The Racial Injustice That Harms Our Democracy," *The Guardian*, June 7, 2018, sec. Opinion. https://www.theguardian.com/commentisfree/2018/jun/07/black-voter-suppression-rights-america-trump
192. Nader, *Unstoppable*, 81–83.
193. Alexis de Tocqueville, *Democracy In America* (New York: Harper Collins, 2000).

Citations

194. Doug Marsh, The Battle of Marathon: The Stunning Victory and Its Contribution to the Rise of Athens Studia Antiqua, Vol 5, no 2, Dec 2007. https://scholarsarchive.byu.edu/cgi/viewcontent.cgi?article=1069&context=studiaantiqua

195. Adam Nossiter, "France's Mayors, Feeling the Pinch, Lead a Quiet Rebellion and Quit," *The New York Times*, November 11, 2018, sec. World. https://www.nytimes.com/2018/11/11/world/europe/france-mayors-quit-macron.html Josh Bavas, "With Several Queensland Councils in Crisis, What Is Going so Wrong?," *ABC News*, March 12, 2018. https://www.abc.net.au/news/2018-03-13/south-east-queensland-councils-in-crisis/9513242

196. Wouter P. Veenendaal and Jack Corbett, "Why Small States Offer Important Answers to Large Questions," *Comparative Political Studies* 48, no. 4 (March 2015): 527–49. https://doi.org/10.1177/0010414014554687

197. John L. Campbell and John A. Hall, *The Paradox of Vulnerability: States, Nationalism, and the Financial Crisis*, Princeton Studies in Global and Comparative Sociology (Princeton: Princeton University Press, 2017).

198. Elisabeth Mahase, "Covid-19: Local Health Teams Trace Eight Times More Contacts than National Service," *British Medical Journal* 369 (June 22, 2020): m2486. https://doi.org/10.1136/bmj.m2486 George Monbiot, "Without Trace," *The Guardian*, October 21, 2020. https://www.monbiot.com/2020/10/23/without-trace/

199. Pope Pius XI, "Quadragesimo Anno," Papal Encyclicals, May 15, 1931. https://www.papalencyclicals.net/pius11/p11quadr.htm

200. Indra Warnes, "How a Swiss Canton Voted to Deny a Vegan Citizenship – Because She Was 'Annoying,'" *New Statesman*, June 9, 2021. https://www.newstatesman.com/politics/2018/03/how-swiss-canton-voted-deny-vegan-citizenship-because-she-was-annoying

201. Justine Verhoeven, "The Effect of Physical Proximity on Empathy and Prosocial Behavior through Reading" (University of Twente, Enschede, 2016). http://essay.utwente.nl/72432/1/Verhoeven_MA_BMS.pdf

202. Kaufmann, Büchi, and Brauneisen, *Guidebook to Direct Democracy in Switzerland and Beyond*, chap. 4.

203. Nassim Nicholas Taleb, "Antifragile," RSA House, London, December 6, 2012. https://www.youtube.com/watch?v=k4MhC5tcEv0

204. "From Thomas Jefferson to William Taylor Barry, 2 July 1822," Founders Online (University of Virginia Press), accessed July 19, 2023. http://founders.archives.gov/documents/Jefferson/98-01-02-2919

205. Max Farrand, ed., "The Founders' Constitution: Volume 4, Article 5, Document 2," in *The Records of the Federal Convention of 1787*, Rev., vol. 4 (New Haven and London: Yale University Press, 1937). http://press-pubs.uchicago.edu/founders/documents/a5s2.html

206. "Is It Best for the States to Unite, or Not to Unite?," Letters of Note, April 26, 2010. https://web.archive.org/web/20200814182729/https://lettersofnote.com/2010/04/26/is-it-best-for-the-states-to-unite-or-not-to-unite/

207. Ginsberg & Melton, "Does the Constitutional Amendment Rule Matter at All? Amendment Cultures and the Challenges of Measuring Amendment Difficulty". *Chicago Unbound*, University of Chicago Law School, 2014.

208. Tom Ginsburg, James Melton, and Zachary Elkins, "The Endurance of National Constitutions," Working Paper, John M. Olin Program in Law and Economics (University of Chicago Law School, 2010), 6.

209. Ginsburg, Melton, and Elkins, 8.
210. Jefferson to Kercheval, Letter.
211. Thomas Jefferson, *The Works (Correspondence and Papers 1816-1826)*, vol. 12 (New York: G. P. Putnam's Sons, 1905).
212. George Mader, "Binding Authority: Unamendability in the United States Constitution—A Textual and Historical Analysis," *Marquette Law Review* 99, no. 4 (2016): 841–91. https://scholarship.law.marquette.edu/cgi/viewcontent.cgi?article=5293&context=mulr
213. Lijphart, *Patterns of Democracy*, chap. 12.

31. How much power should each institution have?

1. Jeff Jefferson Looney, ed., "John Adams to Thomas Jefferson, 9 July 1813," in *The Papers of Thomas Jefferson: 11 March to 27 November 1813*, vol. 6, Retirement (Princeton: Princeton University Press, 2009), 227–80. https://founders.archives.gov/documents/Jefferson/03-06-02-0230

32. Awakening the democratic instinct

1. David Detzer, *Donnybrook: The Battle of Bull Run, 1861* (Orlando, Florida: Harcourt, 2004), 233.
2. Bret Weinstein, "The Social Brain: Culture, Change and Evolution," *Big Think*, accessed August 23, 2023. https://bigthink.com/the-present/bret-weinstein-the-social-brain-culture-change-and-evolution-big-thinks-long-take/
3. "Support for Trump Fed by Near-Universal Frustration That Government Ignores the People," *World Public Opinion*, November 18, 2016. https://worldpublicopinion.net/support-for-trump-fed-by-near-universal-frustration-that-government-ignores-the-people/
4. "Support for Trump Fed by Near-Universal Frustration That Government Ignores the People."

VI. Teaching the democratic arts

1. Walt Whitman, *Democratic Vistas and Other Papers* (London: Walter Scott Publishing, 1888), 5.

33. The two-way street

1. Hansen, *The Athenian Democracy in the Age of Demosthenes*, 396.
2. Jack Crittenden and Peter Levine, "Civic Education," in *The Stanford Encyclopedia of Philosophy*, ed. Edward N. Zalta and Uri Nodelman, Fall 2023 (Metaphysics Research Lab, Stanford University, 2023). https://plato.stanford.edu/archives/fall2023/entries/civic-education/
3. W. David Stedman and La Vaughn G. Lewis, eds., *Our Ageless Constitution* (Asheboro, NC: W. David Stedman Associates, 1987). https://nccs.net/blogs/our-ageless-constitution/the-responsibility-of-citizens

34. The worship of jackals by jackasses

1. Aristophanes, *The Knights* (Cambridge: Cambridge University Press, 1901).
2. Xenophon, *Xenophon*, trans. Edgar Cardew Marchant and Glen Warren Bowerstock, vol. 7 (Cambridge, Massachusetts: Harvard University Press, 1984). http://www.perseus.tufts.edu/hopper/text?doc=Perseus:text:1999.01.0158
3. Marcus Cicero, *Treatise on the Commonwealth* (London: Edmund Spettigue, 1841). https://oll.libertyfund.org/title/cicero-treatise-on-the-commonwealth-5
4. Anthony Grafton, Glenn W. Most, and Salvatore Settis, *The Classical Tradition* (Harvard University Press, 2010).
5. Keane, *The Life and Death of Democracy*, 82.
6. Sir Thomas Browne, *Pseudodoxia Epidemica* (London: A. Miller, 1650), chap. 3. http://archive.org/details/BrownePseudodoxia1650Clark
7. Keane, *The Life and Death of Democracy*.
8. Thomas Babington Macaulay, "Curious Letter from Lord Macaulay on American Institutions and Prospects.," *The New York Times*, March 24, 1860, sec. Letters.
9. H. L. Mencken, *Notes on Democracy* (London: Jonathan Cape, 1926), 218.
10. Paul Street, "Divide and Rule: Class, Hate, and the 2016 Election," *CounterPunch*, January 20, 2017. https://www.counterpunch.org/2017/01/20/divide-and-rule-class-hate-and-the-2016-election/
11. Bruce Gilley, "Is Democracy Possible?," *Journal of Democracy* 20, no. 1 (January 2009). https://www.journalofdemocracy.org/articles/is-democracy-possible/
12. Henry E. Hale, "25 Years After The USSR: What's Gone Wrong?," *Journal of Democracy* 27, no. 3 (2016): 24–35. https://doi.org/10.1353/jod.2016.0035
13. Jason Brennan, "Is This the End of Democracy?," *New Statesman*, December 21, 2016. https://www.newstatesman.com/politics/uk-politics/2016/12/end-democracy
14. Steven Pinker, *Enlightenment Now: The Case for Reason, Science, Humanism, and Progress*, Business Book Summary (New York: Viking, 2018), 204.

35. 'A mode of associated living'

1. John Dewey, *Democracy and Education: An Introduction to the Philosophy of Education* (Urbana, Illinois: Project Gutenberg, 1997). https://www.gutenberg.org/ebooks/852
2. Robert D. Putnam, Robert Leonardi, and Raffaella Nanetti, *Making Democracy Work: Civic Traditions in Modern Italy*, 5th ed. (Princeton, NJ: Princeton Univ. Press, 1994).

36. What to teach

1. Christopher Hitchens, "Goodbye to All That: Why Americans Are Not Taught History," *Harper's Magazine*, November 1998, pp. 37–47. https://scrapsfromtheloft.com/history/goodbye-to-all-that-why-americans-are-not-taught-history-by-christopher-hitchens/

Citations

2. Ulrich Chaussy, Franz Josef Müller, and Britta Müller-Baltschun, *The White Rose: The Student Resistance against Hitler Munich 1942/43* (München: Ludwig-Maximilians-Universität, 2006), 40. https://www.bls.org/downloads/MFL/White%20Rose.pdf
3. Edward Bernays, *Propaganda* (New York: Horace Liveright, 1928), 9.
4. David Remnick, "Trump vs. the Times: Inside an Off-the-Record Meeting," *The New Yorker*, July 30, 2018. https://www.newyorker.com/news/news-desk/trump-vs-the-times-inside-an-off-the-record-meeting
5. Benwell, "John Bolton's Bombshell Trump Book."
6. Mike Mariani, "Is Trump's Chaos Tornado a Move From the Kremlin's Playbook?," *Vanity Fair*, March 28, 2017. https://www.vanityfair.com/news/2017/03/is-trumps-chaos-a-move-from-the-kremlins-playbook
7. Edward Docx, "The Death of 'Boris' the Clown," *New Statesman*, July 13, 2022. https://www.newstatesman.com/long-reads/2022/07/death-boris-johnson-clown
8. Peter Pomerantsev, "The Hidden Author of Putinism," *The Atlantic*, November 7, 2014. https://www.theatlantic.com/international/archive/2014/11/hidden-author-putinism-russia-vladislav-surkov/382489/
9. Pomerantsev.
10. Mariani, "Is Trump's Chaos Tornado a Move From the Kremlin's Playbook?"
11. John Macgregor, "Blinded by the Light," *The Sydney Morning Herald*, August 31, 2002.
12. Oliver Carroll, "Putin Advisor Says 'Russia Is Playing with the West's Minds,'" *The Independent*, February 12, 2019, sec. News. https://www.independent.co.uk/news/world/europe/putin-russia-kremlin-vladislav-surkov-grey-cardinal-moscow-a8773661.html
13. Karlina Orlova, "The futile search for a Russian ideology". The American Prospect, Feb 14, 2019. https://www.the-american-interest.com/2019/02/14/the-futile-search-for-a-russian-ideology/
14. Yoni Appelbaum, "Americans Aren't Practicing Democracy Anymore," *The Atlantic*, September 13, 2018. https://www.theatlantic.com/magazine/archive/2018/10/losing-the-democratic-habit/568336/
15. Appelbaum.
16. Quoted in Appelbaum.
17. Eitan D. Hersh, "Listen Up, Liberals: You Aren't Doing Politics Right," *The New York Times*, January 28, 2020, sec. Opinion. https://www.nytimes.com/2020/01/27/opinion/liberals-politics.html
18. Butler, *War Is a Racket*, 1.
19. Patricia Cohen and Liz Alderman, "'The World's Largest Construction Site': The Race Is on to Rebuild Ukraine," *The New York Times*, February 16, 2023, sec. Business. https://www.nytimes.com/2023/02/16/business/economy/ukraine-rebuilding.html
20. Alan Greenblatt, "All or Nothing: How State Politics Became a Winner-Take-All World," *Governing*, December 17, 2018. https://www.governing.com/archive/gov-state-politics-governors-2019.html
21. Lilliana Mason, *Uncivil Agreement: How Politics Became Our Identity* (Chicago, Illinois: The University of Chicago Press, 2018), chap. 3.
22. William Galston, "The 2016 U.S. Election: The Populist Moment," *Journal of Democracy* 28, no. 2 (April 2017): 21–33.

Citations

23. Garry Kasparov [@Kasparov63], "The Point of Modern Propaganda Isn't Only to Misinform or Push an Agenda. It Is to Exhaust Your Critical Thinking, to Annihilate Truth.," Tweet, *Twitter*, December 13, 2016. https://twitter.com/Kasparov63/status/808750564284702720

24. "Our Conception of Critical Thinking," Foundation for Critical Thinking, accessed July 18, 2023. https://www.criticalthinking.org/pages/our-conception-of-critical-thinking/411

25. Robb Sheffield, Paul Is Dead: The Bizarre Story of Music's Most Notorious Conspiracy Theory; Rolling Stone, Oct 11, 2019. https://www.rollingstone.com/music/music-features/paul-mccartney-is-dead-conspiracy-897189/

26. Cognitive Bias; J.E. (Hans) Korteling, Alexander Toet, in Encyclopedia of Behavioral Neuroscience, 2nd edition, 2022. https://www.sciencedirect.com/topics/neuroscience/cognitive-bias

27. Elizabeth Kolbert, "Why Facts Don't Change Our Minds," *The New Yorker*, February 19, 2017. https://www.newyorker.com/magazine/2017/02/27/why-facts-dont-change-our-minds

28. Steven Pinker, "Why Heterodoxy Matters in the World," *Heterodox Academy*, June 20-21, 2019. https://www.youtube.com/watch?v=zzK3jS209GI

29. Arthur Conan Doyle, "The Adventure of Silver Blaze," *The Memoirs of Sherlock Holmes* (Urbana, Illinois: Project Gutenberg, 1997). https://www.gutenberg.org/ebooks/834

30. Ajai Sreevatsan, "British Raj Siphoned out $45 Trillion from India: Utsa Patnaik," *Mint*, November 19, 2018, sec. Companies. https://www.livemint.com/Companies/HNZA71LNVNNVXQ1eaIKu6M/British-Raj-siphoned-out-45-trillion-from-India-Utsa-Patna.html Jason Hickel, "How Britain Stole $45 Trillion from India," *Al Jazeera*, December 19, 2018. https://www.aljazeera.com/opinions/2018/12/19/how-britain-stole-45-trillion-from-india

31. Sreevatsan, "British Raj Siphoned out $45 Trillion from India."

32. "Historians Call for a Review of Home Office Citizenship and Settlement Test," *History Journal*, July 21, 2020. https://historyjournal.org.uk/2020/07/21/historians-call-for-a-review-of-home-office-citizenship-and-settlement-test/ Angelique Richardson, "H. and I Are Going to Rebel," *LRB Blog*, July 31, 2020. https://www.lrb.co.uk/blog/2020/july/h.-and-i-are-going-to-rebel Lorena Allam and Nick Evershed, "The Killing Times: The Massacres of Aboriginal People Australia Must Confront," Information Clearing House, March 4, 2019. http://www.informationclearinghouse.info/51206.htm

33. The speeches of Adolf Hitler, 1921-1941; Berlin, Reichstag -- Speech of May 4, 1941. https://identityhunters.files.wordpress.com/2017/07/the-speeches-of-adolf-hitler-1921-1941.pdf

34. "Biden Promise Tracker," *PolitiFact*, accessed June 26, 2023. https://www.politifact.com/truth-o-meter/promises/biden-promise-tracker/promise/1580/introduce-constitutional-amendment-eliminate-priva/

35. Adam Andrzejewski, "$1.4 Billion Forgiven PPP Loans Paid To Wealthiest Law And Accounting Firms," Substack newsletter, *OpenTheBooks*, December 2, 2022. https://openthebooks.substack.com/p/14-billion-forgiven-ppp-loans-paid

36. Alexander Solzhenitsyn, *The Gulag Archipelago* (London: Collins, 1974), 168.

37. Yeray Lopez, Noam Chomsky on activism and climate change. https://www.moonleaks.org/noam/

38. John Adams to Hezekiah Niles, Letter, 13 February 1818, *Founders Online,* National Archives. https://founders.archives.gov/documents/Adams/99-02-02-6854

39. Katherine Dahlsgaard, Christopher Peterson, and Martin E. P. Seligman, "Shared Virtue: The Convergence of Valued Human Strengths across Culture and History," *Review of General Psychology* 9, no. 3 (September 2005): 203–13. https://doi.org/10.1037/1089-2680.9.3.203

40. Plutarch, *Plutarch's Lives, Volume 1 (of 4).*

41. "Civility in America 2019: Solutions for Tomorrow" (Weber Shandwick, 2019). https://web.archive.org/web/20190713112130/https://www.webershandwick.com/wp-content/uploads/2019/06/CivilityInAmerica2019SolutionsforTomorrow.pdf

42. Niraj Chokshi, "Thanksgiving Got Shorter After the 2016 Election, Study Says. You Can Guess Why," *The New York Times,* May 31, 2018, sec. Science. https://www.nytimes.com/2018/05/31/science/thanksgiving-political-views.html

43. Matt Flegenheimer, "Group Therapy and Chastened Lawmakers at Raucous Town Halls," *The New York Times,* April 20, 2017, sec. U.S. https://www.nytimes.com/2017/04/20/us/politics/group-therapy-and-chastened-lawmakers-at-raucous-town-halls.html

44. Kolbert, "Why Facts Don't Change Our Minds."

37. How to teach

1. Vaclav Havel, "Forgetting We Are Not God," *First Things,* March 1, 1995. https://www.firstthings.com/article/1995/03/forgetting-we-are-not-god

2. "Polis," in *Merriam-Webster,* accessed August 25, 2023. https://www.merriam-webster.com/dictionary/polis

3. Sherry Turkle, "Reclaiming Conversation in Relationships," Reclaiming Conversation, accessed July 17, 2023. https://soundcloud.com/user-157577938/reclaiming-conversation-1

4. Michael Dean McGinnis, *Polycentric Games and Institutions: Readings from the Workshop in Political Theory and Policy Analysis* (Ann Arbor, Michigan: University of Michigan Press, 2000), 483.

5. Pallavi Singhal, "UN Agency Ranks Australia 39 out of 41 Countries for Quality Education," *The Sydney Morning Herald,* June 16, 2017, sec. National. https://www.smh.com.au/education/un-agency-ranks-australia-39-out-of-41-countries-for-quality-education-20170615-gwrt9u.html

6. *The Finland Phenomenon* (True South Studios, 2011).

7. Peter Gray, "The Evolutionary Biology of Education: How Our Hunter-Gatherer Educative Instincts Could Form the Basis for Education Today," *Evolution: Education and Outreach* 4, no. 1 (March 2011): 28–40. https://doi.org/10.1007/s12052-010-0306-1

8. J Helliwell et al, World Happiness Report 2023 (11th ed.); Sustainable Development Solutions Network. https://happiness-report.s3.amazonaws.com/2023/WHR+23.pdf

9. Singhal, "UN Agency Ranks Australia 39 out of 41 Countries for Quality Education."

38. Who to teach

1. "The Facts and Figures of International Students in Australia," Study in Australia, accessed June 19, 2023. https://www.studiesinaustralia.com/Blog/australian-education-news/the-facts-and-figures-of-international-students-in-australia

2. Inbound internationally mobile students by continent of origin, UNESCO Institute for Statistics. Nov 13, 2023. http://data.uis.unesco.org/index.aspx?queryid=3804

3. Alina Mungiu-Pippidi et al., "The Quest for Good Governance," *Journal of Democracy* 27, no. 1 (2016). https://www.journalofdemocracy.org/wp-content/uploads/2016/01/Mungiu-pippidi-27-1.pdf

39. The hidden superpower

1. Walter Lippmann, *The Phantom Public*, The Library of Conservative Thought (New Brunswick, N.J., U.S.A: Transaction Publishers, 1993).

VII. The invisible consensus

1. Gessen, "What Happens When a Group of Strangers Spends a Day Debating Immigration?" The New Yorker. July 23, 2019.
   https://www.newyorker.com/news/dispatch/what-happens-when-a-group-of-strangers-spends-a-day-debating-immigration

40. Why do we have political differences?

1. John R. Alford, Carolyn L. Funk, and John R. Hibbing, "Are Political Orientations Genetically Transmitted?," *American Political Science Review* 99, no. 2 (May 2005): 153–67. https://doi.org/10.1017/S0003055405051579 Chris Mooney, "Why Right-Wingers Think the Way They Do: The Fascinating Psychological Origins of Political Ideology," *Alternet*, April 28, 2014. https://web.archive.org/web/20140502052844/http://www.alternet.org/why-right-wingers-think-way-they-do-fascinating-psychological-origins-political-ideology Kevin B. Smith et al., "Linking Genetics and Political Attitudes: Reconceptualizing Political Ideology: Linking Genetics and Political Attitudes," *Political Psychology* 32, no. 3 (June 2011): 369–97. https://doi.org/10.1111/j.1467-9221.2010.00821.x Benedict Carey, "Some Politics May Be Etched in the Genes - The New York Times," *The New York Times*, June 21, 2005. https://www.nytimes.com/2005/06/21/science/some-politics-may-be-etched-in-the-genes.html

2. R. Chris Fraley et al., "Developmental Antecedents of Political Ideology: A Longitudinal Investigation from Birth to Age 18 Years," *Psychological Science* 23, no. 11 (November 2012): 1425–31. https://doi.org/10.1177/0956797612440102

3. Mathilde Maria Van Ditmars, "Family and Politics: The Enduring Influence of the Parental Home in the Development and Transmission of Political Ideol-

ogy" (San Domenico di Fiesole, European University Institute, 2017). https://data.europa.eu/doi/10.2870/158529

4. Jeffrey Lyons, "The Family and Partisan Socialization in Red and Blue America," *Political Psychology* 38, no. 2 (2017): 297–312. https://doi.org/10.1111/pops.12336

5. Scott Eidelman et al., "Low-Effort Thought Promotes Political Conservatism," *Personality and Social Psychology Bulletin* 38, no. 6 (June 1, 2012): 808–20. https://doi.org/10.1177/0146167212439213

6. Linda J. Skitka et al., "Dispositions, Scripts, or Motivated Correction? Understanding Ideological Differences in Explanations for Social Problems.," *Journal of Personality and Social Psychology* 83, no. 2 (August 2002): 470–87. https://doi.org/10.1037/0022-3514.83.2.470

7. "Presidential Job Approval Center," *Gallup*, accessed August 25, 2023. https://news.gallup.com/interactives/507569/presidential-job-approval-center.aspx

8. Chris Mooney, "5 Ways to Turn a Liberal Into a Conservative (At Least Until the Hangover Sets In)," *Discover Magazine*, April 20, 2012. https://www.discovermagazine.com/mind/5-ways-to-turn-a-liberal-into-a-conservative-at-least-until-the-hangover-sets-in

9. Alford, Funk and Hibbing, "Are Political Orientations Genetically Transmitted?"

10. Tim Dean, "Evolution and Moral Diversity," *Baltic International Yearbook of Cognition, Logic and Communication* 7, no. 1 (January 1, 2012). https://doi.org/10.4148/biyclc.v7i0.1775

41. How meaningful are 'left' and 'right'?

1. Grant, "The Social Nature Of Australian Nationalism," *The Nativist Herald*, July 31, 2017. https://nativistherald.com.au/2017/07/31/the-social-nature-of-australian-nationalism/ "The Labor Party and 'White Australia,'" in *The Historical and International Foundations of the Socialist Equality Party (Australia)*, by Socialist Equality Party (Mehring Books, 2010). https://www.wsws.org/en/special/library/foundations-aus/04.html E. W. Campbell, *History of the Australian Labor Movement - A Marxist Interpretation by CPA* (Current Book Distributors, Communist Party of Australia, 1945). https://www.marxists.org/history/australia/comintern/sections/australia/1945/history-labor/ch04.htm

42. How real is our famous polarization?

1. "'Kill or Be Killed': Inside Australia's Postcode Gang Wars," *ABC Listen*, September 21, 2022. https://www.abc.net.au/listen/programs/abc-news-daily/postcode-gang-wars/101462304

2. Philip E. Converse, "The Nature of Belief Systems in Mass Publics (1964)," *Critical Review* 18, no. 1–3 (January 2006): 1–74. https://doi.org/10.1080/08913810608443650

3. Pamela Johnston Conover, "The Influence of Group Identifications on Political Perception and Evaluation," *The Journal of Politics* 46, no. 3 (August 1984): 760–85. https://doi.org/10.2307/2130855

4. Lilliana Mason, "Ideologues without Issues: The Polarizing Consequences of

Citations

Ideological Identities," *Public Opinion Quarterly* 82, no. S1 (April 11, 2018): 866–87. https://doi.org/10.1093/poq/nfy005

5. Carroll, "Evolutionary Social Theory: The Current State of Knowledge," *Style* 49, no. 4 (2015): 512. https://doi.org/10.5325/style.49.4.0512

6. Lilliana Mason, "The Rise of Uncivil Agreement: Issue Versus Behavioral Polarization in the American Electorate," *American Behavioral Scientist* 57, no. 1 (January 1, 2013): 140–59. https://doi.org/10.1177/0002764212463363

7. "Trump-O-Meter: Tracking Trump's Campaign Promises," *PolitiFact*, accessed July 2, 2023. https://www.politifact.com/truth-o-meter/promises/trumpometer/

8. Linda Qiu, "Donald Trump's Top 10 Campaign Promises," *PolitiFact*, July 15, 2016. https://www.politifact.com/article/2016/jul/15/donald-trumps-top-10-campaign-promises/

9. Aidan Quigley, "Trump Says He's 'looking at' Breaking up Big Banks," *POLITICO*, May 1, 2017. https://www.politico.com/story/2017/05/01/trump-break-big-banks-237836

10. "US Election 2020: Has Trump Delivered on His Promises?," *BBC News*, November 14, 2016, sec. US & Canada. https://www.bbc.com/news/world-us-canada-37982000

11. Jenna Johnson, "Here Are 76 of Donald Trump's Many Campaign Promises," *Washington Post*, November 26, 2021. https://www.washingtonpost.com/news/post-politics/wp/2016/01/22/here-are-76-of-donald-trumps-many-campaign-promises/

12. "Trump Campaign Promises," AOL, accessed July 2, 2023. https://web.archive.org/web/20200409102008/https://www.aol.com/news/trump-campaign-promises/

13. Jane C. Timm, "The 141 Stances Donald Trump Took During His White House Bid," *NBC News*, November 28, 2016. https://www.nbcnews.com/politics/2016-election/full-list-donald-trump-s-rapidly-changing-policy-positions-n547801

14. "Donald Trump Explains All," *Time*, August 20, 2015. https://time.com/4003734/donald-trump-interview-transcript/

15. "Trump on Trade, NAFTA," *ABC News*, November 9, 2016. https://www.youtube.com/watch?v=gepaJum69CI

16. Tepper, "The Conservative Case for Antitrust."

17. Lilliana Mason, *Uncivil Agreement: How Politics Became Our Identity* (Chicago, Illinois: The University of Chicago Press, 2018), chap. 1. Michael Billig and Henri Tajfel, "Social Categorization and Similarity in Intergroup Behaviour," *European Journal of Social Psychology* 3, no. 1 (1973): 27–52. https://doi.org/10.1002/ejsp.2420030103. Rajiv Jhangiani and Hammond Tarry, *Principles of Social Psychology*, 1st ed. (Surrey: BCcampus, 2022). https://opentextbc.ca/socialpsychology/

18. Billig and Tajfel, "Social Categorization and Similarity in Intergroup Behaviour."

19. A. B. Cryer, "Henri Tajfel," in *Everything Explained Today*, n.d. https://everything.explained.today/Henri_Tajfel/

20. Mason, *Uncivil Agreement*, 2018, chap. 1.

21. David J. Lynch, "Democrats and Republicans Have Traded Places in Their Views of the Economy's Direction," *Washington Post*, December 28, 2020.

https://www.washingtonpost.com/business/2020/12/28/biden-trump-econ omy-confidence/

22. Bruce Drake, "Where Republicans Are United, Divided on the Economy," *Pew Research Center*, accessed July 17, 2023. https://www.pewresearch.org/ short-reads/2015/10/28/where-republicans-are-united-divided-on-the-econ omy/ Andrew Kohut, "Obama Job Approval Improves, GOP Contest Remains Fluid" (Pew Research Center, November 17, 2011).

23. Lara Seligman, "The Hill Poll: Voters: Pentagon Should Bear the Brunt of Deficit Cuts," *The Hill*, February 25, 2013. https://thehill.com/polls/284579- the-hill-poll-voters-pentagon-should-bear-the-brunt-of-deficit-cuts/ Donna Cassata, "Tea Partiers: Defense Budget in the Mix for Cuts," *NBC News*, January 23, 2011. https://www.nbcnews.com/id/wbna41219824

24. Ben Casselman and Jim Tankersley, "Democrats Want to Tax the Wealthy. Many Voters Agree.," *The New York Times*, February 20, 2019, sec. Business. https://www.nytimes.com/2019/02/19/business/economy/wealth-tax-eliza beth-warren.html

25. "Progressive Movement Stirs Democrats," *Reuters*, August 23, 2018. https:// www.reuters.com/investigates/special-report/usa-election-progressives/

26. Jocelyn Kiley, "60% in US Say Health Care Coverage Is Government's Responsibility," *Pew Research Center*, October 3, 2018. https://www.pewre search.org/short-reads/2018/10/03/most-continue-to-say-ensuring-health- care-coverage-is-governments-responsibility/

27. Carrie Dann, "NBC/WSJ Poll: Support for Roe v. Wade Hits New High," *NBC News*, July 23, 2018. https://www.nbcnews.com/politics/first-read/nbc- wsj-poll-support-roe-v-wade-hits-new-high-n893806

28. Justin McCarthy, "Record-High Support for Legalizing Marijuana Use in U.S.," Gallup.com, October 25, 2017. https://news.gallup.com/poll/221018/ record-high-support-legalizing-marijuana.aspx

29. Abigail W. Geiger, "How Republicans and Democrats View Federal Spend- ing," *Pew Research Center*, April 11, 2019. https://www.pewresearch.org/poli tics/2019/04/11/how-republicans-and-democrats-view-federal-spending/

30. Peter Beinart, "Why America Is Moving Left," *The Atlantic*, December 22, 2015. https://www.theatlantic.com/magazine/archive/2016/01/why-america- is-moving-left/419112/ Marriage equality, Gallup, Feb 12, 2024. https://www. gallup.com/Search/Default.aspx?q=marriage+equality Gallup Inc, "Larger Majority Says Racism Against Black People Widespread," *Gallup*, July 23, 2021. https://news.gallup.com/poll/352544/larger-majority-says-racism- against-black-people-widespread.aspx

Frank Newport, "Continuing Change in U.S. Views on Sex and Marriage," *Gallup*, June 18, 2021. https://news.gallup.com/opinion/polling-matters/351326/continuing- change-views-sex-marriage.aspx

Lydia Saad, "Gallup Vault: A History of Reluctance to See Women Work- ing," *Gallup*, March 26, 2021. https://news.gallup.com/vault/341822/gallup-vault-history-reluctance- women-working.aspx

31. Abel Gustafson et al., "The Green New Deal Has Strong Bipartisan Support," *Yale Program on Climate Change Communication*, accessed July 17, 2023. https://climatecommunication.yale.edu/publications/the-green-new-deal-has- strong-bipartisan-support/

Citations

32. BRENNAN CTR. FOR JUSTICE, DEMOCRACY: AN ELECTION AGENDA FOR CANDIDATES, ACTIVISTS, AND LEGISLATORS 20 (Wendy Weiser & Alicia Bannon eds., 2018). https://www.brennancenter.org/sites/default/files/2019-08/Report_ Democracy%20Agenda%202018.pdf [https://perma.cc/4C4U-ZFA2]
33. Abigail W. Geiger, "From Universities to Churches, Republicans and Democrats Differ in Views of Major Institutions," *Pew Research Center*, September 26, 2016. https://www.pewresearch.org/short-reads/2016/09/26/from-universities-to-churches-republicans-and-democrats-differ-in-views-of-major-institutions/
34. "Join the Movement. Support Tea Party," Tea Party, accessed September 11, 2023. https://teaparty.org/ Richi Jennings, "Revealed: Mass Spying by Governments, Says WikiLeaks," *Computerworld*, December 2, 2011. https://www.computerworld.com/article/2471577/revealed--mass-spying-by-governments--says-wikileaks.html
35. Gilens, "Inequality and Democratic Responsiveness."

43. Divide et impera

1. "Let's stay chummy, Chomsky" by Pat Kane, *The Independent*. June 22, 1997.
2. Markandey Katju, "The Truth about Pakistan," *The Nation*, March 2, 2013, sec. Analysis. https://www.nation.com.pk/02-Mar-2013/the-truth-about-pakistan
3. Clive Boddy, *Corporate Psychopaths: Organisational Destroyers* (Houndmills, Basingstoke; New York: Palgrave Macmillan, 2011).
4. Ron Synovitz, "Facebook Manipulation Echoes Accounts From Russian 'Troll Factory,'" *Radio Free Europe/Radio Liberty*, 10:58:24Z, sec. Russia. https://www.rferl.org/a/us-russia-facebook-manipulation-echoes-troll-factory-accounts/28722595.html
5. David A. Broniatowski et al., "Weaponized Health Communication: Twitter Bots and Russian Trolls Amplify the Vaccine Debate," *American Journal of Public Health* 108, no. 10 (October 2018): 1378–84. https://doi.org/10.2105/AJPH.2018.304567
6. John Perkins, "The New Confessions of an Economic Hit Man," *Economics*, August 21, 2016. https://evonomics.com/the-new-confessions-of-an-economic-hit-man-perkins-reality/
7. Carter C. Price and Kathryn A. Edwards, "Trends in Income From 1975 to 2018" (RAND Corporation, September 14, 2020). https://www.rand.org/pubs/working_papers/WRA516-1.html Nick Hanauer and David M. Rolf, "The Top 1% of Americans Have Taken $50 Trillion From the Bottom 90% —And That's Made the U.S. Less Secure," *Time*, September 14, 2020. https://time.com/5888024/50-trillion-income-inequality-america/
8. Hughes, "It's Time to Break Up Facebook."
9. Victoria Grant "Public Banking in America," Public Banking in America Conference, Philadelphia, April 27, 2012. https://www.youtube.com/watch?v=Bx5Sc3vWefE

44. Common ground

1. Yuval Noah Harari, "Who Really Runs The World?," interview by Russell Brand, *Under the Skin*, October 13, 2018. https://www.youtube.com/watch?v= ta4U8G03q98
2. Nader, *Unstoppable*, chap. 2.
3. Brigitte Sebbah et al., "Les Gilets Jaunes, des cadrages médiatiques aux paroles citoyennes" (Université de Toulouse, November 26, 2018). https://fr.scribd. com/document/394250648/Rapport-Gilets-Jaunes
4. Lucy Williamson, "The Gilets Jaunes," *BBC News*, December 14, 2018. https://www.bbc.co.uk/news/resources/idt-sh/yellow_vests
5. "'Gilets jaunes': le soutien des Français au mouvement gagne sept points (84%) malgré les annonces d'Emmanuel Macron sur l'écologie, selon un sondage," *Franceinfo*, November 28, 2018. https://www.francetvinfo.fr/ economie/transports/gilets-jaunes/gilets-jaunes-le-soutien-des-francais-au-mouvement-gagne-sept-points-84-malgre-les-annonces-d-emmanuel-macron-sur-l-ecologie-selon-un-sondage_3075995.html
6. Lawrence Mishel, "Causes of Wage Stagnation" (Economic Policy Institute, January 6, 2015). https://www.epi.org/publication/causes-of-wage-stagnation/ "Food Dollar Application," accessed June 20, 2023. https://data.ers.usda.gov/ reports.aspx?ID=17885 The Editorial Board, "The Jobs We Need," *The New York Times*, June 24, 2020, sec. Opinion. https://www.nytimes.com/2020/06/ 24/opinion/sunday/income-wealth-inequality-america.html
7. "LIVE: House Weaponization of the Federal Government Subcommittee Holds Hearing on 'Twitter Files.'"

VIII. The Bill of Change

1. Havel, "Forgetting We Are Not God."
2. Aldous Huxley, *Brave New World Revisited* (London: Vintage, 2004), 143.

46. The deliberation stage

1. "Home," Citizens' Assembly, accessed June 19, 2023. https:// citizensassembly.ie/

47. The referendum

1. 1800.0 - Australian Marriage Law Postal Survey, 2017, Australian Bureau of Statistics, Nov 15, 2017. https://www.abs.gov.au/ausstats/abs@.nsf/mf/1800.0
2. The road to MMP, New Zealand History. NZ Ministry for Culture and Heritage, Jun 9, 2021. https://nzhistory.govt.nz/politics/fpp-to-mmp
3. Richard Shaw, "MMP in New Zealand Turns 30 at This Year's Election – a Work in Progress, but Still a Birthday Worth Celebrating," The Conversation, January 2, 2023. http://theconversation.com/mmp-in-new-zealand-turns-30-at-this-years-election-a-work-in-progress-but-still-a-birthday-worth-celebrat ing-194622

48. Dealing with anti-democratic roadblocks

1. Tweet by Jon Stone, June 8, 2020. https://twitter.com/joncstone/status/1269961630940631041?lang=en
2. Tom Ginsburg and James Melton, "Does the Constitutional Amendment Rule Matter at All? Amendment Cultures and the Challenges of Measuring Amendment Difficulty," SSRN Scholarly Paper (Rochester, NY, May 3, 2014). https://doi.org/10.2139/ssrn.2432520
3. "Universal Declaration of Human Rights - Human Rights at Your Fingertips - Human Rights at Your Fingertips," Australian Human Rights Commission, accessed June 27, 2023. https://humanrights.gov.au/our-work/commission-general/universal-declaration-human-rights-human-rights-your-fingertips-human
4. International Covenant on Civil and Political Rights; United Nations Human Rights Instruments. Dec 16, 1966. https://www.ohchr.org/en/instruments-mechanisms/instruments/international-covenant-civil-and-political-rights
5. Our Ageless Constitution, W. David Stedman & La Vaughn G. Lewis, Editors (Asheboro, NC, W. David Stedman Associates, 1987) Part III: ISBN 0-937047-01-5. National Center for Constitutional Studies, Sep 17, 1987. https://nccs.net/blogs/our-ageless-constitution/natural-law-the-ultimate-source-of-constitutional-law
6. Corwin, E, The Natural Law and Constitutional Law; Natural Law Institute Proceedings Vol. 3, Notre Dame Law School, 1950. https://scholarship.law.nd.edu/cgi/viewcontent.cgi?article=1003&context=naturallaw_proceedings
7. Alexander Hamilton and Richard B. Vernier, *The Revolutionary Writings of Alexander Hamilton* (Indianapolis, Ind: Liberty Fund, 2008).
8. James Wilson, "Speech to the Pennsylvania Convention, November 24, 1787," Speech, Teaching American History, November 24, 1787. https://teachingamericanhistory.org/document/speech-to-the-pennsylvania-convention/
9. "State Constitution - Bill of Rights," New Hampshire Government, accessed June 27, 2023. https://www.nh.gov/glance/bill-of-rights.htm
10. Akhil Reed Amar, "The Consent of the Governed: Constitutional Amendment Outside Article V," *Columbia Law Review* 94, no. 2 (March 1994): 457. https://doi.org/10.2307/1123201
11. "Is the US Declaration of Independence Illegal?," *BBC News*, October 19, 2011, sec. Magazine. https://www.bbc.com/news/magazine-15345511

49. The Democracy Commission

1. Stephen Hawkins et al., "Hidden Tribes: A Study of America's Polarized Landscape" (New York: More in Common, 2018). https://hiddentribes.us/media/qfpekz4g/hidden_tribes_report.pdf
2. Patrick Gathara, "How Kenya's 'Second Republic' Failed to Materialise," *Al Jazeera*, August 27, 2020. https://www.aljazeera.com/opinions/2020/8/27/how-kenyas-second-republic-failed-to-materialise
3. Francis Fukuyama, "The Emergence of a Post-Fact World," *Project Syndicate*, January 12, 2017. https://www.project-syndicate.org/magazine/the-emergence-of-a-post-fact-world-by-francis-fukuyama-2017-01

50. Cost savings from the Bill of Change

1. Ober, *The Rise and Fall of Classical Greece*, chap. 1.
2. Christopher Leonard, Lockheed Martin's $1.7 trillion F-35 fighter jet is 10 years late and 80% over budget—and it could be one of the Pentagon's biggest success stories; Fortune magazine, Aug 2, 2023. https://fortune.com/long form/lockheed-martin-f-35-fighter-jet/
3. Dan Sabbagh, "MoD Procurement Disasters, Delays and Overspends," *The Guardian*, November 3, 2021, sec. UK news. https://www.theguardian.com/uk-news/2021/nov/03/mod-procurement-disasters-delays-and-overspends
4. David Vine et al., "Creating Refugees: Displacement Caused by the United States' Post-9/11 Wars," Costs of War (Providence, Rhode Island: Watson Institute for International & Public Affairs, September 21, 2020). https://watson.brown.edu/costsofwar/files/cow/imce/papers/2020/Displacemen t_Vine%20et%20al_Costs%20of%20War%202020%2009%2008.pdf
5. "2008 Recession: What It Was and What Caused It," in *Investopedia*, April 30, 2023. https://www.investopedia.com/terms/g/great-recession.asp
6. Sarah Childress, "How Much Did the Financial Crisis Cost?," *FRONTLINE*, May 31, 2012. https://www.pbs.org/wgbh/frontline/article/how-much-did-the-financial-crisis-cost/
7. Andrzejewski and Smith, "Federal Funding of Fortune 100 Companies."
8. Aimee Picchi, "Billionaires Got 54% Richer during Pandemic, Sparking Calls for 'Wealth Tax' - CBS News," March 31, 2021. https://www.cbsnews.com/news/billionaire-wealth-covid-pandemic-12-trillion-jeff-bezos-wealth-tax/ Chuck Collins, "Global Billionaires See $5.5 Trillion Pandemic Wealth Surge," Institute for Policy Studies, August 12, 2021. https://ips-dc.org/global-billion aires-see-5-5-trillion-pandemic-wealth-surge/
9. Matt Taibbi, "The S.E.C. Rule That Destroyed The Universe," *Racknet News*, April 10, 2020. https://www.racket.news/p/the-sec-rule-that-destroyed-the-universe
10. Henry, "The Price of Offshore Revisited"; Henry, "Taxing Tax Havens."
11. The Visual Capitalist: Visualizing the $105 trillion world economy in one chart; Aug 9, 2023. https://www.visualcapitalist.com/visualizing-the-105-tril lion-world-economy-in-one-chart/

52. Homeostasis

1. "What's Gone Wrong with Democracy," *The Economist*, February 27, 2014. https://www.economist.com/essay/2014/02/27/whats-gone-wrong-with-democracy

53. Society is ready for wholesale change

1. Tuchman, *The March of Folly: From Troy to Vietnam*, 236. Aiden Bradford, ed., "Letter from the House of Representatives to D. De Berdt, Esq. Agent for the Province, in England, January 12 1768," in *Speeches of the Governors of Massachusetts, from 1765 to 1775; and the Answers of the House of Representatives, to the Same; with Their Resolutions and Addresses for That Period, and Other Public Papers, Relating to the Dispute between This Country and Great Britain, Which*

Citations

Led to the Independence of the United States, Early American Imprints (Boston: Russell and Gardner, 1818), 124–33. https://books.google.co.uk/books?id= AEZfAAAAcAAJ

2. "Confidence in Institutions," *Gallup*, June 22, 2007. https://news.gallup.com/ poll/1597/Confidence-Institutions.aspx

3. Noah Feldman, "This Is the Story of How Lincoln Broke the U.S. Constitution," *The New York Times*, November 2, 2021, sec. Opinion. https://www. nytimes.com/2021/11/02/opinion/constitution-slavery-lincoln.html

4. George Eaton, "Is the World Really Better than Ever? Steven Pinker on the Case for Optimism," *The New Statesman*, March 1, 2018. https://www. newstatesman.com/culture/2018/03/world-really-better-ever-steven-pinker-case-optimism

5. Katherine Schaeffer, "6 Facts about Economic Inequality in the U.S.," *Pew Research Center*, accessed June 21, 2023. https://www.pewresearch.org/short-reads/2020/02/07/6-facts-about-economic-inequality-in-the-u-s/

6. "As Putin Threatens Nuclear Weapons Use, What's Next in the Ukraine War?" *Wall Street Journal*, September 22, 2022. https://www.youtube.com/watch?v= b0lzn3FSJNs "Putin Says 'No Need' for Using Nuclear Weapons in Ukraine," *PBS NewsHour*, October 27, 2022. https://www.pbs.org/newshour/world/ vladimir-putin-rules-out-using-nuclear-weapons-in-ukraine Brendan Cole, "Fact Check: Did Volodymyr Zelensky Call on NATO to Start Nuclear War?," *Newsweek*, October 7, 2022. https://www.newsweek.com/zelensky-nuclear-putin-russia-war-pre-emptive-1749781 "Cheers as Liz Truss Says She's Ready to Press Nuclear Button and Unleash 'Global Annihilation,'" *Yahoo News*, August 24, 2022. https://au.news.yahoo.com/audience-liz-truss-ready-press-nuclear-button-unleash-global-annihilation-103552126.html

7. Lijphart, *Democracy in the Twenty-First Century*.

8. Larry Jay Diamond, *Developing Democracy: Toward Consolidation* (Baltimore: Johns Hopkins University Press, 1999). http://www.gbv.de/dms/sub-hamburg/ 249103761.pdf

9. Jamelle Bouie, "Constitutional Change Will Be Here Sooner Than We Think," *The New York Times*, November 2, 2021, sec. Opinion. https://www.nytimes. com/2021/11/02/opinion/change-constitution-articles-confederation.html

10. Hawkins et al., "Hidden Tribes: A Study of America's Polarized Landscape."

11. Hawkins et al.

12. Lilliana Mason, "Ideologues without Issues: The Polarizing Consequences of Ideological Identities," *Public Opinion Quarterly* 82, no. S1 (April 11, 2018): 866–87. https://doi.org/10.1093/poq/nfy005

13. Plutarch, *Plutarch's Lives, Volume 1 (of 4)*.

14. You Don't Need To Call It A Conspiracy - Michele Tafoya Mike Benz 11-30-23; Rumble video Nov 30, 2023. https://rumble.com/v3zfq93-you-dont-need-to-call-it-a-conspiracy-michele-tafoya-mike-benz-11-30-23.html

15. Jordan Press, "Canadian Economy Adds 953,000 Jobs in June, Unemployment Rate Falls," *CTVNews*, July 10, 2020. https://www.ctvnews.ca/business/ canadian-economy-adds-953-000-jobs-in-june-unemployment-rate-falls-1. 5018613

16. Mathias Brotero, "Mais de 600 mil pequenas empresas fecharam as portas com coronavírus," *CNN Brasil*, April 9, 2020. https://www.cnnbrasil.com.br/econo mia/mais-de-600-mil-pequenas-empresas-fecharam-as-portas-com-coronavirus/

Citations

17. Matthew Yglesias and Christina Animashaun, "Chart: New Unemployment Claims Soar to 3.3 Million, Shattering Record," *Vox*, March 26, 2020. https://www.vox.com/2020/3/26/21195171/new-unemployment-claims-march-21

18. "Policy Responses to COVID19," *IMF*, accessed June 27, 2023. https://www.imf.org/en/Topics/imf-and-covid19/Policy-Responses-to-COVID-19

19. "Vicentin, una empresa en concurso de acreedores con una deuda de 1.350 millones de dólares," *TÉLAM*, June 8, 2020. https://www.telam.com.ar/notas/202006/473931-vicentin-una-empresa-en-concurso-de-acreedores-con-una-deuda-de-1350-millones-de-dolares.html

20. Sudha Ramachandran, "The COVID-19 Catastrophe in Bangladesh," *The Diplomat*, April 29 2020. https://thediplomat.com/2020/04/the-covid-19-catastrophe-in-bangladesh/

21. "Singapore Airlines Posts First Annual Net Loss in 48-Year History after COVID-19 Cripples Demand," *Channel News Asia*, May 14, 2020, sec. Business. https://web.archive.org/web/20211121015210/https://www.channelnewsasia.com/business/singapore-airlines-sia-q4-full-year-results-covid-19-coronavirus-940016

22. Michelle Toh, "HSBC Results: Bank Posts Sharp Fall in Profits and Warns of US-China Tensions," *CNN Business*, August 3, 2020. https://edition.cnn.com/2020/08/03/business/hsbc-results-2020-intl-hnk/index.html

23. "Dismal Employee Engagement Is a Sign of Global Mismanagement," *Gallup*, December 20, 2017. https://news.gallup.com/opinion/gallup/224012/dismal-employee-engagement-sign-global-mismanagement.aspx

24. Lucia Binding, "Coronavirus: Only 9% of Britons Want Life to Return to 'normal' Once Lockdown Is Over," *Sky News*, April 17, 2020. https://news.sky.com/story/coronavirus-only-9-of-britons-want-life-to-return-to-normal-once-lockdown-is-over-11974459

25. Stefanie Valentic, "Most Americans Expect Life to Never Return to Normal," *EHS Today*, June 4, 2020. https://www.ehstoday.com/covid19/article/21133121/study-most-americans-expect-life-to-never-return-to-normal

26. "Around the World, People Yearn for Significant Change Rather than a Return to a 'Pre-COVID Normal,'" *Ipsos*, September 16, 2020. https://www.ipsos.com/en/global-survey-unveils-profound-desire-change-rather-return-how-life-and-world-were-covid-19

27. Aidan Connaughton, Nicholas Kent, and Shannon Schumacher, "How People around the World See Democracy in 8 Charts," *Pew Research Center*, accessed June 28, 2023. https://www.pewresearch.org/short-reads/2020/02/27/how-people-around-the-world-see-democracy-in-8-charts/

28. Roberto Stefan Foa et al., "The Global Satisfaction with Democracy Report 2020" (Cambridge: Bennett Institute, January 2020). https://www.bennettinstitute.cam.ac.uk/wp-content/uploads/2020/12/DemocracyReport2020.pdf

29. Jessica Irvine, "'In Freefall': Satisfaction with Democracy Hits New Low," *The Sydney Morning Herald*, December 4, 2018, sec. Federal. https://www.smh.com.au/politics/federal/in-freefall-satisfaction-with-democracy-hits-new-low-20181204-p50k4d.html

30. Neil Gross, "Is the United States Too Big to Govern?," *The New York Times*, May 11, 2018, sec. Opinion. https://www.nytimes.com/2018/05/11/opinion/sunday/united-states-too-big.html

31. Daniele Archibugi, "European Poll Shows Democracy Still Needs a Bit of

Work," *The Conversation*, September 15, 2014. http://theconversation.com/european-poll-shows-democracy-still-needs-a-bit-of-work-31592

32. "Americans' Views on Money in Politics," *The New York Times*, June 2, 2015, sec. U.S. https://www.nytimes.com/interactive/2015/06/02/us/politics/money-in-politics-poll.html

33. Nicholas Confessore and Megan Thee-brenan, "Poll Shows Americans Favor an Overhaul of Campaign Financing," *The New York Times*, June 2, 2015, sec. U.S. https://www.nytimes.com/2015/06/03/us/politics/poll-shows-americans-favor-overhaul-of-campaign-financing.html

34. "Beyond Distrust: How Americans View Their Government" (Pew Research Center, November 23, 2015). https://www.pewresearch.org/politics/2015/11/23/6-perceptions-of-elected-officials-and-the-role-of-money-in-politics/

35. Luke Tryl et al., "Democratic Repair: What Britons Want from Their Democracy" (More in Common, 2021). https://www.moreincommon.com/media/uimo2edp/democratic-repair_what-britons-want-from-their-democracy_more-in-common_oct-2021.pdf

36. "Indicators of News Media Trust," *Knight Foundation*, accessed June 28, 2023. https://knightfoundation.org/reports/indicators-of-news-media-trust/

37. Nick Visser, "Hardly Anyone Trusts the Media Anymore," *Huffington Post*, April 18, 2016, sec. Media. https://www.huffpost.com/entry/trust-in-media_n_57148543e4b06f35cb6fec58

38. "Americans' Trust in Media Remains at Historical Low," *Gallup*, September 28, 2015. https://news.gallup.com/poll/185927/americans-trust-media-remains-historical-low.aspx

39. "Poll: Mainstream Media Continues to Lose the Public's Trust," *WJLA*, February 14, 2017. https://wjla.com/news/nation-world/main-stream-media-continue-to-lose-the-publics-trust

40. Richard Fletcher, "Trust Will Get Worse before It Gets Better," *Reuters Institute Digital News Report*, January 9, 2020. https://www.digitalnewsreport.org/publications/2020/trust-will-get-worse-gets-better/

41. "Edelman Trust Barometer 2021" (Edelman, 2021). https://www.edelman.com/sites/g/files/aatuss191/files/2021-03/2021%20Edelman%20Trust%20Barometer.pdf

42. Richard Wike and Shannon Schumacher, "Democratic Rights Popular Globally but Commitment to Them Not Always Strong," *Pew Research Center's Global Attitudes Project*, February 27, 2020. https://www.pewresearch.org/global/2020/02/27/democratic-rights-popular-globally-but-commitment-to-them-not-always-strong/

43. "Beyond Distrust: How Americans View Their Government."

44. Russell Dalton, Wilhelm Burklin, and Andrew Drummond, "Public Opinion and Direct Democracy," *Journal of Democracy* 12, no. 4 (October 2001). https://www.journalofdemocracy.org/articles/public-opinion-and-direct-democracy/

45. Wilf Day, "Wilf Day's Blog: Poll Results on Canadian Public Support for Proportional Representation," *Wilf Day's Blog*, January 5, 2011. https://wilfday.blogspot.com/2011/01/poll-results-on-canadian-public-support.html

46. The road to MMP, New Zealand History. NZ Ministry for Culture and Heritage, Jun 9, 2021. https://nzhistory.govt.nz/politics/fpp-to-mmp

47. "Public Supports Reforming How Members of Congress Are Elected," *World*

Public Opinion, April 12, 2018. https://worldpublicopinion.net/public-supports-reforming-how-members-of-congress-are-elected/

48. Toby S. James, "Fewer Costs, More Votes? United Kingdom Innovations in Election Administration 2000–2007 and the Effect on Voter Turnout," *Election Law Journal: Rules, Politics, and Policy* 10, no. 1 (March 2011): 37–52. https://doi.org/10.1089/elj.2009.0059

49. J. Manza, "Public Attitudes Toward Felon Disenfranchisement in the United States," *Public Opinion Quarterly* 68, no. 2 (June 1, 2004): 275–86. https://doi.org/10.1093/poq/nfh015

50. "Support for Civics Education Initiative" (table), Civics Education Initiative (2017). https://www.leg.state.nv.us/App/NELIS/REL/79th2017/ExhibitDocument/OpenExhibitDocument?exhibitId=31627&fileDownloadName=SB%20322%20Handout_Civics%20Education%20Initiative_Karen%20Summers.pdf

51. Diana Owen, "Public Attitudes About Civic Education," *SSRN Scholarly Paper* (Rochester, NY, 2013). https://papers.ssrn.com/abstract=2303540

52. "Edelman Trust Barometer," *Edelman*, accessed August 27, 2023. https://www.edelman.com/trust/trust-barometer

53. "Edelman Trust Barometer 2019" (Edelman, 2019). https://www.edelman.com/sites/g/files/aatuss191/files/2019-02/2019_Edelman_Trust_Barometer_Executive_Summary.pdf

54. "Edelman Trust Barometer 2021."

55. Plutarch, *The Lives of the Noble Grecians and Romans* Vol 1, ed. Arthur Hugh Clough, trans. John Dryden (New York: Random House, 2000).

56. Kevin Gray, "Addiction on Wall Street," *The Fix*, March 26, 2012. https://web.archive.org/web/20150328035226/http://www.thefix.com/content/wall-street-addiction-finance-cocaine-meltdown7456

57. Thomas Frank, "David Graeber: 'Spotlight on the Financial Sector Did Make Apparent Just How Bizarrely Skewed Our Economy Is in Terms of Who Gets Rewarded,'" *Salon*, June 1, 2014. https://www.salon.com/2014/06/01/help_us_thomas_piketty_the_1s_sick_and_twisted_new_scheme/

58. Deborah Copaken, "What I Learned About Life at My 30th College Reunion". The Atlantic, October 24, 2018. https://www.theatlantic.com/education/archive/2018/10/what-my-harvard-college-reunion-taught-me-about-life/573847/

59. Nick Hanauer, "The Pitchforks Are Coming… For Us Plutocrats," *POLITICO*, May 8, 2020. https://politi.co/2KTghlP

60. Louise Tickle, "Should Politicians Have Their Mental Health Monitored?," *The Guardian*, January 23, 2012, sec. Education. https://www.theguardian.com/education/2012/jan/23/politicians-stress-mental-health-monitor   Ashley Weinberg, "Should the Job of National Politician Carry a Government Health Warning?: The Impact of Psychological Strain on Politicians," in *The Psychology of Politicians*, ed. Ashley Weinberg (Cambridge: Cambridge University Press, 2011), 123–42. https://doi.org/10.1017/CBO9781139026482.010

61. Tuchman, *The March of Folly: From Troy to Vietnam*, chap. 5.

62. "Politicians and Mental Health," *Palgrave*, accessed June 27, 2023. https://www.palgrave.com/gp/campaigns/mental-health-awareness/politicians-and-mental-health

63. Tucker Carlson, "Life, Death, Power, the CIA and the End of Journalism,"

interview by Tulsi Gabbard, *The Tulsi Gabbard Show*, December 13, 2022. https://www.youtube.com/watch?v=SKEWD4-nwyA

64. Laura Spinney, "History as a Giant Data Set: How Analysing the Past Could Help Save the Future," *The Guardian*, November 12, 2019, sec. Technology. https://www.theguardian.com/technology/2019/nov/12/history-as-a-giant-data-set-how-analysing-the-past-could-help-save-the-future

65. Tom Ginsburg and Aziz Huq, "Democracy's 'Near Misses,'" *Journal of Democracy* 29, no. 4 (October 2018): 16–30. https://www.journalofdemocracy.org/articles/democracys-near-misses/

66. Mark Tran, "Cambodian Soldiers Accused of Land Rights Abuse in Prey Trolach Forest," *The Guardian*, August 3, 2012, sec. Global development. https://www.theguardian.com/global-development/2012/aug/03/cambodian-soldiers-land-rights-prey-trolach

67. Vault 7: CIA Hacking Tools Revealed; WikiLeaks, Mar 7, 2017. https://wikileaks.org/ciav7p1/

68. Ex-CIA software engineer who leaked to WikiLeaks sentenced to 40 years; Al Jazeera, Feb 2, 2024. https://www.aljazeera.com/news/2024/2/2/ex-cia-software-engineer-who-leaked-to-wikileaks-sentenced-to-40-years

69. Dorfman, Naylor, and Isikoff, "Kidnapping, Assassination and a London Shoot-Out."

70. Mark Sancher, The People Power Revolution, Philippines 1986; Orogons. OSU.EDU. https://origins.osu.edu/milestones/people-power-revolution-philippines-1986?language_content_entity=en

54. The campaign

1. Daron Acemoglu and James A. Robinson, "The Constitution Won't Save American Democracy," *Project Syndicate*, September 24, 2019. https://www.project-syndicate.org/commentary/only-social-mobilization-can-save-american-democracy-by-daron-acemoglu-and-james-a-robinson-2019-09

2. John J. Dinan, "The Political Dynamics of Mandatory State Constitutional Convention Referendums: Lessons from the 2000s Regarding Obstacles and Pathways to Their Passage," *Montana Law Review* 71, no. 2 (2010). https://scholarship.law.umt.edu/mlr/vol71/iss2/6

3. Liz Sly, The unfinished business of the Arab Spring, Washington Post, Jan 24, 2021. https://www.washingtonpost.com/world/interactive/2021/arab-spring-10-year-anniversary-lost-decade/

4. Don Emmert, The Occupy Movement did more than you think; The Atlantic, Sep 14, 2021. https://www.theatlantic.com/ideas/archive/2021/09/how-occupy-wall-street-reshaped-america/620064/ Simon Rogers, Occupy protests around the world: full list visualized; The Guardian, Nov 14, 2011. https://www.theguardian.com/news/datablog/2011/oct/17/occupy-protests-world-list-map

55. Bringing the third draft to a non-democracy

1. Will Todman, "A Coup in Tunisia?," *CSIS*, July 27, 2021. https://www.csis.org/analysis/coup-tunisia "Tunisian Constitutional Court Bill Hits Constitu-

tional Snag," *AW*, April 8, 2021. https://thearabweekly.com/tunisian-constitu tional-court-bill-hits-constitutional-snag

2. "Egyptian Parliamentary Elections, Part 1: The Rules," *FairVote*, February 13, 2012. https://fairvote.org/egyptian-parliamentary-elections-part-1-the-rules/ "Egypt and the Winner-Take-All Distortion," *FairVote*, March 8, 2012. https://fairvote.org/egypt-and-the-winner-take-all-distortion/

3. Tarek Masoud and Wael Nawara, "Will Egypt's Liberals Ever Win?," *Slate*, December 4, 2012. https://slate.com/news-and-politics/2012/12/egypts-liber als-can-defeat-mohammad-morsi-if-they-ignore-the-muslim-brotherhoods-conservative-agenda-and-focus-on-the-presidents-autocratic-policies.html

4. "Egypt: President Morsi Changes to the Constitution Trample Rule of Law," *Amnesty International*, November 23, 2012. https://web.archive.org/web/20121130114406/http://www.amnesty.org.uk/news_details.asp?NewsID=20468

5. Robert Kuttner, "Was Putin Inevitable?," *The American Prospect*, January 30, 2020. https://prospect.org/api/content/7740923c-42e1-11ea-b6fe-1244d5f7c7c6/

6. Zeynep Tufekci, *Twitter and Tear Gas: The Power and Fragility of Networked Protest* (Holborn: Yale University Press, 2017).

7. Dingxin Zhao, *The Power of Tiananmen: State-Society Relations and the 1989 Beijing Student Movement* (Chicago: University of Chicago Press, 2001).

8. "The Gate of Heavenly Peace," *Frontline*, April 16, 1997.

9. "六四图片、资料," *Boxun News Network*, n.d. https://web.archive.org/web/20210703022236/https://blog.bnn.co/hero/64/27_3.shtml

10. Kevin McSpadden, June 4, 1989 Is Not Just the Date of the Tiananmen Massacre but of Many Other Bloody Crackdowns Across China; TIME Magazine, June 3, 2015. https://time.com/3908456/tiananmen-massacre-china-chengdu-june-4-1989/

11. James P. Sterba, "Class Struggle: China's Harsh Actions Threaten to Set Back 10-Year Reform Drive — Suspicions of Westernization Are Ascendant, and Army Has a Political Role Again — A Movement Unlikely to Die," *The Wall Street Journal*, June 5, 1989. https://www.wsj.com/articles/BL-CJB-22543

12. John Burgess, "Images Vilify Protesters; Chinese Launch Propaganda Campaign," *Washington Post*, June 12, 1989.

13. Nicholas D. Kristof, "Units Said to Clash: Troops in Capital Seem to Assume Positions Against an Attack," *The New York Times*, June 6, 1989.

14. Xu Zhangrun, "Viral Alarm: When Fury Overcomes Fear," trans. Geremie R. Barmé, *Journal of Democracy* 31, no. 2 (April 2020): 5–23. https://www.jour nalofdemocracy.org/articles/viral-alarm-when-fury-overcomes-fear/

15. Paul Bischoff, "Surveillance Camera Statistics: Which City Has the Most CCTV Cameras?," *Comparitech*, May 23, 2023. https://www.comparitech. com/vpn-privacy/the-worlds-most-surveilled-cities/

16. Paul Mozur, "Inside China's Dystopian Dreams: A.I., Shame and Lots of Cameras," *The New York Times*, July 8, 2018, sec. Business. https://www. nytimes.com/2018/07/08/business/china-surveillance-technology.html

17. Muyi Xiao et al., "Video: China's Surveillance State Is Growing. These Documents Reveal How.," *The New York Times*, June 21, 2022, sec. World. https:// www.nytimes.com/video/world/asia/100000008314175/china-government-surveillance-data.html

Citations

18. Nick Davies, "The $10bn Question: What Happened to the Marcos Millions?," *The Guardian*, May 7, 2016, sec. World news. https://www.theguardian.com/world/2016/may/07/10bn-dollar-question-marcos-millions-nick-davies

19. Tom Phillips, "Fresh Details of 'savage' Tiananmen Massacre Emerge in Embassy Cables," *The Telegraph*, January 27, 2015. https://www.telegraph.co.uk/news/worldnews/asia/china/11372052/Fresh-details-of-savage-Tiananmen-massacre-emerge-in-embassy-cables.html

20. Marina Walker Guevara et al., "Leaked Records Reveal Offshore Holdings of China's Elite," *ICIJ*, January 21, 2014. https://www.icij.org/investigations/offshore/leaked-records-reveal-offshore-holdings-of-chinas-elite/

21. "Xi Jinping Millionaire Relations Reveal Elite Chinese Fortunes," *Bloomberg*, June 29, 2012. https://www.bloomberg.com/news/articles/2012-06-29/xi-jinping-millionaire-relations-reveal-fortunes-of-elite

22. Minxin Pei, "Transition in China?: More Likely than You Think," *Journal of Democracy* 27, no. 4 (2016): 5–19, https://doi.org/10.1353/jod.2016.0057

23. Natasha Kassam, "2021 Report - Lowy Institute Poll," *Lowy Institute*, accessed August 25, 2023. https://poll.lowyinstitute.org/report/2021/ Laura Silver, Kat Devlin, and Christine Huang, "Unfavorable Views of China Reach Historic Highs in Many Countries" (Pew Research Center, October 6, 2020). https://www.pewresearch.org/global/2020/10/06/unfavorable-views-of-china-reach-historic-highs-in-many-countries/

24. Macabe Keliher, "The Power of the Party," *Boston Review*, May 25, 2021. https://www.bostonreview.net/articles/the-power-of-the-party/

25. Willy Wo-Lap Lam, "Xi Facing Opposition on Different Fronts in Run-Up to Key Party Plenum," *China Brief* 21, no. 18 (September 23, 2021). https://jamestown.org/program/xi-facing-opposition-on-different-fronts-in-run-up-to-key-party-plenum/

26. Adrian Zenz, "China's Domestic Security Spending: An Analysis of Available Data," *China Brief* 18, no. 4 (March 12, 2018). https://jamestown.org/program/chinas-domestic-security-spending-analysis-available-data/

56. Leaders

1. Nick Allen, "Busboy Describes Bobby Kennedy's Final Moments," *The Telegraph*, August 30, 2015. https://www.telegraph.co.uk/news/worldnews/northamerica/usa/11834126/Busboy-describes-Bobby-Kennedys-final-moments.html

57. Numbers

1. Erica Chenoweth, "My Talk at TEDxBoulder: Civil Resistance and the '3.5% Rule,'" *Rationalinsurgent*, November 4, 2013. https://web.archive.org/web/20140213034550/https://rationalinsurgent.com/2013/11/04/my-talk-at-tedxboulder-civil-resistance-and-the-3-5-rule/

2. "Paul Hawken," in *Green Wiki*, accessed August 13, 2023. https://green.fandom.com/wiki/Paul_Hawken

58. Collaboration

1. John Hudson, "Tea Party and ACLU Call on Congress to Let Patriot Act Expire," *Foreign Policy*, May 29, 2015. https://foreignpolicy.com/2015/05/29/tea-party-and-aclu-call-on-congress-to-let-patriot-act-expire/
2. "ACLU And Other Privacy Groups Ask Lawmakers To Oppose 'Pass ID Act'"; ACLU press release, July 2013. https://www.aclu.org/press-releases/aclu-and-other-privacy-groups-ask-lawmakers-oppose-pass-id-act
3. Nader, *Unstoppable*, 89–90.
4. Robert Krebsbach, review of *Unstoppable: The Emerging Left-Right Alliance to Dismantle the Corporate State* by Ralph Nader, *Amazon*, May 18, 2014. https://www.amazon.com/gp/aw/review/B00HTQ31TA/R1CTKWHFX9YLGY?ie=UTF8&ASIN=156858525X

59. Planning

1. Becky Bond, *Rules for Revolutionaries: How Big Organizing Can Change Everything* (White River Junction, Vermont: Chelsea Green Publishing, 2016).
2. Pankhurst, *My Own Story*, 54.
3. Records of the Nuclear Disarmament Party, 1984-1985. National Library of Australia. https://catalogue.nla.gov.au/catalog/6540483
4. Gene Sharp, *From Dictatorship to Democracy: A Conceptual Framework for Liberation* (London: Serpent's Tail, 2012).
5. *How to Start a Revolution* (TVF International, 2011). Documentary on Gene Sharp. https://tvfinternational.com/programme/14/how-to-start-a-revolution?trailer=1#:~:text=With%20exclusive%20footage%20and%20unprecedented,and%20the%20ongoing%20Syrian%20uprising
6. Sharp, *From Dictatorship to Democracy*, chap. 6.

60. Symbols

1. Ursula K Le Guin, "Books Aren't Just Commodities" (Acceptance Speech, The 65th National Book Awards, New York, November 20, 2014). https://www.theguardian.com/books/2014/nov/20/ursula-k-le-guin-national-book-awards-speech
2. Matthew Alice, "The True Color of Athena's Eyes," *San Diego Reader*, June 5 1997. https://www.sandiegoreader.com/news/1997/jun/05/straight-did-athena-have-gray-eyes/
3. ATHENE; THEOI GREEK MYTHOLOGY. https://www.theoi.com/Olympios/Athena.html Athena; Livius: Literatuur, geschiedenis en cultuur. https://www.livius.org/articles/religion/athena/

62. Don't expand government power

1. Peter Walker, "Boris Johnson a Pundit Who Stumbled into Politics, Says Cummings," *The Guardian*, June 21, 2021, sec. Politics. https://www.theguardian.com/politics/2021/jun/21/boris-johnson-a-pundit-who-stumbled-into-politics-says-dominic-cummings

2. Scott Brennan, "Constitutional Referenda in Australia," Law and Bills Digest Group (Parliament of Australia, August 24, 1999). https://web.archive.org/web/20210120200750/http://www.aph.gov.au/About_Parliament/Parliamentary_Departments/Parliamentary_Library/pubs/rp/rp9900/2000RP02

63. Non-violence

1. Sharp, *From Dictatorship to Democracy*, chap. 1.
2. Maria J. Stephan and Erica Chenoweth, "Why Civil Resistance Works: The Strategic Logic of Nonviolent Conflict," *International Security* 33, no. 1 (July 2008): 7–44. https://doi.org/10.1162/isec.2008.33.1.7
3. Erica Chenoweth, "The Success of Nonviolent Civil Resistance," TEDxBoulder, November 4, 2013. https://www.youtube.com/watch?v=YJSehRlU34w
4. Sharp, *From Dictatorship to Democracy*, chap. 5.

64. Keep political parties armslength

1. Mads Qvortrup and Matt Qvortrup, *A Comparative Study of Referendums: Government by the People* (Manchester University Press, 2002).
2. Micah L. Sifry, "The Obama Disconnect: What Could Have Been?," *TechPresident*, January 3, 2010. https://web.archive.org/web/20201005203856/https://techpresident.com/blog-entry/obama-disconnect-what-could-have-been
3. Thorvaldur Gylfason, "Democracy on Ice: A Post-Mortem of the Icelandic Constitution," *openDemocracy*, June 19, 2013. https://www.opendemocracy.net/en/can-europe-make-it/democracy-on-ice-post-mortem-of-icelandic-constitution/
4. Tom Fairless and Gabriele Steinhauser, "Greece Requests Three-Year Bailout in First Step Toward Meeting Creditors' Demand," *Wall Street Journal*, July 8, 2015, sec. World. http://www.wsj.com/articles/greek-prime-minister-pledges-concrete-proposals-to-bridge-creditor-impasse-1436348229

65. Expect major opposition

1. "The Parallel Society vs Totalitarianism | How to Create a Free World," Academy of Ideas, February 26, 2022. https://academyofideas.com/2022/02/parallel-society-vs-totalitarianism-how-to-create-a-free-world/
2. Gylfason, "Democracy on Ice."
3. Stephen Kinzer, Ervand Abrahamian, "50 Years After the CIA's First Overthrow of a Democratically Elected Foreign Government We Take a Look at the 1953 US Backed Coup in Iran," interview by Amy Goodman, *Democracy Now!*, August 25, 2003. http://www.democracynow.org/2003/8/25/50_years_after_the_cias_first
4. Pankhurst, *My Own Story*, chap. 1.
5. Micah White, "I Started Occupy Wall Street. Russia Tried to Co-Opt Me," *The Guardian*, November 2. 2017, sec. Opinion. https://www.theguardian.com/commentisfree/2017/nov/02/activist-russia-protest-occupy-black-lives-matter
6. Hannes Grassegger and Mikael Krogerus, "Weaken From Within," *The New Republic*, November 2, 2017. https://newrepublic.com/article/145413/

weaken-within-moscow-honing-information-age-art-war-how-free-societies-protect-themselves

7. Rosalind Adams Brown Hayes, "These Americans Were Tricked Into Working For Russia. They Say They Had No Idea.," *BuzzFeed News*, October 18, 2017. https://www.buzzfeednews.com/article/rosalindadams/these-americans-were-tricked-into-working-for-russia-they How the "troll factory" worked in US elections; RBC Magazine, Oct 17, 2017. https://www.rbc.ru/technology_and_media/17/10/2017/59e0c17d9a79470e05a9e6c1

8. O'Rourke, Lindsey A, The Strategic Logic of Covert Regime Change: US-Backed Regime Change Campaigns during the Cold War. *Security Studies.* **29**: 92–127, Nov 29, 2019. doi:10.1080/09636412.2020.1693620 Dov H. Levin, "Partisan Electoral Interventions by the Great Powers: Introducing the PEIG Dataset," *Conflict Management and Peace Science* 36, no. 1 (January 2019): 88–106. https://doi.org/10.1177/0738894216661190 Lindsey A. O'Rourke, "The Strategic Logic of Covert Regime Change: US-Backed Regime Change Campaigns during the Cold War," *Security Studies* 29, no. 1 (January 1, 2020): 92–127. https://doi.org/10.1080/09636412.2020.1693620

66. Use the next crisis

1. William F. Ward, "The Movement for American Independence," ed. Daniel Gaido, *Fourth International* 11, no. 4 (1950): 122–26.
2. Kristinn Már Ársælsson, "Real Democracy in Iceland?," *OpenDemocracy*, November 12, 2012. https://www.opendemocracy.net/en/real-democracy-in-iceland/

68. Interim Bill option

1. David Broder, "'We Have Nothing to Lose but Our Debts': An Interview with Yanis Varoufakis," *Jacobin*, July 6, 2019. https://jacobin.com/2019/06/yanis-varoufakis-interview-greece-european-elections

69. Bedding down a post-Bill society

1. Alexander Solzhenitsyn, *The Gulag Archipelago* (London: Collins, 1974), 168.
2. Noam Chomsky, "Manufacturing Consent: The Political Economy of the Mass Media," Wisconsin Union Theater, University of Wisconsin, March 15, 1989. https://www.youtube.com/watch?v=jxhT9EVj9Kk "Functions of the Supreme Economic Council," *Seventeen Moments in Soviet History*, August 26, 2015. https://soviethistory.msu.edu/1917-2/economic-apparatus/economic-apparatus-texts/functions-of-the-supreme-economic-council/
3. Leon Trotsky, *Our Political Tasks* (London: New Park Publications, 1904). https://www.marxists.org/archive/trotsky/1904/tasks/
4. Claude Lefort, "The Contradiction of Trotsky"; Libcom.org, July 2005. https://libcom.org/article/contradiction-trotsky-claude-lefort
5. Micah L. Sifry, "Obama's Lost Army," *The New Republic*, February 9, 2017. https://newrepublic.com/article/140245/obamas-lost-army-inside-fall-grass roots-machine
6. Sifry, "The Obama Disconnect."

70. Possible trajectories

1. Sharp, *From Dictatorship to Democracy*.
2. "How the World Votes: 2019," *Al Jazeera*, accessed June 19, 2023. https://inter active.aljazeera.com/aje/2019/how-the-world-votes-2019/index.html Women and the vote: World suffrage timeline; NZ History website. https://nzhistory. govt.nz/politics/womens-suffrage/world-suffrage-timeline Katherine Schaeffer, Key facts about women's suffrage around the world, a century after U.S. ratified 19th Amendment; Pew Research Center, Oct 5, 2020. https://www.pewre search.org/short-reads/2020/10/05/key-facts-about-womens-suffrage-around-the-world-a-century-after-u-s-ratified-19th-amendment/
3. Tom Ginsburg, Nick Foti, and Daniel Rockmore, "'We the Peoples': The Global Origins of Constitutional Preambles," SSRN Scholarly Paper (Rochester, NY, November 27, 2013). https://doi.org/10.2139/ssrn.2360725

71. The sharpest weapon

1. Walter E. Weyl, *The New Democracy; an Essay on Certain Political and Economic Tendencies in the United States* (New York: The Macmillan company, 1913). http://archive.org/details/newdemocracyessa00weylrich
2. "Confidence in Democracy and Capitalism Wanes in Former Soviet Union," *Pew Research Center's Global Attitudes Project*, December 5, 2011. https://www. pewresearch.org/global/2011/12/05/confidence-in-democracy-and-capitalism-wanes-in-former-soviet-union/

72. Inferior binaries

1. Jeffrey M. Jones, "Confidence in U.S. Institutions Down; Average at New Low," *Gallup*, July 5, 2022. https://news.gallup.com/poll/394283/confidence-institutions-down-average-new-low.aspx
2. Jon Clifton, "The Global Rise of Unhappiness," *Gallup*, September 15, 2022. https://news.gallup.com/opinion/gallup/401216/global-rise-unhappiness.aspx
3. "The Good News Hidden inside Today's 'Polycrisis,'" *Zurich*, March 9, 2023. https://www.zurich.com/en/knowledge/topics/global-risks/the-good-news-hidden-inside-todays-polycrisis

73. Fateful complexity

1. Russian/Chechnya: THE "DIRTY WAR" IN CHECHNYA: FORCED DISAPPEARANCES, TORTURE, AND SUMMARY EXECUTIONS; Human Rights Watch, Mar 2001. https://www.hrw.org/reports/2001/chech nya/RSCH0301.PDF
2. "UN: Unprecedented Joint Call for China to End Xinjiang Abuses," *Human Rights Watch*, July 10, 2019. https://www.hrw.org/news/2019/07/10/un-unprecedented-joint-call-china-end-xinjiang-abuses
3. Max Fisher, "U.S. Allies Drive Much of World's Democratic Decline, Data Shows," *The New York Times*, November 16, 2021, sec. World. https://www. nytimes.com/2021/11/16/world/americas/democracy-decline-worldwide.html

Citations

4. Aleksandra W. Gadzala, "Global Reach: Information Is a Weapon," *Democracy Journal*, no. 52 (March 12, 2019). https://democracyjournal.org/magazine/52/global-reach-information-is-a-weapon/ Melanie Hart and Blaine Johnson, "Mapping China's Global Governance Ambitions," *Center for American Progress*, February 28, 2019. https://www.americanprogress.org/article/mapping-chinas-global-governance-ambitions/

5. Zhang Zhixin, "Election Game Mirrors Failure of US Democracy," *China Daily*, October 11, 2016. http://www.chinadaily.com.cn/opinion/2016-10/11/content_27018105.htm

6. Fan Zhengkun, "对西方的制度迷信该醒醒了_社会 (It's Time to Wake up from the Superstition of the Western System)," *China Education News*, December 10, 2020, 5th ed. https://www.sohu.com/a/437343080_243614

7. "A Landmark Night in US History: Capitol Riots Nation's Waterloo, Destroy Global Image," *Global Times*, January 7, 2021, sec. Diplomacy. https://www.globaltimes.cn/page/202101/1212139.shtml

8. "After Capitol Riots, Russia Slams US's 'Archaic' Electoral System," *Al Jazeera*, January 7, 2021. https://www.aljazeera.com/news/2021/1/7/russian-officials-say-us-democracy-limping-after-capitol-riot

9. Jamie Seidel, "Russian and Chinese Media Are Celebrating US Capitol Riots," *News.Com.Au*, January 8, 2021, sec. US Politics. https://www.news.com.au/world/north-america/us-politics/russian-and-chinese-media-are-celebrating-us-capitol-riots/news-story/b125a44d03c393e8141cc5108fde72ab

10. Eric Cline, "1177 BC: The Year Civilization Collapsed," National Capital Area Skeptics, Bethesda, Maryland, October 8, 2016. https://www.youtube.com/watch?v=bRcu-ysocX4

74. Third draft efficiency

1. Henry David Thoreau, *Walden, and On The Duty Of Civil Disobedience* (Urbana, Illinois: Project Gutenberg, 1995). https://www.gutenberg.org/ebooks/205

2. Cameron Keith Murray and Paul Frijters, *Game of Mates: How Favours Bleed the Nation* (Brisbane, Qld.: Cameron Murray, Cameron Murray, 2017), chap. 13.

3. Shreya Sheth, "America's Top Fears 2019," Survey, Chapman Survey of American Fears (Orange, California: Chapman University, November 11, 2019). https://www.chapman.edu/wilkinson/research-centers/babbie-center/_files/americas-top-fears-2019.pdf

4. Price and Edwards, "Trends in Income From 1975 to 2018"; Rick Wartzman, "'We Were Shocked': RAND Study Uncovers Massive Income Shift to the Top 1%," *Fast Company*, September 14, 2020. https://www.fastcompany.com/90550015/we-were-shocked-rand-study-uncovers-massive-income-shift-to-the-top-1 Nick Hanauer, "Inequality Is Costing Workers $50 Trillion (with Carter Price)," Podcast, Pitchfork Economics, September 15, 2023. https://pitchforkeconomics.com/episode/inequality-is-costing-workers-50-trillion-with-carter-price/

5. "World Bank Open Data," World Bank Open Data, accessed June 16, 2023. https://data.worldbank.org Sara Atske, Abigail W. Geiger, and Alissa Scheller, "The Share of Women in Legislatures around the World Is Growing, but They Are Still Underrepresented," *Pew Research Center*, March 18, 2019. https://

www.pewresearch.org/short-reads/2019/03/18/the-share-of-women-in-legisla tures-around-the-world-is-growing-but-they-are-still-underrepresented/

6. Abdurashid Solijonov, *Voter Turnout Trends around the World* (Stockholm: International Institute for Democracy and Electoral Assistance, 2016).

75. Syzygy

1. "Lynn Margulis," in *New World Encyclopedia*, accessed June 22, 2023. https:// www.newworldencyclopedia.org/entry/Lynn_Margulis
2. Campaign contributions: Ralph Nader website. https://nader.org/1980/01/11/ campaign-contributions/

76. Giant-killing

1. "John Adams to Thomas Jefferson, 9 July 1813."
2. George Bernard Shaw, Pygmalion (Urbana, Illinois: Project Gutenberg, 2003). https://www.gutenberg.org/ebooks/3825

Glossary

1. Jack Seale, "The Anthrax Attacks: In the Shadow of 9/11 Review – the Lethal Letters That Brought America to Its Knees," *The Guardian*, September 12, 2022, sec. Television. https://www.theguardian.com/tv-and-radio/2022/sep/ 12/the-anthrax-attacks-in-the-shadow-of-911-review
2. Fred Charatan, "Anthrax and the US Media," *British Medical Journal* 323, no. 7318 (October 20, 2001): 942. https://www.ncbi.nlm.nih.gov/pmc/articles/ PMC1121464/
3. Angela Liegey Dougall, Michele C. Hayward, and Andrew Baum, "Media Exposure to Bioterrorism: Stress and the Anthrax Attacks," *Psychiatry* 68, no. 1 (2005): 28–42. https://doi.org/10.1521/psyc.68.1.28.64188
4. Glenn Greenwald, "The Largely Forgotten—And Still-Highly Suspect—2001 Anthrax Attacks That Enabled the Iraq War & Shine Light COVID's Origins," *System Update*, vol. 86, May 22, 2023. https://rumble.com/v2pcs3i-system-update-85.html
5. "BREAKING: Tucker Carlson Makes Unexpected Announcement," Brian Taylor Cohen, May 10, 2023. https://www.youtube.com/watch?v= eylbtjut3Uk
6. Asch, S. E. (1951). Effects of Group Pressure on the Modification and Distor-tion of Judgements. In H. Guetzknow (Ed.), Groups, Leadership and Men (pp. 177-190). Pittsburgh, PA: Carnegie Press. https://gwern.net/doc/psychol ogy/1952-asch.pdf
7. *How to Start a Revolution* (documentary on Gene Sharp), transcript. The Media Education Foundation. https://www.mediaed.org/transcripts/How-to-Start-a-Revolution-Transcript.pdf
8. George Bernard Shaw, *Pygmalion* (Urbana, Illinois: Project Gutenberg, 2003). https://www.gutenberg.org/ebooks/3825
9. Shane Wright, "Economy to Recover Strongly, but Wages and Jobs Will Not," The Sydney Morning Herald, July 5, 2020, sec. Federal. https://www.smh.

Citations

com.au/politics/federal/economy-to-recover-strongly-but-wages-and-jobs-will-not-20200705-p5594c.html

10. Binyamin Appelbaum, "The Founders of a Nation Should Not Have the Last Word," *The New York Times*, September 2, 2022, sec. Opinion. https://www.nytimes.com/2022/09/02/opinion/chile-new-constitution-referendum.html

11. David Welch et al., "Democracy Spreads in Waves – but Shared Cultural History Might Matter More than Geography," *The Conversation*, November 1, 2022. http://theconversation.com/democracy-spreads-in-waves-but-shared-cultural-history-might-matter-more-than-geography-189959

12. Raphael, *Jewish Views of the Afterlife*.

13. Alexander Solzhenitsyn, *Rebuilding Russia* (New York: Farrar, Strauss and Giroux, 1990).

14. Nick, Mōri Motonari: The Strategic Genius of Feudal Japan; Medium, Dec 9, 2023. https://medium.com/@spunkthecat101/m%C5%8Dri-motonari-the-strategic-genius-of-feudal-japan-05abe31bd762

15. 59 days to go: Syzygy; EarthSky (video). https://www.youtube.com/watch?v=iPZov5w6934&ab_channel=EarthSky

Sources for Figures

1. Zach Dorfman, Sean D. Naylor, and Michael Isikoff, "Kidnapping, Assassination and a London Shoot-out: Inside the CIA's Secret War Plans against Wiki-Leaks," Yahoo News, September 26, 2021. https://au.news.yahoo.com/kidnapping-assassination-and-a-london-shoot-out-inside-the-ci-as-secret-war-plans-against-wiki-leaks-090057786.html

2. "Largest Anti-War Rally," Guinness World Records, September 4, 2004. https://web.archive.org/web/20040904214302/http:/www.guinnessworldrecords.com/content_pages/record.asp?recordid=54365

3. "Inside VETERANS ROW: Homeless Vets Outside Los Angeles's VA", Invisible People, June 14, 2021. https://www.youtube.com/watch?v=5S943965QQE Gwynedd Stuart, "Inside Veterans Row, the Tent City That's Sprung Up Outside the VA," Los Angeles Magazine, July 10, 2020. https://www.lamag.com/citythinkblog/veterans-row-homeless-los-angeles/ Robert Reynolds, "Sign the Petition: West Los Angeles Veterans Affairs Land Fraud," Change.org, January 30, 2020. https://www.change.org/p/west-los-angeles-veterans-affairs-land-fraud Office of Audits and Evaluations, "VA's Management of Land Use Under the West Los Angeles Leasing Act of 2016," Audit (Los Angeles, California, September 28, 2018). https://www.va.gov/oig/publications/report-summary.asp?id=4578

   Thom Mrozek, "Parking Lot Operator Arrested for Allegedly Failing to Pay Dept. of Veteran's Affairs at Least $11 Million While Paying Bribes to VA Official," U.S. Attorney's Office, Central District of California, November 8, 2017. https://www.justice.gov/usao-cdca/pr/parking-lot-operator-arrested-allegedly-failing-pay-dept-veteran-s-affairs-least-11 "Individual Donors Gave 187 Large ($200+) Contributions to This PAC in the 2001-2002 Election Cycle," Open Secrets, 2002. https://www.opensecrets.org/political-action-committees-pacs/la-pac/C00095059/donors/2002 "Declaration of Ryan-Thompson Re UCLA Veteran Research," Google Docs, April 20, 2020. https://drive.google.com/file/d/1HOX9NjZ1vasGFmWhrN5yngslFXOBjd4o/view?usp=embed_facebook

Citations

4. "Rough Ride for the F-35," The New York Times, July 27, 2014, sec. Opinion. https://www.nytimes.com/2014/07/26/opinion/Rough-Ride-for-the-F-35.html Dave Majumdar and Marcus Weisgerber, "Kendall: 'Putting the F-35 into Production Years before the First Test Flight Was Acquisition Malpractice,'" Atlantic Organization for Security (AOS), February 6, 2012. https://www.aofs.org/2012/02/06/kendall-putting-the-f-35-into-production-years-before-the-first-test-flight-was-acquisition-malpractice/

5. Christopher Leonard, Lockheed Martin's $1.7 trillion F-35 fighter jet is 10 years late and 80% over budget—and it could be one of the Pentagon's biggest success stories; Fortune magazine, Aug 2, 2023. https://fortune.com/long form/lockheed-martin-f-35-fighter-jet/

6. Keynes, The General Theory of Employment, Interest, and Money, chap. 12.

7. Sally Denton and Roger Morris, The Money and the Power (Meyer Lansky); New York Times, 2001. https://archive.nytimes.com/www.nytimes.com/books/first/d/denton-power.html

8. Savranskaya and Blanton, "NATO Expansion: What Gorbachev Heard."

9. "Tsar Bomba," Atomic Heritage Foundation, Aug 8, 2014. https://ahf.nuclear museum.org/ahf/history/tsar-bomba/ Alex Wellerstein, An Unearthly Spectacle; Bulletin of the Atomic Scientists, Oct 29, 2021. https://thebulletin.org/2021/11/the-untold-story-of-the-worlds-biggest-nuclear-bomb/

10. "Summary Results from the National Deliberative Poll in Mongolia on Constitutional Reform," (Stanford: Center on Democracy, Development and the Rule of Law, April 29-30, 2017. https://deliberation.stanford.edu/mongo lias-first-national-deliberative-poll-constitutional-amendments

11. America in One Room: A "deliberative polling" experiment to bridge American partisanship; Stanford University. https://www.norc.org/research/projects/america-in-one-room.html America in One Room, Stanford Deliberative Democracy Lab, July 5, 2019. https://deliberation.stanford.edu/news/america-one-room "Polling results on immigration before and after deliberation," Helena Foundation, April 20, 2021. https://www.flickr.com/photos/192803194@N03/51127750743/

12. World Wide Views on Global Warming policy report; Danish Board of Technology, Nov 2009. https://globalwarming.wwviews.org/files/AUDIO/WWViews%20Policy%20Report%20FINAL%20-%20Web%20version.pdf

13. Silke Koltrowitz, Switzerland votes to make same-sex marriage legal by near two-thirds majority; Reuters, Sep 27, 2021. https://www.reuters.com/world/europe/swiss-vote-allowing-same-sex-marriage-referendum-2021-09-26/

14. Rachel M. Cohen, "Local Governments Lead the Charge on Safe Voting by Mail," The Intercept, April 20, 2020. https://theintercept.com/2020/04/20/vote-by-mail-wisconsin-pennsylvania-elections/ Akela Lacy, "Milwaukee Documents Seven Coronavirus Cases Linked to In-Person Voting," The Intercept, April 20, 2020. https://theintercept.com/2020/04/20/milwaukee-coron avirus-voting-election/ Chad D. Cotti et al., "The Relationship Between In-Person Voting And Covid-19: Evidence From The Wisconsin Primary," Working Paper (Cambridge: National Bureau of Economic Research, May 2020). https://www.nber.org/system/files/working_papers/w27187/w27187.pdf

15. Illinois' 4th Congressional District Elections, 2012. BALLOTPEDIA. https://ballotpedia.org/Illinois%27_4th_Congressional_District_elections,_2012

Citations

16. PEACE IN NO MAN'S LAND? THE TRUTH BEHIND THE CHRISTMAS TRUCE; Commonwealth War Graves, Dec 15, 2022. https://www.cwgc.org/our-work/blog/peace-in-no-man-s-land-the-truth-behind-the-christmas-truce/

17. The Citizens' Assembly, Previous Assemblies. https://citizensassembly.ie/over view-previous-assemblies/

18. Howard H Peckham, "Independence: The View from Britain," American Antiquarian Society 85, no. 2 (October 1975): 387–403; "Parliament and the War in the American Colonies 1767-83," UK Parliament, accessed June 27, 2023. https://www.parliament.uk/about/living-heritage/evolutionofparliament/legisla tivescrutiny/parliament-and-empire/parliament-and-the-american-colonies-before-1765/parliament-and-the-war-in-the-american-colonies-1767-83/ Richard Howe and William Howe, "A Response to the American Declaration of Independence, 1776," in Founding Documents of the United States of America (Williamstown: Chapin Library, 2017). https://librarysearch.williams. edu/discovery/delivery/01WIL_INST:01WIL_SPECIAL/ 12289215360002786 Emily Sneff, "September Highlight: Extravagant and Inadmissible Claim of Independency," September 4, 2016. https://declaration. fas.harvard.edu/blog/september-kings-speech

19. Jeffrey Wasserstrom, The fallen goddess; Perspectives on History, Dec 14, 2023. https://www.historians.org/research-and-publications/perspectives-on-history/december-2023/the-fallen-goddess-a-different-sort-of-statue-story Remembering Tiananmen: Why the 'Goddess of Democracy' still stands tall in a Sydney suburb; SBS Mandarin, June 9, 2017. https://www.sbs.com.au/language/chinese/en/article/remembering-tiananmen-why-the-goddess-of-democracy-still-stands-tall-in-a-sydney-suburb/1e4crkifv

20. "China's Repression of Uyghurs in Xinjiang," Council on Foreign Relations, accessed July 14, 2023. https://www.cfr.org/backgrounder/china-xinjiang-uyghurs-muslims-repression-genocide-human-rights "China: Big Data Program Targets Xinjiang's Muslims," Human Rights Watch, December 9, 2020. https://www.hrw.org/news/2020/12/09/china-big-data-program-targets-xinjiangs-muslims

21. Max Benwell, John Bolton's bombshell Trump book: eight of its most stunning claims; The Guardian, Jun 18, 2020. https://www.theguardian.com/us-news/2020/jun/17/john-bolton-book-trump-china-dictators-saudi-arabia

22. Lyndsey Jenkins, Annie Kenney and the Politics of Class in the Women's Social and Political Union; Twentieth Century British History, Volume 30, Issue 4, December 2019, Pps 477–503. Sep 13, 2019. https://doi.org/10.1093/tcbh/hwz021

Printed in Great Britain
by Amazon

48431975R10380